NOVELS
for Students

Advisors

Erik France: Adjunct Instructor of English, Macomb Community College, Warren, Michigan. B.A. and M.S.L.S. from University of North Carolina, Chapel Hill; Ph.D. from Temple University.

Kate Hamill: Grade 12 English Teacher, Catonsville High School, Catonsville, Maryland.

Joseph McGeary: English Teacher, Germantown Friends School, Philadelphia, Pennsylvania. Ph.D. in English from Duke University.

Timothy Showalter: English Department Chair, Franklin High School, Reisterstown, Maryland. Certified teacher by the Maryland State Department of Education. Member of the National Council of Teachers of English.

Amy Spade Silverman: English Department Chair, Kehillah Jewish High School, Palo Alto, California. Member of National Council of Teachers of English (NCTE), Teachers and Writers, and NCTE Opinion Panel. Exam Reader, Advanced Placement Literature and Composition. Poet, published in *North American Review, Nimrod,* and *Michigan Quarterly Review,* among other publications.

Jody Stefansson: Director of Boswell Library and Study Center and Upper School Learning Specialist, Polytechnic School, Pasadena, California. Board member, Children's Literature Council of Southern California. Member of American Library Association, Association of Independent School Librarians, and Association of Educational Therapists.

Laura Jean Waters: Certified School Library Media Specialist, Wilton High School, Wilton, Connecticut. B.A. from Fordham University; M.A. from Fairfield University.

NOVELS
for Students

Presenting Analysis, Context, and Criticism on Commonly Studied Novels

VOLUME 29

GALE
CENGAGE Learning

Detroit • New York • San Francisco • New Haven, Conn • Waterville, Maine • London

Novels for Students, Volume 29

Project Editor: Sara Constantakis

Rights Acquisition and Management: Mollika Basu, Leitha Etheridge-Sims, Jacqueline Flowers, Barb McNeil

Composition: Evi Abou-El-Seoud

Manufacturing: Drew Kalasky

Imaging: John Watkins

Product Design: Pamela A. E. Galbreath, Jennifer Wahi

Content Conversion: Civie Green, Katrina Coach

Product Manager: Meggin Condino

For product information and technology assistance, contact us at
Gale Customer Support, 1-800-877-4253.
For permission to use material from this text or product,
submit all requests online at **www.cengage.com/permissions.**
Further permissions questions can be emailed to
permissionrequest@cengage.com

Gale
27500 Drake Rd.
Farmington Hills, MI, 48331-3535

ISBN-13: 978-0-7876-8686-4
ISBN-10: 0-7876-8686-7

ISSN 1094-3552

This title is also available as an e-book.
ISBN-13: 978-1-4144-4945-6
ISBN-10: 1-4144-4945-3
Contact your Gale, a part of Cengage Learning sales representative for ordering information.

Printed in the United States of America
1 2 3 4 5 6 7 13 12 11 10 09

Table of Contents

The Informed Dialogue: Interacting with Literature

When we pick up a book, we usually do so with the anticipation of pleasure. We hope that by entering the time and place of the novel and sharing the thoughts and actions of the characters, we will find enjoyment. Unfortunately, this is often not the case; we are disappointed. But we should ask, has the author failed us, or have we failed the author?

We establish a dialogue with the author, the book, and with ourselves when we read. Consciously and unconsciously, we ask questions: "Why did the author write this book?" "Why did the author choose that time, place, or character?" "How did the author achieve that effect?" "Why did the character act that way?" "Would I act in the same way?" The answers we receive depend upon how much information about literature in general and about that book specifically we ourselves bring to our reading.

Young children have limited life and literary experiences. Being young, children frequently do not know how to go about exploring a book, nor sometimes, even know the questions to ask of a book. The books they read help them answer questions, the author often coming right out and *telling* young readers the things they are learning or are expected to learn. The perennial classic, *The Little Engine That Could,* tells its readers that, among other things, it is good to help others and brings happiness:

"Hurray, hurray," cried the funny little clown and all the dolls and toys. "The good little boys and girls in the city will be happy because you helped us, kind, Little Blue Engine."

In picture books, messages are often blatant and simple, the dialogue between the author and reader one-sided. Young children are concerned with the end result of a book—the enjoyment gained, the lesson learned—rather than with how that result was obtained. As we grow older and read further, however, we question more. We come to expect that the world within the book will closely mirror the concerns of our world, and that the author will *show* these through the events, descriptions, and conversations within the story, rather than *telling* of them. We are now expected to do the interpreting, carry on our share of the dialogue with the book and author, and glean not only the author's message, but comprehend how that message and the overall affect of the book were achieved. Sometimes, however, we need help to do these things. *Novels for Students* provides that help.

A novel is made up of many parts interacting to create a coherent whole. In reading a novel, the more obvious features can be easily spotted—theme, characters, plot—but we may overlook the more subtle elements that greatly influence how the novel is perceived by the reader: viewpoint, mood and tone, symbolism, or the use of humor. By focusing on both the obvious and more subtle literary elements within a novel, *Novels for Students* aids readers in both analyzing for message and in determining how and why that message is communicated. In the discussion on Harper Lee's *To Kill a Mockingbird* (Vol. 2), for example, the mockingbird as a symbol of innocence is dealt with, among other things, as is the importance of Lee's use of humor which "enlivens a serious plot, adds depth to the characterization, and creates a sense of familiarity and universality." The reader comes to understand the internal elements of each novel discussed—as well as the external influences that help shape it.

"The desire to write greatly," Harold Bloom of Yale University says, "is the desire to be elsewhere, in a time and place of one's own, in an originality that must compound with inheritance, with an anxiety of influence." A writer seeks to create a unique world within a story, but although it is unique, it is not disconnected from our own world. It speaks to us *because* of what the writer brings to the writing from our world: how he or she was raised and educated; his or her likes and dislikes; the events occurring in the real world at the time of the writing, and while the author was growing up. When we know what an author has brought to his or her work, we gain a greater insight into both the "originality" (the world of the book), and the things that "compound" it. This insight enables us to question that created world and find answers more readily. By informing ourselves, we are able to establish a more effective dialogue with both book and author.

Novels for Students, in addition to providing a plot summary and descriptive list of characters—to remind readers of what they have read—also explores the external influences that shaped each book. Each entry includes a discussion of the author's background, and the historical context in which the novel was written. It is vital to know, for instance, that when Ray Bradbury was writing *Fahrenheit 451* (Vol. 1), the threat of Nazi domination had recently ended in Europe, and the McCarthy hearings were taking place in Washington, D.C. This information goes far in answering the question, "Why did he write a story of oppressive government control and book burning?" Similarly, it is important to know that Harper Lee, author of

To Kill a Mockingbird, was born and raised in Monroeville, Alabama, and that her father was a lawyer. Readers can now see why she chose the south as a setting for her novel—it is the place with which she was most familiar—and start to comprehend her characters and their actions.

Novels for Students helps readers find the answers they seek when they establish a dialogue with a particular novel. It also aids in the posing of questions by providing the opinions and interpretations of various critics and reviewers, broadening that dialogue. Some reviewers of *To Kill A Mockingbird,* for example, "faulted the novel's climax as melodramatic." This statement leads readers to ask, "Is it, indeed, melodramatic?" "If not, why did some reviewers see it as such?" "If it is, why did Lee choose to make it melodramatic?" "Is melodrama ever justified?" By being spurred to ask these questions, readers not only learn more about the book and its writer, but about the nature of writing itself.

The literature included for discussion in *Novels for Students* has been chosen because it has something vital to say to us. *Of Mice and Men, Catch-22, The Joy Luck Club, My Antonia, A Separate Peace* and the other novels here speak of life and modern sensibility. In addition to their individual, specific messages of prejudice, power, love or hate, living and dying, however, they and all great literature also share a common intent. They force us to *think*—about life, literature, and about others, not just about ourselves. They pry us from the narrow confines of our minds and thrust us outward to confront the world of books and the larger, real world we all share. *Novels for Students* helps us in this confrontation by providing the means of enriching our conversation with literature and the world, by creating an *informed* dialogue, one that brings true pleasure to the personal act of reading.

Sources

Harold Bloom, *The Western Canon, The Books and School of the Ages,* Riverhead Books, 1994.

Watty Piper, *The Little Engine That Could,* Platt & Munk, 1930.

Anne Devereaux Jordan
Senior Editor, TALL (Teaching and Learning Literature)

Introduction

Purpose of the Book

The purpose of *Novels for Students* (*NfS*) is to provide readers with a guide to understanding, enjoying, and studying novels by giving them easy access to information about the work. Part of Gale's "For Students" Literature line, *NfS* is specifically designed to meet the curricular needs of high school and undergraduate college students and their teachers, as well as the interests of general readers and researchers considering specific novels. While each volume contains entries on "classic" novels frequently studied in classrooms, there are also entries containing hard-to-find information on contemporary novels, including works by multicultural, international, and women novelists.

The information covered in each entry includes an introduction to the novel and the novel's author; a plot summary, to help readers unravel and understand the events in a novel; descriptions of important characters, including explanation of a given character's role in the novel as well as discussion about that character's relationship to other characters in the novel; analysis of important themes in the novel; and an explanation of important literary techniques and movements as they are demonstrated in the novel.

In addition to this material, which helps the readers analyze the novel itself, students are also provided with important information on the literary and historical background informing each work. This includes a historical context essay, a box comparing the time or place the novel was written to modern Western culture, a critical essay, and excerpts from critical essays on the novel. A unique feature of *NfS* is a specially commissioned critical essay on each novel, targeted toward the student reader.

To further aid the student in studying and enjoying each novel, information on media adaptations is provided (if available), as well as reading suggestions for works of fiction and nonfiction on similar themes and topics. Classroom aids include ideas for research papers and lists of critical sources that provide additional material on the novel.

Selection Criteria

The titles for each volume of *NfS* were selected by surveying numerous sources on teaching literature and analyzing course curricula for various school districts. Some of the sources surveyed included: literature anthologies; *Reading Lists for College-Bound Students: The Books Most Recommended by America's Top Colleges*; textbooks on teaching the novel; a College Board survey of novels commonly studied in high schools; a National Council of Teachers of English (NCTE) survey of novels commonly studied in high schools; the NCTE's *Teaching Literature in High School: The Novel*; and the Young Adult Library Services Association

(YALSA) list of best books for young adults of the past twenty-five years.

Input was also solicited from our advisory board, as well as from educators from various areas. From these discussions, it was determined that each volume should have a mix of "classic" novels (those works commonly taught in literature classes) and contemporary novels for which information is often hard to find. Because of the interest in expanding the canon of literature, an emphasis was also placed on including works by international, multicultural, and women novelists. Our advisory board members—educational professionals—helped pare down the list for each volume. If a work was not selected for the present volume, it was often noted as a possibility for a future volume. As always, the editor welcomes suggestions for titles to be included in future volumes.

How Each Entry Is Organized

Each entry, or chapter, in *NfS* focuses on one novel. Each entry heading lists the full name of the novel, the author's name, and the date of the novel's publication. The following elements are contained in each entry:

Introduction: a brief overview of the novel which provides information about its first appearance, its literary standing, any controversies surrounding the work, and major conflicts or themes within the work.

Author Biography: this section includes basic facts about the author's life, and focuses on events and times in the author's life that inspired the novel in question.

Plot Summary: a factual description of the major events in the novel. Lengthy summaries are broken down with subheads.

Characters: an alphabetical listing of major characters in the novel. Each character name is followed by a brief to an extensive description of the character's role in the novel, as well as discussion of the character's actions, relationships, and possible motivation.

Characters are listed alphabetically by last name. If a character is unnamed—for instance, the narrator in *Invisible Man*—the character is listed as "The Narrator" and alphabetized as "Narrator." If a character's first name is the only one given, the name will appear alphabetically by that name.

Variant names are also included for each character. Thus, the full name "Jean Louise

Finch" would head the listing for the narrator of *To Kill a Mockingbird*, but listed in a separate cross-reference would be the nickname "Scout Finch."

Themes: a thorough overview of how the major topics, themes, and issues are addressed within the novel. Each theme discussed appears in a separate subhead and is easily accessed through the boldface entries in the Subject/Theme Index.

Style: this section addresses important style elements of the novel, such as setting, point of view, and narration; important literary devices used, such as imagery, foreshadowing, symbolism; and, if applicable, genres to which the work might have belonged, such as Gothicism or Romanticism. Literary terms are explained within the entry but can also be found in the Glossary.

Historical Context: this section outlines the social, political, and cultural climate *in which the author lived and the novel was created*. This section may include descriptions of related historical events, pertinent aspects of daily life in the culture, and the artistic and literary sensibilities of the time in which the work was written. If the novel is a historical work, information regarding the time in which the novel is set is also included. Each section is broken down with helpful subheads.

Critical Overview: this section provides background on the critical reputation of the novel, including bannings or any other public controversies surrounding the work. For older works, this section includes a history of how the novel was first received and how perceptions of it may have changed over the years; for more recent novels, direct quotes from early reviews may also be included.

Criticism: an essay commissioned by *NfS* which specifically deals with the novel and is written specifically for the student audience, as well as excerpts from previously published criticism on the work (if available).

Sources: an alphabetical list of critical material used in compiling the entry, with full bibliographical information.

Further Reading: an alphabetical list of other critical sources which may prove useful for the student. It includes full bibliographical information and a brief annotation.

In addition, each entry contains the following highlighted sections, set apart from the main text as sidebars:

Media Adaptations: if available, a list of important film and television adaptations of the novel, including source information. The list also includes stage adaptations, audio recordings, musical adaptations, etc.

Topics for Further Study: a list of potential study questions or research topics dealing with the novel. This section includes questions related to other disciplines the student may be studying, such as American history, world history, science, math, government, business, geography, economics, psychology, etc.

Compare and Contrast: an "at-a-glance" comparison of the cultural and historical differences between the author's time and culture and late twentieth century or early twenty-first century Western culture. This box includes pertinent parallels between the major scientific, political, and cultural movements of the time or place the novel was written, the time or place the novel was set (if a historical work), and modern Western culture. Works written after the mid-1970s may not have this box.

What Do I Read Next?: a list of works that might complement the featured novel or serve as a contrast to it. This includes works by the same author and others, works of fiction and non-fiction, and works from various genres, cultures, and eras.

Other Features

NfS includes "The Informed Dialogue: Interacting with Literature," a foreword by Anne Devereaux Jordan, Senior Editor for *Teaching and Learning Literature* (*TALL*), and a founder of the Children's Literature Association. This essay provides an enlightening look at how readers interact with literature and how *Novels for Students* can help teachers show students how to enrich their own reading experiences.

A Cumulative Author/Title Index lists the authors and titles covered in each volume of the *NfS* series.

A Cumulative Nationality/Ethnicity Index breaks down the authors and titles covered in each volume of the *NfS* series by nationality and ethnicity.

A Subject/Theme Index, specific to each volume, provides easy reference for users who

may be studying a particular subject or theme rather than a single work. Significant subjects from events to broad themes are included, and the entries pointing to the specific theme discussions in each entry are indicated in **boldface**.

Each entry may include illustrations, including photo of the author, stills from film adaptations, maps, and/or photos of key historical events, if available.

Citing Novels for Students

When writing papers, students who quote directly from any volume of *Novels for Students* may use the following general forms. These examples are based on MLA style; teachers may request that students adhere to a different style, so the following examples may be adapted as needed.

When citing text from *NfS* that is not attributed to a particular author (i.e., the Themes, Style, Historical Context sections, etc.), the following format should be used in the bibliography section:

> "*Night*." *Novels for Students*. Ed. Marie Rose Napierkowski. Vol. 4. Detroit: Gale, 1998. 234–35.

When quoting the specially commissioned essay from *NfS* (usually the first piece under the "Criticism" subhead), the following format should be used:

> Miller, Tyrus. Critical Essay on "*Winesburg, Ohio*." *Novels for Students*. Ed. Marie Rose Napierkowski. Vol. 4. Detroit: Gale, 1998. 335–39.

When quoting a journal or newspaper essay that is reprinted in a volume of *NfS*, the following form may be used:

> Malak, Amin. "Margaret Atwood's *The Handmaid's Tale* and the Dystopian Tradition." *Canadian Literature* 112 (Spring 1987): 9–16. Excerpted and reprinted in *Novels for Students*. Vol. 4. Ed. Marie Rose Napierkowski. Detroit: Gale, 1998. 133–36.

When quoting material reprinted from a book that appears in a volume of *NfS*, the following form may be used:

> Adams, Timothy Dow. "Richard Wright: 'Wearing the Mask.'" In *Telling Lies in Modern American Autobiography*. University of North Carolina Press, 1990. 69–83. Excerpted and reprinted in *Novels for Students*. Vol. 1. Ed. Diane Telgen. Detroit: Gale, 1997. 59–61.

We Welcome Your Suggestions

The editorial staff of *Novels for Students* welcomes your comments and ideas. Readers who wish to suggest novels to appear in future volumes, or who have other suggestions, are cordially invited to contact the editor. You may contact the editor via e-mail at: **ForStudentsEditors@cengage.com.** Or write to the editor at:

Editor, *Novels for Students*
Gale
27500 Drake Road
Farmington Hills, MI 48331-3535

Literary Chronology

1478: Thomas More is born on February 6, in London, England.

1516: Thomas More's *Utopia* is published.

1535: Thomas More dies of execution by beheading on July 6, in London, England.

1775: Jane Austen is born on December 16, in Steventon, Hampshire, England.

1814: Jane Austen's *Mansfield Park* is published.

1817: Jane Austen dies of unknown medical causes on July 18, in Winchester, Hampshire, England.

1875: Thomas Mann is born Paul Thomas Mann on June 6, in Lübeck, Germany.

1883: Anzia Yezierska is born circa 1883 in Plotsk (or Plinsk), Poland.

1905: Ayn Rand is born Alice Rosenbaum on February 2, in St. Petersburg, Russia.

1908: Pat Frank is born on May 5, in Chicago, Illinois.

1918: Glendon Swarthout is born Glendon Fred Swarthout on April 8, in Pinckney, Michigan.

1920: Isaac Asimov is born on or around January 2, in Petrovichi, Russia.

1920: Ray Bradbury is born on August 22, in Waukegan, Illinois.

1924: Thomas Mann's *The Magic Mountain* is published in German as *Der Zauberberg*.

1925: Anzia Yezierska's *Bread Givers* is published.

1927: Thomas Mann's *Der Zauberberg* is published in English as *The Magic Mountain*.

1928: Robert Newton Peck is born on February 17, in Vermont.

1929: Thomas Mann is awarded the Nobel Prize for Literature.

1937: Sook Nyul Choi is born in Pyongyang, North Korea.

1938: Ayn Rand's *Anthem* is published.

1942: Isabel Allende is born on August 2, in Lima, Peru.

1947: Paulo Coelho is born on August 24, in Rio de Janeiro, Brazil.

1948: Alan Lightman is born on November 28, in Memphis, Tennessee.

1950: Isaac Asimov's *I, Robot* is published.

1955: Thomas Mann dies of atherosclerosis in Zurich, Switzerland, on August 12.

1959: Pat Frank's *Alas, Babylon* is published.

1962: Ray Bradbury's *Something Wicked This Way Comes* is published.

1964: Pat Frank dies on October 12, in Atlantic Beach, Florida.

1970: Anzia Yezierska dies on November 22, in Ontario, California.

1970: Glendon Swarthout's *Bless the Beasts and Children* is published.

1972: Robert Newton Peck's *A Day No Pigs Would Die* is published.

1982: Ayn Rand dies of heart failure on March 6, in New York, New York.

1985: Isabel Allende's *Eva Luna* is published in Spanish and will be published in English in 1988.

1988: Paulo Coelho's *The Alchemist* is published in Brazil as *O Alquimista*. The English version will be published in 1993.

1991: Sook Nyul Choi's *Year of Impossible Goodbyes* is published.

1992: Isaac Asimov dies of complications of AIDS on April 6, in New York, New York.

1992: Glendon Swarthout dies of emphysema, in Scottsdale, Arizona.

1993: Alan Lightman's *Einstein's Dreams* is published.

2007: Ray Bradbury receives a special citation for a distinguished career from the Pulitzer Board.

Acknowledgements

The editors wish to thank the copyright holders of the excerpted criticism included in this volume and the permissions managers of many book and magazine publishing companies for assisting us in securing reproduction rights. We are also grateful to the staffs of the Detroit Public Library, the Library of Congress, the University of Detroit Mercy Library, Wayne State University Purdy/Kresge Library Complex, and the University of Michigan Libraries for making their resources available to us. Following is a list of the copyright holders who have granted us permission to reproduce material in this volume of *NFS*. Every effort has been made to trace copyright, but if omissions have been made, please let us know.

COPYRIGHTED EXCERPTS IN *NFS*, VOLUME 29, WERE REPRODUCED FROM THE FOLLOWING PERIODICALS:

Clearing House, v. 64, July-August, 1991. Copyright © 1991 by Helen Dwight Reid Educational Foundation. Reproduced with permission of the Helen Dwight Reid Educational Foundation, published by Heldref Publications, 1319 18th Street, NW, Washington, DC 20036-1802.—*College Literature*, v. 29, fall, 2002. Copyright © 2002 by West Chester University. Reproduced by permission.—*Doctoral Forum: National Journal for Publishing and Mentoring Doctoral Student Research*, v. 4, 2007. Reproduced by permission.—*English Journal*, v. 61, January, 1972; v. 78, March, 1989. Copyright © 1972, 1989 by the National Council of Teachers of English. Both reproduced by permission of the publisher.—*English Review*, v. 11, April, 2001. Copyright 2001 Philip Allan Updates. Reproduced by permission.—*Explicator*, v. 56, summer, 1998; v. 57, summer, 1999. Copyright © 1998, 1999 by Helen Dwight Reid Educational Foundation. Both reproduced with permission of the Helen Dwight Reid Educational Foundation, published by Heldref Publications, 1319 18th Street, NW, Washington, DC 20036-1802.—*Foundation*, autumn, 2000 for "Reiterated Plots and Themes in the Robot Novels: Getting Away with Murder and Overcoming Programming" by Donald Palumbo. Reproduced by permission of the author.—*German Quarterly*, v. XXXVIII, November, 1965. Copyright © 1965 by the American Association of Teachers of German. Reproduced by permission.—*Germanic Review*, v. 74, spring, 1999 for "Magic Science on the Mountain: Science and Myth in Thomas Mann's 'Der Zauberberg'" by Malte Herwig. Copyright © 1999 Heldref Publications. Reproduced by permission of the author.—*Journal of Modern Literature*, v. 30, summer, 2007. Copyright © Indiana University Press. Reproduced by permission.—*Journal of Popular Culture*, v. 13, spring, 1980. Copyright © 1980 Basil Blackwell Ltd. Reproduced by permission of Blackwell Publishers.—*Kirkus Reviews*, v. 73, June 1, 2005. Copyright © 2005 by The Kirkus Service,

Inc. All rights reserved. Reproduced by permission of the publisher, *Kirkus Reviews* and Kirkus Associates, L.P.—***Lion and the Unicorn***, v. 28, 2004. Copyright © 2004 The Johns Hopkins University Press. Reproduced by permission.— ***MELUS***, v. 17, fall, 1991-1992. Copyright *MELUS: The Society for the Study of Multi-Ethnic Literature of the United States*, 1991. Reproduced by permission.—***Moreana***, v. 40, March, 2003. Reproduced by permission.— ***Mosaic: A Journal for the Interdisciplinary Study of Literature***, v. XIII, spring-summer, 1980. Copyright © Mosaic 1980. Acknowledgment of previous publication is herewith made.—***PMLA***, v. 78, June, 1963. Copyright © 1963 by the Modern Language Association of America. Reprinted by permission of the Modern Language Association of America.—***Publishers Weekly***, v. 238, December 20, 1991. Copyright © 1991 by Reed Publishing USA. Reproduced from *Publishers Weekly*, published by the Bowker Magazine Group of Cahners Publishing Co., a division of Reed Publishing USA, by permission.—***Romance Quarterly***, v. 51, fall, 2004. Copyright © 2004 by Helen Dwight Reid Educational Foundation. Reproduced with permission of the Helen Dwight Reid Educational Foundation, published by Heldref Publications, 1319 18th Street, NW, Washington, DC 20036-1802.—***Social Theory and Practice***, v. 33, October, 2007 for "Courageous Humility in Jane Austen's 'Mansfield Park'" by Jeanine M. Grenberg. Copyright © 2007 by Social Theory and Practice. Reproduced by permission of the publisher and the author.— ***Technology Review***, v. 96, May-June, 1993. © 1993 by the Association of Alumni and Alumnae of MIT. Reproduced by permission.— ***UNESCO Courier***, v. 51, March, 1998. Reprinted from the UNESCO Courier.—***Voice of Youth Advocates***, v. 14, December, 1991. Reproduced by permission.—***West Virginia University Philological Papers***, v. 53, fall, 2006 for "Magical Places in Isabel Allende's 'Eva Luna' and 'Cuentos de Eva Luna'" by Barbara Foley Buedel. Copyright © 2006 West Virginia University, Department of Foreign Languages. Reproduced by permission of the publisher and author.

COPYRIGHTED EXCERPTS IN *NFS*, VOLUME 29, WERE REPRODUCED FROM THE FOLLOWING BOOKS:

Reid, Robin Anne. From ***Ray Bradbury: A Critical Companion***. Greenwood Press, 2000. Copyright © 2000 by Robin Anne Reid. All rights reserved. Reproduced by permission of Greenwood Publishing Group, Inc., Westport, CT.—Valliant, James S. From ***The Passion of Ayn Rand's Critics: The Case Against the Brandens***. Durban House, 2005. Copyright © 2005, James S. Valliant. All rights reserved. Reproduced by permission.

Contributors

Susan Andersen: Andersen holds a Ph.D. in English and teaches literature and writing. Entry on *Bread Givers*. Original essay on *Bread Givers*.

Bryan Aubrey: Aubrey holds a Ph.D. in English. Entries on *Anthem* and *A Day No Pigs Would Die*. Original essays on *Anthem* and *A Day No Pigs Would Die*.

Catherine Dominic: Dominic is a novelist and a freelance writer and editor. Entries on *The Magic Mountain* and *Utopia*. Original essays on *The Magic Mountain* and *Utopia*.

Joyce M. Hart: Hart is a freelance writer and the author of literary essays and several books. Entries on *Alas, Babylon* and *Year of Impossible Goodbyes*. Original essays on *Alas, Babylon* and *Year of Impossible Goodbyes*.

Diane Andrews Henningfeld: Henningfeld is a professor of English who publishes widely on novels, short stories, and poetry. Entry on *I, Robot*. Original essay on *I, Robot*.

Sheri Metzger Karmiol: Karmiol has a doctorate in English Renaissance literature. She teaches literature and drama at the University of New Mexico, where she is a lecturer in the University Honors Program. Karmiol is also a professional writer and the author of several reference texts on poetry and drama. Entry on *Bless the Beasts and Children*. Original essay on *Bless the Beasts and Children*.

David Kelly: Kelly is a writer and instructor of creative writing and literature at two colleges in Illinois. Entry on *The Alchemist*. Original essay on *The Alchemist*.

Laura Pryor: Pryor has been a professional and creative writer for more than twenty years. Entry on *Eva Luna*. Original essay on *Eva Luna*.

Bradley A. Skeen: Skeen is a classics professor. Entry on *Mansfield Park*. Original essay on *Mansfield Park*.

Leah Tieger: Tieger is a freelance writer and editor. Entries on *Einstein's Dreams* and *Something Wicked This Way Comes*. Original essays on *Einstein's Dreams* and *Something Wicked This Way Comes*.

Alas, Babylon

PAT FRANK

1959

Pat Frank's *Alas, Babylon*, written almost fifty years ago, is considered a classic nuclear holocaust story. The novel is set in the 1950s during the cold war between the United States and the U.S.S.R. (Union of Soviet Socialist Republics, also known as the Soviet Union, which consisted of the country now known as Russia and numerous smaller, neighboring countries). In writing the novel, Frank used his knowledge of war and the potential consequences of a nuclear fallout, which he gained from years of working as a war correspondent and also as a special consultant on issues of war for President Franklin Roosevelt. The story remains relevant today, as the threat of nuclear devastation of the world continues to be a possibility.

At the novel's outset, Randy Bragg has recently failed to win the state senate election in the small town of Fort Repose, Florida, because he is considered too liberal. Randy is nice to the black people in town, and the majority of the white town folk are worried about the recent talk of civil rights. However, when the bombs start falling and scattering radioactivity and thugs begin using force to take whatever they want, Randy is the only person in town who is willing to reinstate order.

Alas, Babylon is a story of death and the horrors of living through a disaster worse than any the United States has ever faced. Yet it is also a story of love and compassion. Over the

course of the novel, Frank strips his characters down to the foundation of basic humanity. Money loses its worth. Communications to distant places are all but completely cut off. And the old social systems are obliterated. Factors like social status, age, and skin color no longer hold the same distinctions that they once did. Because of the disaster, people are forced to come together and face the challenge of survival.

AUTHOR BIOGRAPHY

Pat Frank is the pen name of Harry Hart Frank, who was born on May 5, 1908, in Chicago. He was the son of Harry Hart Frank, Sr., and Doris Cohen Frank. Frank attended the University of Florida for two years but dropped out to become a journalist. His first job as a reporter was for the Jacksonville, Florida *Journal*.

In 1929, Frank moved to New York so that he could work for the *New York Journal*. Next he moved to Washington, D.C., where he become involved in politics and government, reporting for the *Washington Herald*. Later, he was sent abroad to head the Washington Bureau of the Overseas News Agency. His work at the agency led to his gaining a position, in 1941, as assistant chief of the Office of War Information. Frank's work at this office, plus his three years as a war correspondent in Italy, Austria, and Turkey, won him a War Department Award in 1945.

After World War II, Frank retired from his journalistic and governmental positions and devoted his remaining years to writing. The topic of his nonfiction books was nuclear technology and weaponry, about which he was considered an expert. His novels include *Mr. Adam* (1946), a story about the only surviving fertile man left on the planet after an explosion in a bomb factory, and *An Affair of State* (1948), which explores the foibles of the U.S. government. In 1952, he published *Hold Back the Night*, based on the war in Korea. This was followed by *Forbidden Area* (1956), about the possibility of nuclear war; his fifth novel, *Alas, Babylon* (1959), takes this concept to fruition. It is for *Alas, Babylon* that Frank is best known.

From 1960 until his death on October 12, 1964, Frank wrote mostly nonfiction, including a book called *How to Survive the H-Bomb, and Why* (1962). Frank died in Atlantic Beach, Florida.

PLOT SUMMARY

Chapters 1–4

Alas, Babylon begins on a normal day in the small southern town of Fort Repose, Florida. Florence Wechek is on her way to work at the local Western Union telegraph station. Shortly after arriving, Florence calls Randy Bragg (the main character) to read an unusual telegram from Randy's brother, Mark. In the telegram, Mark, a U.S. Air Force colonel, tells Randy to meet him in Orlando the next day, as he has very important news to relate to his brother. The very end of the telegram reads, "Alas, Babylon." From these two closing words, Randy knows that disaster is pending, as the phrase was a boyhood code of theirs. The brothers had often heard this biblical phrase from Preacher Henry, the black minister of a local church. The preacher used this phrase to predict disasters he believed were imminent.

Mark is involved with Air Force intelligence. He lives in Omaha, Nebraska, with his wife, Helen, and their two children, Ben Franklin and a daughter named Peyton. In Omaha, the Air Force maintains a defense and communications center that is located in a deep hole in the earth, fortified against attack. When Randy meets Mark the next day, he learns that Mark is sending his wife and children to Florida to stay with Randy. Military intelligence is expecting a nuclear attack from Russia.

When Randy gets back to Fort Repose, he buys huge amounts of food and supplies. Some of the townspeople start talking about him, leaving Randy unsure as to how much he should tell them. He is concerned about causing a panic, but he does decide to tell the Henrys, an African American family living nearby, about the expected attack. Lib McGovern, who has become a close friend of Randy's, comes to visit, as does Dr. Dan Gunn, and Randy also tells both of them about the threat.

The story moves from Florida to the air over a U.S. aircraft carrier ship in the Mediterranean. A pilot, Ensign James "Peewee" Cobb, is surveying an enemy plane from his own jet. Cobb tries to get a fix on it. When he succeeds, he fires a missile, but the missile does not follow the path intended but rather falls to the ground and hits the Syrian port of Latakia, setting off a series of explosions. In the next scene, Mark is in Omaha. He and his fellow officers hear the news and begin initial procedures in preparation for retaliation by Russia.

Chapters 5–8

Everyone at Randy's house is suddenly awakened. Randy rushes outside and sees a light to the west, bright as the sun. Then there are more bomb blasts. Peyton, who was staring toward one of the bomb explosions, is temporarily blinded. In a short period of time, other blasts are felt. Randy drives to town to find Dr. Gunn for Peyton. Chaos has erupted in town. The doctor promises to come to Randy's house as soon as he can. While in town, Randy learns that all communications with the outside world have been destroyed. A rush of people attempt to withdraw their money from the bank. Stores are quickly emptied, and gas stations have run out of fuel. Soon the electricity is cut off.

Back home, Randy has a small battery-operated radio. On it he hears a message from Mrs. Josephine Vandruuker-Brown, who announces that she has been named the acting chief executive of the United States. She also announces that Washington, D.C., has been destroyed, along with most of the executive, legislative, and judicial members.

After the doctor treats Peyton's eyes, he and Randy discuss Fort Repose's radiation threat. They conclude that they might be safe, as the town enjoys a strong ocean breeze blowing in from the east that might keep radiation levels low. Later, Randy and Helen visit Admiral Sam Hazzard, who has a shortwave radio. He tells them that he has not heard any announcements coming out of Omaha since the bombs were dropped. He implies that there is little chance that Mark could have survived.

The next day, the dire conditions the people are under have begun to sink in, and people are panicking. They break into stores and loot everything they can find, including all of the medicine from the pharmacy. Randy has cash but realizes that soon money is not going to be worth anything, so he does not mind paying ridiculously high prices for the remaining staples, like salt, that the grocer was saving. While in town, Randy finds the doctor at his clinic. A local policeman is lying at the doctor's feet, having been shot dead. Thugs have broken into the clinic and demanded all the doctor's drugs.

That night, Randy insists that the doctor stay with them so as to be protected. After dinner, they

hear a broadcast that enumerates all the U.S. cities that have been destroyed. The whole state of Florida has been classified as a contaminated zone—no one can leave without going through an official health check to determine their level of radioactivity.

In the following days, Randy, the McGoverns, and the Henrys, along with Florence and Dr. Gunn, pool their strengths and skills to ensure the group's survival. They develop a plumbing system that takes advantage of an old artesian well. They catch fish and hunt armadillos and quail. The Henrys share their chickens and eggs. And the librarian, Alice, teaches them how to identify edible mushrooms and wild plants.

Chapters 9–13

Randy hears a bulletin on the radio that suggests that people in the military reserves who are not on active duty should organize their towns and enforce the laws. Because Randy was an officer in the reserves, he takes this message as his cue to administer authority in town. This comes none too soon, as one night the doctor goes missing. He has been beaten by some thugs, and his car and remaining supplies are gone. Randy goes to the admiral to get advice on how to catch the men who attacked the doctor. The admiral, before he retired, had been involved in war intelligence and battle tactics. Randy and the admiral work through several plans. Lib suggests they go to Rita, an old girlfriend of Randy's. Rita is the biggest trader in town and has stored huge supplies of everything she could get her hands on. They know that Rita has an old grocery delivery truck and some gasoline. They will use the truck to help them catch the criminals.

Randy and his men drill holes in the back of the truck through which they can see and shoot their guns. The plan is for Malachai Henry to drive, while Randy, the admiral, and Bill McGovern ride in the back. A couple of days later, they see the thugs following them in a car. In a matter of minutes, Randy and his men attack. All the outlaws are killed except for one. Randy temporarily spares the man's life so that he can hang him and use him as an example of what will happen to anyone else who breaks the law. Unfortunately, Malachai was also shot, and he dies.

Near the story's end, Randy and Lib are getting married. There is also a suggestion that Helen and the doctor are in love. In November, about one year after the bombs fell, a U.S.

military helicopter circles Randy's house. When it lands, Colonel Paul Hunt, whom Randy met in Orlando when he went there to meet his brother, steps out. Hart tells Randy about all the U.S. cities that have been destroyed, and he tells Helen that there is no chance that her husband, Mark, could have survived. Hart also tells them that they are establishing a headquarters at Patrick Air Force Base on the east coast of Florida. He says that they are all invited to start a new community there, but no one in Randy's group wants to go. Just before Hart leaves, Randy asks him who won the war. The colonel tells Randy that the United States did but that it really does not matter, referring to the fact that much of the world has been destroyed.

CHARACTERS

Ben Franklin Bragg
Ben Franklin is the son of Mark and Helen Bragg. He is thirteen years old when he is first introduced. Ben is forthcoming in his conversations with adults. His parents have been very honest and direct with him, which pleasantly surprises his uncle Randy when Ben goes to live in Florida.

Helen Bragg
Helen is Mark's wife and Ben Franklin and Peyton's mother. Normally, Helen has a clear head, strength in the midst of calamity, and a willingness to do more than her share of the work. Helen becomes weakened, however, in the middle of this story when she must face the realization that her husband has died in the nuclear explosion in Omaha. She transfers her feelings for her husband to Randy. She tries to insist that Randy has become Mark. This is only a temporary madness that passes. Later, Helen falls in love with Dr. Gunn, but she insists on waiting for an official declaration of her husband's death before she gives in to her love.

Mark Bragg
Mark is Helen's husband and Randy's older brother. Mark is a high-ranking officer in the Air Force, specializing in military intelligence. Suspecting that a war is pending, he insists that his wife and children leave Omaha and move in with Randy in Florida. Mark is involved in only two scenes in the story, but his influence is felt through his brother and his wife throughout the remaining chapters.

Peyton Bragg
Peyton is the ten-year-old daughter of Mark and Helen Bragg. She is often lost in the shadow of her older brother, Ben Franklin. This is due not only to the fact that she is younger but also to her being a girl.

Randy Bragg
Randy is the main character of the story. He is the younger brother of Mark. Randy is in his thirties and has never been married. At the beginning of the story, Randy does not know what to do with himself. Lib tells him he should move to a bigger city and find something he wants to do. She likes Randy but is afraid the town is killing him psychologically. Randy has started to drink too much.

Once Randy is forced to face the nuclear destruction and fight for his survival, he turns a corner. He stops drinking and begins caring about the people around him. He takes charge when no one else is willing to do so. As Randy's image of himself improves and he finds ways to keep the people put in his charge alive, his feeling of pride helps him accept Lib's love. Although Colonel Hart gives Randy a chance to leave Fort Repose and return to the twentieth century by living in a better-structured community on the coast, Randy decides to stay right where he is. Something about having to figure out how to do the most basic things, like frontier people had to do, brings Randy alive. He loves the challenges and the sense of accomplishment he gets from facing them.

Ensign James "Peewee" Cobb
Cobb is the young Air Force pilot who chases an enemy spy plane away from a U.S. military ship. In the process of trying to shoot the spy plane down, Cobb accidentally fires a missile that makes impact on a Syrian harbor. That event is the excuse that Russia needs to start the nuclear war.

Alice Cooksey
Alice is the local librarian and Florence's good friend. Before the disaster the library was mostly ignored, but after all communications are shut down, people flock to the library to help pass the time away and to learn about survival. Alice moves in with Florence for company. She becomes involved with Randy's extended family by helping to teach Ben Franklin, Peyton, and Caleb.

Dr. Dan Gunn

Dr. Dan Gunn is Fort Repose's only surviving doctor. Gunn is a close friend of Randy's, and like his friend, Gunn helps to keep the town functioning after the bombs have been dropped. He suffers a brutal beating from some thugs who want his car and his drugs. Gunn has limited knowledge about radioactivity and knows specific procedures that must be followed to deal with it. After moving in with Randy's family, Dr. Gunn falls in love with Helen.

Colonel Paul Hart

Hart appears only briefly in the story. At the end, Hart lands in Fort Repose in a helicopter, the first outsider to come to the town after the devastation. He tells Randy that Patrick Air Force Base is untouched and invites Randy and his family to move there if they want to.

Admiral Sam Hazzard

Hazzard was once a leader in the U.S. Navy. Besides fighting naval battles, Hazzard was also involved in military intelligence. His background helps Randy and the others understand what might be going on in the world despite their lack of direct contact with officials. Hazzard has a shortwave radio and because of his military background is able to decipher the military code used in communications. Hazzard also helps Randy make a plan for snaring the criminals who beat up the doctor.

Reverend Clarence Henry

Clarence Henry, most often referred to as the Preacher, is the patriarch of the Henry family. He is a wise old man, especially when it comes to surviving off the land. He is especially good at fishing. It was the Preacher who used the phrase "Alas, Babylon" during his Sunday sermons. Whenever the Preacher mentioned the sins of the common person, he would then warn his congregation that if these sins were perpetuated, cities would be destroyed, as stated in the Bible. Though they did not attend church, Randy and Mark, as young boys, used to sit outside the Preacher's church and listen to his sermons. This is how they picked up the phrase, which then became their secret code for impending trouble.

Hannah Henry

Hannah is the Preacher's wife. She only appears in the scene of her son Malachai's death.

Malachai Henry

Malachai Henry is about Randy's age. He is a quiet man who goes out of his way to help those around him. When it comes time to catch the men who have beaten up the doctor, Malachai volunteers to take on the driver's position. He successfully plays the role of a submissive black man, luring the thugs into believing he is an easy target. This costs Malachai his life.

Missouri Henry

Missouri is Two Tone's wife. She is the cleaning woman in the neighborhood, a good-natured woman who respects Randy and his family.

Two Tone Henry

Two Tone, so named because of discolored patches on his otherwise dark face, is the Preacher's oldest son and Missouri's husband. Two Tone comes up with a plan for raising sugar cane, which he will later mix with some corn to create a homemade liquor. After the devastation, a good strong drink is better than money in the bartering system that is established in the town.

Rita Hernandez

Rita is an old girlfriend of Randy's. She is described as beautiful and seductive. Having been poor most of her life, Rita collects superfluous material objects that the townspeople give away almost for free after the bombings. Randy turns to Rita when looking for a vehicle and some gasoline in order to catch the criminals who are stalking the community.

Bill McGovern

Bill is Lib's father and Lavinia's husband. Bill is not very happy in his retirement, but when Randy tells him, after the bombs have fallen, that the group needs his mechanical skills, Bill snaps back to life. Prior to this, he was feeling suicidal. He is a rather grouchy old man until he is put to use. Bill even grabs a gun when necessary and goes on the hunt for the thugs who beat up the doctor.

Elizabeth "Lib" McGovern

Elizabeth, or Lib, is the adult daughter of Bill and Lavinia. She has fallen in love with Randy. She encourages Randy to leave Fort Repose so that he might find some kind of job that excites him. She thinks that Fort Repose is too small for him. She promises to follow him once he becomes established, but then the war comes. Lib turns out to be very resourceful in finding food in unlikely places, like at the tops of tall palm trees that she climbs. Lib comments, at least once, that she does not feel that the men really know her or respect her ideas. This is the late 1950s, when women were supposed to take on rather submissive roles. However, Lib comes up with the idea for how the men can entrap the criminals who beat up Dr. Gunn. Like Peyton, who also feels neglected and disregarded by the men, Lib proves that she has a brain and can think up creative solutions for the good of the group.

Lavinia McGovern

Lavinia's role is very minor. She is a sickly woman and succumbs to death because of diabetes fairly soon after the war has started.

Patricia Vanbruuker-Brown

Patricia, who has been the head of Health, Education and Welfare, is suddenly thrust into the role of acting chief executive of the United States. This is due to the total destruction of Washington, D.C., and all the other major heads of government. She makes announcements over the shortwave radio about what has happened to the United States.

Florence Wechek

Florence is a neighbor of Randy's who works at the local Western Union station. In the beginning of the story, she does not like Randy. She thinks he is lazy and spoiled. She also believes that he has been spying on her with his binoculars. Florence is in her forties and has never been married. She is a bit nosey and likes to spread gossip. After the bombs fall, she becomes almost heroic in her commitment to keeping the cable office open in case communications are restored. She also pitches in by using her creative problem solving to help make ends meet and by providing goods for her neighbors.

THEMES

War

Although the superpowers of the 1950s, the Soviet Union and the United States, thankfully realized that a nuclear war could not be won by either side because of the resultant destruction, Frank's novel *Alas, Babylon* imagines what would have happened if those two countries had decided to play out such a nuclear scene. In Frank's book, the war begins with a somewhat innocent accident—an errant missile hitting a Soviet-protected country. That event is all that is needed in the tense situation; war quickly ensues.

Frank's book was written after fifty years of intense wars. Between the early 1900s and 1959, when the novel was published, three major wars took place: World War I, World War II, and the Korean War. Afterward, another war was also looming—the war in Vietnam. Thus, the possibility of a nuclear holocaust was not too hard to envision. Frank uses the imminent threat of such a war to promote peace. He demonstrates through his novel the concept that the leaders of the United States and the Soviet Union fully understood: no one wins a nuclear war. Both countries in this novel are devastated by war. Frank claims that because of the radiation caused by the bombs, the affected areas might not be inhabitable for another thousand years. As the characters fight for their survival, they realize that civilization has been forced to retreat back into the Dark Ages, living without most of the conveniences and inventions that were created throughout the years. They are set back to primitive times, with their main focus in life being on finding food and keeping warm. Can people survive war? Yes, this story points out. But at what cost? And in what condition?

Breakdown of Society

Societies are formed to protect inhabitants and provide services. In Frank's novel, the author shows how quickly a society can break down under extreme pressure caused by a holocaust. Many basic things are affected, like communications and infrastructure. Electricity is shut off, so no broadcasts are available through radio or television. No mail arrives, and no mail or telegrams can be sent out. With the loss of electricity comes the loss of refrigeration, a convenient means of keeping food and medicine fresh. Money, the currency with which almost all transactions are conducted, comes to hold little or no worth, such that those who count on money as their safeguard against hunger or for self-protection can no longer rely on it. Food, which once was so readily available at the neighborhood grocery store, is no longer there and will not be brought by trucks or trains from other parts of the state or country. The only food that residents can count on is the food they catch or raise. This increases

TOPICS FOR FURTHER STUDY

- Fort Repose is a fictional city in Florida. However, the author provides geographical clues to where the city might have existed. Create a map of Florida that demarcates the devastation that occurs in this story, and place Fort Repose where you think it might have been located. Research the Air Force bases that are mentioned and find out why these places were targeted. Present your findings to your class.

- Reread *Alas, Babylon*, paying particular attention to the issues of race that are an undercurrent in the novel. How are the Henrys depicted? Are they treated similarly to the white characters? What roles do the Henrys play? Do you notice any stereotypes in how they are described? What are the relationships between the whites and the blacks in this story? Jot down notes as you are reading, and then lead a discussion group in your class. Be prepared to keep the discussion on track and to provide stimulating questions should the discussion die out.

- Recreate of the town of Fort Repose on a map or as a three-dimensional model. Identify the following places: all the houses on River Road, including the houses of Florence, Randy, the Henrys, and the McGoverns; Marines Park; Rita's house; and the major businesses in town (grocery store, doctor's clinic, the bank, the mortuary, the library, and the Western Union station). Many of these places are described in the novel. If you cannot find precise locations in the text, use your imagination.

- Read Cormac McCarthy's Pulitzer Prize-winning book *The Road*, another novel about catastrophe. Then compare this novel with Frank's *Alas, Babylon*. Provide your class with a synopsis of McCarthy's novel, then give a presentation in which you explain and analyze the two books' similarities and differences. Some questions you may choose to address in your presentation include: What are the overall tones of the two novels? Do either of them offer hope? How do the authors' writing styles compare? Would you recommend these books to your classmates? Why or why not?

---

competition, as hungry residents vie for whatever their surroundings give them. Those who lack the skills needed to stave off their hunger must learn to beg or steal.

As these shortages or absences of supplies and resources become more and more familiar, law and order fall apart. There are no longer any universal or enforced codes by which to live, as all aspects of life have been rearranged or redefined. Those people who lack or choose to ignore morals will take from those around them who are weaker than they are. As such, any possessor of a gun may be motivated to create his or her own rules. Randy owns a gun and, rather than acting immorally, demonstrates the courage not only to bring his society back to a functional level but

also to demand that others see him as the moral authority. Ben Franklin does the same when he asserts with a gun that the animals on the farm are meant for humans, not for the dog that has gone wild. Both Ben Franklin and Randy attempt to restructure society by creating new rules.

Survival

The main emphasis in this story is on survival. Randy, thanks to his brother's warning that a huge disaster is about to happen, is a step ahead of everyone else. He thus thinks ahead about what the impending disaster will mean. Though he has money, he knows it will be worth very little after supplies become scarce. He also knows too that some supplies will be worth more than

Chain gang (*Ed Clark | Time & Life Pictures | Getty Images*)

others. He figures out which ones will be most necessary to help him and his family to survive and buys them before there is a rush on the stores.

As the story progresses, Randy uses the knowledge that pulling family and friends together will give them a better chance of surviving. His friends and neighbors all have special gifts through which they can provide needed materials or intelligence. Randy and most of the others have creative intelligence, so when they have no means of obtaining necessary objects, they are clever enough to improvise. Some of the people in his

group also have a keen understanding of what nature can supply them, and they research books to help them locate necessities such as salt and proteins in unusual places and forms. The author demonstrates through this story that adaptability and cooperation are traits that are needed for survival under pressure.

Love

Through all the carnage in this novel and the ongoing fight to live, there is an undercurrent of love. This is first exposed as Mark and Randy meet in Orlando. Mark suspects that there is a good chance he will not make it through a nuclear war, as he works in one of the enemy's main targets. Mark expresses to Randy how much he loves his wife, Helen, and asks Randy to take good care of his family, knowing that he may never see them again. Mark sacrifices his life out of love for his country and his family.

In the midst of this catastrophe in her life, Helen, emotionally overburdened, thinks she has fallen in love with Randy. This occurs because she transfers her feelings of love for her presumed-dead husband to Randy. Randy, who has respect and love for both Helen and his brother, does not take advantage of Helen's weakened spirit. He senses that something is wrong and tries to make Helen understand that he is not his brother. Helen eventually comes back to her senses. Later, she develops a friendship with Dr. Gunn but refuses to allow herself to fall in love with him because she does not officially know if her husband is dead. She honors her love for her husband by controlling her emotions this time.

The main love story is that between Randy and Lib McGovern. Theirs is also a strong love, as well as a very rational one. In the beginning of the story, Lib shows that she is willing to sacrifice her need to be with Randy when she tells him to get out of Fort Repose because she thinks the small town is hurting him psychologically. Then, after the bombing, Lib and Randy work as a team to protect their families and the neighbors who live close by. They share their love for one another with those who are in need around them. Not until others are taken care of do they take the time to enjoy the privacy of their feelings for one another.

STYLE

Transitions in Point of View

Frank uses an omniscient third-person narrator in *Alas, Babylon*. The author switches back and forth from one scenario to another, from one character to another, telling the story from different points of view. For example, Frank begins his novel with the narrator telling the story from Florence Wechek's point of view. The narrator recounts not only Florence's actions but also her feelings, suspicions, and memories. This use of an omniscient narrator—one who is privileged to know characters' inner dialogues—is

not unusual; indeed, many authors use this technique. However, the manner in which Frank transitions from one character to another is fairly unique.

The first transition occurs between Florence and Randy in the early stages of the first chapter. Florence has noticed Randy sitting on his front porch, holding a pair of binoculars and looking Florence's way. She then leaves to go to work. There is a space break in the narration (an extra few lines of space between paragraphs), and then the story picks up from Randy's point of view. The first line narrated through Randy's perspective tells readers that Randy sees Florence's car drive by the front porch of his house. Thus, the author connects the two different points of view by linking them. First, the narrator is with Florence, looking at Randy, and then the narrator is with Randy watching Florence.

In the second chapter, the narrator observes two characters together: Florence and Alice are having lunch. Most of the text in this section is the dialogue between the two friends, but when there is a reflection or thought, the narrator relates only Florence's inner dialogue. A little later on, after another space break, the narrator leaves Florence and follows Alice back to her place of work, the library. At this point the narrator is now privy only to Alice's thoughts.

Another example of such a relational transition in point of view occurs at the end of the third chapter. The narrator relates that at 7 p.m., Randy is listening to the news on the radio before falling asleep for the night. Then there is a space break. The next paragraph begins with a statement of the corresponding time in the Mediterranean (where a U.S. Navy ship is watching a spy plane), thus connecting the two different points of view, from one side of the world to the other.

Historical Flashback

To provide a deeper understanding of the setting of Fort Repose, Florida, as well as to give a fuller account of the lives and the relationships of some of the characters, the author uses flashbacks to the time when Fort Repose was first established by Randy's ancestor, Lieutenant Randolph Rowzee Peyton. This storyline signifies Randy's deep roots in the town, helping to introduce Randy and his situation. By providing the historical flashbacks, the author gives Randy's predicament more meaning. One of the reasons for Randy's political defeat is his friendship and support of the African American population in the town. In the traditions of the South, Randy is considered a traitor to his heritage for his support of civil rights for black people. Randy's support of the Henrys, his black neighbors, becomes more interesting when readers learn that the Henrys arrived in Fort Repose at the same time as Randy's ancestors; the Henrys were Randy's family's slaves.

Another benefit of this storyline told through historic flashbacks is that it helps to explain why, at the end of the story, Randy does not want to leave Fort Repose, despite the hardships he and his family are experiencing. Although Colonel Hart offers his family the opportunity to start a new life on the east coast of Florida, near Patrick Air Force Base, Randy wants to stay in his ancestral home.

Southern Setting

The southern setting influences the story in several ways. First, as the novel opens, Randy has been defeated in his bid for the Florida State Senate. One of the reasons for his defeat was his friendship and support of the African American population in the town. Randy believed in integration, which the federal government was supporting. Nevertheless, there in Florida, deep in the South, the white voters distanced themselves from Randy for his so-called radical stance. In the South in the 1950s, before integration, there was a very strict divide between whites and blacks, not only in school but also in most aspects of public life.

One other condition of the southern setting is that survival through the winter is challenging but not as devastating as if the story had been set in a northern location like New England. In central Florida, a fireplace is enough to keep the chill of a winter night at bay. For most of the winter, cool weather crops can be grown, and wild plants can still be harvested, whereas in the North, all plant life is dormant. Because the author lived in Florida, the state might have been a natural choice for a setting rather than a choice designed to make the characters' challenges easier. Nonetheless, the decision to set the story in the South affected both the plot of the story and the tone.

HISTORICAL CONTEXT

The Creation, Use, and Effects of the Nuclear Bomb

When the U.S. government learned that Nazi Germany was working on the creation of a nuclear bomb, President Franklin D. Roosevelt ordered a focused and expedited project run by U.S. scientists to do the same. Thus the Manhattan Project was established.

For the creation of the bomb, a labor-intensive process to extract the isotope uranium-235 was needed. To this end, the government supported the construction of a secret laboratory at Oak Ridge, Tennessee. One of the principal participants at this lab was Harold Urey, of Columbia University, who helped devise the extraction process through which the isotope would be obtained. Working with him was Ernest Lawrence, from the University of California at Berkeley. Another scientist, Robert Oppenheimer, became the head of a lab at another site, in Los Alamos, New Mexico. Oppenheimer was in charge of testing the first nuclear explosion. This first test of an atomic bomb occurred on July 16, 1945.

The atomic bomb was dropped twice by the United States as a weapon of war. On August 6, 1945, one bomb was dropped on Hiroshima, Japan, causing the deaths of approximately 66,000 people; another 69,000 people were immediately injured. Physical damage to the area stretched out some three miles, with everything in sight burning. Three days later, the United States dropped another atomic bomb, on Nagasaki, Japan. This time, 39,000 people died instantly, and over 25,000 others were immediately injured. The next day, Japan surrendered.

The Cold War and the Nuclear Arms Race

A cold war (referring to a type of conflicted state relationship without actual warlike confrontation) developed between the United States and the U.S.S.R. after World War II. Ironically, the United States and the Soviet Union had fought as allies during World War II. Although some might imagine that the two nations had been friendly toward one another during that war, this was not the case. The two countries came together because they had a common enemy—Nazi Germany. The Germans had invaded the Soviet Union and Europe. And after Japan attacked the American fleet at Pearl Harbor, the

COMPARE & CONTRAST

- **1950s:** What becomes known as the cold war between the United States and the Soviet Union threatens the peace and safety of the world, as both countries vie for military dominance.

  Today: After the terrorist attacks on September 11, 2001, several countries join forces in what is called the War on Terrorism, a unified effort to stop further terrorist attacks.

- **1950s:** Huge stockpiles of nuclear weapons exist in both the Soviet Union and the United States.

  Today: Although their supplies are small, countries such as North Korea develop their nuclear plants and weapons capabilities.

- **1950s:** Segregation in the South leads African Americans to engage in civil disobedience in attempts to secure their civil rights.

  Today: Although segregation was outlawed through the Civil Rights Act of 1964, racial divides still exist in neighborhoods and schools in both the North and the South.

United States was pulled into the war, to fight Japan in the Pacific and Germany on the European continent.

Although the Soviet Union supported the Allied troops, the United States did not trust the Soviet Union. This lack of trust continued after the war. The U.S. government was concerned that the Soviets were attempting to spread Communism throughout the world, including in the United States. Although labor unions slowly but successfully grew during the 1950s and 1960s in the United States under the influence of communist theory, the Communist Party did not thrive. Communism is a socioecomonic system in which the public owns the means of production and wealth is shared equally, as opposed to a capitalist system, in which private individuals own the means of production and are free to accumulate wealth. As the United States is a capitalist system, philosophically the two countries were at odds.

After the United States dropped the two atomic bombs on Japan to end World War II, the Soviet Union feared the military power of the United States. The Soviet Union thus began to develop a stockpile of weapons of mass destruction of their own. This amounted to an arms race, as both countries continued to top the other in mass and in power in terms of weaponry. Some use the date of the signing of the Intermediate-Range Nuclear Forces Treaty in 1987 by the Soviet Union and the United States to mark the end of the cold war. On that date, Mikhail Gorbachev, the leader of the Soviet Union, and U.S. President Ronald Reagan met to sign a historic agreement by which they both agreed to eliminate certain nuclear and conventional missiles.

Life in the 1950s

Many younger readers can have only a limited understanding of how much life has changed in the United States over the past fifty or so years; many facts of daily life were much different in the 1950s. On the economic side, incomes and expenses were scaled dramatically lower. A family could buy an average house for about twelve thousand dollars. To go to the movies, an adult ticket cost one dollar. At the grocery store, a loaf of regular bread cost twenty cents. A gallon of gas cost a quarter.

It was in the 1950s that the first Barbie doll was produced. Two new states were added to the Union that decade: Alaska in 1958 and Hawaii the following year. The Soviet Union outpaced the United States in space exploration by launching the first satellite to circle the earth in 1957. Jack Kilbyk, in 1959, received a patent for the design of the first microchip. The 1950s also brought the birth of rock and roll and the rising

Mushroom cloud (*National Archives and Records Administration [NARA]*)

popularity of a radical new singer, Elvis Presley. The fourteen-year-old Bobby Fischer became the U.S. chess champion and would later go on to beat the Soviets' best player, Boris Spassky.

CRITICAL OVERVIEW

Frank's *Alas, Babylon* is considered by critics and many readers to be a classic atomic holocaust novel. Whenever this genre is mentioned, Frank's novel is one of about four or five that are named as must-reads. *Alas, Babylon* is also often considered the author's best work of fiction.

Though Frank's novel carries this reputation, some critics have found fault with the book. The general sentiment among reviewers is that *Alas, Babylon* provides a detailed glimpse into what might happen after a nuclear bomb is dropped and how people might survive the aftermath. However, Orville Prescott remarks in his 1959 review for the *New York Times* that Frank demonstrates "minimum competence in characterization and no ability whatever to convey the emotional atmosphere of a time of supreme crisis." Prescott does admit that "Frank commands a crisp, readable style and has an inventive imagination for practical details and small incidents."

A similar sentiment is expressed by David Dempsey, writing for the *New York Times Book Review*, also in 1959. Dempsey refers to Frank's novel as a "manual for survival," which he says "might just be worth keeping around." Dempsey's criticism is that even though Frank's book is "provocative," it "never comes to grips with the more important question of just what kind of guilt his modern Babylonians are paying for." This is a reference to the biblical phrase that is used as the title, alluding to its use by Preacher Henry to warn his parishioners to live a good life without sin. In other words, if the biblical Babylon was destroyed for the breaking of moral rules, then what sins were committed to lead to the nuclear devastation in the novel?

In a more recent review as well, written by Viv Holmes for the publication *Countryside and Small Stock Journal* in 2003, the emphasis is on *Alas, Babylon* being more like a survival guide than a novel. Holmes states, "To me this is a resource book and will always be in my home library." Holmes does call the book "enlightening," but she uses this word in reference to learning what the characters in Frank's novel have to do to survive, not in reference to Frank's literary style.

CRITICISM

Joyce Hart

Hart is a freelance writer and author of literary essays and several books. In this essay, she explores the roles of women as depicted by Pat Frank in Alas, Babylon.

Given that Frank's novel *Alas, Babylon* was published before the second wave of feminism (roughly in the 1960s and 1970s), the female characters in his novel are somewhat dated. For the most part women are cast as stereotypes, such as the gossip, the homemaker, the maid, the seductress, the good wife, the cook, and the grieving mother. They are incapable of creative thoughts; they are frail; they have no leadership qualities. The stereotypes are not always blatant, as some are colorfully and carefully concealed. Nonetheless, they are there. And if one takes the time to look for them, they are quite easy to see.

WHAT DO I READ NEXT?

- Frank's *Hold Back the Night* (1952) provides readers with a detailed account of the Korean War. The story follows a group of U.S. Marines who refuse to give up on their assignment in a difficult war.

- In 1985, Larry Niven published *Footfall*, which was nominated for the Hugo Award for best science fiction novel of the year and remains a science fiction favorite. The story is about an alien invasion. Unlike some other fictional alien characters, Niven's aliens are actually very strange; they are not just altered human beings.

- Stephen King's *The Stand* (1978) is an apocalyptic horror story, with the main action revolving around the consequences of a killer flu being accidentally released from a military compound. The virus wipes out almost the entire population of the world. The people who are left assemble into two distinct groups, the good versus the evil.

- In 1987, Robert McCammon published his *Swan Song*, which went on to become the co-winner of that year's Bram Stoker Award for best horror novel. Often compared to King's *The Stand*, the catastrophe in this novel is nuclear fallout. Interesting characters fight for their survival against powerful enemies.

- Cormac McCarthy's *The Road*, published in 2006, is a Pulitzer Prize–winning postapocalyptic novel. In sparse prose, McCarthy tells the story of a father and son who work their way across America to the southern part of the East Coast, searching for tidbits of food, scraps of clothing, and anything else to help keep them alive.

- In 2005 the Carnegie Endowment for International Peace published a study called *Deadly Arsenals: Nuclear, Biological, and Chemical Threats*, written by Joseph Cirincione, Jon B. Wolfsthal, and Miriam Rajkumar. The authors list and define various weapons that readers may have heard mentioned in news stories. This reference book also discusses the governments around the world that may have developed and stockpiled these weapons.

The story begins with Florence Wechek, who is labeled a gossip within the first four lines of the novel. The narrator later adjusts this pronouncement slightly by stating that Florence is prudent about choosing the topics of her gossip. She censors herself and does not tell anything scandalous. However, the narrator then dismissively excuses Florence's inclination to spread stories: she gossips, the narrator suggests, because she is an unmarried woman—a spinster—and an old one at that. She has nothing better to do with her time but gossip, it is implied, because she has no life. Randy, the main character, on the other hand, is also unmarried, but there are no derogatory references to his single status. He drinks too much, but that is merely bad for his health. Randy is not a menace to his community, at least not like Florence; he is only a menace to himself.

Besides being a gossip, Florence also has a wild imagination, the narrator continues. Her imagination is not wild in a good sense that suggests a positive and creative intelligence. Rather, Florence's imagination is used to think up stupid fantasies. The stupid fantasy that Florence has that morning is that Randy is trying to catch a Peeping-Tom glimpse of Florence as she is dressing. Randy is actually bird-watching, readers learn later, which confirms the impression that Florence is a fool.

The author does give Florence one positive attribute. This occurs after the bomb has destroyed all communications to the outside world. Florence

> FOR THE MOST PART WOMEN ARE CAST AS STEREOTYPES, SUCH AS THE GOSSIP, THE HOMEMAKER, THE MAID, THE SEDUCTRESS, THE GOOD WIFE, THE COOK, AND THE GRIEVING MOTHER."

is dutiful to an extreme then, riding her bike down unpoliced roads in her commitment to keep the cable lines secure should a message finally come through. She also makes socks. Everyone is running out of socks, and she saves their poor feet. Yet this act places Florence back into the domestic arena, the stereotypical realm of duty for women.

Another woman who is cast in a domestic role is Missouri, the black cleaning woman. According to the narrator, she loves cleaning. She loves it so much that she wraps rags around her feet and dances as she waxes the floor. The narrator also refers to her as the maid. She cleans her own home, Randy's, and the McGoverns'.

Missouri is also the stereotypical long-suffering woman. She has a no-good husband, Two Tone, who is usually drunk. She also suffers through Mrs. Lavinia McGovern, who is a racist. Mrs. McGovern drives Missouri crazy, following her around the McGovern house while wearing white gloves and wiping her fingers across everything that Missouri has touched. She wants to make sure that Missouri has caught every particle of dust. Indeed, Mrs. McGovern is another stereotypical female. She and Missouri sit on opposite ends of a spectrum. Missouri has been downtrodden all her life, living in the segregated South; Mrs. McGovern is a rich, spoiled, white woman from the North who has nothing better to do than intimidate and belittle Missouri.

Mrs. McGovern's daughter, Lib (which is supposedly a shortened version of her formal name, which is Elizabeth, though it could be a shortened version of the word *liberated*) is nothing like her mother. But even Lib is a rather stiff, cardboard figure of a woman. Randy, who has fallen in love with Lib, tends to discount Lib's strengths: "She bewildered him. She was brash, unpredictable, and sometimes uncomfortably outspoken." In other words, Lib has an intelligence

and a mind of her own. Randy is threatened by her, so he turns her assets into something negative.

The narrator then describes Lib in terms of her physicality. This is where the narrator describes Lib's true assets as both Randy and Lib see them. She is not a great beauty, the narrator (or Randy) thinks, but she does have a great pair of legs, it is reported. The author even has Lib define herself in terms of what parts of her body lure men and what parts do not. And when Lib tells Randy something serious, when she is not being playful with him like a child, he sees her mouth as being "drawn into a taut, colorless line"—something that sounds unattractive.

At one point in the story, when Randy is scheming with Admiral Hazzard about how to catch the men who beat up the doctor, Lib wants to assert herself, but she resists. She states, to herself, that the admiral makes her feel like a member of the kitchen staff bringing in the coffee and serving the men, as if that is all she is good for. Then she tells herself that these thoughts of hers are "silly," and she curls up on a couch and tries to make herself "inconspicuous." Soon after comes the line "Lib started to speak but decided it would be unwise." Readers have to wonder where these feelings of inferiority and hesitation are coming from. If this is a liberated, outspoken woman, would she be having these types of thoughts? Or do these comments come from a male author who wants to keep his female characters in their place—a quiet, subdued place?

In another scene with Lib, the author places her on the top of a palm tree. Lib has discovered that the tree bears an edible fruit, and she rejoices over her ingenuity. What response does she receive from the men? She is told not to go up the tree again because she might fall and hurt herself. On one hand, there is a good reason to be concerned: they have few medical supplies or services, so a broken leg could be a lot more complicated than it would be under normal conditions. However, none of the women tell the men not to go out with their guns to capture or kill the criminals who have been ravaging the town. In this particular incident, Randy talks to Lib as if she is a child.

In another incident that is telling, Ben Franklin, Helen and Mark's son, is encouraged to take a gun and keep guard behind the barn, waiting to catch whoever has been stealing the

Henrys' pigs. Ben is only thirteen, not quite a man. When he kills the wild dog who has been stealing their food, everyone calls him a hero. Still a child, Ben cries once he realizes he has killed the dog; yet he proudly takes the compliments. His sister, Peyton, on the other hand, also wants to win the praise of her elders. She goes to Preacher Henry, the most successful fisherman in the area, and asks him why the fish are not biting. The Preacher helps Peyton figure out the problem: the river water is too hot along the shoreline, so the fish have gone out to the deeper water to keep cool. Peyton thanks the Preacher and decides to go out in the boat alone to the middle of the river, where the fish are biting. In the process, she catches three huge fish, but she also gets caught in the river's current. It takes her a long time to row home, and her family grows worried about her. Her mother, instead of praising her wisdom and skill, spanks her and sends her to bed. In essence, Peyton's mother signals that she is a bad girl. Nothing is said about the bounty she brought home with her, the fish that no one else was able to catch. There is no hero worship for Peyton. One has to wonder if this would have been the case if she were a boy.

The women in Frank's novel play out traditional female roles as nurturers and caretakers. They cut the men's hair, cook, and wash and mend the men's clothes. They soften the men by giving them attention. They strengthen the men with their love. They bite their tongues when they are around the men but let their thoughts run free when they are in one another's company. Maybe these were just the roles that women were expected to take on in the 1950s, before the liberation marches and demands for equality. Maybe the female characters just seem like stereotypical images of women because modern readers are encountering them from another century, one that has been influenced by a renewed feminism. But there is another possibility: Frank may have simply created his female characters as models of how he saw women—docile, submissive, quiet, and dumb human beings.

Source: Joyce M. Hart, Critical Essay on *Alas, Babylon*, in *Novels for Students*, Gale, Cengage Learning, 2009.

Jacqueline Foertsch

In the following excerpt, Foertsch uses Alas, Babylon *to explore the role of African American and ethnic characters in literature.*

AS IF THEIR IGNORANCE OF AND INDIFFERENCE TO WORLD AFFAIRS HAD MIRACULOUSLY PRESERVED THEM AGAINST EVEN THE BOMB'S PHYSICAL EFFECTS, THE HENRYS OCCUPY AN EXTRA-TEMPORAL POCKET-PARADISE OF ORDER AND EASE YET AT THE EXPENSE OF THEIR MEMBERSHIP IN HISTORY—IN HUMANITY—AT THIS MOMENTOUS MOMENT."

... The title of Frank's novel, *Alas, Babylon* is not only a quote from Revelations but from the sermons of a black minister, Preacher Henry, overheard by the story's white protagonist, Randy Bragg, and his brother Mark as boys. Listening outside (instead, of course, of occupying a pew within) Preacher's ramshackle church, the boys gain anyway from his apocalyptic perspective, trading the expression "Alas, Babylon" between them throughout childhood whenever a situation seemed hopeless. When Randy receives a telegram from Mark, now a SAC officer in Omaha, with the words "Alas, Babylon," he understands that nuclear war is imminent and makes the preparations that will eventually save his extended family (including Preacher and his family, who are neighbors) from nuclear destruction. Thus it is Preacher Henry's "long view"—his eye to the end of time, even should this occur tomorrow—that enables Randy to the heroism he eventually achieves. Randy's devotion to the Henrys, and his enlightening experience in the integrated ranks in Korea, instilled in him the respect for black Americans that doomed his pro-"Constitution" campaign for the state legislature months earlier. Meanwhile, he is independently wealthy and better off mulling over his options in the Florida countryside rather than losing his life in the state capitol of Jacksonville, demolished along with the other U.S. major cities, at the hour of attack. We recall that this same set of circumstances—the main white figure fortuitously sidelined on bomb day due to enmeshments with the serving class—opened [Judith] Merril's *Shadow on the Hearth*.

In the days following "The Day," Randy integrates his commune of neighbors and relatives, despite the misgivings and outright hostilities of the more segregationist among them. Randy's future father-in-law, who began the story by referring to African Americans as "dinges" and must function as assistant to Malachi Henry (Preacher's son)—"mechanic second class"—when the company's few autos need repairing, has his consciousness raised in the process. Despite the emotional trauma and new limitations in diet, Randy admits to himself, after a few weeks of laboring alongside his black neighbors, that "he was leaner and harder, and truthfully, felt better than before The Day." Many months into their ordeal, the old social divides—and the city services that supported them—have dissolved. In town, Randy observes that "[t]here were two drinking fountains in Marines Park, one marked 'White Only' and the other 'Colored Only.' Since neither worked, the signs were meaningless." The meaninglessness of segregated drinking facilities, revealed to the town only in the rocket-red glare of nuclear Armageddon, enables the vision of "Carleton Hawes . . . vice president of the county White Citizens Council" taking a drink from "a Negro's jug." While the social order has not declined to such a degree that Randy actually knows the name and club affiliations of the generous "Negro," it is the case that the novel's "vision" of the post-nuclear world—to the degree that it is a vision, a fantasy come true—has its radical edge: recall that, where [Philip] Wylie envisioned a racially, politically homogenous suburban new city in the wake of nuclear annihilation, Frank's post-bomb utopia features blacks and whites drinking from the same jug in an environment too naturally and politically broken down to sustain the old mores and "civilities."

In a dramatic later episode, Malachi drives a decoy truck that enables Randy and several other white characters to dispatch a band of deadly highwaymen. Seeing past the glimmer of hope represented by the interracial jug-sharing downtown, Malachi recognizes the persistence of racist sentiments on the highway and takes the wheel so as to function as an irresistible target to those they hope to capture. Indeed, he has read his adversaries like a book and is fatally wounded in the takedown; I will read the significance of his passing momentarily but note here that his death also results in the incapacitation of the last racist element in the narrative frame, furthering progress toward the interracial utopia Frank seems to be reaching for. We must note, however, that both

Malachi and especially Preacher, despite their potentially subversive features, serve ultimately *as* servants, supporting the interests of white masters. Acknowledging the somewhat enlightened qualities of Malachi, the Henrys otherwise abound in racial stereotypes, with Preacher the classic tom, his daughter (and Randy's maid) Missouri the eternal mammy, and her disaffected husband Two-Tone figuring as "the coon"—identified by Bogle (7–8) as another recurrent type in popular narrative.

The proximity of the Henry homestead to the many whites who also own property along the river may not seem to be a function of the family's former attachment to an antebellum plantation. However, their very integration in the neighborhood already serves those around them, especially tolerant whites like the retired Admiral Hazzard, who are pleased to snap up waterfront property at reduced rates—the only drawback being [their black neighbors]. While the novel roundly condemns the racist sentiments of the white realtor who phrases the situation thus, the Admiral does capitalize on his investment at the Henrys' surely under-compensated expense:

> Sam Hazzard found that the Henrys were extraordinarily convenient neighbors. Malachi tended the grounds and helped design and build the dock. Two-Tone, when in the mood—broke and sober—worked in the grove. The Henry women cleaned, and did his laundry. Preacher Henry was the Admiral's private fishing guide, which meant that *the Admiral* consistently caught more and bigger bass than anyone on the Timucuan, and possibly all of Central Florida.

(emphasis added)

Note the ways in which the Henrys' various labors are all for improving the leisure and "convenience" of the Admiral's post-retirement life. Especially significant is the arrangement by which Preacher's talents as a master fisherman are transferred to the Admiral to secure his catch (and his fame as a fisherman) instead of accruing in any way to Preacher himself. Throughout the story, the Henrys will donate their skills and expertise—without complaint and without credit—to the cause of securing white well-being.

Following the blast, Randy approaches Malachi and announces matter-of-factly: "We don't have water in our house. I want to take up some pipe out of the grove and hook it on to the artesian system." Though he adopts a confident, possessive tone, Randy has already admitted to white family members that he has no idea how to tap into the artesian water system that will save their lives, but that luckily "Malachi will know how to do it." Later in the story, Preacher shares more of his knowledge of fishing to enable young, white, female Peyton Bragg to save the day by finding the fish that will bite, never receiving credit for the role he has played. In this unofficial servant capacity, he is only doing his job.

As their essential contribution to post-nuclear survival is persistently unacknowledged by the narrative's white viewpoint, so the black figures are depicted—as Veda was in [Judith] Merril's novel—as oblivious and in some ways impervious to (outside of) the bomb's threat and the seriousness of the response it requires. Missouri, whom Randy calls by the childish name Mizoo, cleans the Bragg household, "shuffling" as she goes, fulfilling various stereotypes with her jollity, size, and dialect speech. Early in the story, she puts on the phonograph and polishes the floor by "dancing" with rags tied to her feet, her light manner as inappropriate to her 11th-hour situation as was Gladys's ignorance of major headlines. When she informs Randy that "nerves" have caused her to lose weight, it is not nuclear news-reporting that induces her anxiety but the demanding standards of another employer, Randy's future mother-in-law. Because Randy and Malachi were boyhood friends (even though Malachi now addresses Randy as "sir" and regards him as a boss), Randy shares with Malachi Mark's vital information regarding the bomb's approach. Malachi, however, is utterly unfazed: "Mister Randy, I've thought about it a lot, but there's not a doggone thing we can do about it. We just have to sit here and wait for it." As opposed to the frantic but effective preparations engaged in by Randy throughout the novel's early chapters, Malachi is content to wait, sitting-duck style, for the bombs to strike, endangering his family by his fatalist (and "no-count") inclination to simply take it easy. Before divulging his secret to Malachi, Randy had wrestled with the prospect of doing so: unlike his white neighbors whom he has no intention of enlightening but whom he assumes will fend well for themselves following attack, the Henrys are a "special problem"—beloved caretakers and helpless "wards" who will surely perish without his support. When Malachi rejects Randy's invitation to swing into panicky action alongside him, it now seems that he and his family deserve any bad luck that befalls them. Malachi has explained his indifference by reminding his boss that "we [Henrys] don't need much" anyway: their lack of most modern amenities, and total acceptance of this lack, suit them better than their white neighbors to any return to the "Dark Ages" that may come their way.

Indeed, preparedness would have been wasted energy for the Henry family, given their remarkably "isolated" situation. In a startling scene, Randy approaches the Henry farm immediately following the blasts and is transported back in time—to a pre-bomb, indeed prelapsarian, scene of rural contentment:

> Fifty yards up the slope, Preacher Henry and Balaam [the mule] solemnly disked the land, moving silently and evenly, as if they perfectly understood each other. Caleb [Missouri's son] lay flat on his belly on the end of the dock, peering into the shadowed waters behind a piling, jigging a worm for bream. Two-Tone sat on the screened porch, rocking languidly and lifting a can of beer to his lips. From the kitchen came a woman's deep, rich voice, singing a spiritual. That would be Missouri, washing the dishes. Hot, black smoke from burning pine knots issued from both brick chimneys. It seemed a peaceful home, in time of peace....
>
> Randy walked over toward the back door and the Henrys converged on him, their faces apprehensive... "Everything okay here?" [Randy asked]
>
> "Just like always" [Malachi replied].

As if their ignorance of and indifference to world affairs had miraculously preserved them against even the bomb's physical effects, the Henrys occupy an extra-temporal pocket-paradise of order and ease yet at the expense of their membership in history—in humanity—at this momentous moment. Randy's approach—the approach of awareness and action in the figure of the white master—elicits their "apprehension," indicating that the Henrys must now rely on Randy to reintroduce them to the passage of time itself—to the awful realities of their present and future. While Randy's yanking the Henrys into the present is a dubious favor to be sure, the Henrys' ability to help Randy and his white relatives adjust to "the past"—the primitive mode of living that is the only option in the devastated post-atomic environment—is a priceless gift that is barely acknowledged, let alone adequately compensated.

One ethnic character—of the many surveyed in all of these works—stands out for her refusal to fill the servant's role and for the consequences she pays for it. As her Otherness stems from ethnicity (and class) instead of the more "alien" qualities of "race," Rita Hernandez, a Minorcan siren from the rundown Pistolville section of town, is closer to Randy both before the bomb (they are lovers in the story's pre-history) and after. As opposed to the Henrys, who serenely disregard the bomb's approach, and despite Randy's attempt to relegate her to his own pre-bomb adolescence by insisting that "Rita is part of the past," Rita, like Randy, is keenly aware of the unfolding future and has been stockpiling wares against the day. Yet Rita's accumulation of resaleable hard goods contrasts to Randy's pre-bomb hoarding in the name of protecting his family (especially his young niece and nephew) and is thus demonized by the narrative. With the advent of the waspy, marriageable Lib McGovern, Randy has cut Rita loose. When she refuses to resign her role . . . by pressing to legitimize their relationship, she is implicitly accused of not knowing her place, and the narrative turns against her. Her aggressive, unkempt brother Pete reinforces our dislike of Rita and all her Pistolville clan. According to Pete, "Rita says this war's going to level people as well as cities"; Frank celebrated this interracial groundbreaking in the instance of white and black sharing the same water jug, but Rita's attempt to level the playing field, which threatens Randy's respectable union with Lib, is castigated.

Because of the large store of supplies Rita has maintained against the thieving gangs of Pistolville, Randy reencounters her during a goods exchange and is recaptivated by her seductive ways. Her crude assessment of Randy's current living situation . . . snaps him out of his spell, and he harshly turns against her. Fittingly, the diamond ring she shows off to entice Randy—as both wealthy and spoken-for—is "hot" property, stolen from a jewelry store in south Florida that had been radiated by an atomic blast. Dan Gunn, the town doctor who accompanies Randy to the meeting diagnoses radiation poisoning: "Her finger was marred by a dark, almost black circle, as if the ring were tarnished brass, or its inside sooty. But the ring was a clean bright white gold." Concluding their visit, Dan observes to Randy that the Hernandez's stolen goods are "[i]mpregnated with fallout . . . Suicide." Cruelly abandoned by Randy in his white, male, middle-class superiority, Rita is forced to make symbolic marriage with the bomb, impregnated not with a child but a monster: radiation poisoning. Her refusal to know her place . . . is the sin for which her terrifying dose of radiation exposure is supposedly

just reward. As opposed to the impervious, oblivious Henry family, Rita has both a firmer grasp of the bomb's social significance and a normal ("human") physical reaction to the bomb's contaminating effects.

As the Henrys were a "special problem" for Randy in the beginning of the story, solved by their exploitative incorporation into the Bragg commune's early days of survival, they along with Rita and her family become the narrative's own special problem as it draws to its triumphant close. Malachi and Rita's nasty brother Pete are the two minority characters who die in the story (Malachi heroically, saving white lives, Pete despicably, swathed in hot gold), yet all characters of color are pushed to the invisible margins of the story in its final pages. Although Randy trades for honey as a treat for Ben Franklin and Peyton (the story's two white children) as well as Missouri's son Caleb, later in the story, there is only typhoid vaccine enough for Peyton and Ben Franklin. The unvoiced presumption perhaps is that Caleb is hearty enough to withstand the infections threatening more delicate, middle-class systems. Following the Henrys' initial heavy infusion of folk wisdom into the Bragg collective, it becomes self-sustaining, and there is less and less for a large cast of supporting characters to do. Again, their last service of any value is to simply fade away; neither the Henrys nor Rita make any appearance in the story's final episode—when a surveillance/decontamination patrol arrives by helicopter from the outside and invites the family (and its white neighbors—"the librarian and the telegraph gal") to vacate to a safer zone. When Randy, on behalf of his familial collective, rejects the pilot's offer, he completes our understanding that the group has already reached, has created for itself, its zone of utopic safety, contentment, and "unmitigated hope" (Hager 323). Again, the Henrys' role at this point in the story is all but nonexistent; they are not referred to during the offer of evacuation nor consulted before the offer is turned down, and their role from then on seems to be one of complaisant invisibility.

Hal Hager observes that as he wrote, Frank was as caught up in headlines that told of school desegregation as those that warned of atomic war (322); while the large role granted African-American and other minority characters in this novel corroborates that argument, it is the case that for Frank, and for white authors and policymakers in general, negroes were a "problem," like the bomb, to be solved as expeditiously as possible. For white America, the answer in both cases was flight to the protected suburb, even as it knew that the solution was provisional at best. Racial integration was as looming a prospect as radioactive contamination, and in only the most farfetched geographic fantasies...would one problem (the bomb) conveniently take care of the other (the Negroes trapped in their ground-zero inner cities). To discern African Americans as "being" a problem in the nuclear-imminent landscape, of course, ignores the reality of their "having" a problem—the same one facing white America (and the world as a whole) at that moment—and the agency with which they would execute their own antinuclear protest, pre-nuclear preparedness and, in the worst case, post-nuclear survival. While the novels read in this discussion each add dimension to their nuclear scenarios by including characters of various ethnicities, races, and social classes, all tend toward the assumptions and conclusions dependent upon black servitude discerned by film and cultural theorists to have been part of a white-authored narrative since at least the end of the Civil War.

Source: Jacqueline Foertsch, "'Extraordinarily Convenient Neighbors': African-American Characters in White-Authored Post-Atomic Novels," in *Journal of Modern Literature*, Vol. 30, No. 4, Summer 2007, pp. 122–38.

SOURCES

Dempsey, David, "H-Bomb's Aftermath," Review of *Alas, Babylon* in *New York Times Book Review*, March 22, 1959, p. 43.

Frank, Pat, *Alas, Babylon*, HarperPerennial, 2005.

Holmes, Viv, Review of *Alas, Babylon*, in *Countryside and Small Stock Journal*, Vol. 87, No. 6, November/December 2003, p. 93.

Kaledin, Eugenia, *Daily Life in the United States, 1940–1959: Shifting Worlds*, Greenwood Press, 2000.

Lawson, Steven F., *Civil Rights Crossroads: Nation, Community, and the Black Freedom Struggle*, University Press of Kentucky, 2003.

Painter, David, *The Cold War: An International History*, Routledge, 1999.

"Pat Frank Dead: Wrote 'Mr. Adam,'" in *New York Times*, October 13, 1964, p. 43.

"Pat (Harry Hart) Frank," in *St. James Guide to Science Fiction Writers*, 4th ed., St. James Press, 1996.

Prescott, Orville, "Books of the Times," Review of *Alas, Babylon*, in *New York Times*, March 20, 1959, p. 29.

Young, William H., *The 1950s*, Greenwood Press, 2004.

FURTHER READING

Gaddis, John Lewis, *The Cold War: A New History*, Penguin, 2005.

> This volume presents a detailed history of the cold war, including how it began, what it signaled, who it involved, what happened, and how it ended. One of the best-known historians on this topic, Gaddis presents an in-depth account in an easy-to-read style.

Gannon, Michael, *Florida: A Short History*, University Press of Florida, 2003.

> Professor Gannon provides a brief yet comprehensive tour through the history of Florida. Gannon looks at topical issues still relevant today, such as the environment, race relations, weather catastrophes, wildlife, and other social issues.

Kelly, Cynthia, ed., *The Manhattan Project: The Birth of the Atomic Bomb in the Words of Its Creators, Eyewitnesses, and Historians*, Black Dog and Leventhal Publishers, 2007.

> This collection presents firsthand accounts of and perspectives on the creation of the atomic bomb, as told by scientists, military personnel, and academics. Some of the accounts are historical; others are reflections from a contemporary point of view.

Wiseman, John, *SAS Survival Handbook: How to Survive in the Wild, in Any Climate, on Land or at Sea*, HarperResource, 2004.

> For readers who might be interested in learning basic skills useful in an emergency, Wiseman has written a book that contains strategies for surviving in any type of stressful situation. This book could be read merely for the fascination of the details provided or for practical knowledge to be used in rugged circumstances.

The Alchemist

PAULO COELHO

1988

When he first published *The Alchemist* in his native Brazil in 1988, Paulo Coelho was known mainly as a writer of popular songs. The book failed to attract public attention and went out of print. A few years later, however, a reissue caught on: readers were transfixed by its simple, parable-like story, and recommended it to their friends, who recommended it to their friends. Fan Web sites popped up, and Coelho was invited to speak at conferences. Celebrities talked about how reading *The Alchemist* had changed their lives. In one country after another the book rose to the top of bestseller lists. It became one of the most astonishing stories in publishing history, joining the top twenty-five selling books of all time, making Coelho one of the most widely read authors living on the planet.

The story concerns a young Andalusian shepherd boy who has a recurring dream of treasures, and the people that he meets on his journey to Egypt, where he knows his treasure is to be found. Deeply allegorical, his adventure introduces him to an ancient king from the Old Testament; a gypsy; a hard-working Muslim crystal merchant; an intellectual; the love of his life; and of course, the alchemist of the title, who has lived for centuries and has been waiting for the boy to show up so that he may guide the boy's spiritual growth. In the course of seeking his Personal Legend, the boy learns that it is the journey, not the reward, that makes a quest like his worthwhile.

Paulo Coelho *(Pascal Le Segretain / Getty Images)*

The Alchemist was published in the United States in 1993, and is available in a paperback edition from HarperSanFrancisco, as well as in several deluxe gift editions for those who would like to explore the book's spiritual insights.

AUTHOR BIOGRAPHY

Paulo Coelho was born in Rio de Janeiro, Brazil, on August 24, 1947. In a city known for its poverty, he grew up in a comfortable middle-class household. His father, Pedro, was an engineer, and his mother, Lygia, was a housewife. He entered a Jesuit school at the age of seven. It was there that he started writing, although he was not to publish his first novel until the age of thirty-eight.

At the age of seventeen, Coelho rejected the course that his parents wanted him to follow. They planned for him to be an engineer: when he stopped attending school, they had him committed to a psychiatric hospital, where he was subjected to electroconvulsive therapy. He still suffered from depression and panic attacks, and was admitted a second and then third time, at the age of twenty.

When he was out of the hospital, Coelho began writing for a living, working as a journalist and writing with a theater group. For two years, he traveled throughout South America, Mexico, North America, and Europe. Upon his return to Rio de Janeiro in 1971, Coelho started a long and fruitful collaboration with popular rock musician Raul Seixas: Coelho wrote the lyrics for several of Seixas's albums, and together they created the "Kring-Ha" comic strip series. He also wrote lyrics for other popular musicians such as Elis Regina and Rita Lee. The comic strip was considered subversive, and Coelho was arrested in 1974 and put in prison for a short time, released, and then rearrested and tortured before gaining his release by claiming to be mentally ill.

Soon after his release, in 1976, Coelho ended his association with Seixas and went to work for a record company. His life changed in 1986, when, at the advice of a friend, he walked the ancient Road of Santiago de Compostela in northern Spain, a journey of more than five hundred miles that led him to a spiritual awakening. His first book, *The Pilgrimage*, published in 1987, describes his trip and the emotional changes that it brought. *The Pilgrimage* was well-received, but did not sell well. Coelho's second novel, *The Alchemist*, sold less than a thousand copies. He did not become an international literary sensation until the publication of his third book, *Brida*, in 1990. The success of *Brida* brought international attention to Coelho's writing, spurring reissues of his first two novels and ensuring that his future publications sold millions of copies. Coelho's popularity has enabled him to lend spiritual and financial support to charitable causes around the world, most notably the Paulo Coelho Institute, a foundation to help children and the elderly citizens of Brazil that is funded solely by the author's book royalties.

PLOT SUMMARY

Prologue

The prologue for *The Alchemist* gives a brief look at the alchemist, a character who will not appear in the story until much later. He opens a

MEDIA ADAPTATIONS

- In 2008, A-Mark Entertainment announced a film adaptation of *The Alchemist*, directed by and starring Laurence Fishburne, for release in 2009.
- An unabridged version of *The Alchemist*, read by Jeremy Irons, was released by HarperAudio on both audio cassette and compact disc in 2001. This release is the R.I.G. Winner of AudioFile Earphones Award.
- The Cornish Theatre Collective's stage adaptation of *The Alchemist* has toured the British Isles with traveling companies since 2002.
- Readers who want to see what Coelho thinks about life on a daily basis can go to his official Web site at http://www.paulocoelho.com/ and read the blog that he updates regularly.

book and reads a story about Narcissus. In the ancient Greek legend, Narcissus is a vain boy who falls in love with his own reflection in the clear water of a lake and falls in and drowns when trying to kiss the beautiful person he sees there. In the version that the alchemist reads, the lake grieves over Narcissus's death, because Narcissus's eyes reflected the lake's own beauty back to itself. The alchemist finds this version of the story touching.

Part One

A shepherd boy named Santiago is traveling the countryside in southern Spain with his flock and arrives at a decaying church with a caved-in roof. A sycamore tree grows in the middle of the church. He spends the night there and has a dream that he had a week before, telling him that his fortune can be found at the pyramid in Egypt. Up to that point, his fondest wish has been to return to see a girl he saw in Tarifa the last time he was there, the daughter of a wool merchant. He takes the sheep to Tarifa, and there he goes to an old woman, a gypsy, to have his recurring dream interpreted. After he tells her the details,

she tells him he must go to Egypt, and that the only payment she will take for her interpretation is one tenth of his fortune once he has gotten it.

On a bench in a square, an old man strikes up a conversation with Santiago. He gives him advice about life, telling him that the greatest thing in the world is to realize one's Personal Legend and that the greatest lie is that one cannot control one's fate. He strangely seems to know details about the boy's life. He says that he is Melchizedek, the king of Salem. He tells the boy to go find his fortune, advises him to heed omens, and gives him two magic stones, named Urim and Thummim, to help him make decisions. The boy pays him with a tenth of his flock, sells the rest, and takes a boat from Spain to Tangier, in northern Africa.

In a café on his first day in Tangier, he meets a young man who speaks the native tongue and offers to rent camels and take him across the desert to Egypt. Walking through a marketplace behind his guide, however, the boy is distracted, and the young man runs off with all of his money.

The next morning, he goes into a shop that sells crystal at the top of a hill and offers to clean the delicate glasses in exchange for food. When he hears that it would take more than a year of working in the crystal shop to earn enough to pay for passage across the desert, he agrees to work until he has enough to cross back to Spain and become a shepherd again.

Part Two

Santiago stays at the crystal shop for a long time and prospers there, thinking of innovations that help bring in more business. He builds a display case to put outside, to attract more customers to the shop, and decides to sell tea, so that thirsty travelers who have climbed up the hill can have a drink and think about buying the glassware it is served in. The merchant tells him that he should not feel bad about abandoning his search for the treasure he dreamed of; as a Muslim, the shop keeper long dreamed of making a pilgrimage to Mecca, and so he knows what it is like to give up on a dream.

Santiago leaves the crystal shop after eleven months and three days. With the commissions he has earned from helping to sell crystal, he could go home, but instead decides to join a caravan that is heading across the desert.

Waiting for the caravan, he talks with an Englishman who is disinterested in the boy until he recognizes that he too is familiar with Urim and Thummim, the divining stones. The Englishman is an intellectual and has a case of books traveling with him. He tells the boy that he is studying to be an alchemist, and that he is joining the caravan in order to go to the oasis at Al-Fayoum, where he has been told that a great alchemist lives who is over two hundred years old, thanks to his use of the Elixir of Life. The alchemist is also reputed to be in possession of the fabled Philosopher's Stone, which is supposed to hold the secret to changing any metal into gold.

The caravan starts out after the leader warns of possible danger out in the desert. While riding, Santiago befriends a camel driver who knows the ways of the desert and talks to him. He finds that he is more interested in reading the signs that present themselves in the world, which he calls the Language of the World, and he throws away the big book that he has brought with him. Later, he tries to learn about alchemy from the books that the Englishman has brought with him, reading biographies of people who have lived out their Personal Legends and performed miracles.

The caravan hears rumors that there are warring tribes in the desert, and that they have to be cautious. They travel day and night without talking. When they finally stop, it is at an oasis of three hundred wells and fifty thousand date trees. They are safe because the warring tribes have a tradition of leaving oases alone. The Englishman is happy because the oasis is Al-Fayoum, the home of the alchemist.

In trying to help the Englishman find where the alchemist lives, Santiago talks to a young woman who is drawing water from a well. The moment that she looks into his face he knows that he is in love with her. He learns that her name is Fatima, and the next day he comes back to the well to see her again. They strike up an acquaintance, and finally he tells her that he has loved her from the first. She tells him that when the war is over and it is safe to leave the oasis he must leave again to find his fortune, that she cannot be responsible for holding him back.

Sitting by himself at the edge of the desert, the boy watches a pair of hawks in the sky. Just as he is starting to fall asleep, he sees one of the hawks turn and attack the other. The vision immediately changes to one of an army riding forward to attack the oasis. The boy goes to his friend the camel driver to tell him of his vision, and he tells the boy that, given the seriousness of the vision, he must go to the tribal leaders and tell them what he saw. So he goes to the most richly appointed tent in Al-Fayoum and, after a long wait, is admitted to tell his vision to the chieftains. The chieftains are unsure whether or not to believe him, but the eldest among them trusts the boy. They will break a long-standing tradition and distribute weapons to the citizens of the oasis, he says, in preparation for the coming invasion. If the oasis is attacked, the boy will be paid a gold piece for every invader killed. If not one invader shows up to be killed, the weapons that were to be used against them will be used to kill the boy.

That night, the boy is walking alone when he is visited by a man in black with a falcon on his shoulder, bearing a sword. He holds the sword against the boy's head and asks why he interpreted the omen of the fighting hawks, and when the boy points out that his action will save many lives, he puts the sword away. As the horseman rides away, the boy realizes that he was talking to the fabled alchemist.

The next morning, five hundred men attack Al-Fayoum, but thanks to Santiago's vision, the residents are prepared, and kill them all. The boy is paid fifty gold pieces.

As they ride in the desert, the alchemist tells him to watch his horse, which can find signs of life in the desert; when the horse stops, the alchemist puts his hand deeply into a hole in the ground and pulls out a huge cobra. He is not harmed by the snake's venomous bite. The alchemist explains how miserable the boy will eventually be if he abandons his quest for his Personal Legend, the treasure that he has been seeking, to stay at the oasis as an official seer and marry Fatima. Over the years, the alchemist says, he will lose the ability to read the omens that he can read now, and he will become resentful. He offers to guide the boy across the desert to find the treasure at the pyramids. The boy goes to Fatima's tent that night and says goodbye.

Crossing the desert, the alchemist tells Santiago that he can learn to understand the world by listening to his heart. Soon, his heart is talking to him, telling him that human hearts require a search for treasure, or else they will lose their happiness.

When they are only two days' ride from the pyramids, the two travelers are stopped in the desert by tribesmen. The alchemist offers them all of the gold that the boy has earned, and then makes a deal with them. They agree to let the captives go if the boy can, as the alchemist claims, turn himself into the wind. After three days, the boy stands on the edge of the desert and has a conversation with the desert. The boy beseeches the desert, saying that he needs to return to the one he loves, and the desert lets him talk to the wind and then to the sun. In the end, a powerful, blinding wind does arise, and the captors are sufficiently impressed to let the alchemist and the boy go free.

At a monastery, the alchemist turns lead into gold and gives one fourth of it to his hosts and one fourth to the boy, then asks the host to keep another fourth of it for the boy's return. He keeps the rest. Before they part, the alchemist tells the boy the Biblical story about a man who has two sons, one a poet and the other a soldier: when a prophesy tells him that his son's words will be recited forever, the man assumes it will be the poet's, only to find after he is dead that it was the other son, who went on to meet Jesus and utter the phrase quoted in the book of Matthew, "My lord I am not worthy that you should come under my roof."

When he reaches the pyramid, the boy sees a scarab beetle, and takes it for an omen. He digs all night at the place where the beetle stood. In the night, some refugees from the tribal wars find him and search him, finding the gold that was on him. He explains that he is there to find his treasure. After they beat him nearly to death, the leader of the group, mocking him, says that a dream once told him to find his personal treasure, too. He was supposed to look in a crumbling church in Spain, where a sycamore tree grew. Though the man ignored his dream, the boy Santiago is delighted, because he knows the place to which the man's dream referred.

Epilogue

Having stopped to retrieve the gold the alchemist left for him at the monastery, the boy is able to return to the crumbling church where he had his dream that led him to the pyramids. Digging under the base of the sycamore tree, he finds a chest of Spanish coins and jewels. The wind from Africa brings him the scent of Fatima's perfume, and he promises to return to her.

CHARACTERS

The Alchemist

The alchemist of the novel's title is a legendary man, said to be over two hundred years old, who lives at the oasis Al-Fayoum. The Englishman with whom the boy travels comes to the desert seeking him, but the alchemist is interested in meeting the boy, whose arrival he has been expecting. He first appears as a threatening figure and holds his sword to the boy's head, but when the boy does not fear him the alchemist offers to accompany him across the desert to the Pyramids, where his fortune can be found.

The alchemist teaches the boy lessons about following his Personal Legend, lessons that were started by Melchizedek, the king of Salem. He shows him that the perceived difference between the solid world and the imagination is just an illusion by showing how he is able to change common metals to gold. After taking Santiago most of the way to the pyramids, he leaves him before reaching the end of the journey, so that the boy can face his fate alone. Before leaving, though, he tells a story from the New Testament about a relatively minor character whose words have lived on for millennia, to illustrate the point that each person holds an important place in the history of the world.

The Boy

See Santiago

The Camel Driver

During his trip across the desert, the boy makes the acquaintance of a camel driver. This man, a simple working man, tells Santiago his philosophy of life. He lives in the present and does not concern himself about the past or the future, which makes his simple life a big festival for him.

The Crystal Merchant

When he finds himself stranded in Tangier after his money has been stolen, Santiago stops into the shop of a crystal merchant and asks if he can work for food. He ends up being useful to the merchant, and stays on for a year, during which the shop prospers.

The merchant serves as an example of someone who has not followed his Personal Legend. He recounts to the boy how he had ambitions to travel when he was a young man, particularly to make a pilgrimage to Mecca, as his Muslim faith commands him to do. He became engrossed in making his shop prosper, and then in keeping it prospering as all of the wealthy shoppers stopped coming to his neighborhood in Tangier and took their business to Ceuta. He knows that he could have made more money by moving his shop, and that he would have gotten more satisfaction in his life if he had made the pilgrimage he had dreamed of, but he also knows that he is settled in his ways. It is from the crystal merchant that Santiago picks up the expression "Maktub," which translates roughly to "It is written." It is an expression he uses often after leaving the crystal merchant when he wants to express his acceptance of events.

The Desert

Throughout the story there are characters who are said to understand the desert. Late in his adventure, when he is crossing the desert, Santiago finds out that this is more than a turn of phrase: the desert is personified as a living, sentient being, and the boy has discussions with it.

Their conversation comes when he is being held by tribesmen who expect him to be able to turn himself into the wind. The desert, lacking emotional ability, asks the boy to explain to it the concept of love. When he does, the desert offers to summon the wind to help him reunite with his love, Fatima.

The Englishman

When he has saved enough money in Tangier to start his trip across the desert to the pyramids, Santiago goes to sign up on a caravan, and it is there that he meets the Englishman. An intellectual, the Englishman has bags of books that he is carrying across the desert with him. He is a student of alchemy and wants to meet the fabled alchemist who lives at Al-Fayoum, in order to learn the alchemist's secrets. He tells the boy the basic principles of alchemy and lends him a book, which the boy struggles with and then returns unread.

Arriving at the oasis, the Englishman asks Santiago to talk to the local people on his behalf in order to find the alchemist. When the alchemist does show up, however, it is not the Englishman that he is interested in meeting but the boy. The Englishman, studying the principles of alchemy by himself, is enthused about his chances of transmuting metal into gold at one point, but he fails.

Fatima

At one of the many wells at the oasis of Al-Fayoum, Santiago is warned that he should not talk to any of the women dressed in black, because they are married and their husbands will be jealous. The first woman he stops who is not in black is Fatima. He falls in love with her the moment he looks into her eyes.

The boy offers to stay at the oasis with this woman that he loves, but she encourages him to go off and fulfill his Personal Legend. She does not want to be responsible for his living a life of resentment. Later, when the alchemist predicts what will happen to Santiago's life if he stays at Al-Fayoum, he foresees the same kind of resentment. By letting Santiago go without having to worry about her, Fatima ensures that he will be able to find his Personal Legend.

The Gypsy Woman

Soon after bringing his sheep to market in Tarifa, Santiago goes to visit a gypsy woman to have his recurring dream interpreted for him. He is skeptical about her, expecting her to cheat him in some way, particularly when she insists on one tenth of the fortune that he will find, but he agrees to her price. She disappoints him by failing to give any specific information. He will find a fortune, she tells him, but that is all she can divine. She cannot tell him how to get there, and in fact admits that she has never heard of the Egyptian pyramids at all.

Melchizedek

Melchizedek is the self-proclaimed king of Salem, who runs into Santiago in a village square in Tarifa and strikes up an acquaintance. He tells the boy that he must follow the dream that he had, that it is his responsibility, as it is with everyone, to follow his Personal Legend. To help him, he takes two stones from the breastplate of the armor that he has hidden under his robe, telling the boy that they are to be used in cases where he cannot make a decision. He says that he will be with the boy in spirit as he goes. One of the last things he does for the boy is tell him the story about a servant boy who was required to view the many splendors of a king's castle while carrying a spoonful of oil, trying to marvel at what he sees but not forgetting to make sure that not a drop is spilled. This story mirrors Santiago's own position as he goes on his quest.

As he goes about his travels, Santiago finds himself in several situations that remind him of Melchizedek. When he is living with the crystal merchant and planning to return to the life of shepherding in Spain, Santiago remembers the old king's admonition that he needs to find his Personal Legend. Later, the Englishman he meets dismisses Santiago until he sees that the boy has Urim and Thummim, the divining stones that Melchizedek gave him. The Englishman is familiar with the ancient legends of the stones, and of Melchizedek.

In the Old Testament of the Bible, Melchizedek is also the king of Salem. He gives his blessing to Abraham. In payment for his blessing, Abraham gives him a tenth of all that he possesses, which is exactly what Santiago promises to do after he finds his fortune.

Santiago

Santiago is the main character of this book, often referred to as "the boy." When the book begins, he is a shepherd, having chosen that career so that he could travel and see the world. His parents objected to his career choice, but eventually gave their blessing. He is driving his sheep to Tarifa, where, a year earlier, he met a shopkeeper's daughter and became infatuated with her. En route, though, he sleeps within a crumbling church that has a tree growing through its open roof and has a dream that he first had the week before, telling him that he can find a fortune if he goes to the ancient pyramids of Egypt. The dream sets him off on the adventure of his lifetime. He goes to a gypsy woman who he assumes can interpret what it means, and soon after that meets Melchizedek, who tells him that the dream is his Personal Legend and he must pursue it. He travels to Africa, is robbed of all of his money, and works in a crystal shop for nearly a year until he has enough to travel across the desert. His trip across the desert puts Santiago in the way of even more challenges and adventures that bring him greater insights into how his life can be led in a meaningful way.

Throughout the first part of his journey, Santiago is watched over by the spirit of Melchizedek. After he arrives at the oasis of Al-Fayoum, however, and eventually makes the acquaintance of the alchemist, he refers less often to Melchizedek's teachings. At the oasis he also meets Fatima, who, being the true love of his life, is a major motivating force in his journey, as shown by the fact that he begs the wind's help so that he can make his way back to her. In the end, when he finds his fortune in the very place where he started, he wonders why he could not have been told that it was there earlier, but a voice carried on the wind, probably that of the alchemist, reminds him of the adventures that he experienced in his journey, making him glad not to have missed them.

Santiago's Heart

When the alchemist tells Santiago to listen to his heart, it comes across as being just a familiar expression. After a while in the desert, however, Santiago ends up listening to actual words that his heart tells him, and ends up having a dialogue with it.

Santiago's heart is presented as an actual, independent character in the story, and reveals that it has thoughts independent of him. It tells him stories of his childhood, of how it took actions that Santiago was not aware of to protect the boy, such as hiding a gun he had found so that he could not hurt himself with it. Knowing Santiago better than the boy knows himself, his heart identifies his two greatest assets, courage and enthusiasm.

The Young Man

When Santiago arrives in Tangier, everything is unfamiliar to him, He does not know the language or the local customs. He thinks that he is fortunate when a young man in a café approaches, speaks to him in his own language, and offers to arrange a trip across the desert to Egypt. When the owner of the café speaks to them harshly, the young man tells Santiago that the man is a thief and intends to rob them. Walking across the crowded marketplace, however, Santiago is distracted when he sees what he thinks is the most beautiful sword he has ever seen, and when he turns to speak to his new friend he finds that the young man, who was holding his money so that he could buy two camels, is gone. This robbery is the first and one of the worst obstacles that Santiago faces on his journey, and it makes him seriously consider giving up and going back home to be a shepherd again.

THEMES

Fortune and Luck

When Coelho uses the word "fortune" in this novel, he uses it in a dual sense: though Santiago often speaks of "a fortune," referring to wealth,

TOPICS FOR FURTHER STUDY

- What recent scientific advances do you think seem related to the book's idea of alchemy? Create a poster that explains your interpretation of what Coelho means by alchemy and show how alchemy applies to three or four advances made in chemistry, physics, or data processing within your lifetime.

- When he last appears in the book, Melchizedek looks to the sky and speaks to "my Lord." At the end of the Epilogue, Santiago speaks to the sky and is answered. Write an essay discussing who you think each of these characters is talking to, whether it is the same entity, and the symbolic significance of the sky.

- Make a list of famous people who you think have spent their lives seeking their Personal Legends and another list of those who you think have merely attained popular success. Write an essay in which you explain what characteristics distinguish the two types from each other.

- Draw or paint portraits that show what you think key characters from this book such as Santiago, Fatima, Melchizedek, the Englishman, the crystal merchant, the gypsy, and the alchemist look like. Alternatively, find pictures in magazines or on the Internet that you believe best represent each character. Mount the photographs or portraits on a display and write a brief statement explaining how the descriptions in the novel led you to picture the specific characters that way.

---

the narrator makes reference to "his fortune," implying the ways that fate will act on the boy. Throughout *The Alchemist* there is a continuous question about just how much one controls one's fate. Simple luck seems to have a hand in the way that Santiago meets his future, but luck is not the only element involved. His successes are also a result of how he meets his luck and responds to it.

Early on in the book, Melchizedek, the king of Salem, tells Santiago that he is going to have Beginner's Luck when he first starts out on his trip because there is a force in the universe that wants each person to be encouraged in the pursuit of his or her Personal Legend, and Beginner's Luck will give the person a taste of what success is like. It is a concept echoed later by the owner of the crystal shop, who refers to it as the "principle of favorability."

Although luck does play a role in the first steps of one's journey, the book does not suggest that people should merely rely on luck and accept whatever might come to them. Melchizedek also tells Santiago that he needs to learn how to read the omens in life, and adjust his behavior according to his readings, giving the boy responsibility for his own fate. The old king does give him the two stones, Urim and Thummim, which he says can be used to make decisions for him if he sees no clear direction, but he also tells Santiago to use them sparingly, and in fact the boy completes his journey only taking the stones out once. He knows that the good fortune that will come to him from Beginner's Luck is limited, and he also knows that leaving his fate entirely up to the random reading of the stones is just a way of avoiding the responsibility he has to lead himself to his own fortune. In the end, Santiago attains a material fortune of gold and jewels, but he has also fulfilled his Personal Legend, thus achieving an even more meaningful fortune. It is because he chooses to pursue his own fortune that good luck befalls him.

Wealth

Though the object of Santiago's quest is a treasure, Coelho makes it clear throughout the story that wealth is not a goal to be pursued for its own sake. At the end, when the treasure is found to be waiting for Santiago at the very place where he began his quest, he questions why he could not simply have found it there without traveling so far, and a voice from the sky makes the point that seeing the ancient pyramids was the important part of the journey, giving the experience more weight than the treasure he gained at the end.

Another place in the book where material wealth and experience are linked to one another is in the basic function of the alchemist, from whom the book takes its title. To some people, alchemy, or the transformation of matter, which

Pyramids and camel, Giza, Egypt *(© BL Images Ltd. | Alamy)*

includes the skill of turning common metals into gold, seems like nothing more than a means of acquiring wealth. Alchemists, however, do not value gold for its market value but for what it represents in ability. Even the Englishman, who is not yet an alchemist but who wishes to become one, knows better than to pursue gold for its own sake. He wants to be able to produce gold for what such an ability can tell him about his own personality; he knows that he must attend to the process of transformation with no fear in his heart if he is going to succeed. He understands that the intellectual process of alchemy means more to him than the gold that will result from it.

The alchemist himself, who has the power to create all of the gold he could possibly ever want, shows no interest in worldly wealth, but instead is interested in the physical process that leads to it. He helps the boy follow his dream because he knows that following dreams is what really matters in the world, just as he knows that seeing the boy transform himself into the wind will be just as impressive to the bandits of the desert as his

own power to change metal to gold. Both come from the same place, an understanding of the Language of the World.

Love

When this story begins, the boy is motivated to take his flock of sheep to Tarifa by his infatuation with the daughter of a merchant, whom he met a year earlier but did not talk to long enough to even find out her name. After his second dream about the treasure he is to find at the pyramids, he realizes that the merchant's daughter will likely forget about him while he is away on his quest. He knows that she will probably take up with someone who has more money, or at least more identifiable prospects, but he takes the chance of losing her in order to pursue his Personal Legend.

Later in the book, this circumstance is mirrored when Santiago meets Fatima at the oasis of Al-Fayoum. Rather than an infatuation, however, the relationship that develops between them is presented as true love, even though they know it is love within moments of their initial meeting. The boy is aware that his parents and grandparents would consider it a false way to approach love because they would want love cultivated more carefully over the course of time, but the feelings that he has are more convincing to him than the logical arguments that anyone might present.

Fatima shows her own love for Santiago by encouraging him to go ahead and pursue his Personal Legend. She is aware that he might be lost to her forever, but she knows that taking that chance is better for their relationship than forcing him to give up his quest, which could keep him there but doom their relationship to a lifetime of resentment.

STYLE

Parable

The rhetoricians of ancient Greece used the word "parable" to refer to a literary illustration. The most common association that the word has comes from the Bible, where it is used to describe a brief story that is meant to convey some spiritual truth. One example of this would be the well-known parable of the prodigal son from the Gospel of Luke, which tells the story of a son who leaves his father's house and wastes his inheritance on extravagant, or prodigal, living. When he returns, broken and impoverished, he is welcomed back into the family, offering a lesson in forgiveness that has become familiar to people of various cultures and religions throughout the ages.

Though, at book-length, *The Alchemist* is longer than parables traditionally are, it does possess qualities of a parable. Coelho uses the book as an instrument to show his readers behaviors that he believes will benefit their lives. Readers can relate events in Santiago's story, such as his encounter with the self-proclaimed king of Salem or his rise from servant to partner in the crystal shop, to their own lives, and draw lessons and generalizations from it that can guide them in how to live their lives.

Religious Allusions

An allusion is a reference to a character or event that readers might recognize. In *The Alchemist*, Coelho uses frequent allusions to works with religious and spiritual significance. The character of

Melchizedek, for example, is not necessarily the king of Salem who is referred to in the Hebrew Tanakh and in the Christian Old Testament, but giving him that name makes readers think of those two books. Other parts of the book allude to the gospel of Saint Matthew, the story of Abraham, and the Koran's five obligations for Muslim life. By alluding to a diversity of traditional, sometimes contradictory, religious texts, Coelho is able to give *The Alchemist* a feeling of tradition and spiritualism, lending the new book some of the gravity that has been earned by the ancient works.

Archetype

An archetype is a literary figure that seems familiar across ages and cultures. One such figure is the person who sets out on a quest. The quest often entails a search for material wealth. While on the way the seeker is bound to find out things about his or her personality that will prove them worthy of accomplishing their goal.

Coelho draws attention to the fact that the main character of *The Alchemist* should be understood by readers as an archetype, rather than as an individual person, by calling him "the boy" throughout the story. He does have a name, which is given in the book's first line, but his function is to represent all people, not just dreaming shepherds. Similarly, though actual locations such as Tarifa and Tangier are used, the specific places are not given with very many details, to emphasize that it is intended to be a universal story.

Pilgrimage Narrative

The trip that Santiago follows in this novel follows the traditional form of a pilgrimage: it entails a long journey to a place of mystic, ancient significance (in this case, the pyramids), during which the protagonist gains spiritual enlightenment. The pilgrimage is a familiar structure for literary works—a famous example is Geoffrey Chaucer's *The Canterbury Tales*—with roots in the some of the major religions of the world. Muslims, for instance, are obliged to make a pilgrimage to Mecca once in their lifetime if they can, a fact that is referenced directly in *The Alchemist*. Hindus travel to Banares, India, to bathe in the sacred River Ganges. Buddhist pilgrimage destinations include the Bodhi tree under which the Buddha attained enlightenment. Christians journey to such places as Lourdes, France, where the Virgin Mary is said to have appeared eighteen times to followers in the 1800s. Jewish pilgrimages to the Temple Wall in Jerusalem are common. Paulo Coelho has said repeatedly that the pilgrimage that he took in 1986 to Saint James of Compostella, Spain, a journey that he later described in detail in his book *The Pilgrimage*, was a turning point in forming his spiritual view of the world. Likewise, Santiago's pilgrimage brings about a spiritual transformation.

HISTORICAL CONTEXT

"New Age" Spirituality

The Alchemist is considered to be an example of the resurgent, independent interest in spirituality that arose during the 1970s and 1980s and is generally identified as "New Age" thinking.

The social movement that is referred to as New Age is not clearly defined. The phrase is frequently used in a derogatory sense; often, people whose works are called New Age would reject being placed into that category. Still, it appears to be a useful term for identifying a distinct social movement.

Throughout history, there have been off-shoots from mainstream religions. One of the most prominent of these in American history, for example, was Transcendentalism, a system of beliefs that was supported by American literary figures such as Ralph Waldo Emerson, Henry David Thoreau, and Margaret Fuller in the early nineteenth century. In the late nineteenth century, Theosophy was developed by Madame Helena Petrovna Blavatsky to unite the physical world with the spiritual world. Mesmerism and Swedenborgianism were other examples of movements that took on the basic shapes of organized religions but engaged in practices, from divination to hypnosis to studies in the paranormal, that had been rejected by older religions.

In the 1960s, cultural changes swept through society and left people questioning tradition. The fall of segregation as a legal social practice due to the civil rights movement of the 1950s and 1960s led to skepticism about other social structures. Feminism made people question why women and men were expected to follow certain distinct social roles; the American Indian movement addressed the segregation of Native Americans to reservations; the gay liberation movement raised skepticism about what was to be considered the norm in sexuality. It was natural, therefore, that a decade so driven toward individual thought would lead people away from traditional religions in their search for spiritual meaning.

The term "New Age" was used earlier in the twentieth century to describe independent religious movements, but it came into common usage during the 1970s when shops across the country began identifying themselves as New Age bookstores and the monthly publication *New Age Journal* began its run. This category, incorporating various movements such as those labeled self-help, spiritualism, paganism, and self-awareness, continued growing throughout the 1980s and 1990s. Bookstores expanded to carry more goods associated with New Age principles, such as incense, crystals, dream catchers, and recordings of New Age music, which grew into a multi-million dollar industry.

Although it is based on diversity, certain characteristics are common to the New Age movement of the late twentieth century. One is an embrace of spiritualism, or a belief that the ordinary understanding of reality sets artificial limits on the abilities of the individual spirit; this is sometimes talked about as the human potential movement. Another is an interest in the religious practices of exotic ancient cultures, usually Native American or Far Eastern: in *The Alchemist*, this desire to incorporate the established power of older traditions shows itself in the use of stories from the Old and New Testaments, and in observance of rules from the Koran. Often, New Age texts also rely on the existence of mystical beings, or spiritual guides, who are aware of the true state of existence that many people cannot or will not see, and are willing to lead special, chosen individuals to their own enlightenment.

By the 1990s, the term "New Age" was seldom used anymore. Still, the beliefs in individual spiritual growth that led to its identity as a movement a quarter of a century earlier continued to grow. Interest in organized religion declined throughout the late twentieth century, but the same religious impulses that drew people toward religions still existed, and those impulses found themselves satisfied by the New Age religions, books, and music that addressed their questions of spirituality.

COMPARE
&
CONTRAST

- **1980s:** Interests in religious practices that diverge from traditional religions are categorized as "New Age." This term covers a wide range of interests, including self-awareness, occultism, holistic medicine, belief in positive thinking and human potential, and music that promotes relaxation.

   Today: The term "New Age" is used infrequently. In many cases this label has become associated with the very same commercialism that many practitioners of New Age thinking sought to abolish.

- **1980s:** To discover the secrets of world wonders like the Egyptian pyramids, one can read books, watch television specials and films, or travel.

   Today: Using the Internet, individuals from all over the world can take a virtual tour of the pyramids.

- **1980s:** Alchemy is viewed as a quaint old religious belief, almost as a superstition.

   Today: While transmutation of metals into other metals has not been reliably achieved yet, scientists have had some success with electrolysis and sonic cavitation, making it a distinct possibility in the near future.

CRITICAL OVERVIEW

When it was first released in Brazil in 1988, *The Alchemist* failed to attract the attention of the reading public and did not even sell out its initial publication of nine hundred copies. Coelho's publisher dropped it from the publication list. When his following book, *Brida*, was able to generate more interest in 1990, *The Alchemist* was reissued. Its subsequent success has made it a publishing phenomenon. The book has been translated into fifty-six languages and has been published in over one hundred and fifty countries. It is one of the best-selling novels in history, with more than sixty-five million copies sold. *The Alchemist* has made Coelho an international literary sensation: his novels generally are met with much pre-publication interest, arriving at the tops of the bestseller lists in dozens of countries. In all, Coelho has sold over a hundred million books. In addition to his publications, his fans' reverence for Coelho is expressed in their enthusiasm for related products such as calendars, diaries, coffee mugs, and picture frames, all carrying his image and quotes from his works. His fans include such diverse international celebrities as former U.S. president Bill Clinton, Nobel Prize-winner Kenzaburo Oe, and pop singer Madonna.

While Coehlo's popular success is undeniable, his reputation as a literary artist has been a subject of much dispute. In 1992, his nomination to the prestigious Brazilian Academy of Letters was fiercely contested by writers across the country, who felt that his competitor, the social scientist Helio Jaguaribe, would be a much more dignified choice; Coelho won, though even members who voted for him admitted that they were reluctant. "I read one of his books and it was poorly written," said the academy's secretary general, Ivan Junqueria, in an article by Andrew Downie published in the newspaper *Scotland on Sunday*. "We can't ignore the biggest selling author Brazil has ever had. We'll have to elect him one day so it's better to resolve the problem now and get it over with." Critics who do not fall under the spell of his charm tend to be excessively harsh, as when David Sexton, reviewing Coelho's book *Eleven Minutes* in an article in the London *Evening Standard* titled "The High Priest of Spiritual Twaddle," took time out of his review to go back to the author's most famous work. "Actually," Sexton wrote, "*The Alchemist*, his world-beating classic, is even worse, an insufferable little yarn about an Andalusian shepherd boy who journeys into the Egyptian desert to be told by a two-hundred-year-old alchemist to follow his destiny and find his treasure in his heart. 'Listen to your heart. It knows all things, because it comes from the Soul of the World, and it will one day return there,' the alchemist instructs the boy—and the slackjawed multitude who have purchased this egregious volume."

> IT IS DIFFICULT TO TELL THE DIFFERENCE BETWEEN A WORK THAT IS UNBALANCED TO ILLUSTRATE THE RANDOMNESS OF THE WORLD AND ONE THAT IS JUST THE WORK OF AN AUTHOR WHO DOES NOT HAVE FIRM CONTROL OF HIS MATERIAL."

CRITICISM

David Kelly

Kelly is a writer and an instructor of creative writing and literature at two colleges in Illinois. In the following essay on The Alchemist, *he looks at the artistic merit of the novel's structure.*

Many discussions of Paulo Coelho's novels, and in particular his breakout book *The Alchemist*, focus on the author himself or his massive worldwide popularity. His sales numbers are indeed astounding—by some counts, *The Alchemist* is included in the top twenty-five best-selling books in all of human history, and it certainly is one of the biggest sellers by any living writer. People across the world say this book changed their lives and realigned the way they viewed the world. The book's impact on the publishing world cannot be doubted.

Being a publishing success does not necessarily make one's work an artistic success, much as the two might seem to be inseparable to people who can see no other standards for judgment. Many people are willing to dismiss the artistic achievement of *The Alchemist* as illusory after-effects of the book's breathtaking sales records, but they need to offer reasonable evidence for their position; it makes no more sense to say that something is not artistically sound because it is popular than it does to say that its popularity proves its artistic worth. Elements of the novel need to be looked at in their own context for evidence of talent and skill.

One way to test a work's artistic sensibilities is to look at its overall structure. The structure is the place where one can see if the author has a sense of the big picture, if he envisions his novel as a canvas that he is working on and not just as a series of events. Legend has it that Coehlo wrote the book over the course of just a few days, working under a manic sense of inspiration, but the furious pace at which it was produced does not indicate whether it has a sound overall structure; some people are simply able to understand what they want to accomplish as soon as they start. Besides, there is nothing that says that a work written through hurriedly cannot be revised; whatever his inspiration, it is the structure of the finished work that counts.

The Alchemist is divided into four sections. The novel itself is split into Part One and Part Two, both of which are sandwiched between a prologue and an epilogue. Since these parts are situated in parallel places to one another, it would be reasonable for a reader to expect each of them to show some relation to its counterpart.

Readers might be surprised to find a break in the novel when they reach the end of Part One, while the boy is working in a crystal merchant's shop. This division does not occur in any obvious breaking point in the plot of the story. A more natural breaking place might have come fourteen pages earlier, for instance, when the book's main character, Santiago, leaves European soil for the first time in his life and ends up in Africa, or twenty pages later, when he sets off, at last, after a year of distraction, to cross the African desert for Egypt. As it is, the break between the two parts comes in the middle of one of the boy's smaller adventures, when the boy takes up work in the shop of the crystal merchant, whom he is still working for in the beginning of Part Two.

The break between the two parts comes at a low point in Santiago's spiritual life. Not only has he suffered a reversal of fortune in losing his money but at the end of Part One he has lost his momentum. He decides to abandon his quest for the treasure he has been told he can find at the pyramids and return to being a shepherd, the life he lived in comfort for years. In this respect, it is a very fitting place to bring the novel to a halt as

WHAT DO I READ NEXT?

- Coelho has said that he drew much of the inspiration for his 2006 novel *Veronika Decides to Die: A Novel of Redemption* from his own experiences with depression and suicidal feelings, for which he was institutionalized several times in his youth. The book has a more realistic setting, but retains his identifiable spiritual tone. It is published by Harper Perennial.

- Readers often compare the style of Coelho's novel to the 1943 book *The Little Prince*, by Antoine de Saint-Exupéry. Saint-Exupéry's Little Prince, like the boy in Coelho's story, goes on a journey in which he finds meaning in the simplest metaphoric relationships, although his trip covers a more cosmic terrain. This book was published in a new sixtieth anniversary edition by Harcourt in 2003.

- The short story "In Baghdad, Dreaming of Cairo: In Cairo, Dreaming of Bagdhad" by the thirteenth-century Persian poet Jalal ad-Din Muhammad Balkhi-Rumi (known in the West as simply Rumi) is said to be one of the clear inspirations for *The Alchemist*. It is available in the Penguin Classics publication of Rumi's *Selected Poems*, published in 2004.

- The principles for living well that Paulo Coelho outlines in this book are explained more directly in the 1997 collection of his teachings titled *Warrior of the Light: A Manual*. Reissued by Harper Perennial in 2004, this book is often described as a companion piece to *The Alchemist*.

- The title character of Herman Hesse's classic work of literature *Siddhartha* also goes on a spiritual journey to find true meaning in his life. Hesse's book is based in the tenets of Buddhism and Hinduism, which Hesse, a German, combined with European sensibilities, just as Coelho drew from several religious traditions to produce his work. Originally published in 1922, *Siddhartha* was re-released by Shambhala Classics in 2000 in a new translation by Sherab Chodzin Kohn.

- Before *The Alchemist*, Richard Bach's novel *Jonathan Livingston Seagull*, first published in 1970, captured the imaginations of millions of readers worldwide with its simple, meaningful fable about a seagull who transcends the basic selfishness of his breed to indulge his love of flight. It is still available from Avon Press, having never been out of print.

- Coelho has listed the Argentine writer Jorge Luis Borges as one of his literary inspirations. Critics note that *The Alchemist* appears to be based on Borges's 1934 story "Tale of Two Dreamers." The story was originally published in Borges's first collection of stories, *A Universal History of Infamy*, which Putnam reissued in 1992.

- Many of Coelho's fans throughout the world are also attracted to the writings of Irish novelist Niall Williams, who also explores spirituality in ordinary life through signs and omens, writing in a similarly graceful, understated style. Williams's first novel, *Four Letters of Love*, published in 1998 by Grand Central Publishing, concerns a man with a steady government job who quits to be a painter because God has spoken to him, and the ramifications for his son after his suicide.

---

well. This is, after all, a book about a quest, and a quest can only be stopped when the person who is conducting it decides to consider it done. But readers know that this will just be a temporary lull, that the quest is not really called off at the end of Part One at all.

When Part Two begins, Santiago's circumstances are not that much different than they were before the break: he is still working in the crystal merchant's shop, still optimistic enough about his life to turn a profit at his job as the merchant's assistant, and the crystal merchant is still glad to have him there. He spends nearly a year in the crystal business, and then decides that he will not return to Tarifa after all, though planning to do so was the climax of Part One. His decision to renew his quest and travel to Egypt is described in such an off-handed, casual way that he actually explains himself by saying, "Why not?" The crisis that ended Part One apparently was not such a personality-changing crisis at all, leaving readers to wonder why that particular spot would warrant the novel's only division.

It is an important moment, but there are other moments in Santiago's life, as it is related in the story, that are at least as important: his arrival at the oasis of Al-Fayoum; his meeting the love of his life, Fatima; or, certainly, his meeting with the alchemist of the novel's title. As it stands, the book is lopsided, with Part Two comprising roughly two and a half as many pages as Part One. If another break had been added later, Coelho could have divided it neatly into near thirds.

There is a good case to be made that the lopsidedness is consistent with the book's message. The shape of the book could be seen as emerging naturally as Coelho followed his own impulse, just as the story chronicles Santiago's spiritual journey as he throws away the book he is carrying and learns to heed the Voice of the Universe. This might justify the unevenness of the book's structure. It is difficult to tell the difference between a work that is unbalanced to illustrate the randomness of the world and one that is just the work of an author who does not have firm control of his material.

The only other sections of the book, the Prologue and the Epilogue, are poised at either end of the work like bookends and are particularly suited to examination as complements of one another. The Prologue begins with a scene that occurs outside of the flow of the novel, at some time before or after the events described. The alchemist has a book that has been left by someone in a caravan; assuming, with no other evidence, that the caravan referred to is the one that brought the boy, then the book would have been brought by the character called the Englishman, who travels with a heavy load of books. He reads a version of the Greek myth of Narcissus, this one taking the point of view of the lake that Narcissus drowns in after admiring his own reflection. The lake proves to be just as vain as the legendary character, having admired its own reflection in his eyes while he admired his image in its water. The alchemist enjoys this story.

The Prologue adds nothing to the development of the book's specific events. Instead, its significance lies in preparing readers for personification of natural phenomena, which plays a big part in the book when Santiago converses with the desert and the wind. The alchemist's pleasure in this story hints at the values that are in play in the book, with a natural world that is ready to interact with humans on an equal footing. It does not say anything about significant characters or events.

The Epilogue, on the other hand, is an important piece of the story. Part Two of the novel ends with the boy, Santiago, lying in the Egyptian sands, having taken a beating from a band of thieves. It is not until the Epilogue that he finally fulfills his quest and holds the treasure he has been seeking in his hands. He makes plans to return to the gypsy woman he met in Part One, to pay her, and to return to Fatima, whom he met in Part Two, to marry her.

The Prologue is all allegory, and the Epilogue is a continuation of the book's action. They are not designed to match one another at all; there is no attempt made to finish the story in the way it started. They are different styles.

This, along with the division of the novel proper into two vastly uneven parts, broken at an arbitrary point, indicates that *The Alchemist* takes its shape from principles other than artistic design. Paulo Coelho may indeed be a master of allegory and sublime symbol, and his book may have touched the hearts of tens of millions of readers, but at least on the level of artistic design, there is no reason to believe that the book is an artistic success.

Source: David Kelly, Critical Essay on *The Alchemist*, in *Novels for Students*, Gale, Cengage Learning, 2009.

Kirkus Reviews

In the following interview, Coelho addresses his religious background and discusses why he believes The Alchemist *has been so well received.*

What role does spirituality play in your books?

I was always a religious person. I grew up, like almost all Brazilians, in a strictly Catholic family. Later, at the age of rebellion, I doubted Catholicism, and felt that I must try something new. Then

I became a hippie. During this time, I traveled a lot, met people of different backgrounds, and had learned different paths to come closer to spirituality. After I did a pilgrimage to Santiago de Compostela, I returned to the Catholic faith—just because it is in my blood, not because it is the best religion (although the current pope may disagree . . .). All religions have advantages and disadvantages.

Humans have always looked for a sense of purpose for their life. And there are essentially three ways to achieve this: art, science and religion. But if science and religion meet, we will have problems. Spirituality has nothing to do with whether you believe in God or not—it is an approach to life. During the twentieth century we experienced the dictatorship of science, which tells us that the world consists only of scientifically provable things. Thus the amazement and surprise of experiencing our souls were lost to us.

What issues do you explore in The Zahir *that you have not explored in previous works?*

This is the story we hear about success: If you are successful, you should buy this brand, go to this restaurant, talk about this book or this opera, drive this car. In fact, this goes back, in my opinion, to Darwin's theory of the survival of the more strong and fit. We try to prove that we are capable of rising above the average. Although we are not in the caverns anymore, we still behave as if we were—struggling to prove that we are the best. One of the most important things in *The Zahir* is that the main characters are constantly thinking about this: Who am I? Am I who I am, or am I believing in a story that was OK some centuries, millennia, ago, but now is totally outdated? This is the main subject: What story did people tell me? Why do I still believe it? Is this story in fact totally outdated?

Why do you think The Alchemist *has been so well received?*

When I wrote *The Alchemist*, I was trying to understand my own life, and the only way that I could do it was through a metaphor. Then, the book—with no support of press coverage, because the media normally refuses to publish anything about an unknown writer—made its way to the readers, and the readers started to discover that we share the same questions. Little by little, the book started to travel abroad, and today is one of the bestselling books of all time. But this success came slowly, based on word-of-

mouth, and this gives me the sensation, the wonderful sensation, that I am not alone. Of course, by being a well-known author, I never feel myself as a stranger in a strange land, and I am pleased with the idea that many people, all over the world, share a similar modern perspective on life.

What question do you wish people would ask you?

"Are you happy?" The answer is: "No." Happiness is like a Sunday afternoon—very boring. I am in my personal turmoil, which is much more interesting than happiness.

If you could only keep one material possession, excluding a writing tool, what would it be?

A lawnmower and enough fuel.

Source: Kirkus Reviews, "Q & A: Paulo Coelho," in *Kirkus Reviews*, Vol. 73, No. 11, June 1, 2005, p. S4.

Stephen M. Hart

In the following essay, Hart details the use of magical realism in The Alchemist, *places the novel in the context of other works of magical realism, and provides an explanation of the work's success.*

> We are nothing: imitations, copies, phantoms; repeaters of what we understand badly, that is, hardly at all; deaf organ grinders; the animated fossils of a prehistory that we have lived neither here nor, consequently, anywhere, for we are aboriginal foreigners, transplanted from birth in our respective countries of origin. (Lihn, *El arte de la palabra* qtd. in Yúdice 8)

O Alquimista (1988) by the Brazilian writer Paulo Coelho is one of the best-selling novels of all time. Coelho's work has to date sold 31 million copies in fifty-one different countries, making him what one reviewer in *The Independent on Sunday* called a "publishing phenomenon" (qtd. on the book's back cover). A reviewer in *The Times* said his books have had a "life-enhancing impact on millions of people," and another in the *Express* observed that *The Alchemist* "gives me hope and puts a smile on my face" (both qtd. on the book's back cover). One possible explanation for Coelho's popularity is that he uses the shorthand of literary cliché expertly. Consider the following passage that occurs halfway through *The Alchemist*:

> The boy couldn't believe what he was seeing: the oasis, rather than being just a well surrounded by a few palm trees—as he had seen once in a geography book—was much larger than many

> THE ALCHEMIST FUNCTIONS IN COELHO'S NOVEL IN A WAY REMINISCENT OF MELQUÍADES IN GARCÍA MÁRQUEZ'S *ONE HUNDRED YEARS OF SOLITUDE*—THAT IS, AS THE SAGE WHO KNOWS THE ANSWER TO ALL OF LIFE'S QUESTIONS."

towns back in Spain. There were three hundred wells, fifty thousand date trees, and innumerable coloured tents spread among them.

"It looks like The Thousand and One Nights," said the Englishman, impatient to meet with the Alchemist.

Here are a young Spanish shepherd boy who has sold all his sheep to look for treasure in the Egyptian pyramids, an oasis worthy of *The Arabian Nights*, and even an English Orientalist looking for the Alchemist: a passage that clearly presses all the buttons of the easy read.

This play with stereotypes, indeed, is one of the reasons Coelho's work has not always endeared itself to academic audiences, who often see it as pandering to popular taste. Coelho has a column in the online version of the Brazilian newspaper *O Globo*, and he regularly includes a horoscope column (see http://oglobo.globo.com). In some ways his fiction expresses the rather simplistic ideology of the horoscope writ large; his novels are *animated horoscopes*.

It is also true that Coelho's work is often full of grammatical errors when submitted to his Brazilian publishers. Coelho resists having his "errors" corrected, because it changes the "numerology" of the text. Publishers routinely give in to his demands. (I am grateful to João Cézar de Rocha for this information provided in an interview in London, June 24, 2003.) Whatever the literary quality of Coelho's fiction—and many argue it is minimal—there is no doubt that Coelho is a sociological phenomenon. His books have changed what it means nowadays to be a Latin American author (for more discussion on this, see Hart, "Isabel").

Coelho's fiction indeed has broken out of the shell of a mere novel. It now is sold routinely in bookshops on the new age philosophy bookshelf; in my local bookshop, *The Alchemist* appears in the "Mind, Body, Soul" section under the heading of "Visionary Fiction," and alongside Richard Bach's *Jonathan Livingston Seagull*.

There are, moreover, a few delicate hints of magical realism in *The Alchemist*. Magical realism possesses a broadly based public appeal. Indeed, it was the only "foreign" fiction genre chosen by Bloomsbury when the publisher launched the new Reading Group Internet books on various aspects of world literature. The genre of J. K. Rowling's hugely successful *Harry Potter and the Philosopher's Stone* is listed as none other than "magical realism" (see http://silicontenge.com/recommendedreading/reviews/philosophersstone.html).

The alchemist functions in Coelho's novel in a way reminiscent of Melquíades in García Márquez's *One Hundred Years of Solitude*—that is, as the sage who knows the answer to all of life's questions. Omens in *The Alchemist* are used similarly to those in *Chronicle of a Death Foretold* (see Hart, *Gabriel* 43–47), and the appearance of the King of Salem to Santiago smacks of the appearance from beyond the grave of Clara's ghost to Alba when she is in prison in Isabel Allende's *The House of Spirits*.

At this point, the inevitable question arises: What is magical realism? My point of departure is the following observation that appears in Julian Barnes's novel, *Flaubert's Parrot*:

> A quota system is to be introduced on fiction set in South America. The intention is to curb the spread of package-tour baroque and heavy irony. Ah, the propinquity of cheap life and expensive principles, of religion and banditry, or surprising honour and random cruelty. Ah, the daquiri bird which incubates its eggs on the wing: ah the fredonna tree whose roots grow at the tips of its branches, and whose fibres assist the hunchback to impregnate by telepathy the haughty wife of the hacienda owner: ah, the opera house now overgrown by the jungle. (Barnes 104)

Though witty, Barnes's point is misleading because he misses a sense of how the genre has evolved over time and place. This is precisely because of the ways in which magical realism has crossed national, linguistic, and genre boundaries. In addition to the Spanish American variety, there have been studies of magical realism in West African fiction (Cooper); in German, Italian, Flemish, Spanish, French, Polish, and Hungarian literatures (see Hart, *Reading*); and in the visual arts, painting, and cinema (Jameson). In fact, quite a strong case can be made for seeing magical realism's favored genre being the visual arts; it had its indisputable roots in the German art movement Neue Sachlichkeit in the 1920s (Weisgerber). But where did the term come from?

The period from the mid 1920s until the mid 1940s might be called the pre-baptismal stage of magical realism. The term was first used by Franz Roh, a German art critic, in his book *Nach Expressionismus* (*Magischer Realismus*) in 1925. Roh argued that post-expressionist artists painted concrete, real objects in such a way as to reveal their hidden mystery, that is, the magic that lies just beneath the surface of everyday things. Roh's work had an impact in Spanish-speaking countries when translated into Spanish by Fernando Vela and published by the prestigious cultural magazine *Revista de Occidente*. However, the idea only bore fruit some twenty years later, not in Spain but Latin America. What Roh identified as the combination of a crisp, sharply defined phenomenal world with a metaphysical dimension—evident, in his view, in the works of Chirico and Otto Dix—emerged some forty years later as the hallmark of Latin America's version of magical realism. Hence the standard definition, which is evident in the work of critics such as Luis Leal (for further discussion, see below), whose influences can be traced back to Roh and which may be summarized thus: "[T]he secret of magical realism lies in its ability to depict reality objectively but with a magical dimension" (Hart, "Magical Realism in the Americas" 115).

Its first real breakthrough came in the form of Alejo Carpentier's classic essay "De lo real maravilloso," published in the Venezuelan newspaper *El Nacional* in 1948 and republished a year later in the preface to Carpentier's novel *The Kingdom of This World*. Carpentier proposed that the marvellous real defines, no less, the most appropriate way of seeing the history of Latin America:

> The marvellous real comes into existence in an undeniable way when it is born from an unexpected change in reality (a miracle), from an enhanced revelation of reality, or from an illumination which is unusual or singularly able to reveal the hitherto unnoticed richness of reality. (Carpentier 108, my translation)

Carpentier went on to say that the marvellous real is not a mere literary fabrication; rather, it is a question of the people in Latin America actually believing in the supernatural, miracles, and ghosts, even in the twentieth century. As if on cue, one of Carpentier's compatriots, Esteban Montejo, gave the following account to Cuban sociologist Miguel Barnet of the most supernatural breed of creature, the Caribbean witch:

> In Ariosa I saw them catch a witch. They caught her with some sesame seeds and mustard, and she was trapped to the spot. As long as there's a little grain of sesame on the floor, they can't move. [...] So they could fly off the witches used to leave their skins behind. They would hang them up behind the door and then they would fly off, just wearing their bare flesh. All of them were from the Canary Islands. I've never seen any Cuban witches. They would fly here every night from the Canary Islands to Havana in a few seconds. (Barnet 125–26, my translation)

During the 1960s the Latin American variant of magical realism finally came into its own. Following Carpentier's 1949 novel, a number of works, including Juan Rulfo's *Pedro Páramo* (1955), José María Arguedas's *The Deep Rivers* (1958), and especially García Márquez's *One Hundred Years of Solitude* (1967) set the mold for years to come. The criticism written about the movement during the 1960s and 1970s was basically concerned with elucidating the formal mechanics of the work, rather in the style of the new critics. Highly influential during this period was Luis Leal's definition of magical realism as "capturing the mystery which palpitates within things" (Leal 234). This interest in the formal qualities of the work also was evident in the structuralist readings of the 1980s (for examples, see Chiampi; Ricci; for discussion of their approaches, see Angulo 8–18).

But as the structuralists reached their conclusions, the carpet was being swept from beneath them. The Chilean journalist turned novelist Isabel Allende asserted a new brand of magical realism. Her *The House of Spirits* became an instant bestseller in 1982, as did its English translation published a year later. The 1980s were a decade of transition for both the critical analysis and creative writing of magical realism; in turn, Allende's feminized version of the magical-realist formula led to a further spin-off version by Laura Esquivel. Her *Like Water for Chocolate*, published in 1989, was an enormous bestseller when published in English, in particular when her (now ex-) husband's film version of the novel came out in 1994. I use the word *transitional* because new theories of magical realism were on the horizon, theories that initially were inspired by cultural studies and later by postcolonial theory. These theories provided new readings that honed in on the portrayal of cultural boundaries, the cross-mixing of cultures, the mixing of races, the mixing of high and low cultural styles, and a whole new gamut of issues that were as far from the structuralist readings of the 1980s as much as the new criticism that preceded it.

A landmark study was Lois Parkinson Zamora and W. B. Faris's edition of *Magical Realism: Theory, History, Community*, which came out to great acclaim in 1995. To make things even more complicated, hot on the heels of this new version of magical realism were the final stages of the internationalization of the movement that had begun in the 1960s with García Márquez and that meant that the term no longer just referred to Latin America. It now included the fiction of various post-colonial nations of the world. As Aijaz Ahmad puts it (with ill-disguised sarcasm):

> The bastion of Englishness crumbles at the sign of immigrants and factory workers. The great Whitmanesque sensorium of America is exchanged for a Warhol blowup, a Kruger installation, or Mapplethorpe's naked bodies. "Magical Realism," after the Latin American boom, becomes the literary language of the emergent post-colonial world. (qtd. in Cooper 30–31)

This internationalization often was accompanied by a flagrant promotion of the mixing of races and cultures, what Salman Rushdie called "mongrelization." As Rushdie said of his masterpiece:

> *The Satanic Verses* celebrates hybridity, impurity, intermingling, the transformation that comes of new and unexpected combinations of human beings, cultures, ideas, politics, movies, songs. It rejoices in mongrelization and fears the absolutism of the Pure. Melange, hotchpotch, a bit of this and a bit of that is how newness enters the world. It is the great possibility that mass migration gives the world, and I have tried to embrace it. *The Satanic Verses* is for change-by-fusion, change-by-conjoining. It is a love-song to our mongrel selves. (qtd. in Cooper 20)

There has been a growth in this approach since the 1990s and beyond of a group of writers whom Timothy Brennan has called the "Third-World cosmopolitans." Brennan began his book on Rushdie "by looking at a group of literary celebrities from the Third World who all seemed to share something in common. Originally, this included Mario Vargas Llosa, Derek Walcott,

Salman Rushdie, Isabel Allende, Gabriel García Márquez, Bharati Mukherjee, and a few others—a group I would call 'Third-World cosmopolitans'" (qtd. in Cooper 20).

So what distinguishes the traditional approach to magical realism and the new cultural studies approach? Are they that different? The traditional approach sees magical realism in terms of a conflation of two literary genres—realism and the fantastic. So in the master narratives of the nineteenth century—Dickens, Balzac, Perez Galdós, for example—the realist mode leaves room for the emergence of the magical, but it is done in such a way that the monofocal vision of the text is not undermined. Prosper Mérimée's *La Statue de Vénus* is an excellent example of what is meant here. Magical events are reported, alluded to, and discussed, but they are separated from the world of the narrator by an invisible line; that is, they occupy the realm of the bizarre, the strange, the "Other" (see Hart, "Magical Realism in Gabriel" 40–42). In a text such as García Márquez's *One Hundred Years of Solitude*, however, it is not immediately clear from which side of the invisible line the narrative speaks. In this novel, what the cosmopolitans regard as fantastic—ghosts, young beautiful girls going up to heaven when hanging the sheets on a line, gypsies disappearing into a puddle of tar—are not seen by the locals as magical in any sense. What is magical for them is what the cosmopolitan sees as ordinary—railways, trains, the cinema, false teeth.

A cultural studies approach to magical realism, by contrast, is one that focuses on the cultural politics underlying the ideology of representation. According to this methodology, the emergence of the magical-real is predicated on the existence of cultural bi- or trifocalism—that is, a cultural system in which no one single system of thought is given precedence over another. It is not that the savage is magical and the nonsavage refuses to see this, or that the narrator—in a gesture of anticolonialist recuperation—brings the savage's worldview to the fore in his or her fiction. For this in itself would still be monofocalism, not colonial but anticolonial. Rather, it is that the novel presents a worldview that is characterized by hybridity, in which no one of the competing visions is accorded preeminence (see Rowe). It is, indeed, from within the jaws of the Lacanian *béance* that the magical-real emerges.

In my view, however, there is an aspect of magical realism that runs deeper than whether one takes a close reading or a cultural studies view of the genre and that concerns the ambiguous way in which magic appears within the economy of the magical real novel. Often it is at odds with stereotypical views about what magic is. The inevitable question arises: What is magic? When a magician does a conjuring trick—creating magic before our eyes—he does something ordinary, hoping we will miss the trick and see the magic. As we all know, the conjurer uses apparatus of three types: apparatus that is exactly as it appears to the audience, equipment that secretly has been prepared to aid the performance of the trick without altering its appearances, and equipment that is hidden from sight and used without the knowledge of the audience. The knowledge possessed by the conjurer is in direct proportion to the audience's ignorance—in other words, if the audience sees behind the scenes, the trick fails and the magic is dispelled. This relationship between the magician and the audience is very different from the "magic"—if such a word is permissible—that is found, for example, in the Old Testament. Here it is as if the conjurer does not know what he is doing but the audience does.

There is a famous story in the Book of Exodus when Joseph correctly divines the meaning of the dreams of the baker and the butcher. Both men tell their dreams to Joseph, but they do not know what the dreams mean. Joseph—who listens to the dreams in the way an audience witnesses a story—does know what they mean and correctly predicts the stories as omens: The baker will be spared and the butcher hanged. The baker and the butcher have no idea what the magic means, although it comes from within them, and yet somebody external to the process does. The unconscious speaks a language that the subject misunderstands but the Other divines. The unconscious, to quote Lacan, is the language of the Other.

It ought to be added that Joseph fulfills the role of Other in the Old Testament in another far more fundamental way. He is a Hebrew in a foreign country (Egypt): "I was stolen out of the land of the Hebrews, and here also I have done nothing that they should put me into the dungeon" (Genesis 40.15). It is not only butchers and bakers who do not understand their dreams, but also the pharaoh of Egypt who is ignorant of the meaning of his dream about the seven fat and the seven lean cows. In the Old Testament the

Hebrew is the one able to see the magic depth within external phenomena, whereas the Egyptian simply sees the surface reality of things and reads dreams literally. To use a metaphor quoted from Luis Leal's definition of magical realism, we could say that Joseph "captures the mystery which palpitates within things" (Leal 234).

Santiago, the protagonist of *The Alchemist*, operates in the story of his own life in a way that is reminiscent of Joseph's role in the Old Testament, although he takes divination one step further. He is able to interpret objective phenomena, rather than simply dreams, as omens of future events. When he sees a hawk swooping down to make a kill, he "knows" the oasis will be attacked:

> Suddenly, one of the hawks made a flashing dive through the sky, attacking the other. As it did so, a sudden, fleeting image came to the boy: an army, with its swords at the ready, riding into the oasis. The vision vanished immediately, but it had shaken him.

What is intriguing about this vision—which turns out to be a correct premonition—is that it came to a boy who only recently arrived in the oasis. Like Joseph, Santiago is a foreigner. The chieftains want to know why this has happened:

> "Who is this stranger who speaks of omens?" asked one of the chieftains, eyeing the boy.
>
> "It is I," the boy answered. And he told what he had seen.
>
> "Why should the desert reveal such a thing to a stranger, when it knows that we have been here for generations?" said another of the chieftains.
>
> "Because my eyes are not yet accustomed to the desert," the boy said. "I can see things that eyes habituated to the desert might not see."

It is precisely because Santiago is a stranger—because he sees with the eyes of a foreigner the land he inhabits—that he is able to divine the future, to see the divine within the everyday.

In various guises this idea—that individuals are often unaware of the magic staring them in the face and need a nudge to see it—weaves its way through Coelho's novel. This is especially evident at the point of anagnorisis when, after years of searching, Santiago suddenly realizes where the treasure is hidden. Thus, when Santiago is discovered digging for treasure near the Pyramids he is attacked and nearly left for dead. But then the leader comes back and says to him:

> You're not going to die. You'll live, and you'll learn that a man shouldn't be so stupid. Two years ago, right here on this spot, I had a recurrent dream, too. I dreamed that I should

travel to the fields of Spain and look for a ruined church where shepherds and their sheep slept. In my dream, there was a sycamore growing out of the ruins of the sacristy, and I was told that, if I dug at the roots of the sycamore, I would find a hidden treasure. But I'm not so stupid as to cross an entire desert just because of a recurrent dream.

Again, while the Egyptian sees nothing in his dream—that is, interprets it as meaningless—the foreigner, the Spaniard, sees that it contains the truth. The real suddenly has burst open to reveal its magic. Santiago discovered his treasure, which was—the whole time—just beneath his feet near the sycamore tree. The leader is the unknowing recipient of treasure, and although the answer comes from within him in the form of a dream, he is unable to decipher its meaning. It is the foreigner who is able to decipher the rebus that comes from the unconscious. The system whereby the subject's unconscious needs to be interpreted by the Other is echoed by the rule whereby the events of a national culture need to be deciphered by a foreigner to function as omens.

There are a number of ways in which *The Alchemist* overlaps with the ideology and techniques of magical realism—in the use of the omen to structure the story and its vision of magic just palpitating beneath the surface of things. But perhaps just as important is the sense in which the novel reenacts the drama of cultural hybridity that lies at the core of magical realism. In an interview Coelho pointed out, "Even if I don't write about Brazil, I see the world with Brazilian eyes. [...] I don't have this wall. I believe that everything is magic and profane at the same time, everything is sacred and mundane" (Coelho, "Interview," http://www.fireandwater. com/microsites/coelho). This admixture of the magical and the profane is echoed in Coelho's novel by the collision of cultures; *The Alchemist*, to use Rushdie's words, is, after all, "a bit of this and a bit of that."

First, it is important to note that Santiago's name is chosen deliberately—alluding to the patron saint of Spain—and yet his journey will take him to the heart of Arabian culture, understood in a generic sense, through Morocco and on toward the Pyramids of Egypt, such that his journey reenacts some of the topoi of *The Arabian Nights* (for more about these topoi, see Irwin). The first person he meets is a mysterious individual who turns out to be a high priest of the Old Testament (because he possesses the

Urim and the Thummin, that is, the divinatory devices contained within the breastplate of judgment worn by the high priest described in the Book of Exodus 28.15). Right from the beginning, therefore, the protagonist is portrayed as standing at the crossroads between various ancient cultures; he simultaneously is intersected by Christian, Hebraic, and Arabian cultures. This is what I think Coelho means when he says that he sees the world with Brazilian eyes. His eyes are those of the hybrid in which there is no single, overriding monofocal vision of reality. Instead, it is a culture of palimpsest in which different cultural surfaces slide over one another, supplanting each other momentarily. Just as one day is followed by its successor in historical time, so each day is proved retroactively to be an omen of the following day, and so the faces of different cultures melt into each other.

In this brief analysis I have shown some similarities between the magical realism in Coelho's fiction and the fiction of, for example, García Márquez. Some differences are in tone. Whereas the Colombian's fiction is predicated on an ideology that verges on the nihilistic, viewing Latin American history as repeating the mistakes of its past with depressing regularity, Coelho's fiction grows from a vision of reality that is, as *The Times* critic put it, "life-enhancing." Coelho's fiction uses the techniques of magical realism, but endows them with a visionary quality, promoting the notion that each of us is destined for treasure, that each of us has a magical dream buried deep down within us, and that it is up to us to search the reality around us until we finally discover where the magic is.

Source: Stephen M. Hart, "Cultural Hybridity, Magical Realism, and the Language of Magic in Paulo Coelho's *The Alchemist*," in *Romance Quarterly*, Vol. 51, No. 4, Fall 2004, pp. 304–12.

Baghat Elnadi and Adel Rifaat

In the following excerpt from an interview conducted by Baghat and Rifaat, Coelho discusses his spiritual background and its influence on The Alchemist.

... In the two centuries since the Enlightenment, man has become the measure of all things. This attitude of mind has changed many things for the better, but it gives short shrift to the spiritual dimension of human existence. People today need to rediscover a relationship with transcendence, but only on condition that it is through their own

> YOU NEED COURAGE TO LAUNCH OUT INTO AN UNKNOWN WORLD, ABANDONING ALL YOU POSSESS. AT THE THRESHOLD OF OUR QUEST, THE FEAR OF STEPPING INTO AN UNKNOWN WORLD AND THE DESIRE TO STAY AT HOME LIE IN WAIT FOR US. IT IS A CRUCIAL MOMENT OF INITIATION."

experience and that they [give] consent to that experience, which should not be subjected to any religious authority. By putting forward a model for an individual spiritual quest in your novel The Alchemist, *you put your finger on this overriding concern of people today. Perhaps this is one of the reasons for its tremendous success.*

Paulo Coelho: The Enlightenment did not prevent people from having their irrational side or rule out intuition or enthusiasm. Humanity gradually turned its back on them for other reasons. Yet I am convinced that humanity is now quietly opening its doors again to things which it had rejected and ceased to respect. The most important of these seems to me to be the idea of mystery. This is something that must be understood—not so much the fact that there is a limit to human knowledge as the fact that mystery is part of the human condition. When I fall in love, it is not because the person I love is the best in the world or even the best person for me. Love is beyond reason, and so is spiritual questing. Why do we need spirituality? I do not know. That's part of the mystery. Some people have sought a recipe for the human condition. "You've got to do this," they tell us. "You've got to do that." I don't trust them. But I do trust those who have sufficient humility to respect the mystery surrounding our lives and to acknowledge that there are major reasons that are beyond our understanding. When I wrote *The Alchemist*, I obviously did not know that it was going to be such a success. I only wanted to write about what I firmly believe, which is that everybody needs to live out their personal legend.

This is what's new, that people who feel the need to get down to essentials no longer have to go through a priest, a rabbi or an imam. The Alchemist *suggests that they can find self-fulfillment by pursuing a personal quest which is a source of fulfillment rather than a curtailment of their freedom. This changes a lot of things.*

P.C.: We all feel an inner need to see the world not only as it appears to our senses but as a vaster intangible reality embracing the Whole. This is what I called the "soul of the world" in *The Alchemist*. Spirituality, which caters for this need, can therefore only be a personal quest. There is a path to God, marked by signs which are so many letters of an alphabet ensuring direct communication with the divine. However, this does not preclude the need at certain times for collective adoration and prayer. At those times, we turn to religion. Religion is there to satisfy a desire to belong to the community, to find brothers and sisters. But it does not show us the path to God. This path starts from within each of us. It is up to us to unravel the thread. ...

Yet your own personal quest first led you in different directions. At one time you were a hippie and then you flirted with left-wing politics. ...

P.C.: Yes. I have tried just about everything. I have wanted to live my life to the hilt. I was raised by the Jesuits, which is the best way of completely losing your faith, because God is forced on you. I left the Catholic church precisely because it had been forced on me. I returned to it later after a pilgrimage to Santiago de Compostela, not because it is the best or ultimate religion but simply because I carry it within me. The world opened up in the 1960s. People, especially young people, started to travel, meet and make contact with each other. It was a magic moment, a moment in the history of humanity when an entire generation set about answering basic questions such as: What am I in this world for? Who am I? Why was I born in Brazil instead of in Egypt? These questions have been pursuing people ever since the dawn of time. They can't be avoided, even if people sometimes feel they have given up on them. In an attempt to answer them, people have explored the three paths of art, science and spirituality. These are three very different things, but they impinge on each other. In fact, the three overlap and blend together. But there are certain things that it is very dangerous to mix up. Spirituality and art can cross-fertilize one another and great scientific geniuses often have poetic intuitions. But when people want to find some kind of scientific basis for religion, the result is catastrophic. The experience of faith belongs to an order of reality that cannot be reduced to the world of concepts or be forced into a scientific mould.

Collective religious experiences are creating many conflicts, instead of prompting people to understand each other better and share things. . . .

P.C.: The experience of true faith always brings us back to the Other. This being so, the first person I see is my neighbour. There is a sense of joy which I want to share with him or her. If that joy is not shared, it ceases to be joy. On the other hand, in sadness that is truly shared there is room for joy. . . .

Even misfortunes are opportunities to learn the price of things.

P.C.: Yes, provided we persevere along the path of our own personal legend, provided that we do not give up. Unfortunately, in the course of their journey, many people betray the dream which connects them to the soul of the world. They sacrifice it to the acquisition of social status. If a person's true vocation is to become a gardener and if by becoming a gardener that person achieves self-fulfillment, nothing should deter him or her. However, in our day, people will be forced more and more often to abandon their dream—often under family pressure—and become lawyers or doctors. They will forget their personal legend, they will lose their sense of belonging, they will no longer have the resources to transform each experience and each misfortune into a fresh opportunity to lift themselves up.

No sooner has the hero of *The Alchemist* decided to follow his dream than he is robbed. You can imagine his disillusionment! He who had found the inner strength to fulfill his personal legend, who thought, as if by right, that the whole world would conspire on his behalf, finds himself alone and penniless. You need courage to launch out into an unknown world, abandoning all you possess. At the threshold of our quest, the fear of stepping into an unknown world and the desire to stay at home lie in wait for us. It is a crucial moment of initiation. But we cannot stand on the threshold for ever. We must dare to move. Only corpses do not move. Life is movement. But where to? This is what we all have to discover for ourselves.

The need to cast off from our moorings. . . .

P.C.: To do this, we have to give free rein to our rebellious side. I am a great believer in inner rebellion—not lifelong rebellion or rebellion without cause or restraint, but rebellion against the force of habit, against the fear of change—which is really fear of living—rebellion that will enable us to make our own way by strengthening our determination. Take the example of the struggles we have to wage with the family from childhood on. My mother was always opposed to my personal destiny. But at the same time she helped me find the strength and skills to control myself, persevere and find my own way. Without this conflict, I would never have developed willpower. These are quite legitimate struggles!

I do not know where this rebellion comes from. It is a force which is liberated in us and which liberates us in turn. It is the quest for personal space and time. We cannot accept that our life span should be measured in terms of so many years of primary school, followed by secondary school and then a job. All this is only our collective space-time and it should on no account stifle our personal space-time. It is necessary to strike a balance between the two.

You say that we do not know where we are going, and yet you speak of rebellion. Isn't there a contradiction in this?

P.C.: Yes there is, fortunately. This is what freedom is all about. There has to be rebellion against the forces of inertia and death in order to liberate the forces of life and creation, which are not programmed in advance. Otherwise, there would be no freedom. By that I mean freedom in its existentialist sense, in other words a compromise. I am free, I can leave this room right now, but I won't because I have freely imposed a certain code of behaviour on myself. I am also free to write a book, but to do so I have to sit at the computer for several hours a day. I impose this constraint on myself in complete freedom. On the other hand, if I am sitting in front of the computer and all the ideas are already in my head, there will be nothing creative about it. We have to leave a space so that inner freedom can express itself.

How did you set about writing The Alchemist? *What ideas did you start out with? Did you know how the story would develop beforehand?*

P.C.: You may be amazed to learn that the story of *The Alchemist* comes from the *One Thousand and One Nights*. It is quite a short tale, only a few lines long, about a hidden treasure for which the hero searches far from home, only to find it eventually within himself. I took four guiding ideas from it: the personal legend, the language of signs, the soul of the world and the need to listen to one's heart. I started the novel with this very short tale as my guide. The rest was vague, like being in a fog. The only thing I knew was that the boy would eventually return to his starting point. There were times—and this is the experience of creation—when I felt as if I was trapped by my own story. At one point, the boy has to transform himself into the wind. It is a matter of life or death. He has to do it. But how do you start describing such a thing? As you can imagine, I myself have never transformed myself into a wind. I panicked. . . . Then I told myself that I had to take the plunge and I went right on to the end of the book.

Hemingway used to say that when he started a novel he had no guiding theme, but that when he stopped writing in the evening, he knew what he was going to write on the following day. . . .

P.C.: In my youth, when I came across quotations like that, I used to say to myself that they were hooey. Now I know they make sense. The wellsprings of creation bubble up in ways that are to some extent unpredictable. In Hemingway's case, the limits of the predictable were on the following day. The day after that was always a blank page. Writers are like pregnant women. . . .

In my own case, I don't write all the time. I let two years go by between one novel and the next. Things happen during those two years which, together with many others that happened long before, beget a novel in me, like begetting a child. Everything we say today may find its way into some future book.

Frederic Rossif, the well-known film director who died some years ago, once met a Sufi mystic in a cave in Iran and asked him: "What is a saint?" The holy man's answer struck everybody to whom Rossif told the story. It was: "A saint is a man who has pardoned God".

P.C.: That was a brilliant answer. It strikes a particular chord with me since my book *The Fifth Mountain* starts out from the idea that we should struggle with God. According to the Bible, God should be accepted as a father. Personally, as I said earlier when talking about my mother, I am rather more inclined to wrestle with Him. It is a legitimate struggle. Pardoning God implies that one has already fought with him, as a way of gradually coming closer to Him.

By raising all these questions, The Alchemist *has gone well beyond the realm of literature.*

P.C.: The novel has inspired a classical symphony, composed in the United States, which will be played at Tarifa in Spain next June. This concert will also be an occasion for an international debate to be held on religions and on ways and means of defusing the religious wars that are threatening us. It is in this capacity, in fact, that I have been appointed an adviser to the Director-General of UNESCO.

Source: Baghat Elnadi and Adel Rifaat, "'The Beyond Is Accessible to Those Who Dare,'" in *UNESCO Courier*, Vol. 51, No. 3, March 1998, p. 34.

SOURCES

"Biography," in *Official Site: Paulo Coelho*, http://www.paulocoelho.com.br/engl/bio.shtml (accessed July 25, 2008).

"Blavatsky, Helena Petrovna Hahn," in *The Oxford Companion to American Literature*.

Coelho, Paulo, *The Alchemist*, translated by Alan R. Clarke, HarperSanFrancisco, 1993.

"Coelho 'Very Happy' with *The Alchemist* Screen Adaptation," in *CBC News*, May 18, 2008, http://www.cbc.ca/arts/film/story/2008/05/18/alchemist-coelho-weinstein.html?ref=rss (accessed July 25, 2008).

Downie, Andrew, "Novelists' Talents Brought to Book in Brazilian Literary Battle," in *Scotland on Sunday*, July 21, 2002, p. 21.

Funk & Wagnalls New World Encyclopedia, s.v. "Parable."

Howe, Peter J., "Martha Stewart's Firm Buys Magazine," in *Boston Globe*, August 13, 2004, http://www.boston.com/ae/celebrity/articles/2004/08/13/martha_stewarts_firm_buys_magazine/ (accessed September 16, 2008).

Memmott, Carol, "Paulo Coelho Builds on His Alchemy," in *USA Today*, May 9, 2007, http://www.usatoday.com/life/books/news/2007-05-09-paulo-coelho_N.htm (accessed July 25, 2008).

Oxford Reference Online, s.v. "Pilgrimage."

Schafer, Jack, "What Does New Age Really Mean?" in *New Age Information*, http://www.newageinfo.com/whatis.htm (accessed September 16, 2008).

Sexton, David, "The High Priest of Spiritual Twaddle," in *Evening Standard* (London, England), August 4, 2003, p. 35.

FURTHER READING

Arias, Juan, *Paulo Coelho*, Thorsons Publishers, 2000.
 This authorized biography of the author's life gives the details of his story in a complimentary way, as Coelho would like them presented; still, it is the only comprehensive overview of his career to date.

Hauck, Dennis William, *The Emerald Tablet: Alchemy of Personal Transformation*, Penguin Press, 1999.
 With simple, direct language, Hauck gives the history of alchemy and outlines seven basic steps for transformation, corresponding with the principles discussed in Coelho's novel.

Ortolano, Glauco, "An Interview with Paulo Coelho: The Coming of Age of a Brazilian Phenomenon," in *World Literature Today*, Vol. 77, No. 1, April–June 2003, pp. 57–9.
 While there are many interviews with Coelho in publication, this one focuses on him as a writer, not as a figure of inspiration. Ortolano keeps the focus on his inspirations and his place in the literary world.

Anthem

AYN RAND
1938

Anthem is a novella by American writer Ayn Rand, first published in Great Britain in 1938 and revised for its first American edition in 1946. The novel is set in some unspecified time and place in the future, many years after human civilization has undergone a cataclysm in which all knowledge was lost and a primitive, rigidly collectivist society was established. In this society, there is no concept of individuality. Even the word "I" has disappeared from the language. The novel describes the efforts of the main character, Equality 7-2521, to reestablish a sense of personal identity and restore the knowledge of the past by objective scientific inquiry. In doing so, he must face many dangers and privations.

Although *Anthem* did not attract much attention on first publication, the success of Rand's later novels gave it a boost, and it has maintained its popularity for nearly half a century. By the early twenty-first century, 3,500,000 copies had been sold, and 100,000 copies are sold every year. *Anthem* is especially popular among young people, including high school and college students, who see in Equality's struggle to attain a meaningful sense of self a model for their own emergence into maturity. The novella remains important as an expression of the dangers of totalitarian societies and the importance of individual creativity and political freedom.

Ayn Rand (New York Times Co. / Getty Images)

AUTHOR BIOGRAPHY

Novelist, philosopher, playwright, screenwriter, and author Ayn Rand was born Alice Rosenbaum in St. Petersburg, Russia, on February 2, 1905. She was twelve years old when the Bolshevik revolution took place in 1917, and she witnessed the early establishment of the Soviet communist state. As a young girl she had already decided to become a writer, but when she entered the University of Petrograd she chose to major in history, graduating in 1924 at the age of nineteen.

Seeing no future for herself in the communist state, she came to the United States in 1926. Hoping to become a screenwriter, Rand went to Hollywood, where Cecil B. DeMille gave her a job as a movie extra and junior writer. In 1929, Rand married the aspiring young actor Frank O'Connor, and two years later she became a naturalized American citizen.

In the 1930s Rand worked as a screenwriter, but her first success was a play, *Night of January 16th*, which had a successful run on Broadway in 1934. In 1936, Rand published her first novel, *We the Living*, which is set in Russia and shows the destructiveness of the Soviet communist system. Rand was a strong supporter of capitalism.

American publishers rejected Rand's next work of fiction, the novella *Anthem*, which was first published in Great Britain in 1938. It did not find an American publisher until 1946, several years after the publication of Rand's third novel, *The Fountainhead*, in 1943. Rejected by many publishers, *The Fountainhead* was finally published by Bobbs-Merrill, slowly became a bestseller, and was made into a movie in 1949. Like Rand's earlier works, the theme of *The Fountainhead* is the superiority of individualism over collectivism.

During the 1950s, Rand gathered around her a group of admirers who helped to promote the philosophical system Rand founded, known as objectivism. In 1957, Rand's last novel, *Atlas Shrugged*, was published. This also became a bestseller, and Rand became well known not only as a novelist but as a philosopher. She was a regular speaker on college campuses and was interviewed on TV talk shows by Johnny Carson, Tom Snyder, and Phil Donahue. One of her followers, Nathaniel Branden, created the Nathaniel Branden Institute, which offered taped courses on objectivism.

Among Rand's best-known philosophical works are *For the New Intellectual: The Philosophy of Ayn Rand* (1961), *The Virtue of Selfishness: A New Concept of Egoism* (1964), *Capitalism: The Unknown Ideal* (1966), *Introduction to Objectivist Epistemology* (1967), *The Romantic Manifesto: A Philosophy of Literature* (1969), and *Philosophy: Who Needs It* (1971).

Rand died of heart failure on March 6, 1982, in New York City.

PLOT SUMMARY

Chapter 1

Anthem begins with the narrator, a young man named Equality 7-2521, writing in his diary. He is alone in some dark, hidden place and he writes by candlelight. He knows that in his society it is considered a sin to write and think alone, and to have an individual will, but he is determined to record his story. Everything in society is under the control of the state. He was raised not by a

MEDIA ADAPTATIONS

- *Anthem* was adapted unabridged for audio CD, narrated by Paul Meier, by HighBridge Audio, in 2002.
- Another unabridged audio CD version, narrated by Christopher Long, was released by Blackstone Audiobooks in 2004.

family but in the Home of Infants, then at the age of five he was sent to the Home of the Students, where he remained for ten years. His daily routine was strictly regulated, and he was taught that the individual counts for nothing: "We exist through, by and for our brothers who are the State." He was unhappy there because he knew he was different from the others, but he was not allowed to acknowledge it. He thirsted for knowledge but found little to interest or stimulate him because all the scientific and other knowledge from the past had been lost. When he was fifteen, he was sent to the Council of Vocations, which allocates an occupation to everyone, regardless of their abilities or interests. He was told he would be a street sweeper. He worked as a street sweeper for four years, living in the collective Home of the Street Sweepers. Then, two years ago, he committed what he calls a "crime," and his life changed dramatically.

One spring day after work, he and his friend, International 4-8818, discover an iron bar covered by weeds in a ravine. They pull it up and find steps going down into a shaft. Equality 7-2521 descends. He finds a long tunnel with iron tracks, and he realizes that it is a remnant of the past, known as the Unmentionable Times, almost all traces of which have been lost. Returning to the surface, he tells International 4-8818 that he has no intention of reporting his find to the authorities. They agree that they own this newly discovered place and will die before they surrender it. Each night thereafter, Equality 7-2521 sneaks away from the House of the Street Sweepers and goes to the secret tunnel. He does

simple scientific experiments and studies manuscripts he has stolen from the Home of the Clerks. He has discovered knowledge that is unknown in the Home of the Scholars. He knows that what he is doing is considered evil because it does not have a clear goal of benefiting humanity, but he feels no guilt or regret.

Chapter 2

Equality 7-2521 finds that he is attracted to a young woman who has been assigned to work in the fields. She lives in the House of the Peasants. For men to take notice of women in this way is forbidden. He keeps watching her, and one day she notices him and smiles at him. Although they do not speak to each other, they develop a secret signal of their mutual interest. He calls her the Golden One, even though it is considered a sin to give someone a name that distinguishes them from others. One day they manage to meet and exchange a few words. They fall in love. He feels happy as he goes home. He also knows that although officially everyone is happy, in fact, everyone is fearful. Suspicion falls upon him because he is so clearly filled with joy. He thinks about all the knowledge that was possessed in the Unmentionable Times and wonders what it was that was lost. All the books from those times were long ago burned. He remembers how he once saw a man burned at the stake because he had uttered the Unspeakable Word, and wonders what that word was.

Chapter 3

Equality 7-2521 reports that after two years of research and thought, he is discovering how to harness the power of electricity. He calls it "the greatest power on earth." Using copper wires and other materials he found in his secret hideout, he has constructed new devices. He is eager to learn more.

Chapter 4

Some time passes before Equality 7-2521 and the Golden One speak again. She reveals that she calls him The Unconquered. They speak affectionate words to each other, knowing that such words and thoughts are forbidden. She gets some water and he drinks it from her hands. They do not understand the emotions they are feeling.

Chapter 5

Equality 7-2521 finishes constructing an electric light. He is delighted with his accomplishment and is inspired when he thinks about how it might be used to benefit humanity. He decides to take his invention to the meeting of the World Council of Scholars, convinced that it will be well-received.

Chapter 6

Thirty days pass before Equality 7-2521 writes in his diary again. He reports that he was captured the night of his last entry. That night he had forgotten to return on time to the Home of the Street Sweepers. His absence was noticed and he was questioned about where he had been. He refused to answer and was sent to the Palace of Corrective Detention, where he was severely whipped. But he still refused to answer. He lay in a cell for many days recovering from the whipping. Then he remembered that the World Council of Scholars would be meeting the next day. He escaped from his cell and returned to his secret hiding place in the tunnel.

Chapter 7

He carries his electric light, which is in a glass box, to the Home of the Scholars, where the Council is meeting. He greets the scholars and tells them about his invention, placing the box on a table in front of them. But when he demonstrates it to them, they are frightened. They tell him he has broken the law by thinking that he has more wisdom as an individual than the collective wisdom of all other men. They condemn his invention in part because it would destroy the Department of Candles and play havoc with the Plans of the World Council. They declare that the box must be destroyed. When he hears this, Equality 7-2521 breaks one of the windowpanes and jumps out of the window, clutching the glass. He runs until he reaches the Uncharted Forest, which is an uncultivated place beyond the reach of the authorities. He knows he is doomed but does not care. He takes courage from the fact that he still has his glass box with him.

Chapter 8

He records in his diary his first day in the forest. He is enjoying a newfound sense of freedom. He managed to kill a bird for food, and for the first time saw his own face in the reflection from a stream. He explored the forest until sunset, then found a hollow between the roots of the trees where he plans to sleep that night.

Chapter 9

More days pass without him writing. Then he records what happened on his second day in the forest. The Golden One found him. She had heard that he had gone to the Uncharted Forest and followed his tracks. She said she would follow him wherever he went. They embraced, and he told her there was nothing to fear. From that day on, they continue to walk through the forest, sleeping at night within a ring of fires to protect themselves from the wild animals. They plan to build a house someday when they have traveled far enough away from the city.

Chapter 10

They are crossing a chain of mountains when they discover a house. They know instantly that it dates back to the Unmentionable Times, protected from the weather by trees. They explore the house and find many things they do not understand and wonder at, such as mirrors and books, which they have never seen before. They decide to make it their home. Settling in to their mountain dwelling, they feel called to a great work but do not yet know what it is.

Chapter 11

Standing on the top of the mountain, Equality discovers the meaning of his life, which lies in the expression of his individual thoughts, will, and desires. In this lies his happiness. He owes nothing to anyone else and has no obligation to share anything with anyone else. He will no longer have to think in terms of "we," which results in slavery, but only in terms of "I," in which lies freedom.

Chapter 12

He reads many books for days and realizes the full significance of the word "I." He decides he wants to be called Prometheus, after the mythological figure who brought light from the gods in order to aid humanity. He wants the Golden One to be called Gaea, who in mythology was the mother of the earth and of all the gods. He is now certain of his mission. He will continue to study and learn the secrets of the past; he will produce a son and teach him "reverence for his own spirit." He plans one day to return to the city and take some like-minded people back to his house and together they will begin a new chapter in the history of mankind. He envisions eventually being able to free the entire world from its condition of slavery.

CHARACTERS

Collective 0-0009

Collective 0-0009 is described as the "oldest and wisest" of the World Council of Scholars. After Equality has demonstrated his electric light to the Council, Collective 0-0009 denounces him as an arrogant lawbreaker and declares that he will be turned over to the World Council who will decide what to do with him. He calls for the box which contains the electric light to be destroyed. In making these judgments, Collective 0-0009 reveals himself to be as small-minded as everyone else is in this society, unable to recognize the value of innovation, or of any idea or piece of knowledge that is not already known and approved by general consent.

Equality 7-2521

Equality 7-2521 is the twenty-one-year-old man who narrates the novel. He is also referred to as The Unconquered by the Golden One, and eventually he renames himself Prometheus. Equality has always known that he is different from the other members of his society, who passively accept their situation and do not question the authorities or the collectivist ideology under which they live. He explains that he was born under a curse, which "has always driven us to thoughts which are forbidden. It has always given us wishes which men may not wish." Although Equality is intellectually gifted, he is assigned by the authorities to a lifetime of labor as a street sweeper.

Equality first disobeys authority when he falls in love with the Golden One; such relations between individual men and women are forbidden. He shows his rebellious, independent qualities again when he decides not to report the discovery of the secret tunnel. This is the moment when he takes his decisive step toward a new way of thinking and living. He spends much time alone in his secret tunnel, researching and conducting scientific experiments, reading manuscripts, and writing in his diary. All these things are forbidden. He shows physical courage when he endures a whipping without giving his interrogators the information they seek. He shows courage again when he defies the verdict of the World Council of Scholars and escapes with his precious invention. This marks another turning point for him. Until this moment, he has not fully understood the nature of his society. He naively expects the scholars to embrace his discovery of electricity and to invite him to live in the Home of the Scholars. But when the scholars refuse to listen to him, he is no longer under any illusions about the nature of the society he lives in, and he finds freedom at first alone and then with the Golden One in the forest, where he practices self-reliance. Throughout his adventures, he shows that he is prepared to take all manner of risks in order to follow his individual desire and creativity, his sense that individual life is better than the dull conformity he is presented with, that knowledge from the past must be revived, that something vital is missing from human life as he experiences it in his repressive collectivist society. He has the courage to be independent, to commit what are considered sins so that he can forge a new path for himself and eventually for humanity as well.

Fraternity 2-5503

Fraternity 2-5503 lives in the Home of the Street Sweepers. He is quiet and cries often, day or night, for no apparent reason.

The Golden One

See Liberty 5-3000

International 4-8818

International 4-8818 is a street sweeper who works in the same brigade as Equality. He is a lively young man with a sense of humor and some artistic talent, which he is not allowed to express. He and Equality become friends, even though it is forbidden to make personal friends, and they discover the secret tunnel together. International is too frightened to go down into it, and he wants to report the find to the City Council and claim a reward. This shows that although International has some spark of individuality, he is still cowed by the prevailing ideology, naively believes in its authority, and is willing to do what is expected of him.

Liberty 5-3000

Liberty 5-3000 is a young woman of seventeen who lives in the Home of the Peasants and works in the fields. When Equality falls in love with her he calls her the Golden One. Like Equality, the Golden One is different from the others. She has an intelligence and wisdom beyond her years and she not been entirely brainwashed by the authorities. When Equality first sees her, he notes that in her eyes there is "no fear in them, no kindness and no guilt," and he cannot get her out of his mind. For her part, when she first sees Equality, she recognizes him for the defiant rebel he really is. She runs away from the Home of the Peasants and follows Equality into the Uncharted Forest. She understands his ideas and wants to share her life with his, and together they begin to plan for their future. She eventually takes the name Gaea, the mythological goddess of the earth.

Solidarity 9-6347
Solidarity 9-6347 lives in the Home of the Street Sweepers. He appears to be a well-adjusted young man, but he has nightmares in which he calls out for help.

The Transgressor of the Unspeakable Word
The Transgressor of the Unspeakable Word is a young man who is burned to death in public by the authorities for uttering the Unspeakable Word. He goes to his death proudly and calmly, even with a smile. Equality, then a child of ten, is in the crowd that watches the burning. The Transgressor looks directly at Equality, as if he is trying to communicate something to him.

The Unconquered
See Equality 7-2521

Union 5-3992
Union 5-3992 is a pale, unintelligent boy whom Equality knows when they are both living in the Home of the Students. He is also sickly and has convulsions. Like Equality, he becomes a street sweeper.

THEMES

Individuality versus Collectivity
Anthem is a hymn to the virtues of individuality, the need for people to express themselves authentically, to follow their own desires and be true to their own individual natures. In this novel, a philosophy that claims to establish the collective good as the sole organizing principle for human society is shown to be counterproductive. It stifles people's natural instincts, creating a kind of robotic conformity that amounts to little better than slavery. In the society depicted in the novel, the indoctrination in the virtue of the collective rather than the individual has drastically affected the language that people speak. The pronoun "I" does not exist.

TOPICS FOR FURTHER STUDY

- Read George Orwell's novel *1984*. Write an essay in which you compare and contrast it to *Anthem*. In what ways does the character Equality resemble Orwell's hero, Winston Smith? Which is the more pessimistic novel?

- Write a diary entry in which you describe your attempts to determine your own course in life, by use of your reason, rather than conforming to what others expect of you. Describe the values you try to live by. In what ways do they resemble or differ from the values that Equality/Prometheus develops in the novel?

- Is Rand's picture of a collectivist, totalitarian society taken to its extreme a fair one? How does it compare to the ideology of the Soviet Union in the 1930s and beyond? Give a class presentation in which you list at least five of the characteristics of the society Equality lives in and then present a historical parallel in the Soviet Union or another totalitarian society.

- What role do feelings, emotions, and intuition play in human life? Should a person's thoughts, decisions, and actions be guided by rational principles only, as Rand's objectivism would dictate? How would society change if this were the case? How would your life change, and the lives of your peers? Give a class presentation in which you discuss the moral and social implications of Rand's objectivist philosophy.

Individuals are referred to in the plural, as "we" or "they." This makes it almost impossible for people to understand themselves as individuals who are different from all other individuals. The paradox is that the attempt to establish a society in which the common good is the only goal has resulted in the opposite—the enslavement of all and the triumph of mediocrity and ignorance. However, for some unknown reason, Equality 7-2521 has managed to grow up in this repressive society with a sliver of individuality; some part of him has escaped the indoctrination that condemns others to a dreary life dominated by fear of doing something that is not approved of by the group. All that is needed, the novel implies, is the unleashing of a single spark of creativity in one individual to reactivate the potential of human life that is otherwise buried under a false ideology that obscures rather than reveals the truth. Equality, on his journey to becoming Prometheus, learns that nothing is more important than his own individual will and creativity, and only by following these inner impulses can he ensure the future of humanity. The sacred word that he finally learns, "ego," is simply the individual self, different from all other selves and the only arbiter of what is right. Once the individual ego relearns how to assert itself, humanity is freed from the chains of conformity. In this sense, the novel is an anthem (that is, a song of praise or celebration) to the unconquerable spirit of humanity that cannot be totally and forever crushed. All that is necessary is that individuals follow the prompting of their own minds, not the official dictates of those who set themselves up as the spokesmen for the group and the arbiters of right and wrong. These so-called leaders are incapable of conceiving a single original thought and therefore pull everyone down to the same level of dullness and weakness. In contrast, Equality, now Prometheus, realizes the secret of life in his declaration, "I shall live my own truth."

Courage

In the group-dominated society depicted in the novel, it is much easier to conform to what others expect than to think and act for oneself. Bringing attention to oneself in any way, whether it is coveting a certain career or cultivating a romantic relationship, invites censure and punishment from those whose job it is to ensure that no one thinks or does anything outside the range of socially approved behaviors. The courage to be different is therefore a significant theme. This involves physical and mental courage. This is seen first in the cruel death of the Transgressor of the Unspeakable Word, which the Transgressor endures calmly, even with a smile on his face. His knowledge that he is right gives him the courage he needs to face death. Equality shows physical courage when he endures a whipping without giving his interrogators the information they want. He shows courage again in venturing into the Uncharted Forest; he is prepared to

Greek god Prometheus (Mansell / Time & Life Pictures / Getty Images)

confront the unknown. His mental courage is apparent throughout the story; he has the nerve to explore the secret tunnel and to pursue genuine scientific inquiry there when he knows it is forbidden. He dares to challenge the basic assumptions of everything he has been taught; therefore, he exhibits a mental toughness that is necessary for any progress to take place. His companion, the Golden One, is also courageous. She is not only prepared to enter a romantic relationship with Equality, challenging the depersonalized relationships between the sexes that is the social norm, she is also prepared to risk her life when she heads off on her own to the Uncharted Forest in order to be with Equality. The message is that those who wish to free themselves from slavery must be willing to risk their own lives in the process. It is better to die than to give up one's freedom; therefore courage is one of the greatest virtues.

STYLE

Symbolism of the Forest

Set against the uniform dullness of the urban setting—in which the sleeping halls are white and devoid of any furniture other than beds, the Home of the Street Sweepers is "a grey house on a narrow street," and all activity is reduced to an orderly, mind-numbing routine—is the wildness of the Uncharted Forest, which serves as a symbol of freedom. People are taught to fear the Forest, but Equality hears rumors that the Uncharted Forest grew over the ruins of the cities that existed in the Unmentionable Times. This leads him to associate the Forest with vital secrets formerly known and now lost. When he flees to it, the Uncharted Forest turns out to be a place of freedom where he can construct for himself a new life. He describes his first day there as a "day of wonder," and the description he gives as he lies on his back looking up at the sky shows the beauty of what he has discovered: "The leaves had edges of silver that trembled and rippled like a river of green and fire flowing high above us." As often occurs in the romantic comedies of William Shakespeare, the "green world" of the forest contrasts with the hypocrisy of life in the city; it is a place where people can discover their true selves.

Mythological Allusions

Equality eventually renames himself Prometheus, but he has been a Prometheus figure long before he realizes it. In Greek mythology, Prometheus, one of the immortal Titans, was a benefactor of humanity, interceding on man's behalf with Zeus, the most powerful of the gods. Prometheus wanted to help men to keep warm and cook their own food, and so he stole fire from the gods and carried it in secret down to earth. Prometheus, who is also sometimes known as the bringer of light, thus contributed to the advancement of human civilization. It is therefore appropriate that Equality, with his grand designs for the regeneration of humanity and his ability to harness the power of electricity to create light, should name himself after the Titan. Equality's role as Prometheus is clear from the dramatic moment when he demonstrates his electric light to the World Council of Scholars. As he connects the wires, "slowly, slowly as a flush of blood, a red flame trembled in the wire. Then the wire glowed."

HISTORICAL CONTEXT

The Soviet Union in the 1930s

Anthem was written in opposition to the kind of collectivist society that Rand had experienced in the 1920s in Russia, and which continued its hold over the peoples of the Soviet Union during the 1930s and beyond. The 1930s were a particularly brutal and tragic time for the Soviet Union. Joseph Stalin, who was the Soviet leader from the mid-1920s until his death in 1953, launched a massive campaign, known as the Great Purge, in which up to two million people died. Victims included members of the Communist Party and other perceived political enemies. From 1936 to 1938, the Moscow Trials were held, in which over fifty Party officials were accused of conspiring with the West to assassinate Stalin and restore capitalism. They were all convicted and most were sentenced to death. Although it was not widely known at the time, the defendants' confessions of guilt were extracted under torture, and the rigged trials were merely for show. Other victims of the Great Purge included peasants, ethnic minorities, and others declared to be against the Soviet regime, such as former members of other political parties. The collectivization of agriculture under Stalin's regime was also responsible for a famine that killed over fourteen million people during the 1930s. It has been argued by historian Robert Conquest in *The Harvest of Sorrow: Soviet Collectivization and the Terror-Famine* that the famine was deliberately created in order to ensure that the peasants would not be able to oppose the communist government.

The Red Decade

In the United States during the 1930s, there was more enthusiasm for socialist and communist ideas than at any other point, before or since, in U.S. history. At the time, the tyrannous nature of the Soviet Union's collectivist system was not as widely known as it later became, and capitalism was proving, as it seemed at the time, to be an unstable economic system that had produced the worldwide Great Depression. For several years in the early 1930s, unemployment in the United States was about 25 percent; the Gross National Product fell by 31 percent between 1929 and 1932; and there were thousands of bank failures. Hardships were widespread since, in those days, there were no government programs to alleviate economic distress; millions of American citizens lost their jobs and their savings and were barely able to survive. As a response to the Great Depression, President Franklin D. Roosevelt, elected in 1932, launched what he called the New Deal. The New Deal marked the beginning of an expansion of the role of the federal government in such a way

COMPARE
&
CONTRAST

- **1930s:** The Great Depression causes hardship for millions of Americans; in nearly half of all households, the breadwinner is either unemployed or underemployed, enduring cuts in hours and wages. President Franklin D. Roosevelt creates the New Deal to alleviate the worst effects of the Depression.

  Today: The U.S. economy is the largest in the world. Gross Domestic Product shows steady growth. However, most of the increase in living standards since 1975 has gone to the top 20 percent of households. Rising oil prices create inflationary pressures; budget and trade deficits, among other factors, cause a decline in the value of the dollar worldwide in 2007.

- **1930s:** The New Deal creates a political coalition that enables the Democratic Party to become the dominant force in American politics. The coalition consists of the urban working class, ethnic minorities, farmers, Southerners, and liberal intellectuals.

  Today: The political coalition established by the New Deal no longer exists. Since the 1980s, the South has become predominantly Republican. The politicization of the Christian evangelical movement, whose adherents overwhelmingly vote Republican, has also eroded support for the Democrats since many of these so-called "values voters" are drawn from the working classes who might otherwise be expected to vote Democratic.

- **1930s:** Under the direction of the Communist International (Comintern) based in Moscow, communism grows as a worldwide political movement. In Germany and Italy, communist parties are banned; communists in European countries and the United States ally with social democratic movements to create the Popular Front, which opposes fascism.

  Today: Communism has significantly diminished worldwide. The only communist countries remaining are China, Cuba, and North Korea. China is no longer a rigidly communist system; its economy is increasingly market-oriented with a growing private sector, although political controls on the population remain significant.

that it affected the life of every American citizen. It included the Social Security Act of 1935, the creation of public sector jobs, welfare, unemployment insurance, and other measures designed to regulate the economy to offset the negative effect of normal business cycles. Ayn Rand regarded Roosevelt as a collectivist who was initiating a socialist program. She even thought that some of his advisors were communists. However, because of the perceived weakness and inequities of capitalism, many intellectuals and journalists admired the Soviet Union, seeing communism as a bold experiment in a new economic system and refusing to acknowledge the seriousness of the crimes committed in the name of Stalinism. In such circles, individualism in a competitive market, which had been the bedrock of American tradition, was looked on less favorably. As a consequence of this way of thinking, during the 1930s the Communist Party of the United States of America experienced a period of growth and was very influential in labor unions, which also grew in strength and influence. Many people believed that it was essential to subordinate individualism to the need for collective action to combat the exploitation of the poor by the rich. It was for these reasons that some historians describe the 1930s as the "red decade" in American history.

CRITICAL OVERVIEW

When first published in England in 1938, *Anthem* received generally positive views. A reviewer for the *Times Literary Supplement* described it as a

Two men working as street sweepers (David Rubinger | Time & Life Pictures | Getty Images)

"fantasia with a moral" about the dangers of "collective tyranny . . . whether labelled Communism or Fascism." In the London *Sunday Times*, Dilys Powell declared that "this parable against the submergence of the individual in the State has the merits of simplicity and sincerity" (quoted in Michael S. Berliner's essay "Reviews of *Anthem*" in *Essays on Ayn Rand's* Anthem). When first published in the United States in 1946 by the small Los Angeles press Pamphleteers, *Anthem* received little attention from reviewers; the 1961 publication of the novel by a major press, New American Library, fared no better. In 2002, an audio version of the novel was reviewed by Mark Pumphrey for *Library Journal*. However, Pumphrey showed little enthusiasm for what he called "this long-forgotten exercise in paranoia," commenting also on "the extremist tone" of the author. Literary scholars have generally followed reviewers in giving short shrift to *Anthem*, although this was partially remedied by the publication in 2005 of *Essays on Ayn Rand's* Anthem, edited by Robert Mayhew, which contained

essays on all aspects of the novel. One of these essays, Harry Binswanger's "*Anthem*: An Appreciation," is the text of remarks Binswanger made at an event in New York City in 1998 that marked the sixtieth anniversary of the publication of the novel. Binswanger writes of the novel's "unalloyed benevolence" in the sense that it recognizes "that great things can be accomplished, and that, ultimately, nothing can hold one back but one's own errors—errors that cannot stand the light of the will to understand."

CRITICISM

Bryan Aubrey

Aubrey holds a Ph.D. in English. In the following essay, he examines how Rand's nonfiction book For the New Intellectual *sheds light on the ideas contained in* Anthem.

If *Anthem* is a hymn to the creative potential of the individual, it is also a hymn to the United

WHAT DO I READ NEXT?

- *The Fountainhead* (1943) is Rand's most popular novel. It follows the career of Howard Roark, an architect and one of Rand's ideal men. Roark is guided by his own values, not those of other people, unlike his rival, Peter Keating, and the villainous newspaperman, Ellsworth Toohey. In this struggle between good and evil, the former, revealing itself through the qualities of individualism and integrity, triumphs.

- George Orwell's novel *1984*, first published in 1948, depicts a totalitarian society of the future in which every aspect of life is controlled by the Party. This was the book in which Orwell introduced such terms as Big Brother and the Thought Police, which have since become part of contemporary language. As in *Anthem*, *1984* features a couple, Winston Smith and Julia, who fight back against the stranglehold that the Party has on their lives.

- *We*, by Yevgeny Zamyatin, is a dystopian, futuristic novel that was first published in the Soviet Union in 1921. It is available in a 2006 Modern Library edition. *We* is set in the thirtieth century in a totalitarian state that denies individual freedom and emphasizes the collective good. As in *Anthem*, characters are given impersonal names; the protagonists are the mathematician D-503 and I-330, a woman he falls in love with.

- *Objectivism: The Philosophy of Ayn Rand* (1991), by Leonard Peikoff, is a comprehensive account of Rand's philosophy of objectivism by one of Rand's followers. Much of the book consists of summaries of Rand's philosophical tracts, and Peikoff explains all her major ideas.

States, Ayn Rand's adopted country. In her youth, Rand admired the United States from afar, seeing it as the land of individualism, rationality, and freedom. She never had any

> THE PRODUCER IS AT ONCE THE PHILOSOPHER, THE SCIENTIST, AND THE INTELLECTUAL. HIS IS THE MOST IMPORTANT ROLE IN SOCIETY BECAUSE HE ALONE CAN STEER HUMANITY ON THE COURSE THAT WILL ENSURE THE FREEDOM OF EACH MAN AND WOMAN."

love for her own country, even before the communist revolution of 1917. She despised Russia as the embodiment of a life-negating mysticism that spoke to the worst aspects of human nature. When Rand came to the United States in 1926, it did not take long for her to fall in love with her new country, which she believed represented endless prosperity and progress. She retained her admiration and love for the United States throughout her life; however, in the 1930s she worried that the United States might be betraying the secret of its success and adopting the ideology of collectivism and altruism that had led the Soviet Union down a path of tyranny. Collectivism is the idea that society matters more than the individual; altruism, the unselfish concern for the welfare of others, emphasizes the virtue of self-sacrifice, which is the opposite of Rand's creed of egoism, which lauds self-interest as the motivating factor in human action. *Anthem* serves as a warning of what Rand saw as the collectivist, altruistic idea taken to its logical extreme—the complete absence of any concept of individuality, and how this allows society to lose everything that is most valuable about human life, including creativity, the search for scientific knowledge, and the essential differences between each human being.

Anthem, and the place of the United States in Rand's thinking, can be further understood by a reading of her nonfiction work, *For the New Intellectual* (1961), in which she explains the outlines of her philosophical system. Much of the book consists of excerpts from her four novels, but she also includes an essay in which she surveys and interprets the history of human societies. She argues that they fall into three main categories, run by three types of men. First is Attila, "the man who rules by brute force" and sees violence as the only solution to problems. Second is the Witch Doctor, the religious man, the man of faith who, unable to act effectively in the world, "escapes into his emotions, into visions of some mystic realm where his wishes enjoy a supernatural power unlimited by the absolute of nature." The third type of man is the Producer, also referred to as the "man of reason," the thinker, the intellectual.

In her survey of history, Rand argues that most societies have been ruled either by Attila or the Witch Doctor, or a combination of the two; however, a profound shift occurred in the Renaissance, which dethroned the Witch Doctor—the controlling power of religion over human affairs—and loosened the hold of Attila, who was unable to understand or control the new tide of intellectual and political freedom that had been unleashed. The Industrial Revolution changed the situation still further. The rise of science and political freedom meant that for the first time, Producers, the men of science and reason, became the leaders in society. This was most fully embodied in the United States. Rand's praise of the Founding Fathers, who rejected the ideas associated with both Attila and the Witch Doctor, is fulsome:

> The Founding Fathers were... *thinkers* who were also men of action... They proclaimed man's right to the pursuit of happiness and were determined to establish on earth the conditions required for man's proper existence, by the "unaided" power of their intellect.

For Rand, the rule of reason was necessarily accompanied by political and economic freedom, in the form of capitalism. She admired capitalism as embodied in the United States during the nineteenth century, when the country was largely free of government regulation. In Rand's view, the capitalistic system produced two kinds of men, "the producer of wealth and the purveyor of knowledge—*the businessman and the intellectual.*" These types working together become the benefactors of mankind: the businessman "carries scientific discoveries from the laboratory of the inventor to industrial plants, and transforms them into material products that fill men's physical needs and expand the comfort of men's existence."

How does this theory apply to *Anthem*? The society against which Equality/Prometheus rebels is clearly dominated by Attilas and Witch Doctors—brute force backed up by an apparently secular ideology that in fact contains strong elements of pseudo-religious faith. The Attila element is not difficult to discern. Those who in any way oppose the governing authorities are subject to torture and death. The Transgressor of the Unspeakable Word—that word being "ego," a word that acknowledges the existence of an individual self—has his tongue cut out and is burned to death on a pyre as the mindless masses hurl insults at him. Even speaking about the Unmentionable Times, that period before humanity regressed and the tyranny of the collective was imposed, would earn a person three years in the Palace of Corrective Detention. Equality learns firsthand about the violence the regime is capable of when he is whipped, and after he shows his invention to the Council of World Scholars, he is threatened with being burned at the stake or whipped "till there is nothing left under the lashes." This is a society that will tolerate no dissent, and as such it resembles Soviet Russia and Nazi Germany, the worst totalitarian regimes of the twentieth century.

In addition to Attila, the Witch Doctors are also in full control in this nightmare society of the future. In communist ideology there is no place for God or religion, but it nonetheless has its dogmas, which are every bit as rigid as any theological system and demand just as much blind faith from its adherents. In *Anthem*, the worship of God has been replaced with a worship of the group, which is declared always to be sovereign, no matter how weak or stupid or cruel it might be. In order to enforce the dogma, the architects of this society have developed a pseudo-religious language with which they have indoctrinated their citizens. Equality, for example, is aware that what he is doing, writing in his diary and thinking thoughts that are not shared by the group, is a "sin." The mere fact of being alone is a "great transgression and the root of all evil." As in a religion, there is a creed, and men and women repeat it to themselves if they are "tempted" to think or do anything that is not sanctioned by the group:

> We are one in all and all in one.
> There are no men but only the great WE,
> One, indivisible and forever.

The collective "we" is therefore presented as a quasi-god and described in terms similar to the Christian creed's description of God. This pseudo-religion has its own hymns, sung in the mandatory Social Meetings, in praise not of God but of Brotherhood, Equality, and the Collective

Spirit. As in any religion, there are saints: the Saints of Labor, the Saints of the Councils, the Saints of the Great Rebirth.

The effect of this kind of mind control within an ideological framework is to inculcate fear, shame, and guilt in people about their own individual natures. They learn to self-censure their own thoughts and actions so that they can avoid transgression. As Rand puts it in *For the New Intellectual*, the Witch Doctor makes a man "reject his own consciousness." In this way, morality is turned "into a weapon of enslavement."

The exception, of course, is Equality, who simply does not feel guilty about his heretical thoughts. At the age of twenty-one, when the novel begins, he is already a free man in the sense that he is capable of thinking his own thoughts, having his own desires, and following his own reason. As the novel progresses, he learns how to break free entirely from the demands of the group and steer his own course in life according to the dictates of his reason. He is therefore, in the terms Rand employed in *For the New Intellectual*, a Producer, the creative genius in society, able to discover new knowledge because he employs the unlimited powers of his intellect to understand the laws of nature. He does this not for any altruistic purpose—altruism, in Rand's philosophy, is a negative thing—but simply because of an innate love of learning, of using his own mind, of being curious about things. He does "work which has no purpose save that we wish to do it." The Producer is at once the philosopher, the scientist, and the intellectual. His is the most important role in society because he alone can steer humanity on the course that will ensure the freedom of each man and woman. He does this by following his own self-interest, which alone makes him happy. Happiness, purpose, and freedom all lie within the individual self, not within the collective: "Whatever road I take, the guiding star is within me; the guiding star and the lodestone which point the way. They point in but one direction. They point to me. "

Source: Bryan Aubrey, Critical Essay on *Anthem*, in *Novels for Students*, Gale, Cengage Learning, 2009.

Rhodena Townsell and William Allan Kritsonis

In the following excerpt, Townsell and Kritsonis reveal the importance of reading Rand's works, placing special emphasis on Anthem.

> THE STUDY OF AYN RAND AND HER WORKS LEADS ONE TO THINK ABOUT HIS OR HER OWN PERSONAL PHILOSOPHY OF LIFE. YOU MUST FIRST KNOW WHAT YOU BELIEVE AND UNDERSTAND AND WHY YOU BELIEVE IT BEFORE YOU CAN LEAD OTHERS."

WHO IS AYN RAND?

Understanding Rand's history is essential to understanding and appreciating her storylines. Ayn Rand (Alissa Rosnbaum) was born in Russia, in 1905. She taught herself to read at the age of six and had decided that she wanted to become a writer by the age of nine.

As a youth, Rand witnessed two Russian wars: The Kerensky Revolution (The February Revolution) and the Bolsheviks Revolution (The October Revolution). The February Revolution brought a victory against communism and The October Revolution restored communism.

During the Bolsheviks Revolution, Rand's family fled to the Crimea (a republic in the Ukraine). Her family, once upper middle class business owners, faced near-starvation. The government seized the family pharmacy. Rand witnessed the shortcomings of communism firsthand. She came to hate collectivism.

Rand loved the romantic fantasy of western style writing. She was introduced to it through American history during her last year of high school. Rand took America as her model of what a nation of free men could be. She felt that this was her destiny.

After the Bolsheviks Revolution, Ayn Rand returned to live in Russia. She attended the University of Petrograd. The communist government was running the university. Opportunity for free inquiry was gone. Rand was not satisfied as she studied philosophy and history. Her one escape was the cinema. She loved western films and plays. She wanted to be free of government censure and pursue her desire to write. When she left Russia in 1925 to visit relatives in the United States she secretly vowed never to return to her homeland. Rand's goal was to live in Hollywood and pursue a career as a screenwriter.

Rand struggled for several years at various non-writing jobs. She sold her first screenplay, *Red Pawn*, to Universal Pictures in 1932. This book is said to be the most autobiographical of her novels. It described the tyranny of Soviet Communism. *Red Pawn* is a dramatic story about a beautiful woman who becomes the adored mistress of a commandant of a Soviet prison for men convicted of political crimes. The heroine becomes the commandant's mistress in order to free her husband who, unknown to the commandant, is one of his prisoners. This work contains philosophical insights that reach their climax in the book *Atlas Shrugged* (Page by Page, 2006). The topic for the screenplay was obviously influenced by Rand's childhood in Communist Russia.

Ms. Rand was able to get many of her books and plays published. *The Fountainhead*, written in 1943, eventually became a movie. It was rejected twelve times before it was published in 1943. It made history by becoming a best seller through word-of-mouth. This is the book that gained author Ayn Rand recognition as a champion of individualism.

Rand's most famous book, *Atlas Shrugged* was published in 1957. In this novel, she dramatized her unique philosophy as an intellectual mystery writer with a story that integrated ethics, metaphysics, epistemology, politics, economics and romance. Although she considered herself primarily a fiction writer, she realized that in order to create heroic fictional characters, she had to identify the philosophy, which makes such individuals possible.

Kritsonis (2007) says that some theorists hold to a natural view of moral constructs. This means that they believe that right conduct can be made on rational grounds. All men are created equally. Their creator gives them the unalienable rights to life, liberty and the pursuit of happiness. All of Ayn Rand's heroes...hold this view.

Every book by Ayn Rand published in her lifetime is still in print. Hundreds of thousands of copies are sold each year, so far totaling more than twenty million. Several new volumes have been published posthumously. Her vision of man and her philosophy for living on earth have changed the lives of thousands of readers and launched a philosophic movement with a growing impact on American culture.

The Anthem was written in 1937, but was not published in the United States until 1946. The book was rediscovered when a dinner guest in Rand's home related that he wished for a book about a collective society. Rand told him that she had already written such a book and the rest is history.

Rand was married to American actor Frank O'Connor for fifty years. She preceded him in death and died on March 6, 1982, in New York City.

HOW IS RAND'S PHILOSOPHY REFLECTED IN *THE ANTHEM?*

To understand how Rand's philosophy is reflected in this novella, one must first know the story. The following is a brief synopsis:

The society described in *The Anthem* (1938) has arisen from the remains of what could have been a great nation that has been destroyed. All of the vestiges of modern conveniences have been buried away and are no longer spoken of by the citizens. The people are figuratively and literally kept in the dark. Great fires had raged over the land. In these fires, the Evil Ones (scientific men of a modern society) and all the things made by them were burned. The fire was called the Dawn of the Great Rebirth. It was the script Fire where all the scripts (books) of the Evil Ones were burned, and with them all the words of the Evil Ones. Great mountains of flame stood in the squares of the Cities for three months. This began the Great Rebirth.

The central character in *The Anthem* (1938), Equality 7-2521, was taken from an anonymous mother at birth and raised in a common institutional building with other boys born in the same year. The same holds true for the female infants born in this society. Equality 7-2521 is ostracized because he fights with the other children. Fighting one's brothers is a sin.

At the age of five, Equality 7-2521 is sent to the Home of the Students to study. Again he stands out because he learns too quickly and asks too many questions. He tries to forget his lessons but he has a scientific mind and it shows. Equality 7-2521's teachers are not pleased with his inquisitiveness and they scorn him. He feels that his only hope is to be chosen to study as a scholar when he turns fifteen. At the age of fifteen, all people are assigned a profession.

Equality 7-2521 is crushed when he is not chosen by the great council to begin further studies. He is instead chosen to become a street sweeper. Street sweeping is one of the lowest jobs to be bestowed to a man. Equality 7-2521 finds that many of his co-laborers are mentally and/or physically handicapped. One other normal man appointed to become a street sweeper is called International 4-8818. He is tall and strong and loves to laugh. It is not proper to smile at others; therefore, the teachers shun International 4-8818. International 4-8818 is artistic and draws with pieces of coal. This creates another problem because only those living in the Home of Art are allowed to draw. Equality 7-2521 and International 4-8818 become friends but they never say so in words nor do they allow others to know because it is a sin to show preference for one brother over another.

Equality 7-2521 relates that the newest discovery in this society was made only a hundred years ago. It was the making [of] candles from wax and string. Before this discovery came the latest technology of making glass. Equality 7-2521 is curious about many things and lets his mind run to the old ones. They are the men who live to reach the age of forty. At forty, men are thought of as being worn out. Men are sent to the Home of the Useless, where the old ones live. The old ones no longer work; the government takes care of them. The old ones do not live much longer. When they do live to age forty-five, they are called the ancient ones. This is as much as one can expect.

Equality 7-2521 accepts his fate and keeps his allegiance to his fellowmen. As he goes about his job as a street sweeper he . . . collects and experiments with the materials that he finds in the yard of the scholars. He hides his collection at the city cesspool until he makes his next discovery. As he [is] cleaning one evening he discovers an iron bar among the weeds. Underneath the iron bar is a black hole. The hole is a tunnel. This tunnel has existed since the unmentionable time. It soon becomes a place where Equality 7-2521 goes to study in secret.

Equality 7-2521 studies in secret for two years and he realizes that he has learned more during this time period than he had learned in all of his years in the Home of the Students. He learned things, which are not in the scripts. He has solved secrets of which the Scholars had made no record. He came to see how great the unexplored was, and to realize that many lifetimes would not bring him to the end of his quest

for understanding. He also realized that he did not wish to end his quest. He wished nothing but to be alone and to learn. It was the first peace that he had known in his twenty years.

Equality 7-2521's next great discovery was a female. The men in this society are forbidden to take notice of women and vice versa. This woman, Liberty 5-3000, had been assigned to work the soil. She was a farmer and she lived in the Homes of the Peasants. Street Sweepers had to keep the road to the Homes of the Peasants clean.

Liberty 5-3000 was young, thin, blonde and strong. She was a perfect match for Equality 7-2521. They both knew it, and thus began to communicate in subtle ways. He began to think of her as the Golden One. He called his interest in her another great sin. It was the sin of preference. It was a sin to give men names that distinguish them from other men. Later in the book she reveals that she has come to think of him as The Unconquered. This would become his name.

The laws after the Great Rebirth say that men may not think of women except for the Time of Mating. This is the time each spring when all the men older than twenty and all the women older than eighteen are sent for one night to the City Palace of Mating. The Council of Eugenics assigns mating partners to each man and woman. Children are born each winter, but women never see their children and children never know their parents. Twice Equality 7-2521 had been sent to the Palace of Mating and he felt that it was an ugly and shameful matter. Equality 7-2521 vows that the Golden One will never be sent to the [Palace of Mating]. He did not yet know how to prevent it but he knew that he must.

Equality 7-2521 realizes that there is a word, one single word, which is not in the language of men, but which had been. It was an unspeakable word, which no men may speak nor hear. Street Sweepers often found it upon scraps of old manuscripts or cut into the fragments of ancient stones. But when they speak it, they are put to death. There is no crime punished by death in this world, save this one crime of speaking the unspeakable word. When he was ten, Equality 7-2521 [saw] a man burned alive in the square of the City. The man's tongue was torn out so that he could speak no longer. He died with a smile on his face. Equality 7-2521 always wondered, what was the Unspeakable Word?

Equality 7-2521 is eventually caught up in his discovery of the light bulb and does not return to his dormitory on time. Once caught, he refuses to tell the secret of his whereabouts. He is beaten and imprisoned. He hopes that the council of great minds will be grateful for his discovery of electricity and make him a fellow council member. This hope [is] short lived because his electric light bulb frightens the council. They tell him that his unwanted discovery would cause chaos in their world. His discovery could not easily be explained nor would it be accepted. They call for his death. I end here to say that the philosophy espoused by the society in *The Anthem* (1938) is total collectivism.

Collectivists believe that the sole purpose of man is to serve one another. Equality 7-2521 repeated the following words whenever he was tempted: "WE ARE ONE IN ALL AND ALL IN ONE. THERE ARE NO MEN BUT ONLY THE GREAT WE, ONE, INDIVISIBLE AND FOREVER."

We believe this book has the power to cause a reader to pause and reflect. We encourage leaders to read this book in its entirety in order to enjoy its nuances and discover the ending.

Objectivism is the philosophy of Ayn Rand. Objectivism is the belief that there is no greater good for man than to seek to satisfy his own desires. In her novels, Rand dramatizes her ideal man as a physically strong, blue-eyed blond who lives by his own effort and does not give or receive the undeserved. Her heroes honor achievement and reject envy. Rand laid out the details of her world-view in nonfiction books such as *The Virtue of Selfishness* (Rand, 1964).

Objectivism holds that there is no greater moral goal than achieving one's own happiness. A person cannot achieve happiness by a wish or a whim. This requires rational respect for the facts of reality, including the facts about human nature and human needs. Happiness requires that one live by objective principles, including moral integrity and respect for the rights of others (Rand, 1964). Again, Kritsonis (2007) calls this belief natural law.

Objectivists believe the following:

1. Reality exists as an absolute. Facts are independent of man's feelings, wishes, hopes or fears.

2. Reason is man's only means of perceiving reality. Reason is his only source of knowledge, his only guide to action, and his basic means of survival.

3. Every man is an end unto his own self. Man exists for his own sake. He must not sacrifice himself for others or accept the sacrifice of others for himself. The pursuit of his own rational self-interest and of his own happiness is the highest moral purpose of his life.

4. Laissez-faire capitalism is the best system of politics. Under this capitalism, a limited government protects each person's rights to life, liberty, and property. It forbids that anyone initiate force against anyone else. Champions of objectivism are achievers who build objectivism as optimistic. They hold that the universe is open to human achievement and happiness and that each person has within him the ability to live a rich, fulfilling, independent life. This is the idealistic message in Rand's novels. Her novels continue to sell by the hundreds of thousands every year to people attracted to their inspirational storylines and distinctive ideas. Individuals run businesses, invent, create art and ideas that depend on their own talents and on trade with other independent people to reach their goals.

WHEN IS IT PERMISSIBLE FOR LEADERS TO BE SELFISH?

In relation to the *Virtues of Selfishness* (Rand, 1964), one comes to understand the importance of shielding himself from those who would rob him of the time and talent that is necessary for ethical behavior. For example, adequate rest is one of the main requirements for the maintenance of a healthy body and a sound mind.

History tells us that great leaders in battles retreated so that they would live to fight another day. The study of Ayn Rand and her works leads one to think about his or her own personal philosophy of life. You must first know what you believe and understand and why you believe it before you can lead others.

If a leader is so busy meeting everyone else's needs that he does not pause to rest then mistakes, burnout and/or collapse will occur. The average principal must respond to an average of 500 questions per day. A leader must take time to reflect or disaster is certain to follow.

WHERE SHOULD ETHICAL LEADERS LOOK FOR GUIDANCE?

The days of, "That's the way we've always done it," are gone. Understanding the ethical decision-making process has become a critical tool for those who lead America's schools. It is not clear that any amount of scientific inquiry can tell us whether a decision is fair, just, or equitable. When making ethical decisions, the decision-maker must also look beyond his own religious beliefs and personal values. This was a problem in *Atlas Shrugged* (Rand, 1957). A grand transportation system eventually collapsed because business matters were not based on the best practices for the business. A decision maker has to consider his rights and beliefs but ethical decisions must take into consideration the rights and interests of other stakeholders. This is the point where it becomes essential for leaders to be strongly rooted. Ethical leaders must balance their beliefs with a plethora of rules and regulations. Everyone needs philosophy. Philosophy is essential in each person's life. Those who do not think philosophically are the helpless victims of the ideas they accept from others (ARI, 2006).

Educators in a democratic society must educate students and attempt to provide them the motivation to be the best that they can be. Educators must attempt to give everyone the same educational opportunities as we wrestle with "No Child Left Behind" legislation. With all of the pressures from the state level, we must also try to resist the temptation to . . . try and apply the cookie cutter method that Rand describes in *The Anthem* (1938).

When making ethical decisions, the decision-maker must also look beyond his religious beliefs and personal values. A decision maker has to consider his rights and beliefs, but ethical decisions must take into consideration the rights and interests of other stake holders. For example, permitting student led prayer at football games was ruled unconstitutional because it did not take into consideration the rights and interests of persons outside . . . Christianity. Decisions must not be based on personal religious beliefs. Decisions should not violate the moral rights of persons with different beliefs.

Decision-makers must be aware of the difference between the right to hold an opinion on a matter of private concern, and the right to use that opinion as the basis for moral decision-making. We must strive to help each student realize his potential as a worthy and effective member of society. Educators, therefore, must work to stimulate the spirit of inquiry, the acquisition of knowledge and understanding, and the thoughtful formulation of worthy goals (NEA, 2006).

There are many sources for guidance that an ethical leader must refer to and adhere to in order to remain employed. Those obvious sources are: the educator's code of conduct, the local board policy (this will include federal, state and local guidelines), district/campus handbooks and district/campus plans. The ultimate source of guidance comes from within the leader himself. This would be his creator's plan. This plan is built experiences and input from many sources, including authors such as Ayn Rand.

CONCLUDING REMARKS

In conclusion, Ayn Rand's childhood experiences resulted in her taking a strong stance against collectivism. This stance is obvious in her novels, especially *The Anthem* (1938). As leaders, our actions and reactions are revealing in many ways. By studying the works of Rand and other philosophers like her, administrators have cause to stop and revisit their own philosophy. It is our personal belief that the study of Rand and her works will lead ethical leaders to reflect on their own personal philosophy of life. We also believe that one must first know what he/she believes before he/she can ethically lead others. "If you don't stand for something, you will fall for anything."

Source: Rhodena Townsell and William Allan Kritsonis, "Who in the World is Ayn Rand?," in *Doctoral Forum: National Journal for Publishing and Mentoring Doctoral Student Research*, Vol. 4, No. 1, 2007.

James S. Valliant

In the following excerpt, Valliant challenges Barbara and Nathaniel Branden's biographical portraits of Rand and argues that, with the publication of such novels as Anthem, *Rand proved to be ahead of her time.*

. . . Ayn Rand came to America at the age of 21—a young woman, alone in the 1920s—halfway around the world to a country where she still barely spoke the language, determined to become a writer, an artist, in that new language. Less than twenty years later, after the publication of *The Fountainhead*, she was selling the movie rights to her best-selling novel, which was being praised by *The New York Times* for its literary mastery.

Rand's novels represent a remarkable achievement. They involve complex plots that can last over a thousand pages and which are

> "
>
> AYN RAND SAW MUCH MORE CLEARLY, AND MUCH SOONER, THAN EVEN ITS MOST CELEBRATED CRITICS THE NATURE AND CAUSES OF TWENTIETH CENTURY TOTALITARIANISM."

explained in long and complex philosophical passages. Yet, they are still "best-sellers" that keep readers in page-turning suspense through exciting twists and turns across vast and thrilling tableaux.

We the Living, Rand's searing indictment of the Soviet Union—indeed, any dictatorship— was based in part on her own experience in Russia. First published in 1936, it predates the assassination of Leon Trotsky by four years, the publication of Boris Pasternak's *Doctor Zhivago* by two decades, and that of Alexander Solzhenitsyn's work by two-and-a-half decades. Of course, with respect to their philosophies these authors are miles apart, and Rand, in contrast to so many anti-communist writers, opposed both socialism and mysticism in *any* form. Although Rand was certainly not the first Russian to complain about Russia's experience with communism, she was among the earliest to gain an audience outside of that country.

Anthem, Rand's depiction of a future totalitarian dark age in which the word "I" has been removed from the human vocabulary, was first published in 1938, eleven years before the publication of George Orwell's *Nineteen Eighty-Four*, and seven years before *Animal Farm*. Unlike Orwell, Rand labored under no illusion that a totalitarian state could long remain a technologically advanced society, and, again, she seemed uniquely able to perceive the dictatorship implicit in *any* form of collectivism. (24)

Ayn Rand saw much more clearly, and much sooner, than even its most celebrated critics the nature and causes of Twentieth Century totalitarianism.

These novels were just etudes in relation to the concerto that would follow, but *The Fountainhead* would be rejected by a dozen publishers. Despite all the advice she received to temper her views, Rand refused to compromise and held fast to her controversial positions. With very little help, Rand was almost entirely a "self-made" success.

Conservatives hated Rand for her atheism, liberals for her defense of capitalism, and everyone objected to her egoism, but Rand refused to modify or moderate her views to please the critics, and she stuck to her beliefs through thick and thin. The battles she waged over her innovative play, *The Night of January 16th*, and the widely anticipated film version of *The Fountainhead* show how hard she was willing to fight, like her hero Howard Roark, for her artistic integrity— as the Brandens admit.

That Rand never surrendered her controversial stances for popularity would be tested again and again throughout her life—as when a "Texas oil man once offered her up to a million dollars to use in spreading her philosophy, if she would only add a religious element to it to make it more popular." (25) She refused.

Rand astonished her own publishers by getting them to agree to print every word she wrote in her magnum opus, *Atlas Shrugged*. With the same energy and acumen, Rand had gotten Jack Warner to film every single word of the climactic courtroom speech of her hero, Howard Roark, in the film version of *The Fountainhead*.

Clearly, Rand could be as "hard-thinking" (Peikoff's term for Rand), hard working and fiercely independent as any of the characters in her novels.

The Brandens contend that Rand was blind—perhaps even dishonest—when it came to certain "personal areas," especially in her relationship with the Brandens. Mr. Branden says that keeping his affair with Rand a secret involved an otherwise undefined "network of lies and deception." (26) That Rand and Branden worked closely together—and (at the time) had the highest admiration for one another—was certainly no secret, however. If nothing else, the original dedication of *Atlas Shrugged* to both O'Connor and Branden makes this obvious.

Actually, the extent to which Rand was serious about honesty can be seen from the fact that only with the full knowledge and consent of both of their respective spouses did Rand begin her affair with Nathaniel Branden.

We shall return to these "personal areas" shortly. On all other matters, they provide substantial evidence of Rand's impressively rigorous honesty.

Ms. [Barbara] Branden repeatedly tells us that a strict respect for the facts was Rand's normal policy, both in theory and in practice. Ms. Branden even reveals that she was "always impressed with the range and exactitude of [Rand's] memory," a capacity Ms. Branden elsewhere calls "remarkable." (27)

Through their research, even scholars who are critical of Rand have almost entirely verified the truth of Rand's various assertions regarding her education and youth, long a subject of doubt and speculation in some quarters. (28) Despite such verification, these scholars persist in treating Rand's statements skeptically while they simultaneously fail to subject the Brandens' assertions to the same testing of credibility. Indeed, most uncritically (and often extensively) rely on them in their own work.

Describing his first impressions of Rand, her husband, Frank O'Connor, is quoted by Nathaniel Branden as follows: "One of the most striking things about [Ayn] was the absence of any trace of deviousness. The total honesty . . ." (29)

Branden writes that "[w]ith the exception of certain personal areas where she could be appallingly unconscious, [Rand] had the most profound and passionate respect for the facts." (30) More than this, he concedes, Rand was an honest writer who strove for clarity, lucidity and precision. Rand wrote exactly what she meant, getting straight to her point, pulling no punches.

Rand was also true to her values, an attitude which today is regarded as downright rude in dry, academic circles. If Rand admired something, her praise was an exultant hymn—when she admired someone, she hero-worshipped. Conversely, if Rand did not think highly of something or someone, her attack could be merciless. Her sense of justice demanded this attitude, according to all sources.

It seems that Rand embodied in her very personality—as well as in her philosophy—a passionate concern for truth and justice.

By Ms. Branden's account, Rand got intoxicated exactly once in her entire life, at the final dress-rehearsal of the disastrous stage adaptation of her first novel, *We the Living*, titled *The Unconquered*, in 1940. She did not like the effects of alcohol, but she did not object to the social drinking of others. . . .

Rand was no socialist; in fact, she regarded taxes as immoral. Yet, unlike many a socialist hypocrite, she was, going by the Brandens' accounts, a tax-paying, law-abiding citizen. (As an egoist, Rand was dubious of self-made martyrs.)

Rand is also repeatedly described by both Brandens as being remarkably generous to others with both her time and her money. Ms. Branden writes that, "Ayn often was warm and generous with her friends, generous with her concern, her time, her attention . . . " (32) She also relates that an old friend of Rand's recalled "that Ayn and Frank, despite their difficult financial circumstances [at the time], loaned small sums of money to out-of-work writers who were having an even more difficult time." (33) We also hear that, in later years, Rand "gave gifts of money, informal scholarships to young people who could not otherwise complete their education and in whom she saw intelligence and promise." (34) Each of the Brandens reports experiencing Rand's various kinds of generosity, personally.

Rand's gratitude was apparently no less than her generosity, "so much so that people who knew her were often startled by the extent of her gratitude, when they did her the smallest of services . . . " (35). Rand's charm, brilliance and, especially, her gratitude were the very attributes Rand's publisher, Bennett Cerf, most recalled of Rand in his own memoir, *At Random*. (36) Ms. Branden reports that this graciousness and charm were felt by people even in the last decade of her life. (37)

Despite her atheism, and surprisingly to those who might not grasp her concept of egoism, Rand loved Christmas, "an excuse to give parties and exchange gifts with friends." (38)

In comparison to the "great minds" Johnson writes about, and even the average Joe, Ayn Rand was a sober, non-promiscuous, peaceful, rights-respecting, honest, hard-working and generous individual. Rand also exhibited a degree of integrity unknown to a majority of the "giants" of modern intellectual history.

The Brandens all but say that Ayn Rand was a genius of the ages, but they fail to give comparison to others who are said to have achieved that status. Was Ayn Rand harsh to questioners following a lecture, as they report? In comparison to Beethoven's social manner, Rand was a pussycat. Was Rand alienated from her culture and those around her? In comparison to Van Gogh,

Rand was a party animal. Was Rand authoritarian with her students? Mullah Rand?

To justify what they were willing to "tolerate," Rand must be portrayed as a genius. To justify their break with Rand, Rand must be portrayed as a monster. Ms. Branden writes of Rand that both her "virtues" and her "shortcomings" were "larger than life." (39) The whole enterprise is suspect in light of their obviously similar agendas.

The Brandens' criticisms of Rand are, mostly, but not exclusively, personal and psychological rather than philosophical. They briefly review several of Objectivism's principal ideas, not always in the language Rand herself used to explain those ideas, but they do so in a generally laudatory manner. In fact, they appear to be repeatedly assuring their readers that they still support most of Rand's ideas—and that they had good reason to be caught up in Rand's spell, as it were. Their thrust is that Rand often did not live up to her own stated ideals because of deep psychological issues which Rand herself never acknowledged.

There are some significant philosophical differences, however. Mr. Branden rejects the use of the term "validate" with regard to metaphysical axioms, thinks Rand's novels subtly but pervasively encourage psychological repression, (40) and thinks Rand gave insufficient attention to benevolence. (41)

Still more profoundly, Branden endorses such assertions as Haim Ginott's "labeling is disabling." (42) Without disputing that it may be counterproductive in a psycho-therapeutic context to pour concrete onto a patient's current self-estimate, surely even the field of psychology is conceptual, and Branden seems to have veered sharply away from the author of *Introduction to Objectivist Epistemology*, if not the necessity and objectivity of concepts themselves.

Branden also now generally rejects making Rand-style ethical judgments about others, and he says that he prefers a non-judgmental, psychological approach to human evaluation. For example, he now rejects the normative evaluations of the great philosophical systems in history—and some of their originators—which Rand had developed in *For the New Intellectual*. (43) Branden does not argue with Rand's evaluations, but he nonetheless claims Rand's approach unnecessarily alienates intellectuals.

Branden asserts that the severity of Rand's moral judgments was a relic of religious thinking—which he had, he suggests, purged from his own psychology completely. He prefers now to see things simply as "harmful" or "beneficial," rather than "good" or "bad." (44) Branden thus appears to accept the modern notion that passionate normative evaluation is "unscientific" or non-objective, hence, religious. Ironically, it is the psychological dimension of evaluations, i.e., emotions, which Branden now emphatically rejects.

Branden's own confessions to having slavishly and "violently" suppressed his "true self" in order to identify with Rand (discussed in chapters three and four) do not suggest any disturbing religiosity on his own part to Branden. Nor does his self-defined role as Rand's "enforcer" (also discussed in chapter three) strike him as "a remnant" of anything of the sort. The fact that in those days Branden could be what he regards as too "judgmental" and "intolerant" does not suggest anything about his own psychology to the famous psychologist, either.

For her part, Ms. Branden uses concepts that Rand would have wholeheartedly rejected. She refers, for example, to Rand's "feminine instincts," (45) the "intuitive aspects of her nature," (46) and areas of "subjective preference." (47) Rand herself would have demanded definitions of these concepts—whether used about her or anyone else—and almost certainly would have rejected the terminology. Ms. Branden does not give definitions and leaves it up to the reader to rely on what Rand herself would have regarded as sloppy modern thinking. It is not too much to ask that Ms. Branden should explain her philosophically contentious terminology to, say, the average student of Rand's philosophy.

In any case, the thrust of their critique is not aimed at Rand's philosophy, but rather at her failure to live up to it. But they do concede that Rand had remarkable qualities, that she was a woman of rationality, artistic integrity and independence, that she conscientiously read her critics but never yielded to them. She made it her policy to respect the rights of her fellow man and to be an exactingly honest person.

And she was exciting to be around. New ideas flowed daily from a mind with a seemingly unlimited range. Her brilliance and charm could be irresistibly compelling. That is why, they say, they devoted their lives to the woman as well as her ideas. . . .

Source: James S. Valliant, "Rand and Non-Rand, at the Same Time and in the Same Respect," in *The Passion of Ayn Rand's Critics: The Case against the Brandens*, Durban House, 2005, pp. 15–52.

SOURCES

Berliner, Michael S., "Reviews of *Anthem*," in *Essays on Ayn Rand's* Anthem, edited by Robert Mayhew, Lexington Books, 2005, p. 56.

Binswanger, Harry, "*Anthem: An Appreciation*," in *Essays on Ayn Rand's* Anthem, edited by Robert Mayhew, Lexington Books, 2005, p. 309.

Central Intelligence Agency, *World Factbook*, https://www.cia.gov/library/publications/the-world-factbook/geos/us.html (accessed July 20, 2008).

Conquest, Robert, *The Harvest of Sorrow: Soviet Collectivization and the Terror-Famine*, Oxford University Press, 1986.

Hall, Thomas E., and J. David Ferguson, *The Great Depression: An International Disaster of Perverse Economic Policies*, University of Michigan Press, 1998.

Kangas, Steve, "Timelines of the Great Depression," http://www.hyperhistory.com/online_n2/connections_n2/great_depression.html (accessed September 16, 2008).

Miller, Laurence, "Ayn Rand," in *Dictionary of Literary Biography*, Vol. 227, *American Novelists since World War II, Sixth Series*, edited by James R. Giles and Wanda H. Giles, The Gale Group, 2000, pp. 251–60.

Powers, Richard Gid, *Not without Honor: The History of American Anticommunism*, Yale University Press, 1998, pp. 117–54.

Pumphrey, Mark, Review of *Anthem* (audiobook), in *Library Journal*, Vol. 127, No. 19, November 15, 2002, p. 116.

Rand, Ayn, *Anthem*, Dutton, 1995.

———, *For the New Intellectual: The Philosophy of Ayn Rand*, Random House, 1961, pp. 8, 9, 13, 14, 18, 23, 24, 26.

Review of *Anthem*, in *Times Literary Supplement*, May 7, 1938, p. 321.

FURTHER READING

Branden, Barbara, *The Passion of Ayn Rand*, Doubleday, 1986.

This is a sympathetic biography of Rand. Branden first met Rand in 1950 and was her close associate for nineteen years.

Brown, Susan Love, "Ayn Rand: The Woman Who Would Not Be President," in *Feminist Interpretations of Ayn Rand*, edited by Mimi Reisel Gladstein and Chris Matthew Sciabarra, Pennsylvania State University Press, 1999, pp. 275–98.

Brown argues that Rand accepted stereotypical gender roles in which men are associated with reason and superiority, and women are defined only in their relations to men. She illustrates how this works in Rand's fiction, including *Anthem*.

Conquest, Robert, *The Great Terror: Stalin's Purge of the Thirties*, Macmillan, 1968.

This was the first book that revealed the full extent of the terror unleashed by Stalin in the Soviet Union in the 1930s, in which millions died. It is essential reading for anyone who wishes to understand more fully the collectivist system that Rand opposed in *Anthem*.

Gladstein, Mimi Reisel, *The New Ayn Rand Companion*, Greenwood Press, 1999.

This guide to all of Rand's works, including fiction and nonfiction, includes a useful chapter summarizing books written about Rand. Gladstein's short section on *Anthem* (pp. 38–40) is mostly a plot summary.

Bless the Beasts and Children

GLENDON SWARTHOUT

1970

Glendon Swarthout's novel *Bless the Beasts and Children* became a bestseller when it was published in 1970. The novel was so popular that a film was made the following year, and it, too, proved a big success. Swarthout wrote many novels and screenplays, both before and after the publication of *Bless the Beasts and Children*, many of which were very successful, but this 1970 book for adolescents, perhaps above all, has remained very popular. It has never been out of print. Swarthout based the idea for the novel on his own son's experience at a summer camp.

Bless the Beasts and Children is a coming-of-age story in which a small group of adolescent boys discover that they are not the misfits they have thought themselves to be all their lives. Swarthout creates a story of sacrifice and honor among this group of boys, who are called the Bedwetters. Each boy's emotional and psychological needs are explored as the plot unfolds. The story is one of personal strength and of individual and group triumphs that change all their lives.

Swarthout's novel happened to publicize the inhumane slaughter of buffalo by the Arizona Game and Fish Department, and as a result, these state-sanctioned slaughters ceased. The buffalo herds still need to be thinned, but the process has been made more humane, and the suffering of the animals is minimized.

Glendon Swarthout (*AP Images*)

AUTHOR BIOGRAPHY

Glendon Fred Swarthout was born on April 8, 1918, in Pinckney, Michigan. His father, Fred, was a banker, and his mother, Lila, was a homemaker. Swarthout attended Lowell High School, graduating in 1935, and then moved to Ann Arbor to attend the University of Michigan, where he earned a B.A. in English in 1939. After graduation, he married Kathryn Vaughn, whom he had known since he was thirteen years old. After a brief stint writing ad copy for Cadillac and Dow Chemical and then writing a newspaper column, Swarthout saw his writing career interrupted by the start of World War I, when he and his wife began working at a bomber plant. Swarthout began writing his first novel at night while working at the plant during the day. *Willow Run* was published in 1943, just as the author was shipped overseas in the infantry. Swarthout was able to serve as a writer in the army and saw little combat. After his return to Michigan, he again enrolled at the University of Michigan, completing an M.A. in 1946. Swarthout began teaching English at the university, and his only child, a son, was born that same year. After he received the Hopwood Award in Fiction in 1948, Swarthout began teaching at the University of

Maryland. In 1951, he returned to Michigan and began teaching at Michigan State University while studying for his doctorate, which he received in 1955. Swarthout continued to write while a graduate student and teacher and sold a number of short stories, but his first successful novel was *They Came to Cordura* (1958), which was nominated for the Pulitzer Prize and became both a best-selling novel and a successful film.

The year 1960 proved especially successful for Swarthout. *Where the Boys Are* was published and became a successful novel and film, and he was nominated for the O. Henry Prize for one of his short stories, "A Glass of Blessings." After he and his family moved to Arizona, Swarthout began teaching English at Arizona State University, and another novel, *Welcome to Thebes*, was published in 1962. In 1963, Swarthout left teaching and began to write full-time. A succession of novels followed, including *The Cadillac Cowboys* (1964) and *The Eagle and the Iron Cross* (1966). *Bless the Beasts and Children* (1970) became Swarthout's second novel to be nominated for the Pulitzer Prize. Several novels followed, with one of them, *The Shootist* (1975) being named Best Western Novel of that year and becoming a very successful film for the movie star John Wayne. Swarthout won the Spur Award for Best Western Novel in 1988 for *The Homesman*, which also won the Wrangler Award. In 1991, Swarthout received the Western Writers of America's Owen Wister Award for Lifetime Achievement at the National Cowboy Hall of Fame. He died the following year at his home in Scottsdale, Arizona, of emphysema, due to a lifelong smoking habit. His last novel, a romantic comedy, *Pinch Me, I Must Be Dreaming* (1994), was published posthumously. During his lifetime, Swarthout published twenty-two novels, including several children's novels co-written with his wife, as well as several short stories.

PLOT SUMMARY

Chapters 1–3
Bless the Beasts and Children opens with a dream. The dreamer is John Cotton, a fifteen-year-old counselor at the Box Canyon Boys Camp in Arizona, where the sons of wealthy families are sent for the summer. In Cotton's dream, he and the other five members of his

MEDIA ADAPTATIONS

- *Bless the Beasts and Children* was filmed in 1971, with Stanley Kramer directing and producing. The screenplay was written by Mac Benoff, and the distributor was Columbia Pictures.

- An audio version of *Bless the Beasts and Children*, narrated by Scott Brock, was released in January 2006 by the Listening Library. This four-hour tape is available from Books on Tape.

group, known as the "Bedwetters," are herded into a corral, where they are slaughtered. In Cotton's dream, he and his friends are buffalos, as the reader soon learns; Cotton is the last of the six buffalo boys to be murdered. He awakes from his dream just after the gun that shoots him is fired by his mother. Once he is awake, Cotton automatically checks on the campers in his charge—Goodenow, Teft, Shecker, and the two Lally brothers. In Cotton's descriptions of the campers, he paints a picture of misfits who share a cabin because no other group will have them. The boys are called by their last names, with the two Lally brothers known as Lally 1 and Lally 2. Each camper has a transistor radio to listen to while going to sleep. The music from the radio helps each boy relax and provides a soothing escape from the activities of the camp, at which none of the boys has excelled. The camp does not assign the boys to their cabins. Instead, the boys self-choose, or the other boys choose for them. The teams are naturally formed, according to Cotton's explanation, by the boys themselves, as they gravitate toward those they judge most like themselves. Those who do not fit in or who are outsiders are excluded by all groups and eventually band together to form their own group.

In this first chapter, Cotton provides a quick characterization of the boys in his group that establishes their vulnerabilities. He explains that the boys dread going to sleep at night and fear their dreams, but they also hate waking up in the morning and leaving the security of their beds. On this night, the night when Cotton awakes from his nightmare, the boys have witnessed something so terrible that they cannot discuss it. What they witnessed was so awful that Goodenow vomited after dinner. The boys were so traumatized by the events witnessed earlier in the day that they quickly climbed into their sleeping bags without any discussion. After Cotton awakes about an hour later, however, he realizes that one of the boys is missing. Lally 2 has run away. Cotton quickly wakes the other four boys, and in spite of protestations from Lally 1 that he does not care if his brother is found, all of the boys leave their cabin to search for Lally 2.

In the second chapter, all five boys begin the search for Lally 2, who is headed for the highway, where he plans to hitch a ride. After the boys find Lally 2, Cotton tries to persuade all of them to return to the camp, but after it becomes clear that no one is willing to return, Cotton and the boys discuss how they can all work together to complete the job that Lally 2 set out to do. Thus far, no one has mentioned their goal, but all of the boys spend a few minutes recalling their failures at camp and wondering if they can succeed at the quest they are about to undertake. At this moment in the narration, the author inserts some background information about the Box Canyon Boys Camp, whose slogan is "Send Us a Boy—We'll Send You a Cowboy." For a large fee, the camp promises to turn any boy into a man-in-the-making. The camp counselors use a series of physical competitions to transform the boys into young men. The six boys whom Cotton leads have no physical talent for sports, a mode of competition that the boys must face. After this brief background information is provided, Cotton tells the boys that they must vote to decide if they will join Lally in his quest. All the boys agree to go, and the chapter ends with the six boys beginning the preparations for their journey.

In chapter 3, the boys quickly return to their cabin to gather coats and supplies for their journey. They attempt to steal a camp truck, but it is necessary to push the truck away from camp so as not to awaken other campers. Even though the key is in the ignition, the slope away from camp is uphill, and soon the boys discover that they cannot push the truck far enough to start it without notice. They thus decide that they will ride their horses into town, where they can steal a car. The reader learns that the competitions at the camp determine the name of each cabin. The strongest cabin of boys is called the Apaches, followed by, in descending order, the Sioux, the Comanche, the Cheyenne, and the Navajo. The last team is called the Bedwetters.

Chapters 4–6

The boys saddle their horses, lead them away from the camp, and then mount them for the ride into town. Cotton reveals that he is concerned that their choice to leave on their journey will bring the summer camp to a ruinous end. As they depart, the boys pause to celebrate their bravery in leaving the camp. All the boys are inspired by Western movies, in which a heroic cowboy rescues someone, usually a woman, who is in danger. It is especially important to the boys that a movie hero is someone who is going to do something dangerous. The boys see themselves as molded in the same image. Their quest is dangerous, but they are bravely determined to succeed. After they are clear of the camp, the boys begin to gallop into town, just as their film heroes would do and as fast as their horses can manage.

The boys' heroic ride into town is halted at the beginning of chapter 5, when Lally 2 drops his pillow and insists that he will not proceed without it. After the pillow is recovered, the boys continue their ride into town, now at a much slower pace. Once the boys arrive in town, they discover that finding a car to steal is not as easy or as quickly done as they had assumed. After rejecting a number of available cars, the boys begin to panic, and their team camaraderie begins to fall apart. Cotton helps them to refocus by calling for "bump time," a moment of closeness, with all the boys touching in a huddle. When they break apart, they finally see the ideal car to steal, a pickup, which Teft does with ease. It turns out that Teft is both an experienced car thief and a good driver, in spite of his young age. The group is careful to duck out of sight in the stolen pickup, but once out of town, they all cheer and are once again a united team.

As the boys continue their drive, Cotton worries about the amount of time that has already passed and whether they can get back

into camp before dawn brings the discovery that they are missing. He also worries about the rifle that Teft brought along and wishes that they were back in their sleeping bags and that the trauma of the previous day had not occurred. Cotton has Teft stop the pickup after an hour so that the some of the boys can ride up front in the cab, where it is warmer. When he steps out of the cab and goes to the back of the pickup, he sees that Shecker, Goodenow, and Lally 1 are asleep, all three carefully nested together for warmth. The sight of this unity moves Cotton almost to tears. Shecker is the only boy who refuses to take a turn in the cab of the truck. A flashback tells the story of the boys' ultimate humiliation after they tried to steal the buffalo head that is the symbol of the Apache cabin. The morning after this very painful episode, Cotton stepped up to be their leader and to unite the boys. The strength of Cotton's personality gave the boys the strength they needed after their loss and allowed them to leave their cabin and face the further humiliation that they would have to endure. Chapter 6 ends with the boys on their journey and with Cotton firmly in charge of his unified group.

Chapters 7–9

Chapter 7 opens with a short mutiny. After they arrive in Flagstaff, Shecker and Lally 1 rebel, as Shecker wants food, and Lally 1 is tired of taking orders from Cotton. Although he initially does not want to stop, Cotton agrees to do so and finds a bowling alley and bar, where the boys order food. After they are accosted by a pair of local drunks, the boys leave without their food, but the two locals follow them and eventually force the boys to pull over. After the locals threaten to call the law and turn in the boys for stealing a truck, Teft takes the gun out of the truck and shoots one of the tires on their car. Teft then tells the locals to begin walking toward town and threatens to shoot them if they do not comply quickly. Once the locals begin walking away, the six boys pile back into the pickup and resume their trip.

In chapter 8 the boys are nearly at their destination, but then they run out of gas, and Teft admits that he never looked at the gas gauge. By the time the truck stops, they are off the highway and in a very isolated spot. The reader learns about one of the boys' previous expeditions, when they decided that they wanted to go into town and to the movies one evening.

Only the top cabin is given movie privileges as a reward for winning competitions, and the Bed-wetters know that they will never be top cabin and so will never be permitted to go the movies. Instead, they sneak out at night, ride their horses to town, and are able to sit through almost all of the movie before the camp director catches them.

Initially after they run out of gas, the boys' unity dissolves, and they become panicked individuals again. Cotton, though, is able to once again turn them into a team. He knows that without gas, there is no way they can complete their mission and get back into camp before dawn. He presents the boys with two choices to consider. They can abandon their mission, get to the road, and perhaps hitch a ride that will allow them to once again steal a car and then arrive back at camp before their absence is detected. Or they can complete their mission, probably be arrested for stealing the truck and for shooting out one of the tires back in Flagstaff, and probably be sent to some sort of juvenile facility. Cotton unites the boys by letting them vote on these two options. When Cotton himself votes to return to camp, the team initially cannot decide what to do. Since he is their leader, they want to follow Cotton, but finishing their job is also deemed important. Cotton's efforts to unite the boys are rewarded when Lally 2 is the first of the boys to challenge Cotton and vote to continue. After Lally 2 begins walking away, Goodenow, Lally 1, Shecker, and Teft begin to follow, leaving only Cotton standing by himself, next to the now useless truck. For only a brief moment, Cotton feels defeated, but then he feels great joy because the boys no longer need him. They are capable of leading their own way. As chapter 9 ends, Cotton follows the boys as they continue their march.

Chapters 10–12

In chapter 10, the boys arrive at their destination, which is some sort of camp, with many buildings, equipment, and cars. The boys climb over the gate that encloses the camp and begin to walk across a corral. Immediately Goodenow falls down and begins to retch. The boys turn back to help him, and they, too, fall down. When the clouds part to allow moonlight to filter in, the boys see that they have fallen down onto a field of blood, which now covers them.

In chapter 11, the reader is finally told the story of what the boys saw the previous day that

upset them so much. Following a campout elsewhere, the boys are in a camp truck being driven back to the Box Canyon Boys Camp when they see a sign along the highway pointing toward the turn off to a buffalo preserve. Wheaties, the boys' ineffective cabin counselor, is driving, and the boys easily persuade him to leave the highway and drive to where they can see the buffalo. When the boys arrive, they encounter a sanctioned civilian slaughter of buffalo. Three well-fed, domesticated buffalo, who are not afraid of humans, are led into a corral, where a woman, a man, and a teenager are each given a turn at killing a buffalo. None of these people are good shots with a rifle, and many of those in attendance are drunk, which makes them worse shots. What ensues is an inhumane slaughter in which the animals are tortured and forced to endure great pain before they finally die in a barrage of rifle shots. The boys from Box Canyon Boys Camp have mistakenly wandered into a "hunt" that is sanctioned by the Arizona Game and Fish Department as a way to thin the herd of buffalo. Thirty buffalo are to be slaughtered in this manner each day for three days. The chapter ends with the narrator's tribute to the majesty of the buffalo and a commentary on the inhumanity of mankind.

After the boys see the first buffalo killed, they beg Wheaties to leave, but he maliciously refuses. He keeps them all there for the six hours that it takes to murder thirty buffalo in as inhumane a manner as can be imagined. There are thirty buffalo remaining in the pens for the third and last day of the hunt, which is the following day. After their return to their camp, the boys do not talk, and Goodenow throws up his meal. This chapter ends where the first chapter began, with the boys sleeping in their cabin after witnessing the brutal slaughter of buffalo earlier in the day.

Chapters 13–15

After telling the story of the buffalo slaughter in the previous two chapters, the narration now returns to the boys' arrival at the site of the buffalo slaughter. After they are all able to crawl out of the blood and onto dry land, they find a small pond, where they are able to wash off some of the blood covering them. They next begin searching for a way to free the buffalo. The corrals are much stronger and better built than any of them had anticipated. They begin to walk around the corrals, searching for a way into the pens and a way to release the buffalo. Cotton's first attempt to open a pen fails, but by the end of the chapter, he is even more determined to find a way to free the animals.

In chapter 14, the boys make one final attempt to free the animals. Each boy is given an assignment, and under Cotton's leadership, the plan begins to work. Using their flashlights and radios, they manage to spook the buffalo sufficiently to cause them to move as a herd toward the open pens and eventually to freedom. Working as a team, the boys succeed in freeing the buffalo, who when they are free begin running from the pens and camp. The narrator makes clear that the boys have used their previous adventures as a way to develop as a team. Besides the midnight trip to the movies, they had also staged a diversion late one night at their camp, when they opened the horse corral and set all the horses free. Then they went into all of the empty cabins and kidnapped the cabin trophies and claimed them as their own. This trip to free the buffalos is the group's third adventure together and clearly their biggest.

The boys are almost stunned by their success in freeing the buffalo. Cotton has brought along a way for them to all celebrate. On the airplane ride to Arizona several weeks earlier, Cotton had taken advantage of two of the distracted flight attendants and stashed away several small bottles of liquor. He brought three of the bottles with him when they left the camp earlier that night and now shares them with the five other boys. Although the boys quickly begin celebrating their triumph, Cotton once again takes control of the group to call their attention to a problem they have not anticipated. The buffalo are free from the pens, but they have not run away. Instead, they are all standing just outside the corrals grazing on the grass, where they can be easily recaptured. Cotton suggests that the boys can use a truck of hay as a way to lead the buffalo away from the camp and toward the open range.

Chapters 16–18

All of the boys quickly take on their assignments one more time. Teft will steal and drive a truck, and Lally 2 will look for any radios or flashlights that still work, while the other boys help load the hay. Once they are ready, the group piles into the truck and begins the drive out to the range where the buffalo are grazing. Once the truck is next to the buffalo, Lally 2 begins speaking to the buffalo in a soothing tone, and the boys begin to drop hay over the side of the pickup bed. As the truck pulls ahead, the buffalo follow. Cotton worries about the time and about whether they can get to the outermost fence before the sun is up and daylight exposes what they have done. The truck continues its very slow march, through chapters 16 and 17, with the herd following slowly behind.

Teft begins chapter 18 by telling a story about his cousin's piranha and the importance of doing a job completely and finishing what is begun. Teft explains the importance of the story and how the analogy and the story apply to what the boys have done this night. As Teft finishes the story, the boys suddenly realize that more buffalo have joined their caravan. They now have more than the thirty buffalo who were in the pens. Soon it is dawn, and Cotton is even more worried that they are running out of time. He knows that the boys will all be punished, and so he wants their punishment to mean something. They must succeed, or their sacrifice will be for nothing.

Chapters 19–20

When they arrive at the fence, the boys are shocked to see that it is not the simple wire fence they have anticipated. Instead, the fence is chain-link iron and will not be easily broken. The boys try pushing the fence, but it does not budge. At that moment, the boys see trucks and a jeep heading their way. Each vehicle is loaded with people. Cotton orders Teft to load the rifle and to begin firing at the trucks. Cotton tells Teft to aim for the radiators and not at people. Although initially reluctant to shoot, Teft eventually begins to shoot, while Cotton disappears. At this point in the story, the narrator intrudes again to tell the story of the Bedwetters' last competition with the group from the Apache cabin, when the boys surmounted great difficulties to win a wager and prove their strength and teamwork. The symbolism is clear—the boys' teamwork will lead them to stand together against the people who are driving toward them, intent on capturing the boys and the buffalo.

While Teft and the rest of the boys try to stop the people in the trucks and jeep, Cotton drives the pickup through the fencing, tearing a large hole in it. Once the hole in the fence is there, Cotton uses the truck and its horn to create a stampede of buffalo in the direction of the torn fence and freedom. Once clear of the fence, the herd splits into two directions and away from the rim of the canyon. The truck, though, with Cotton still driving, keeps to its course and heads right for the rim. The last vision that Teft, Shecker, Goodenow, Lally 1, and Lally 2 have of Cotton is a glimpse of him sitting in the driver's seat as the truck drives straight over the rim. The boys hear the sounds of the crash and do not know if Cotton was unable to stop or chose not to do so. When the men from the camp arrive, they are stopped in their tracks at the sight of the five boys at the rim; they are crying for Cotton but also rejoicing at their accomplishments, as they honor their leader.

CHARACTERS

Bowlers

The bowlers are two local young men that the boys meet in Flagstaff. They try to hassle the six boys, and when they discover that the boys have stolen a truck they threaten to turn them in to the authorities. Their role in the book is to create tension and cause a small detour. After Teft shoots one of the tires of their car, they are left to walk back into Flagstaff.

Camp Director

The camp director is often referred to but not often seen. His efforts to intimidate the Bedwetters and force their compliance amount to his most notable achievement. He is responsible for the competitive environment that humiliates any boy who lacks the physical abilities that the camp director values. His primary threat is that he is the boys' parental surrogate, and as such, running away from him is the same as running away from their parents. Such an action makes them juvenile delinquents. He uses threats and select rewards to maintain control at Box Canyon Boys Camp.

John Cotton

Cotton is fifteen years old, a teenager. He begins the book as one of the camp counselors but soon becomes the unofficial leader of the group of boys collectively known as the Bedwetters, a title bestowed on them when they fail to win any cabin challenges and end up in last place. Cotton's mother has been married and divorced three times. She is narcissistic—completely selfish and focused only on her own needs. Cotton's only experience with positive parenting was with his mother's second husband, the only one of his stepfathers to spend time with him; after their divorce, this stepfather disappeared from his life. Cotton grew up watching the Vietnam War broadcast on television. He was fixated on the war and planned to become a soldier fighting in Vietnam after joining the Marine Corps at the age of seventeen. As the oldest of the group of six boys, he is also the strongest and the most stoic. Cotton is proud and tenacious in pursuing what he thinks is the right choice. He is also compassionate and accepting of the outsiders in the camp, which is demonstrated early in the book, when he offers several of the boys a place in the cabin that he shares. Cotton is a natural leader who knows that the boys will only succeed and survive by using their group strength and uniting, which he encourages. As a team, the boys are stronger. At the conclusion of the book, Cotton sacrifices his life to complete the group's quest.

Gerald Goodenow

Goodenow is fourteen years old. His father died when he was only four years old. Goodenow is insecure, suffers from panic attacks, and has a poor sense of his own value. He slept in a bed with his mother until he was twelve years old, which was when she remarried. Goodenow does not get along with his stepfather, who displaced him from his position in his mother's bed. When Goodenow's serious emotional problems resulted in his being unable to function at school, the counselor recommended counseling and a special school for disturbed children. Goodenow was pulled from this school as soon as he began to show improvement, but once away from the school, he quickly regressed. After the stepfather discovered that his stepson was wetting the bed, Goodenow was severely punished. At camp, he is teased for being too weak and sissified and because he wets the bed. He cries easily, is homesick, and has attempted suicide. When he tried to drown himself, other campers and counselors laughed at him. Cotton intervened and invited Goodenow to move into his cabin. The special school in which he was enrolled used a technique called "bumping," which was used when a child was in danger of an emotional collapse. Bumping entails a huddle in which all participants bond closely together, touching one another for strength. Goodenow introduces the Bedwetters to bumping after his second suicide attempt, in which he tried to hang himself. This suicide attempt was interrupted by Cotton, who convinced Goodenow that he deserves to live. Goodenow gains confidence and strength of character with the help of the other boys in the Bedwetters' group.

Lally 1

See Stephen Lally, Jr.

Lally 2

See Billy Lally

Billy Lally

At twelve years old, Billy is the youngest boy at camp, and he is usually referred to as Lally 2. His parents are wealthy, which is true for the parents of all six boys. Lally's parents have many marital problems, which account for yearly separations and reconciliations and long vacations together, without their sons. Lally 1 and Lally 2 are left home alone with the servants. Both boys are lonely and neglected. Lally 2 hides in his parents' long-neglected sauna, where he turns up the temperature and sleeps until one of the servants finds him there. He copes with his parents' neglect by withdrawing into fantasies and into an infantile world of bed-wetting and thumb sucking. Lally 2 suffers from night terrors. His parents' erratic parenting and lack of common sense have interrupted his schooling and several attempts at counseling. It is Lally 2 who encourages the rest of the boys in his cabin to run away with him. Lally 2 demonstrates bravery and strength during their quest, especially once the boys arrive at the buffalo camp. He takes the lead several times, and his ability to talk to the buffalo seems to calm them. By the end of the book, Lally 2 is willing to give up his security pillow and stand on his own.

Stephen Lally, Jr.

Stephen is fourteen years old and is called Lally 1. He is jealous of his parents' affection for his younger brother, Lally 2. In actuality his parents are too busy to be bothered with either of their sons, who have been raised by the family servants. The boys are always given two of everything whenever they receive gifts. Because they are treated identically, they have become competitors for their parents' affection. Lally 1 is mean-spirited and vicious and torments Lally 2.

In one example of the older brother's cruelty, after Cotton destroyed a letter that Lally 1 wrote home to his parents, in retaliation Lally 1 tormented and murdered all of the animals that the boys had brought to their cabin. In an uncontrolled fit of anger, he stomped on or beat to death all of the pets he could find. Although he has spent most of his life competing with his younger brother for his parents' love and attention, Lally 1 recognizes his brother's strength by the conclusion of the book, and the two become friends.

Sammy Shecker

Sammy is fourteen years old and, like the other boys in his group, has many emotional problems. Shecker's problems are caused by his comedian father, who uses his son as the object of jokes to impress his friends. Shecker is fat, a glutton who eats to fill the emotional void in his life. Shecker's father once bet a thousand dollars that his son could eat a dozen pieces of pie in four minutes. His father did not care that his son was humiliated. When Shecker's father dropped him off at the camp seven weeks earlier, he spread around bribe money to make sure that his son had extra food. He also gave money to one of the camp counselors and asked him to be his son's friend, and he attempted to bribe the camp director to give Shecker the best horse. Shecker was thrown out of four cabins in his first two days at camp. Cotton offered him a home but quickly began to regret doing so. Shecker is loud and nervous, and he is a braggart who mimics his father's comedy routines. He is a compulsive overeater who also chews on his fingernails, and he generally irritates everyone who is around him. When asked by the other members of the Bedwetters cabin to calm down, Shecker accuses them of targeting him because he is Jewish. He tells Cotton that the boys are all Nazis. By the time the boys arrive at the buffalo camp, Shecker has discovered that he no longer needs to live in his famous father's shadow to succeed.

Lawrence Teft III

Lawrence is fourteen years old. He has a criminal past that proves helpful for his cabin group's needs. Like other adolescents who are bored, Teft easily finds ways to get into trouble. He has stolen his mother's purse, although he does not need money. He also stole his father's car and then a neighbor's car. When his father tried to get his son admitted to the same exclusive school that he had attended, Teft managed to sabotage the application interview. The headmaster recommended the Box Canyon Boys Camp as a way to force discipline on Teft. He was flown from New York to Arizona like a prisoner; he was so disruptive on the plane that he had to be physically confined to a seat. Teft is brave and foolhardy, and he is also determined and tenacious. His boldness is demonstrated several times in the novel, such as when he steals a pickup and also when he shoots out the tire of a car to prevent the group's capture.

Wheaties

Wheaties is supposed to be the Bedwetters cabin counselor. He is abusive and controlling of the boys, labels them as useless, and attempts to punish them. After Teft exposes Wheaties's secret stash of alcohol, cigarettes, and dirty magazines, the counselor abdicates any possible authority over the boys, and Cotton becomes their unofficial counselor. Wheaties takes the boys to the buffalo slaughter and then refuses to take them away until it is completed and all the animals have been killed. Wheaties thrives on the blood and gore of the slaughter and uses the boys' misery as a way to retaliate against them.

THEMES

Heroism

The purpose of the Box Canyon Boys Camp is to turn boys into cowboys. The camp's motto is "Send Us a Boy—We'll Send You a Cowboy." The image of the cowboy was one carefully crafted by Western films in the last half of the twentieth century. The promise inherent in the camp's motto is that the camp can create the same strong heroic figure that has been defined by the Western cowboy. The cowboy is an iconic figure of heroism who faces risks and rescues those in need of saving. The six boys who compose the group called the Bedwetters do not begin their journey to the buffalo camp as any sort of heroes; the camp has failed to turn them into heroic cowboys. They are ordinary boys who have to prove that they can be ordinary heroes, and it takes them the entire journey to do so. In confronting their fears, the six boys find that they are stronger and braver than they thought. Cotton's sacrifice at the end of the

novel is not the kind of heroic choice expected from cowboys. In Western films, the cowboy always triumphs and always survives. Swarthout makes clear that these boys, and Cotton in particular, find their heroism within themselves and not through the artifice of the cowboy motif.

Humanity versus Nature

The slaughter of the buffalo in *Bless the Beasts and Children* serves as an example of mankind's inhumane treatment of animals. Swarthout describes the slaughter of these animals in great detail in chapter 11. The author feels so strongly about the subject that he includes a short lecture about the destruction of the buffalo at the conclusion of that chapter. Swarthout says that the living buffalo, those who remain on the prairies in the twentieth century, are only a remnant of the many that used to live there. That small remnant serves as a reminder of the slaughters that occurred during the nineteenth century. According to Swarthout, this reminder "stirs in us the most profound lust, the most undying hatred, the most inexpiable guilt." Rather than learn from the inhumanity of the past, mankind continues to treat animals as less significant than humans and thus less deserving to live.

Being Outsiders

All six boys in the Bedwetters cabin are outcasts; they do not fit into the Box Canyon Boys Camp social structure. Most of the boys lack the physical acuity and emotional resources that the camp requires of them. Even before they arrive at camp, though, the boys are outcasts within their own families. The parents of Lally 1 and Lally 2 have no interest in parenting. They are so involved in their own lives and their marriage that their sons are excluded from their family. The other four boys come from families that are not much different. Shecker's father identifies himself so completely as a comedian that he cannot be a father, since it is not part of his act. When Goodenow's mother remarries, her new husband forces her to choose between her son and her husband. Goodenow is rejected and displaced and becomes an outsider in his own family. Teft's father is unable to deal with his rebellious son and so his solution is to cast him out of the family. When he fails to have his son admitted to a boarding school, he sends him away to camp. Teft's exclusion by his family is very much like what happens to Cotton. Cotton's mother is a wealthy divorcée who does not

TOPICS FOR FURTHER STUDY

- Camps that are designed to teach discipline to teenagers are quite common. There have been problems with a number of these camps, however, and some children have even died. Research such teenage "boot camps" and prepare an oral presentation in which you discuss what you learned about the way these camps operate and whether they are considered effective at instilling discipline in teenagers.

- *Bless the Beasts and Children* was made into a film the year after the book was published. Rent or borrow a copy of the film and then write an essay in which you compare the film and book. Be sure to include some analysis of the changes that the director made in filming the book and what those changes contribute to the viewer's understanding of the story.

- The broadcasting of the Vietnam War on television was an important influence on Cotton's ideas about manhood. Research the role of television in broadcasting war. Write an essay in which you discuss whether televising a war creates unrealistic or distorted expectations for viewers or if it perhaps makes viewers feel more patriotic.

- The buffalo is an iconic image of the American West. Find at least four different images featuring buffalo that are representative of the role of the buffalo during the nineteenth century. Look for images of the buffalo as they are depicted in Native American life, as they appeared during buffalo hunts, as part of staged Western shows, and as they lived while on the range. Prepare a poster presentation in which you explain to your classmates what each image suggests about the life of the buffalo and what the images teach people about the American West.

- The kind of buffalo "hunt" that Swarthout describes in *Bless the Beasts and Children* was quite common at one time. Research the role of the government in staging public hunts to thin herds of animals. Prepare an oral presentation in which you explain how these hunts were staged, the kinds of animals involved, and how the hunts have changed since Swarthout's novel was published.

- Summer camps for boys date from at least the 1880s. There are a number of photos from early camps as well as other illustrations that depict summer camps. Look through art and photography books in a library and try to select a picture or illustration that you feel best depicts Swarthout's portrayal of Box Canyon Boys Camp. Then write an essay in which you discuss the image that you have selected and explain how your image captures at least one of the themes of this story.

---

want her teenage son to serve as a reminder of how old she is. All of the six boys have been outcasts within their own families, and when they arrive at Box Canyon Boys Camp, the counselors, campers, and even the camp director make clear that they do not fit into the camp hierarchy either.

Teamwork

The six camp rejects who work together to save the buffalo from slaughter are only able to succeed because they work together. Goodenow introduces the boys to a counseling technique that he learned called bumping, in which the boys huddle together, with eyes closed, touching their faces together in a moment of complete trust and bonding. Working together as a team is not easy for the boys. They are accustomed to being rejected and therefore isolated, and it takes practice to learn how to work together. The boys demonstrated that they could work together when they created a diversion at camp that allowed them to steal each of the separate cabin trophies. On the journey to rescue the buffalo, the boys' teamwork falters at times. For instance, in chapter 9, after they run out of gas, the boys' unity dissolves, and they become individuals again. When they arrive at the camp and must work together to release the buffalo, each boy becomes part of the team, with each one performing the job assigned. Only through this teamwork do they achieve their goal.

STYLE

Authorial Intrusion

Authorial intrusion occurs when the author of a novel or story stops the narration to step into the story and insert his or her own comments. Swarthout does this a number of times throughout *Bless the Beasts and Children*. In chapter 11 the author interrupts the narration to provide a history of the kind of state-sponsored slaughter of buffalo that he describes happening in the book. He does more than provide a history lesson, however. Swarthout sermonizes, telling readers that mankind is "born with buffalo blood upon our hands." What follows is a digression from the boys' story that links humankind's obligation to nature with the violence of humans, whose thirst for blood can govern their actions.

Young-Adult Novel

A young-adult novel usually focuses on an adolescent character or a character with whom an adolescent can identify. Literature directed toward an adolescent audience also tends to contain themes that appeal to teenagers and that address issues in which they are interested. In addition, the vocabulary and sentence structure are likely to be easily accessible for adolescents.

Bless the Beasts and Children addresses several concerns of adolescent readers, including bullying, lack of self-esteem, and being an outsider. Swarthout's novel offers six boys whose age makes them ideal for youthful readers who are looking for character types that they recognize and with whom they might identify. Many teenagers have experienced the trauma of not fitting in with other teenagers. In addition, the author is careful to include several exciting episodes in which the boys rebel against authority, a subject of particular interest for many teenagers.

Coming-of-Age Novel

Bless the Beasts and Children can be described as a coming-of-age story. Typically in a coming-of-age novel, a character or characters endure great trials and difficulty, at the end of which the protagonists have grown stronger and matured. It is typical for the characters to suffer and undergo hardships that test their strength and will to succeed. The six boys in *Bless the Beasts and Children* undergo many difficulties and endure many hardships in attempting to succeed. They grow from misfits whose insecurities and fears hamper their efforts into more confident young men who have learned that they are strong and brave. Other coming-of-age novels include Mark Twain's *Huckleberry Finn* and Charles Dickens's *Great Expectations*.

Quest Narrative

In a quest narrative, a hero undertakes a journey in search of something, and after the mission is accomplished, the hero returns home. The quest typically requires traveling a long distance and overcoming many obstacles along the journey. Oftentimes, the quest story includes a great deal of description of the land and of objects encountered by the hero during the journey. *Bless the Beasts and Children* contains many of the descriptive elements of a quest story. Instead of one heroic figure, Swarthout provides six heroic figures who must overcome many obstacles during their journey. The object that the heroes seek is the freedom of the buffalo being held at the buffalo camp. In literature a quest is often a mythic adventure, and indeed, there is a sense of myth in the story that Swarthout tells. The boys, several of whom lack determination and stamina, are able to complete a journey that involves sneaking out of the Box Canyon Boys Camp, stealing a pickup, surviving a confrontation with two local men who accost them, and continuing on foot after their truck runs out of gas. They also survive frequent bouts of fear that threaten to incapacitate them. When they arrive at their destination, they must devise a way to free the buffalo, which requires physical and emotional strength that most of the boys lacked when the journey began. The quest story is a very old literary format, used in epics such as Homer's *Odyssey* and Virgil's *Aeneid*.

Animal Symbolism

Symbolism is the use of a concrete object to represent an abstract concept. In *Bless the Beasts and Children*, each cabin of boys was given the head of an animal to symbolize the strength of the boys in that cabin. The Apaches received a buffalo head, while the Sioux received the head of a lion. The remaining cabins also received animal heads, with the positioning and status of the animals dependent upon the cabins' placement in the camp hierarchy after a series of competitions. The cabin in last place became the Bedwetters, who received a metal chamber pot instead of an animal head, symbolizing their low position in camp. The chamber pot was designed to humiliate the boys in last place, and it represents the protagonists' status as losers.

HISTORICAL CONTEXT

The Development of Summer Camps for Boys

When Swarthout set his novel *Bless the Beasts and Children* in a summer camp for boys, he used a setting that would be familiar to many readers. Summer camps for boys date from at least the 1880s. The goal of early camps was to help middle- and upper-class boys learn skills and develop emotional resources that would help them grow into morally strong young men. Like the Box Canyon Boys Camp in Swarthout's novel, many of the early camps were designed to make a profit and catered to the needs of wealthy families. While many public camps used tents to house the campers, the for-profit private camps were more likely to use wooden cabins, in which several boys would live together. In addition to the sleeping quarters, which were often arranged in group dormitories, camps would also contain a dining hall and kitchen building, as well as a chapel. There would also be a headquarters building, which housed the camp director and featured areas in which the campers could socialize and write letters home to their parents.

The creation of summer camps at the end of the nineteenth century coincided with an increased emphasis on naturalism and a realization of the importance of nature in forming strong young men. At a time when more people were moving to cities, summer camps provided a way to take city boys to the country, where they could develop both physically and mentally in naturalistic ways. Rural boys could gain such experience simply working alongside their fathers, but such was not the case for boys raised in the cities. Consequently, there was a fear that city boys, who were being raised primarily by their mothers while their fathers worked, would either become sissies or be corrupted by the influences of city life. As a result, the first camps were designed primarily to get boys out into the country and away from their mothers. A secondary reason for sending boys to summer camp was to give their lives purpose and structure during the summer months when they were not in school. Mandatory education laws that required children to attend school for much of the year, combined with restrictions on child labor, meant that when school ended at the start of summer, there was little for children to do in the cities. Summer camps provided diversion from city streets, where boredom could lead to discipline problems.

Although the first summer camps provided little structure, they quickly developed very ordered programs to teach boys moral lessons such as the importance of work. Boys were divided by age and assigned duties that were based upon teamwork. In many camps the structure was modeled upon a military system of organization. In some camps, boys wore uniforms, and each group of boys had a leader who assigned work chores for each boy. Boys took turns cooking, cleaning, and maintaining order. When not performing their chores, they took long hikes, exercised, and engaged in competitive sports and games. Boys also learned survival skills, such as how to build a fire and how to fish for food. They also learned how to swim and how to survive if a boat capsized. Although the goal was for the boys to work together as teams, cliques also formed, just as they would in any other environment. As the boys in the Bedwetters' cabin learn, if a boy was an outsider in his ordinary life, he would be an outsider at summer camp as well. Camps run by the Young Men's Christian Association, the Boy Scouts, the Girl Scouts, and the Camp Fire Girls evolved in the wake of the popularity of the first private boys' camps. The first girls' camps opened late in the nineteenth century, while coed camps for adolescents did not become common until after World War II.

Staged Buffalo Hunts

American bison or buffalo, as they are more commonly known, were nearly eradicated in the nineteenth century, when the systematic slaughter of buffalo herds reduced numbers

COMPARE
&
CONTRAST

- **1970s:** In 1973, eighty nations, including the United States, sign the Convention on International Trade in Endangered Species (CITES). Each country agrees to control the import and export of animals appearing on an endangered species list. The agreement is designed to protect animals like the African elephant, which is hunted for its ivory. In 1970, there are an estimated two million elephants in Africa.

  Today: In spite of CITES and other similar accords, and in spite of a ban on international trade in ivory in place since 1989, the illegal trade of ivory continues, and in fact, this trade has increased in recent years. By 2000, it was estimated that the number of African elephants had decreased to about five hundred thousand.

- **1970s:** Corral buffalo hunts, such as the hunt depicted in Swarthout's novel, have been common in Arizona since the 1940s as a way to control herd size. By the early 1970s, after the publication of *Bless the Beasts and Children*, the widespread negative publicity generated by the novel results in a change in the way these hunts are managed. The Arizona Game and Fish Department ceases to stage corral hunts, and hunters are forced to kill buffalo out in the fields instead of in the corrals.

  Today: So-called "canned hunts" on private ranches have increased in popularity. One ranch in Michigan charges three thousand dollars for a hunter to shoot a buffalo, while a Texas ranch advertises prices of twenty-five hundred dollars and up. A number of animal rights organizations, such as the Humane Society of the United States, are working to stop canned hunts. It is estimated that more than one thousand private hunting operations exist in the twenty-eight states that allow this practice.

- **1970s:** The Vietnam War, which Cotton watched on his television with such fervor, officially ends in March 1973, after fifteen years of military involvement and the loss of nearly fifty-eight thousand U.S. soldiers. This highly controversial war has divided the American people and resulted in many public protests.

  Today: The United States is involved in a war abroad that, like Vietnam, is being covered on the television news. Like the Vietnam War, the Iraq War is also highly controversial and has resulted in many protests that have divided families and friends.

---

from an estimated sixty million to only a few hundred. By the late 1800s, the American bison had been placed on a government endangered species list, and slaughters were halted. Since that time, herds of buffalo have continued to grow, and in most cases the animals remain protected from indiscriminate hunting. It is estimated that populations have grown to more than 150,000, and as a result, buffalo are no longer on the endangered species list. In an effort to manage herd size, buffalo hunts, such as the staged hunt in *Bless the Beasts and Children*, have been used for many years as a way to limit the sizes of buffalo herds. In fact, many states, including Montana, Arizona, Oregon, Iowa, and numerous others, now sell buffalo-hunting permits as a way to reduce the sizes of herds. In many cases, the permits allow hunters to participate in staged hunts similar to that described by Swarthout in *Bless the Beasts and Children*, though with less barbarity since that book's publication. However, there is always opposition to staged hunts when they are held. In January 2008, a newspaper in Waterloo, Iowa, the *WCF Courier*, reported a great deal of opposition to an announcement that a staged hunt was to be held.

Yet since staged hunts are legal in many states, opposition has had little effect on the practice. Arizona's staged hunts, the subject of Swarthout's novel, have changed since the novel was published. Staged hunts still occur, but the Arizona Game and Fish Department has modified the hunts so that hunters are forced to take the animals into the field before they can shoot them. Shooting buffalo confined to corrals has not been permitted since the early 1970s.

CRITICAL OVERVIEW

Although Swarthout wrote many novels, *Bless the Beasts and Children* was his bestseller. Following its release in 1970, *Bless the Beasts and Children* was nominated for the Pulitzer Prize. The book became a selection of the Literary Guild and of the Doubleday Book Club as well as a Reader's Digest Condensed Book. Reviews upon the book's release in 1970 were generally positive. In an April 1970 review for *Harper's* magazine, Richard Schickel enthusiastically praises Swarthout's thoughtful, lively writing. One of the elements of the novel that Schickel likes best is "the juxtaposition of the primal innocence of the great animals with that of the boys." He also praises the book's message, noting that Swarthout "is a stylist who also entertains and instructs." Schickel believes that the brevity of the novel creates a tension in the story that, combined with the engaging characters, makes the book the kind of novel that will continue to hold the attention of young readers.

In his 1972 review of *Bless the Beasts and Children* for the *English Journal*, John W. Conner calls Swarthout's novel "tautly written" and duly notes the excitement of the night journey to the buffalo killing camp. Conner states that Swarthout "understands the anxiety accompanying illegal flight and carefully selects incidents and language to enhance this anxiety." Although he expresses skepticism about whether or not the book is intended for adolescents, he finds it to be an "excellent example of literature *about* adolescents." Regardless of Conner's uncertainty about the most appropriate audience for Swarthout's novel, it has remained popular with readers of all ages. A twenty-fifth anniversary edition was published in 1995, and the book has now been published in many foreign language editions.

CRITICISM

Sheri Metzger Karmiol

Karmiol has a doctorate in English Renaissance literature and teaches literature and drama at the University of New Mexico. In this essay, she discusses Bless the Beasts and Children *as a book that inspires imagination, sympathy, and social responsibility in young readers.*

Swarthout's novel *Bless the Beasts and Children* offers important lessons about the nature of individual strength, the ability to face challenges, and the importance of friendship. One of the novel's greatest assets is the way it challenges young readers to consider the world in which they live and what they might do to make the world a better place for all living things. For this reason, books like *Bless the Beasts and Children* fill an important need for young readers. Such books allow their readers to imagine a world in which they can create change.

In his essay "A Plea for Radical Children's Literature," Herbert Kohl suggests that books can help young readers see beyond their own world and limited experiences and thus help them to see that they can be more than their own personal experiences might suggest. Books can feed the imagination and manifest "the possibility of personal, social, and political change." It is the imagination, according to Kohl, that leads the young to consider "the idea of possibility" and "the contrast between what is and what might be." It is easy to see how *Bless the Beasts and Children* accords with Kohl's ideas about the importance of imagination in literature as an agent of change. When Lally 2 runs away at night and imagines that he can find his way back to the buffalo encampment and somehow save the buffalo, he is using his imagination to seek to change what might be to what is. When all six boys decide that they will join Lally 2 and that they are capable of journeying halfway across the state to set free a corral's worth of buffalo, they are using their imaginations to fight injustice. And although the sheer size of the buffalo initially intimidates them, all of the boys know that they can succeed in setting the animals free. Their imaginations tell them that what they envision is possible. They imagine a better world and set out to create it. Radical stories such as Swarthout's inspire young imaginations and permit young student readers the opportunity to understand that they have the

WHAT DO I READ NEXT?

- The 1966 novel *Whichaway*, by Glendon and Kathryn Swarthout, is the story of a fifteen-year-old boy who struggles to survive after being injured and left to die.

- *Easterns and Westerns* (2001) is Swarthout's only collection of short fiction. There are thirteen stories, including "A Glass of Blessing," which was nominated for the O. Henry Prize for short fiction, and one novella. The collection was edited and published by his son, Miles Swarthout.

- William Golding's novel *Lord of the Flies* (1954) tells the story of a group of boys stranded on an island after a plane wreck. Unlike the boys in Swarthout's novel, these boys become less civilized and more barbaric as time passes.

- *The Catcher in the Rye* (1951), by J. D. Salinger, is the story of a teenage outsider that captures adolescent cynicism and rebellion so well that it has appeared on banned book lists since its release.

- John Knowles's novel *A Separate Peace* (1959) is about adolescent boys at a New England prep school. A mystery surrounding two of the boys is left up to readers to solve.

- *Father Sky* (1979), a novel by Devery Freeman, tells a story about what happens when students resist a decision to close a military school. The book asks serious questions about what happens when teenagers are subjected to a form of brainwashing instituted by adults in charge. The book was made into a successful film, *Taps*, in 1981.

power to change the world. Imagination can erase the fear of failure with the possibility of action.

Kohl defines a radical story as one that involves a community or group's efforts to address an injustice, that also involves an enemy

> SWARTHOUT'S NOVEL PRESENTS YOUNG ADULT READERS WITH THE OPPORTUNITY TO THINK CRITICALLY ABOUT THE CHOICES THEY MAKE AND THE IMPLICATIONS OF THOSE CHOICES."

who has abused power and who is real, and that "illustrates comradeship as well as friendship and love." When the other five boys in his cabin join Lally 2 on his quest, they are fulfilling Kohl's suggestion that radical literature for young readers allow them to go beyond their own experiences and build bridges to others, to understand the creation of a community with others in a common struggle. This is exactly what Swarthout's six protagonists do when they unite to save the buffalo. They become strong enough as a community to accomplish their goal; in Kohl's words, they become "a group working toward unity and focusing on solving a problem of inequity." The boys' unity permits them to challenge the cruel system of slaughter that they have witnessed. There is no guarantee that they will succeed, but the experience of uniting against a common enemy makes each boy a stronger member of the community.

In his depiction of the buffalo slaughter, Swarthout shows what really happened during such unsportsmanlike amateur hunts. His depiction of these hunts helped to publicize and eventually change the ways in which the herds were thinned. The novel inspires an empathy in readers that extends to both nature and humanity. Although the six boys in *Bless the Beasts and Children* are not in physical danger of being killed, as the buffalo are, they have been tormented and cast aside as if they have no value. Cotton, Teft, Goodenow, Shecker, Lally 1, and Lally 2 are outsiders who seem to have no place at camp. They do not excel at sports or at camper competitions. They are weaker, either physically or emotionally, than the other thirty boys at camp. Many students are often bullied at school because they do not fit in well with their classmates. Swarthout's novel allows all readers to fully see and understand how it feels to be an outsider. *Bless the Beasts and Children* provides a hopeful resolution for readers who are outsiders, since it presents the six boys as finding the inner strength to finish their quest and help the buffalo survive.

Swarthout also inspires readers to question unjust and unfit systems of authority. He reveals the repressive and demeaning structure of the Box Canyon Boys Camp in such a way that readers sympathize with the boys and condemn the camp leadership, from the camp director down to the camp counselors, who thrive on torturing the boys whom the counselors have defined as social misfits. At Box Canyon Boys Camp, whose slogan is "Send Us a Boy—We'll Send You a Cowboy," camp counselors use a series of physical competitions as a mechanism to transform each boy camper into the kind of strong heroic figure that the cowboy image of their slogan promises is possible. By their very nature, competitions have both winners and losers—and at Box Canyon Boys Camp, losers become the subject of ridicule. As can be expected, boys who lack physical prowess are at a disadvantage in the kind of environment created at this camp. The six boys who serve as protagonists in Swarthout's book become the object of harassment and bullying. The ridiculing includes the title given to the boys—the Bedwetters—as well as their cabin trophy—a chamber pot. Humiliation, rather than growth, is the inevitable outcome of this kind of competition. From the history Swarthout provides for each boy, readers know that the parents of all six are neglectful, unloving, and self-centered. From their parents, the boys have learned what it means to feel undeserving of love. They have learned that in failing to please their parents, they are failures. The quest they undertake in *Bless the Beasts and Children* replaces their histories of personal failure with the experience of success. Once the boys break free of the oppressive environments that have devalued them, they learn that they are not misfits, that they are not incapable of success, and that they are not without friends. The lesson that Swarthout's six boys teach young readers is that by working together as a community, people can transform their own lives and find inner strength they did not know existed.

According to Kohl, a radical book should not be preachy or dogmatic and should be "honest about pain and defeat." Because Swarthout integrates flashbacks into the story, readers see how damaged the boys have been by their parents' neglect. Readers know that Lally 1 is so jealous of his younger brother that he tortures and kills his brother's pets and that Lally 2 hides from the world in his parents' sauna and that he wets the bed and sucks his thumb. Readers also understand that Goodenow is suicidal and that Shecker's compulsive behaviors are an effort to compensate for his father's abuse. Teft's father and Cotton's mother, in turn, have banished their sons to Box Canyon Boys Camp rather than parenting them. By the time readers finish Swarthout's novel, they know the emotional pain these boys have endured and are thus very cognizant of how bravely they have faced the challenges that they have surmounted in their journey to save the buffalo. Readers learn the lessons that Swarthout presents, not because the author delivers a sermon about the perils of poor parenting but because he tells a story in which six young boys learn through their own hard work that they can achieve something important in their lives.

Reading can open doorways into new experiences for readers, as books are able to present worlds never before experienced; books have the ability to show young readers that there are many ways in which they might experience the world. Well-constructed narratives with engaging characters and compelling plots tempt readers of all ages to return again and again to reading, which is what makes novels for children and young adults the perfect venue for inspiring youth toward change. Kohl is correct about the importance of providing radical literature to children and adolescents. *Bless the Beasts and Children* proves that literature for young adults can provide important lessons. The value of such literature far exceeds the obvious strengths that reading always offers, such as the chance to improve upon language and vocabulary skills. Swarthout's novel presents young adult readers with the opportunity to think critically about the choices they make and the implications of those choices. If young readers are not exposed to the uncomfortable realities of the world, how will they learn to understand and sympathize with the tragedies that other people and animals suffer? The chance to engage in critical thinking about a relevant dramatic story is exactly why students should be encouraged to read *Bless the Beasts and Children*.

Source: Sheri Metzger Karmiol, Critical Essay on *Bless the Beasts and Children*, in *Novels for Students*, Gale, Cengage Learning, 2009.

Patricia Sanders

In the following excerpt, Sanders notes that Bless the Beasts and the Children *serves to introduce adolescent readers to William Golding's classic novel* Lord of the Flies.

A novel of contemporary culture which serves to introduce adolescent readers to Golding's *Lord of the Flies* is Glendon Swarthout's *Bless the Beasts and Children*. Set in the turbulent 1970s, it is both a social-problem novel about neglected youth and social criticism with an environmentalist bent. Additionally, it has an accessible set of symbols, including a savior figure, which prepare students for the Christian allegorical proposition of Golding's novel. Specifically, the religious and allegorical aspect of *Bless the Beasts and Children* is set up in a simple and uncomplicated way which delights young readers because it fits together neatly and prepares them for the more subtle and complex symbolism of Golding.

The symbols of *Bless the Beasts and Children* are as obvious as a hymn refrain. The hero's name is John Cotton, whose ultimate fate is at the wheel of a Judas truck. His six disciples wear the initials "B. C." (for Box Canyon) on their backs. The modern American West is called the "Land of Canaan." And the sacrifice of the buffalo, the Beasts, about which the novel centers, is called "the Blood of the Lamb." The novel's theme is more ambiguous than Golding's and not as controlled. Swarthout's theme is egalitarian. Those extraordinary leaders like Cotton carry salvation for the ordinary; the spirit of brotherhood is triumphant. Students find this reassuring; it reaffirms what they want to believe. Although they support the idea of competition, cooperation is the method which they turn to most naturally.

Source: Patricia Sanders, "Using Adolescent Novels as Transitions to Literary Classics," in *English Journal*, Vol. 78, No. 3, March 1989, pp. 82–84.

Millicent Lenz

In the following excerpt, Lenz examines the alienation displayed by characters in several works of young-adult fiction, including the characters of John Cotton and his friends in Bless the Beasts and the Children.

In *Anna Karenina*, Tolstoy observed, "All happy families resemble one another; every unhappy family is unhappy in its own way."

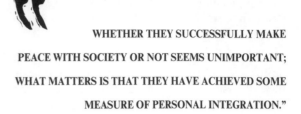

WHETHER THEY SUCCESSFULLY MAKE PEACE WITH SOCIETY OR NOT SEEMS UNIMPORTANT; WHAT MATTERS IS THAT THEY HAVE ACHIEVED SOME MEASURE OF PERSONAL INTEGRATION."

Similarly one could say with some justification that though the socially accepted characters in children's literature resemble one another greatly, the loners are highly individualized, both in the reasons for their loneliness and in the ways they cope with it. We are all familiar with the loner in modern adult fiction, but it still surprises some of us to find children's literature, the proper domain of the Happy Ending and Joy, becoming rapidly overpopulated with loners. All the lonely children, where do they all come from? Particularly in today's fiction for early teenagers, one finds an unremitting epidemic of alienation.

Every loner is by definition unique. Nonetheless, it is possible to show certain relationships, grouping loners together on the basis of a principle of classification and relating them to a literary ancestor. I have chosen to classify loners according to the factors that precipitate their alienation and to point out any identifiable patterns in their plights. I shall also note key images expressive of alienation, images that body forth the loners' own perceptions of their situations. Finally, I shall identify both the positive and negative results of alienation in each case. By "positive" aspects of alienation I mean the ways that alienation serves as a stage through which the character passes on the way to further growth and reintegration, so that this experience as a loner finally enriches him as a human being. By "negative" aspects, I refer to the ways that alienation may diminish or destroy the loner's humanity, ending with his disintegration or destruction. For it is evident that the experience of alienation, like any human experience of suffering, may lead either to final affirmation or to final negation of human values. Through my survey, I hope to discover whether alienation as it is presented in contemporary young people's fiction can be said to be shown in a predominantly positive or a predominantly negative light. Does the loner usually succeed in salvaging something of value from his loneliness, or is he more often defeated and destroyed by it? The contrast here is between the "tragic" loner, who passes beyond tragedy into affirmation, and the "pathetic" loner, who is stranded upon the treacherous rocks of Carlyle's Everlasting Nay.

The first type of loner, for convenience called Type A, is best seen in fantasy. This loner is actually different in kind from the rest of humanity, having some characteristic that could be called "trans-human" or "extra-human." Helpful paradigms can be drawn from myth, for example, the selkie—half seal, half human—or the ondine—half fish, half human. Will Stanton in Susan Cooper's *The Dark Is Rising* exemplifies this type of loner, for he has extra-human powers, being one of the Old Ones, distinguished from humankind in general, as Merriman tells him, in being "bound by nature to devote yourself to the long conflict between the Light and the Dark." Merriman also points out to Will the advantages and the drawbacks of his special gift:

> It is a burden.... Any great gift or power or talent is a burden, and this more than any, and you will often long to be free of it. But there is nothing to be done. If you were born with the gift, then you must serve it, and nothing in this world or out of it may stand in the way of that service....

Will's situation is metaphorically expressed through the image of "The Great Doors," "...The tall carved doors that led out of Time," through which Merriman disappears at the close of the book. Will also moves in and out of time, to and from the timeless realm of the immortal Old Ones. Enchanted music heralds the opening of the Great Doors "...or any great change that might alter the lives of the Old Ones...." The "sweet beckoning sound" expresses "the space between waking and dreaming, yesterday and tomorrow, memory and imagining." The central symbols of Will's quest are the Six Signs of Fire, Water, Iron, Bronze, Wood and Stone—elemental signs that must be joined together on a chain of gold to reaffirm the power of the Light over the Dark. His success in joining the Six Signs represents not only a victory over the Dark but also an ordering of reality and the achievement of a wholeness of vision. In an illuminated moment, Will, who has earlier suffered from loneliness because of his isolation

from the human community, realizes that the Old Ones "are my people. This is my family, in the same way as my real family." He thus transcends loneliness and expands his humanity to embrace his extra-human experiences.

Not all loners of Type A achieve this happy amalgam of their humanity and trans-humanity. For instance, consider the Tuck family of Natalie Babbitt's *Tuck Everlasting*. The entire Tuck family has unwittingly drunk the immortalizing water of a mysterious spring, thereby forfeiting their human claim to mortality. Their story is told through the eyes of a young girl, Winnie Foster, who resists the temptation to drink of the water herself. The Tucks' pathetic plight is expressed through their inability to "climb back on the wheel" of human experience in time. As Mr. Tucks says to Winnie:

> "Everything's a wheel, turning and turning, never stopping.... Being part of the whole, that's the blessing.... You can't have living without dying. So you can't call it living, what we got. We just *are*, we just *be*, like rocks beside the road."

Also symbolic of the "otherness" of the Tucks is the "elf music" of their music box, which leads the ill-willed man in the yellow suit to discover their whereabouts, resulting in calamity for both him and them. Their breach with humanness is not healed; no happy denouement is possible for them. In contrast to Will Stanton, they must live forever outside the magic circle of humanity.

The loner of Type B is alienated by physical isolation resulting from an accident or a natural catastrophe. At the outset of the story, the Type B loner comes close to the norm, but he endures a traumatic experience that leaves him stranded, outcast from society. Robinson Crusoe provides a paradigm for this type. A current example is Albie, the protagonist of Chester Aaron's *An American Ghost*, who finds himself, as the result of a massive flood, afloat on the Mississippi in a house that he shares with a mountain lion. Through their mutual struggles to survive, Albie and the mountain lion (which he names Alice after his sister) develop a close emotional tie. Albie needs the lion because he identifies with her will to live: "As long as this lion breathed and lived, he could draw from its strength and will a strength and will of his own."

The major symbol in the book is the house, paradoxically both a lifeboat and a prison. At one point in the book, after Albie has encountered and escaped from the ruffians of the Delta Belle, whose intent has been to kidnap him and hold him for ransom, he ponders the meaning of houses and the word *home*. He thinks of "the shell of what had once been a home" that now carries him down the river, and his imagination conjures up the theme of the human will to endure as he pictures the new house his father will now build. "Would a new house promise new life? This old house in which he now sat . . . had been nourished on myths of human endurance." He remembers how his mother likened their house to a pitcher, from which her children "would take out to the world what this house had poured into them" and also to a church, because it was a refuge of spiritual, aesthetic values in the midst of wilderness. The meanings that cluster around the symbol of the house are primarily positive, life-affirming ones, but the book as a whole stresses the naturalistic pessimism engendered by Albie's isolation as well as by the degradation he suffers at the hands of the Delta Belle crew. In a scene evocative of keen nausea, Albie hides from his persecutors by crawling among the tethered livestock, knowing that if he succumbs to despair and sickness, he will die like the untended cattle. This knowledge spurs his will to fight against death: "In the midst of this heavy presence of death, Albie chose to fight to live." From his experience *in extremis* Albie gains an ironic insight into both the inestimable value of all life—human and non-human—and the need nonetheless to sacrifice some lives (like those of the shivering goats he feeds to Alice) to sustain others. The vision of life that proceeds from the book can scarcely be called affirmative; it is rather keenly ironic; the line usually separating human and animal life is curiously blurred in Aaron's naturalistic vision. It finds its final symbol in the cougar skin Albie sees nailed to the side of the barn at the end of the book. With the keen perception that he owes to his survival of a descent into a psychic hell, Albie senses what those around him do not—the carnivorous, predatory basis of even so-called civilized society. Small wonder that he sobs uncontrollably. He owes his life to a cougar, yet his family considers a slain cougar a triumph. The gap between him and them seems unbridgeable, and a reader must suppose that Albie will remain alone with his terrible knowledge.

Another Type B loner, Karana of Scott O'Dell's *Island of the Blue Dolphins*, is isolated as the result of two events. First, she is accidentally stranded on the island with her small brother, Ramo, who then meets death at the fangs of the wild dogs. Karana adjusts to her aloneness, finding comfort in relationships with the animals; ironically, the leader of the wild dogs becomes her closest companion. Dolphins play a symbolic part as figures of hope. They appear around Karana's canoe as she struggles to return to the island in a storm, seeming like "friends." At the end of the book they swim ahead of the ship that carries her to the mainland. The symbol most expressive of her isolation may well be the ritual she goes through when she realizes she has been found: she makes the mark of her tribe on her face, and below it "the sign which meant I was still unmarried." Her sensitivity to animals develops gradually. She must kill some in order to survive, yet later she determines never to kill cormorants, seals, wild dogs, or sea elephants, feeling they are all potential if not actual friends. " . . . Animals and birds are like people, too, though they do not talk the same or do the same things. Without them the earth would be an unhappy place." With a little help from her friends, Karana copes with loneliness successfully. Her alienation becomes transformed into an experience of worth, somewhat in the manner of that of a mystic. Her journey back to society at the close is tinged with sadness because one suspects society has little to offer her; she seems to have achieved a spiritual peace that one hopes she can maintain in her new setting.

The loner of Type C, closely related to Type B, becomes alienated through the absence or failure of primary human relationships. He suffers from homelessness or from the death or absence of parents; sometimes his alienation is compounded by poverty or the accident of being born into an oppressed minority.

This type abounds in current fiction; for convenience in discussion I shall organize my characters into two sub-groups. Type C1 describes the loner who in the absence of primary human relationships turns to animals to fill an emotional need, whereas C2 seeks attachment to another human being.

Miyax-Julie of *Julie of the Wolves* by Jean George qualifies as a C1 loner. She becomes isolated in the Arctic wastelands when she attempts to flee from an unbearable child-marriage but misses her intended destination, San Francisco. Her experience parallels that of Karana in several ways: like Karana, Julie becomes emotionally linked to animals, in this case the wolf-pack that adopts her. But Julie's alienation has deeper roots. She despises "gussak" society, symbolized in the plane that carries the hunters that kill Amaroq, leader of the pack, Julie's surrogate father. All the ugliness of the white man's civilization—its materialism, its voracity, its deadliness and insensitivity to nature—come to her through the vision of the plane's black exhaust. Julie faces severe self-conflict when she must choose between the pure wolf society, where good and evil are clearly defined, and human society, where good and evil are inextricably and fearsomely entangled.

The conflict between cultures is reflected in Julie's dual name: she is "Julie" to the English-speaking people, "Miyax" to the Eskimoes. A symbol of her treasured Eskimo heritage is her *i 'no Go tied* n house of the spirits made for her by the bent old woman, discarded by Julie in a frenzy when her Americanized friends poke fun at her for thinking a charm bracelet serves the same purpose. The plover, named "Tornait" or "bird spirit" by Julie, seems to embody the fragile Eskimo way of life. When he succumbs to death and Julie buries him, she sings her song to the spirit of Amaroq in "*her best English.*" This is her moment of decision. She acknowledges the sad truth: "'... The hour of the wolf and the Eskimo is over'," and she points "her boots toward Kapugen," her Americanized father. Julie's alienation has positive value, for through it she clarifies her own values, yet her choice is in part a capitulation. She accepts reintegration into a sullied, far from satisfactory human society. This is the price she must pay to retain her humanness.

John Cotton and his group of "Bedwetters" in Swarthout's *Bless the Beasts and Children* share the status of outcasts; none of the others at the Box Canyon Boys' Camp will associate with them. It is their reaction to a buffalo kill that gives them a common motive and spurs them into action. They are filled with nausea at the spectacle of slaughter and determine to turn the remaining buffalo loose. The buffalo are the prime symbols in the book, reminders of the white man's guilt—of the violence he has done to "the land of Canaan into which we were

led. ..." Again, the pattern is the familiar one: the outcast boys are sensitized to the plight of the persecuted animals. When they return to the camp after seeing the kill, they collectively avoid the others, and instead seek the company of their horses, "currying them and feeding them and talking to them and dallying until the supper gong clanged. It was as though they could not abide the company of humans." (One is reminded of Gulliver at the close of *Gulliver's Travels*, seeking out the company of horses in preference to that of humans.) The boys' experience of alienation is complex, intermingled with their experience of communion with one another in dedication to their anti-social act that is paradoxically superior in its motivation to the motives of the society they flout. The effects of their communal alienation are positive, for they experience a momentary vision of prelapsarian life, life as it must have been before the fall, when man lived in harmony with all creatures. Their freeing the buffalo costs John Cotton's life, and whether he is a willing martyr to the cause or not, the ending suggests his transfiguration, with a glimpse of his "red hair flaming like a torch as the truck seemed to soar and dive and disappear." The sight of Cotton soaring to his death "cracked their hearts even as it freed them, too, forever." Whether they successfully make peace with society or not seems unimportant; what matters is that they have achieved some measure of personal integration.

The main character of Donovan's *Wild in the World* lives alone in the New England mountains after the members of his family die one after the other. A stray dog (or wolf, he is never sure) becomes his only companion. John calls him "Son" and grows greatly attached to him. The picture of this man-dog relationship conveys the degree of John's isolation; so also does his habit of going to his dead brothers' graves and "talking" with them. He says on one occasion, "'It's easier to talk to you now you're dead than it was when you were alive. Son taught me a lot. Human critters hold back'." A key theme in the book is the failure of human communication; for instance, the men who discover John's body, when he dies from pneumonia, think he has been killed by the dog, which they take for a wolf and try to destroy. There is nothing positive resulting from alienation here; the emphasis is on the tragedy of human isolation. An image expressing the futility of life arises out of John's strange recurring dream. He dreams that he is a boy, taken to a graveyard by his father, and walking upon the dead leaves. When he tries to read the names on the tombstones, he finds them covered with moss, indecipherable. So small is the mark of humanity on the world. The picture of human futility seems unrelieved; this is naturalism at its purest and most depressing.

A book similar in its naturalistic despair is *A Wild Thing* by Jean Renvoize. Morag flees from the "home" where she has been placed after being orphaned. She takes with her in her flight a newspaper clipping, a treasured photograph of a herd of deer seen against the background of a mountain and valley. To her, the picture symbolizes a land of promise, but it contains death as well, for in the corner is "the whitened skull of an old stag...." The scene arouses both joy and fear, and she searches for terrain that resembles that in the photograph. Ironically, in search of freedom, she finds a new kind of bondage, for though she had wanted independence, "to stop being in debt, to give no one the right to own her because they had fed her...," she finds she must steal in order to exist. A primary image of her loneliness is the "Mossman," a skeleton she finds in the woods, about whom she invents an elaborate fantasy, imagining he is a prince with whom she falls in love, then progressively comes to worship as an idol. Throughout the book, the author compares her frequently to an animal, and like many loners she becomes sensitive to animals and draws close to the goats she adopts when she finds them running in the wild. Morag seems "very like an animal" to the young man she rescues after an accident on the mountain. He, in exchange for her kindness, rapes her, then wins her passionate devotion, and finally abandons her, leaving her pregnant. Before he leaves, she senses his intent to withdraw and tries to share her treasures with him—a pink pearl found in a mussel, and the Mossman; he, however, is revolted by the latter and abruptly departs. She seeks human help to save her unborn child, but the village people scream at her and pursue her with guns. Horrified, she is forced to flee, and her child, arriving prematurely, is stillborn in the open air. Shortly after, Morag herself dies. The one comforting element in the ending is her dying vision: she sees the scene represented in the treasured photograph before her eyes and dies satisfied: "With total love and familiarity she unclenched her hands and entered her own land." Because of her faithfulness to her dream, the ending cannot be called

hopeless; however, it is difficult to find much that is positive or hopeful in it, for Morag finds her place and her peace only through death.

A book presenting a more positive experience of alienation is Julia Cunningham's *Dorp Dead*. The protagonist, a ten-year-old orphan named Gilley Ground, is isolated not only by his lack of family but also by his intelligence and sensitivity. He hides his high intelligence because "it is a weapon for defense as comforting as a very sharp knife worn between the skin and the shirt." His isolation has the advantage of affording him privacy, which he sorely wants. Realistic on the surface, this novel is full of symbolic meaning. A major symbolic character is the Hunter, who appears early in the book at Gilley's tower (itself symbolic of his dreaming, aspiring nature). The mysterious Hunter carries a gun without bullets; he asks Gilley what plans he has for the future. To Gilley, the Hunter is "like an eagle whose wingspread shadows the eyes for a moment and then vanishes forever. He does not fly the same way twice." It is hard to say what the Hunter represents, but he is obviously an influence for good in Gilley's life.

When Gilley is taken to live at the house of the laddermaker, Kobalt, he is struck by its security; he also senses that Kobalt "has not created this shiny, absolute precision out of love but because it creates safety for him." Kobalt represents a stultifying, fear-based approach to life; his one book, from which he reads a set number of lines each evening, is entitled *Time Patterns and How to Control Them*. Kobalt's spiritless, drab-colored dog, Mash, arouses sympathy in Gilley, and he resolves "to treat him with honor. This works sometimes with orphans. I've seen it happen. They get to believe they are somebody better than just themselves." When Kobalt reveals that he has beaten Mash because "'He is getting old. I will soon need another dog and Mash must learn to die'," and Gilley discovers Kobalt has made a cage just the size for a boy, Gilley realizes the man's murderous nature and manages to escape by using one of Kobalt's own ladders. During his climb up the ladder, Gilley focusses his eyes constantly on a star that becomes a substitute for the picture of his Grandmother he has had to leave behind. When the mad Kobalt pursues him, it is Gilley's own resolve to fight for his life, plus the sudden appearance of Mash, that saves him. Gilley's last message to Kobalt before going to live with the Hunter is the defiant "Dorp Dead" that [he] scrawls on Kobalt's door. The misspelling is symbolic of Gilley's refusal to be "the same as everyone else."

The book's symbolic texture is much richer than this short survey can indicate; however, it should be evident that Gilley succeeds in growing through his experience of alienation, that he even finds positive value in his aloneness, and that he moves beyond it into personal relatedness, first by involving himself in Mash's fate, then by responding to the Hunter's invitation to make something of his life, to shape it actively instead of trading his freedom for the deadening security offered by Kobalt.

A pattern emerges for the Type C1 loner: cut off from human relationship, he compensates by forming an emotional link with animal life, sometimes developing a hyper-sensitivity to all forms of life. This tendency to seek non-human friendship receives a lightly satirical treatment in Donovan's picture story-book, *Good Old James* where the protagonist, alienated by age and homelessness, becomes attached to a fly, which he names Gwen. The point is perhaps too obvious: in a pinch, even a fly will do as a love-object, if nothing better is available.

Loners of Type C2 are very much like those of Type C1, except that they turn more directly toward humans for companionship. The boy of Ester Wier's *The Loner*, nameless until adopted by Boss, a woman sheepherder, is a good example. He finally wins self-integration and is granted the name David (after the Biblical David) plus acceptance into a family. This happy ending is foreshadowed early in the book when the man Tex tells him that living as a loner is "selfish," and also a needless kind of suffering: "'There's always people who need you as much as you need them. Don't you forget that. All you got to do is find 'em'." The image most expressive of the boy's alienation is the one coined by Tex, who calls him "'A bum lamb'." His lack of a name is also significant; early in the book, Raidy, a young girl who is the first to show him kindness (who dies tragically when her hair is caught in a digging machine), tells him "'Even dogs have names'." David wins acceptance by Boss when he proves his proficiency as a sheepherder. It is Boss who relates to the sheep emotionally, in compensation for the death of her son Ben, a peerless shepherd who has been killed by a grizzly bear. She blames humanity for breeding "'all the wild animals' independence and cunning out of them for his own gain, to have their meat and their wool with the least possible bother from them'." It is Ben's widow, Angie, who makes David realize he must be himself, not try to take Ben's place, to "'be a copy of someone you never knew'."

Alienation here is viewed as an unnecessary burden, because of the possibility of finding people with a mutual need for relatedness. Since David achieves self-integration and acceptance into society, the overall impact of the book is a positive, affirmative one.

Buddy and Angela of June Jordan's *His Own Where* are alienated from their parents and in effect homeless. They are also socially and economically nearly powerless. Although they are black, their blackness does not seem a prime factor in their alienation; the reasons are deeper, more nearly existential. Buddy's father is "dying lonely" in a hospital, and Angela endures life with a suspicious, domineering mother and a father who beats her. There are several images that very effectively express Buddy's feelings of alienation. The first occurs where, thinking of the hospital where his father is, he imagines what the world would be like if it were one big hospital:

> Buddy sure the whole city should be like a hospital and everybody taking turns to heal the people. People turning doctor, patient, nurse. Whole city asking everybody how you are, how you feel, what can I do for you, how can I help.

This dream is of course in ironic contrast to the actual situation that prevails in Buddy's world, which finds its appropriate image in the picture of an emergency room: "Buddy leaning on the wall be thinking that the whole city of his people like a all-night emergency room. People mostly suffering, uncomfortable, and waiting." The two loners, Buddy and Angela, find comfort and love together; in the final, symbolic scene, they make love in the cemetery where they have found what Buddy calls "his own where"—his "own place for loving made for making love, the cemetery where nobody guards the dead." The last line of the book, after Buddy and Angela have expressed the hope that she may be pregnant, reads thus: "And so begins a new day of the new life in the cemetery."

Alienation in this novel is painful, yet productive, because the two loners identify in their plight and are able to communicate meaningfully to shape a new life together. But in order to do so they must turn their backs upon parents and established society; their hut at the side of the cemetery becomes their new and brave little homestead in an uncaring world.

Fifteen-year-old Tink of James Fritzhand's *Life is a Lonely Place* is alienated from his parents and older brother, chiefly because his achievements have been constantly measured against the older brother's athletic accomplishments and found wanting. In his loneliness, Tink turns for friendship to David Hastings, a writer-in-residence at a nearby college, who has recently taken residence in a beach house. It is only to David that Tink can talk meaningfully. He tells David, "'It's hard trying to live up to other people's expectations, especially parents!'" A jealous, bullying classmate, Rick Camero, calls Tink a "'fairy',", an accusation that hurts less than Amy Bailey's term for him, "'kid.'" In his loneliness, Tink draws close to Margie Blanchard, a girl about whom a rumor has been spawned, to the effect that she has had an abortion. Tink comes to appreciate her worth, despite his eventual knowledge of the truth of the rumor. The image used to express the nature of intolerance and ignorance is that of sheep.

Camero's accusations and taunts against David and Tink lead to a heated confrontation with Tink's father, Willard (Tink calls both his parents by their first names), who is finally convinced that Camero is lying, and if any doubt remains it is dissipated when David's wife, hitherto unmentioned, is belatedly brought into the story to squelch any lingering doubts of his heterosexuality.

The book is flawed, yet it expresses with considerable power the loneliness of a boy whose own family has unwittingly forced him to turn elsewhere for meaningful relationships. Tink's alienation, though painful, is an occasion for his growth, mainly because he is fortunate enough to find two people of depth—David and Margie—in his otherwise shallow world.

The heroine of Marilyn Harris' *Hatter Fox* is alienated in almost every way possible. She is a Navajo orphan, the victim of child-abuse, an experienced prostitute at a tender age, when she is arrested and taken to the State Reformatory for Girls outside Albuquerque. Her story is told from the viewpoint of Dr. Teague Summer, who becomes involved in her destiny and attempts to help her, going so far as to live in at the Reformatory during the period of her incarceration. Several images stand out as expressive of her situation. The first is the "dog pen" into which rebellious girls are placed until their will is broken. The dog pen fails to work on Hatter Fox, as do all the other types of treatment and therapy, with the exception of the love of Summer and Rhinehart, the obese, good-natured nurse who aids Summer's attempts to help the girl. An image symbolic of Hatter Fox's dreams of a free and beautiful life grows from her words on the mountainside, where she tells Summer she wishes they (the white people) would go away and leave nature alone, "'let the field and sky and mountains fill the empty space until it isn't empty any longer...'." But the most striking image in the book has to do with the narrator's recognition. He insisted that Hatter Fox, now out of prison and employed, return to her place of work to retrieve her paycheck, her first; after all, he reasons, she must learn responsibility. She does not see a Greyhound bus approaching, and is run down as she rushes toward him, clutching a check for $41.28 in her hand. He reflects on his mistake, which he recognizes as springing from some deep wrong in the fabric of his world. Her alienation was of value only because Summer could help her grow beyond it, but he could not overcome the wrong in himself and the world that led to her destruction. The ending is highly ambiguous; even the one person who has loved Hatter Fox and gained her love has finally been an unwitting instrument in her death....

From such a variety of experiences, it is possible to draw few general conclusions. Of the twenty loners examined, twelve achieve some measure of reintegration, either within themselves, or into society, or both. Eight do not achieve either a new personal wholeness or acceptance into their societies: instead they die (John of *Wild in the World*, Morag of *A Wild Thing*, Dummy of *Hey, Dummy*, the Motorcycle Boy of *Rumble Fish*, and Hatter Fox) or they face very uncertain futures (Albie of *An American Ghost*, Chau Li of *Man in the Box*). The Tucks are a special case—condemned as they are to an immortality that is worse than death.

Of the characters winning a measure of reintegration, two would seem to be fully successful—Will Stanton of *The Dark Is Rising* and David of *The Loner*. Karana's case, in *Island of the Blue Dolphins*, is marginal: can she possibly be as happy among people of a strange culture as she was on her island among her feathered, finny, and four-footed friends? All of the others have unquestionably grown from their experiences of alienation. Yet their peace with society and in some cases with themselves seems tentative: Julie will surely miss her wolves and continue to find much of gussak society repugnant; Gilley Ground of *Dorp Dead* will never fit easily into any society, given his need for uniqueness; Buddy and Angela are bound to find *His Own Where*, their cemetery Eden, full of briars; Tink's family and Margie will never fully fill the emptiness that makes his life a lonely place; Patty Ann may or may not prove herself as a long-distance swimmer, though she has certainly grown during her summer of the German soldier; Jean of *Diving for Roses* may or may not find happiness with Andrew Curtin, though she seems secure within herself. The prognosis for Junior Brown is hopeful, but the survival of his planet is by no means certain, and surely Ann Burden's chances of finding what she desires on a depopulated and radioactive planet are minimal; her inner belief in her search, however, makes her quest worthwhile. John Cotton is a very special case, for although he undergoes a spectacular self-immolation, he does so happily, having experienced a moment of beatitude among the beasts and children.

Two other generalizations seem permissible. One, it appears that the human needs to love and be loved, and to venerate something above oneself, are so universal and pressing that they will find expression even in the most extreme isolation—witness Morag and her Mossman. Secondly, all of the loners considered come out of the fiery furnace of their experiences clutching the gold of some special insight, some new truth or vision, that is theirs alone. All of these books urge a reader to reconsider the old question, does suffering ennoble? A case might be made for the view that it does, if it is not so severe that it shatters the human spirit utterly. *Man in the Box* depicts such a shattering, making reintegration, a new wholeness, impossible, unless it be by means of a miracle.

On the basis of this study, it seems safe to conclude that alienation, as presented in contemporary young people's fiction, more often than not shows the loner as salvaging something of value from his experience. The number of those stranded on the rocks of negation is small, but

still large enough to keep us from any unwarranted complacency. We have seen how an ending can be affirmative even though it is unhappy, and paradoxically, a character may win an inner victory in an apparent defeat. The important thing is, surely, that the mystery and wonder of human suffering and human endurance be preserved.

The risk of failure, of despair or madness or death, must be acknowledged; to eliminate these possible "loser's" fates for every loner would be to falsify the human condition. The failures, paradoxically, give the victories their grandeur. . . .

Source: Millicent Lenz, "Varieties of Loneliness: Alienation in Contemporary Young People's Fiction," in *Journal of Popular Culture*, Vol. 13, No. 4, Spring 1980, pp. 672–88.

John W. Conner

In the following review, Conner summarizes Bless the Beasts and the Children *and categorizes it as an exciting book that may be better directed at adults than adolescents.*

The misfits of Box Canyon Boys Camp become a single force in pursuit of ecological justice in this tautly written brief novel. Horrified by the slaughter of buffalo at a government-sponsored extermination site, six boys steal away from their summer camp, confiscate an old truck, and set out to free the remaining buffalo.

Each boy is a peculiar bundle of psychoses which are carefully explained in interesting if occasionally tedious flashbacks. But the boys are unified in their pursuit of justice for the buffalo. They are directed by fifteen-year-old John Cotton who needs to command as desperately as his followers need someone to command them.

The night journey from the camp to the government extermination site is an exciting one. Glendon Swarthout understands the anxiety accompanying illegal flight and carefully selects incidents and language to enhance this anxiety. Perhaps the author's most perceptive comment on man and his relationship to nature occurs when the boys finally arrive at the pens containing the buffalo. Still wanting to free the buffalo, the boys are temporarily stymied by their own fears of the mammoth bison.

I'm not at all certain that *Bless the Beasts and Children* is a book for adolescents. It is about adolescents, their concerns, their values. But each boy is so filled with personal doubts that he scarcely has an opportunity to react genuinely to his peers. The author gathers six diverse personalities and concentrates their activities on one major event. Theoretically, it ought to work, but it doesn't. Each boy is a psychiatric case study, interesting to observe but impossible to be concerned about.

John Cotton's death near the end of the novel releases the tension created by the government authorities' discovery of the boys in the act of releasing the buffalo. The author needed an event of this magnitude to culminate the escapade. I can appreciate the author's technical prowess, but I regret the lack of an empathic response.

Bless the Beasts and Children is an exciting adventure yarn using adolescents as major characters. It is an excellent example of literature *about* adolescents rather than literature *for* adolescents.

Source: John W. Conner, "Book Marks," in *English Journal*, Vol. 61, No. 1, January 1972, p. 139.

SOURCES

"American Bison: Are Bison an Endangered Species?" Web site of the Leon M. Lederman Science Foundation Center, http://ed.fnal.gov/entry_exhibits/bison/endangered.html (accessed August 1, 2008).

Beane, Linda, J., ed., "Canned Hunts: The Other Side of the Fence," *Animals in Print: The On-Line Newsletter*, October 31, 2001, http://www.all-creatures.org/aip/nl-31oct2001-canned.html (accessed June 9, 2008).

Brantley, Margaret, Introduction to *Bless the Beasts and Children*, by Glendon Swarthout, Pocket Books, 2004, pp. xi–xxi.

"Buffalo," Web site of the Arizona Game & Fish Department, http://www.azgfd.gov/h_f/game_buffalo.shtml (accessed June 9, 2008).

Conner, John W., Review of *Bless the Beasts and Children*, in the *English Journal*, Vol. 61, No. 1, January 1972, p. 139.

"Illegal Ivory Trade Driven by Unregulated Domestic Markets," Web site of the Convention on International Trade in Endangered Species of Wild Fauna and Flora, October, 4, 2002, http://www.cites.org/eng/news/press/2002/021004_ivory.shtml (accessed June 9, 2008).

Kohl, Herbert, "A Plea for Radical Children's Literature," in *Should We Burn Babar? Essays on Children's Literature and the Power of Stories*, New Press, 1995, pp. 57–93.

Maynard, W. Barksdale, "'An Ideal Life in the Woods for Boys': Architecture and Culture in the Earliest Summer Camps," in *Winterthur Portfolio*, Vol. 34, No. 1, Spring 1999, pp. 3–29.

Nelson, Josh, "Animal Welfare Activists Decry Proposed Buffalo 'Hunt,'" in *WCF Courier*, January 19, 2008, http://www.wcfcourier.com/articles/2008/01/19/news/regional/2276948810186d9a862573d400836bb4.txt (accessed August 1, 2008).

Norris, Diana, Norm Phelps, and D. J. Schubert, "Canned Hunts: Unfair at Any Price," Michigan State University College of Law, Animal Legal & Historical Center Web site, July 19, 2002, http://www.animallaw.info/articles/arusfund22002.htm (accessed June 9, 2008).

"Petition to List the Yellowstone Bison as Endangered," Web site of the Buffalo Field Campaign, http://www.buffalofieldcampaign.org/legal/petition.html (accessed August 1, 2008).

Schickel, Richard, Review of *Bless the Beasts and Children* in *Harper's*, Vol. 240, No. 1439, April 1970, p. 105.

"Stop Canned Hunts," Web site of the Humane Society of the United States, http://www.hsus.org/wildlife/stop_canned_hunts/ (accessed June 9, 2008).

Swarthout, Glendon, *Bless the Beasts and Children*, Pocket Books, 2004.

"The Vietnam War: The Bitter End, 1969–1975," in *History Place*, http://www.historyplace.com/unitedstates/vietnam/index-1969.html (accessed June 9, 2008).

FURTHER READING

Eisner, Michael D., *Camp*, Warner Books, 2005.
Former Walt Disney Company chief executive officer Eisner writes about the lessons that he learned as a young boy when he attended summer camp in Vermont, including what he learned about working as part of a team.

Falke, Terry, *Observations in an Occupied Wilderness: Photographs*, Chronicle Books, 2006.
Falke's volume is a collection of photographs of the American Southwest. There are brief essays by William L. Fox to accompany the photographs.

Louv, Richard, *Last Child in the Woods: Saving Our Children from Nature-Deficit Disorder*, Algonquin Books, 2005.
The author, a child advocacy expert, argues in this book that children are spending too little time at play outdoors and that more time spent outdoors learning about nature would create healthier children. This book offers a number of suggestions for teaching children about nature.

McCullough, David, *Mornings on Horseback: The Story of an Extraordinary Family, a Vanished Way of Life, and the Unique Child Who Became Theodore Roosevelt*, Simon & Schuster, 2001.

This biography tells the story of one of America's first conservationists. As president, Roosevelt worked to pass legislation that would protect America's natural resources.

Punke, Michael, *Last Stand: George Bird Grinnell, the Battle to Save the Buffalo, and the Birth of The New West*, Smithsonian Books/Collins, 2007.

Grinnell was an early conservationist who founded the Audubon Society. This biographical study focuses on how Grinnell became a naturalist and on his efforts to preserve the American wilderness.

Van Slyck, Abigail A., *A Manufactured Wilderness: Summer Camps and the Shaping of American Youth, 1890–1960*, University of Minnesota Press, 2006.

Van Slyck's book is the only thorough study of summer camps and their role in shaping American youth. The author describes camp design, including the housing and feeding of children, and also discusses how many of these camps appropriated Native American culture as part of their programs.

Bread Givers

ANZIA YEZIERSKA
1925

Anzia Yezierska came to America with her Polish immigrant family in the 1890s. She never forgot the hunger and hardship of their early days in the Jewish ghetto on the Lower East Side of Manhattan. Her struggle to escape from the slums to an independent American life is fictionalized as Sara Smolinsky's journey in *Bread Givers* (1925), originally subtitled, "A Struggle Between a Father of the Old World and a Daughter of the New." It is the most closely autobiographical of Yezierska's early works.

Yezierska was at the height of her fame in the 1920s when she wrote *Bread Givers*. She had already been exploring similar themes of surviving in a foreign culture in her short stories and novels. Her first collection of short stories, *Hungry Hearts* (1920), had been made into a successful film, and she had been accepted by Hollywood as "the Sweatshop Cinderella," a rags-to-riches stereotype she came to resent as oversimplified. Returning to her roots in New York, she continued to pour out fiction about the hope, guilt, anger, and determination of the immigrant in America. All but forgotten after the Great Depression, she enjoyed a mild revival with her autobiographical novel about being a writer, *Red Ribbon on a White Horse* (1950). Not until interest in ethnic literature rose in the 1960s, however, was she rediscovered. *Bread Givers*, which had been out of print, was republished by Persea Books in 1975, and it has remained the author's most popular work. Yezierska's fame

seems assured the second time around. Her primary topic, the clash of conflicting values in a multicultural world, is a timely theme in contemporary society.

AUTHOR BIOGRAPHY

Anzia Yezierska was born in Plotsk (or Plinsk), a small town in Russian Poland, around 1883 to a family with ten children. Her father was a Talmudic scholar. The family immigrated to New York around 1893, where the eldest son had moved first, changing his name to Max Mayer. The rest of the family changed their last name to his, with Anzia becoming Harriet (Hattie) Mayer, only later changing her name back. They lived in the Jewish ghetto on the Lower East Side of Manhattan. Yezierska left her family to live on her own in 1900, going to night school to learn English and working in sweatshops during the day. She lived at the Clara de Hirsch Home for Working Girls, a settlement house that helped immigrant girls train as servants. She was given a scholarship to study domestic science at Columbia University's Teachers College and became a teacher of cooking in the New York public schools from 1905 to 1913.

To compensate for the intellectual education she had not gotten, she read and attended lectures, living in Rand School, a Socialist gathering place. There she met feminist activists and writers. In 1911 she married Jacob Gordon, an attorney, but quickly got an annulment and then married Arnold Levitas, the father of her only child, Louise, born in 1912. Finding marriage too confining, she tried to be a working single mother but finally let Levitas have custody of Louise so that she could devote herself to writing. Her first story, "The Free Vacation House," was published in 1915 in *Forum*.

In 1917 Yezierska met the philosopher John Dewey, who enrolled her in his Columbia class on social philosophy. He inspired her to write and helped her publish. Dewey also wrote love poems to her but broke off the relationship. Yezierska included older Dewey figures throughout her work, representing the wise American who accepts the immigrant woman for her gifts. In 1918 Dewey got her a job as a translator for a research project studying the Polish community of Philadelphia. Her story "The Fat of the Land" won the O. Henry Award as best short story of

1919. A collection of stories was published as *Hungry Hearts* in 1920. Hollywood made a film of it, and Samuel Goldwyn signed Yezierska to write scripts. Uncomfortable with Hollywood, however, she returned to New York.

This was Yezierska's period of fame as "the Sweatshop Cinderella" who worked her way out of the slums. She wrote realistic scenes of ghetto life in an anglicized Yiddish idiom. *Salome of the Tenements*, a novel that was also made into a film, and *Children of Loneliness*, a collection of short stories, followed in 1923. *Bread Givers* (1925), with the original subtitle "A Struggle Between a Father of the Old World and a Daughter of the New," is her most famous work. *Arrogant Beggar* (1927) was her last novel of this prolific time. From 1929 to 1930 she was a writer in residence at the University of Wisconsin. During the Depression years, when there was less interest in her work, she became poor again, working for the Federal Writers Project of the Works Progress Administration. *All I Could Never Be* (1932) continued themes of her relationship with John Dewey.

Her work was criticized as being repetitive and emotional, but after an eighteen-year period of oblivion, Yezierska made a brief comeback with her fictionalized autobiography *Red Ribbon on a White Horse* (1950), with an introduction by W. H. Auden. In the 1950s she reviewed books for the *New York Times*, and in the 1960s she was rediscovered by university students. Seen as a pioneer of Jewish literature, she was given grants by the National Institute of Arts and Letters in 1962 and 1965. In her last years of declining health, she was tended by her daughter; she died in 1970 in a nursing home in California. *Bread Givers* was republished in 1975. *The Open Cage: An Anzia Yezierska Collection* (1979) includes her best and previously unpublished stories. *How I Found America: Collected Stories of Anzia Yezierska* (2003) includes all of the author's short fiction. With the public catching up to her timely feminist and immigrant themes, Yezierska's fame has been re-established.

PLOT SUMMARY

Book I: Hester Street

CHAPTER 1: HESTER STREET

In the 1890s in the Jewish ghetto on the Lower East Side of Manhattan, on Hester Street, the immigrant Smolinsky family gathers for dinner.

MEDIA ADAPTATIONS

- *Bread Givers* was not made into a film, but Yezierska's first collection of short stories, *Hungry Hearts*, with similar ghetto vignettes, was made into an eighty-minute silent film in 1922 by Samuel Goldwyn Pictures, directed by E. Mason Hopper. Still photos from this film are used as illustrations in the 2003 Persea edition of *Bread Givers*. The film has been restored by the National Center for Jewish Film, Samuel Goldwyn Pictures, and the British Film Institute. It is available for institutional rental from the National Center for Jewish Film at Brandeis University.

While ten-year-old Sara, the youngest daughter of Rabbi Smolinsky, is peeling potatoes for dinner, the other sisters tell of how they could not find work. The eldest sister, Bessie, the main breadwinner of the family, is discouraged because the family needs her wages or they will be thrown out for not paying the rent. Mashah, the pretty and vain sister, comes in having bought roses for her hat instead of having found work. Fania, another sister, says there are lines of girls for each job. The mother comes in saying the shopkeepers will give her no more credit.

Sara resents poverty and hates hunting through ash cans for wood and coal. The house is dirty and packed with too many people and things. The front room is reserved for the father and his holy books, which he studies all day while the other members of the family support him, as is the old tradition for a scholar in the family. The father reminds the women that according to Jewish law, they must serve him so that they will find a place in heaven, for a woman cannot get there by herself. The women are starving but give all the best food to the father. Sara's mother tells her husband that he must move out of the front room into the kitchen so that they can rent the room. When the angry rent collector does not get the rent, she throws the father's holy book to the floor, telling him to get a job. He slaps her, and a policeman takes him to jail. Muhmenkeh, the herring seller, gives little Sara some herring to start her own business, and she begins to make money, hollering along with the pushcart sellers on the street.

CHAPTER 2: THE SPEAKING MOUTH OF THE BLOCK

The neighbors, revering the rabbi as a holy man, pool their money to bail Smolinsky out and pay a lawyer. The lawyer tells the court that the rabbi is the community's religious man and displays the landlady's footprint on his Bible. The judge lets him go, and he is the hero of the neighborhood as the speaking mouth of the block who stood up to a rent collector.

With Reb Smolinsky's fame, it proves easy to rent the front room, and the family gets credit to buy things to fix up the house. The three older girls get work, Sara sells herrings, and there is some ease for the family. The mother stops yelling and cursing and tells her girls stories of the Old World, when they had plenty and she was as beautiful as Mashah. Her father was wealthy and wanted a scholar for a son-in-law, and that was how she married the high-minded Reb. When they became poor and the pogroms threatened them, they sold everything to get to America, where Reb thought everything would be free.

CHAPTER 3: THE BURDEN BEARER

The mother worries about marrying off Bessie, who is getting old. She is the one who bears the burden of the house, bringing in the most wages and giving them all to her father. The boarders, whom the family hoped would want to marry the girls, have eyes only for Mashah, who spends all her money on herself. Fania, the third daughter, is the first to get a young man, but he is poor and goes to night school. He writes poetry to Fania.

One night Bessie comes home with a new tablecloth and some odds and ends to decorate the house. She makes everyone help scrub the house and tidy it up. The next evening, Bessie waits until everyone is gone and then puts on Mashah's pink dress. She is fat, and Sara has to help her get into it, but the seam rips out. She entertains a young man from work, Berel Bernstein, who wants to marry Bessie because she is a strong worker, and he wants to open his own clothing shop.

Berel offers to marry Bessie without a dowry, but Reb says that he cannot afford to let her go because of all the money she brings in. He insists that Berel pay him for marrying his daughter by setting him up in business. Berel refuses, and Bessie gives him up. Six weeks later, Berel is engaged to another woman, and Sara, enraged, curses him at his engagement party.

CHAPTER 4: THE "EMPTY-HEAD"

Mashah, whom Reb calls the "Empty-head," falls in love with Jacob Novak, a refined piano player and the son of a wealthy department store owner. He lives on the corner, and the music he plays attracts Mashah. Mashah woos him by cooking and creating beauty around him when he comes over to the house.

When Jacob's father meets the ghetto girl his son is in love with, he puts pressure on his son to dump her. She hears of his concert, to which she is not invited. In despair, Mashah sends Jacob a letter of reproach. The lovers almost make up, but Reb finds them and pushes Jacob out of his house. Jacob keeps trying to see Mashah, but she is too weak to go against her father's will. Reb continues to browbeat Mashah, and Sara begins to hate him.

CHAPTER 5: MORRIS LIPKIN WRITES POETRY

Reb intercepts a love letter to Fania from Morris Lipkin, who says he has no money to give her, only his poems called "Poems of Poverty." Fania and Reb argue, and she insists that she will marry someone she loves. Sara joins in the fight, debating with her father, and he calls her "Blood-and-iron" for daring to question him.

When Mrs. Smolinsky accuses Reb of driving suitors away, he says he will find suitors for his daughters by going to Zaretsky, the matchmaker. Morris comes to the house to ask for Fania's hand, and Reb ignores him until he leaves. Reb finds another suitor for Fania, Moe Mirsky, a supposed diamond salesman. Moe takes a fancy to Mashah, and Reb is ready to marry her off to him, despite the fact that he knows nothing about the man. Fania fights with her father over Morris, but he brings her a suitor from the matchmaker as well, Abe Schmukler, a clothing manufacturer from Los Angeles. Moe gives Mashah diamonds, and Abe gives Fania clothes and takes her to the theater. Both girls give in to get out of poverty and out of their father's house. There is a double wedding, and Bessie is jealous.

A month after the wedding Mashah comes home with the news that she is starving and needs food. She admits Moe is not a diamond salesman; he borrowed the diamonds from the jewelry store where he worked and was fired for it. Now he is a shoe clerk. The father berates the daughter for her misfortune. Sara finds Morris Lipkin's love letters to Fania under the mattress, reads them, and falls in love with him. She follows Morris around, finally confessing her love. He calls her a silly kid, and she tears up his letters and her hope of finding love.

CHAPTER 6: THE BURDEN BEARER CHANGES HER BURDEN

Though Sara is thin, she is known as a good worker because of her passion. She works in a paper-box factory and gets paid more than larger women. She gives it all to her father, who will not let her have any for herself. He gives part of the money to charity but will not buy his daughter a coat. Reb becomes a matchmaker, thinking he is good at it. The wife of Zalmon, the fishmonger, dies, and Zalmon wants a replacement to care for his six children. Reb decides that this is Bessie's chance, though Zalmon is fifty-six.

Mrs. Smolinsky defends Bessie, but Reb has his own plan to get money from Zalmon to start his own business. They shake hands on the matter and then tell Bessie. She hates Zalmon and the smell of fish and has a fit of crying. Zalmon comes courting, having bathed and shaved and bringing Bessie presents of his former wife's fur coat and gold watch.

Bessie is wretched until Zalmon brings his youngest, five-year-old son, who has hurt his knee. Bessie takes care of him, and the boy, Benny, says he is waiting for his mother to come home, but she does not. Bessie cries and hugs him. Zalmon begins to use the child to bargain for himself, but Bessie feels trapped. When Bennie falls sick, one of the children finds Bessie, who cares for him, and he calls her "mother." She gives in to Zalmon.

CHAPTER 7: FATHER BECOMES A BUSINESS MAN IN AMERICA

Mrs. Smolinsky tells her husband to put the four hundred dollars from Zalmon in the bank, but he says the cash must be ready for a bargain. He sees an ad for a grocery in Elizabeth, New Jersey, and rushes off to look at it. Reb sends word for his wife and Sara to come to Elizabeth to see the store. When they arrive, there are crowds buying food, and the store looks successful. Reb has already bought it. They begin to dream about being rich but then discover they were swindled. The store is not really stocked, and the people came in because the man had reduced the prices below cost. Reb is shocked, because he had believed what the man told him. His wife is frantic, but Reb remains calm, trusting in God.

CHAPTER 8: THE HARD HEART

The family prays for a miracle. They sleep in the store and buy supplies on credit, but they can never keep enough stock to pull in customers. Sara is bored and longs for the fast life of the city, where she earned money. Her mother is happy for the green grass and blue sky at least. When Sara sees the incompetence of her parents, how her father drives away customers with preaching and insults, she loses her temper. She grabs her things and explains that she is leaving and not coming home again.

CHAPTER 9: BREAD GIVERS

Sara gets off the train in New York and goes to stay with Bessie. She is shocked to see Bessie standing next to her husband peddling fish to crowds of desperate ghetto women. In Zalmon's house, five boys sleep on a mattress on the floor, and the fat daughter takes up a sofa. Bessie congratulates Sara for getting free and says that she would run, too, except for Benny. Bessie and Sara sleep together on the floor; in the morning, Zalmon sends Sara away, claiming she is a bad example to his daughter.

Next Sara tries her sister Mashah's home but runs into Moe Mirsky in the street. Wearing a new suit, he looks like a gentleman. In her doorway, Mashah is arguing with the milkman over the unpaid bill. Sara cannot believe that Moe has spent their money on himself instead of food for the children. Sara sees the attempts Mashah has made to create beauty in her home, but she herself looks old and shabby and hopeless. When the gas goes out, Sara puts a quarter in the gas meter and helps the children to bed. They wait at dinner for the bread giver (wage earner), Moe, but he comes in after they have finished, saying he ate in a restaurant. He abuses his wife for being shabby and overworked. Sara says that she would kill him if he were her husband and walks out.

Book II: Between Two Worlds

CHAPTER 10: I SHUT THE DOOR

Sara remembers a story in the newspaper about a girl who went to night school and then college and became a teacher. She looks for a room to rent, but many landlords do not want working girls. She finds a cheap, dirty room and exults because closing the door and being alone is the first step in becoming a person.

She finds a job ironing in a laundry. In night school she studies English and arithmetic in a class of fifty students. She begins a demanding schedule of ten hours of work, two hours of class, and two hours of homework every day. The neighborhood is loud with noise as she tries to study, but she blocks it out with discipline.

CHAPTER 11: A PIECE OF MEAT

Sara does not have enough money for food and is always hungry. Thinking of food when she is ironing, she burns a shirt, and the boss takes three dollars out of her salary. In the cafeteria, she buys some stew, asking for a lot of meat, and is angry when the worker gives her mostly potatoes. The man behind her is given stew with big chunks of meat. Furious, she says she wants a dish like the man's. She is told they always give the men more.

She goes home, eats bread, and tries to study, but it is so cold that she cannot. Suddenly, there is a knock on the door, and it is her mother, who has walked all the way from Elizabeth with a feather bed. She has brought a jar of pickled herring, and Sara feels pain at her mother's love because she cannot give her mother the one thing she wants: a visit from her daughter. Sara says that she will visit after she gets her degree. She cannot waste her youth; she must become a person. Her mother holds her for a moment, disappointed, and leaves.

CHAPTER 12: MY SISTERS AND I

Sara tires of being alone. Suddenly, her sisters Fania and Bessie burst through the door. Fania has come from California in silks and diamonds, while Bessie is in her rags. Fania tells Sara to come to California with her, but Sara says she has to finish college. She notices that Fania has shadows under her eyes. Fania confesses her loneliness, as her husband is gone all the time, gambling, and she has no friends. She has to lie to him to get money. She can only think of Morris Lipkin.

Bessie talks about her cruel stepchildren, whom she cannot please. Sara thinks that Bessie looks older than their mother. Sara decides that she does not want to marry because she has a goal to her life. She refuses to stop studying and go home with them. Fania compares her to their father with his Torah.

CHAPTER 13: OUTCAST

In the laundry Sara feels outcast from the other girls because they gossip about their boyfriends and tell about their love lives. The girls make fun of her purity and lack of a boyfriend. In school she is different, too. She is hungry for knowledge and asks endless questions, annoying both the teacher and students. In the mirror she sees that her face is sad and lifeless, even at twenty-three. Deciding to dress like the other girls, she spruces up her wardrobe and buys makeup. The laundry girls see her attempts and make fun of her. She longs to get to college with loftier thinkers.

CHAPTER 14: A MAN WANTED ME

Sara fails geometry and worries that she is not smart enough. A letter from Fania warns her that Max Goldstein, a rich young businessman from California, is coming to see her. She is trying to get Sara married to him. It is spring, and Sara is lonely, so when Max knocks on her door, she is ready for company. She likes him and goes out with him. He seems to like her as she is, innocent and plain. He flatters her, and she likes being touched. He tells her his success story, how he worked his way up to buying real estate in Los Angeles. He takes her to a dance, and she dances to the rhythms of jazz for the first time. She feels alive and gives in to the experience. Although she hates how Max talks of money all the time, she likes the affection. She is finally disillusioned when he does not respond to her desire to study. He cannot think of anything beyond money; he wants to buy a wife, and though she has been awakened by his attention, she knows they have nothing in common. She goes back to her geometry.

CHAPTER 15: ON AND ON—ALONE

Sara's father arrives and yells at her for refusing Max Goldstein. She is hurt by his abuse and wishes he could see that she needs his support. Instead, Sara is goaded into saying she hates her father, and he curses and disowns her. She knows it is merely a conflict between the Old World and the New World but determines to go on without family, love, or approval.

CHAPTER 16: COLLEGE

The long-awaited day arrives when Sara leaves for college. She takes the train to a quiet college town, marveling at the green trees, pretty houses, and glorious buildings. There is beauty without poverty; the young people are tastefully dressed, not gaudy. They seem to be at ease laughing and playing. She imagines that these are the real Americans she has been waiting to meet. In class she tries to make conversation, but the students are cold to her.

Sara gets a job at a laundry and settles in. She gets along in her classes but is always the outsider. Although she flunks geometry, she comes to life in Mr. Edman's psychology class because she understands her own behavior for the first time and learns how to control her raging emotions. She wants to be inspired and tries to get him to teach her outside class, but he is too busy and overworked. When summer comes, the other students go home, while she gets a job in a canning factory.

Sara begins to idolize Mr. Edman. In the fall, he is friendly to her. She finds out where he lives and gets a room in the same house. She makes overtures to him, and he gets annoyed, telling her he does not like her manner. She is crushed. Sara finds that she is best understood by older men like the dean, and he takes her under his wing. He appreciates her hard journey and encourages her to be a pioneer.

In her senior year, Sara wonders what will become of her after college. She enters an essay contest on the topic of what college has done for her. At graduation, her name is called out. She has won.

Book III: *The New World*

CHAPTER 17: MY HONEYMOON WITH MYSELF

Sara returns to New York with new clothes, a new career, and a new image of herself. She travels in first class on the train, has proper table manners, walks on Fifth Avenue, and has a checking account with her thousand-dollar essay prize money. She buys a dark blue suit for teaching and all new accessories, priding herself on her quiet, dignified manner. She rents a room with windows and sunlight. Sara has power and feels she can go as high as she wants in life.

CHAPTER 18: DEATH IN HESTER STREET

Sara has been away from her family for six years and decides to visit them. Her parents are back on Hester Street, and as she goes in the door there she hears her mother and father arguing. Her mother is ill and begs her husband to stay with her. He claims he cannot miss prayers at the synagogue and says he will call the widow Feinstein upstairs to help her. The mother gets angry and says that the widow is only waiting for her death to get Reb for herself.

Her mother is so ill that Sara hardly recognizes her, and Sara feels guilty. Mrs. Smolinsky is overjoyed to see Sara. She is proud that her daughter looks and acts like a lady, a real teacher. Sara shows her mother money from her purse and says she will help them and visit every day. Her mother says that she is dying and her one last wish is that Sara be good to her father because he is helpless. She shows Sara her foot, full of spreading gangrene.

All the sisters are home as the mother dies. The doctor says that she needs to have her foot amputated to live, but the mother is afraid of an operation. She continues to nag her husband about eating his meals upstairs with the widow Feinstein. Reb soothes his wife with his touch. The mother introduces her daughters to the doctor, with special pride in the daughter who became a teacher, smart like her father.

Suddenly Mrs. Smolinsky's eyes are full of light, which she transfers directly to Sara just as she dies, a last blessing. Sara sees her father suffering like a child, wondering who will take care of him. The neighbors all come to mourn, and the undertaker takes a knife and makes a tear in the clothes of all the family members, as is the mourning custom, but Sara will not let him cut her new suit, and people are shocked.

CHAPTER 19: LODGE MONEY

Sara goes to see her father every day, but he does not seem to be mourning. He wears his best clothes and eats with Mrs. Feinstein. He praises her and says that God has sent him some luck. Sara wants to tell him to beware and is disgusted with her father for forgetting her mother's true devotion. Reb tells Sara that legally he can remarry after a month, and that is what he will do. She knows now that her mother had seen what was coming. Sara warns her father that the widow wants his lodge money. He says it is too late; he has already married her.

Sara goes to inform her sisters, and in shock, they denounce him for the insult to their mother. They do not visit him. One day Sara receives a note from the new Mrs. Smolinsky saying that there is trouble. She rushes to Hester Street thinking her father is ill. The woman has taken her mother's death money (insurance) and redecorated and bought new clothes, and now she wants the children to pay for their keep. She wants to have diamonds for herself. She threatens to get Sara fired by the board of education if she does not help. She threatens to take Reb to court for non-support. Reb pleads with Sara to help him get rid of the cursed woman. The daughters refuse to help, but Sara worries.

CHAPTER 20: HUGO SEELIG

Sara is teaching in the same neighborhood where she sold herring as a child. She is lonely and thinks of all her father's sayings about a woman being nothing without a man. The other teachers are unattractive old maids. Only the principal, Hugo Seelig, has kept a spark of life in him. He is kind to everyone. He comes into her class and helps her correct the children's pronunciation.

When the new Mrs. Smolinsky sends Hugo Seelig a letter explaining that Sara is not helping her parents and half her wages should be sent to them, Sara is terrified that she will be fired. Instead, Hugo comes to her with a compliment from a parent who is pleased with how her child is learning. The two become friends and find they have much in common. They come from villages a few miles apart in Poland and have had similar experiences growing up in America. Sara feels a release from the burden of her past and confesses that she has had to make her heart hard to survive. Hugo says that she is not hard but strong.

CHAPTER 21: MAN BORN OF WOMAN

Sara is happy but feels guilty over her success whenever she walks down Hester Street. She has not seen her father for months. One day she bumps into an old man in the street selling chewing gum. The packages fall to the ground, and she helps pick them up. As she looks up at him, she is shocked to recognize her father. He pitifully bewails that his children have abandoned him. His new wife has forced him to the street to sell gum. Sara takes him to his house. She cares for him and sees how he has aged since her mother died. She calls a doctor, and he is put to bed.

Reb's wife waits on him during the day, and Sara comes after school. Her father refuses to take medicine from his wife because he is afraid of her. She is waiting for him to die. When Sara hears his wife trying to discover where his lodge papers are kept, she knows that she cannot leave him with this woman. She gets a leave of absence from school to nurse him. The daughters get together and provide an allowance so that his wife will be happy. The wife softens, as she finally gets diamond earrings.

Sara takes Hugo to meet her father. Hugo impresses Reb, especially when he asks him to teach him Hebrew. Reb lights up with pride. Sara has wanted a home of her own with Hugo, but she cannot cast off her father. She asks Reb to live with her, and he agrees only on the condition that she will keep the old sacred laws. Hugo agrees that Reb should live with them when they marry. Sara worries that Reb will tyrannize their home, but she cannot rid herself of her father's influence over her or of the weight of her inherited Old World tradition.

CHARACTERS

Benny
Benny is the fish peddler Zalmon's five-year-old son. Bessie marries Zalmon to be a mother to Benny. Benny is also the reason she stays in the marriage rather than running away.

Berel Bernstein
Bessie Smolinsky's chosen suitor is Berel, who works with her in the clothing factory and lives in Mumenkeh's house. He is a cutter, making good wages, and he wants Bessie because she could be his partner in the business he wants to set up for himself. When Reb tells him he has to pay to marry Bessie by setting him up in business to make up for her lost wages, Berel tells him off. He explains that he is desirable to many women with dowries, and he will not support the whole Smolinsky family. He tells Reb to get a job because in America the only thing that counts is working for money. Berel chooses to marry the forewoman in the factory, and when Bessie is desolate, Sara curses him at his engagement party.

The Dean
The dean of Sara's college is an older man who appreciates her Hester Street background and encourages her journey out of the ghetto as a pioneer effort. Having someone to believe in her makes a difference. She wins the senior essay contest and its prize of a thousand dollars.

Mr. Edman
Mr. Edman is a psychology professor at Sara's college. He is a good teacher who motivates Sara, but when she wants extra attention outside of class, he says he is too busy. She discovers that he is overworked but manages to walk with him sometimes to converse. When she discovers where he lives, she gets a room in the same house and tries to become friends with him. He epitomizes the higher life of learning to her. He only sees her as a nuisance, however, and asks her to leave him alone.

Widow Feinstein
The widow upstairs from the Smolinskys on Hester Street schemes to marry Reb so as to get his lodge money after his wife dies. She assumes that the daughters will support them. She threatens Sara's job and threatens to take Reb to court to get support. He had assumed that all women were worshipful like his wife had been, ready to wait on him so that he could study. She bullies Reb and forces him out on the street to sell chewing gum. When she sends a letter to Sara's principal asking him to divert her wages on her father's behalf, however, her plan backfires and brings Sara together with her future husband, Hugo. They remove the ailing father from the clutches of the greedy and heartless woman who only married Reb Smolinsky to get diamond earrings.

Shprintzeh Gittel
A neighbor to the Smolinksys in Hester Street, she puts down her baby and proudly acts out Rabbi Smolinsky's attack on the rent collector, on the front stoop.

Max Goldstein
Max is a self-made man, rich and successful, sent by Fania from California to woo her sister Sara. He falls in love with Sara and takes her out, and they have fun. She likes his touch and the intimacy, since she is starved for affection. He asks her to marry him. She is tempted for a moment, to have a home and to get out of poverty, but he

can only talk about money and himself, and she wants a more cultured life. She wants independence, and he makes fun of her learning. When Sara turns him down, her father, who would have thus been provided for, reminds her of the shame of being an unmarried woman and disowns her.

Hannah Hayyeh

Hannah is the washwoman on Hester Street who complains about slum landlords to the neighbors.

Morris Lipkin

Morris is Fania Smolinsky's choice for a husband, a poor boarder at Zalmon's place. He sweeps the corner drugstore, goes to night school, and spends time at the library. He writes Fania love poems that she reads to the girls on the stoop. He says that he cannot give her gifts but will give her his collection "Poems of Poverty." When he tries to ask for Fania's hand, Reb Smolinsky ignores him and shames him until he leaves. Reb finds another suitor for Fania, Moe Mirsky, a supposed diamond salesman. Later, Sara reads all of Morris's love letters to Fania and gets a crush on him. When she follows Morris around and confesses her love, he calls her a kid, and she has her first broken heart.

Moe Mirsky

Moe Mirsky is the vain and selfish salesman who pretends to be a diamond seller and woos Mashah Smolinsky with diamonds borrowed from the jewelry store where he works. After Moe is fired, he gets a job as a shoe salesman. Although Mashah and the children are hungry, he spends money on new clothes and restaurants and abuses his wife for looking shabby. She loses her beauty and freedom and is unhappy at not having married the man of her choice, Jacob Novak.

Muhmenkeh

Muhmenkeh is the old herring seller of Hester Street. She is kind and helps the Smolinsky family by loaning them a feather bed so that they can rent out their front room. She shows them how to furnish the room with boxes and barrels, and she helps ten-year-old Sara start selling herring by giving her a few from the bottom of her barrel.

Jacob Novak

Jacob is the young pianist living on the corner who is supported by his father to study music.

Mashah Smolinsky falls in love with him when she hears him play as he prepares for his first concert. His father owns a big department store on Grand Street and persuades his son to ignore Mashah. She is not invited to the big concert. When Mashah is heartbroken, Jacob tries to woo her again, but Reb Smolinsky puts his foot down and throws him out of the house. Mashah is too scared to go against her father, and so she never sees him again.

Abe Schmukler

Abe, a rich clothing manufacturer from Los Angeles, marries Fania Smolinsky. Fania is rich but lonely, and her husband gambles. She has to lie to him because he is tight with money.

Hugo Seelig

Hugo is the handsome principal of the school where Sara Smolinsky teaches, young and full of energy, unlike the old-maid teachers. He is kind and attentive to all the teachers and students. He helps Sara's class with pronunciation, and when Reb's second wife sends a letter of complaint to him about Sara not supporting her father, he does not pay attention but instead becomes friends with her. They date and find that they are from villages in Poland only a few miles apart. His background of making his way in America as a Jewish immigrant parallels Sara's, but it has not hardened him. He has lost the desperate greed of the ghetto but has remained a dreamer with refined sensibilities. He makes friends with Sara's father by asking for Hebrew lessons, and he agrees to take the old man into the house when he marries Sara. He is portrayed as the ideal Jewish American.

Bessie Smolinsky

The eldest daughter, Bessie is called the burden bearer by her father because she is the main support of the family. She does not have time to think of herself or of marrying because Reb wants her wages to support him. She is jealous of her younger sisters, who do not have to work so hard and are encouraged to marry. She is older and unattractive and used to being a martyr like her mother. Her father finally marries her off to the older widower Zalmon, and she only agrees because the little boy Benny needs her as a mother.

Fania Smolinsky

The third Smolinsky daughter, Fania, falls in love with Morris Lipkin, the poet. She goes to night school and meets him at the library. When her father will not let her marry the man she loves, she marries his choice, Abe Schmukler from California, so she can be rich and get away from her father. She is miserable, however, with loneliness in her loveless marriage, though she looks grand in silks and diamonds. She tries to marry off Sara to another rich Californian.

Mashah Smolinsky

Mashah, the beautiful second Smolinsky daughter, has long golden hair and a love of cleanliness and beauty. She spends her wages on herself to be attractive to young men and is never concerned with her family's troubles. Liking to hear free music in the park, she is attracted by the piano music of Jacob Novak. Yet his rich father and her proud father team up to prevent the marriage, and she ends up living in poverty with Moe Mirsky, who is abusive to her and their three children.

Mrs. Smolinsky

Old before her time from working for the family and waiting on her husband, Mrs. Smolinsky alternates yelling at Reb and worshipping him. Worrying constantly about money, she nags and scolds everyone but is a good mother, even walking in the cold winter night to bring a feather bed to her freezing daughter Sara. Although his wife has good sense, Reb never listens to her, as he insists on making the decisions as the head of the family. She tells the girls tales from the old country when she was a beautiful young girl and a good dancer. Then she was healthy and had life in her, compared to her careworn face and shapeless body now. In Poland her wealthy father wanted a scholar for a son-in-law and was willing to support him. She fell in love with Reb when she heard him recite the books of the Bible and saw how his learning radiated from him. She brags about her rich dowry of feather beds, embroidered sheets, curtains, and tablecloth and tries to impress upon her daughters her belief that old handmade items are better than machine-made goods from stores. The tsar's pogroms on the Jews made them have to sell everything and escape to America. As Mrs. Smolinsky is dying of gangrene and blood poisoning, she becomes conscious of the plotting of the widow upstairs to take her place and warns her husband.

Rabbi Reb Smolinsky

The main antagonist of the story, Reb is an otherworldly scholar who loves studying and chanting the Torah all day, and he is also a tyrant who runs the lives of his overworked wife and four daughters, who are pressured into supporting him. His holy life both inspires and exasperates his family, for he earns no money and does not feel it is his duty to do so. As a man, according to Jewish tradition he is the only one in the family who can study the scriptures. He frequently reminds his family that only a woman who serves a man can get into heaven. When the rent is not paid, the rent collector steps on his Bible, and when he slaps her, he is arrested but let off because he is a religious man. The people see him as a hero, a David who fought a Goliath of a landlord. Coming from the Old World, where rabbis were treated with respect and supported by family and neighbors, he stands up for his religion and tradition. In Poland, he was a teacher who gave lessons in Hebrew and on the Torah, but in America, people are interested only in making money, not in his wisdom. Alternately admiring of the American dream and disillusioned by the godless America he finds, he, unlike the Jews around him, will not adapt to the New World. He is able to intimidate every daughter except Sara, whose will matches his. Reb is vulnerable when it comes to worldly matters. He is swindled when he buys a grocery store with no goods in it and when he marries a greedy widow, thinking she will take care of him. He bullies everyone in the family, beating them down and destroying their self-confidence. When Sara finds him on the street selling gum, forced by his wife to forsake his religious calling, she is indignant and helps him get back on his feet. He is like a helpless child in the world, and that is why Sara finally asks him to live with her and her husband, Hugo. He is a man both hated and loved. The sole link to the family's rich traditions, he is not easily dismissed, and in fact, Sara finds she can throw out neither her father nor their traditions.

Sara Smolinsky

The main character and first-person narrator of her own story, Sara is ten when the story starts and in her later twenties at the end. A fiery, determined girl with red hair, she takes after her father in terms of her love of learning, strong will, and ambition for a higher life. He calls her Blut-und-Eisen, "Blood-and-iron," for she is the only one who resists his will and tries to become a person or individual, instead of a servant to the family. After witnessing the brutal way in which her father bullies her sisters into marrying men they do not love, she runs away from home at the age of seventeen, determined to live her own life and be an American. She supports herself working in a laundry ten hours a day, goes to night school, and then comes home to a dingy room to study late into the night. Hungry and cold, she does not give in to hardship because her hunger to better herself is greater. Sara gives up seeing her family while studying, and when her mother begs her to visit, she says she has to spend her youth on her education. She is lonely but self-disciplined, always envying the lifestyle of the rich Americans and desiring education, which can lift a person from the cycle of poverty. She suffers frequently from casting off her tradition, which nourishes her on a deep level, as she tries to embrace the American dream. Like her father, she is disillusioned by the shallowness and coldness of the New World, rejecting a rich suitor, Max Goldstein from California, because he is too self-centered and materialistic. While she does not want riches, she does want to avoid poverty so that she can have a life of culture and independence. She studies in college to become a teacher, battling the scorn of the richer students. She is crushed by the indifference of Mr. Edman, her psychology teacher, on whom she dotes, but finds understanding and encouragement from the older dean. Winning a college essay contest, she enters the world as an independent lady with a little money, teaching for a living, having the refined life she fought for. Her mother is proud of the teacher in the family, but her father casts her out when he finds she refused to marry a rich man who could have helped support him. She makes friends with the principal, Hugo Seelig, and they date. She decides to marry him, but her father needs her after her mother's death, for he is helpless in the world and becomes ill. Hugo Seelig agrees to care for the father in their home. Sara worries that he will take over their home and be a tyrant, but she knows that he represents the whole weight of the tradition she has not been able to throw off, and she gives in.

Rosy Stein

Rosy is one of Sara's ghetto students whose mother is happy with her progress under Sara's care.

Yenteh

Zalmon's oldest daughter, Yenteh, wanted her deceased mother's fur coat that was given to Bessie. She does not like her stepmother, Bessie, and gives her a hard time, rejecting a dress that Bessie sewed for her as being too old-fashioned.

Zalmon

Zalmon, the old fish peddler, loses his wife and marries Bessie Smolinsky to care for his six children. She is miserable because he is fifty-six and smells of fish. She finally gives in because she loves his youngest child, who wants her to be his mother. Zalmon claims that his wife will not have to work, but Bessie has to sell fish all day, with fish scales in her hair, and she cares for the house and children as well. Zalmon pays Smolinsky four hundred dollars for Bessie so that Reb can buy a business for himself. Reb is swindled out of this money.

Zaretsky

Zaretsky is the old matchmaker who arranges marriages for the ghetto people. He finds Moe Mirsky and Abe Schmukler for Mashah and Fania Smolinsky, respectively.

Aby Zuker

Aby is one of Sara's ghetto students, a bright boy of eleven whom she corrects when he says, "ain't it?" He wants to be a lawyer.

THEMES

Immigrant Life in America

The high expectations of immigrants coming to America, and their subsequent disillusionment from living in poverty, are a major focus in *Bread Givers*. The Polish Smolinskys, like other immigrants from different parts of the world, are drawn to the United States by the promise of a better life. Persecuted in the Old World, they have heard glorious tales of freedom. Reb Smolinsky, in particular, is full of myths about the American dream. He tells his wife that she should not bring anything with her, for "in the new golden country," "milk and honey flow free

TOPICS FOR FURTHER STUDY

- Research at least two films that deal with challenges faced by any immigrant group in this country or another country. Give a talk, with film clips, comparing and contrasting the lives of the immigrants in the films with the lives of the Smolinskys in *Bread Givers*.

- Write an immigrant story from your own family's history or the family history of an acquaintance. Read the story aloud to the class, and then invite your classmates to share similar anecdotes from their family histories.

- Write a paper comparing and contrasting the Jewish perspective in *Bread Givers* with one or two other Jewish American works, such as Denise Levertov's poem "The Jacob's Ladder," Tillie Olsen's story "Tell Me a Riddle," Isaac Bashevis Singer's story "Gimpel the Fool," or Grace Paley's story "A Conversation with My Father."

- Write a paper on the economic and political repercussions of the Jewish Pale of Settlement, established in 1791, in imperial Russia in the nineteenth century. What conditions led to the mass emigration of Jews to America?

---

in the streets" and "all America will come to my feet to learn."

Continually inspired by the notions that anyone can be successful or a millionaire in America and that his daughters can marry rich men without dowries, Reb easily falls prey to scams, such as that of the suitor who pretends to be a diamond merchant, Moe Mirsky, and the ready-made grocery store he buys in Elizabeth with no groceries in it. He soon realizes that no one is impressed with his holiness and scholarship. The father is not respected as infallible in America. He is furthermore disappointed to find that America is a land of materialistic rather than spiritual values.

Sara describes the crowded tenement buildings with their lack of fresh air, standing in line at public baths, scrounging coal from garbage cans for the stove, the pushcart peddlers out in all weather selling their wares for a few pennies, the starvation, the sweatshops, the dirt, the constant threat of eviction if the rent is late, and the great fatigue and bitterness as people struggle to survive. Instead of getting out of the ghetto, many are stuck there for generations. Mashah's children are starving, even as she did, and as her mother did.

The positive memories of the immigrant's life are preserved in the form of the traditions they bring and maintain. Even though Sara rebels against her father's strict Old World ways, there are times when she is charmed by his stories from the Torah, his chanting, and his high-mindedness. His face shines from within because of his devotion to his faith. Contrasted to the coldness of Americans toward her is the devotion of her mother, who walks in a cold winter night to bring her a homemade feather bed. The mother instills in her daughters pride in the beautiful hand-crafted sheets, tablecloths, and quilts of the old country. Neighbors sticking together as a community is a cultural value Sara does not find when she leaves the ghetto. Her life demonstrates the difficulties faced by the immigrant who is forever in between two worlds, the old and the new.

Gender Inequality

Feminist themes are strongly presented throughout Sara's journey to independence. Reb, the patriarchal father, repeats to her over and over, "It says in the Torah: *A woman without a man is less than nothing*. No life on earth, no hope of Heaven." The woman's place in traditional Judaism is subservient to the man's. Sara reflects on the fact that her father is bitter at having no son, for there will be no one to pray for his soul when he dies: "The prayers of his daughters didn't count because God didn't listen to women. Heaven and the next world were only for men." Reb tells his wife and daughters that they should support his holy studies, and in this way, by waiting on him, they will earn their place in heaven.

The Smolinsky wife and daughters are the bread givers, or wage earners, of the family, but they are not allowed to keep their own earnings. All must go to the father for the household. He also receives the best food, as though he is the only valuable person in the family. He expects to be given the only morsels of meat, while he sees his family eating thin soup. Sara sees this same prejudice when she is living on her own and starving. She goes to a cafeteria and orders stew but gets mostly potatoes. The man behind her gets large chunks of meat. She is told: "Don't you know they always give men more?" Similarly, when she tries to rent a room, she is told that landlords do not like to rent to single females because women are more trouble. She is treated like a prostitute for wanting to live alone.

Although Bessie, Mashah, and Fania initially pick out men whom they love as husbands, they are threatened and bullied by their father until they give in to his miserable choices for them. Each is terribly unhappy but stuck with an unsuitable mate. When Sara hears her sisters describe their sad marriages, she declares that she will never get married: "At least I've no boss of a husband to crush the spirit in me."

The father and the matchmaker arrange the marriages for the daughters. Sara is aware, even as her sisters are caving in to their father's will, that in America, "girls pick out for themselves the men they want for husbands." This is regarded as open rebellion by the father, and Sara has to run away to make her own life. She is cursed by her father when she does not accept Max Goldstein, a rich suitor found for her by her sister: "Woe to America where women are let free like men. . . . All the evils of the world come from them."

Reb's wife accepts her subservience, but she voices her dissatisfaction at times, yelling at her husband when he forces Bessie to marry the old fishmonger for his own convenience. Sara, on the other hand, creates a new pattern by finding her own husband, marrying Hugo Seelig for love. They meet on equal ground as professionals, accepting each other's past and going forward as partners.

Becoming an Individual

From childhood Sara is proud and ambitious. When the family is in financial trouble, the ten-year-old insists on earning money. Her father has named her Blut-und-Eisen ("Blood-and-iron") because of her determination. Her mother says, "When she begins to want a thing, there is no

rest, no let-up till she gets it." This trait is Sara's ticket to individuality. She does not turn aside when she wants something, as her sisters do.

Mumenkeh helps Sara find something to sell and gives her blessing: "Go, make yourself for a person." This is Sara's main quest in the novel, to become a person, someone of respectability and independence. When her father condemns her for wanting to "live for yourself," Sara replies, "I've got to live my own life. It's enough that Mother and the others lived for you." He tells her that she would have been stoned in the old days, but she knows that "this is America, where children are people."

Solitude, the author shows, is an important ingredient for becoming a person. When Sara runs away at the age of seventeen and eats breakfast at a bakery, she notes that it is the first time she has eaten alone in her life. Poverty and overcrowded conditions go together. Sara's first luxury on her own is to have a room by herself, like her father has, for study. Self-sufficiency means not only supporting herself, working her way through school, but also mastering loneliness, which is the price she must pay to think her own thoughts.

Sara has to learn to accept herself as an individual. She fails at first, wanting to fit in. The other girls working at the laundry exclude her because she is not silly over boys, as they are; she studies on her breaks. When she wears makeup to look like them, she quickly wipes it off as a false mask. She thinks she will find her kind at college but is surprised by the carefree gaiety of the rich students. She is still the poor immigrant who has to work her way through school. Not until she receives encouragement from the dean as one of the "pioneers" and wins the essay contest does she begin to feel the fruit of her efforts.

The biggest temptation to turn aside from her goal comes when Max Goldstein proposes. He is rich and shows her a good time, and she is lonely. When he ridicules her study, however, she pulls back, thinking, "All great people have to be alone to work out their greatness." Sara becomes a teacher and has her honeymoon with herself, "a person among people." Her mother's dying pride in her achievement allays her guilt: "You shine like a princess."

An orthodox Rabbi lights the Chanukah candelabrum (© World Religions Photo Library / Alamy)

STYLE

Bildungsroman

Bread Givers is fashioned primarily as a bildungsroman, or a coming-of-age novel, showing the emergence of a young person into adulthood. In the bildungsroman, the main character's growth is chronicled, step by step, from innocence to experience. The hero or heroine must discover how to negotiate the opposite qualities of life—success and failure, hope and disappointment, love and loneliness. The character must learn to accept responsibility for his or her own life, rather than living a life fashioned by society or parents. Often, the boundaries of class, gender, or background must be overcome. The formation of individuality is a key feature.

This novel form became popular in nineteenth-century Europe with such works as *The Sorrows of Young Werther*, by Johann Wolfgang von Goethe; *Sentimental Education*, by Gustave Flaubert; *David Copperfield*, by Charles Dickens; and *Jane Eyre*, by Charlotte Brontë. A young man's journey might show the path to his place in society through temptations, obstacles, a search for meaningful work, and marriage. A woman's journey traditionally revolved around her moral education, her trials, and finding a husband. Yezierska's novel is emotionally more complex because Sara is overcoming the several barriers of gender, race, religion, and culture. It has a feminist angle in that she is more interested in her education and career than marriage, and she nevertheless finds a husband. She takes on herculean tasks to become herself and forge her own unique way to adulthood, from an immigrant waif selling herrings on the street to an American professional. The author shows us the price Sara pays for daring to be a self-made woman in an unsupportive environment.

Autobiographical Novel

Bread Givers is an autobiographical novel. An autobiographical novel is a piece of fiction modeled on the life of the author but fictionalized or changed in certain details. It is distinct from straight autobiography, which proposes to be a truthful account. Although most authors draw on their own lives to some extent for fictional material, the autobiographical novel depends heavily on the author's life in terms of the plot and protagonist. Some autobiographical novels, such as *A Portrait of the Artist as a Young Man*, by James Joyce (1916), use a third-person point of view, as though witnessing the story from outside. Stephen Dedalus, the main character of Joyce's novel, however, is basically a fictionalized Joyce. It is common for authors to use first-person narrative in the autobiographical novel, as Yezierska does. The "I" is thus the protagonist telling his or her own story from inside the story. This gives greater immediacy and a closer feeling of identification of the author with the main character. Sara Smolinsky, then, can tell the reader what it feels like to grow up in poverty, and these are likely Yezierska's own feelings and experiences. Since it is fiction, the author is free to change incidental details around for the sake of better telling the story. For instance, Yezierska had brothers, but she makes the Smolinsky family have only daughters. She wanted to focus on the condition of the immigrant Jewish girl, and the boys would have diluted the circumstances and her message. Other examples of autobiographical novels include *David Copperfield*, by Charles Dickens (1850); *Of Human Bondage*, by William Somerset Maugham (1915); and *Invisible Man*, by Ralph Ellison (1952).

Jewish American Novel

The bulk of early Jewish American literature was written in Yiddish (a dialect, or nonstandard regional language, combining Hebrew and German) between 1885 and 1935 by immigrants, although there were other Jewish languages used for literature, such as Ladino (Judeo-Spanish), Hebrew, and Judeo-Arabic. Yiddish authors produced poetry, fiction, plays, newspapers, and journals for other Yiddish-speaking immigrants. These writers were influenced by the Jewish enlightenment, Haskalah, a secular movement brought over from Europe. This tradition laid the groundwork for the emerging Jewish writers in English. In *Bread Givers*, Yiddish expressions are translated into English for the ghetto speakers, while the narrator uses standard English.

Mary Antin's *The Promised Land* (1912) was a landmark novel in which a Jewish immigrant tells of the process of becoming American. Antin portrays a girl who successfully assimilates into the American culture. The most important early Yiddish writer in America was Abraham Cahan, founder of a successful Yiddish newspaper, the *Jewish Daily Forward*, which was read by Yezierska's family. He wrote the novella *Yekl* (1896) in an attempt to translate the Yiddish dialect into English, and this appealed to a wider audience. His novel *The Rise of David Levinsky* (1917) is important for outlining the familiar themes being explored at the same time by Yezierska and later writers concerned with assimilation. The hero, Levinsky, a Jewish immigrant, becomes a millionaire in America but finds that his life is empty when he divorces himself from his ethnic past. Sally Ann Drucker, in her article "Yiddish, Yidgin, and Yezierska: Dialect in Jewish-American Writing," acknowledges Cahan's groundbreaking work as having created the hybridization of American and Yiddish culture, but she finds that no Jewish writer of the time created a Yiddish-English dialect as convincing as Yezierska's.

Together, Antin, Cahan, and Yezierska are often credited as founders of Jewish American literature, but as the *Norton Anthology of Jewish American Literature* points out, "They were transitional figures, lifting one foot out of their native Yiddish-speaking immigrant culture while, with the other, stepping toward the English-speaking American culture they aspired to." After 1935, most Jewish American authors were born in America, and they continued to explore the secular themes and ethnic character types of immigrant literature. Except for Isaac Bashevis Singer, the Nobel Prize-winning Yiddish writer whose stories were translated, these authors wrote in English. Prominent Jewish novelists of the twentieth century include Bernard Malamud, whose novel *The Fixer* (1967) is about antisemitism in tsarist Russia, and Saul Bellow, whose *Mr. Sammler's Planet* (1970) is set in contemporary New York with a misanthropic Jew who has been through the Holocaust. Tillie Olsen, Grace Paley, Joseph Heller, and Philip Roth are other well-known Jewish mainstream writers. These authors separate Jewishness from Judaism and discuss issues outside of Jewish history, such as the problem of finding meaning in the modern world. American Jewish authors before World War II disconnected themselves from European Judaism and focused primarily on American issues. After World War II, another avenue of Jewish literature explored the Holocaust and its aftermath for Jews and for humanity as a whole.

Characters in Jewish American novels often question, explore, love, hate, and celebrate their background, as does Sara Smolinsky. They are often ambivalent about their Jewishness and divided within themselves. Like Sara, they look for love and approval but face rejection, prejudice, and misunderstanding. Even for those born as Americans, being a Jew in its positive or negative aspects is consciously addressed as an act of identity, for ethnicity no longer means an inherited place (outside of Israel, established in 1948), as it had to Jews in previous centuries. Like Sara, characters decide for themselves who they are. Yezierska must be credited as a first-generation writer of the Jewish American novel who set the stage for the subsequent secular expression of what it means to be Jewish in America.

HISTORICAL CONTEXT

East European Immigration to America
More than twenty-three million immigrants came to America from eastern Europe, Italy, and Greece between 1880 and 1920, resulting in the largest influx of immigration in American history. These immigrants were largely seeking refuge from upheavals in their native lands. For the Jews in Russian Poland, many hardships contributed to one-third of the Jewish population's coming to America, the largest Jewish immigration that had ever taken place. The Russian tsar had confined Jews to the Pale of Settlement, covering part of Poland, Byelorussia, the Ukraine, and Lithuania. Yezierska's family came from a shtetl, or small town, in Poland within this region. Economically the people were squeezed out of their professional roles and wealth, and jobs became more menial and harder to find. Universities were closed to Jews. Famine, cholera, and starvation were common. Pogroms, or attacks of violence, committed by Cossacks, troops loyal to the tsar, disrupted and destroyed the towns. In *Bread Givers*, Mrs. Smolinsky describes how much of her father's wealth was used in bribing the Cossacks to leave them alone. Conscription into the Russian army was another way the tsar broke up the shtetls, for a Jewish boy would be forced to serve for twenty-five years, thus taking him away from his religious practices. The latter point, more than famine or the feared pogroms, was the reason Reb Smolinsky left for America—to avoid conscription and preserve his religion.

Orthodox Rabbinic Judaism
In America, there are several branches of Judaism: Reform Judaism, the mainstream Jewish religion of nineteenth-century America until the eastern European immigration; Orthodox Judaism, shown in *Bread Givers*; Conservative Judaism, combining practices of the first two types; and Hasidism, or Jewish mysticism. In *Bread Givers*, Reb Smolinsky is a rabbi, or religious teacher, who studies and teaches Orthodox Jewish law, the predominant tradition of eastern European Jews. The ancient oral traditions of Judaism were written down once Jews began dispersing all over the world, and rabbis taught and interpreted through their study to other Jews. The Torah, or Jewish scripture, along with the Talmudic commentaries on religious practice and the codified Mosaic law in the Mishnah and Gemara, are the holy books Reb Smolinsky studies. Every detail and aspect of life is covered in rabbinical writings (called halacha, or "the way"), hence Reb's constant lecturing on his family's behavior. In the Polish Jewish village, closed to outsiders, the father, as head of the house, and rabbi, as respected teacher, were expected to be learned upholders of the prescribed practices. Later Reform movements in Judaism softened the strictness of these laws to fit contemporary life. Smolinsky, however, threatens his daughter by asserting that he will not live with her in her home unless she agrees to the strictness of Jewish law. This worries her, for she had hoped to create her own home.

Lower East Side of Manhattan
New York was the port that immigrants came through on their way to settling in the United States, and many were forced to stay there because they had no means for moving elsewhere. The immigrants in Yezierska's day were not like many of the well-educated immigrants today, who are world citizens, traveling back and forth from America to their homelands. The late nineteenth-century immigrants fled from intolerable situations in their countries and could never return. They fled from poverty into poverty. Many were peasants and laborers without skills who brought no savings and spoke no English. They settled in ghettos with their own kind.

The Lower East Side of Manhattan was dominated by east European Jews after 1880. They were crowded into tenement buildings, described by Moses Rischin in *The Promised*

COMPARE
&
CONTRAST

- **1890s:** Poor working girls without education or skill, like Sara Smolinsky, can only find jobs as domestics, or in sweatshops, factories, or home businesses, or as pushcart vendors on the streets. Most upper-class women do not go to college and are still supported by husbands or family; if they work, they usually do so as volunteers for charities and causes.

  1920s: Women of all classes begin to seek professional careers, but they are still a minority. They attend schools or colleges, like Sara does, to qualify as secretaries, teachers, nurses, actresses, and writers. In general, however, like Yezierska, they have to choose between career and family.

  Today: All professions are open to qualified women. It is the norm for women to juggle families and careers at the same time.

- **1890s:** Unregulated immigration to the United States reaches a peak volume, with millions of refugees coming from eastern and southern Europe.

  1920s: In 1924, the National Origins Act sets up national immigration quotas to control ethnic populations in the United States,

  especially those from southern and eastern Europe.

  Today: The Immigration and Nationality Act of 1965 abolished national quotas. Most immigrants coming to the United States are from Asia and South and Central America. Illegal immigration is a frequently discussed problem.

- **1890s:** The Lower East Side of Manhattan is crammed with poor immigrants living in unhealthy conditions in tenements.

  1920s: The Lower East Side gains mythic status with the release of Yezierska's hit film *Hungry Hearts*. Conditions in the ghetto there inspire urban reform movements, with professors at Columbia, like John Dewey, leading the way.

  Today: The Lower East Side, also called "The Big Onion," is a trendy area with a mix of ethnic cultures whose residents increasingly include students and young professionals. Although one can visit the Lower East Side Tenement Museum, in 2008 the neighborhood is put on an endangered list by the National Trust for Historic Preservation.

City: New York's Jews, 1870–1914 as multistory buildings with four apartments to a floor and little ventilation. The buildings were jammed together along city blocks with only air shafts between buildings. *Bread Givers* speaks of the windows that look out on air shafts, with no view but other buildings. There were no green places, and the dirt and odor and heat were oppressive. There were shared toilets, and one had to take a bath at a public bathhouse. The tenements were owned by slum landlords who made substantial profits because housing was short. They evicted anyone unable to pay, and the fear of this was always hanging over the heads of the poorest residents, as it does with

the Smolinskys. Like them, families seldom used all the rooms in a flat, instead having to sublet to boarders to make the rent, creating extremely dense numbers in small spaces. As a working girl, Sara is willing to pay extra for a room of her own, having never been alone through her first seventeen years.

East European Jews were small in build compared to other immigrants and, like Sara, had trouble persuading employers to use them for physical work in factories. They most often sold wares from pushcarts or worked home industries, making clothing and other items. Sara Smolinsky describes the settlement houses in the ghetto that offered relief to the poor in the form of various social services and education. They were charitably established by rich donors to help new immigrants settle and assimilate. Sara and Fania take advantage of the night-school programs to learn English and other subjects that their parents think are a waste of time, for old-timers like Reb Smolinsky do not want to assimilate into the American culture.

American Attitude toward Immigrants in the Late Nineteenth and Early Twentieth Centuries

The myth of the American melting pot, which imagined the races of other countries being blended together into a new American stew, made it easier for early immigrants to be accepted. Many of these were the pioneers who settled the West and earned their places as Americans. The late-nineteenth-century refugees from eastern Europe, however, had to face greater barriers and prejudices. They did not farm and settle in the West because the frontier was closed, and they were not farmers. They were not welcomed by other groups in the cities because they competed for jobs. Furthermore, they were strange, with different religions, customs, and languages.

The melting pot idea began to change. New racial theories developed by European writers gave superiority to the northern white races and were adopted in America as well. Americans began to believe that the truest American was a white Anglo-Saxon Protestant and that immigrants who wanted to be assimilated had to learn how to look and act as such. *Bread Givers* shows Sara Smolinsky dealing with these problems, as Anzia Yezierska did when she had to anglicize her name to Hattie Mayer. Sara is aware that to be an American she must shed her Old World look, her native tongue, her emotional reactions, her ethnic markers. At college she sees the clean-cut kids who seem rich and carefree but cold. She has to learn reason and restraint to be accepted. This, in turn, makes her alternately yearn for and hate her own heritage. Cleansing herself of her upbringing makes her into a woman, but she has to chop off a lot of herself to fit into what she perceives as a shallow stereotype.

White Americans, feeling threatened and overwhelmed by other racial types, through the National Origins Act of 1924, set quotas on how many could enter the country from different regions. These quotas were only liberalized after the 1960s, when multiculturalism began to be a new norm in America as well as in the rest of the world, with boundaries being shattered by technology.

John Dewey

In 1917 when John Dewey, the famous philosopher and educator, was teaching at Columbia, Anzia Yezierska went to him for help in getting certified to teach full-time. She was in her late thirties, and he was twenty years older. Yezierska was still attractive and a magnetic woman, and he apparently fell in love with her as she attended his classes. Although it is not certain what the relationship was, his love poems to her have been published (*The Poems of John Dewey*, edited by Jo Ann Boydston, 1977). He became a mentor, and his encouragement was the push she needed to become a serious writer. They were very different—he the cold New Englander, she the passionate and exotic Polish Jew with flaming red hair. He did not tell her to become Americanized and fit in; he encouraged her to write about her ghetto experience. Married to an activist wife who was his partner, Dewey believed in rights for women. He liked Yezierska's strength and honesty. While Dewey felt love, Yezierska idealized Dewey as the older wise man. She began to use an older Dewey figure in almost all of her stories. In *Bread Givers*, he is glimpsed in the dean of Sara's college, who opens his home to Sara and tells her that she is a pioneer who will succeed. Dewey helped Yezierska publish, and after that she quickly became famous.

Dewey participated in debates on educating immigrants. There was fear in the country about the loyalties of so many foreigners, and one school of thought was that the immigrant should be Americanized in school, to have the foreign elements taken out. Dewey took a different stand, believing that immigrants brought their own gifts to the country and could enrich the culture.

Dewey's personal encouragement and his liberal thinking, partly derived from Ralph Waldo Emerson, emphasized the process of becoming an individual. He preached self-reliance. Dewey believed that education could bring about social justice. One of his poems ("Generations") describes Yezierska as a spokesperson for the mute masses of immigrants; her life could have the purpose of informing Americans and encouraging those immigrants following in her footsteps. This is the calling she indeed embraced, as inspired by Dewey's sympathy and recognition.

CRITICAL OVERVIEW

Bread Givers, published in 1925, came on the wave of Yezierska's fame in the 1920s following her recognition for *Hungry Hearts* and *Salome of the Tenements*, both of which were made into films. At the time of the publication of *Bread Givers*, critics generally had the same points of praise and criticism as they did for her earlier work. *New York Tribune* contributor Samuel Raphaelson, quoted in Carol B. Schoen's book *Anzia Yezierska*, lauds her ability to render Yiddish into poetic English but feels that the story repeats from her earlier works "a theme of which we have grown weary—the story of a poor East Side girl who Americanized herself by sheer force." The Jewish audience was less pleased by the Yiddish dialect. Joseph Goer, writing in the *Menorah Journal*, complains that the book is "pandering" to Americans who want to laugh at the Yiddish dialect and at Judaism (quoted in Schoen). *International Book Review* contributor William Lyons Phelps, quoted in Alice Kessler-Harris's introduction to *Bread Givers*, summarizes the depth and realism that many critics admired in Yezierska's work: "One does not seem to read. One is too completely inside."

The book went out of print with the loss of interest in Yezierska in the 1940s and 1950s. At that time, she was not thought to be a serious author. Not until the 1960s, when ethnic and women's literature became important, was she rediscovered. Kessler-Harris, the scholar from Columbia responsible for getting *Bread Givers* reprinted, remarks in her foreword to the book, "Persea's edition of *Bread Givers* appeared in 1975 not to wild acclaim but to steady success." Yezierska was finally justified after her death, becoming the spokeswoman of immigrants for later generations, who began to study her novels in their classes. *Bread Givers*, however, has continued to draw divided opinions on its artistic merit. Schoen, in *Anzia Yezierska*, calls it her finest early work, with unforgettable characters, even the minor ones "sharply rendered," and the author "willing to let the story speak for itself" rather than moralizing. Laura Wexler, in her essay in *Women of the Word: Jewish Women and Jewish Writing*, is among those who try to defend the author's vivid but awkward storytelling on the ground that it is her passion that counts, but Wexler admits that "she struggled so with form, and often lost." To the constant charges that Yezierska is overemotional and unrestrained in her use of language, Sally Ann Drucker explains in her essay in *Yiddish* that the author is faithfully replicating the emotion in the Yiddish ghetto language. This point reinforces Yezierska's own complaint that her work has been misunderstood because of ethnic differences. Laura Wexler concludes that Yezierska has a better chance of being understood "in her revival than she was the first time around."

CRITICISM

Susan Andersen

Andersen holds a Ph.D. in English and teaches literature and writing. In this essay, she explains why Yezierska kept writing and rewriting fictionalized versions of her ghetto origins, including Bread Givers.

Anzia Yezierska wrote version after version of the archetype she could not erase from memory. She describes this image in *Red Ribbon on a White Horse*: "I saw myself, a scrawny child of twelve, always hungry, always asking questions." Yezierska had a need to create a myth for herself through writing, a bridge between the Old World and the New. She kept retelling the story of the immigrant waif, because by focusing on the difficulties of assimilation into a new culture, she could be the mouthpiece of the ghetto. She was a skillful storyteller and did not feel compelled to tell her life exactly as it happened. She had two failed marriages, a daughter, and six successful brothers who were left out of her fictional plots because they were not an important part of the story she wished to tell. Mary Dearborn states in *Love in the Promised Land: The Story of Anzia Yezierska and John Dewey* that Yezierska imaginatively "distorted" the facts in her semiautobiographical writings: "Facts simply did not matter to her; what she was after was the emotional truth." This explains why she felt that her mission would be lost in the luxury of California and why she refused to sign a Hollywood contract that would make her rich but take her away from her roots: "Writing is

WHAT DO I READ NEXT?

- *How I Found America: Collected Stories of Anzia Yezierska* (1991) contains all of Yezierska's short fiction, including the stories from the collections *Hungry Hearts* and *Children of Loneliness* as well as her stories about old age. Of note is "The Fat of the Land," which won the author the O. Henry Award for the best short story of 1919.

- Mary Antin's *The Promised Land* (1912) is a landmark work in immigrant writing, an autobiography describing the flight from Russian Poland to Boston, where Antin became educated and happily assimilated as an American. This optimistic account of Americanization contrasts with the ambivalence of Yezierska's experience.

- *The Jewish Woman in America*, by Charlotte Baum, Paula Hyman, and Sonya Michel (1976), gives an in-depth look at the woman's traditional place in Judaism and her historical place in eastern Europe, the American ghetto, and contemporary mainstream America. Showing the heroism and achievement of Jewish women, the book was a response to the critical stereotype of the Jewish mother in Philip Roth's 1969 novel *Portnoy's Complaint*.

- Abraham Cahan's *The Rise of David Levinsky* (1917) has been called the most important early immigrant novel in America, addressing the difficulties of assimilation into another culture. David Levinsky, a self-made millionaire, grows bitter and empty with his financial success, which comes at the cost of his spiritual heritage.

everything I am. . . . It's my search for a meaning" (*Red Ribbon on a White Horse*).

All of Yezierska's writings are heavily autobiographical. Sara Smolinsky's journey in *Bread Givers* (1925) is the earliest and fullest account of her ghetto upbringing. Her later struggles as a

> SHE KEPT RETELLING THE STORY OF THE IMMIGRANT WAIF, BECAUSE BY FOCUSING ON THE DIFFICULTIES OF ASSIMILATION INTO A NEW CULTURE, SHE COULD BE THE MOUTHPIECE OF THE GHETTO."

writer are detailed in the fictionalized autobiography *Red Ribbon on a White Horse* (1950). Sara, like Anzia Yezierska, determines early in her life to avoid the limited and tragic stories of the Jewish women around her and to make her own stories. Sara's goal is to "make [herself] for a person."

Rabbi Reb Smolinsky, Sara's father, is the main antagonist to her desire to live for herself. Reb is the most powerful storyteller of the family, one whose tales Sara must fight with her own. Reb's wife and daughters truly are charmed by his tales from the Torah, by the folktales he tells at supper, and by his chanting of the beautiful and poetic verses in Hebrew that are Sara's earliest lessons in literature. He is further celebrated as "the speaking mouth of the block" when he wins the court case against the landlord. The neighbors are so delighted that they act out his David-versus-Goliath victory on the tenement stoops.

Reb's high-handed way of using his wife and daughters to support him is excused by his belief in his calling: "Am I not their light? The whole world would be in thick darkness if not for men like me who give their lives to spread the light of the Holy Torah." He not only creates his role but also designates the role of his children by naming them Burden Bearer, Empty-head, and Blood-and-iron. He tells them their place: "It says in the Torah, only through a man has a woman an existence. Only through a man can a woman enter Heaven." Sara is at first intimidated by this story, for her father looks "as if he just stepped out of the Bible" in his coat, skullcap, and beard.

Mrs. Smolinsky believes in her husband's religion and holiness; Sara reports, "Mother licked up Father's every little word, like honey."

On the other hand, when he forces Bessie to marry the fish peddler, Mrs. Smolinsky cries out, "Woe to us women who got to live in a Torah-made world that's only for men." The women are inscribed into a story that does not honor them but makes them subservient. In an essay in *Women of the Word: Jewish Women and Jewish Writing*, Judith Dishon gives examples of the kind of stories Reb Smolinsky might have told his household about women in Hebrew proverbs and tales and other medieval texts. In these stories, women are lazy, deceitful, fickle, light-headed, rebellious, and vain, and they take men away from God.

In traditional Rabbinic Judaism only men could study the Torah, and Hebrew, the language of learning, was likewise for men. The women had their own religious books in the vernacular Yiddish that taught them their duties. In fact, Yiddish was considered something of a woman's language, since it was the language spoken in the home for everyday matters. According to Shmuel Niger, in "Yiddish Literature and the Female Reader," much of the literature in Old Yiddish was written by or for women. In the Jewish enlightenment, called Haskalah in the later nineteenth century in eastern Europe, Yiddish rather than Hebrew became the primary language of Jewish secular literature. Sara's father tells the religious Hebrew tales, while her mother tells historical stories of the Old World dances, weddings, and pogroms in Yiddish. These are the inherited stories from mother and father.

Martin Japtok explains in "Justifying Individualism: Anzia Yezierska's *Bread Givers*" how Yezierska's language in the novel illustrates her piecing together of her own story. Ghetto speech is portrayed in the Yiddish idiom, rendered in English, while the narration is in American English. These two languages represent the integration of the ethnic world she comes from and the American world she aspires to. Both English and the Yiddish dialect are secular tongues, however, as opposed to the strict, religious Hebrew world of her father. This attempt at making a hybrid language that can tell her story is analogous to her making a hybrid self.

When Sara leaves home for good she tells her father, "I'm going to make my own life.... I'm American!" Trying to find her own place in America, however, proves more than she imagined. She does not get along with the other working-class girls in the laundry, who scorn her for studying on her breaks. When she finally goes to college, looking for the Americans she thinks will understand her, she finds she has nothing in common with their squeaky-clean lives, their materialism, their lack of sympathy, and their time to play. And yet, the study of psychology opens a door in her, as she learns that her years in the slums were not wasted; they contain "treasure chests of insight," her buried treasure. Just as Yezierska mined her ghetto years as her personal treasure, so Sara finds that her background has made her who she is.

She learns what to do with her treasure when the dean of the college befriends her. He is an older man who influences Sara, the way John Dewey influenced Yezierska. The author puts Dewey's message in the dean's mouth: "Your place is with the pioneers. And you're going to survive." Dewey had written love poems to Yezierska, envisioning her as speaking for generations of mute immigrants. Dewey's confidence in her gave her the push she needed to be a writer. She would make her own story, and it would speak for all the ghetto dwellers that could not tell theirs. Similarly, Sara finds her voice and is able to tell her history to an American audience in the essay contest.

Yezierska won fame and success when Samuel Goldwyn bought the film rights to her first bestseller, *Hungry Hearts*, in 1920. She was brought to Hollywood, was given a huge salary and office, oversaw the making of the film, and was signed on to be a salaried writer. She was promoted as "the Sweatshop Cinderella," a pose that she helped create but that imprisoned her at the same time. As she tells in *Red Ribbon on a White Horse*, "I felt like the beggar who drowned in a barrel of cream." The screenwriters trivialized her work, making it into a stereotype with comic jokes, and she was too numb to write in such an atmosphere. In an amusing scene in *Red Ribbon*, between Yezierska and the ever-cheerful Will Rogers, he tells her to drop the sad Cinderella act and have a good time now that she's rich and famous: "Gal! You're like a punch-drunk prize fighter, striking an opponent no longer there. You've won your fight." Critics said similar things every time Yezierska published another book about the ghetto.

She fled Hollywood and settled in New York, closer to the life that gave her creative material. She lived in poverty and loneliness for much of her life and turned it into fiction. Although she was in touch with other intellectuals, at times she would get a job as a waitress or visit the ghetto. Why did she hold on to this story of deprivation? Blanche Gelfant's essay "The City's 'Hungry' Woman as Heroine" suggests that "the hungry heroine feels passionately alive." Yezierska felt not alive in Hollywood but drowned in a barrel of cream.

In *Bread Givers*, instead of assimilating completely into American culture, Sara Smolinsky returns to the hungry masses of the Lower East Side to teach ghetto children, as Yezierska had. Sara feels guilt when she sees the hungry push-cart sellers. She wants to help raise others. There is another guilt as well. She cannot completely reject her parents' stories and write hers as if there is no relationship: "Can a tree hate the roots from which it sprang?" As Alice Kessler-Harris writes of the author in her foreword to *Bread Givers*, "She never did reconcile the dichotomies in her life," such as trying to be both American and Jewish, both writer and woman, and that is precisely the value of her message. She writes of a life in process. When the author first began to write, as she says in *Red Ribbon*, she saw herself in the ghetto people: "I plucked out of the contradictions of a human being the living seed of a story."

Yezierska may have fudged facts, like her age, or withheld facts, like the existence of her daughter. Why, then, did she not fantasize a resolution to the immigrant's contradictions? The ending of *Bread Givers* does come close to such a resolution. It suggests that Sara and her fiancé, Hugo Seelig, both Americanized Jews who teach in the ghetto they escaped, are trying to work out an equal marriage and to honor both the past and the future. But Sara makes it clear that it will continue to be a juggling act when her father insists on living by the old Jewish law in her house. He symbolizes "the shadow of the burden" she will always carry as a Jew.

Yezierska thus did not consider her struggle or story of ghetto origins to be over once she had won public recognition. Her point was, how does a person create a hybrid identity in a new country? The only way that she could exist as a person was through her writing, and therein she was constantly exploring and creating that delicate bridge between the Old World and the New. She had to stay on that bridge and avoid the temptation of simple closure that Hollywood held out to her: "Nothing would stop me. I'd live my life writing and rewriting my story" (*Red Ribbon*).

Yezierska's quest as a writer is better understood by an audience of the twenty-first century, as many face the problem of creating hybrid identities in an increasingly multicultural world. The idea of ethnic identity as a constant that one must preserve is upheld by Reb Smolinsky, but this notion from the Old World could not help Sara with her challenges in the New, for in America and the modern world, ethnicity is, as Werner Sollors explains in "The Invention of Ethnicity," a constructed or invented reality, ever shifting. Mary Dearborn details in "The Making of an Ethnic American Self" how "Yezierska's life provides a case study of the invention of ethnicity in American culture." Yezierska and her generation of immigrants were indeed pioneers in this effort. As Magdalena Zaborowska, in "Beyond the Happy Endings: Anzia Yezierska Rewrites the New World Woman," concludes, "By persisting in her defiance of the official narrative inscribing her as a woman, a Jew, and a writer, she opened a possibility of happier endings for the women writers to come after her."

Source: Susan Andersen, Critical Essay on *Bread Givers*, in *Novels for Students*, Gale, Cengage Learning, 2009.

Renny Christopher

In the following excerpt, Christopher uses Bread Givers *as a basis for explaining an interpretation of an insatiable appetite for rewards in American culture.*

... Sara Smolinsky, Anzia Yezierska's semi-autobiographical heroine in *Bread Givers*, has, like many of the characters in Yezierska's novels and short stories, an insatiable hunger. Ellen Golub best interrogates Yezierska's use of the

> central metaphor of her generation: hunger. For the promise of America, its language, its natives, and her rapidly Americanizing Lower East Side of New York, she has but one metaphor. For beauty, language, love, achievement — for all the desires she confronts in the immigrants' name, issues of the mouth color and define her prose. (Golub 1983, 51–52)

As Sara says at one point during her struggle for upward mobility, "I hated my stomach. It was like some clawing wild animal in me that I had to stop to feed always."

Golub goes on to describe Yezierska's heroines as speaking,

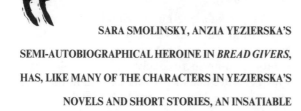

SARA SMOLINSKY, ANZIA YEZIERSKA'S
SEMI-AUTOBIOGRAPHICAL HEROINE IN *BREAD GIVERS*,
HAS, LIKE MANY OF THE CHARACTERS IN YEZIERSKA'S
NOVELS AND SHORT STORIES, AN INSATIABLE
HUNGER."

in a communal voice, of a fire that cannot be quenched in their souls, of a hunger that food cannot sate. Theirs is a permanent sense of alienation and aloneness. And though they insist on breaking down the barriers to their desire, their tragedy remains the paradoxical desire which is fed on hunger...The saddest moment [for these heroines] is when that dream is achieved and yields little more than longing for the old days when the heroine was young and hopeful. (Golub 1983, 53)

The similarity to Martin Eden is clear: his saddest moment is the same as theirs. Further, this insight points out one of the great problems with "the American Dream": it is one built of hope, but it is none too specific about what is to be hoped for. Any definition of a goal is going to be unsatisfactory, since the only attainable goals within American culture are material, and, as Golub points out, Yezierska's heroines, "with their bellies full...hunger even more intensely. Still wailing their desires in the language of the mouth, they betray their longings to be more psychological than physiological" (1983, 54). Each of these heroines,

attempts to attach herself to America by filling her hungry mouth with American culture and language.... Those who hunger for beauty in Yezierska's world are twice as hungry as those who hunger for mere food. Theirs is a spiritual yearning of the heart and soul to possess an American aesthetic, to achieve the clean spareness which they deem patrician. (Golub 1983, 58)

But nothing will ever satisfy these hungers, because the only real rewards in American culture, and the only ones American language is designed to describe, are material, not psychological or spiritual. Further, they are rewards granted only to individuals who, in order to achieve them, must do so alone, leaving behind the people they were once a part of.

The structure of the novel reflects the protagonist's upward mobility: Book I, "Hester Street," consists of chapters that describe the life of the family—the stories of Sara's sisters, into which Sara as a character (rather than as narrator) actually enters very little. This section of the book is situated in the collectivity of working-class life. It is the story not of an individual, but of a family, and that family's struggles with poverty, and the conflict between the old-world father and his new-world daughters. The focus of the narrative turns to Sara herself only in Book II, "Between Two Worlds," which describes her lonely struggle for upward mobility, which is achieved, but not happily, in Book III, "The New World." Thus the narrative goes from the family to the individual, from the working class to the middle class, from community to solitude, following the trajectory of the protagonist's life.

When Reb Smolinsky protests his wife's plan to take in boarders because it means he will have to give up having a room to himself to study in, she replies, "Only millionaires can be alone in America," but it is precisely a desire for aloneness (perhaps first inspired by her father's desire) that impels Sara on her journey. When she tells her father she's leaving, he says, "I didn't send you to work at the age of six like some poor fathers do. You didn't start work until you were over ten. Now, when I begin to have a little use from you, you want to run away and live for yourself?" This is precisely what Sara wants. She answers, "I've got to live my own life." Her core value is possessive individualism: to break away from the collectivity of her working-class family and pursue her own self-determined goals. When she sets out in the city to find work, a room of her own, and schooling, she thinks, "I, alone with myself, was enjoying myself for the first time as with the grandest company." Her quest for a room isn't easy: "For the first time in my life I saw what a luxury it was for a poor girl to want to be alone in a room," but she finally succeeds. "This door was life. It was air. The bottom starting-point of becoming a person. I simply must have this room with the shut door." Once she starts school, she has to close that door and shut her surroundings out of herself; she has trouble concentrating through the noise of the building and the neighborhood, and tells herself she simply must "shut your ears to the noise,"— that is, isolate herself from the community.

This aloneness, a positive value for study, also costs her dearly, because it results in a permanent isolation and sense of outsiderness. Once, when her mother travels all the way in to the city to see her just briefly, she reflects, "How much bigger was Mother's goodness than my burning ambition to rise in the world!", and when she says she can't come visit her mother because she has to study for college, her mother asks, "Is college more important than to see your old mother?" Although Sara doesn't admit it outright, yes, it is more important to her, as she goes on with her solitary struggle and does not visit her mother for six years.

She's tempted when a man sent by her sister courts her; she's overwhelmed by him because, "My one need of needs, stronger than my life, was my love to be loved." Yet clearly Sara's assessment of herself is wrong; she does not give in to that need, but rejects the suitor, because his values are purely materialistic. This disillusions Sara: "The man seemed to turn into a talking roll of dollar bills right there before my eyes." Her father comes to castigate her for refusing her suitor. He says to her, "Why do you hold yourself better than the whole world?", and although Yezierska seems to endorse Sara's answer, "I have to live and die by what's in me," her father's perspective has truth to it. Sara does try to be "better" than the others of her world. When she finally returns to her family after her absence of six years, she wonders, "would they understand that my silent aloofness for so long had been a necessity and not selfish indifference?" Why should they understand any such thing? When she returns to find her mother dying, her sister Fania asks her, "Was that what they taught you in college, to turn your back on your own people?", and indeed, this is what she has been taught in college—to value middle-class mores, materialism, and the habit of abstract thought over the close family ties she cut in order to achieve those things.

Yezierska emphasizes throughout Books II and III Sara's incurable aloneness. The title of chapter 15 is "On and on—alone." That chapter ends with these lines: "Knowledge was what I wanted more than anything else in the world. I had made my choice. And now I had to pay the price. So this is what it cost, daring to follow the urge in me. No father. No lover. No family. No friend. I must go on and on. And I must go on—alone." In the next chapter Sara arrives in college, only, once again, to find out that she does not fit in. The other students are not poor immigrants, and she is always set apart from them. She reflects, "Maybe I'd have to change myself inside and out to be one of them" (50 years later Richard Rodriguez will echo this: "education requires radical self-reformation"). Sara does not succeed in fitting in: "I was nothing and nobody. It was worse than being ignored. Worse than being an outcast. I simply didn't belong. I had no existence in their young eyes.... Even in college I had not escaped from the ghetto."

She does transform herself, however, and learns to devalue the person she was before, in the same way that Martin Eden learned. "I had learned self-control. I was now a person of reason," which means that she's learned to distance herself from herself: "The fight with Father to break away from home, the fight in the cafeteria for a piece of meat—when I went through those experiences I thought them privations and losses, now I saw them as treasure chests of insight." She makes one friend at college, the dean. One day she asks him, "Why is it that when a nobody wants to get to be somebody she's got to make herself terribly hard, when people like you who are born high up can keep all their kind feelings and get along so naturally well with everybody?" This is the closest that Sara comes to a class critique. What she is noting is the effect of privilege and lack of privilege, but she doesn't carry that analysis further than this single comment. The dean answers "All pioneers have to get hard to survive.... And you're going to survive." His answer is misleading—pioneers blaze the way for others to follow; Sara, however, is pursuing individual mobility, blazing a trail for no one. All working-class people who become educated and "successful" do so without leaving a trail behind them for a large segment of the working class to follow, because to do so would be structurally impossible. Capitalism requires a working class and can allow some, but not all, to move out of it. The dean's metaphor smacks of the American myth, and Sara buys into it because, for all her oppositional consciousness, she doesn't really have a political analysis, any more than Martin Eden did.

The dean tells her she will survive. Survive, however, in what sense? She triumphs by finishing college successfully and returning to the city as a teacher, "changed into a person!" That is, a "person" of middle-class manners, means, and education. For all her earlier rejection of materialism, this seems to be the main meaning of her upward mobility: she goes shopping for appropriate clothes for work, and for "the first time in my life I asked for the best, not the cheapest," and when her mother dies, she defies custom by refusing to tear her clothes—the new suit she has bought. When Sara gets the beautiful room of her own she has longed for, it is, significantly, empty, as is the life she's worked so hard to achieve: "nothing but a clean, airy emptiness." Even her attitude toward solitude, which she saw before as a punishment, has changed: "The routine with which I kept clean my precious privacy, my beautiful aloneness, was all sacred to me."

The novel does not have a happy ending. Although Sara has achieved upward mobility, the ending is, as Gay Wilentz calls it, "a Jewish lament rather than . . . a happy-ever-after" (1991, 35). Sara asks herself, "Now I was the teacher. Why didn't I feel as I had supposed this superior creature felt? Why had I not the wings to fly with? Where was the vision lost?" Perhaps because she's discovered that teachers are not "superior creatures" after all—that the very idea of superiority is hollow and false. When she meets a kindred spirit in Hugo Seelig, the school principal, she tells him, "Years ago, I vowed to myself that if I could ever tear myself out of the dirt I'd have only clean emptiness," and although what she's describing is her apartment, she is also describing her life.

Wilentz points out that most critics of the novel, in particular Alice Kessler-Harris and Carol Schoen, have interpreted the ending as representing reconciliation, "with Sara having it both ways." Wilentz reads it not as a "neatly packaged" happy ending, but as one which exposes the "elements of incongruity" in Sara's trajectory. Sara, like Yezierska herself, is uneasy in America, not accepted, as an immigrant Jew, as an equal. "Just as Yezierska herself never resolved the conflict, the novel also does not reconcile difference, although it appears to superficially. The sense of loss and the tone of lament which pervade the novel are not easily mitigated by Sara's triumphs at the end" (Wilentz 1991, 39). Further, he insists that even "mediated cultural assimilation inscribes loss throughout the novel, and dialectically, it is precisely in the apparent resolution of the last chapter that *Bread Givers'* 'fairytale' ending

deconstructs" (39). I would suggest, further, that any reading of the ending of the novel as "happy" is simply a reading which overlays upon the text the fulfillment of the myth we've been so conditioned to expect in American narratives. But to read Yezierska's text in this way is to ignore the details of the text itself in favor of the myth. Wilentz goes on to quote the crucially important passage in which Sara looks at the people she's left behind, those still in the ghetto, still poor, still suffering:

> But as I walked along through Hester Street towards the Third Avenue L, my joy hurt like guilt. Lines upon lines of pushcart peddlers were crouching in the rain. Backs bent, hands in their sleeves, ears under their collars, grimy faces squeezed into frozen masks. They were like animals helpless against the cold, pitiless weather.

In the midst of this reflection, Sara runs into her own father peddling chewing gum, thus emphasizing the fact that Sara's journey has been one of only individual upward mobility. Nothing of the hard world she left has changed. If "joy hurt[s] like guilt" for the narrator, any happiness imputed to this ending must be read into it over the evidence that the narrator presents most forcefully.

Wilentz points out that "Sara's lament for her people is not only for the cruelty of a system that locks people in poverty, but also for what one must leave behind to succeed" (1991, 40). Indeed yes. Thus Sara shares Martin Eden's problem—she was well-fitted for the struggle, but the end of the struggle leaves her unsatisfied with what she has achieved, leaves her lost and as metaphorically at sea as Martin Eden is literally at sea. When Sara goes home to her empty room, there are roses which Hugo has given her. "I didn't want them if they were only for me," she thinks, but of course they are only for her, because she's become an individual, a middle-class model of possessive individualism. And there is no happiness to be found in this state, when the ghetto still exists so nearby.

Thomas J. Ferraro writes that "In narrating Sara's life story, Yezierska seems to be as drawn as her protagonist to a conservative denouement: it is Yezierska, after all, who seems incapable of imagining for her any other solution to the disappointments of teaching" (1990, 579). I see this, however, not as a conservative ending but a radical one—a refusal to capitulate to the

Horatio Alger myth (the novel might have ended with Sara's triumphant graduation, at which she wins a prize and receives the acclaim of her classmates; this is where a true Horatio Alger story would have ended), an exposure of the structural problem of individual upward mobility in a class-based society. A refusal of a resolution for the protagonists of both of these novels constitutes on the part of the writers a refusal of the American myth of happy upward mobility, and makes these novels oppositional texts which call for a different way of reading, and for a discourse which, contrary to the celebratory tone of the dominant American discourse, recognizes loss within "." ...

Source: Renny Christopher, "Rags to Riches to Suicide: Unhappy Narratives of Upward Mobility: Martin Eden, *Bread Givers, Delia's Song*, and *Hunger of Memory*," in *College Literature*, Vol. 29, No. 4, Fall 2002, p. 79.

Gay Wilentz

In the following essay, Wilentz classifies Bread Givers *as Jewish immigrant writing and defines its place and impact on the genre as a whole.*

In "Immigrant Fiction as Cultural Mediation," Jules Chametzky examines the interaction between the Jewish immigrant and American culture through the literature. "Mediation," in this case, reflects the dialectical relationship of Jewish historicity and the demands of a new national identity. While the desire to assimilate was strong—especially for those coming from restricted *shtetls*—the immigrants were aware that attempts to assimilate into the dominant culture often precluded adherence to a centuries-old culture which has existed only because of its adherents. Exposing this clash of cultures, Jewish immigrant fiction functioned "as mediator and creator of culture, a meaningful way of being in the [new] world" (59). Chametzky presents an interpretive model for examining the oppositional nature of much Jewish immigrant writing, particularly that of generational conflict within the Jewish community. Unfortunately, he does not include any Jewish women writers in his study—although he does suggest that someone should examine "fathers and daughters, starting with the intensity of Anzia Yezierska's *Bread Givers*" (67).

Unequivocally, Chametzky reads immigrant discourse as male and, along with other Jewish [male] critics, has set up a male paradigm for immigrant experience: "The gender-specificity of the language of fathers and sons cannot be written

> *BREAD GIVERS—WHICH CHALLENGES NOTIONS OF INDEPENDENCE AND THE RIGHTS OF WOMAN ALONG WITH WHAT IS LOST IN THE JOURNEY TOWARD ASSIMILATION—IS FINALLY NOT A TALE OF RECONCILIATION BUT A NOVEL OF LAMENTATION. AND THIS LAMENT IS BORN OF THE COLLECTIVE MEMORY OF DIASPORA JEWS."*

off merely as linguistic shorthand" (Dearborn 73). Using female-centered discourse to expose Jewish immigrant experience, we can discern how intricately that experience was tied to the immigrant's gender. Exploring the experience of women as well as men enhances our perception both of how male writers mediated between Jewish immigrant and American culture and of how Jewish women attempted—not always successfully—gender as well as cultural mediation in the New World. Appropriating Chametzky's notion of "cultural mediation," I examine how Yezierska illustrates the dilemma of the Jewish immigrant woman whose conflict between living her life as an *Americanerin* and retaining the strength and sustenance she receives as part of the Jewish community is further exacerbated by her desires for independence as a woman. Moreover, I (re)read the novel's contradictory ending in relation to Yezierska's dis-ease with any possibility of mediated existence in the "promised" land.

In "America and I," Yezierska wrote of her conflicting feelings for this supposed paradise for beleaguered Eastern European Jews: "Where is America? Is there an America? What is this wilderness in which I am lost?" (*Open Cage* 25–26). For the Jewish immigrant, the New World promised freedom from the racial/religious oppression of European society. This oppression, which ranged from exclusion to pogrom, remained as bitter memories in the hearts of immigrant Jews who believed in the chance for a better life in spite of ghetto life, abject poverty, and Anglo-American prejudice. But as many Jewish immigrant writers have recorded, the price of Americanization was high—the loss of Jewish traditions and the rich, cultural life of the *shtetl*. For the Jewish woman immigrant, this conflict of culture took on an added dimension: not only was she forced to deal with the prejudices of the dominant culture but also with the patriarchal traditions of the Ashkenazi Jewish community. In *Bread Givers*, Anzia Yezierska transforms her own paradoxical experiences as an immigrant daughter of America to expose us to the double bind of the Jewish woman, whose freedom from the rigid strictures of traditional Jewish culture left her rootless and thrust her into a hard and prejudiced world which kept her always a stranger. It is through the protagonist's stormy relationship with her Old World father that Yezierska presents the dialectics of mediation for the Jewish woman and gives us special insight into these immigrant daughters for whom the quest for identity entails both gender and cultural considerations.

Bread Givers has its place as part of the genre of Jewish immigrant writing; it shares a tradition with such positivist works as Henry Roth's novel, *Call it Sleep*, and Mary Antin's autobiography, *The Promised Land*. All are concerned with the Jewish immigrant's experience in the New World and the possibility of a successful and fulfilling life in this alien culture. The title is a direct translation of the Yiddish term, *broit gibbers* (the women who make both physical and metaphorical "bread" for the home), and much of the dialogue incorporates both Yiddish words and syntax. Sara Smolinsky, Yezierska's persona, is the youngest daughter of a Talmudic scholar who believes that "only through man can a woman enter heaven." In this way, he justifies marrying off his first three daughters to apparently rich men they don't love while stifling any suitors without money. The core of the novel is the cultural/generational conflict between father and this youngest daughter who has inherited his "Blood and Iron" personality. The other women, the mother and other daughters, bow down to his will and support his Hebraic study as they try to rise out of the poverty of the ghetto. Unwilling to succumb to her father's demands, Sara breaks with her father. She leaves behind her suffering mother, and works her way through dirt, despair, sweat shops, and night school to finally gain a college degree. As a *teacherin* she fulfills her ambitions to be part of America, falls in love with an Americanized Jew who feels a desire to retain his Jewish culture, and after the death of her mother, is reconciled to her father. Through familial and cultural mediation, she finds a way to be true both to her culture and the American

ideal of independence, at least on the surface. But it is here that Yezierska breaks with the two works mentioned above. Yezierska's "fairy-tale" text has strong elements of incongruity inscribed in it, and the novel ends as a Jewish lament rather than in a happy-ever-after.

Encoded in the novel are the cultural conflicts at the heart of Jewish immigrant experience. The promised land, as Mary Antin hopefully called it, turned out for many to be a furthering of cultural isolation and poverty. For the men of stature—that is, the scholars of the community—life in America was poverty without the status of community leader and spiritual guide. The dominant capitalist culture hardly prized a learning of Torah or the scholar's position as community exemplar. Nevertheless, Sara's father, Reb Smolinsky—or, revealingly, Yezierska's own father—held on to these values and traditions, and as in the European *shtetls*, the burden of financial responsibility fell on the women and children. In contradistinction to the *shtetl*, however, one (especially a woman) could make even a subsistence living only with great difficulty in America. In the old country the women gained little status for their economic role; in America, where the ability to make money constitutes success, the women still remained subservient—the only difference was that the traditional scholars were also denied an esteemed place in society. Irving Howe comments on how the Jewish woman's role as economic provider questioned the mandate of Anglo-American society that woman be solely wife and mother. Jewish expectations emphasized maternal roles, but "the position of the Jewish woman was rendered anomalous by the fact that Jewish tradition enforced a combination of social inferiority and business activity" (265). Counterpoised in this novel are the duty of the wives and daughters to support the family and their acceptance of the secondary status consigned to them. The duty of the daughters also includes marrying men who have been successful materially or remaining at home to work if no suitor rich enough appears—a distortion of the Jewish tradition of extended family involvement in mate selection. Against this rigid system that insists "God did not listen to [the prayers of] women," Sara revolts.

In *Bread Givers*, Reb Smolinsky represents the rich traditions of Old World Jewry as well as the hypocritical and patronizing airs of Jewish patriarchy in the New World. (Here, the use of the term "patriarchy" is inscribed by its gendered "other," since Judaism is a matrilineal culture).

It is understandable that modern readers (particularly feminist ones) might dismiss Reb Smolinsky as a petty tyrant who sells off his daughters and respects nothing but a distorted love of Torah and a hypocritical desire for material wealth. Even the younger "Americanized" Jews within the context of the novel show little respect for these patriarchs. When a young man, Berel Bernstein, asks to marry Smolinsky's eldest daughter Bessie, they begin to barter about "price"—what Reb will lose if Bessie marries. Bernstein responds angrily: "Aint it enough that your daughter kept you in laziness all these years? You want yet her husband to support you for the rest of your days? In America they got no use for Torah." We might feel sympathy for this older man, so insulted, if he weren't himself so money-grubbing. His attitude is that his children are there to make sure his study is uninterrupted; he appears to care little about their own welfare. Even with his wife he is both condescending and verbally abusive. As they argue, he yells: "Woman! Stay in your place! You're smart enough to bargain with the fish-peddler. But I'm the head of this family."

Although this narrow depiction of Reb Smolinsky is a valid one, it may very well ignore Yezierska's purpose as well as the dialectical structure of the novel. More than a hypocritical petty tyrant, Reb is a portrait of the learned scholar described earlier in this essay—lost in an America that has no respect for Talmudic pedagogues and that sees Jewish culture in general as negative and alien. There is another side of this man that Yezierska takes great pains to show us. He is described by Sara as "a picture out of the bible" and his language is full of the parables that have been passed on for generations. In Yezierska's earlier short story, "Children of Loneliness" (1923), a precursor to Reb Smolinsky is portrayed as a "mystic stranger from some far-off land" with a "thousand years of exile, thousand years of hunger, loneliness and want" sobbing in his voice (*Open Cage* 155). Reb is perceived by his family as a prophet of old; in spite of his treatment of his wife, she reveres him because, in some ways, he encapsulates the Jewish collective spirit which has allowed them to survive generations of persecution. As her father prays, Sara watches her mother: "Mother's face lost all earthly worries. Forgotten were beds, mattresses, boarders, and dowries. Father's holiness filled her eyes with light." He becomes a hero after a fight with the landlady and stories resound about him in the Jewish community. As they elaborate on the reason he hit her, they reveal that in their minds his bravery was an act against the Americanized Jews who have forgotten their people: "She stepped on the Holy Torah." After Sara leaves home and is isolated from her community, her father comes to see her. She characterizes him thus: "He seemed to me like Isaiah, Jeremiah, Solomon, and David, all joined together in one wise old face. And this man with all the ancient prophets shining out of his eyes—my father."

This scene reinforces the dialectical quality of the tensions developed in the novel, for it is at this point—when Sara is finally open to her father—that he once again attempts to force her into marriage and the strictly defined roles for women. He refuses to understand how closely bonded in spirit he and his daughter are. This conflict eerily foreshadows Yezierska's own life when, after the publication of *Bread Givers*, she returned to her father's home only to hear him tell her: "He who separates himself from people buries himself in death. A woman alone, not a wife and not a mother, has no existence" (*Red Ribbon* 217). For the protagonist Sara, this last attack from her father gives her the strength to respond to him in kind. Her eyes have his "stony hardness" and she appears to us as obsessed as he is with her own dreams of independence in a world "where women don't need men to boss them." To some extent, Sara is as fanatical as her father, and her rift with him and her community is tied to this ideal vision of America and American women. She flings her angry farewell at her father: "Thank God, I'm living in America! You made the lives of the other children! I'm going to make my own life!"

In leaving her tyrannical father, however, she must also give up the rest of her family, particularly her mother. When her mother comes to see her, she asks Sara: "Is college more important than to see your old mother?" Sara answers, "I could see you later. But I can't go to college later." Sara's sisters, who beg her unsuccessfully to visit their mother with them, clearly indicate which parent she takes after: "Let's leave her to her mad education. She's worse than Father with his Holy Torah." Within the historicity of the immigrant self-made American compounded by the scholarly traditions of Judaism, Sara runs headlong into her studies, ignoring the other aspects of her life. It is significant to note that both these symbols of fulfillment (even though they represent opposing cultural values) are inscribed as male. As many early feminists, Sara sees her way toward success within a male-structured environment; one might go so far as to say that Americanization, in addition to the denial of Jewish culture, is seen in this work as a denial of a community of women supporters. Kessler-Harris notes: "On the way to successful Americanization lay another kind of anguish. Becoming an American cut women off from their culture and their past. It brought the fearful recognition that they were adrift in the world" (xiv). For Sara, this feeling of being adrift from her community is exacerbated by the attitudes and, at times, overt racism of the Americans. They ridicule her at her ironing job, and the teacher at night school ignores her. Most painfully, the students at the college where she has worked so hard to win acceptance, look right through her as though she doesn't exist: "[I was] like a lost ghost. I was nothing and nobody.... Even in college, I had not escaped from the ghetto." Pertinently, Sara is at a dance when she realizes the extent of her outsider status. Because of her childhood of poverty, her physical presence, and her perceived "Jewish" difference, Sara is isolated from the happy dancers—she is not one of them. Her sexual identity is then marked by her cultural difference.

Much of Jewish fiction worldwide has focused on the outsider status of the Jew; as with other "minority" literatures, Jewish immigrant fiction has also addressed the loss of culture in the attempt to assimilate. Often, the shocking irony is that no matter what one gives up, s/he still remains an outsider to the dominant culture. What adds to the complexity of *Bread Givers* is that Sara's flight towards Americanization is intricately bound to her fight for independence as a woman. And as I noted above, her identity as woman has been developed by her cultural/ethnic background, isolating her even more from the world she hopes to attain. For on the surface of this novel, Sara succeeds in the Anglo-American world she longed to penetrate, but like Yezierska, Sara finds the rewards empty because of the loss of her cultural identity. The subverted vision of Sara's apparently successful integration into American culture and the layers of loss ascribed to it is brought into stark relief by the novel's ending. At the end of the novel, *teacherin* Sara finds happiness with Hugo Seelig, a native-born Jew and the principal at her school; through his love and desire to learn Hebrew from Reb Smolinsky, she is reconciled to her father and

has mediated a place between her own culture and the dominant one. In this way, she gains her rights as an independent woman choosing the man and career that she wants and is still a part of her ancient heritage. As an old man, her father finally begins teaching her "the wisdom of Torah" and glows once more with the possibility of passing on the traditions to her Americanized Jewish lover:

> "I thought that in America we were all lost.... And yet my own daughter who is not a Jewess and not a gentile—brings me ... an American. And for what? To learn Hebrew. From whom? From me. Lord of the universe! You never forsake your faithful ones."

Even in his joy, the father sees his own daughter as a double-self, to paraphrase W.E.B. DuBois, in spite of her and her husband's adherence to Judaic traditions.

The tensions of Jewish immigrant experience, so graphically portrayed, appear to be relieved by the end of the novel. Sara has mediated between cultures as the narrative resolves difference. Most critics of *Bread Givers* agree that the novel ends in reconciliation—with Sara having it both ways. In fact some critics, like Alice Kessler-Harris and Carol Schoen, see the ending as too pat, too happy-ever-after to be believable; they do not see the conflicts in the novel appropriately resolved by the neatly packaged ending. But is the ending so neatly packaged? I pose a (re)reading of this ending by exposing the elements of incongruity in Sara's successful move towards Americanization. As a persona for the author Yezierska, Sara's experience reflects the dis-ease that Yezierska felt in her adopted land. As an immigrant daughter of America, Yezierska did manage for a time to fulfill her goal for success in America, yet as an alien and a Jew, she was never accepted into that world as an equal. Both the biography written by her daughter, Louise Levitas Henriksen, and Yezierska's own autobiography, *Red Ribbon on a White Horse*, attest to the alienation she suffered. Just as Yezierska herself never resolved the conflict, the novel also does not reconcile difference, although it appears to superficially. The sense of loss and the tone of lament which pervade the novel are not easily mitigated by Sara's triumphs at the end. Earlier moments in Sara's linear move towards her goal expose hidden opposition to her progress. One such event is the death of Sara's mother. When Sara finally returns home after college to be with her mother, she finds her dying. Sara's belief that she could regain the lost time away from her family is shattered by her mother's death, and she is further estranged from her community by her refusal to tear a rent in her only suit, as is Jewish burial custom. The loss of her mother is symbolic of the other losses Sara suffers as she makes her uneven journey toward the dominant culture. Living away from her community, she feels disconnected, homeless, apart from life. She thinks back to the kitchen in Hester Street: "Even in our worst poverty we sat around the table, together, like people."

Even mediated cultural assimilation inscribes loss throughout the novel, and dialectically, it is precisely in the apparent resolution of the last chapter that *Bread Givers*'s "fairytale" ending deconstructs. The title of this chapter is "Man Born of Woman," taken from a Torah passage Reb Smolinsky recites: "Man born of woman is of few days and full of trouble." At the opening of this chapter, Sara walks through the ghetto and sees her own happiness as an affront to her people who still suffer the degradations of poverty:

> But as I walked along through Hester Street towards the Third Avenue L, *my joy hurt like guilt*. Lines upon lines of pushcart peddlers were crouching in the rain. Backs bent, hands in their sleeves, ears under their collars, grimy faces squeezed into frozen masks. They were like animals helpless against the cold, pitiless weather. (emphasis added)

Sara's lament for her people is not only for the cruelty of a system that locks people in poverty, but also for what one must leave behind to succeed. The melancholy tone of this chapter is oppressive, hardly the cadences of young love and familial/cultural reconciliation. But it is the last paragraph of the novel which most forcefully undercuts the narrative's conclusion, unraveling the chapter's neatly tied ends and collapsing the ideology of mediated assimilation. We close the book with Hugo and Sara questioning whether her father, unhappy in his surroundings, should come and live with them. She leaves the decision and "the problem of father—still unresolved." But as they walk away, they hear the "sorrowful cadences" of her father's voice, and Sara utters the last line of the novel as she hears the "fading chant": "I felt the shadow still there, over me. It wasn't just my father, but the generations who made my father whose weight was still upon me."

The ending of the novel deconstructs the notion of cultural mediation which, for Sara, is finally untenable. Referring to the character David Levinsky in Abraham Cahan's novel as one who has attempted mediation, Chametzky acknowledges those for whom mediation did not work: "He tried to put together the phenomenon of biculturality; trying to see if the two parts of his life might fit together. Levinsky at the end of his narrative concludes that they do not comport well—and so the feeling of fragmentation and cultural unease we are left with" (63). This "cultural unease" that Chametzky refers to is starkly manifest in Yezierska. For Sara—and for Yezierska—as for many immigrant Jewish women and their descendents, the desire to diassociate oneself from those generations and that historicity is impossible. Sara's recursive memory of the culture that both sustained and restricted her as a woman is posited in contradistinction to a hegemony which has sought to efface her and her community. This dis-ease with which Sara moves into the margins of the dominant culture signifies an (un)mediated difference that resists the external reconciliation of the text.

In her poem, "Yom Kippur 1984," Adrienne Rich poses the question, "What is a Jew in solitude?" (75). Over fifty years earlier, Anzia Yezierska wrestled with the same question, attempting to reconcile the Jewish immigrant woman's desire for assimilation (Americanization) with the rich but constricting life of her community and culture. For Yezierska, and perhaps for her literary daughter Rich, culture (and gender) identity cannot be mediated to erase difference. *Bread Givers*—which challenges notions of independence and the rights of woman along with what is lost in the journey toward assimilation—is finally not a tale of reconciliation but a novel of lamentation. And this lament is born of the collective memory of diaspora Jews. For the author, and for the generations of (women) Jews "in solitude," the conflict is still left unresolved.

Source: Gay Wilentz, "Cultural Mediation and the Immigrant's Daughter: Anzia Yezierska's *Bread Givers*," in *MELUS*, Vol. 17, No. 3, Fall 1991, pp. 33–41.

SOURCES

Chametzky, Jules, et al., eds. *Jewish American Literature: A Norton Anthology*, Norton, 2001, p. 120.

Dearborn, Mary V., *Love in the Promised Land: The Story of Anzia Yezierska and John Dewey*, Free Press, 1988, pp. 86, 87, 144.

————, "Anzia Yezierska and the Making of an Ethnic American Self," in *The Invention of Ethnicity*, edited by Werner Sollors, Oxford University Press, 1989, p. 109.

Dishon, Judith, "Images of Women in Medieval Hebrew Literature," in *Women of the Word: Jewish Women and Jewish Writing*, edited by Judith R. Baskin, Wayne State University Press, 1994, pp. 39–45.

Drucker, Sally Ann, "Yiddish, Yidgin, and Yezierska: Dialect in Jewish-American Writing," in *Yiddish*, Vol. 6, No. 4, 1987, pp. 99, 108.

Gelfant, Blanche H., *Women Writing in America: Voices in Collage*, University Press of New England, 1984, p. 220.

Japtok, Martin, "Justifying Individualism: Anzia Yezierska's *Bread Givers*," in *The Immigrant Experience in North American Literature: Carving Out a Niche*, edited by Katherine B. Payant and Toby Rose, Greenwood Press, 1999, p. 17.

Kessler-Harris, Alice, Foreword and Introduction to *Bread Givers*, by Anzia Yezierska, Persea Books, 2003, pp. vii, xi, xxvii.

Niger, Shmuel, "Yiddish Literature and the Female Reader," in *Women of the Word: Jewish Women and Jewish Writing*, edited by Judith R. Baskin, Wayne State University Press, 1994, p. 71.

Payant, Katherine B., "Introduction: Stories of the Uprooted," in *The Immigrant Experience in North American Literature: Carving Out a Niche*, edited by Katherine B. Payant and Toby Rose, Greenwood Press, 1999, pp. xvii–xviii.

Rischin, Moses, *The Promised City: New York's Jews, 1870–1914*, Harper, 1962, pp. 76–86.

Schoen, Carol B., *Anzia Yezierska*, Twayne Publishers, 1982, pp. 10–13, 61, 68, 74, 75.

Sollers, Werner, "Introduction: The Invention of Ethnicity," in *The Invention of Ethnicity*, edited by Werner Sollors, Oxford University Press, 1989, pp. x, xiii.

Wexler, Laura, "Looking at Yezierska," in *Women of the Word: Jewish Women and Jewish Writing*, edited by Judith R. Baskin, Wayne State University Press, 1994, pp. 157, 178.

Yezierska, Anzia, *Bread Givers*, 3rd ed., Persea Books, 2003.

————, *Red Ribbon on a White Horse*, Scribner, 1950, pp. 38, 41, 68, 78, 87, 118.

Zaborowska, Magdalena, "Beyond the Happy Endings: Anzia Yezierska Rewrites the New World Woman," in *How We Found America: Reading Gender through East European Immigrant Narratives*, University of North Carolina Press, 1995, p. 163.

FURTHER READING

Dearborn, Mary V., *Pocahontas's Daughters: Gender and Ethnicity in American Culture*, Oxford University Press, 1986.

Dearborn considers the possibility of a female ethnic literature as part of mainstream American literature. Dearborn discusses the "Pocahontas marriage" between the exotic ethnic woman and the white American man, a pattern in the fiction of Anzia Yezierska, making her relationship with John Dewey part of a myth of acceptance.

Goldsmith, Meredith, "Dressing, Passing, and Americanizing: Anzia Yezierska's Sartorial Fictions," in *Studies in American Jewish Literature*, Vol. 16, 1997, pp. 34–45.

Goldsmith discusses the symbolism of character dress in Yezierska's fiction as representing the desire of the immigrant to assimilate into the new culture. A large portion of the essay addresses *Bread Givers*.

Handlin, Oscar, *Adventure in Freedom: Three Hundred Years of Jewish Life in America*, Kennikat Press, 1971.

Handlin's influential and award-winning scholarship on immigrants in America is here focused on Jewish immigration and assimilation in the United States. Chapters 5, 6, 7, and 8 deal particularly with Yezierska's generation: why they fled Eastern Europe, the conditions in America, and antisemitism.

Henriksen, Louise Levitas, *Anzia Yezierska: A Writer's Life*, Rutgers University Press, 1988.

This biography by Yezierska's daughter draws on personal and family memories of the author's life and work. Here is detailed what Yezierska left out of her autobiographical fiction: her two husbands, daughter, and other family members. Although it was difficult having a mother like Anzia, Louise recalls their warm and intimate relationship.

A Day No Pigs Would Die

ROBERT NEWTON PECK

1972

A Day No Pigs Would Die is a novel for young adults by the American author Robert Newton Peck. Published in 1972, it was Peck's first novel, and it soon became widely read and admired. It is currently available in a paperback edition published by Laurel Leaf. The story is about a twelve-year-old boy named Robert Peck who is growing up on his father's farm in rural Vermont in the mid-1920s. The family adheres to the principles of the Shakers, a Protestant sect that flourished in the nineteenth century but had almost died out at the time the story is set. The combination of the austere Shaker beliefs and the family's poverty ensures that Rob learns to do without any luxuries in his life. He is thrilled when a neighbor repays him for a good deed by giving him a piglet, which he calls Pinky. In the ten months covered by the story, Rob learns many things about life as he quickly grows into manhood. He must endure heartbreak and loss, and he learns to be self-reliant and aware of his responsibilities toward himself, his family, and his neighbors. *A Day No Pigs Would Die* has endured for thirty years as a much-loved book because of its simple, direct style, its humor, its emotional honesty, and its ability to authentically recapture a certain time and place in American history.

AUTHOR BIOGRAPHY

Robert Newton Peck was born on February 17, 1928, in Vermont, the youngest of seven children born to F. Haven and Lucile Peck. His father was a farmer who made his living slaughtering pigs, and Robert grew up working with his father on the farm. Neither his father nor his mother could read or write, and Robert, though the youngest child, was the first in the family to go to school—a one-room school on a dirt road in rural Vermont.

Peck's high school education was interrupted by World War II, and from 1945 to 1947 he served as a machine gunner with the U.S. Army's 88th Division in Italy, Germany, and France. He was awarded a commendation. On his return to the United States he enrolled in Rollins College, Florida, graduating with an A.B. in 1953. Afterward, he entered Cornell Law School in New York but did not graduate. In 1958, he married Dorothy Ann Houston, a librarian, and they had two children.

Before Peck became a writer, he worked in a variety of occupations. He was a lumberjack and a hog butcher; he worked in a paper mill and also as an advertising executive in New York City. In 1972 he published his first novel for young adults, *A Day No Pigs Would Die*, which won many awards, including a Best Books for Young Adults citation from the American Library Association in 1973 and a Colorado Children's Book Award in 1977.

From the publication of his first book onward, Peck produced a steady stream of books for children and young adults. One of the earliest of these was *Soup* (1974), about a boy named Soup who was based on Peck's best friend during his childhood. Between 1974 and 1995, Peck wrote fourteen novels featuring the adventures of Soup. In 1981, Peck was awarded the Mark Twain Award by the Missouri Association of School Librarians for his novel *Soup for President* (1978). In total, Peck has written over fifty young-adult novels. Many of these are set in Vermont, but after Peck moved to Florida he set some of his work in that state. Some of the novels have historical settings in the colonial and Revolutionary periods.

Peck has also written a novel for adults, *The Happy Sadist* (1962); an autobiography, *Weeds in Bloom* (1995); and two nonfiction books for aspiring writers about how to write fiction. In addition, he has written songs, television commercials, and advertising jingles and has adapted three of his novels for television.

His first marriage having ended, Peck married Sharon Ann Michael in 1995. As of 2008, Peck was living in Longwood, Florida.

PLOT SUMMARY

Chapter 1

A Day No Pigs Would Die begins on an April day in the mid-1920s on the Peck family farm in the town of Learning, Vermont. Twelve-year-old Rob has had an argument with a boy at school and failed to return to class after recess. He sees Apron, a cow belonging to their neighbor, Mr. Tanner, and realizes that she is having great difficulty giving birth to her calf. He runs toward her and, as she runs away, tries to pull the calf from her body, but he loses his grip and falls. He then removes his pants and ties one pant leg to the head of the calf. Apron runs off again, pulling the boy with her. He manages to tie the other pant leg around a tree. This time when Apron moves, the calf comes out. Apron struggles to breathe, and Rob pulls a goiter from her throat. The cow bites him hard in the arm and runs off, dragging him behind her.

Chapter 2

Rob is back at home, and his mother and father are tending his injured arm. His Aunt Carrie is there, also. They lay him on a table, and Mama puts many stitches in his arm. His father, Haven Peck, carries him upstairs to his bedroom. His right hand is numb. Later, his father brings him an apple and some spruce gum, and Rob explains further what happened to him. When Papa pulls the quilt up around his throat, Rob can tell by the smell that his father has slaughtered pigs that day.

Chapter 3

After staying in bed for a week, on a Sunday Rob helps his father mend a fence that separates their property from that of Mr. Tanner. Papa explains the importance of fences for good relations between neighbors. Mr. Tanner arrives carrying two bull calves—Apron's offspring. Mr. Tanner thanks Rob for what he did and gives him a piglet. Rob loves the piglet and calls it Pinky. It is the first thing he has ever owned. Papa tells

MEDIA ADAPTATIONS

- *A Day No Pigs Would Die* was adapted unabridged for audio cassette and released by Recorded Books in 1995.

him that he must make a pen for her, since the piglet must be housed apart from the cow and Solomon, the family ox.

Chapter 4

Pinky follows Rob everywhere, and he enjoys looking after her. His father decides that an old corn cratch close to the barn would make a comfortable home for the pig, except that is it too close to the barn. Haven then explains that with the use of a capstan, Solomon will be able to move the cratch. As Solomon does his work, father and son discuss what they call Shaker Law. The family is steeped in the traditions of the Shakers. Robert says he would like to go to baseball games on Sundays, but Shaker Law forbids it. He says he wants to see the Green Mountain Boys play. He is making a mistake. The Green Mountain Boys was the name given to the Vermont militia around the time of the Revolutionary War, and they were led by a man named Ethan Allen. Rob, however, thinks Allen is a baseball player, although he can find nothing written about him in a baseball book at school. Instead, the book mentions Abner Doubleday as the leading baseball player. Because of this error, Rob has recently incorrectly answered a question on a history test. His father cannot correct him because he is illiterate and knows nothing about baseball or history. Rob tells his father that his schoolteacher, Miss Malcolm, says that as Vermonters they should be proud of their history and also proud of President Calvin Coolidge. (Coolidge was U.S. president from 1923 to 1929.) Haven Peck replies that he is not allowed to vote because he cannot read or write. He says that he and his family are simple folk who live by the Book of Shaker. They work hard and are thankful for what they have. That night Rob sleeps with Pinky in her new crib.

Chapter 5

One Sunday, Rob takes Pinky with him on a walk on a ridge near the edge of their farm. Rob cracks open a butternut for the pig and then builds a flutterwheel in a stream. Pinky finds a frog and chases it, but the frog is devoured by a swooping crow. Rob thinks it will be a good idea to have frogs for supper, so he takes Pinky to the sump to look for some, with no luck. As they walk farther along the ridge, Rob sees the Tanner farm below them, looking prosperous. He also sees the two bull calves, named Bob and Bib. Then he reflects on the origin of his own name, Robert. He was named after a Shaker named Major Robert Rogers, who was famous for his exploits against the Indians. As it is getting late, Rob and Pinky run back home. They find that their barn cat, Miss Sarah, has given birth to three kittens.

Chapter 6

On a hot day in June, Rob comes home from the last day of school with his report card. Pinky, now weighing about as much as Rob, runs after him as he races for the house. At home Rob finds that his Aunt Matty is visiting. She is not really his aunt but a distant cousin. Rob shows his report card to Mama and Aunt Carrie, neither of whom can read well. The card shows an A for all subjects except English, for which he got a D. Aunt Matty, who is a former schoolteacher, is shocked that he would get a D in English and says that what he needs is a tutor. She decides to tutor him herself and gives him a simple grammar lesson on the spot. She provides a sample sentence and then draws a diagram that divides the sentence up into its grammatical components.

Chapter 7

After working all day on the hay wagon, Rob takes a rest as evening approaches. Pinky is with him. Rob watches as a hawk circles the sky and then swoops down on a rabbit, kills it, and flies off with it. This gets Rob thinking about food, and he comments about how well he feeds Pinky. The pig is very well cared for. Rob is expecting that Pinky will be bred with Mr. Tanner's boar and produce many litters.

Chapter 8

One night Rob awakens during a thunderstorm late at night. He hears voices downstairs and recognizes them as Mama, Aunt Carrie, and a neighbor, Mrs. Hillman. Mrs. Hillman says that her husband has gone off to the graveyard, but she does not explain fully what she means. Papa summons Rob, and Rob gets Solomon, the ox, hitched up to the wagon. They go out in the rain to the church graveyard in Learning, where they find Sebring Hillman digging up a grave. It transpires that Letty Phelps, a relative of Haven Peck, was once employed as a maid by the Hillmans. Mr. Hillman fathered her baby, who died in infancy. Sebring now wants to claim the child as his own and bury her remains on his own property. Haven agrees to allow him to do this, as long as Letty's coffin remains in the church graveyard. Rob, Papa, and Mr. Hillman then return to the Peck home. It is dawn, and they have breakfast together.

Chapter 9

Aunt Carrie and Mama argue in the kitchen. Aunt Carrie is shocked because she thinks that Widow Bascom, who lives nearly a mile down the road, is living with the man she hired as a worker. Mama disagrees with her, saying that it is none of their business. As Rob listens to them talk, he remembers his own encounters with Widow Bascom. He once ran through her backyard and her strawberry patch, and she beat him with a broom. The second encounter was only a couple of days ago, when at her request he helped her move some heavy flowerpots. She gave him buttermilk and gingersnaps, and he met Ira Long, the hired hand. Rob mentioned that he would love to take Pinky to the upcoming Rutland Fair, but the family does not have a horse. Back in the present, it transpires that Widow Bascom told Mrs. Tanner about Rob's desire to go to the fair, as Papa tells Rob that Mr. Tanner has offered to take him there. Mr. Tanner needs Rob to work the two young oxen in the ring, and he says Rob can take Pinky, too. Rob hopes Pinky will win a blue ribbon.

Chapter 10

Rob goes with Mr. and Mrs. Tanner in a horse-drawn wagon to Rutland. At the fair, Rob is in awe of the crowds and all the unfamiliar sights. He takes the two young oxen around the ring three times as the crowd applauds. Rob is excited and proud. Then it is time to show Pinky. Rob is appalled to see that the pig has been rolling in some dirt, and he has to buy some soap to get the pig clean. He takes Pinky around the circle but then catches a whiff of pig manure that makes him feel ill. Just as the judge pins a blue ribbon on Pinky, Rob vomits. Mr. and Mrs. Tanner take him back to Pinky's pen and clean him up. Then they point to Pinky, and Rob sees that on the blue ribbon it says, "FIRST PRIZE FOR BEST-BEHAVED PIG."

Chapter 11

Rob returns home and excitedly tells his parents about all the events at the fair. In the morning, as he starts on his chores, Papa brings a dead hen from the coop. A weasel killed it, and Papa captured the weasel, which is in a sack in the tack room. He has yet to decide what to do with it. Rob says that Ira Long has a terrier, so Rob goes to fetch him. The terrier is to be trained to hate weasels and so protect the hen house. Papa puts the dog into an empty apple barrel. Then he throws in the weasel and puts the top on the barrel. The dog kills the weasel, but is so badly injured in the fight that he has to be put down. Papa swears he will never weasel a dog again.

Chapter 12

Papa examines Pinky and thinks she may be barren. Rob is upset at this news, since he wanted Pinky to have many litters. Mama sends him out to shoot a squirrel, and when he returns Papa tells him that the apple yield this year is not good. It transpires that Rob made a mistake in the procedure he followed for killing the spanner worms that attacked the buds. Papa is kind to him, saying that he will get it right next spring. After supper, Papa confides in Rob that he is dying, and that Rob must learn how to manage the farm. There is nobody else to do it.

Chapter 13

In November, Mr. Tanner brings over his boar named Samson to mate with Pinky to see if she is barren or not. Mr. Tanner inquires about the health of Rob's father, but Rob just says he is fine. Mr. Tanner, who suspects Haven may be ill, says that he should ease up a bit, but Rob says his father is always working. Mr. Tanner asks how Rob is doing in school, and then he talks about how Pinky will produce twenty pigs a year, and that will bring in a lot of money with which they can pay off the mortgage on the farm.

Rob wonders whether he should want much money, since as a Shaker his family lives simply. Mr. Tanner lets on that he and his wife are not Shakers but Baptists.

Chapter 14

In the winter, Rob's father's health deteriorates. His lungs are bad and he coughs a lot. Pinky fails to produce a litter; she is barren. Since they cannot afford to keep Pinky as a pet, she has to be slaughtered, which Rob's father does one day in December, with Rob's assistance. Rob knows this has to be done and accepts it, but he cries nonetheless.

Chapter 15

Papa dies in his sleep early next May. Rob, now thirteen, finds him lying on his straw bed in the barn. Rob does his chores and then informs his mother and Aunt Carrie of the death. Rob takes charge of the situation. He takes Solomon into town and informs Mr. Wilcox, the undertaker and county coroner, of his father's death. He then informs some other people and returns home, to find Mr. Wilcox already there with a coffin. Rob digs a grave in the family plot, and at noon the mourners arrive. Rob says a few words about his father, and then the coffin is lowered into the ground. After the mourners leave, Rob does some chores and then has supper with his mother and Aunt Carrie. After supper he walks to his father's grave and says, "Goodnight, Papa."

CHARACTERS

Iris Bascom

Iris Bascom, known as Widow Bascom, is a widow who lives nearly a mile down the road from the Peck farm. Her husband died several years ago, and some people in the community gossip disapprovingly about her because she appears to be living with a man she hired as a worker, Ira Long. Eventually, Iris and Ira marry. Iris can be fierce—she beat Rob with a broom when he trespassed on her backyard—but she can also be kind, as when she offers him buttermilk and gingersnaps after he helps her with some heavy flowerpots. Iris likes Rob and makes sure that Bess Tanner learns about his desire to attend the Rutland Fair.

Bib and Bob

Bib and Bob are the two young oxen owned by Ben Tanner. Bob, whom Rob Peck pulled from the body of his mother, Apron, is named after Rob, who is often called Bob. Rob gets to show Bib and Bob in the ring at the Rutland Fair.

Aunt Carrie

Aunt Carrie is Rob Peck's aunt, the oldest sister of his mother. Nearly seventy years old, she lives with Rob and the family. Like the Pecks, she is unable to read or write.

Jacob Henry

Jacob Henry is Rob's close friend at school. Jacob makes only one direct appearance in the novel, when he attends the funeral of Rob's father. He seems to come from a family that is better off than Rob's, since he owns a cornet, which he plays in the school band, as well as a store-purchased overcoat.

May Hillman

May Hillman is the wife of Sebring Hillman. They are neighbors of the Pecks. May comes to the Peck farm one stormy night, distressed because she thinks that her husband has gone to the graveyard to dig up the graves of Letty Phelps, their former maid, and the baby he fathered out of wedlock. It appears that May knew of her husband's infidelity and the trouble it caused, but she decided to stay with him.

Sebring Hillman

Sebring Hillman is May's husband. It appears that he is deeply troubled by the affair he had with Letty Phelps, the maid. One night he goes to the graveyard determined to dig up the casket that holds the remains of the baby he had with Letty. He wants to rebury it on his own land and give it the Hillman name, a belated admission that the baby was indeed his.

Ira Long

Ira Long is the man Iris Bascom originally hires as a worker, but they are soon living together, and they eventually marry. Ira is a big man, and when Rob meets him at Iris's house, Ira is friendly toward him. Ira meets Haven Peck when he brings his terrier named Hussy to the Peck farm so that the dog can learn how to kill a weasel.

Aunt Matty

Aunt Matty is a distant cousin of Rob's. Her full name is Martha Plover. Aunt Matty lives in Learning and visits the Pecks about once a month. Aunt Matty is an educated woman, a former English teacher, and she is shocked when she learns that Rob has received a D for English. She resolves to become his tutor and gives him a grammar lesson on the spot. Unlike the Pecks, Aunt Matty is a Baptist. Her policy as a teacher is to never get angry.

Haven Peck

Haven Peck is Rob Peck's father. Nearly sixty years old, he is a serious, hardworking, unsentimental man, a responsible husband and father who makes his living by slaughtering pigs. He believes in strict discipline but he is also a kind, loving father to his son, although he does not show Rob any physical affection. Living according to the simple, no-frills ways of the Shakers, Peck is a good neighbor to Ben Tanner, and he instills in Rob the need for good manners, honesty, and politeness. Peck cannot read or write, and his family is poor, but he is a proud man who does not envy others their riches. He is grateful for the things that he and his family do have. By some measures he is an ignorant man, since he knows nothing of history, and because he is illiterate he is not allowed to vote. He claims that he does not resent this discrimination, but he does tell Rob that he thinks a man should be valued for his practical skills in life, not based on whether he can sign his name or not. By those standards, Haven is an accomplished man, and he also possesses an abundance of common sense and wisdom. When the time comes to slaughter Pinky, Haven, as with all things, gets the job done efficiently and without fuss, taking no pleasure in doing so. Haven has foreknowledge of his own death, and he instructs Rob to take over the management of the farm. The fact that so many people from the town attend his funeral shows the respect held for him among the people of Learning.

Lucy Peck

Lucy Peck is Rob's mother. She loves and is dedicated to her husband and son, and she does everything she can to support them. Rob says that her voice is "soft and sweet like music." Like her husband, she cannot read or write, but she is a very capable woman who makes all her son's clothes, and she puts stitches in his arm after he is injured by the cow. Lucy is a compassionate woman who is also tolerant; she is not interested in hearing gossip from her sister, Aunt Carrie, about Iris Bascom. She is devastated by her husband's death but carries herself with dignity at the funeral.

Robert Peck

Robert Peck, Haven Peck's son, is twelve years old when the novel begins. He is an intelligent, capable, respectful boy who not only learns how to do a variety of tasks on the farm but also does well in school, getting A's in every subject except English, in which he receives a D. Rob has a strong sense of duty, which has been instilled in him by his father. He knows, for example, that it is his duty to help his neighbor's stricken cow, even though he gets badly injured in the process. He respects his parents and his elders, and adults in turn approve of him. He is clearly going to develop into a man of high principles, like his father. When Ben Tanner gives Rob a piglet, he lavishes care and affection on it. It is the first thing he has ever owned. As he approaches his thirteenth birthday, Rob goes through his most testing experiences. First he must accept that he is going to lose his beloved pet pig and must also assist his father in slaughtering it. Then he has to assume the role of head of the family in the wake of his father's death, even though he is only thirteen years old. He passes each test with flying colors.

Pinky

Pinky is the pig that is given to Rob by Ben Tanner. Rob thinks she is prettier than any other animal he knows: "She was clean white all over, with just enough pink to be sweet as candy." Rob gets very attached to Pinky, feeding her carefully and getting to know all her habits. She is affectionate and playful. Rob expects Pinky to be a brood sow and produce hundreds of pigs and enjoy a long life. When Pinky turns out to be barren, the Pecks reluctantly slaughter her, since they cannot afford to keep her as a pet.

Clay Sander

Clay Sander employs Haven Peck to slaughter pigs. He appears only once in the novel, when he attends Haven Peck's funeral.

Benjamin Tanner

Benjamin Tanner is a neighbor of the Pecks. He is a decent man and a good neighbor. He is also an excellent farmer; Haven Peck holds him in high regard, believing that Ben is the better farmer of the two. Haven praises Ben to his son, saying, "His fence is straight and white as virtue. All the critters are clean. Mark how he cuts his hay." Ben rewards Rob with the gift of a piglet after Rob helps his cow, Apron, deliver her calf. He also allows Rob to accompany him and his wife to the Rutland Fair. Unlike the Pecks, Ben Tanner is a Baptist.

Bess Tanner

Bess Tanner is Benjamin Tanner's wife. She is a large, friendly woman who takes a liking to Rob and ensures that he is able to go to the Rutland Fair.

Mr. Wilcox

Mr. Wilcox is the undertaker and county coroner in Learning. Like the Peck family, he is a Shaker, and he makes the arrangements for the funeral of Haven Peck.

THEMES

Death and the Transition into Manhood

When the novel begins in April, Rob Peck is a twelve-year-old boy who is completely dependent on the love and care of his parents. When he is out in the fields helping his father mend a fence, he learns much from the instructions of his father, who teaches him practical skills as well as moral values. Rob is in all respects just a boy, still learning about the world around him; he asks his father questions and his father answers them. His pleasure in acquiring a pet pig is another indication of his young age, as is the thrill he gets from attending the Rutland Fair for the first time.

Nevertheless, during the course of the ten months over which the story takes place, Rob is forced into a rapid maturation. This occurs mostly through his two encounters with death. When the time comes to slaughter Pinky, he learns that sometimes he must sacrifice the thing he loves. He has learned from his father that "you got to face what is." Haven Peck sees Rob's acceptance of the necessity of slaughtering Pinky as a test of his attaining manhood: "You got to face up to it. You can't be a boy about it." Although he is heartbroken by the loss of his pet, Rob accepts what his father says, and in doing so

he makes a big leap from child to man. Then, when his father dies, Rob is ready to assume the responsibility of becoming the head of the household. He does not react emotionally or expect to be comforted by his mother or Aunt Carrie. He takes it upon himself to go into town to inform Aunt Matty and Mr. Wilcox, the county coroner, about the death, as well as to write to tell his married sisters about it. He even digs his father's grave.

Two other moments on the day of the funeral show Rob's transition to manhood. The first occurs when Ben Tanner, his neighbor, whom Rob has up to then called Mr. Tanner, tells Rob that from now on he should call him by his first name: "I think two men who are good friends ought to front name one another." The second moment comes after supper, when Rob notices how tired his mother and Aunt Carrie look. He takes it upon himself to send them upstairs to bed. Early in the novel, the same exchange occurs the other way around, but now Rob has matured to the point where he can take charge and look out for the welfare of others.

Being an Outsider

As simple, poor folk who live by the old Shaker ways, the Pecks are in some respects outsiders in the wider community. This is made clear in the very first paragraph in the novel, in which Rob reveals how upset he is by the persistent taunting he receives from Edward Thatcher, another boy at school. Edward mocks Rob because of his old, homemade clothes and makes fun of the "Shaker ways." Although Rob does have a friend at school, Jacob Henry, he is clearly lonely, since he adopts Pinky as his best friend, spends as much time with her as he can, and talks to the pig as if it is almost human. Although his father tells him that they, being Shakers, are not worldly people and are content with the necessities of life, Rob still longs to be more like the other boys he knows. He learns to suppress his desire for a bicycle, but he cannot resist telling his father that he would love to own a store-bought coat, just as Jacob Henry does.

Although Rob's father is on good terms with his neighbors, being poor and illiterate makes him something of an outsider, too. He is unable to fully participate in society, not being allowed to vote, for example, because he cannot read or write. He complains, "When a man

TOPICS FOR FURTHER STUDY

- There were a number of utopian-minded communities in the United States in the nineteenth century, including the Shakers. Prepare a presentation for the class that describes the characteristics of a utopian community. Compare the Shakers to other such communities of the period, including the Church of Jesus Christ of Latter-Day Saints at Nauvoo, Illinois; the Oneida Community, in New York; the Amana Colonies, in Iowa; and others you may read about in your research.

- Find out as much as you can about raising pigs, showing them, and auctioning them. How do you evaluate the healthiness of a pig? What do pigs eat? What is their proper weight? How do you groom a pig? How much does it cost to raise a pig? If possible, interview a farmer to answer these questions and learn about other aspects of raising pigs. Give a class presentation in which you share your findings.

- Write a short memoir about losing a beloved pet. Describe the circumstances of your pet's death, what the pet meant to you, what you felt at the time of the loss, and how you dealt with it.

- Reread the first few pages of the third chapter in *A Day No Pigs Would Die*, in which Rob helps his father repair a fence. Then read Robert Frost's poem "Mending Wall." Compare what Haven Peck says, that "A fence sets men together, not apart," with the theme of Frost's poem. Why does Rob think that keeping up a fence is like a war? Does the speaker in "Mending Wall" have a similar opinion? What does the speaker's neighbor say? Write an essay in which you discuss your comparison of these two works.

cannot do those things, people think his head is weak." He counters this sense of being misunderstood and excluded by developing strong beliefs in the virtues of hard work and competence in practical matters. He convinces himself that on his own terms he is better off than those who have more material possessions: "I am rich and they are poor," he tells Rob. He passes these values on to his son, but even at the end of the novel, Rob, realizing that he has no decent clothes to wear for his father's funeral, reflects that "it's hell to be poor."

STYLE

Symbolism for the Value of Work

Haven Peck struggles to live his life in the best way he knows. His is a life of simplicity and hard work, dedicated to upholding the core values he has inherited from the Shaker tradition. In this sense he lives a rich life, though outwardly he is poor. After Haven Peck dies, Rob notices something in the tackroom that he has never observed before. As he looks at his father's tools, which are all dark with brown handles, he notices the places where his father's hands had touched the tools: "They were lighter in color. Almost a gold. The wear of his labor had made them smooth and shiny, where his fingers had held each one. . . . It was real beautiful the way they was gilded by work." The tools therefore become a symbol of the value and dignity of Haven Peck's life. He may not have earned much money in his life, but his tools were nonetheless like gold. He used them honestly and well, and they repaid him handsomely.

Nonstandard Grammar and Regional Dialect

The sometimes ungrammatical language in which Rob tells his tale is often appropriate, given the fact that his parents are illiterate and he is getting a D in English at school. For example, in the first sentence, he says, "I should of been in school that April day." He is confusing the similarity of sound between the abbreviated form of "should have" ("should've") and the preposition "of," such that he incorrectly uses the preposition instead of the verb "have." He repeats this several times, notably in the triple-negative statement "There couldn't of been nobody in Vermont who weren't there." Expressions used by other characters capture what appears to be a rural dialect in Vermont at the time. For example, Mr. Tanner says, about Rob's injured arm, "It got tore up worse than proper. May be broke," while Mama later says, "I'm preferenced to mend busted pants than a busted

Pig *(Jana Leon | Stone | Getty Images)*

boy." Expressions such as these, along with similes that perhaps were well-known at the time ("clean as clergy," "true as a taproot") effectively convey the rural and regional flavor of the story.

Bildungsroman

A bildungsroman is a novel that traces the moral, intellectual, and emotional development of the protagonist from childhood to maturity. This growth usually involves some crisis that is decisive in shaping the protagonist's sense of identity and determining the path he or she is to take in life. Such novels are also known as coming-of-age novels. *A Day No Pigs Would Die* covers only a short period in the life of the protagonist, young Robert Peck, but in that time he goes through several experiences that lead him to make a leap from childhood to a more adult sensibility and role in the world.

HISTORICAL CONTEXT

The Shakers

The Shakers were a Protestant sect that originated in Manchester, England, as an offshoot of the Quakers. They were called Shakers because

of their habit of shaking, trembling, dancing, and shouting during their religious services. One of their early leaders was Ann Lee. Born in 1736, Lee was given to having religious visions, and in 1772 she declared that she was the embodiment of the female aspect of Christ. In another vision she was told to go to America and establish a church there. She and eight other believers arrived in New York City in 1774, just before the outbreak of the Revolutionary War. They soon began to attract followers. Mother Ann, as she had become known, died in 1784, but the small sect flourished in spite of the death of its leader. Eleven Shaker communities were set up in New York, Massachusetts, New Hampshire, Connecticut, and Maine. Interestingly, although *A Day No Pigs Would Die* is set in Vermont and contains characters who identify themselves as Shakers, there were in fact never any Shaker communities in that state.

In Shaker communities, all property was held in common, and men and women lived separately, in buildings that could house up to a hundred people. Celibacy was the rule. By the early nineteenth century, Shaker communities were also found in Ohio and Kentucky, and by the middle of the century, just before the Civil War, there were an estimated six thousand Shakers living in organized societies. The Shaker communities were run in an orderly and efficient way, and they soon prospered. The Shakers had a strong work ethic. As L. Edward Purcell writes in his book *The Shakers*, "Work was sacred—and not just any work, but work done to the utmost skill and energy of the worker. Perfection in work reflected a perfection of spirit." (This view accounts for the reverence with which Haven Peck regards work in *A Day No Pigs Would Die*.) The Shakers' dedication to work was the reason they excelled at whatever they did, whether it was agriculture or making furniture or other household goods. They also developed great knowledge of herbs and herbal medicine, which explains Rob's remark in the novel that his mother had all kinds of remedies for whatever ailed a person: "Mama had give me a spoonful of remedy for one thing or another almost every winter and spring."

After the Civil War, as the nation became more urbanized, the agrarian life of the Shakers became harder to maintain, and it became more difficult for them to attract new converts. Because they practiced celibacy there were no

COMPARE
&
CONTRAST

- **1920s:** According to the U.S. Census Bureau, in 1920, 6 percent of the U.S. population over fourteen years old is illiterate.

  1970s: According to the National Assessment of Adult Literacy (NAAL), less than 1 percent of the U.S. population over fourteen years old is illiterate. However, there is a new emphasis on functional literacy, defined as how well a person is able to function in society. Using that measure, there is widespread concern over falling educational standards and growing functional illiteracy.

  Today: According to the National Assessment of Educational Progress (NAEP), among seventeen-year-olds, only one-half of Caucasians, one-quarter of Latinos, and under one-fifth of African Americans are able to read and understand at a level high enough for them to function successfully in college and in the workplace.

- **1920s:** Although the U.S. economy prospers for most of the 1920s, many people, especially in rural areas, cannot afford the new consumer items.

  1970s: As a result of the "War on Poverty" begun by the administration of President Lyndon B. Johnson in 1964, poverty falls to a record low level of 11.1 percent in 1973.

  Today: According to the 2008 Statistical Abstract produced by the U.S. Census Bureau, in 2005 there are 36,950,000 people living below the official poverty line. This represents 12.6 percent of the population. This figure includes over twelve million children.

- **1920s:** Shaker communities still exist in very small numbers in Mt. Lebanon, New York, and in Connecticut and New Hampshire.

  1970s: Only about a dozen Shakers remain, living in two villages that go back two hundred years. However, there is a strong interest in the Shakers, and eight original Shaker villages attract thousands of visitors who want to learn about the Shaker past.

  Today: As of 2006, there are four Shakers left in the world, two men and two women who live in Sabbathday Lake Shaker Village in southern Maine. Interest in Shaker craftsmanship remains high, and Shaker furniture items are considered valuable American antiques.

---

children to whom they could pass on their traditions, so it was always necessary to draw new people into the sect. But as the nineteenth century wore on, it became clear that this was not happening in sufficient numbers for the Shakers to survive for long. By the early twentieth century, Shaker communities began to close, and by the 1920s, there were few remaining Shakers.

CRITICAL OVERVIEW

Reviews of *A Day No Pigs Would Die* were generally positive. For Arthur Cooper, in *Newsweek*, Peck's narrative is "suffused with wit" and "glowing with warmth." Cooper expresses admiration for the way in which Peck manages to evoke "a sense of a vanished America," and he holds that the author effectively portrays the transition from childhood to manhood in the narrator. Cooper warmly identifies the novel as a "love letter to a father long dead but never missing." In the *New York Times Book Review*, Jonathan Yardley calls the novel a "modest and affecting little book," praising it as "sentiment without sentimentality" and suggesting that it might appeal to adults as well as older children. However, Richard Todd, in the *Atlantic Monthly*, disagrees with this verdict, commenting that the novel is "ruinously sentimental." In his opinion, there is a discrepancy between the youthfulness of the narrator and the sophistication of some of his observations: "The book . . . is full of dialogue and images that are too clever by half, that let the author's self-approval show through." This opinion is echoed by a reviewer for the *Times Literary Supplement*, who suggests that the story might be regarded as "treacly." The reviewer feels that the more poetic passages about nature seem to come from a voice other than that of the "first-person vernacular which . . . saltily conveys Shaker turns of speech."

CRITICISM

Bryan Aubrey

Aubrey holds a Ph.D. in English. In this essay on A Day No Pigs Would Die, *he discusses the many ways in which Rob Peck grows from boy to man during the course of the story.*

A Day No Pigs Would Die is a novel about the growth to maturity and wisdom of a young boy, set against a background of nature's eternal cycle of life and death. On the Peck family farm in Vermont in the 1920s, young Rob learns early about the mysteries of being born and of dying. The very first scene in the novel is about the painful and difficult birth, assisted by Rob at great cost to himself, of a calf. During the course of the story, as the cycle goes on, Rob learns of the cruelties of nature as well as its beauties. He observes with pleasure that the barn cat, Sarah, has given birth to three kittens, which, as Mama puts it, is "always a wondrous thing to see." He witnesses the painful death of a rabbit, caught in the talons of a swooping hawk, as well as a crow making short work of killing and eating a frog. Moreover, he learns about the necessary cruelties of the interactions between humans and animals on a farm—through the smell of the butchered hogs on the clothes and skin of his father, which never seems to go away; through the ferocious fight between the weasel and the dog (deliberately initiated by Haven Peck and Ira Long), which results in the death of both animals; and of course through the slaughter of his own pet pig, Pinky, whom the family cannot afford to keep.

Shortly after enduring the sorrow that accompanied the painful death of his pig, Rob must learn how to deal with an even greater blow, the death of his father. He is forced to grow up very quickly, and the reader may feel

WHAT DO I READ NEXT?

- Peck's novel *A Part of the Sky* (1994) is a sequel to *A Day No Pigs Would Die*. Following his father's death, Rob has to work in a store to pay for the upkeep of the family farm. But times are hard, and he has to contemplate selling the farm.

- *The Shaker Experience in America: A History of the United Society of Believers* (1992), by Stephen J. Stein, is a comprehensive history of the rise and decline of the Shakers. Stein discusses issues such as schisms and doctrinal disputes within the Shaker communities and profiles their charismatic leaders. He takes a revisionist view that questions how successful Shakerism was in living up to its ideals. He takes the story up to the 1980s, describing the Shaker community at Sabbathday Lake, Maine.

- *The Giver* (1994), by Lois Lowry, won the Newbery Medal in 1994. It is set in a seemingly utopian society in the future, but twelve-year-old Jonas gradually discovers that it is not as utopian as it claims to be. Facing disillusionment, he is forced to examine his own beliefs and make a momentous decision.

- *Hatchet* (1987), by Gary Paulsen, is the story of a thirteen-year-old boy who survives when the small plane in which he is flying crashes in the Canadian wilderness. All he has with him is a hatchet, and he must somehow summon all the inner and outer resources he needs in order to survive fifty-four days in the wilderness. Like Robert in *A Day No Pigs Would Die*, he is obliged to undergo a rapid process of maturation.

that this is a boy who never really had a childhood. Part of this is due to the poverty of the family, which imposes severe restrictions on the extent to which they can participate in the pleasures that money can buy. Rob never even asks his parents for a bicycle, for example, and the

> " HE REALIZES THAT NOT EVERYTHING HE HAS
> BEEN TOLD IS TRUE, THAT HE CAN MAKE JUDGMENTS
> FOR HIMSELF, AND THAT WHAT MATTERS IS NOT THE
> RELIGIOUS DENOMINATION TO WHICH PEOPLE MIGHT
> BELONG BUT WHAT IS IN THEIR HEARTS AND HOW
> THEY BEHAVE TOWARD OTHERS."

family is unable to attend the Rutland Fair because they do not own a horse. But Rob's restricted childhood is also due to the strict upbringing that Haven Peck gives his son because of his adherence to what he calls "Shaker Law." Although the Shakers had virtually died out by the 1920s, when the novel is set, Haven Peck remains true to many of their precepts, which he believes in with a passion. The Shaker creed is a somewhat austere one. According to Haven, Shakers do not believe in what he calls "frills," and he is even reluctant to allow Rob to accept Ben Tanner's gift of the piglet. Rob has learned early that "in a Shaker household, there wasn't anything as evil as a frill." The Shakers also frown on baseball being played on Sunday, which is why Rob is not able to attend the games he would love to watch, as his friend Jacob Henry does.

There may be much that Rob gains from this strict Shaker upbringing, but he seems to miss out on a lot as well. This is why his trip to the Rutland Fair is an important milestone for him. Up to this point, his life has been very isolated, but he has learned to make the best of it. Before he realizes that he has a chance to actually go to the fair, he is content to put a ribbon around Pinky's neck and pretend that he is taking her. Where his physical horizons are limited, he tries to make up for the lack by using his imagination. But Jacob Henry has told him that the Rutland Fair is a sight to behold, and Rob is thrilled when the Tanners ask him to go with them. Even his father has never been to the Rutland Fair. So in a sense, Rob, at the age of twelve, is already expanding his horizons further than Haven Peck has ever been able to.

Rutland, in fact a smallish town, seems to Rob as if it is almost as big as London, which he has been told at school is the biggest city in the world. He is so excited by all the bustle of the fair that he fears that if he so much as blinks he will miss some of it. One of the moments he will treasure most comes when he enters the show ring with Bib and Bob, the two young oxen belonging to Mr. Tanner. He hears his name announced over a loudspeaker as "Mr. Robert Peck," and he hears the applause of the crowd. In the show ring he is in the limelight for the first time in his life, and it is a moment of triumph for him: "It was sinful, but I wanted the whole town of Learning to see me just this once." This event provides a huge boost to Rob's self-esteem; "It was just like I was somebody," he says. He wants not only his family and his friend Jacob Henry to see him but also Edward Thatcher, the boy who taunts him at school about his poverty and his Shaker ways. Rob's remarks are very revealing. They show how he must have felt up to this point in his life: that because of his humble circumstances he did not really amount to much. It is interesting also that he feels that his thoughts on this occasion might be considered sinful. Perhaps he has learned from his religious upbringing that it is not a good thing to seek or take pleasure in the attention of others; perhaps he thinks this might be considered a sin of pride, of putting oneself above others. But that is not what Rob is doing. He is merely finding for the first time some affirmation of the value of his own life, and he wants others to see it, too. Another interesting point is that he appears not to care that some might regard his desire to be seen in a moment of triumph as sinful; he is quietly ready to reject what he has been told in favor of what he instinctively feels is a good thing for him. This is evidence of the maturing process that his mind is undergoing.

Another lesson that Rob learns during the course of the novel is also connected with religion. He learns the virtue of religious tolerance in a small community in which, it would appear, there is a fair amount of intolerance. He has heard, for example, Jacob Henry's mother talking about the Baptists:

> According to her, Baptists were a strange lot. They put you in water to see how holy you were. Then they ducked you under the water three times. Didn't matter a whit if you could swim or no. If you didn't come up, you got dead and your mortal soul went to Hell. But if you did come up, it was even worse. You had to be a Baptist.

When he first discovers that Aunt Matty is a Baptist, he is alarmed to be in the same room with her, even though he is fond of her. Toward the end of the novel, Ben Tanner, who with his wife Bess has been so kind to Rob, tells him that both he and Bess are Baptists. This takes Rob by surprise, but on this occasion, instead of feeling alarmed, he bursts out laughing. He knows that the Tanners, as well as Aunt Matty, love him, and now he knows also that "all of them were good shouting Baptists. It just goes to show how wrong I could feel about some things." This acknowledgment is a humbling experience for him. He realizes that not everything he has been told is true, that he can make judgments for himself, and that what matters is not the religious denomination to which people might belong but what is in their hearts and how they behave toward others. From this point on it is hard to imagine the rapidly maturing Rob condemning others on the basis of what people say about them.

Rob has already been exposed to some of the moral complexities that life presents. By overhearing a conversation between his mother and Aunt Carrie about Iris Bascomb and Ira Long, he has learned that sometimes a man and a woman will live together even though they are not married. Some people, like Aunt Carrie, think this is shocking and sinful; others, like his mother, express a more tolerant view. Rob finds that his mother's attitude is the one that most appeals to him, since he thinks of Iris and Ira as married, whatever the legal niceties of the situation might be. Rob has also discovered, in the episode involving Sebring Hillman's desire to dig up the coffin of the infant daughter he fathered with the family maid, that people do not always stay true to their spouses; that babies are born out of wedlock and that such affairs can lead to suffering and remorse. Rob learns still another level of complexity from his father, both in life and after his death. His father teaches him the virtues of acceptance—of his place in life and of the tasks he is called upon to perform: "Every man must face his own mission," Haven Peck tells his son. He teaches him of the necessity of self-reliance within the context of community responsibility, and it is a lesson Rob learns well.

After Haven dies, a chance discovery by Rob brings a new challenge into focus for him. Rob finds in an old cigar box a scrap of paper on which his illiterate father had been practicing writing his own name. One of the "Haven Pecks" had come out almost perfect. Symbolically, this suggests that in spite of the harsh circumstances in which he lived, Haven Peck's dedication to work, to the Shaker way, and to his family allowed him to live as perfect a life as could be imagined. He had succeeded against the odds. But his careful, repeated practice at writing his own name also poignantly suggests something else. It would appear that Haven may not have been entirely honest when he told Rob that he was not disturbed by the fact that he was denied the right to vote and looked down on by others because of his illiteracy and poverty. On the contrary, this poor treatment must have pained him greatly, as his secret efforts to learn how to write his name show. He did want to better himself in that respect.

Now Rob, in turn, must face an issue that is not dissimilar. Because of the death of his father, he is in all likelihood going to have to give up his education in order to manage the farm. How will he survive? Will he, too, end up like his father, worn down by an honorable life of hard work on the economic margins of society, or will he be able to reach for something better, something that eluded his father? His challenge over the next period of his life is to discover how to write a perfect Robert Peck—how to live the life that most suits his talents, abilities, and desires. At the age of thirteen, thanks to his solid upbringing in a loving home, he has a good basis on which to work.

Source: Bryan Aubrey, Critical Essay on *A Day No Pigs Would Die*, in *Novels for Students*, Gale, Cengage Learning, 2009.

Teresa J. Lucie-Nietzke

In the following essay, Lucie-Nietzke relates her experience teaching metaphors from A Day No Pigs Would Die.

Imagine this sunset—" . . . like when Mama poured peach juice on the large curds of white potcheese"—and you will know why Rob, the character who uttered that simile, snared my affection (as did his creator, Robert Newton Peck). Such language is perfect for a farm boy gently metamorphosing into a man. It helps us see what Rob saw—as he saw it. With just his simple Shaker upbringing between him and his experiences, Rob could only describe things in terms farmy and austere.

Teaching *A Day No Pigs Would Die* to a contemporary literature class, I wanted my students to experience the perfection, simplicity, and honesty that I did in its metaphorical language. But they were jaded juniors and seniors who thought Rob's language was as queer and as backwards as the plastic pocket liners they stuffed into their shirts on nerd day. Like most adolescents, they were threatened by anything very different from their own values and styles. To this group of sophisticated, upper-middle-class teenagers, Rob was a mud-splattered pick-up truck in their parking lot of BMWs, classic Mustangs, and sporty foreign cars.

Maybe my cherished farm background made me feel a bit defensive at their responses, but I decided two things: (1) I would help them appreciate Rob's language (not necessarily like it—just appreciate it), and (2) I would help them examine their own metaphorical language (and its implications) and the concept of metaphor without the technical jargon of the traditional poetry lesson.

Before I could address these two goals, I had to place Rob in a context; my students needed background information about the Shakers. In a lecture, I told them about Anne Lee (who founded the Shaker society in the United States), about the shaking and dancing that characterized Shaker prayer meetings, about the surprising fact that the Shakers were a celibate communal group, about Shaker furniture design, and about their numerous inventions, such as garden seeds and circular saws. We listened to a recording of traditional Shaker music and skimmed through books laden with photos of Shaker dwellings. Then I put my students to work. I asked each of them to compile a Book of Shaker Laws as they read the novel. Haven Peck (Rob's father) frequently refers to the Book of Shaker, and I thought this assignment—actually making a list of these Shaker rules—would clearly show students the guidelines and beliefs by which Rob lived.

Once my students began to understand and appreciate (and even like!) Rob's character, I could address my first goal. Most still thought Rob talked "like, y'know, queer." Telling them that Rob was influenced by his farm surroundings the way they were influenced by Madonna and Bart Simpson would only lead to looks calculated to show me that I was not as hip as I thought. So, I divided the class of twenty-two

into five groups and distributed a handout (see figure 1).

Most groups responded to the handout's first question—How are the metaphors similar?—with little variation, stating that all the comparisons are about simple, ordinary things or are associated with the farm or country. One of the better responses to the second question—Why are these metaphors used so frequently?—was that as Rob is maturing he is encountering new things; by comparing the new to something old, he understands the new things better. (One of the poorer responses: "That's how the backwoods people talked back then." I still had work to do!) The class agreed that the country/religious metaphors were much more effective in communicating the Shaker lifestyle, Rob's limited experiences, and the world as Rob saw it than other words might be. For example, "lumpy and apricot-colored" would not help us see a very pretty sunset, nor would those words do double duty and show us a simple treat the Shakers might eat. "Perfectly straight and white" does not make us feel the Shaker's rigid adherence to the religious life the way that "straight and white as virtue" does.

Once students realized that Rob's language revealed Rob's lifestyle, the discussion moved naturally to my second goal. I asked students to find two or three of their own metaphors in their journals; then we discussed what their language revealed about them, listing some examples on the board. It was easy for the students to discern the influences in their lives. For example, in the college town where I teach, some animosity exists between the college students and the high school students; one junior girl described college students in a local semi-fast-food restaurant "who act as if their feet have been cemented." Other examples revealed the influence of advertising and material goods on students' lives: "She's as soft as a tube of toothpaste" or "Your face looks like a Big Mac." And, of course, the influence of popular music was readily apparent: "Tina Turner's hair is a mane"; "after his tackle, his nose looked like Michael Jackson's did before his plastic surgery." Students began to glimpse what their metaphorical language revealed about them and their culture at the same time that they more clearly saw Rob as a product of his Shaker culture.

These were two lessons really as simple as Shaker life—only the favorite teacher tools of the chalkboard, chalk, and ditto machine were needed—but learning, as evidenced by a change in awareness and understanding, occurred.

FIGURE 1. Metaphor in Dialogue Based on *A Day No Pigs Would Die*

Below is a list of metaphors found in the dialogue of Robert and Haven and the pages [Dell paperback edition, 1979] on which they are found. As a group, answer the following questions and be prepared to share your responses with the class:

1. How are the metaphors similar?
2. Find the metaphors in your text. Why are they used so frequently in the dialogue of Rob and Haven?
3. Write a different way of communicating the information provided in each metaphor. Compare it with the metaphor listed. Which method of communicating seems most appropriate for Rob and Haven? Why?

Group 1

7 bleed like a stuck pig
11 as wrong as sin on Sunday
15 clean as a cat's mouth
20 smell like Sunday morn
21 fence up like it was war
22 clean as clergy

Group 2

22 alike as two peas
23 like a chin napkin
25 sweet as candy
26 nervous as a long tail cat in a room full of rocking chairs
35 like you'd wind a kite string around a spool
39 true as a taproot

Group 3

41 hard as winter
48 like her motor was running and wouldn't stop
50 dry, as dust
58 like a hill of barbwire
61 like when Ma poured peach juice on white pot-cheese
70 frosted the wheels like they was cake

Group 4

75 like a potato dug up on a rainy day
80 ugly as sin
83 clean as an archangel
93 like somebody broke eggs all over the hillside
108 sassy as salt

Group 5

110 straight and white as virtue
116 colors as pretty as laundry on a line
125 tasted like soap
127 colder than death
128 quite like Christmas morning

Source: Teresa J. Lucie-Nietzke, "As Simple as Shaker Life: Teaching Metaphor in *A Day No Pigs Would Die*," in *Clearing House*, Vol. 64, No. 6, July–August 1991, p. 399.

SOURCES

Cooper, Arthur, Review of *A Day No Pigs Would Die*, in *Newsweek*, March 12, 1973, p. 98.

"National Assessment of Educational Progress," Web site of the National Institute for Literacy, http://www.nifl.gov/nifl/facts/NAEP.html (accessed July 17, 2008).

Peck, Robert Newton, *A Day No Pigs Would Die*, Knopf, 1975.

Purcell, L. Edward, *The Shakers*, Crescent Books 1991, p. 11

"Robert Newton Peck," in *UXL Encyclopedia of World Biography*, 2003, http://findarticles.com/p/articles/mi_gx5229/is_/ai_n19149312 (accessed September 17, 2008).

"Swine Fever," Review of *A Day No Pigs Would Die*, in *Times Literary Supplement*, August 17, 1973, p. 945.

Todd, Richard, "Psychic Farming: Country Books," in *Atlantic Monthly*, Vol. 231, No. 4, April 1973, p. 114.

U.S. Census Bureau, "Historical Poverty Tables," http://www.census.gov/hhes/www/poverty/histpov/hstpov2.html (accessed July 17, 2008).

U.S. Census Bureau, "The 2008 Statistical Abstract," http://www.census.gov/compendia/statab/cats/income_expenditures_poverty_wealth/poverty.html (accessed July 17, 2008).

U.S. Department of Education, "National Assessment of Adult Literacy," Web site of the Institute of Education Sciences, National Center for Education Statistics, http://nces.ed.gov/naal/lit_history.asp (accessed July 17, 2008).

Yardley, Jonathan, Review of *A Day No Pigs Would Die*, in *New York Times Book Review*, May 13, 1973, p. 37.

FURTHER READING

Hartvigsen, M. Kip, and Christen Brog Hartvigsen, "Haven Peck's Legacy in *A Day No Pigs Would Die*," in *English Journal*, Vol. 74, No. 4, April 1985, pp. 41–45.
    The authors of this essay highlight the positive values embodied in the book, including the

notions of duty to others and dedication to everyday tasks. They also point out the appreciation Haven Peck has for nature and how he passes this on to his son.

Klyza, Christopher McGrory, and Stephen C. Trombulak, *The Story of Vermont: A Natural and Cultural History*, University Press of New England, 1999.

This is an exploration of the history of Vermont from the prehuman era to the present. The authors describe the interconnectedness of the geological, biological, and cultural aspects of the region.

Peck, Robert Newton, *Weeds in Bloom: Autobiography of an Ordinary Man*, Random House, 2005.

In telling his life story, Peck includes some lively anecdotes about his childhood growing up on the family farm in rural Vermont. Much of the book consists of stories about people who shaped his life.

Stein, R. Conrad, *Ethan Allen and the Green Mountain Boys*, Children's Press, 2003.

Stein tells the story of Vermont's Ethan Allen, who led the Green Mountain Boys in their capture of Fort Ticonderoga from the British in 1775.

Einstein's Dreams

ALAN LIGHTMAN

1993

Alan Lightman's *Einstein's Dreams* was first published in 1993 by Warner Books. Despite the fact that the book was Lightman's first work of fiction—he had only written non-fiction books on physics, astrophysics, and astronomy up until that point—the book was an instant critical and popular success, becoming an international bestseller. Set over the course of April 1905 to June 1905, the novel presents a fictional version of the physicist Albert Einstein as he forms his famed theory of relativity. Quite literally a book of Einstein's dreams, nearly every chapter depicts a world in which the laws of time operate under different conditions. Each of the physicist's dreams thus illustrates how humankind's various experiences of time affect their experiences of the world and also of one another. The book, then, is a meditation on the nature of time and of being human. At intervals throughout the book, Einstein is depicted in his waking life as he works towards perfecting the theory of relativity, which will bring him worldwide renown. Given its weighty topic, *Einstein's Dreams* is one of the few contemporary novels about science to be studied in high schools and colleges nationwide. The original edition of the novel remains in print, and a 2004 edition was released by Vintage Books.

Alan Lightman (*AP Images*)

AUTHOR BIOGRAPHY

Alan Lightman was born November 28, 1948, in Memphis, Tennessee. His father, Richard Lightman, owned a movie theater chain, and his mother, Jeanne Garretson Lightman, was a dance teacher who also volunteered as a Braille typist. Lightman's scientific talent was apparent early on, and as a young student, he entered (and won) several science fairs and competitions at state and national levels. Lightman attended White Station High School in Memphis, and though he continued his scientific studies, he also began writing poetry. He earned the state-level National Council of Teachers of English literary award for his efforts. Lightman graduated from high school in 1966, and then graduated magna cum laude with a bachelor of arts degree from Princeton University. In 1974, he received his Ph.D. in theoretical physics from the California Institute of Technology. Lightman went on to conduct his post-doctorate work in astrophysics at Cornell University from 1974 to 1976, publishing his poems in literary magazines at the same time. Lightman married the painter Jean Greenblatt in 1976, and the couple has two daughters, Elyse and Kara.

After working as assistant professor of astronomy at Harvard University from 1976 to 1979, Lightman became a lecturer in astronomy and physics there from 1979 to 1989. He also worked at the Smithsonian Astrophysical Observatory, as a staff astrophysicist from 1979 to 1989. During this time, Lightman published his first scientific textbooks, including *Problem Book in Relativity and Gravitation* (1975) and *Revealing the Universe: Prediction and Proof in Astronomy* (1982), which Lightman edited with James Cornell. By 1981, Lightman began writing essays about the more human aspects of science, most of which were published in a *Science* column from 1982 to 1986. These essays were also collected and published as *Time Travel and Papa Joe's Pipe: Essays on the Human Side of Science* (1984) and *A Modern-Day Yankee in a Connecticut Court, and Other Essays on Science* (1986). In 1989, Lightman joined the Massachusetts Institute of Technology (MIT) as professor of science and writing and senior lecturer in physics. He was the first person to be assigned a post in both the sciences and humanities at MIT. In 1995, Lightman was named the John E. Burchard Professor of Humanities. He resigned from the position in 2001 in order to have more time to pursue his writing, although he remained employed at MIT as an adjunct professor of humanities, a post he still held as of 2008.

During his early career at MIT, Lightman published several nonfiction books, including *Ancient Light: Our Changing View of the Universe* (1991) and *Time for the Stars: Astronomy in the 1990s* (1992). The former won the *Boston Globe* Critics' Choice award. The following year, Lightman published his first novel, *Einstein's Dreams*, to immense success. The book was nominated for the PEN New England/*Boston Globe* Winship award and was translated into thirty languages, earning the rare status of international bestseller. Lightman followed up on the success of *Einstein's Dreams* with the novels *Good Benito* (1995) and *The Diagnosis* (2000). The latter was a finalist for the National Book Award.

In 1999, Lightman founded the Harpswell Foundation, an organization dedicated to making education available to women and children in Cambodia. For his philanthropy work, Lightman was awarded the Gold Medal for humanitarian service from the government of Cambodia. Returning to fiction writing in 2003, Lightman released his fourth novel, *Reunion*. Aside from his novels, Lightman has continued to write books on science and on the intersection between science and humanities, such as *A Sense of the Mysterious: Science and the Human Spirit* (2005). Lightman's professional focus on this intersection led to his cofounding the Graduate Program in Science Writing at MIT in 2001. He is also the first author to have an essay on language published in the science periodical *Nature*, and to have a short story published in the physics journal *Physics Today*.

PLOT SUMMARY

Prologue

It is 1905, late June in the Alps at a pre-dawn hour. A young patent clerk (presumably Albert Einstein) sits at his desk having just finished a twenty-page paper that he's been writing through the night. The paper is on the clerk's new theory of time. It is based on the dreams he has been having since April.

14 April 1905

This is the book's first dream, taking place two months before the prologue. It opens with the statement: "Suppose time is a circle, bending back on itself. The world repeats itself, precisely, endlessly." What follows is a description of what this kind of world would be like. Notably, this format can be seen in most of the dreams.

In this world, people live their lives as if every moment is unique, unaware that it will repeat itself. Those who have lived "unhappy lives" are "vaguely aware" of this repetition; they feel a sense of déjà vu at each bad decision, and a sense of resigned chagrin at each consequence.

16 April 1905

Time here is like "water" flowing, moving along until parts of it are diverted in other directions, namely the past. People who are tragically swept into the past are afraid to act for fear of changing the future. A person like this is a "ghost" who has "lost his personhood" and "is an exile of time."

19 April 1905

This chapter opens as a man decides not to go see the woman he is interested in dating. Based on this decision, he meets a different woman and has a happy future with her. But, this world has "three dimensions, like space." In the remaining two dimensions the man does decide to go see the first woman. In one of the two dimensions, they

fall in love, and though she does not treat him well, he is still happy. In the other, they do not fall in love, and the man returns home, feeling "empty." In this world, every time a decision is made, no matter how minor, "the world splits into three worlds," with different scenarios for each decision. Because of this, "there are an infinity of worlds."

24 April 1905

There are two kinds of time in this world, "mechanical time" and "body time." Those who live by the latter do not use clocks; they eat, sleep, and work whenever they feel like it. Those who live by mechanical time wake, eat, and work at the same exact time each day. Both worlds can simultaneously exist "in one," but when they come together, they cause "desperation," and when they move apart, they cause "contentment." Though "each time is true," their "truths are not the same."

26 April 1905

People here only live in the mountains because time moves more slowly the farther one is from the center of the earth, and they can increase their longevity by doing so. Some do not care about extending their lives for a few minutes. They enjoy the empty valleys and swim in the deserted lakes. Over time, people forget "why higher is better," but they stay and continue to teach their children to do the same. They suffer in the cold, thin mountain air and they "have become thin like the air, bony, old before their time."

28 April 1905

Here "time is absolute." There are regular and daily celebrations of time. Religious people think time is the "evidence for God." Philosophers have also "placed time at the center of their belief," and they use time as a moral touchstone. All over this world, people are comforted by time. They take "refuge" in it and in the thought that the moment of their birth is "recorded," as are all of the moments of their lives.

3 May 1905

In this world, "cause and effect are erratic." One may come before or after the other with no discernible pattern. Despite this, the "future and past are entwined." For instance, a man does not understand why his friends want nothing more to do with him. A week later, he is unkind to them. In the "acausal" (without cause) world,

MEDIA ADAPTATIONS

- A musical composition titled "In This World," based on *Eisntein's Dreams*, was written by Paul Hoffman and performed in the Boston metro area by the Silverwood Trio in 2000. Their independently recorded concert is available from http://CDBaby.com in compact disc format.

- *Einstein's Dreams* has been adapted as a play, which was produced and directed by Patrizia Acerra and Dawn Arnold at the National Pastime Theater (Chicago, IL) in 2000; a revised adaptation was staged there in 2005.

- A separate stage adaptation of the book was produced at the Paradise Theater (New York, NY) in 2001, produced and directed by Paul Stancato and Brian Rhinehart.

- A musical composition based on the book, titled "When Einstein Dreams," was written by Nando Michelin and performed by the Nando Michelin Group in 2003. Produced by record label Double-Time, this composition is available on compact disc.

- *Einstein's Dreams* was independently adapted to the stage by the Culture Project Theater (New York, NY) in 2003, directed by Rebecca Holderness.

- A stage adaptation of the novel by Brian Niece and David Alford was produced at the People's Branch Theater (Nashville, TN) in 2003.

- A musical adaptation of the book, with music and lyrics by Joshua Rosenblum and Joanne Lessner, was staged at the Martin Segal Theater (New York, NY) in 2003.

- Yet another unique stage adaptation of *Einstein's Dreams* was produced at the University of Memphis (Memphis, TN) in 2006, directed by Gloria Baxter.

- A dance/theater adaptation of *Einstein's Dreams* was staged at the Dance Theater Workshop (New York, NY) in 2006.

- A choral production based on the novel, with music and lyrics by Lorraine L. Whittlesey, was staged in Baltimore, MD, in 2006.

- *Einstein's Dreams* was further adapted for the stage by Wesley Savick and produced at the Catalyst Collaborative and Underground Railway Theater (Cambridge, MA) in 2007.

---

the past and the future become meaningless. The present thus becomes ever more meaningful.

4 May 1905

Two couples are on their traditional annual vacation together. Their conversation is banal, and they do nothing of interest. In this world, "little happens." Either it is time that does not move or it is the people. This chapter also asks whether "time and the passage of events are the same."

Interlude

The narrative shifts back to Einstein in the waking world. He and his friend Besso are on the way to Besso's house to have dinner with Besso's wife, Anna. Occasionally, when Einstein stays too long at their house, Einstein's wife, Mileva, comes with

their "infant" to retrieve him. At dinner, Einstein tells Besso, "I want to understand time because I want to get close to The Old One." Besso says that "perhaps The Old One is not interested in getting close to his creations." He also adds that "it is not obvious that knowledge is closeness."

Besso thinks that Einstein, who is only twenty-six years old, may be too young to come up with a theory of time. Besso then thinks of all that Einstein has already achieved and begins to believe it may be possible. Besso tells Einstein that he won't be able to see him for a while because his brother is coming from Rome for a visit. Afterwards, Besso thinks that Einstein is very independent; he does not go anywhere with his wife, and often sneaks away from her at home to work on his "equations." Thinking about what Einstein said earlier about "The Old One," it occurs to Besso that "for such a recluse and an introvert, this passion for closeness seems odd."

8 May 1905

The narrative returns to the dream worlds, and this chapter opens with the statement "The world will end on 26 September 1907. Everyone knows it." A year before this date, the schools and businesses close. People are more honest with themselves and one another. They are also more polite; no one seems upset about the end because it will happen to everyone: "A world with one month is a world of equality." At the last minute of time, everyone gathers together silently, holding hands. In the "last seconds" it seems as if everyone has jumped from a mountain and "the end approaches like approaching ground."

10 May 1905

Areas of the village in this world are stuck in different time periods. The architecture of each neighborhood reflects this. Time can "hypothetically" be "smooth or rough, prickly or silky, hard or soft." Here, it is "sticky," so objects and people sometimes get stuck. In this world "no one is happy" and "everyone is alone." This is because "a life in the past cannot be shared with the present." People who become "stuck in time" are "stuck alone."

11 May 1905

In this world, everything is neat and orderly. For instance, the leaves fall from the trees in organized patterns, the paint on the buildings does not peel and grows brighter instead. Here, "the passage of time brings increasing order. Order is the law of nature." Instead of spring cleaning, people make a mess every spring. They break things and throw away their watches and appointment books. This goes on all through spring and winds down as summer begins.

14 May 1905

Here, "time stands still"; everything is frozen in stillness; raindrops and clock pendulums are stuck in midair. People who get closer to this place begin to slow down until they come to "dead center" and "stop." This happens because time does not move at "the center of time." Instead, it ripples "outward in concentric circles" like a stone thrown in a pond.

There is very little light at the center of time. It cannot travel through time as it normally would and therefore dims. People just outside the center move "at the pace of glaciers." A single action can take years to complete. Not surprisingly, some feel that the center should be avoided, believing that "life is a vessel of sadness, but it is noble to live life, and without time, there is no life." Those that disagree "would rather have an eternity of contentment, even if that eternity were fixed and frozen, like a butterfly mounted in a case."

15 May 1905

This world has "no time," only "images," perhaps of what might be thought of as frozen moments. What follows in this chapter is a long list of these images, brief snapshots of people and nature. This world is nothing but individual tableaus of life.

20 May 1905

The inhabitants of the city in this world walk around disoriented, using maps to find their way or writing down their experiences as they happen for future reference. Although the people have lived in this city since they were born, they are always discovering it anew because "in this world, people have no memories." Husbands and wives return home to meet each other and their children as if for the first time. "A world without memory is a world of the present."

22 May 1905

Morning breaks in the city and reveals a road that goes nowhere, a house removed from its lot, and a church depicting images of both a religious and non-religious nature. A man walking down the road suddenly turns around, shrieking "excitedly." All of these oddities are a result of the fact that, in this world, "time flows not evenly but fitfully." Because of this people can catch "fitful glimpses of the future." People who see themselves in new careers in the future, immediately leave their current jobs. Parents who see where their children will live in the future move their houses there today. People feel there is no point "in continuing the present when one has seen the future." Those who have seen their future are successful in all that they do, knowing which choices to make and which to avoid. Those who have not are unable to make decisions for fear of making the wrong one.

Some people, however, try to avoid their futures. A man sees himself working as a barrister, so he decides to become a gardener. Eventually, he gets tired of his low pay and becomes a barrister. A woman falls in love with a man who is not the man she sees herself marrying. He leaves, and then she marries the other man. The chapter ends with the questions: "Who would fare better in this world of fitful time? Those who have seen the future and live only one life? Or those who have not seen the future and wait to live life? Or those who deny the future and live two lives?"

29 May 1905

Everything in this world moves at a swift speed; the buildings are on rails, moving along like locomotives. People run around and even their office desks constantly move about. Here, time moves "more slowly for people in motion." Everyone moves about in order "to gain time." Unfortunately, "the motional effect is all relative." The faster a person is going, the faster their neighbor appears to be going, and the slower they themselves seem to be going. Because of this, "some people have stopped looking out their windows." These people live peaceful lives.

Interlude

The narrative returns once again to Einstein in the waking world. He is at an outdoor café with Besso. Einstein does not look well, but repeatedly says he is "making progress." He tells Besso, "I think the secrets will come." The two men discuss a colleague's paper, which neither of them likes. The men silently fiddle with their food and coffee. Einstein gazes at the Alps, but he is really looking "into space," a practice that sometimes gives him headaches.

Besso invites Einstein, Mileva, and the baby, Hans Albert, over for dinner. He is worried about his friend, though Einstein has been like this before. Einstein says he cannot come to dinner, but his wife and baby can. Neither Besso or Einstein knows why Einstein married. Einstein thought his wife would take care of the housekeeping but that has not been the case. The two men then discuss a patent application that Einstein intends to revise. He has anonymously volunteered amendments to several inventions without taking any credit. Nevertheless, when Einstein's first paper was published "he imitated a rooster for fully five minutes."

2 June 1905

Here, "time flows backward." A man who could be Einstein accepts the Nobel Peace Prize for physics. He thinks of when he will be younger

and learn "things about Nature that no one has ever known." He thinks of a "time when he will be young and unknown and unafraid of mistakes." A man at the grave of his friend "does not weep." He knows the days he will spend with his friend are still ahead of him. He waits for his friend to return and remembers the time they will spend together.

3 June 1905

In this world, people only live for one whole day. This is either due to the fact that their experiences have sped up to the point where a lifetime is compressed into one day, or because the earth has slowed down to the point where a full lifetime can be lived in one day. Because of this, people only learn about seasons in books. People born in winter never see flowers. People born in summer never see snow.

People are mindful of each moment and they hurry to live their lives in the brief time allotted them, forever watching "the change in the light." Everything happens so swiftly that seniors begin to doubt how anything that has happened to them could have been real, how they could have truly experienced anything or truly known anyone.

5 June 1905

Here, "time is a sense"; each individual experiences time differently. Three people looking at the boats as they pass by see three very different scenes. One person sees them moving so swiftly they look as if they are skating on ice, one person sees them moving so slowly they are almost still, and another sees them as floating alternately forwards and backwards. Philosophers "argue whether time really exists outside human perception." They wonder if events can be said to "happen at all." They sit together and "compare their aesthetics of time."

9 June 1905

People in this world live forever, and they react to this fact in one of two ways. "The Laters" believe they have all the time in the world to accomplish things, so they take their time doing everything. They wander about in cafés, have easy conversations, and read whatever is around to read. "The Nows," however, believe that they can experience everything, and they rush about attempting to do just that, learning new trades, and rushing through conversations, always on to the next thing.

The downside to immortality is that no one is "whole" or "free." Some, then, feel that "the only way to live is to die." They commit suicide and by dying are finally "free of the weight of the past." This is how "the finite has conquered the infinite."

10 June 1905

Here, "time is not a quantity but a quality." It "exists, but it cannot be measured." A man meets a woman on a train and urgently asks her to go on a date with him. She waits for him to arrive, though they did not set a time. He appears and they walk through a garden. It feels as if they could have been together for a lifetime. They go to a restaurant and the man's mother waits outside, believing that her son is still a child because to her it feels as if he is still a child. Because time is immeasurable, there are no watches or calendars. "Events are triggered by other events, not by time."

11 June 1905

Two men attempting to part are unable to do so. They feel as if it is the last time they will see one another. A lonely woman cries as if she will always be lonely. This is because this world has no future. People are unable to "imagine the future," just as they cannot see colors outside of the "visible end of the spectrum." That is why people act the way the do.

A man sitting on the patio at a café sees a rain cloud but does not go inside because he is unable to imagine the coming rain. He is awed at how dark it is at "the end of the world." It rains and the man goes inside. The storm passes, the sun comes out, and the man goes outside, awed "that the world ends in sunlight." Indeed, "in a world without future, each moment is the end of the world."

15 June 1905

Here, "time is a visible dimension"; people are able to see it and move through it at will, going as slowly or as rapidly as they desire. Some people stick to one time, afraid to venture out into the distance. Others race into the future, though they are unprepared for it when they arrive. A young man attending the polytechnic in Zurich, Switzerland, meets with his professor. (This man could be Einstein; he graduated from that school in 1900.) The young man works on his equations and meets his professor monthly, afraid of how he will manage once he has graduated and will no longer be able to rely on such guidance. The man could skip ahead to other meetings, but he

does not. Everyone in this world "continue[s] on to the future at their own paces."

17 June 1905

The world moves in fitful stops and starts. "Time is a stretch of nerve fibers: seemingly continuous from a distance but disjointed close up." The breaks in time are small, fractions of fractions of a second, and for the most part, everything runs along smoothly despite these gaps. However, sometimes that is not the case.

A man who was left by his lover begins to fall in love with another woman, but he is still hurt by the other woman's unexpected leave-taking. He searches his new lover's face for a sign that she will leave him too. The new woman does love him and will not leave him. Time stops just as a vague thought occurs to her, and when time resumes, the man sees a hesitant look on her face. He takes this to mean that she will leave him, so he leaves her instead. The woman "wonders why the young man did not love her."

Interlude

Once more the narrative finds Einstein and Besso together in waking life. They are sitting in a boat in the river and fishing. Besso eats a sandwich and Einstein smokes his pipe. Einstein says he's never caught any fish in the river and asks Besso for a sandwich. Besso feels bad about tagging along; he knows Einstein was planning to go fishing alone so he could think. The two men look at the clouds and Einstein asks Besso what shapes he sees. For the first time, Einstein refers to Besso by his first name, Michele.

Besso tells Einstein that he believes Einstein's theory of time will be successful. He tells Einstein that once it is complete they will go fishing again and Einstein can tell him about it. "When you become famous, you'll remember that you told me first, here in this boat," Besso says. "Einstein laughs."

18 June 1905

In what can be seen as a parody of the Vatican, ten thousand people stand in line outside of a cathedral in the middle of Rome. The cathedral is the "Temple of Time," and it houses the "Great Clock." It is the only clock on earth, and every person must make a pilgrimage to it at least once in their lives.

Before the clock was invented, people measured time by the stars, sun, and moon, by the seasons and the tides. It was measured "by heart-beats, the rhythms of drowsiness and sleep, the recurrence of hunger, the menstrual cycles of women, the duration of loneliness." When the clock was invented, people were "spellbound" and "horrified." Nevertheless, it "could not be ignored," and so they decided to worship it. The man who invented the clock was pressed to build the Great Clock. Afterwards, all of the other clocks were obliterated and the inventor was murdered. People returned to living their lives the way they always had, with the exception of the pilgrimage. Nevertheless, everything they did was changed by the knowledge that it was being measured. "Every action, no matter how little, is no longer free." The people "have been trapped by their own inventiveness and audacity. And they must pay with their lives."

20 June 1905

"Time flows at different speeds in different locations." Clocks next to one another tick at the same pace, but the farther apart they are in distance, the more varied their rates of progress. Because business can only be reasonably conducted in places where time passes at the same rate, business in each city is isolated. "Each city is an island," self-sustaining and alone. There are occasional travelers, but they do not notice the changes in time because everything happens "proportionally." Travelers are only aware of the changes when they contact their homes. A young daughter may have already grown old and died, or only a split second may have passed. Travelers are "cut off in time, as well as in space." They never go back to where they came from.

22 June 1905

Boys graduate from school; parents gather to watch. No one is excited by the happy occasion. They move through it as if it does not matter. Some of the boys go to college and others go to work, but no one cares about the distinction because everything is preordained. Time here is "rigid," the future will happen the way it has been planned to happen since the dawn of time. No one can do anything to change their future; they are "spectators" in their own lives.

A man who owes his friend money decides to buy himself a coat instead of paying his friend back. He is not wrong for doing so because "in a world of fixed future, there can be no right or wrong." Moral distinctions such as these require "freedom of choice," which does not exist in a

world where the future is preordained. Nevertheless, the man walks along in his new coat feeling "oddly free to do as he pleases, free in a world without freedom."

25 June 1905

There is a scene of the town on Sunday afternoon. A young man plays his violin and thinks about his wife and infant son. He contemplates leaving his wife but then remembers how they met at the polytechnic. (This figure again mimics biographical details from Einstein's life.) The man is slightly aware that there are other men identical to him playing identical violins and thinking identical thoughts. Here, "time is like the light between two mirrors," moving to and fro and "producing an infinite number of images."

27 June 1905

A quarryman lives a routine life, working at the quarry and dining with his wife. His children are grown. On Tuesdays, the quarryman goes to market, and although people greet him, he does not make eye contact with them or respond. In fact, he does not make eye contact with anyone. This is because the man is stuck in a memory of himself as a schoolboy who peed in his pants. His classmates made fun of him endlessly, and in his head, he is still that ashamed little boy.

However, this is a world with a "shifting past." The past is an "illusion," but no one is aware that the past is constantly changing. If the shift is universal, how could anyone know that it has even occurred? Thus, one day the quarryman wakes up and is no longer the boy who wet his pants. He remembers that very same day in class as being uneventful; after class he went out to play with his schoolmates. Now the quarryman visits with his friends and takes strolls with his wife. Each person in this world has their memories, but "in a world of shifting past, these memories are wheat in wind." And no one is the wiser.

28 June 1905

A family picnics on the riverbank; a man, his wife, his mother, and his children. The children are playing as the adults eat and converse. A flock of birds appears and the man, his wife, and his mother, all chase after the birds, futilely attempting to catch them. The children ignore them and continue playing. The birds make their way through the city, and all of the adult townspeople stop whatever they are doing, also attempting, without success, to catch the birds.

The reason people do this is that the birds are made of time; if a bird is caught, the moment in which it is caught becomes frozen and preserved.

On rare occasions when a bird is caught, the catcher is able to "savor" the moment, its sights and smells. However, they "soon discover that the nightingale expires, its clear, flutelike song diminishes to silence, the trapped moment grows withered and without life."

Epilogue
The narrative returns to the scene portrayed in the prologue. Einstein sits at his desk, having just completed his theory of time. It is no longer dawn but now eight o'clock in the morning. A clerk comes in and begins working. The typist comes in, sees Einstein and his papers. He gives them to her. Einstein paces and looks out the window. "He feels empty." He does not want to talk to Besso or think about physics. He stares vacantly out the window.

CHARACTERS

Anna Besso
In the novel, Anna is married to Michele Besso, who is referred to by his last name. She often cooks dinner for both Besso and Einstein. It appears that Anna and Besso have no children, as no mention is made of any. It also seems that they have a happy marriage. This is somewhat implied by the peaceful domestic scene of Anna and Besso hosting Einstein at dinner. By contrast, Einstein wonders why he is married, contemplates leaving his wife and child, and constantly avoids them, preferring instead to work or spend time with Anna and Besso. Anna's character is based on the historical figure Anna Besso-Winteler, who was married to the historical figure of Michele Besso. Notably, the "real" Anna's brother, Paul, married Einstein's sister Maja.

Michele Besso
Michele Besso, referred to primarily by his last name, is Einstein's friend. Besso appears in all of the novel's interludes; Einstein dines with Besso and his wife, Anna, has lunch with Besso at a café, and goes fishing with him. In each episode, Einstein hints that he is working on his theory of time, or relativity, and also mentions his progress. Besso is supportive, although the two men do not discuss Einstein's work. Besso predominantly serves as a

means to give readers insight into Einstein's character. For instance, Einstein tells Besso, "I want to understand time because I want to get close to The Old One." But Besso thinks that "for such a recluse and an introvert, this passion for closeness seems odd." Besso also thinks that Einstein, who is only twenty-six years old, may be too young to come up with a theory of time. Through his eyes, however, readers see that Besso knows what Einstein has already achieved, and thus begins to believe it may be possible. In a later interlude, Besso tells Einstein that once his theory is complete they will go fishing again and Einstein can tell him about it. "When you become famous, you'll remember that you told me first, here in this boat," Besso says. "Einstein laughs."

It is through Besso's eyes that readers are first given a glimpse into Einstein's dysfunctional marriage. Besso thinks that Einstein is very independent; he does not go anywhere with his wife, and often sneaks away from her at home to work on his "equations." Besso wonders why Einstein is married, and Einstein wonders the same thing about himself. Einstein contemplates leaving his wife and child, and constantly avoids them, preferring instead to work or spend time with Anna and Besso. By contrast, Besso and his wife Anna seem to have a happy marriage. Besso's circumstances are used as a foil, or contrast, to Einstein's, thus serving to define Einstein's character rather than demonstrating his own. In fact, there is only one instance in which Einstein comments on Besso's character. While fishing, Einstein asks Besso what he sees in the clouds. When Besso replies, "I see a goat chasing a man who is frowning," Einstein responds, "You are a practical man, Michele." This is also the only instance when Einstein refers to his friend by his first name, or any name at all for that matter.

Besso's character is based on the historical figure of Michele Angelo Besso (1873–1955), who was the "real" Einstein's friend. Besso was an engineer who knew Einstein as a student (they both studied at the Zurich polytechnic) and who also worked with him at the patent office. Besso often argued with Einstein as the physicist worked on his emerging theories, helping to shape them before they were finalized. Besso was the only individual Einstein credited as contributing to his theory of relativity. Thus, the novel presents a marked departure from the facts. It does not portray Besso's contributions or the two friends' arguments.

Besso's Brother

In the novel's first interlude, Besso tells Einstein that he won't be able to see him for a while since his brother will be visiting from Rome. This mention can likely be attributed to the historical figure Beniamino Besso, mostly cited as Besso's uncle (not his brother). Beniamino did live in Rome and he worked with Augusto De Pretto, Olinto De Pretto's brother. Notably, in 1903, Olinto De Pretto published a paper that touched upon the relationship between mass and energy, one of the cornerstones of Einstein's theories of relativity. Scholars have suggested that Einstein may have learned of this through Besso's connections to De Pretto.

Dream Figures

The bulk of the novel's narrative is comprised of varying dream worlds populated by unnamed people; men, women, boys, girls, quarrymen, husbands, wives, lovers, daughters, sons, classmates, and so on. These dream figures are not characters per se but rather serve as part of the extended metaphor that each dream world depicts. The dream figures are representative not only of humanity at large but also of the human experience. Given that the human experience is largely based upon perception, particularly upon the perception of time, the dream populace exists to portray varying perceptions and experiences of each world. The dream figures give each world, each law of time, a human face, allowing the reader to imagine what each world might be like for a human to live in it.

Interestingly, different groups of people react to the same worlds differently, which gives each world a more complex, realistic feel. For instance, in the world where time slows down at higher elevations, most people live ascetic lives in the mountains, hoping to gain longevity. The remainder enjoy their somewhat shorter lives in the warm valleys, swimming in the lakes. In the world without memory, some people study the books recording their lives incessantly. Others have stopped reading their books because they do not think that knowing who they were is essential to their being. These are the people who "have learned to live in a world without memory." In the world where each city's time proceeds at different speeds, some are content to live their entire lives within the borders of their city; they think nothing can be as good or as grand as the city they live in. Others burn with curiosity and become travelers who never return.

There are also several instances in which a single figure gives readers an immediate glimpse into the conditions of living under the law of time. Such examples are set by the woman transported back in time as she anxiously watches over the great-great-great grandfather of the man responsible for forming the European Union; the man who both does and does not decide to go see a love interest; and the quarryman who wet his pants as a child, and then did not.

Einstein

Obviously based on the historical figure of Albert Einstein (1879–1955), the fictional Einstein is only referred to by his last name. Since *Einstein's Dreams* is not a conventional novel, it is difficult to describe Einstein as the protagonist, though he is the main character. At the same time, the dreams are even more of a main character than the dreamer. Regardless, the narrative opens with Einstein having just finished his theory of time, and ends in the same way, albeit a few hours later. The interim describes a series of dreams and flashbacks.

Readers catch mere glimpses of Einstein in the book's interludes, but each glimpse is telling. In the first interlude, Einstein dines with Besso and his wife, Anna. Occasionally, when Einstein stays too long at their house, Einstein's wife, Mileva, comes with their "infant" to retrieve him. In fact, Einstein routinely avoids his wife. At dinner, Einstein tells Besso, "I want to understand time because I want to get close to The Old One." Besso tells him, "Perhaps The Old One is not interested in getting close to his creations." Besso also adds that "it is not obvious that knowledge is closeness."

In the second interlude, overtaken by work, Einstein does not look well, though he repeatedly says he is "making progress." He tells Besso, "I think the secrets will come." Einstein gazes at the Alps, but he is really looking "into space," a practice that sometimes gives him headaches. Einstein's dysfunctional marriage is again referenced, and neither Besso nor Einstein knows why Einstein married. Einstein thought his wife would take care of the housekeeping but that has not been the case. Additionally, readers learn that Einstein has anonymously volunteered amendments to several inventions without taking any credit. Nevertheless, when Einstein's first paper was published "he imitated a rooster for fully five minutes."

In the third interlude, Einstein tells Besso he's never caught any fish in the river, though he goes fishing often. Einstein does not literally fish; instead, he contemplates his work. When Einstein reappears in the epilogue, he gives his papers to the typist. Afterwards, he paces and looks out the window. "He feels empty." He does not want to talk to Besso or think about physics. He stares vacantly out the window.

Einstein also appears in his own dreams in various guises, most notably as a physicist about to receive the Nobel Peace Prize, a student at the polytechnic, and as a man playing violin as he contemplates leaving his wife. In each instance the biographical details of the "real" Einstein align with the fictional dream version.

Hans Albert Einstein

Hans Albert is the infant son of Einstein and Mileva. He never actually appears in the narrative, though he is mentioned in passing on several occasions, particularly in reference to his father's avoidance of him and his mother. The character is based on the historical figure of the same name (1904–1973). Notably, the novel makes no mention of Hans Albert's younger sister, Lieserl, who was born in 1902 before Einstein and Mileva were married and was thus kept a secret (Hans Albert was the couple's first legitimate child). Lieserl's existence was not public knowledge until 1986 and what became of her is not known. Lightman chose not to reference her in the novel.

Mileva Einstein

Mileva is Einstein's wife and Hans Albert's mother. Like Hans Albert, Mileva never actually appears in the narrative, though she is mentioned in passing on several occasions, particularly in reference to her husband's avoidance of her and their son. It is clear that Einstein does not like being with his wife. She is not a good housekeeper, and readers can infer that she is also not a good cook. Einstein often eats at Besso's house, and when the two men are fishing Einstein asks Besso for a sandwich. The character is based on the historical figure of Mileva Marič (1875–1948), who became Einstein's wife in 1903. The couple separated in 1914 and divorced in 1919.

Typist

In the prologue, Einstein has just completed his theory of time. It is dawn and he is sitting in the deserted patent office waiting for the typist to arrive later that morning. In the epilogue, the typist arrives, sees Einstein and his papers and "smiles." She has typed up many of his papers for him before. "He always gladly pays what she asks.... She likes him."

THEMES

Being and Time

What is time? What is the nature of time? How do we perceive time? Is how we perceive time inherent to how we perceive everything else? These and similar questions are set forth by Einstein and his theory of relativity. More ostensibly, they are set forth in the novel under this guise and further under the guise of the physicist's dreams. By setting the tone in this manner, Lightman avoids writing what would otherwise be deemed science fiction. Furthermore, what Lightman's exploration of time reveals is that it can only be understood in terms of being in time—in other words, the experience of time. This is where the dream figures prove their purpose; it is through their examples that one is able to picture a world in which time moves backwards or at different speeds. The dream figures are the humanizing aspects of what would otherwise be a dry introduction to physics; they literally give life to the physics of time, portraying their varying perceptions and experiences of each world. Thus, perhaps unintentionally, the novel's exploration of time becomes an exploration of being in time. It bears repeating that it is impossible for the novel to be otherwise without becoming a book of equations. In a sense, this aligns with Einstein's theory of relativity, large parts of which require an observer in order to hold true.

Free Will and Destiny

Many of the worlds in *Einstein's Dreams* indirectly address free will and destiny. An example is the world in which the end of time is about to take place. A world in which time is about to end is one in which people feel free to do the things they would otherwise have never done, such as take a lover despite being happily married. By completely removing destiny from the equation (in the form of the end of the future, for destiny cannot exist if there is no future), all that is left is free will, and the people exercise it to the utmost. In the world in which people see the future, free

TOPICS FOR FURTHER STUDY

- Einstein's theories could not have been developed without the theoretical foundations established by Isaac Newton. Study Newton's life and work and give a class presentation based on your findings.

- Mimicking Lightman's writing style, create another dream that Einstein could have had. As you write, think of what new constraints on time, or lack thereof, you can imagine. How would humans live in such a world?

- Which other well-known physicists were contemporaries of Einstein? Research their lives and their work, and write a report on your findings.

- Study Einstein's theory of relativity. Which dreams (i.e., chapters) align most with his theory? Which are the most contradictory? Conduct a class debate on this topic.

Einstein's formula for the equivalence of mass and energy (Dominique Sarraute | Getty Images)

will is predominantly removed from the equation, even for those who attempt to exercise it. People who have had their vision of the future cease whatever they are doing and devote themselves to their future self. Those who have not received their vision do nothing but wait for it to arrive. A rare few ignore their vision and choose a different path, only to find that all paths ultimately lead to their vision. Thus, the only will that can be exercised in this world is to choose to arrive at one's destiny directly or via a more circuitous route. In the world where time "is a circle" that "repeats itself, precisely, endlessly" people are entirely at the mercy of destiny and free will does not exist. Yet, the populace is unaware of the law of time in their universe, or of its consequences. Except perhaps for an unhappy few, the people labor under the illusion that they have free will.

In the world where time "has three dimensions," giving rise to three new worlds with each decision that is made, people question how their choices can matter. How can one truly exercise free will if every possible outcome will come to

pass anyhow? This world questions whether or not free will has to do with the reasoning behind a choice (which is still valid in this world), or choosing an outcome to the exclusion of others (which is not a possibility in this world). Those who believe that it is the former are "content to live in contradictory worlds, so long as they know the reason for each." Those who believe the latter feel that their choices are robbed of meaning. Overall, based on these examples, it seems fair to say that free will and destiny are intertwined in the nature of time, as perceived by human beings.

STYLE

Vignettes

Vignettes is a literary term for brief passages that provide a snapshot of a particular place, person, object, emotion, or idea. They tend to be written with a great deal of imagery. They are also very evocative, which means that they capture a sense of place or emotion without explicitly addressing that place or emotion. Vignettes tend to address their subject indirectly rather than directly, writing around their main idea, rather than of it. In this way, they are rather lyrical and poetic, and they do closely resemble prose poems. In fact, the largest difference between a prose poem and a vignette is that prose poems are generally stand-alone pieces whereas vignettes are series of related pieces. All of these qualities are true of the chapters in *Einstein's Dreams*. Not only are the dreams vignettes, but so too are the interludes, the prologue, and epilogue. The former are vignettes of different worlds, and the latter are vignettes of Einstein and his life.

Extended Metaphors for Time and the Human Experience

A metaphor suggests an idea or object through another image or object. Thus, two things that seem unlike are made to seem alike. An extended metaphor does this on a longer and more complex level. For instance, the entirety of *Einstein's Dreams* is an extended metaphor for time and its many modes of being. On a smaller scale, each dream world is also an extended metaphor for a specific mode of time, and the experience of that time is ultimately a metaphor for what it is like to be human.

Dream Figures as Synecdoches

A synecdoche is a form of symbolism, but it is more specifically a literary term that describes the practice of using a part to describe a whole, or a single characteristic to represent a larger related concept. A popular example of this is the phrase "All hands on deck." "Hands" in this phrase are the parts used to represent the entire ship's crew. In a sense, the dream figures that populate each chapter are a synecdoche. The elderly woman who wishes to capture a bird and freeze time is representative of all elderly people, and also of old age in general. Each individual mentioned in the dream worlds becomes a stand-in for all of the people who are conceivably like them. Their individual experience of time is a synecdoche for all experiences of time.

HISTORICAL CONTEXT

Albert Einstein

Albert Einstein was born in Ulm, Germany, on March 14, 1879. His mother was Pauline (Koch) Einstein, and his father, Herman Einstein, was an engineer and salesman. The family, though Jewish, was not actively religious. In 1880, the family moved to Munich, and in 1881, Einstein's sister, Maja, was born. Einstein did not speak until the age of three, and his parents feared he was impaired in some way. At the behest of his mother, Einstein learned to play the violin at a young age. He did not enjoy doing so, however, until later in his life. Einstein was a poor student who disliked school, though he convinced a math teacher to write a recommendation for college, despite the fact that he left high school without graduating. The Einstein family moved to Milan in 1894, and Einstein left high school the following year to join them. Einstein then renounced his German citizenship in 1896, which meant that he would be exempt from compulsory military service. He was then nationless until he became a citizen of Switzerland in 1902. Einstein completed high school in Switzerland and entered the technical school in 1896. He did not do well there, and he barely graduated, taking a degree in teaching in 1900.

Unable to secure a teaching job, Einstein worked as a tutor and then at the Swiss Patent Office in Bern in 1902. Without having worked at the patent office, Einstein's life would have been very different, and it is unlikely that he would have written his theory of relativity. The patents Einstein worked with related to electro-magnetic inventions, and thus dealt with electric signals and electrical-mechanical interaction. These two issues led directly to Einstein's concepts of the way light travels and the relationship between time and space; the very foundations of his theory of relativity. In 1903, Einstein married Mileva Marič, but not before the two had an illegitimate daughter, Lieserl, in 1902. Lieserl's existence remained hidden until 1986, and what happened to her is not known. The couple then had their son Hans Albert in 1904. Their son Eduard was born in 1910. The marriage was an unhappy one, and after separating in 1914, the couple divorced in 1919. Later that year, Einstein married his cousin Elsa Löwenthal. Elsa had two daughters from a previous marriage, and she and Einstein did not have any children together.

In 1905, Einstein wrote three landmark papers that ultimately secured his place as a preeminent physicist. In 1908, he began working as an unpaid instructor at the University of Bern in Switzerland, and as a barely paid one at the University

COMPARE
&
CONTRAST

- **1905:** Einstein publishes his theory of relativity, one of the most groundbreaking physics concepts to date. The theory posits that objects moving at or around the speed of light will appear to move faster or slower relative to their distance from a viewer on earth. It remains one of the leading theories about time for decades to come.

  Today: The latest groundbreaking theory of time is string theory, a still-developing theory that posits that the building blocks of the universe form one-dimensional strings. The theory also posits that the universe is not three-dimensional but may instead contain up to eleven dimensions. Several scientists and physicists are credited with contributing to the theory, including Leonard Susskind and Michio Kaku.

- **1905:** The world is on the cusp of World War I, World War II, and the Holocaust. These events will result in Einstein's immigration to America and his inadvertent role in the creation of the atomic bomb.

  Today: Though the atomic bomb is used to end and prevent war, it is also used to incite war. The perceived threat of nuclear weapons in Iraq incites the Iraq War in 2003.

- **1905:** The intellectual questions of the day center around humanity and its place in the universe. It is commonly believed that all manner of technological progress is inherently good for humanity at large.

  Today: The intellectual questions of the day center around the impacts of globalization on humanity. The focus of technological development has shifted from progress for its own sake to progress that is environmentally sustainable.

---

of Zurich. Over time, Einstein gained recognition for his earlier achievements, and his career began to flourish; he won the Nobel Peace Prize in 1922. After having joined the Kaiser Wilhelm Institute for Physics in Berlin as director of scientific research in 1914, Einstein held the post until he left the country in 1933. Einstein was not only a Jew but also a pacifist, and the Nazi party indicated that Einstein's work did not serve their philosophies. Thus, when the opportunity presented itself, Einstein emigrated, taking a post at the Institute for Advanced Study in Princeton, New Jersey. He remained at the Institute until his death on April 18, 1955. While he was there, he convinced Franklin D. Roosevelt that the atomic bomb could become a reality, contributing to the founding of the Manhattan Project. The scientists working under the project were successful, developing the atom bomb that ultimately played a part in ending World War II. Given his pacifism, Einstein did not actually take part in the development of the bomb. He was naturalized as a U.S. citizen in 1940.

The Theory of Relativity

In 1905, Einstein wrote three landmark papers that secured his place as a preeminent physicist. The first one was on Brownian Motion (the random movement of particles suspended in gas or liquid, also called particle theory). The second was written using the then emerging field of quantum mechanics, and it explored the photoelectric effect (which is what happens when metals transmit electrons when they are under different kinds of light). The last of the three papers was the inception of what eventually came to be known as the theory of relativity. A translation of the title of this paper is "On the Electrodynamics of Moving Bodies," and it includes the world-famous equation $E = mc^2$. The equation means that energy (E) is equal to the mass of an object (m) multiplied by the speed

Albert Einstein (AP Images)

CRITICAL OVERVIEW

Both popular and critical reception of *Einstein's Dreams* was exceedingly warm. The book was on the *New York Times* bestseller list and was almost immediately translated into several foreign languages, becoming an international bestseller as well. Critics predominantly commented on the lyrical nature of the novel, as well as its creativity. For instance, *Hudson Review* critic Thomas Filbin calls the novel "a religious event of secular physics which couples mystical vision with the scientific fervor to explain." Overall, Filbin concludes that "this brief but relentlessly beautiful book ... is literature of realization and transcendence." Lightman "embodies the concept" of time "in brilliant, folkloric tales with extraordinary assurance," states *New Statesman & Society* writer Guy Mannes-Abbott. "Behind it is a formal intelligence and formidable capacity for magic, which he synthesises into prose like bottled air," adds Mannes-Abbott. Another laudatory assessment is proffered by an *Economist* reviewer, who calls the novel "a joy." Explaining this opinion, the reviewer notes that *Einstein's Dreams* "bridges disciplines by linking intellectual understanding with the kind of relaxing enjoyment to be expected from a good novel. The message is simple: like literature, science at its best must take great leaps of the imagination."

Aside from these approbations, some reviewers also commented that the novel stays true to many scientific principles. For instance, Bryce Milligan, writing in the *National Catholic Reporter*, observes that "this collection of speculative moments does, in several ways, reflect Einstein's actual process of inquiry." Additionally, Dennis Overbye, writing in the *New York Times Book Review*, observes that many of the dream worlds demonstrate various theories of time. For instance, he notes that "the fantasy of a world where time has three dimensions instead of one" is representative of "one view of quantum theory, known as the 'many worlds' interpretation." All in all, Overbye found that "Lightman spins these fantasies with spare poetic power, emotional intensity and ironic wit."

CRITICISM

Leah Tieger

Tieger is a freelance writer and editor. In the following essay, she examines the relationship between free will and destiny as it is portrayed in Einstein's Dreams.

of light squared (c^2). This paper set forth the special theory of relativity—"special" indicating that it was only applicable in some, not all, circumstances. It was not until 1916 that Einstein finalized the theory set forth in his third 1905 paper, now referring to it as the general theory of relativity because the revised version proved the equation to be true in more wide-ranging circumstances.

Notably, Einstein's special theory of relativity was not initially greeted with acclaim; it took several years for it to gain popularity. It was not until 1919 that concrete results proving Einstein's theory of relativity were obtained by the Royal Society. The discovery that the planet Mercury did travel in closer proximity to the Sun than Isaac Newton's theory of gravitation predicted, and that light from a star did bend when it came near a massive object such as the Sun, immediately validated Einstein's theory of relativity and brought him worldwide acclaim. Three years after these discoveries, Einstein received the Nobel Peace Prize. Two years later, more proof bolstering Einstein's theory was discovered; not only does light from a star bend when it comes near the Sun, it also lengthens.

WHAT DO I READ NEXT?

- Alan Lightman's *Good Benito* (1995) is also told in vignettes and is also about a physicist, albeit a fictional one. However, this novel focuses on characterization and the protagonist's familial and romantic relationships.

- *The House on Mango Street* (1983), by Sandra Cisneros, is one of the best-known and most-studied collections of vignettes. It is a coming-of-age novel about a Latino girl growing up in Chicago.

- The fifth edition of *Physics for Poets* (2003), by Richard H. March, is a classic layman's introduction to physics. The original edition was published in 1970.

- Walter Isaacson's *Einstein: His Life and Universe* was published in 2007. It is the only biography that addresses Einstein's correspondence.

Einstein's Dreams is a meditation on time, but above all else, it is a meditation on the human experience of time. Lightman shows that time in and of itself can only be comprehended in terms of being in time. The varied perceptions and experiences of the dream figures in each world give life to time in its many guises; however, an unintended consequence of this is the emerging question of free will and destiny as it relates to the experience of being in time. Over the course of the novel, the examples set by each law of time appear to prove that free will and destiny are inextricably entangled in the nature of time (or, at the very least, they are at the heart of the experience of time). Several of the dreams underscore this in interesting ways, especially the dreams of May 11, May 15, June 9, June 18, and June 22. These particular dreams indicate that free will and destiny are symbiotic; yet, where one holds a strong influence, the other is far weaker (and vice versa). Each, in fact, circumscribes the other.

In the dream of May 11, a world of "increasing order" is depicted. The paint on the buildings

> WITHOUT DEATH (THE ULTIMATE DESTINY) ACTING AS THE FOIL THAT SHAPES AND DEFINES LIFE, THE RESULTING PLETHORA OF FREE WILL IRONICALLY MEANS THAT NO ONE IS 'WHOLE' OR 'FREE.'"

does not peel and, instead, grows brighter. People lay in bed as their houses clean themselves. Gardens don't need to be maintained. Everything, it seems, pretty much takes care of itself. Because of this, philosophers believe "that without a trend toward order, time would lack meaning." This may be true of time in this world, but one could posit that just the opposite is true for the human beings in this world. What is the meaning of life in a world in which everything resolves itself to orderliness? How does one exercise free will in a world where even the leaves fall from trees in an orderly fashion? This trend toward order is an all-encompassing destiny in and of itself. Furthermore, it appears that people can only suffer under their tidy destinies for brief periods of time. In a world in which the equivalent of order is meaning, the people respond by causing disorder. They make a mess every year, breaking things and throwing away their watches and appointment books. They drink to excess. This goes on throughout spring and winds down as summer begins.

The May 15 dream is an anomaly, even in a book filled with anomalies. This is because the world portrayed in this dream, unlike all of the others, has "no time." Instead, it has only "images." These images appear to be frozen moments (even though a "moment" in a world without time is impossible). Nevertheless, the dream consists of a long list of images, mostly brief snapshots of people and nature. This world is nothing but individual tableaus of life. In a world such as this one, there can be no destiny and no free will. This is because neither can exist without time. The world explored in this dream further underscores that destiny and free will cannot exist outside of the experience of time.

In the June 9 dream world, destiny is eradicated by immortality, which leads to an abundance of free will. People react to this in one of two ways. "The Laters" believe they have all the time in the world to accomplish things, so they take their time doing everything. They wander about in cafés, have easy conversations, and read whatever is around to read. "The Nows," however, believe that they can experience everything, and they rush about attempting to do just that; learning new trades, and hurrying through conversations, always on to the next thing. Yet, humans aren't equipped to handle unmitigated free will, and thus it becomes diminished in startling ways. Since everyone's relatives are still alive, most people feel compelled to get advice from their infinite list of elders, and this means that "no one ever comes into his own." So much time is spent gathering advice that "life is tentative." Plans are started and abandoned halfway through. Without death (the ultimate destiny) acting as the foil that shapes and defines life, the resulting plethora of free will ironically means that no one is "whole" or "free." Some, then, feel that "the only way to live is to die." They commit suicide and by dying are finally "free of the weight of the past." This is how "the finite has conquered the infinite." And it is also how destiny has conquered unmitigated free will. The only true exercise of will in this world is suicide, creating a destiny where none existed before.

The world that is depicted in Einstein's June 18 dream seems to be indicating that measuring time diminishes free will and amplifies destiny. In this world, every person must make a pilgrimage at least once in their lives to the "Temple of Time" that houses the "Great Clock," paying homage to the clock by chanting off each minute for an hour. Before the clock was invented, people measured time by the stars, sun, and moon, by the seasons and the tides. It was measured "by heartbeats, the rhythms of drowsiness and sleep, the recurrence of hunger, the menstrual cycles of women, the duration of loneliness." In other words, the time before *time* was poetic and intuitive, closely related to the movements of the universe, of the body, and of the soul. This was once a world largely ruled by free will, so much so that it seemed as if time was directed by the natural world (and not vice versa). The invention of the clock thus inverted this state of affairs, and people were rightly "spellbound" and "horrified" by the device. Although all of the clocks (along with their inventor) were destroyed—save the one in the temple—every attempt to return to life as it once was has proved futile. Everything

the people do is forever changed by the knowledge that it is being measured. "Every action, no matter how little, is no longer free." The people "have been trapped by their own inventiveness and audacity. And they must pay with their lives." Thus, they have become slaves to destiny, to the measured inevitability of time passing.

Yet another fascinating take on the relationship between free will and destiny appears in the June 22 dream. In this world, there is no free will, only destiny. Boys graduate from school; parents gather to watch. No one is excited by the happy occasion. In a world where everything is preordained, what is there to be excited about? The people move through the graduation ceremony as if it does not matter. But of course, nothing matters in a world without free will. People in this world are nothing more than automatons; powerless "spectators" of their own lives. Time here is "rigid," the future will happen the way it has been planned to happen since the dawn of time. No one can do anything to change their future. A ballerina dances mechanically, for "there is no room to float" in a world with "no uncertainty." Yet, something truly remarkable occurs; a sense of free will (which may or may not be illusory) occurs when a man abdicates personal responsibility in the face of his own powerlessness. The man in question owes his friend money and decides to buy himself a coat instead of paying his friend back. He is not wrong for doing so because "in a world of fixed future, there can be no right or wrong." Moral distinctions such as these require "freedom of choice" (i.e., free will), which does not and cannot exist in a world where the future is preordained. Nevertheless, the man walks along in his new coat feeling "oddly free to do as he pleases, free in a world without freedom."

While several of the worlds explored in *Einstein's Dreams* subtly address the various correlations between free will and destiny, those explored in this essay do so in the most peculiar or extreme fashion. Some, like the June 22 dream, are even blatantly contradictory. It seems that the only consistency between these examples is the indirect correlation between free will and destiny. It appears that both can not exist without the experience of time, yet they exist in varying degrees of influence depending on the exact nature of the law of time in which they occur.

Source: Leah Tieger, Critical Essay on *Einstein's Dreams*, in *Novels for Students*, Gale, Cengage Learning, 2009.

> EINSTEIN IS A BIT PLAYER IN LIGHTMAN'S OPUS; HE AND HIS THEORY OF RELATIVITY ARE THE FRAME, AN EXCUSE TO FANTASIZE ABOUT TIME. BUT EINSTEIN WAS ALSO THE INSPIRATION FOR THE BOOK."

David Brittan

In the following essay, Brittan interprets Einstein's Dreams *as a work in which Lightman argues with himself.*

A physicist and a poet meet at a cafe on the Kramgasse in Bern, Switzerland, and contemplate the nature of time. "Time is unyielding, predetermined," says the physicist.

"Yet," the poet counters, "it squirms and wriggles like a bluefish in a bay."

"What if time passes more slowly for people in motion?" says the physicist. "To gain time, everyone must travel at high velocity."

"Or," says the poet, "suppose that time is not a quantity but a quality, like the luminescence of the night above the trees just when a rising moon has touched the treeline. It exists, but it cannot be measured."

As their musings grow wilder and wilder, it becomes apparent that the physicist and the poet are in fact the same person. They are Alan Lightman, arguing with himself.

Throughout his life, the Memphis-born physicist and poet has struggled to balance his two selves, going so far as to divide his time at MIT between teaching physics and running the Program in Writing and Humanistic Studies. *Einstein's Dreams*, his best-selling first novel, brings the two Alan Lightmans together for 30 meditations on time. The setting is Bern—where the young Einstein worked as a patent examiner—in the months leading to the completion of the special theory of relativity in 1905. Every few nights, Einstein dreams about time. In each dream, the citizens of Bern go about their lives as shopkeepers or lawyers, lovers or parents, sippers of coffee or writers of letters. Yet in each dream, they have had to accommodate some grave alteration in the way time works.

In a world where time passes slower the farther one gets from the center of the earth, people take to the high ground to preserve their youth. In a world without memory, notebooks are indispensable. Where time is a sense, like sight or taste, some see life whizzing by as in a Chaplin film, others feel it pass with the slow progress of clouds. Where time is a visible dimension, people have the option of sticking close to a comfortable moment or rushing blindly into the future.

One of the dreams hands Einstein the vision of time he will incorporate into his special theory, but it is camouflaged among the other visions, just as it is camouflaged in this review. "An insider joke in the book is that the true theory of relativity is at least as fanciful as all the other dreams," says Lightman in his office at MIT. "Twentieth-century physics has gone into such incredible realms that our new view of nature appears fantastic and unbelievable."

Through *Einstein's Dreams*, the human mind is revealed to be no less fantastic and unbelievable. At first glance, the dreams are bizarre distortions of time as we know it. But on closer inspection, they are time as we know it.

PATHOLOGIES OF TIME

Physicists see time as a straightforward affair—it flows in one direction, from past to future. "The second law of thermodynamics says that systems become more and more disordered in time," Lightman explains patiently. Why not the reverse? Probability, he says. Odds are great that a pendulum will gradually cease to swing as its energy is absorbed by the surrounding air molecules. Odds are slim that the air molecules will spontaneously organize themselves to nudge a still pendulum into motion. Time as nature offers it to us is simple.

But what physicists know—or think they know—about time is almost irrelevant to our actual experience of it. The past, even though in the physical sense it has vanished irretrievably, stays alive in our memories. The present, which has no special cosmological significance, is the conduit for our senses and the stage for our actions. The unknowable future is the foundation of all hope, will, and sense of progress. Time is life, as the saying goes.

Time is also the subject of endless refractions as it filters through the human mind. Here the straight line of the physicist can become a tangle of detours and U-turns that render past, present, and future indistinguishable. In this regard, *Einstein's Dreams* is a laboratory for studying pathologies of time. Its instruments are the metaphors and insights of the poet.

In a dream where "imagining the future is no more possible than seeing colors beyond violet," people are paralyzed. "They lie in their beds through the day, wide awake but afraid to put on their clothes. They drink coffee and look at photographs," Lightman writes, perfectly describing the narrowed horizons of the depressive. In fact, who hasn't been so overwhelmed buy the pressures of the moment that the future seems to evaporate?

An obsession with the future can be just as debilitating. In one dream, time is a river with back eddies that sometimes sweep people into the past. A woman displaced in this way crouches in the shadows at no. 19 Kramgasse, frozen at the thought of altering the future. She huddles in a corner, then quickly creeps across the street and cowers in another darkened spot, at no. 22. She is terrified that she will kick up dust, as a Peter Klausen is making his way to the apothecary on Spitalgasse this afternoon of 16 April 1905. Klausen is something of a dandy and hates to have his clothes sullied. If dust messes his clothes, he will stop and painstakingly brush them off, regardless of waiting appointments. If Klausen is sufficiently delayed, he may not buy the ointment for his wife, who has been complaining of leg aches for weeks. In that case, Klausen's wife, in a bad humor, may decide not to make the trip to Lake Geneva. And if she does not go to Lake Geneva on 23 June 1905, she will not meet a Catherine d'Epinay walking on the jetty of the east shore and will not introduce Mlle. d'Epinay to her son Richard. In turn, Richard and Catherine will not marry on 17 December 1908, will not give birth to Friedrich on 8 July 1912. Friedrich Klausen will not be father to Hans Klausen on 22 August 1938, and without Hans Klausen the European Union of 1979 will never occur.

This sort of precognition is not exactly universal, but the fear of setting off a chain of ever more significant events may well be. Lightman finds this fear dehumanizing: "If you feel you have to tiptoe around everywhere and not disturb anything, you can't participate in the world," he says.

The same holds true in a world where time is "sticky," trapping people in some moment of their live from which they can never free themselves. Here a man speaks only of his school days, years after his friends have moved on to successful careers. Another is doomed to relive a dinner long ago at which he failed to tell his father he loved him. Elsewhere, a woman gazes at an old photo of her son in the pink of his youth. She writes to him at a long-defunct address, imagines the happy letters back. When her son knocks at the door, she does not answer. When her son, with his puffy face and glassy eyes, calls up to her window for money, she does not hear him. When her son, with his stumbling walk, leaves notes for her, begging to see her, she throws out the notes unopened. When her son stands in the night outside her house, she goes to bed early. In the morning, she looks at his photograph, writes adoring letters to a long-defunct address. The tragedy of this existence, Lightman concludes, is that "each person who gets stuck in time gets stuck alone."

It would be easy to dismiss the inhabitants of Lightman's dreams with mutterings of "there but for the grace of God." But viewing these familiar neurotics as specimens under glass, we should not be surprised if we sometimes glimpse our own faces reflected back.

DECISIONS, DECISIONS

The dreams do more than just catalog our neuroses. They also underscore some fundamental conflicts in the human relationship to time: the unpredictability of people versus the predictability of time, the fluidity of minds and bodies versus the rigidity of clocks, and, above all, the agony of decisions. If time were three-dimensional—having a vertical, a horizontal, and a longitudinal direction like space—decisions would lose much of their momentousness. You could, like a character in one of the dreams, travel down each axis and see the consequences of a decision played out three different ways: a happy marriage, an unhappy marriage, a marriage to someone else. But because time is one-dimensional, giving us but a single shot, we are forever gauging the possible results of our actions.

Lightman hates this sort of predicament. "I don't like getting in situations where no matter what you do, you're trying to calculate its effect—how people will react, whether it will have a long-term payoff for you," he says. "Even though I myself have a lot of difficulty being spontaneous, I value it. And I value sincerity."

His answer to a world without spontaneity and sincerity is a world without cause and effect—where cause sometimes precedes effect but often succeeds it. In this world, the cosmos is irrational and scientists find themselves without meaningful employment. Yet clerks speak their minds to their bosses without fear of retribution, and people are loved for themselves rather than for the rewards they can bestow. Lightman writes: "It is a world in which every word spoken speaks just to that moment, every glance given has only one meaning, each touch has no past or no future, each kiss is a kiss of immediacy." If *Einstein's Dreams* has a single clear message—and Lightman swears it doesn't—then this is it: people are happiest living in the moment.

What does living in the moment have to do with Einstein? Nothing, and yet everything. Einstein is a bit player in Lightman's opus; he and his theory of relativity are the frame, an excuse to fantasize about time. But Einstein was also the inspiration for the book. "I was captivated," says Lightman, "by the idea of Einstein dreaming, which expresses a lot of the dialectic in the book: 'Einstein' on the one side—this rational being who deals quantitatively with the laws of nature—and then 'dreams' on the other side, which has an ambiguous, poetic, hazy feeling to it. The antithesis of these two ideas—these two words—seemed to spawn all sorts of rich possibilities."

Einstein and dreams. Physics and poetry. "The tide descended on me from I don't know where, though I was certainly thanking the muses when it came," says Lightman, perhaps unaware that it refers to himself.

Source: David Brittan, Review of *Einstein's Dreams*, in *Technology Review*, Vol. 96, No. 4, May–June 1993, p. 69.

SOURCES

"Alan Lightman," Web site of the MIT Program in Writing and Humanistic Studies, http://www.mit.edu/~humanistic/faculty/lightman.html (accessed June 27, 2008).

Falotico, Michael, "Albert Einstein and Olinto De Pretto," in *Italian American Web Site of New York*, http://www.italian-american.com/depretreview.htm (accessed June 27, 2008).

Filbin, Thomas, "Eurofiction, Interest Rates, and the Balance of Trade Problem," in the *Hudson Review*, Vol. 46, No. 3, Autumn 1993, pp. 587–92.

Lightman, Alan, *Einstein's Dreams*, Warner Books, 1994.

Mannes-Abbott, Guy, Review of *Einstein's Dreams*, in the *New Statesman & Society*, Vol. 6, No. 237, January 29, 1993, p. 46.

Milligan, Bryce, Review of *Einstein's Dreams*, in the *National Catholic Reporter*, Vol. 29, No. 30, May 28, 1993, p. 35.

Neffe, Jürgen, *Einstein: A Biography*, translated by Shelley Frisch, Farrar, Straus and Giroux, 2007.

Overbye, Dennis, "A Kiss Is Just a Kiss of Immediacy," in the *New York Times Book Review*, January 3, 1993.

Review of *Einstein's Dreams*, in the *Economist*, Vol. 326, No. 7794, January 16, 1993, p. 90.

FURTHER READING

Bodanis, David, $E=mc^2$: *A Biography of the World's Most Famous Equation*, Walker, 2000.
    This volume not only explains Einstein's theory of relativity to general readers, but also provides biographical details pertaining to Einstein at the time. Bodanis also discusses other theories from the lesser-known physicists who were Einstein's contemporaries.

Levi, Primo, *The Periodic Table*, translated by Raymond Rosenthal, Schocken Books, 1984.
    Like Lightman, Levi was both a writer and a scientist. His novel presents vignettes of a chemist's life, each based on elements from the periodic table.

Lightman, Alan, *A Sense of the Mysterious: Science and the Human Spirit*, Pantheon, 2005.
    This collection of essays is a meditation on various scientific concepts and their human aspects. It sheds light on the underlying themes of Lightman's fiction.

Popovič, Milan, ed., *In Albert's Shadow: The Life and Letters of Mileva Marić, Einstein's First Wife*, Johns Hopkins University Press, 2003.
    This collection of letters by Mileva Marić provides insight into Einstein's first marriage, as well as the time period referenced in *Einstein's Dreams*.

Eva Luna

ISABEL ALLENDE
1985

Eva Luna, the third novel by the Chilean author Isabel Allende, was first published in Spanish in 1985. An English translation was published in the United States in 1988. The story is narrated by the title character, who first tells the tale of Consuelo, her mother, and then proceeds through the rest of her own adventurous and sometimes bizarre life. The novel has a mythic, fairy-tale quality, though much of it is set against a backdrop of political unrest and violence that closely resembles the realities of several South American nations.

On the page before the story begins, Allende includes this quote from *A Thousand and One Tales of the Arabian Nights* (a classic collection of Arabian folktales written over several centuries): "Then he said to Scheherazade: 'Sister, for the sake of Allah, tell us a story that will help pass the night....'" Like Scheherazade, Eva Luna uses her storytelling ability to help her survive a succession of hardships, and she eventually makes her living as a writer. The transformative power of words and stories is one of the major themes of the novel. Allende also explores themes such as women's rights and the abuse of power.

Readers should be advised that some scenes in *Eva Luna* are sexual in nature, and there are references to violence in both the story of the South American guerrilla fighters and the story of Lukas Carlé, the abusive father of Rolf Carlé.

Isabel Allende (*AP Images*)

In the end, however, *Eva Luna* is an uplifting tale that celebrates the redemptive powers of both love and the imagination.

AUTHOR BIOGRAPHY

Isabel Allende was born on August 2, 1942, in Lima, Peru. Her father and mother were Chilean; her father, Tomás Allende, was a diplomat and first cousin of Salvador Allende, the president of Chile from 1970 to 1973. When Isabel was two years old, her parents divorced. Isabel's mother, Francisca, took her to live with her grandparents in Chile.

After several years in Chile, Allende's mother remarried another diplomat, who took Allende and her two brothers abroad. During these years Allende lived in Bolivia, the Middle East, and various cities in Europe. In 1957 the family was living in Lebanon; political unrest and violence in the country prompted Allende's parents to send her back to Chile to finish her high school education at a private school. She finished at sixteen, and three years later, in 1962, married her first husband, Miguel Frías. During this time she worked as a secretary for the United

Nations' Food and Agriculture Organization, until 1965. Interested in work as a journalist, she then took a job with a radical feminist magazine titled *Paula*, working for several years as a reporter, editor, and advice columnist. She also edited a children's magazine and worked as an interviewer on a weekly television show.

Allende's life changed dramatically in 1973 when President Salvador Allende was assassinated in a military coup that installed General Augusto Pinochet Ugarte as Chile's new leader. Appalled by the oppression and violence supported by this new regime, Allende did her best to help, aiding many to escape military persecution, even driving some to safety in her own car. Soon, however, her family was warned that their close family connections to Salvador Allende put all of their lives at risk, and in 1975 Isabel Allende and several of her relatives fled to Venezuela (a democratic country).

Despite her wealth of experience, Allende was unable to find work as a journalist in Venezuela, and so she worked instead as a teacher. By this time Allende and her husband had two children, Paula and Nicolás. (The couple separated in 1978.) After several years' hiatus from writing, Allende began writing long letters to her dying grandfather in Chile, letters that eventually became the basis for her first novel, *The House of the Spirits* (published first in Spanish as *La casa de los espiritus* in 1982). Though Chile is not named as the setting of the novel, the similarity between political events in the book and those in Chile's recent history resulted in the book being banned in Chile (though many copies were smuggled in). *The House of the Spirits* became a bestseller in Europe, was eventually translated into fifteen languages, and was nominated for the Quality Paperback Book Club New Voice Award in 1986.

Allende's second novel, *De amor y de sombra*, published in Spanish in 1984 and later released in English as *Of Love and Shadows*, tells the story of a woman journalist investigating the political murder of a girl whose body is found in an abandoned mine. This novel was nominated for the Los Angeles Times Book Prize in 1987.

Eva Luna, Allende's third novel, was published in Spanish in 1985 and in English translation in 1988. It follows the title character through both personal and political adventures in an unnamed South American country. Eva

Luna's abilities as a storyteller help her survive heartbreak and tragedy until she is united at the end with her soul mate, Rolf Carlé, the son of an abusive Austrian Nazi. In 1990, Allende followed the novel with a book of short stories titled *The Stories of Eva Luna*, in which Eva tells a series of tales to her lover, Rolf Carlé. She wrote the collection shortly after marrying her second husband, the attorney William Gordon, and settling in San Francisco.

The Eva Luna books were followed by, among other works, the novels *The Infinite Plan* (1991), *Daughter of Fortune* (1999), *Portrait in Sepia* (2000), *My Invented Country* (2003), *Zorro* (2005), and *Inés of My Soul* (2006) and the memoir *The Sum of Our Days* (2007). She has also written several young-adult novels and a memoir of her twenty-nine-year-old daughter's illness and death, titled *Paula*. As of 2008, Allende was living in California with her husband, William Gordon, and continuing to write.

PLOT SUMMARY

Chapter 1

The novel opens with Eva Luna introducing herself and then narrating the story of her mother's childhood. Missionaries in a jungle region take in an abandoned baby and name her Consuelo. They raise her until she is twelve and then send her to a convent. After she spends three years there, the Mother Superior finds Consuelo a job as the servant of a professor who has invented a new method for preserving dead bodies. Though eccentric and bad-tempered, Professor Jones is not unkind or abusive, and Consuelo is content living in his estate with the other servants.

Many years pass. One day a poisonous snake bites the estate's gardener, a Native American man whom Consuelo finds attractive. Consuelo nurses the gardener in his sickness, and they fall in love. Their love has a miraculous effect on the gardener, who recovers completely. Once he is well, he tells Consuelo good-bye, unaware that she is pregnant. Consuelo has the baby by herself and names her Eva, which means life, and Luna, for the Indian tribe the gardener belongs to. The household cook volunteers to be Eva's godmother, or *madrina*.

Eva spends her early years in the professor's mansion, helping her mother with her daily

MEDIA ADAPTATIONS

- While no audiobook version of *Eva Luna* was available as of 2008, the story collection *The Stories of Eva Luna* is available at http://www.audible.com as a purchasable audio download.

chores. When she and her mother are alone, her mother tells Eva tale after tale, sharing her gift for storytelling. She teaches Eva that when reality is difficult, "it is legitimate to enhance it and color it to make our journey through life less trying."

Chapter 2

In this chapter, Eva narrates the childhood of Rolf Carlé, an Austrian boy whose family is headed by a tyrannical, abusive father. Rolf is just a baby when his father joins the army to fight in World War II, allowing him to grow up without the abuse his older siblings had to endure.

When Rolf is ten years old, Russian soldiers order all the residents of his village to come to a nearby prison camp to help bury the dead. A week later, Rolf's father returns from the war and resumes his job as a schoolmaster at the village school. One night Rolf and his brother suspect that their father is abusing their mother; Jochen bursts into his parents' bedroom and hits his father hard enough to break his jaw. Before his father can regain consciousness, Jochen bids his mother farewell and leaves the house forever.

Chapter 3

In chapter 3, Eva tells the story of her mother's death. Consuelo unknowingly swallows a chicken bone at Christmas dinner and later begins bleeding internally. Three days later, realizing that she is dying, she calls in Eva's godmother and tells her to care for Eva; then, with Eva by her bedside, she passes away.

Eva remains at the professor's estate, now under the care of her madrina, the cook. The cook is a robust mulatto Catholic woman with precise ideas of good and evil, though her ideas are eccentric, due in part to her drinking large quantities of rum.

Not long after the death of Eva's mother, the professor dies as well, and Eva's madrina tells her that she must make her own living now. So at seven years of age, she becomes a servant in the household of an elderly woman.

Eva is unhappy about leaving the professor's mansion for this new household, but fortunately she is befriended by Elvira, the cook. Elvira makes sure Eva is well fed, tells her stories, and gives her money to buy candy when they go to the market. Like Eva's madrina, Elvira has her quirks; for instance, in her bedroom she keeps a wooden coffin that she bought for herself, fearing that if she died a pauper she would be buried in a common grave.

One day Eva has a fight with her strict, unforgiving employer and runs away into the city. When she stops to rest in a plaza, she meets a boy named Huberto Naranjo, who lives on the streets and survives as a con artist and pickpocket. Eva stays with Huberto for three days, and then, becoming homesick, she asks him to help her find her godmother. When they find her, she abuses Eva for running away and takes her back to her job.

Eva resumes her relationship with Elvira, whom she calls *abuela*, or grandmother. Eva works for the elderly woman for several years, during which time the country has "a brief interval of republican freedom," as followed by yet another dictatorship. Eva thinks often of Huberto Naranjo and their time together, which was so much more exciting than her life as a servant. She consoles herself by listening to soap operas on the radio and casting Huberto as the hero of her fantasies.

Chapter 4

In this chapter, it is revealed that five students killed Lukas Carlé, Rolf's father, in the forest. Rolf's mother sends Rolf to South America to stay with her cousin. The cousin and his wife, whom Rolf calls Uncle Rupert and Aunt Burgel, run an inn in La Colonia, a town which looks like a European village. While living in La Colonia, Rolf meets Señor Aravena, the inn's best client, a famous and highly respected newspaperman. Aravena teaches Rolf to use a camera and encourages him to see more of the world. Rolf

tells his aunt and uncle that he is leaving La Colonia to study cinematography at the university in the city.

Chapter 5

Chapter 5 resumes Eva's story. Eva's madrina begins going mad after she gives birth to a deformed stillborn baby. She drinks even more heavily than before and pesters Eva's employer for loans and higher wages for Eva (as she has been collecting Eva's pay for years, as her guardian). Finally, Eva's employer loses patience with the whole situation and fires Eva.

Now Eva moves from employer to employer, wherever her madrina finds her work. One of her many employers teaches her to make a substance dubbed Universal Matter, which can be molded and painted to resemble almost anything. Another is a cabinet minister who insists on using an old-fashioned chamber pot instead of a toilet. Unable to find Elvira, and afraid of her mad godmother, Eva eventually goes into the city to look for Huberto Naranjo. When she finds him, he welcomes her warmly and takes her to meet a madam called La Señora. La Señora, a cheerful and flamboyant woman, takes her to a hairdresser and then shopping for clothes. When they return home, Eva meets La Señora's best friend, Melesio, a softhearted schoolteacher who insists that he is not homosexual but a woman trapped in a man's body. Eva and Melesio become fast friends.

Eva's happy time with La Señora comes to an end when a new police sergeant is assigned to the red-light district. Late one night, El Negro, a local bar owner and friend of Huberto, knocks on La Señora's door to warn her that the sergeant is doing a house-by-house search and has arrested Melesio in the cabaret where he performs. Eva flees with La Señora through an underground parking garage, but when La Señora realizes Eva has come with her, she tells her to go away.

After this incident, Eva lives on the streets for days. One evening a kindly Turkish man with a cleft lip buys her some food. After learning that Eva has no home or family, he takes her home with him to be a companion for his wife. The man's name is Riad Halabí.

Chapter 6

Riad Halabí had come to South America at fifteen to seek his fortune and send money back to his family in the East. He settled down in the small town of Agua Santa and built a home and a shop, which became the center of commerce in the village. Then he wrote to his mother and asked her to find him a bride. Riad's mother arranged a match with Zulema, a beautiful twenty-five-year-old. They married, but Zulema found Riad's cleft lip repulsive and was disappointed to find that he was not rich. Even after many years of marriage, Zulema remained disappointed and miserable in Agua Santa, spending most of her time lying in bed eating.

To this household Riad brings Eva Luna, who entertains Zulema with stories as she lies in bed. Riad arranges for Eva to have private reading and writing lessons with a schoolteacher named Inés. Compassionate and generous, Riad becomes like a father to Eva. Eva works in his store and does the housework; Zulema, utterly self-absorbed, has no interest in either of the two.

After Eva has lived with Riad and Zulema for about a year and a half, Riad's twenty-five-year-old cousin Kamal comes to stay with them. When Riad Halabí goes away on business, Zulema and Kamal have an affair. Afterward, Kamal packs his suitcase and leaves. Zulema, despondent, takes to her bed, losing interest in life.

Chapter 7

Rolf Carlé now works as a television reporter for Señor Aravena. After an obviously fraudulent popular election in which the current leader is reelected, the people begin to revolt. When the government is overthrown, Rolf makes a name for himself as a reporter, recording the events with his camera.

A new government is formed, but in a few short years, there is already discontent among students at the university, who feel betrayed by the new president. The Cuban Revolution gives them new hope, and the guerrilla movement is born. Rolf asks Aravena to let him cover the movement for television.

Huberto Naranjo, the leader of a feared gang in the city, first hears of the guerrilla movement when his friend El Negro invites him to a secret meeting. Identifying deeply with their cause, Huberto joins them. He becomes one of the most respected guerrilla fighters in the movement.

Chapter 8

Meanwhile in Agua Santa, two years have passed since Kamal's departure, and Zulema still keeps to her bed like an invalid. Eva continues to study with the schoolteacher and spends so much time writing stories that her characters seem more real to her than does reality.

One weekend Riad Halabí goes on a business trip and leaves Eva to watch over Zulema. On Saturday morning, Eva finds that Zulema has committed suicide. The police come to the house and take Eva to jail, where she is beaten. Word of what has happened reaches Riad in the city, and he immediately returns. He arrives at the police station and demands that Eva be released; when they refuse, he offers them a bribe, and they relinquish her. Once safe at home with Riad, Eva is finally able to speak, and she tells him the story of what has happened. Riad comforts her, and together he and the schoolteacher Inés treat her bruises and injuries.

Three months later, rumors have begun to spread about Riad and Eva (now seventeen) living alone together in his house. In addition, the police lieutenant threatens to reopen the investigation if Riad does not pay him more money. Riad decides that it is best for Eva to go away and have a chance at a new life. Eva realizes that she loves Riad, and she begs him to let her stay. Riad insists that she go, giving her money and an address for a good boardinghouse. She throws the address away, determined to make her own way.

She arrives at the capital in the midst of another coup d'état; with the sound of gunshots in the distance, she manages to find a hotel. One day, while looking for work, she is caught in a street riot and ducks into a church for safety. There she sees a beautiful woman in a nearby pew who recognizes her; it is Melesio, who is now living as a woman, Mimí. After being arrested in the police lieutenant's raid, Melesio was taken to the brutal penal colony at Santa Maria. He stayed there for a year, until La Señora managed to get him out through a combination of bribes and blackmail.

Delighted to see her, Mimí asks Eva to come live with her. Eva does and stays there for years, throughout Mimí's many stormy relationships with men. Mimí is always searching for love, though neither she nor Eva have much luck at this time in their lives.

Chapter 9

One day Eva, now in her twenties, runs into Huberto Naranjo in the city. In seconds she falls in love with him all over again, just as she did when she was a girl. After a short time together, Huberto disappears; unaware of his activities as a guerrilla fighter, Eva wonders what has become of him. He returns again and again, always disappearing afterward. Often when he returns he has new scars or fresh wounds. Eva begins to suspect the truth about Huberto.

During this time Eva and Mimí are living in luxury, thanks to Mimí's success as an actress. She appears on stage and in television shows and is approached on the street for autographs. Mimí disapproves of Eva's relationship with Huberto and suspects that he is a smuggler or drug dealer. Eva's suspicions, however, are confirmed when he admits to Eva that he is part of the guerrilla movement. Eva wants to be a part of it, but Huberto insists, "This is a man's war." Eva realizes that even if the revolution is successful, Huberto will never see her as an equal.

Chapter 10

As the chapter begins, guerrilla activities are escalating, and Señor Aravena wants more information on the men in the mountains. He asks Rolf Carlé to try to re-establish contact with Huberto Naranjo, whom he had met the first time he reported on the guerrillas. Through Huberto's friend El Negro, Rolf contacts him, and the guerrillas agree to let Rolf film their activities. Rolf lives with them for months. He is impressed with Huberto, who commands the respect and admiration of his men, endures hardships without complaint, and is a courageous leader. Knowing they can never show the guerrilla footage without endangering the lives of the fighters, Rolf puts the film in a locked suitcase and has his Uncle Rupert hide it at his inn.

During this time, Eva works at a factory that manufactures equipment for the military. The factory is regularly inspected by Colonel Tolomeo Rodriguez; he notices Eva, and he invites her to dinner. At dinner, Eva tells the colonel that she is not interested in a romance with him, though she finds him a pleasant companion. Determined, the colonel vows to pursue Eva.

Wanting to avoid the colonel, Eva quits her job at the factory, and Mimí buys her a typewriter so that she can dedicate herself full-time to her writing. She begins writing a script for a telenovela, the kind of televised melodrama that Mimí often stars in. She writes almost continuously for three weeks, weaving in characters from her own life. Mimí takes the script to Aravena, now the director of national television, who is inattentive and says that he will read the script later. Mimí turns on the charm and invites him to a dinner party at their home.

When Aravena comes to the party he brings along Rolf Carlé. After dinner, Mimí asks Eva to tell a story, and she spins a tale about a pair of Australian lovers. Rolf compliments her on the story, and they talk together for hours. The next week Aravena calls Eva to his office to sign a contract for the script, partly because he finds it intriguing and partly because he is smitten with Mimí.

Shortly after, days and days of rain cause massive flooding in the country. While watching the news on television, Eva hears of a woman found safely floating in a wooden coffin; it is Elvira. Eva immediately races to the shelter for the flood victims, finds Elvira, and brings her home to live with her and Mimí.

After returning home from an assignment, Rolf takes Eva to the seaside for the day, and they exchange life stories. It is the first time Rolf has told anyone about his abusive father and the way he died.

Chapter 11

El Negro comes to see Eva, and he takes her to see Huberto in the city. Huberto tells her that the guerrillas are planning to break several of their comrades out of the penal colony at Santa Maria; their plan is to steal government uniforms from the factory where Eva works, to disguise themselves as prison guards. Eva tells him that she has quit her job, but she tries to draw the guerrillas a layout of the factory. Mimí is outraged that she is getting involved in the plan, but for Eva's sake, she comes to meet Huberto. Mimí draws Huberto a map of Santa Maria, a place she remembers all too well.

Huberto enlists the help of a tribe of Native Americans who live near the prison. The plan is that the prisoners will be rescued from the prison yard, but the problem lies in how to get the prisoners out of the cells and into the yard. Then Eva remembers the Universal Matter that one of her employers taught her to make, and she devises a plan.

El Negro drives Eva to the town of Agua Santa, which is close to Santa Maria. Eva cannot resist stopping at Riad Halabí's shop. He does not recognize her, and she does not reveal her identity. She discovers that he has married a teenage girl, who is helping him in the shop.

El Negro takes Eva to the tribe's camp, where they will stay during the attempted rescue of the guerrillas. Huberto's men arrive one by one, and then to Eva's surprise, Rolf arrives in a jeep with his camera. He is just as surprised to see Eva, because Eva never told him of her relationship with Huberto. Rolf tells her that Huberto asked him to come film the operation.

Now Eva carries out her part of the plan: she prepares a large batch of Universal Matter, dyed to exactly match the color of a hand grenade. The dough will be sent to the prisoners, who have already been sent instructions for making fake grenades, which they will use to force the prison guards to release them from their cells.

The night before the operation, neither Eva nor Rolf can sleep. They sit together by the fire all night, quiet. The next morning, Eva says goodbye to Huberto and Rolf and takes the bus back to her home. Two days later, Rolf arrives at Eva and Mimí's home with good news: the operation was successful. Rolf tells Eva that he wants her to come away with him for a while, in case someone in Agua Santa might have seen her and recognized her as the girl who used to live with Riad Halabí. He takes her to La Colonia to stay with his Aunt Burgel and Uncle Rupert.

The news of the rescue is told, but the real truth of it is censored. Rolf wants the real story of the guerrillas' struggle and the rescue at Santa Maria to be revealed, so he comes up with a plan: Eva will write the story into her telenovela, and they will use some of the real guerrilla footage that Rolf has hidden away. So Eva weaves fact and fiction together to tell the story of Huberto and the guerrillas. Not long after, she is summoned to the Ministry of Defense, where she is brought to the office of General Tolomeo Rodriguez, who is now commander in chief of the armed forces. He has read the entire script of her telenovela and has just one request: that she remove the part in the story about the fake grenades, because it makes the officers look ridiculous and also is "unrealistic."

The general then tells Eva that the guerrillas have been defeated and that the president will offer amnesty to those who agree to lay down their weapons and live peacefully. He knows about Eva and Huberto's friendship and asks Eva to persuade Huberto to accept amnesty; if Huberto does, his comrades will follow his lead. Eva refuses to lead Huberto into a trap, but Rodriguez convinces her of his sincerity.

Rolf leaves La Colonia for a few days to cover the public reaction to the escape from Santa Maria; Eva stays behind at the inn. When he returns, he finally confesses his love for Eva, which is requited, and the couple then announce the happy news to the rest of the family. Eva and Rolf Carlé live happily ever after— or not; the reader is left unsure whether Eva's rosy picture is reality or simply the result of her penchant for painting a more pleasant picture of life with her gift for storytelling.

CHARACTERS

Señor Aravena

Aravena is a famous and highly respected newsman who guides Rolf Carlé into his career as a reporter and filmmaker. He is honest, shrewd, and hedonistic, with a big appetite for the pleasures of life. Aravena's reputation as a newsman is so well known that even the corrupt government hesitates to censor his stories too heavily. His years of reporting have honed his instincts in political matters, and his predictions are usually accurate regarding government decisions and the public's reactions.

Aunt Burgel

Burgel is the first woman in Rolf's life to show him unabashed, unrestrained affection; his own mother was shy and feared the reaction of Rolf's father, who felt that too much affection would make his son "soft." She is also a prolific cook, constantly churning out baked goods and her own secret stew. Through her love, humor, and cooking, she helps nurture Rolf back to health both physically and emotionally.

Cabinet Minister

The last in the long line of Eva's employers, the vulgar cabinet minister achieved his high position mainly by fawning over others in power. He spends many hours seated on a plush armchair with a hole in the seat, so that he may relieve himself into a basin beneath; it is Eva's unenviable job to empty the basin.

Frau Carlé

Rolf Carlé's mother is a quiet woman who despises her husband, a man who takes every opportunity to humiliate her. Still, she is able to maintain her faith in God and an inner reserve of strength until her husband returns from serving his sentence at a labor camp (having been convicted of desertion); she then loses faith, unable to believe in a God who would allow Lukas Carlé to return despite all her prayers to the contrary. She loves her children but feels helpless to protect them from their father. Still, Rolf discovers that she has not been completely resigned to her fate; when Lukas is murdered by his own students, she tells Rolf, "I am grateful they did it, because if they hadn't, we would have had to do it ourselves one day."

Jochen Carlé

Rolf's older brother, Jochen is not as bright as Rolf but is enormously strong, loyal, and protective of his mother and siblings. His father views him as a complete disappointment. Jochen leaves home after knocking his father unconscious with a single punch in protecting his mother.

Katharina Carlé

Katharina, Rolf's older sister, was born with a heart defect and is also mentally disabled. Whenever Lukas Carlé is in the house, she hides under the kitchen table, behind the tablecloth; Rolf often keeps her company, even sleeping under the table with her. Katharina is not expected to live a very long life, due to her heart defect.

Lukas Carlé

Lukas Carlé is the abusive, tyrannical father of Rolf Carlé. As a schoolteacher, he once broke a boy's hands when disciplining him with a ruler. Lukas Carlé harbors no affection for his wife; he considers her "an inferior being, closer to animal than to man, God's only intelligent creation." A violent man, he dies a violent death, murdered by his own students.

Rolf Carlé

Rolf's life is a study in contradictions: he has a loving mother but a cold, abusive father, and he experiences childhood in Austria before coming of age in South America. His personality reflects these contradictions: "He prided himself on his coldness and pragmatism . . . but in truth he was an incorrigible dreamer. . . . He denied his emotions, but at any unguarded moment was demolished by them." His strong sense of truth and justice makes him an indefatigable reporter, while observing events through the lens of his camera allows him to maintain an emotional distance from the tragedies he sees.

Consuelo

Eva gets her storytelling gift from Consuelo, her mother. The identity of Consuelo's parents is a mystery; as a baby, alone and covered with mud, she was discovered by missionaries and taken in. She later tells Eva that she was set adrift in a rowboat by a Dutch sailor, a romantic invention to stop Eva's many questions. There are many parallels between Eva and her mother; for instance, as an adolescent, Consuelo spent hours in the convent chapel, daydreaming and inventing stories in her mind; later Eva does the same thing, staring at the seascape in her elderly *patrona's* (employer's) dining room.

Consuelo's most important lesson for Eva is that when life becomes too hard, she can transform her experience through her imagination, to make it more pleasant. This lesson leaves the reader in some doubt as to how much of Eva's life story is true and how much is just a product of her fondness for weaving a colorful tale.

The Daughters

Uncle Rupert and Aunt Burgel have two cheerful, rosy-cheeked, blue-eyed daughters, who always smell of spice and vanilla due to their many hours in the kitchen with their mother. Both girls have romantic feelings for Rolf.

Elvira

With Eva's mother gone and her godmother mentally unstable, Elvira becomes the guiding force in Eva's life. Eva meets Elvira when she comes to work in the house of an elderly woman and her bachelor brother; Elvira is the household cook. Eva becomes so attached to Elvira that she calls her abuela, or grandmother. Elvira makes sure Eva eats well, does the harsher household chores for her, plays with her, and comforts her when she is the object of the patrona's wrath. After Eva attacks her employer and rips off her wig (with Eva, unaccustomed to wigs, thinking she has scalped the woman), Eva's godmother gives her a beating, but Elvira approves of the feat; she tells Eva, "You have to fight back. No one tries anything with mad dogs, but tame dogs they kick. Life's a dogfight." Eva calls this "the best advice I ever received."

Eva's Godmother
See Madrina

The Gardener
Professor Jones's gardener, a Native American man from the Luna tribe, is Eva's biological father, though she never meets him. When Eva's godmother insists that Eva should have a last name, Consuelo chooses Luna in honor of the gardener's tribe.

Riad Halabí
Riad Halabí is a kind, compassionate Turkish man who takes Eva, who is living on the streets, home to live with him and his wife. Riad has a cleft lip that he keeps covered with a handkerchief, not so much because he is ashamed but out of concern that he might make others uncomfortable. He is much admired and beloved in the town of Agua Santa, by everyone except his own wife, who is repulsed by his deformity and disappointed that he is not rich. His shop is both the center of commerce and a social meeting place for the small village. Riad is a quiet man but is not afraid to take charge in a crisis or stand up for his beliefs. He becomes like a father to Eva, and gives her the greatest gift of her life: reading and writing.

Eva becomes both a daughter and a sort of substitute wife to Riad, as she does the housework, irons his shirts, helps in the store, accompanies Riad to the movies, and discusses the news, eats meals, and plays games with him. Because of his upbringing, Riad does not speak of his feelings, though he is deeply wounded by Zulema's rejection of him and is starved for love and affection. His tendency to put all others' needs ahead of his own allows him to ignore the failure of his marriage.

Inés
Inés is the schoolteacher who teaches Eva to read and write, at Riad Halabí's request. On the day that Riad first came to Agua Santa, Inés's son was killed for trespassing on a wealthy outsider's property to pick a mango. Riad takes charge and arranges the wake and burial of the son. After leaving Agua Santa, Eva imagines that Riad and Inés will someday marry.

Professor Jones
Consuelo's first and only employer, Professor Jones is a scientist who has invented a system for preserving the dead. Eva grows up in the professor's house, and because he has no interest in national or world events, she and the other occupants are mainly ignorant of the political unrest of the times. Professor Jones is from Europe and is "as handsome as a picture of Jesus, all gold, with the same blond beard as the Prince of Peace, and eyes of an impossible color." Obsessed by his work, the professor has concern for little else. When government officials order the burial of his most famous preserved cadaver, he has a stroke; when the gardener is bit by a snake, Professor Jones's reaction to the news is, "As soon as he dies, bring him to me." When the professor is dying, however, Eva cares for him, and during his last days, he becomes very fond of her and asks that all his property be willed to her. This request is ignored by the local minister, who disposes of all his assets after his death.

Kamal
Kamal is Riad Halabí's cousin, who comes to live with Riad about a year and a half after Eva does. Though Kamal is of slight build, with delicate features, he has a way with women; according to Eva, "the whole street felt his magnetism; he enveloped everyone in a kind of spell." Fifteen-year-old Eva falls desperately in love with Kamal, but he ignores her.

Eva Luna
Eva Luna is the central character and narrator of the novel. Eva uses her imagination as a way to cope with the many hardships she has to face; following her mother's advice, she uses storytelling to put a more positive spin on her life's events. Thanks to the love of her mother, Eva has an innate sense of her own worth as a human being; the mistreatment she receives at the hands of her godmother, her employers, and the police in Agua Santa only serve to make her more determined to triumph and live life on her own terms. Eva also has a generous and compassionate nature and so often makes excuses for the bad behavior of the people she loves. For instance, her godmother sometimes hits her, but Eva excuses her: "That was the only way she knew, because that was how she had learned." Later she spends hours at Zulema's bedside, devotedly caring for her, even though the cause of her

ailment is lovesickness for Kamal, with whom she has had an adulterous affair. When Zulema speaks to Eva, it is usually to scold her or order her around, yet Eva says, "In her own way Zulema was good to me; she treated me like a lapdog." By taking such a compassionate, optimistic view of the people in her life, she paints a world in which she is surrounded by those who care for her, and in the end, this vision becomes truth.

Eva grows up without much formal religion; her godmother's understanding of Catholicism is so eccentric, and Eva's limited exposure to the church is such a negative experience, that Eva goes through life with her own personal moral code rather than one dictated to her. She does heed the teachings of the kindly Elvira, who encourages her to fight back when oppressed. Eva's life experiences are so varied and peculiar that her personal code is truly unique, a patchwork of philosophies taken from different religions, countries, and ideologies.

Madrina

Eva's godmother, or madrina, takes care of Eva after her mother dies. In agreeing to be Eva's godmother, she believes she has a sacred obligation, saying that "anyone who neglects a godchild is damned to hell." Vast quantities of rum, and perhaps a lack of education, make her practice of Catholicism eccentric at best. She prays to a variety of saints, including one that she petitions for relief from hangovers, and believes that they can contact her via the telephone. Her devotion to religion does not prevent her from drinking heavily or treating Eva harshly; Eva's godmother sees religion as a series of black-and-white punishments and rewards. Her inability to live up to the standards of her religion hastens her descent into madness (as does her rum intake).

Melesio

Eva first meets Melesio, a man who says he is a woman trapped in a man's body, when she comes to live with La Señora, Melesio's best friend. Melesio teaches Italian by day and performs as a woman in a cabaret at night. Eventually he decides to become Mimí, his cabaret alter ego, permanently. He becomes a strikingly beautiful woman who is devoted to the teachings of her spiritual guide, the maharishi, and also seeks guidance from astrology and tarot cards. Mimí is on a quest for her romantic soul mate,

but finding a man who is open minded enough to love her for who she is proves difficult.

Mimí

See Melesio

Huberto Naranjo

Huberto, Eva's first love, grows up on the streets of the capital city, surviving on his wits. Later, as a teenager, he becomes the leader of a feared gang, originally formed for the purpose of opposing a gang of privileged youths from wealthy neighborhoods who entertain themselves by tormenting others. After this he joins the guerrilla movement. In short, Huberto has spent his whole life as an underdog, fighting despite the odds against him. With the guerrillas, he discovers the satisfaction of fighting for a cause greater than his own survival. Though he loves Eva, the guerrilla cause is his true devotion. His tough-guy, macho persona is so ingrained that he is unable to see women as equals in this fight, a failing which, in the end, dooms his relationship with Eva.

El Negro

El Negro is Huberto Naranjo's mixed-race friend who works at a bar in the city. Throughout the story, El Negro always knows where Huberto can be found, even when he is in the mountains with the guerrilla fighters. El Negro first introduces Huberto to the guerrilla movement by taking him to a secret meeting.

The Patron

Eva's first pair of employers are an elderly woman, the patrona, and her bachelor brother, the patron. Eva's patron is a hedonistic man with little ambition who spends most of his time and money at the racetrack. He drinks too much and is irresponsible but is much kinder to Eva than is his sister, who runs the household.

The Patrona

Eva's patrona is a strict, unforgiving, and humorless woman who spends most of her time shouting at the household servants. After Eva attacks her and tears off her wig, however, she backs off; she fears Eva's defiance and self-confidence.

Colonel Tolomeo Rodriguez

Colonel Rodriguez (who by the end of the book becomes General Rodriguez) is an anomaly in *Eva Luna*: an honorable government official. He pursues Eva, but when she refuses him, he honors her refusal. When he tells Eva that he will offer Huberto amnesty for his guerrilla activities, Eva believes his sincerity.

Comandante Rogelio
See Huberto Naranjo

Uncle Rupert
Uncle Rupert, the cousin of Rolf Carlé's mother, takes in Rolf after Lukas Carlé's death. A good-natured, robust, overweight Austrian, Rupert makes a good living in La Colonia; in the company of his wife and two daughters, he runs an inn, builds and sells cuckoo clocks, and breeds dogs. Rolf becomes the son Rupert never had, with Rupert showing Rolf all the kindness and pride that Lukas Carlé was incapable of.

La Señora
La Señora is the flamboyant madam of an upscale brothel. When Eva has lost her job and is homeless, Huberto takes her to La Señora to live with her. La Señora is first and foremost a survivor. Though she is kind to Eva and fond of her, when the police are raiding the red-light district, her primary concern is for her own escape, and she leaves Eva to fend for herself. For Melesio, La Señora makes her one selfless exception: she goes to great lengths to free him from the prison at Santa Maria, even putting herself in jeopardy.

Zulema
Zulema, the wife of Riad Halabí, is a completely self-absorbed individual. When Eva meets her, Zulema has been lying in bed eating for most of the ten years that she has been married to Riad. Despite his kindness and devotion, Riad does not measure up to Zulema's ideal for a husband. She is obsessed with personal hygiene, her collection of jewels, and the stories of romance that Eva tells her. After Kamal abandons her, Zulema becomes even less involved in life than before; as Eva puts it, "We grew accustomed to thinking of Zulema as a kind of enormous and delicate plant." In a way, she is the opposite of Eva, who makes the best of all that life gives her, whereas Zulema spends her life pining for what she does not have.

THEMES

The Transformative Power of Words
Eva uses her words and stories to paint her life experiences in more appealing hues. She helps Rolf do the same; in one scene, when Rolf tells Eva that his sister died "a sad death, alone in a hospital," Eva retells the story in a happier way, saying that Katharina died with a smile, repeating Rolf's name and feeling the warmth of their love for each other. Eva paints a vivacious and compassionate picture of her godmother, even though the woman abuses Eva and takes the wages she earns. While living with Riad Halabí, Eva says, "I developed a tolerable image of my *madrina*, and suppressed bad memories so I could remember my past as happy."

Eva is not the only one who uses words to reshape experience; the government regularly spins its own version of events in the fight against the guerrillas, including their account of the rescue at Santa Maria, calling the guerrillas "terrorists." And when Eva tells Huberto about the murder of a policeman near the factory where she worked, Huberto says, "They executed him . . . The people executed him. That isn't murder. You ought to choose your words more carefully. The murderers are the police." Each side chooses the words that paint their view as righteous and just. In Eva's case, she aims to improve only her own view of events, whereas Huberto and the government look to sway others to their side with the right choice of words.

Similarly, the boys who murder Lukas Carlé use words to transform their deed into something noble: "The story passed from mouth to mouth, enhanced at every telling, until it was transformed into a heroic feat." By showing both the positive and negative ways that words can transform experience, Allende demonstrates the importance of language, of storytelling, and of choosing one's words carefully.

Perception versus Reality
Closely related to the theme of transforming experience with words is the idea that because we each perceive events from our own inherently biased viewpoint, there is no such thing as a fixed reality. As Eva puts it, "Maybe Zulema, Riad Halabí, and others had a different impression of things; maybe they did not see the same colors or hear the same sounds I did. If that were true, each of us was living in absolute isolation." Eva's

TOPICS FOR FURTHER STUDY

- *Eva Luna* is often described as a "picaresque" novel. What is the definition of picaresque? What other novels, stories, or movies do you think could be called picaresque? Make a list of ten titles that could be considered picaresque and explain your choices in a class presentation.

- Research the history of Venezuela. What similarities and differences can you find between the history of this country and the events in the novel? Write an essay about what you discover.

- In the novel, Eva enjoys taking stories from the radio or from books and changing the endings or rearranging events. Write a new beginning, middle, or end for *Eva Luna*, using the same characters but altering the events for a different outcome.

- Allende mentions *A Thousand and One Tales of the Arabian Nights* more than once in the novel. How is *Eva Luna* similar to this tale? Does Eva Luna use her storytelling abilities in the same way, or differently? Write a paper comparing and contrasting the two works.

- How many Latin American authors have won the Nobel Prize for Literature? Choose one of these authors, research his or her life, and write a short biography.

---

vivid imagination and the long hours she spends writing contribute to her impression that reality is an amorphous, shifting entity: "I began to wonder...whether reality wasn't an unformed and gelatinous substance only half-captured by my senses."

The connection between perception and reality, and the difficulty of separating the two, is a recurring theme in the novel. Eva works with one employer who teaches her to make Universal Matter, or *porcelana*. The employer has actually become addicted to creating objects from Universal Matter; as Eva explains, "*Porcelana* is a dangerous temptation, because once its secrets are known, nothing stands in the way of the artist's copying everything imaginable, constructing a world of lies, and getting lost in it." Coincidentally, the same thing happens to Eva when she writes her stories. She says, "At times I felt that the universe fabricated from the power of the imagination had stronger and more lasting contours than the blurred realm of the flesh-and-blood creatures around me." Words are Eva's Universal Matter. At the end of the book, Eva makes even the reader uncertain of what is real; she first states that she and Rolf Carlé loved each other "until that love wore thin and nothing was left but shreds." In the very next sentence, she contradicts herself: "Or maybe that isn't how it happened. Perhaps we had the good fortune to stumble into an exceptional love." Which version is reality, and which is Eva's creation? And does it matter? These are questions that Eva brings to mind with her intentionally ambiguous description. If no one can accurately perceive reality anyway, why should it not be perceived in the most pleasant light possible?

Abuse of Power

Throughout the novel, the government of the country changes hands numerous times, but all the governments have two common threads: corruption and violence. During Consuelo's time with Professor Jones, the country is run by El Benefactor, a dictator and tyrant. When El Benefactor dies, the government actually uses military force to make the citizens come out and pay their respects. The people celebrate his death, but their rejoicing is cut short when El Benefactor's minister of war steps in and takes over. The new government vows to be more progressive, but this brief period of democracy gives way to another dictatorship; this dictator is known only as the General, a man "so harmless in appearance that no one imagined the extent of his greed." The General becomes very wealthy from the country's oil boom, maintaining order through military force: "While those in power stole without scruple, thieves by trade or necessity scarcely dared practice their profession: the eyes of the police were everywhere." Some years later, an obviously fraudulent election angers the public, and rebellion begins; fearing for his life (and his fortune), the General escapes on a plane provided by the United States. A new democracy forms.

In the course of all this turmoil, little changes in the lives of ordinary people like Eva and Riad Halabí. In fact, according to Eva, "In many places people did not learn of the overthrow of the dictatorship because, among other things, they had not known that the General was in power all those years." Eva herself does not learn of the rebellion until years later; when she asks Riad what it means, he answers, "Nothing that involves us." The people of the country have grown so accustomed to corrupt governments in which they have no say that only those with power are truly affected by the transfer of power. Eva mentions political upheaval, riots, rebellions, and coups, but none of these seem to affect the story of her own life, with the exception of the guerrilla movement, and in that case only because of her personal relationship with Huberto Naranjo. Mimí's attitude sums up the people's disillusionment with those in power; when Eva tells her that they cannot ignore what is going on in the country, Mimí replies, "Yes, we can. We've done it up till now, and because we have, we're doing fine. Besides, no one in this country cares about those things; your guerrillas don't have the slightest chance." When Eva counters by espousing Huberto's philosophies, Mimí says, "In the unlikely event that your Naranjo wins his revolution, I'm sure in a very short time he would be acting with the arrogance of every man who attains power." In a country where today's government may be gone tomorrow, Eva and Mimí have learned to focus on their own lives and on the lives of those they love; anything beyond that familial realm is beyond their control.

Women's Rights

The second-class status of women in this patriarchal, or male-dominated, society is frequently referred to in the novel; just as the people of the country are resigned to the corruption of the government, the women in the book are resigned to this reality as well. Because women have few rights, they are even less affected by changes in government than men, because even though the government may change, it is always run by men who bear the same ingrained attitudes toward women. For example, when a new democracy comes to the country, the only difference Consuelo notices is "occasionally being able to attend a Carlos Gardel movie—formerly forbidden to women" (Gardel was a popular, suave Latin American singer who specialized in songs

Clouds above Avila Mountain and Caracas, Venezuela (*David Evans | National Geographic | Getty Images*)

of the tango and who made several movies in the 1930s).

Later, after Consuelo dies, Eva's godmother tells her, "If you were a boy, you could go to school and then study to be a lawyer and provide for me in my old age." She believes that men have it best in life: "Even the lowest good-for-nothing had a wife to boss around." Whatever power women may gain is achieved through the help of men. (For example, Eva is able to influence others through her telenovela—under the direction of Aravena and Rolf Carlé.) Although Huberto gallantly struggles to free the people, Eva realizes that his definition of "the people" is actually just men: "We women should contribute to the struggle but were excluded from decision-making and power." Even if the guerrillas succeed, it will mean little to Eva, Mimí, and other women. Eva sums up the plight of women in the country when she says, "I realized that mine is a war with no end in view; I might as well fight it cheerfully or I would spend my life waiting for some distant victory in order to be happy."

STYLE

First-Person Point of View

Eva Luna is written in the first person, from the point of view of Eva. This choice is important for several reasons. First, Eva's prowess as a story-teller and her love of writing are key elements of the novel. Simply by reading the way she tells her own story, the reader is given proof of her abilities. Second, Eva gives us several examples of the ways in which she alters reality to make it more palatable—for instance, when she retells the story of Katharina's death for Rolf to ease his grief. After reading these examples, the fact that the story is told from Eva's point of view leaves the reader to wonder if it is the character's real life story or just another tale spun from the raw material of her experiences. This is one of the points Allende is making in the novel: a person's story is just his or her own perception of the events, and it may be vastly different from another person's perception of the same events. In that sense, all of life is fiction, so it does not matter if Eva is telling the truth or a tall tale; it is all fiction.

Magical Realism

The term magical realism is used to describe a genre of literature in which magical, bizarre, and illogical events take place in an otherwise realistic setting. Allende uses this technique to give a fairy-tale quality to a story that also contains some very grim real-life issues. Wars rage; political leaders imprison, torture, and murder those who oppose them; ethnic groups are oppressed and persecuted; and yet within the same story, the vision of a palace appears from nowhere and then disappears, fictional characters come to life and wreak havoc in a real-life household, and Eva regularly summons the spirit of her dead mother to accompany her in lonely times. Another element that contributes to the fairy-tale feel of the story is Allende's technique of giving characters generic, conceptual names. The country's dictators do not have actual names but rather titles such as El Benefactor and the General; one corrupt official is known only as the Man of the Gardenia.

Rolf Carlé's story in particular is reminiscent of a tale from the Grimm Brothers. La Colonia, the town where Rolf Carlé's relatives live, is described as "a fairy-tale village preserved in a bubble where time had stopped and geography was illusory. Life went on there as it had in the nineteenth century in the Alps." Yet when Rolf leaves La Colonia to see more of the world, he witnesses atrocities, riots, wars, and corruption. This juxtaposition of the unreal with the only-too-real is typical of the genre of magical realism.

Foreshadowing

Allende often hints at events to come or even overtly states what will happen later in the story. When Eva first meets Huberto Naranjo, she drops a hint of his future as a guerrilla: "At sixteen he would be the leader of a street gang, feared and respected... until other concerns took him off to the mountains." Similarly, after Eva first meets Melesio, she foreshadows his troubled future: "He never talked about his family and it would be years later, during his time in the penal colony on Santa María, that La Señora learned anything about his past." These hints of future events keep the reader turning pages, eager to discover how they will come about.

HISTORICAL CONTEXT

Corruption in Venezuelan Government

Although Allende never specifies the country in which *Eva Luna* takes place, the political events Eva describes closely parallel the history of Venezuela. The government corruption that is rampant in the novel is also a part of Venezuelan history. *Eva Luna* was first published in 1985 during the presidency of Jaime Lusinchi, whose administration was even more rife with corruption than those of many of his predecessors. It is estimated that as much as thirty-six billion dollars was stolen from the country through government corruption during Lusinchi's time as president.

The dictator that Eva refers to as "El Benefactor" bears a strong resemblance to Juan Vicente Gómez, who effectively ruled Venezuela from 1908 until his death in 1935, after which his minister of war took over temporarily, just as El Benefactor's does in the story. "The General," who flees the country by jet later in the novel, is

COMPARE & CONTRAST

- **1960s:** In the 1960s, there are no female heads of state in Latin America.

  1980s: Lidia Gueiler Tejada serves as the interim president of Bolivia from 1979 to 1980, becoming only the second female head of state in South America; the first was the Argentinian interim president Isabel Martínez de Perón, who succeeded her husband, Juan Perón, after his death in office in 1974. Neither woman was elected.

  Today: As of 2008, there are two female heads of state in South America: Michelle Bachelet of Chile, elected in 2006 (the first female president in Chile's history), and Cristina Kirchner, elected in 2007 (the first female elected president of Argentina).

- **1960s:** The Cuban Revolution of 1959 results in social reforms for health and education, giving hope to oppressed peoples in other Latin American countries and inspiring an upsurge in guerrilla activities.

  1980s: Although Fidel Castro established better education and health care, Cuba's economy relies heavily on aid from the Soviet Union throughout the 1970s and most of the 1980s. Guerrilla activity continues in many Latin American countries, most notably in Guatemala, El Salvador, Nicaragua, and Peru.

  Today: Although guerrilla activity is not as prevalent in Latin America as it was in earlier decades, guerrilla organizations are still active in some countries. In 2008, a Colombian military assault killing seventeen members of the guerrilla group FARC (in English, Revolutionary Armed Forces of Colombia) draws the ire of the Venezuelan president Hugo Chávez, who usually supports the group, and also angers the Venezuelan allies Ecuador and Nicaragua. The United States supports the Colombian president Álvaro Uribe in his fight against the guerrillas.

- **1960s:** By 1960, Latin American countries export a significant percentage of the world's oil supply. An oversupply of oil on the market has led to lower and lower oil prices; in response to this situation, the world's main exporters of oil form the Organization of Petroleum Exporting Countries (OPEC) in 1960.

  1980s: The Middle East oil embargo of the 1970s was a boon to Latin America's oil industry, but in the 1980s, due to OPEC countries breaking their production quotas, the price of oil once again plummets to record lows (under ten dollars a barrel). This is especially problematic for net oil exporters such as Venezuela and Ecuador.

  Today: With oil prices well over one hundred dollars per barrel, Latin America's oil industry has enjoyed a recent boom.

---

likely meant to be Marcos Pérez Jiménez, another dictator who became wealthy at the expense of the people. Though Venezuela later developed into one of South America's more stable democracies, corruption in government has remained a lingering problem for the nation.

Women's Rights in Venezuela

The advancement of women's rights has come more slowly in South America than in the United States. As late as the 1970s, married or cohabiting women in Venezuela were not allowed to work, own property, or sign official documents without spousal consent. The advent of democracy in the 1960s was essentially a democracy for men only; women still had limited rights.

In 1982, just three years before *Eva Luna* was first published, the Ministry for the Participation of Women in Development brought women together to achieve the reform of the

Guerrilla with machine gun rounds (© guatebrian / Alamy)

civil code in Venezuela. This reform improved the legal standing of women in the country but still stopped short of achieving true equality. Three years later, in 1985, a new group called the Coordinator of Women's Non-Governmental Organizations united women from a wide array of socioeconomic backgrounds and political persuasions. This group would help achieve labor reforms for women, but not until 1990.

The Latin American Boom in Literature

Following World War II, improving economies in many Latin American countries helped bring about a boom in Latin American literature. The most celebrated novel of this period was *One Hundred Years of Solitude*, by Gabriel García Márquez, of Columbia, published in 1967. That same year, the Nobel Prize for Literature was given to the Guatemalan writer Miguel Ángel Asturias. Other significant authors active during this boom include Julio Cortázar, of Argentina; Carlos Fuentes, of Mexico; and Mario Vargas Llosa, of Peru. This fertile period in Latin American literature coincides roughly with the time in

the novel when Eva Luna is first discovering the joy of writing and is beginning to write down the stories of her own life. Allende's style of writing is sometimes compared to that of Márquez; Allende's first novel was not released until 1982, well after the boom period.

CRITICAL OVERVIEW

The critical reception of Allende's third novel, *Eva Luna*, was mixed. Reactions ranged from the wildly enthusiastic (the novelist Margaret McClusky, in a review in the *Sydney Morning Herald*, calls it a "perfect novel") to the decidedly negative (in a review in the London *Sunday Times*, Peter Kemp complains that the novel is "devoid of even the most elementary narrative skills.") More reactions, however, fall between the two extremes. Several reviewers, though not wholly negative, disparage Allende's tendency toward sentimentality; the reviewer Jill Neville of the *Independent* writes, "Occasionally it veers close to Mills and Boon [a British publisher of romance novels] and there are moments of sentimentality, even carelessness." Nicci Gerrard of the *New Statesman* agrees: "Isabel Allende used to translate Barbara Cartland novels.... Perhaps she was slightly corrupted in the process." John Krich of the *New York Times* says that Allende has "yielded to her worst tendencies," including "sentimentality" and "pat judgments."

Most of these same reviewers, however, found things to praise in Allende's work. Gerrard calls *Eva Luna* "an immensely likeable book, more interesting in its failure than are many books in their success." Neville writes, "Isabel Allende makes a plucky Scheherezade; she can spin a tale out of a pebble and a piece of string." John Krich comments that Allende has "an evident affection for words . . . and a nearly maternal approach to narrative that bathes characters in a warm, milky light." Allende's apparent love of language is noted also by the reviewer Susan Benesch of Florida's *St. Petersburg Times*: "What glows from the pages of this novel is the pleasure with which Allende writes. She rubs herself against the language like a cat."

Although *Eva Luna* did not garner the overwhelmingly positive reviews of Allende's first book, *The House of the Spirits*, many reviewers agree that it is good enough to keep the author's followers coming back for more. Writing for *Washington Post Book World*, Alan Ryan concludes, "Reading this novel is like asking your favorite storyteller to tell you a story and getting a hundred stories instead of one."

CRITICISM

Laura Pryor

Pryor has been a professional and creative writer for more than twenty years. In this essay, she debates whether or not Eva Luna *is a picaresque novel and compares Eva's story to that of Charles Dickens's* Oliver Twist.

Isabel Allende's novel *Eva Luna* is often called a "picaresque" novel. Though it does share many qualities with picaresque adventures, Eva Luna herself arguably does not live up to the definition of a *picaro*, the Spanish term from which picaresque is derived, meaning rascal or rogue. The main character of a picaresque novel is usually a wily, cynical, and clever one who must live on his wits, using them to extricate himself from the various predicaments in which

> IN FACT, *EVA LUNA* IS MOST DICKENSIAN IN THIS ASPECT: THE NOVEL HAS AT ITS CENTER A LESS COLORFUL BUT RELIABLE MAIN CHARACTER WHO IS SURROUNDED BY A SUPPORTING CAST OF QUIRKY, EVEN FREAKISH PEOPLE WHO LEND INTEREST TO THE TALE."

the author places him. In addition, the picaresque hero often has scant or questionable morals and often survives through theft and deception, though he may be charming enough for the reader to excuse such transgressions.

By contrast, while Eva finds herself in many predicaments throughout her story, she is rescued from these perhaps more often by others than through her own cunning, though she is by no means a helpless or unintelligent character. In this aspect—and many others—Eva's story is more comparable to that of Oliver Twist, Charles Dickens's hapless orphan, than that of a true picaro. Like Oliver, Eva is an orphan, though she benefits from knowing her mother until the age of six. Both Eva and Oliver are cared for after their parents' demise by individuals whose child-rearing skills are less than ideal. While Eva insists that her godmother has her best interests at heart, the madrina's tenuous grasp of reality, vast consumption of alcohol, and use of corporal punishment hardly recommend her as an ideal guardian. Luckily for Eva, she is delivered into the hands of the kindly Elvira at her next place of employment. Oliver begins life under the care of the self-serving Mrs. Mann, who receives money from the local parish to care for several children too young to go to the workhouse, where older poor children are usually sent. At the age of nine, Oliver, too, is sent to the workhouse. Compared to Oliver's lot in life at this point, Eva's situation with her irritable patrona is a veritable paradise.

Oliver is then sent to work for an undertaker, to spend his nights sleeping among coffins. Interestingly, Eva spends a good deal of her youth surrounded by death also, first in living with the embalmer Professor Jones, who in his

WHAT DO I READ NEXT?

- *The House of the Spirits*, published first in 1982 in Spanish, then in English in 1985, is Allende's first novel. It tells the epic tale of one family, the Truebas, through many years in South America. Many of the same elements found in *Eva Luna* (political strife, characters with unusual powers, an unspecified South American setting) are present in this novel as well.

- Gabriel García Márquez's novel *One Hundred Years of Solitude* (1967) is considered not only a central work of the Latin American boom but also a quintessential example of the magical realism genre. Allende's style is often compared to that of Márquez.

- Allende has written a trilogy of adventure books for older kids (ages ten and up), in which the teenager Alexander Cold and his grandmother, an intrepid reporter for the *International Geographic*, venture first into the Amazon rain forest (in the first book, *City of the Beasts* [2002]), then into the Himalayas (in the second book, *Kingdom of the Golden Dragon* [2004]), and finally to

Kenya (in the third book, *Forest of the Pygmies* [2005]).

- The character Eva Luna is compared to Scheherezade, the heroine of *A Thousand and One Tales of the Arabian Nights*. This classic collection of folktales was written over centuries, with the earliest known partial manuscript dating back to the 800s. In the tales, Scheherezade is the new bride of the King, a man who kills a new wife every night, for fear that each will eventually stop loving him. Scheherezade spins such fascinating stories for the King that he postpones her execution each night, eager for the next story. The tales include well-known characters such as Ali Baba (and his forty thieves) and Sinbad the Sailor.

- Like Scheherezade, Eva Luna has her own collection of tales, in Allende's 1989 book *The Stories of Eva Luna*. Though some of the same characters from *Eva Luna* appear in this book, it is not really a sequel but a collection of different stories that Eva tells to her lover, Rolf Carlé.

---

house keeps corpses that are awaiting his preparation, and then in performing mock funerals with Elvira, who keeps a coffin in her room as a precaution against being buried in a pauper's common grave.

Eva and Oliver find themselves homeless in very similar manners. Eva, pushed too far by her unforgiving patrona, attacks her and snatches off her wig; thinking she has "scalped" her, she runs away, preferring to take her chances on the street than to be arrested. Oliver, likewise, is driven to the brink, by Noah Claypole, his fellow employee, who insults the memory of Oliver's dead mother. Oliver attacks Noah, after which his employer beats him as punishment. Oliver decides to take to the open road rather than endure more mistreatment.

In a true picaresque tale, the hero (or heroine) spends much of his time living by his wits and not much else. Eva, on the other hand, spends the majority of the novel cared for by well-meaning, if somewhat bizarre, characters. Oliver's companions are equally eccentric, but unfortunately, not all are so well-intentioned. Still, regardless of Fagin's evil designs, he and his band of thieves do keep Oliver from starving on the street, and their behavior is far more interesting to read about than that of the bland but lovable Oliver. In fact, *Eva Luna* is most Dickensian in this aspect: the novel has at its center a less colorful but reliable main character who is surrounded by a supporting cast of quirky, even freakish people who lend interest to the tale.

These characters rescue Eva time and again. First, Huberto Naranjo cares for Eva after her attack on her employer, protecting her, providing her with food, and finally helping her find her godmother, who promptly beats her and sends her back to her place of employment. Huberto rescues Eva a second time after she rebels against another employer, now placing her in the care of La Señora, a madam, and Melesio, a future transsexual. Later, when Eva is on the streets again, Riad Halabí comes to the rescue, providing her with not only food and shelter but also love and literacy. Finally, when she is almost out of the money Riad has provided her with, Melesio—now Mimí—appears and takes her in.

Likewise, it is the kindness (or avarice) of strangers that keeps Oliver alive, not his wits. First it is Fagin who keeps him from starvation (though later delivering him into the hands of those who would see him dead). Then the kindly Mr. Brownlow saves him briefly from Fagin and also from illness. Snatched back by Fagin, he is then again rescued, by the kindly Mrs. Maylie and Rose.

Eva, of course, is a far more complex character than Oliver Twist; a boy as guileless, loving, and saintlike as Oliver perhaps never existed, in Dickens's time or any other. While Dickens uses Oliver more as a symbol of the poor and oppressed in British society than as a real character, Eva has her own set of quirks, talents, and opinions that enable her to thrive despite her hardships, and she also is far more rebellious and defiant to her persecutors than Oliver. Her fierce loyalty to her friends and repeated kindnesses toward them establish her not as the rascal or rogue of a picaresque tale but as the novel's moral center. In any other story, Eva would appear eccentric, but when surrounded by a Turkish merchant with a cleft lip, an obese wife who never leaves her bed, a man who goes on to become a famous actress, a mad godmother who gives birth to a two-headed baby, and a fierce guerrilla boyfriend, Eva is a paragon of normality.

Another characteristic that separates Eva from the decidedly unpicaresque Oliver Twist is her ability to transform her miserable experiences through the use of her imagination. While Oliver spends his first night at the undertaker's terrified of a coffin in the room with him, Eva has a wonderful time lying in Elvira's coffin and pretending to be a corpse. Similarly, if Eva's

patrona had told Oliver to stay away from the seascape in the dining room, certainly Oliver would have placidly obeyed, but it holds too strong a pull for Eva's vivid imagination: "That painting of the sea with its foaming waves and motionless gulls was essential to me; it was the reward for the day's labors, the door to freedom." In fact, in her imagination and in her zest for life and adventure, Eva is very nearly a picaro, but in actions she is not. In her most daring adventure, she becomes part of a guerrilla plot to free prisoners from a penal colony. But even this adventure is undertaken somewhat reluctantly, at the request of Huberto Naranjo, and her part in the plot is to make a large batch of dough that can be used by the prisoners to make faux grenades. After this, she rides the bus home, before the actual prison break takes place, and waits at home for news of the outcome.

At the end of *Oliver Twist*, Oliver is still just twelve years old, whereas Eva is a grown woman by the end of her story. At Oliver's tender age, it is no great surprise that he is unable to outwit the conniving Fagin and his cronies, as a picaro might have done. In Eva's case, it is interesting to note that although Allende makes comments on the inequality of women in South American society and has written the character as an independent thinker who resists being dependent on a man, at no time in the novel does Eva actually have to survive independently, without the help of others. She does make her own money while living with Mimí, but she works in a factory, which surely would not support her in the style to which she and Mimí are accustomed, and so she is still dependent on Mimí's fame as an actress. Then she quits her job at the factory to avoid Colonel Rodriguez, an option that would have been unavailable to her if she were on her own. Only near the close of the novel, when she writes her telenovela, does she make a good living. She has barely achieved this when she is united with Rolf Carlé, who, like Mimí, is also conveniently famous and well-off.

Most of Eva's adventures are visited upon her rather than being sought after. Is Allende telling us that because of the inequality of women in South America, the only way they can have adventure is to have it foisted upon them? Certainly Dickens's intention was to show the helplessness and misery inflicted upon the poor by the British poor laws; to have Oliver be too plucky or spirited would have blunted the point he was trying to make. In Eva's vivid imagination, and in her stories, she is no doubt the fearless heroine, outwitting and vanquishing foes at every turn; she creates "a world where I imposed the rules and could change them at will." In her life, however, Eva must live by the rules that men in power impose upon her, necessitating that her greatest, most picaresque adventures remain on the page.

Source: Laura Pryor, Critical Essay on *Eva Luna*, in *Novels for Students*, Gale, Cengage Learning, 2009.

> THUS, WHILE ALLENDE'S FICTION, AS REPRESENTED BY *EVA LUNA* AND *CUENTOS DE EVA LUNA* IS INDEED ACCESSIBLE, A CLOSE EXAMINATION OF ITS MAGICAL PLACES AND THEIR INHABITANTS DEMONSTRATES A COMPLEXITY THAT MAY NOT BE READILY APPARENT."

Barbara Foley Buedel

In the following excerpt, Buedel analyzes five "magical places" found in Allende's novel Eva Luna *and her short story collection* Cuentos de Eva Luna *(Stories of Eva Luna).*

Widely recognized as a major contributor to Latin American literature, Isabel Allende holds a preeminent place in its literary history. In *The Post-Boom in Spanish American Fiction* (1998), Donald Shaw writes, "Without question the major literary event in Spanish America during the early eighties was the publication in 1982 of Isabel Allende's runaway success *La Casa de los Espíritus*" (53). Similarly, in his recent book, *Literature of Latin America* (2004), Rafael Ocasio identifies Allende as "the woman writer from Latin America with the greatest international readership," noting also that "she has a significant influence on an increasingly popular, worldwide literature written by women" (168). Linda Gould Levine in her Twayne book (2002) succinctly assesses the author's status: "Isabel Allende is the most acclaimed woman writer of Latin America" (ix).

Shaw maintains that the "emergence of strong female characters" is what made Allende's first work a "genuinely 'inaugural' novel" (59, 58). This feminist perspective continues throughout her fiction and is especially apparent in her third novel, *Eva Luna* (1987). As numerous critics observe, this work displays aspects of the picaresque tradition: a pseudo-autobiography with an episodic structure, Eva's marginalized status as an orphan and domestic servant who serves a series of oftentimes unkind masters, a streetwise survival instinct promoted by her friendship with Huberto Naranjo, a variety of experiences in different economic classes during which she experiences both hunger and abundance,

and frequent demands for her to be self-reliant and inventive. Yet acts of kindness are more numerous than acts of cruelty, and benevolent mother and father figures often replace tyrannical masters. By the end of the novel, the protagonist is a successful writer, a political activist who has participated in a guerrilla raid and escaped without harm, and the lover of an intelligent journalist. Overall, the tone is optimistic, a characteristic of other Post-Boom narratives that contrasts with the negative visions typically developed in Boom novels (Shaw 10, 65). Levine views the novel as a "female bildungsroman, a novel of a young woman's psychological, intellectual and moral development" (60), and Shaw describes it as "a feminist . . . quest for selfhood" (64). Above all, *Eva Luna* is a "celebratory novel that bears tribute to the power of words and the imagination, the joys of sensuality and friendship, the ability of human beings to overcome social barriers, and the re-creation of reality through the lens of fiction" (Levine 55).

The present study will analyze five magical places that appear in *Eva Luna* and in the collection of short stories that followed two years later, *Cuentos de Eva Luna* (1989). Four are named places: El Palacio de los Pobres, Calle Republica, Agua Santa, and La Colonia, and all but the first receive extensive development in the novel and reappear frequently in the stories. Spanning multiple works, these fictional places recall Garcia Marquez's Macondo and Faulkner's Yoknapatawpha County. A fifth magical place is the lugar ameno, the safe haven where the act of writing takes place. This space is specified in only one story—"Cartas de amor traicionado"—but is emblematic of the novel and of many of the stories which center on storytelling, writing, and the dialectic between art and life. An overview of these magical places will enrich our understanding of Allende's documented focus in her early fiction on the themes of love, social activism, and storytelling (Jehenson 100–01; Levine 55–56; Shaw 59). In addition, my reading of these spaces will allow us to consider ways in which Allende's fiction may be more complex than its commercial success leads some critics to surmise. In particular, it will be demonstrated that although Allende's fiction in these two works is grounded in human emotions arising from the drama of everyday life, it is simplistic to label her work as melodrama as some critics have done (Jehenson 100; Invernizzi [1991], cited in Shaw 58).

Of the five magical places, the summer estate known as El Palacio de los Pobres in the novel and El Palacio de Verano in the short story, "El palacio imaginado," is the most ostensibly marvelous. Eva Luna records that it was built by El Benefactor (a code name for General Juan Vincent Gomez, the Venezuelan dictator who was in power from 1900 to 1935) and that upon his death, it was reclaimed by the natives and the jungle. . . . The night that Eva Luna travels to Agua Santa with Riad Halabi, she sees the enchanted palace for the first time and recounts that experience as follows: "El viaje duro toda la noche a traves de un paraje oscuro, donde las unicas luces eran las alcabalas de La Guardia, los camiones en su ruta hacia los campos petroleros y el Palacio de los Pobres, que se materializo por treinta segundos al borde del camino, como una vision alucinante." The second time Eva witnesses the magical apparition is the day she returns by bus to the capital after participating in a guerrilla raid near Agua Santa: "En un recodo de la ruta, la vegetacion se abrio de subito en un abanico de verdes imposibles y la luz del dia se torno blanca, para dar paso a la ilusion perfecta del Palacio de los Pobres, flotando a quince centimetros del humus que cubria el suelo." Strikingly similar is the description that closes "El palacio imaginado." . . .

These depictions of an enchanted palace that materializes briefly and floats above the ground are undoubtedly several instances where the marvelous is most obvious, yet they are not without ambiguity. For example, the fortress appears "como una vision alucinante" and "como un espejismo"; does it "truly" matenalize or only in Eva's imagination? Similarly, the second time

Eva "sees" the palace she calls it "la ilusion perfecta del Palacio de los Pobres." In addition, the multiple meanings of "imaginado" in the short story's title also contribute to the sense of wonder that elicits the following question: within the world of fiction, is the apparition a dream, an illusion, or does it magically "appear"?

In analyzing the tradition of magical realism in *La casa de los espiritus*, Laune Clancy notes a real tension between realism and fantasy and questions whether or not Allende is somewhat ambivalent about its use: "Are we to believe in 'hidden forces' or the laws of science? Sometimes Allende hedges her bets: Rosa, for instance does not actually float but seems to float; she seems to be a mermaid but is not finally, as she lacks a scaly tail" (40). In *Eva Luna* and "El palacio imaginado," the narration of the construction of the summer palace and its subsequent transformation blends social realism with the extraordinary in order to highlight a sociopolitical truth: marginalized indigenous people are able to retake their land only when the invaders (or their descendants) abandon it. Allende underscores this idea in *Eva Luna* when her narrator explains why the Indians help the guerrilla fighters. . . .

In this passage, the plight of indigenous cultures is established via didactic summary. In the same way, "El palacio imaginado" begins with a didactic introduction of the social injustices suffered by indigenous cultures and then employs magical realista, a blend of social realism and the extraordinary, to narrate the origin and outcome of the summer palace.

Whereas El Palacio de los Pobres (El Palacio de Verano) epitomizes the historical reality of indigenous cultures in Latin America, Calle Republica functions as a microcosm of the cultural institution known us the red-light district. It is magical not in the sense of the extraordinary or the supernatural but because of its allure as a site of transgression. . . . Although Eva is not a "working girl" of the neighborhood, she lives there twice: once briefly when she is about thirteen and later during her twenties.

When Eva Luna rebels from one of her last masters, a government official on whose head she deliberately overturns the chamber pot she has been summoned to empty, she finds herself alone, hungry, and in the street once again. But her childhood friend Huberto Naranjo, local gang leader and petty thief, takes her to reside in an establishment run by La Senora on Calle Republica. Telling everyone that Eva is his sister, Huberto pays for her lodging and meals and instructs La Senora to insulate her from the sordid aspects of the brothel. In turn, he confirms that Eva will be a delightful young companion who will use her talent for storytelling to amuse her guardian. The arrangement works well for several months. Eva is adopted and cared for by La Senora and her best friend, Melesio, a transgendered man who by day is an Italian teacher and by night the best artist in the cross-dressing cabaret theatre. Business runs smoothly and peacefully on Calle Republica because of the cooperation of local police officials who collect their weekly commissions from the establishments, but when a new police sergeant takes over and creates trouble for the residents, their response forces the Chief of Police and the Minister of the Interior to intervene. Calle Republica becomes a war zone which the press names "Guerra al Hampa" and which the locals rename "Revuelta de las Putas." La Senora barely escapes, Melesio is imprisoned, and Eva finds herself in the street once again.

Rescued by un Arab merchant, Riad Halabi, Eva spends the next five years of her adolescence in Agua Santa, a third magical place. She describes it as "uno de esos pueblos adormilados por la modorra de la provincia"; "una aldea modesta, con casas de adobe, madera y cana amarga, construida al borde de la carretera y defendida a machetazos contra una vegetacion salvaje que en cualquier descuido podia devorarla." In general, the inhabitants seem kind and pleasures are simple in this "pueblo olvidado" and "perdido" (EL) "donde nadie se queda y cuyo nombre los viajeros rara vez recuerdan" (CEL 68). In this almost idyllic town unscathed by modern inventions, isolated from political upheavals that characterize the capital, and joined to the rest of the world by only one phone line and a curvy road, Eva is protected and nurtured by the most respected inhabitant of the town: Riad Halabi, her Turkish-born father figure. Through his intervention, Eva acquires two things that will be invaluable in the future: a fraudulent but legal birth certificate and literacy.

Taught to read and write by the schoolteacher Ines, Eva can now complement her oral storytelling with the written word. Though her daytime hours are spent reading, working in the successful merchant's store, and attending his infirm wife, Eva devotes most nights to writing her stories, an activity that she later recalls as "mis mejores horas." Routine and tranquility thus characterize life in Agua Santa.... The only exception occurs on Saturdays when the guards from the nearby prison known as the Penal de Santa Maria visit the local brothel and when the Indians from a nearby settlement enter town to beg for alms. Eva lives in Agua Santa until gossip unfairly implicates her in the suicide of Riad Halabi's wife. Before she leaves, the merchant, who has already given her the tool (literacy) to become a writer, also introduces her to her own sensuality.

When Eva returns to the neighborhood surrounding Calle Republica, she goes to work in a factory and shares an apartment with the transsexual Mimi, the former Melesio. She also reunites with Huberto Naranjo, now Comandante Rogelio and leader of the guerrillas, and for a while, the friends become lovers. Eventually, however, their relationship moves full circle, and they end as friends. Meanwhile, with Mimi's support and encouragement, Eva leaves the factory to devote herself to her writing. She also meets Rolf Carle, and the final chapters of the narrative focus on their social activism and budding romance. The novel closes with a celebration of their union, a conclusion that is set in motion in chapter 2 when the narration of Rolf's life story begins. The narrative makes clear that while Eva lives a portion of her childhood on Calle Republica and all of her teenage years in Agua Santa, Colonia is the town where Rolf Carle spends his adolescence after emigrating from Austria.

Eva Luna identifies this fourth magical place as a "pueblo de fantasia" originally founded by a rich South American landowner with utopian goals who, in the mid nineteenth century went to Europe to secure a group of eighty impoverished families who were willing to move half way around the world with the express purpose of creating "una sociedad perfecta donde reinara la paz y la prosperidad." Distant cousins of Rolf Carie's mother moved to La Colonia to escape the war in Europe, and it was to them that Rolf was sent as a teenager.... A safe harbor, La Colonia offers Eva and Rolf temporary asylum after they help Huberto Naranjo free nine guerrilla prisoners from the prison near Agua Santa.

Turning to the last magical place analyzed in this study, it is emblematic of the storytelling motif extensively treated in *Eva Luna* and *Cuentos de Eva Luna*. For example, as narrator of her pseudo-autobiography (the novel) and as author of a television script entitled *Bolero* and based on her life, Eva Luna is the consummate storyteller. She reprises this role in *Cuentos de Eva Luna*, a collection of short narratives that purport to be her response to Rolf Carle's request that she tell him a story. In addition, a number of the female protagonists in this collection are storytellers of writers. Belisa Crepusculario of "Dos palabras" epitomizes the teller of tales who has learned the power of words. Elena Mejias of "Nina perversa" invents stories and attributes them to the guests who lodge in her mother's boarding house. Maurizia Rugieri of "Tosca" tries to live life as the fictional heroine of an opera. Abigal McGovern of "Con todo el respeto debido," along with her husband, invents a fantastic story of kidnapping and ransom as a strategy to climb the social ladder. And, finally, Analia Torres of "Cartas de amor traicionado" retreats to a special place to invent stories, read, and write.

Raised in a convent because of her parents' death, Analia finds quiet refuge in the attic. Unlike the attic or upstairs room that imprison, respectively, Bertha Mason Rochester of *Jane Eyre* and the narrator-protagonist of Charlotte Perkins Gilman's "The Yellow Wallpaper," the attic in "Cartas de amor traicionado" recalls Emily Dickinson's upstairs bedroom as a place to which the female writer voluntarily retreats in order to cultivate her imagination. In Allende's story, Analia repeats the journey of Eva Luna and Belisa Crepusculario, who first begin as storytellers in the oral tradition and later become readers and writers. As a child, Analia relishes the solitude that the attic affords her, escaping there to amuse herself with invented stories. But as an adolescent, she returns to her lugar ameno to savor the epistles she receives from her cousin and to enter into a clandestine relationship of amorous letter writing. . . .

Analia's enjoyment of the multiple layers of meaning made possible by words recalls a crucial lesson on the magical nature of words that Eva Luna learns from her mother. . . . Thus, the attic is a magical place, a sacred space, where the writer uses her imagination to celebrate and cultivate the creative possibilities of language.

This reading of magical places in *Eva Luna* and *Cuentos de Eva Luna* has identified four named places as well as a generic space. El Palacio de los Pobres (El Palacio de Verano), Calle Republica, Agua Santa, and La Colonia span multiple works and function, respectively, as microcosms of a historical condition (the plight of the indigenous), a cultural institution (prostitution), and the Latin American town geographically isolated from the political battles waged in the capital and other large cities. Magical realism is the predominant mode used to portray the four named places, although the marvelous is most obvious in the narration of the enchanted palace. The fifth place—the attic—serves as a safe haven for the artist who retreats there to celebrate the magic of words. These special places are essential in the portrayal of three major themes: love and friendship, social activism and politics, including social satire, and storytelling and writing.

As a way of conclusion, I would like us to consider how three of these magical places undermine the charge that Allende's fiction is based on melodrama. Classic melodrama creates a simplified moral universe in which the conflict between good and evil is embodied in stock characters and operates according to a series of conventions: the villain poses a threat, the hero or heroine escapes, and the work has a happy ending (Rios-Font 10, 19–49). With Allende's focus on storytelling, both her third novel and her collection of short stories display characteristics frequently associated with melodrama: plot centeredness, highly dramatic incidents, and strong emotionalism. In addition, El Palacio de los Pobres clearly reflects the polarization between good and evil: reclaimed by the Indians and the jungle, the enchanted palace returns to its rightful owners, and justice is served. Calle Republica, La Colonia, and Agua Santa, however, are more complicated.

Although Huberto Naranjo wants to insulate Eva Luna from the illicit world of prostitution located on and around Calle Republica, it is the community he knows, and he places her there in the care of La Senora. The inhabitants of the neighborhood foster a sense of community that allows them to survive and at times to prosper. The polarization between good and evil blurs because the narrative does not rigorously censor their activities. In fact, La Senora's entrepreneurial skills are celebrated. . . .

The true objects of satire are the "banqueros, magnates y encumbradas personalidades del Gobierno" who pay for her services with "fondos publicos" and the police who receive weekly payoffs. Furthermore, Mimi's response to the neighborhood is ironic. In spite of being a marginalized individual who finds social acceptance on Calle Republica, Mimi views the neighborhood as flawed: as soon as she and Eva can afford to move, Mimi finds them a house in the most prestigious neighborhood of the capital city. Her decision to leave the neighborhood depicts the extent to which she is affected by traditional bourgeois values and prejudice.

Rolf Carle's adolescent home, La Colonia, is consistently portrayed as a utopia of refuge from the political and social evils of the outside world. Nevertheless, La Colonia's fairy-tale existence as a safe harbor is undermined by its self-isolation. It is "a place where no one speaks Spanish, and where many of the children have defects because of inbreeding, another reference, perhaps, to the Nazi policy of the 'pure race'" (Diamond-Nigh 37). Thus, whereas in the context of El Palacio de los Pobres magical realism honors the rights of indigenous cultures, in the case of La Colonia it portrays outsiders (Europeans) with a fantastic desire to live in a cultural bubble intended to marginalize Latin America. In short, the representation of La Colonia as a utopia is subverted by satire.

The polarization between good and evil also blurs in Agua Santa. Although it appears to be an idyllic community, integrating Hispanic, Arabic, and indigenous cultures, it is characterized by a number of social flaws. First, most of its inhabitants are illiterate, a condition that contrasts sharply with the importance Eva attributes to her own ability to read and write. Some humor is created at the expense of these simple townspeople when in the story "Tosca" they cannot distinguish between art (the opera that Maurizia is performing) and life (Maurizia's real situation). Second, the townspeople are not always charitable: founded on the mistaken belief that Eva contributed to the death of Riad Halabi's wife, gossip forces Eva to leave town. Third, patriarchal traditions such as domestic abuse are sanctioned in Agua Santa....

Finally, Allende's characters, or at least many of them, are not the one-dimensional stock characters of melodrama. Eva's memory portrays Riad Halabi as an incredibly generous and nurturing father figure, but at the same time he sleeps with her on the eve of her departure from Agua Santa. In addition, when Eva begs him to allow her to stay, he says he cannot marry someone as young as she. Yet when she secretly visits Agua Santa several years later, Eva discovers that his second wife is even younger than Eva.

The schoolteacher Ines is beloved by all her former pupils. Together with Riad Halabi, she generously helps a number of needy children in *Eva Luna* and "El oro de Tomas Vargas," and in "El huesped de la maestra" she is described as "la matrona mas respetada de Agua Santa" (CEL 163). Nevertheless, when the schoolteacher avenges her son's death by killing the man who accidentally shot her boy twenty years ago, the whole community, led by Riad Halabi, joins together to help her dispose of the body. Halabi enjoys significant prestige in Agua Santa and is known as a fair man, but the system of justice operating in the town clearly reflects old laws (and for some readers, outdated traditions), as Ines notes when she defends her own actions and seeks Halabi's approval....

"La esposa del juez" portrays both Casilda, the protagonist, and Nicolas Vidal, the violent outlaw, as multifaceted characters. Although a criminal, Vidal is also a victim of birth and circumstance: "no conocia la intimidad, la ternura, la risa secreta, la fiesta de los sentidos, el alegre gozo de los amantes" (CEL 147). His crimes are not condoned, but his psychological make-up cultivates the reader's sympathy. Similarly, in spite of the story's title that minimizes the protagonist as subject and insinuates she is merely an extension of her husband, Casilda's actions depict her as an intelligent individual with a strong will. Both Vidal and the townspeople are initially deceived by the demure and soft-spoken exterior that masks her inner strength.... The outlaw who initially appears more cunning and powerful loses his life at the end of the story to a woman who is stronger and smarter than he. Traditional stereotypes are subverted in favor of more complex characters.

Although justice is served in El Palacio de los Pobres and the attic is celebrated as the writer's lugar ameno, three magical places—Caile Republica, La Colonia, and Agua Santa—blur the polarization between good and evil. In addition, many of Allende's characters are far more complicated than the one-dimensional stock characters of melodrama. Thus, while Allende's fiction, as represented by *Eva Luna* and *Cuentos de Eva Luna* is indeed accessible, a close examination of its magical places and their inhabitants demonstrates a complexity that may not be readily apparent.

Source: Barbara Foley Buedel, "Magical Places in Isabel Allende's *Eva Luna* and *Cuentos de Eva Luna*," in *West Virginia University Philological Papers*, Vol. 53, Fall 2006, p. 108.

SOURCES

Allende, Isabel, "About Isabel," Web site of Isabel Allende, http://www.isabelallende.com/roots_frame.htm (accessed June 30, 2008).

———, *Eva Luna*, Dial Press, 2005.

Benesch, Susan, Review of *Eva Luna*, in *St. Petersburg Times*, December 11, 1988, Perspective sec., p. 7D.

Coronel, Gustavo, "The Corruption of Democracy in Venezuela," Web site of the Cato Institute, http://www.cato.org/pub_display.php?pub_id=9254 (accessed June 29, 2008).

Dickens, Charles, *Oliver Twist*, Modern Library, 2001.

Encyclopaedia Britannica Online, s.v. "Latin American Literature," http://www.britannica.com/EBchecked/topic/331811/Latin-American-literature (accessed June 28, 2008).

Encyclopaedia Brittanica Online, s.v. "Venezuela," http://www.britannica.com/EBchecked/topic/625197/Venezuela (accessed June 28, 2008).

Erro-Peralta, Nora, "Isabel Allende," in *Dictionary of Literary Biography*, Vol. 145, *Modern Latin-American Fiction Writers, Second Series*, edited by William Luis and Ann Gonzalez, Gale Research, 1994, pp. 33–41.

Gerrard, Nicci, Review of *Eva Luna*, in *New Statesman*, March 24, 1989, p. 38.

Jones, Rachel, "Boom Times Wane in Oil-Rich Venezuela," in *Seattle Times*, June 8, 2008, http://seattletimes.nwsource.com/html/businesstechnology/2004465586_apvenezuelaeconomictroubles.html?syndication=rss (accessed July 6, 2008).

Kemp, Peter, Review of *Eva Luna*, in *Sunday Times* (London), March 26, 1989.

Krich, John, Review of *Eva Luna*, in *New York Times*, October 23, 1988, sec. 7, p. 13.

McClusky, Margaret, Review of *Eva Luna*, in *Sydney Morning Herald*, June 10, 1989, Spectrum sec., p. 87.

Neville, Jill, Review of *Eva Luna*, in *Independent*, March 25, 1989, Weekend Books sec., p. 33.

Ryan, Alan, Review of *Eva Luna*, in *Washington Post Book World*, October 9, 1988, p. X1.

Wagner, Sarah, "Women and Venezuela's Bolivarian Revolution," http://www.venezuelanalysis.com/analysis/877 (accessed June 29, 2008).

FURTHER READING

Allende, Isabel, *My Invented Country: A Nostalgic Journey through Chile*, HarperCollins, 2003.

> This is Allende's memoir of her native country, Chile. The book includes her own experience of the assassination of President Salavador Allende, a cousin of hers (which necessitated her emigration to Venezuela), as well as the story of how she became a writer.

Chasteen, John Charles, *Born In Blood and Fire: A Concise History of Latin America*, 2nd ed., Norton, 2006.

> This book provides a history of Latin American countries from the first arrival of Europeans to the present day. Chasteen analyzes the significant events, ideas, and trends that have shaped Latin America over the centuries.

Jaquette, Jane, ed., *The Women's Movement in Latin America: Participation and Democracy*, 2nd ed., Westview Press, 1994.

> This book analyzes the women's movement in several Latin American countries; the case studies of the movement in Brazil, Argentina, Uruguay, Chile, Peru, Nicaragua, and Mexico are written by different contributors and treat women's struggles to participate in the political process as well as what they have accomplished through that participation.

Swanson, Philip, *Latin American Fiction: A Short Introduction*, Blackwell, 2005.

> This book describes the history of significant developments in modern Latin American fiction and includes sections on regional differences, the boom, the post-boom period, and Latin American literature in the United States. Swanson also provides analyses of some of the most prominent works by Latin American authors.

I, Robot

ISAAC ASIMOV

1950

I, Robot is one of the most influential works of science fiction ever written. During the 1930s, young Isaac Asimov found himself bored with the common science fiction plot that included robots destroying their creators, akin to the destruction of Dr. Frankenstein by his own monster. A precocious and prolific writer, Asimov addressed his boredom by writing his first robot story, "Robbie," in 1940, when he was just nineteen years old. He published it in *Super Science Stories* magazine. Over the next ten years, he wrote and published at least twelve more robot stories.

Asimov's robots were equipped with positronic brains and governed by the Three Laws of Robotics, as articulated in "Runaround," first published in 1942 and later included as the second chapter of *I, Robot*. Each of Asimov's subsequent robot stories explored some aspect of the Three Laws, pushing the boundaries of human/machine interaction. In 1950, Asimov selected what he considered to be his best stories, wrote a framing device to link the stories together into a novel, and published the work as *I, Robot*. Even Asimov recognized that this might be his most lasting work. He wrote in the introduction to *Robot Visions*, "If all that I have written is someday to be forgotten, the Three Laws of Robotics will surely be the last to go." More than fifty years after its first publication, *I, Robot* is still easily available in several editions,

age of fifteen. Asimov was a voracious reader, and became acquainted with science fiction by reading the pulp magazines stocked in the candy store. He was soon writing letters to the editors of several publications.

In 1935, he entered Seth Low Junior College, a division of Columbia University, where he pursued his love of chemistry. During this period, he began writing science fiction stories, and in 1938, with his first completed science fiction story in hand, he met the legendary John W. Campbell, Jr., who had just begun his long tenure as editor of *Astounding Science Fiction*. Campbell became an important mentor and friend to Asimov, and the two worked closely together for the rest of their lives.

Asimov sold his first story, "Marooned Off Vesta," to *Amazing Stories* in 1938. In the same year, he became active in the Futurian Literary Society, a group that included such well-known writers as Frederick Pohl, Donald Wollheim, and Cyril M. Kornbluth.

By 1939 Asimov had completed his bachelor's degree in chemistry and by 1941 a master's degree in the same field. World War II interrupted his work on his Ph.D. During the war years he worked alongside fellow science fiction writer Robert A. Heinlein at the Naval Aircraft Laboratory in Philadelphia. In 1942, he married Gertrude Blugerman. Meanwhile, Asimov had begun working on his robot stories, publishing the first, "Strange Playfellow," in 1940. Retitled as "Robbie," the story became the first chapter of *I, Robot* when it was published in 1950 by Gnome Press. Indeed, after 1940, Asimov sold every story that he ever wrote; nearly all of them have remained in print in the years since his death.

Asimov returned to Columbia University and completed his Ph.D. in chemistry in 1948. In 1949, Asimov moved his family to Boston, where he accepted a position as an instructor of biochemistry at the Boston University School of Medicine. By 1958, Asimov's side career as a science fiction writer was providing a sufficient income that he was able to leave teaching and devote himself to full-time writing. In 1970, Asimov and his wife separated; in 1973, he married Janet Jeppson. Asimov died from complications of AIDS, contracted from a blood transfusion during an earlier heart surgery, on April 6, 1992.

Asimov wrote some five hundred books in the fields of science fiction, popular science, literature, and literary criticism. In addition, he

Isaac Asimov (AP Images)

most notably in a 2008 edition by Bantam Dell publishers.

Well into the twenty-first century, science fiction writers, movie directors, and artificial intelligence engineers continue to take into account Asimov's prescient consideration of what it means to be human and what it means to be machine.

AUTHOR BIOGRAPHY

Isaac Asimov was born on or around January 2, 1920, in Petrovichi, Russia, to Juda and Anna Rachel Berman Asimov. Because the Asimov family was Jewish, and few official records exist in Russia about Jews during this period, the date is nothing more than an approximation made by Asimov. The family left Russia and moved to Brooklyn, New York, in 1923.

The family purchased a candy store in 1926, and soon expanded the business to include additional stores. Young Asimov and the other members of his family devoted many hours to working in the stores. An intelligent and quiet boy, Asimov entered Boys High School in Brooklyn in 1932, and graduated just three years later at the won countless awards for his work, most notably several Hugo and Nebula awards, the most prestigious honors in science fiction. He continued to win awards for his work after his death, and his popularity remains unabated in the twenty-first century. There is little doubt that he will be long remembered as one of the most influential science fiction writers of all time.

PLOT SUMMARY

Introduction

I, Robot is not a novel in the usual sense, with a plotline and consistent characters throughout. Rather *I, Robot* is more like a closely connected set of short stories held together by a frame story that allows Asimov to trace the history of robotics over a fifty-year period.

The novel opens with the first segment of the frame story, set in italic type. Readers are introduced to Susan Calvin, a robopsychologist who is retiring from her position at U.S. Robots & Mechanical Men after a career of some fifty years. The first-person narrator of the frame story is a young, brash journalist who is writing a feature article on Calvin for Interplanetary Press. He is looking for human interest in the story; therefore he urges Calvin to recall some of the most memorable moments of her career. Her memories, then, form the basis of each of the subsequent chapters.

Chapter 1: Robbie

In this chapter, Calvin tells the story of Robbie, one of the first robots constructed to interact with and serve humans. Robbie functions as a nursemaid for a little girl named Gloria; although he cannot speak, Robbie plays with Gloria and seems to enjoy the stories she tells him. Gloria is devoted to Robbie; however, her mother does not like the robot and finally succeeds in convincing her husband to get rid of the mechanical man. Asimov uses the mother to represent one of his common themes—the hostility of some people toward technology.

The parents get rid of Robbie while Gloria is out of the house, and the little girl is heartbroken when she finds her playmate gone. She sickens and loses weight. Finally her parents decide to take her to New York City for a trip to try to cheer her up. She believes that they are going to try to find Robbie. Finally, on a visit to

MEDIA ADAPTATIONS

- An audiobook of *I, Robot*, read by Scott Brick, was produced and distributed by Random House Audio (2004).

- In 1997, InforMedia produced a CD-ROM set called *Isaac Asimov's Ultimate Robot*. Several of the stories from *I, Robot* were included in the set.

- In 2008, Pan Macmillan Publishers produced and distributed the audiobook *I, Robot for Learners of English*, narrated by Tricia Reilly.

- *I, Robot* is the title of a film produced and distributed on DVD by Twentieth Century Fox in 2004. Starring Will Smith and directed by Alex Proyas, the film shares little with Asimov's book other than the title and the names of a few characters.

the U.S. Robots factory, a situation emerges in which Robbie (who is working there) saves Gloria's life. The mother relents, and Robbie goes home with the family.

The second segment of the frame story appears just after the story of Robbie. In her discussion with the journalist, Calvin recalls two important early robotic trouble shooters, Gregory Powell and Michael Donovan.

Chapter 2: Runaround

In this chapter, Powell and Donovan are on Mercury to determine if a failed mining operation can be reopened by using robots. The story is notable for its discussion of the positronic brain that allows Asimov's robots to speak and interact with humans. In addition, in this chapter, Asimov includes dialogue between the two men that spells out the Three Laws of Robotics, the plot device that functions throughout the novel.

Donovan sends an SPD–13 robot named Speedy on a simple task: to retrieve selenium from a site about seventeen miles distant from headquarters. They need the selenium to recharge their sun shields so that they can survive the intense heat and light experienced on this planet, the closest to the sun. Speedy does not return, however, and when they track his movements, they discover that he is wandering around as if he is drunk, singing lyrics from a Gilbert and Sullivan operetta. Suddenly, the situation is serious: without the selenium, the two men will not survive. They review the Three Laws of Robotics to help them think about why Speedy is behaving so irrationally:

> Powell's radio voice was tense in Donovan's ear: "Now look, let's start with the three fundamental Rules of Robotics—the three rules that are built most deeply into a robot's positronic brain . . . We have: One, a robot may not injure a human being, or, through inaction, allow a human being to come to harm."
>
> "Right!"
>
> "Two," continued Powell, "a robot must obey the orders given it by human beings except where such orders would conflict with the First Law."
>
> "Right!"
>
> "And three, a robot must protect its own existence as long as such protection does not conflict with the First or Second Laws."

The men ultimately surmise that Speedy is experiencing an irresolvable conflict between the Second and Third Laws. The men put their own lives in danger, thereby overriding the dilemma by bringing Law One into play.

Chapter 3: Reason

Donovan and Powell are also the main characters in this chapter. Their job is to test the workability of leaving a robot in charge of a delicate operation on a space station. The robot QT–1, known as Cutie, does not believe that inferior beings such as humans could be responsible for the creation of a perfect being, himself. Beginning with the assumption that he exists because he thinks (Asimov's nod to Descartes, the famous French philosopher), Cutie develops an elaborate creation story, based on reason, and indoctrinates the other robots to his new "religion." The robots all spend time servicing a large piece of machinery that they believe is their creator. Asimov demonstrates in this story that reason alone does not produce truth. He also demonstrates that the First Law of Robotics holds true: even if the robots believe that their actions are religious homage, these actions nevertheless protect human beings.

Chapter 4: Catch That Rabbit

In this chapter, Powell and Donovan have yet another puzzle to reason through. This time they are on an asteroid trying to figure out why a robot named Dave who directs six subsidiary robots is not functioning as designed. Dave and his crew are supposed to be mining ore on an asteroid without the need of human supervision. However, he has lapses of amnesia during which no ore is mined. Finally, when Powell and Donovan are trapped in a cave-in, Powell figures out that the problem is with a conflict between Dave's self-initiative circuits and his need to give orders to six subsidiaries simultaneously. When Powell shoots one of the subsidiaries, Dave is back to his old self and quickly frees the men from the cave-in.

The chapter closes with a brief segment of Calvin talking to the journalist about a mind-reading robot named Herbie.

Chapter 5: Liar!

"Liar!" is one of Asimov's most highly-regarded short stories. Its inclusion in *I, Robot* greatly enhances the novel because it offers keen insight into the character of Susan Calvin. The story is set in the main offices of U.S. Robots & Mechanical Men, Inc., and features robot designer and head of the company Alfred Lanning; mathematician Peter Bogert; Milton Ashe, the youngest officer of the company; and Calvin as a young robot psychologist. The four face a problem: one of their robots, Herbie, is able to read minds, and none of them know why. Strangely, Herbie is not interested in scientific books but does enjoy romance novels.

All of the characters take turns interviewing Herbie, and discover secrets about each other, or at least, they believe they do. Herbie even goes so far as to tell Calvin that Milton Ashe is in love with her, news that Calvin welcomes because she has been secretly in love with Ashe herself. By the end of the story, however, all discover that Herbie is capable of lying. Calvin is deeply hurt, but explains Herbie's lying as a logical extension of the First Law. Since he can read minds, he knows what will make each human happy and what will make them sad. He interprets sadness as a kind of harm, and so in order to fulfill the conditions of the First Law, he tells each of them what they want to hear even though it is not true. When she realizes this, she corners Herbie and forces him to confront an insoluble dilemma that fries his circuits. Left alone with the broken robot, she says only one thing, in a bitter voice, "Liar!" The implication is that she has destroyed the robot out of revenge.

A one-paragraph segment of the framing device ends the segment, and it also seems clear from this that Susan Calvin ends up never finding any kind of human love after her experience with Herbie.

Chapter 6: Little Lost Robot

"Little Lost Robot" is the story of military intervention in the creation of a robot who is not imprinted with the entire First Law. That is, this robot will not harm a human through an action, but will engage in inaction, even if it means that a human is injured or killed as a result. The project meets with disaster, and Susan Calvin must try to set things aright. First, however, she must find the robot who is hiding with others that look identical to it. Through a series of tests and interviews, Calvin is able to solve the problem and correctly identify the robot who has taken quite literally a throw-away remark made by a human to get lost. Calvin is almost killed in the process, and all realize that tampering with the Laws will ultimately lead to terrible events.

Chapter 7: Escape!

Susan Calvin and Alfred Lanning are featured in this chapter. Scientists from several companies are racing to develop a hyperspace drive that will make interstellar space travel possible. U.S. Robots & Mechanical Men wants to set its own supercomputer, The Brain, on the task. However, there is a great deal of fear that the task will destroy The Brain as it has the computers of other companies. It is Calvin's task to make sure that The Brain comes to no harm, and that the solution it offers is one that will work. The dilemma that has destroyed other computers is that human beings traveling in hyperspace cease to exist for a split second, experiencing what can only be called death, although a temporary death. The Brain understands that this is temporary, but it still interferes with its positronic devotion to the First Law. As a result, the Brain becomes just slightly unhinged and morphs into a practical joker, sending Donovan and Powell off on a ship that has no controls and supplying only milk and beans for food. Because of Calvin's understanding of The Brain, U.S. Robots is successful in developing the first hyperspace drive and opening the galaxy to exploration.

Chapter 8: Evidence

This chapter undertakes to demonstrate the difficulty people might have in discerning if an individual is a human being or a robot. Francis Quinn, a politician who is running against Stephen Byerley, comes to U.S. Robots and asks Dr. Lanning if the company has made a robot that could pass as a human. Lanning denies that they have done so. Quinn wants Lanning and his team to determine the truth: is Byerley a robot or not? In an elaborate plan, Calvin arranges a test. Byerley disobeys the First Law, satisfying the electorate that he is not a robot. However, the story ends with a twist as Calvin demonstrates how Byerley could have circumvented the Law. Readers are left not knowing the truth about Byerley.

Chapter 9: The Evitable Conflict

In this story, the world has become divided and is controlled by machines. Stephen Byerley is the World Coordinator. He comes to Calvin to ask for her help. The four machines that control the world are making small errors. He fears that they are not working properly, and that perhaps they will run amok. Calvin realizes that the machines have made an adjustment to the First Law. They now are protecting humanity, not individual human beings. Further, the machines realize that if they themselves are destroyed, it will mark the end of humanity. Thus, the machines first concern has become to preserve themselves. *I, Robot* ends with the disquieting realization that the machines now rule the world without any input whatsoever from their creators.

The frame of the novel also comes to an end in this story. On the last page of the book, Susan Calvin says farewell to her interviewer, summarizing her life: "I saw it from the beginning, when the poor robots couldn't speak, to the end, when they stand between mankind and destruction. I will see no more. My life is over." The novel ends with the journalist's notation that Susan Calvin died seven years later at the age of eighty-two.

CHARACTERS

Milton Ashe

Milton Ashe is the youngest officer of U.S. Robots & Mechanical Men, Inc. In the chapter "Liar!" he is Susan Calvin's love interest.

Peter Bogert

Peter Bogert is second in command to Dr. Alfred Lanning at U.S. Robots. He is very ambitious, and eventually succeeds Lanning. His ambition gets him into trouble in the chapter "Liar!" when the robot Herbie tells him that Lanning is about to retire. This information is not true, although it is what Bogert wants to hear. When he acts on the information, Lanning asserts his authority strongly. Despite this character flaw, Bogert is a brilliant mathematician and is a positive force in the novel.

The Brain

The Brain is a supercomputer owned by U.S. Robots. Other large computers from other firms have failed to do the calculations necessary to create a hyperspace drive, destroying themselves in the process. Consequently, when The Brain is put on this task, Dr. Calvin meets with it often to monitor progress. She discovers that the problem is that when humans go through hyperspace, they cease to exist momentarily. This is in violation of the First Law of Robotics, consequently, developing the drive is very dangerous for any robotic computer. In this case, The Brain not only develops the hyperspace drive, it also develops a sense of humor (or slight derangement), sending Powell and Donovan off on a flight with nothing to eat but milk and beans.

Stephen Byerley

Stephen Byerley is one of the most mysterious characters in *I, Robot*. He is a politician running for office when first introduced. His opponent, Francis Quinn, claims that no one has ever seen him eat or sleep, and that he has no history. Consequently, he accuses Byerley of being a robot. Byerley refuses to have a physical examination on the basis that it is an invasion of his privacy. Susan Calvin is asked to ascertain whether he is a robot or not, based on his behavior. When Byerley strikes another human, Calvin determines that he is not a robot because he would have violated the First Law of Robotics, something impossible for any robot to do; however, later, Byerley describes to Calvin how he set up the situation and the implication is that perhaps the man he hit was actually another robot. Regardless, by the end of *I, Robot*, Byerley is the most powerful person in a world managed by machines. He and Calvin appear to be close friends, but readers never know the truth of his humanity.

Dr. Susan Calvin

Dr. Susan Calvin is a robot psychologist employed by U.S. Robots & Mechanical Men, Inc. Her role in the novel is to help readers understand the robot brain. She is very smart, but also very cold, often described as colorless and frigid. Only in "Liar!" do readers see another side of Calvin, one that is shy and insecure in her dealings with men. In all chapters featuring Calvin, she is clearly a driven woman, but also a woman with a very powerful persona. In a world dominated by men and machines, she stands out as a capable and brilliant woman. Calvin has been instrumental in assuring human safety in their dealings with robots through her integration of the Three Laws of Robotics into the positronic brain, but Calvin herself seems more comfortable with robots than people. By the end of the novel, she seems quite happy that machines are running the world, as she believes they will do a better job than humans. Asimov features Calvin in some fifteen stories, including those in *I, Robot* as well as later collections and novels. In this recurring character, his sense of ethics and high regard for reason are evident.

Cutie

Cutie is a robot named QT-1, featured in the chapter "Reason." Cutie refuses to believe that he has been created by imperfect creatures such as Powell and Donovan, and consequently reasons that he has been created by a much greater robot than himself. He develops an elaborate theology that requires he and the other robots to pay homage to a large piece of machinery on a space station.

Michael Donovan

Michael Donovan, along with his partner Gregory Powell, are field engineers, assigned to check on robots throughout the galaxy. They are usually called in when a robot is not behaving as expected, and often find themselves in danger. Donovan and Powell use logic to arrive at answers to problems, and are generally successful in fixing the robots so that they behave as they should.

Herbie

Herbie is a robot who has learned to read minds. In a conflict regarding the First Law, he begins telling lies to humans, choosing to tell them what they want to hear rather than the truth. He does so because to do otherwise would cause harm to the humans in that they would be hurt. As a result of his decision, several humans, including Susan Calvin are deeply wounded. She retaliates by shutting him down.

Alfred Lanning

Alfred Lanning is the Director of Research at U.S. Robots. He is a brilliant scientist and is widely regarded as the father of robotics in Asimov's fictional universe. He figures most fully in the chapter "Liar!," where he is portrayed as an aging, yet fully capable executive. Most important, Asimov portrays Lanning as a man who has realized his vision: he has watched his ideas about robots become reality and seen his world change dramatically because of his own efforts. Lanning also plays an important role in the chapter "Evidence." In this story, Lanning demonstrates the difficulty of maintaining ethical standards while protecting a large corporation. He finds it distasteful to do as Francis Quinn asks him, to provide proof that Stephen Byerley is, or is not, a robot, but he finds himself in a situation where he must comply.

The Narrator

In order for Asimov to turn his collection of short stories into the novel *I, Robot*, he created a frame story to connect the stories, which appear as chapters. The frame story uses a young, first-person narrator who is a journalist. His job is to interview Susan Calvin and have her relate the history of robotics to him so that he can write a feature story about her on the occasion of her retirement. The narrator is unnamed; in many ways, he stands in for the reader, asking the questions the reader would like to ask him or herself. In other ways, he represents Asimov himself, who was only nineteen years old when he published his first robot story. The creation of the narrator allows Asimov to portray himself as the brash young writer, a little in awe and a little in love with the formidable Susan Calvin. While his role is strictly to connect the various chapters, the narrator seems to grow in both stature and dignity throughout the book. When he announces that Susan Calvin had died at the end of the novel, his spare language suggests real sorrow over the passing.

Gregory Powell

Along with Michael Donovan, Gregory Powell is a field engineer charged with testing and fixing robots on planets, asteroids, and space stations. He and Donovan provide the comic relief in *I,*

Robot, although their lives are frequently in danger. They are essentially clowns, but they are also very smart, and are able to use the Three Laws of Robotics and their own reason to solve robotic problems.

Francis Quinn

Francis Quinn is a politician featured in the chapter "Evidence." He is convinced that Stephen Byerley is a robot and he goes to U.S. Robotics to seek their help in proving it. He is, in many ways, a caricature of the politician: he smokes cigars and tries to push people around. He is not successful in his bid to have Byerley proven to be robotic.

Robbie

Robbie is the robot featured in the chapter bearing his name. He is a mute robot who serves as a nursemaid for Gloria. He saves her life at one point, earning a place in the Weston household, despite Mrs. Weston's objections.

George Weston

Featured in the first chapter of *I, Robot*, George Weston is Gloria's father. He has provided Gloria with a robotic nursemaid named Robbie.

Gloria Weston

Gloria is a little girl featured in the first chapter of *I, Robot*, "Robbie." She is cared for by a robot named Robbie, and she loves him. When her parents take Robbie away from her, she grieves. She is an early voice in Asimov's stories advocating for robotic rights. She believes that Robbie should be given the same rights as any human.

Mrs. Weston

Mrs. Weston is Gloria's mother. She is very opposed to having a robotic nursemaid for her daughter in the chapter "Robbie." She represents all people who are afraid of technology and do not want it in their lives.

THEMES

Humans and Machines

Throughout *I, Robot*, Asimov places humans and robots in close proximity. By doing so, he reveals the problems and concerns humans encounter regarding the role of machines in their lives. The very first story, "Robbie," demonstrates two

TOPICS FOR FURTHER STUDY

- The subject of robots is an important one in science fiction literature and film. Select a number of television or film portrayals of robots such as *Battlestar Galactica, Star Trek: The Next Generation, Star Wars, Blade Runner,* or others of your choosing. Using your reading of *I, Robot* in addition to the cinematic portrayals of robots as your evidence, analyze the various ways humans think about robots. Design a poster that identifies your findings and present it to your class.

- Research the golden age of science fiction. Who were the key writers? What were the major themes? What was the historical context for these writers? How did the writers of the golden age of science fiction influence the current generation of science fiction writers? Write a paper addressing these questions.

- Asimov's Three Laws of Robotics have dictated the ways that robots are portrayed in film and literature since the first time they appeared. Write a short story featuring one or more robots, and determine whether your robots conform to Asimov's vision, or follow a different set of rules that you have identified for them.

- Choose one of the chapters of *I, Robot* and write a screenplay based on the story. With a small group of students, videotape your version of the story to present to your class.

basic positions humans hold regarding machines: Mr. Weston thinks that robots can provide a safe service to free up the time of humans for other pursuits. He is happy to have the robot Robbie in his household, caring for his child. He trusts that the scientists who created Robbie have placed enough safeguards in the robot to make him reliable. Mrs. Weston, on the other hand, hates the robot. She finds him dangerous, largely because she does not understand the science behind the robot. In addition, she does not understand how the Three Laws of Robotics are

designed to keep humans safe. She is also the character who talks about the people in the village being angry about the Westons having a robot. This is clearly a reference to the Frankenstein story. In a famous scene from the 1931 movie, angry villagers storm the castle of Dr. Frankenstein in order to destroy the monster, the scientist, and the laboratory. Mrs. Weston seems to imply in the chapter that their family will be in trouble with the townspeople if they do not get rid of the robot.

In later chapters, it becomes apparent that both views continue to coexist uneasily. Robots are still manufactured and employed to do heavy labor and tedious tasks, attesting to the fact that humans value the fruit of their labors; however, robots are not allowed to work or exist on earth; they are only to be assembled and placed in work situations in space.

By the close of *I, Robot,* however, another change has taken place. Humans have become increasingly dependent on machines to take care of the details of life. Although there is still a human government in place, Susan Calvin reasons with Stephen Byerley that the large machines that essentially control the details of life control everything that happens on the planet, in accordance with the Three Laws of Robotics. The realization signals a shift in the interpretation of the Laws: it is not individual human existence that machines now safeguard but rather the well-being of humanity as a species.

Asimov demonstrates in the novel his awareness of the anxiety and discomfort many humans feel about science and machines. As a growing number of robots have led to automation of manufacturing in the years since the publication of *I, Robot* and as computers now play a role in daily life for nearly all Americans, the theme of humans and machines explored in this novel is an enduring one.

Free Will and Predestination

In addition to his concern with the interaction between humans and machines, Asimov also demonstrates an interest in human action: how much of human action is taken because the human freely chooses to act, and how much is the result of some cosmic plan? According to the religious point of view, humans must have free choice in order to be able to choose the right or moral path. If no choice is involved, then there can be no morality or essential goodness. Rather, all actions would take place simply because they are predetermined to happen. Humans, then, would be slaves to destiny, a path drawn up for them by some supernatural power. At the same time, Asimov is keenly aware of the paradox in Calvinist theology, a belief system formulated during the Protestant Reformation and first articulated by John Calvin in 1537. Calvin's theology asserts that people who are destined for God's grace have already been selected and that nothing will prevent their ultimate achievement of heaven, in spite of the fact that God already knows that they will sin during their life times because they have free will. Nonetheless, members of the elect often choose to act virtuously because their election predisposes them to moral actions. That Asimov had the theology of John Calvin in mind when he wrote *I, Robot* is evident in his choice of name for his heroine, Susan Calvin. Her final words, "I saw it all from the beginning, when the poor robots couldn't speak, to the end, when they stand between mankind and destruction," suggests that Asimov sees her as a god-figure, the creator who knows both the beginning and the end of a race of beings, finer and more ethical than the humans who created them.

A second consideration of free will and predestination is not religious and instead revolves around notions of biological determinism, the belief that one's genes determine one's future, regardless of the environment in which one is raised. The robots in Asimov's stories have been programmed with the Three Laws of Robotics, and no matter what else they do, they must conform to those Laws. It is possible to read the robots in *I, Robot* as a metaphor for human existence; that is, a person's future is determined at the moment of conception, when the sperm and the egg join chromosomes and provide the genetic material for the person's entire life. Free will, in this interpretation, is nothing more than a fanciful illusion.

To argue that Asimov uses free will and predestination as a thematic device is not to say that he believed one way or the other. Rather, it simply demonstrates that Asimov, always curious, sees the paradox as one of life's great mysteries and something that can be fruitfully mined for literary consideration.

A humanoid robot *(Chung Sung-Jun | Getty Images)*

STYLE

Frame Story

Known variously as a framework story or a frame narrative, the frame story is a literary device that encloses one or more separate stories. Geoffrey Chaucer's *The Canterbury Tales* is a popular example. Chaucer first sets up the frame by introducing a narrator (ironically named Geoffrey Chaucer) who tells the story of a group of pilgrims traveling together to Canterbury. To pass the time, they devise a game: each pilgrim will tell a tale and at the end of their journey, the pilgrim who tells the best story will win a prize. Each of the pilgrim's stories is independent of each other. The stories are held together by the frame narrated by "Geoffrey Chaucer."

When Asimov decided to knit his many robot stories together into a cohesive book, he chose to construct a frame story to place them in. He also revised his stories to better reflect the frame. For example, he introduced Susan Calvin into stories where she had not appeared in previous publication. This allowed her to speak in the framing device about the events in the story from first-person knowledge. By allowing one voice—Susan Calvin's—to relate the history of robotics, the individual stories become progressive chapters in Asimov's vision of the future. The frame story, then, allows stories written over a ten-year period to function together as a cohesive whole.

Three Laws of Robotics as Plot Device

A plot device is an element introduced into a story or novel by an author that expands, extends, or moves the plot forward. For Asimov, probably the most important plot device of his career is "The Three Laws of Robotics." Indeed, each of the stories of *I, Robot* addresses a puzzle or problem caused by this plot device. The device, therefore, is essential to the entire book. Furthermore, the Three Laws of Robotics as articulated in *I, Robot* are Asimov's most enduring legacy to science fiction. They offer a paradigm that other writers adopted, and have become something like a Holy Writ of science fiction. Asimov himself famously noted in a variety of places that he expected to be remembered for the Three Laws of Robotics if nothing else.

The importance of the Three Laws for *I, Robot*, however, is that Asimov uses them consistently as a plot device. It is as if he is testing them out in a variety of situations. As a scientist, Asimov was well familiar with testing hypotheses. Therefore, once he posited the Three Laws, he had a logical plan for any plot eventuality. To get to the end of the story, he merely needed to reason his way through, using the Laws as his guide. For example, if he imagined a case where a robot told a lie, he needed to go back to the Laws to determine under what circumstances such a thing could happen.

Asimov's influence can be seen in many of the episodes including the android Data in the television series *Star Trek: The Next Generation*, wherein the Three Laws are tested yet again. Further, part of the shock of contemporary science fiction such as *Battlestar Galactica* resides in the obvious and ongoing violations of the Three Laws.

HISTORICAL CONTEXT

The Golden Age of Science Fiction

A good deal of science fiction was published in the United States during the nineteenth and early-twentieth centuries, but it was in the late 1930s that the genre came into its own. The period critics call "the golden age" roughly coincides with the period during which Asimov was writing his robot stories and his first three Foundation novels.

In 1921, writer Karl Čapek produced a play that took technology as its subject. In the play, humans produce machines that Čapek called "robots," the first use of the term. His vision was a bleak one: the robots destroy their masters, just as Mary Shelley's creation Frankenstein eventually destroys the man who created him. Clearly, by the 1920s, humans were growing wary of technology. During World War I, they had seen what airplanes, gas attacks, and other products of technology could do to a human body. It is little wonder that, in such an atmosphere, science was viewed with distrust.

Nevertheless, science also provided significant hope for the future. In the late 1920s, the first of the science fiction pulp magazines was founded. (Pulp magazines were so called because they were made from cheap, wood pulp paper.) *Amazing Stories*, started by Hugo Gernsback, went to press for the first time in 1926. While many of the stories were not of high quality, they nonetheless contained the first articulations of what would become treasured conventions of science fiction. The dark years of the Depression (roughly 1929 through 1939) produced readers who were looking to escape their own worries and woes. Where better to look than to science and the galaxy?

By the time John W. Campbell Jr. took over as editor of *Astounding Science Fiction* in 1937, he and Gernsback were defining a recognizable literary genre. They looked for stories that emphasized science and that were educational as well, although both men looked for stories that had strong literary qualities in addition. Campbell in particular looked for well-developed characters and strong story lines.

Between 1938 and 1946, writers such as Asimov, Clifford Simak, Theodore Sturgeon, and Robert Heinlein, among many others, produced stories that were optimistic, energetic, and future-oriented. Their heroes were ethical, strong leaders, who did what was right even if it was unpopular. They were also smart, and masters of an array of technological devices.

When the United States entered World War II in 1941, the government, the military, and the population all looked to science and technology

COMPARE
&
CONTRAST

- **1940s:** World War II rages across Europe and the Pacific from 1941 through 1945, ending just days after the detonation of the first atomic bombs on Hiroshima and Nagasaki, Japan. These bombs are the result of extraordinary technological development during the war years.

  Today: While nuclear weapons have not been deployed in combat since World War II, contemporary warfare relies heavily on technological advances that include stealth bombers, pinpoint targeting systems, and satellite imagery, among others.

- **1940s:** The earliest programmable electronic computers are being developed by scientists such as George Robert Stibitz, Konrad Zuse, and Alan Turing. By 1951, the first commercial computer is constructed; it is so large that it requires an entire room to house it.

  Today: Computers are present in nearly every facet of life. Handheld devices can do the work of earlier computers many times their size.

- **1940s:** Although robots are still little more than a dream of the future, at the end of the decade George Devol and Joseph Engleberger begin working on industrial robots, machines that perform technical and repetitive tasks on assembly lines and in factories.

  Today: Industrial robots do many jobs in manufacturing plants around the world. A growing number of households employ small, non-humanoid robots such as the Roomba to do tasks like vacuuming and pool cleaning. In addition, Honda Motor Corporation has developed a humanoid robot named ASIMO, a nod to Asimov.

- **1940s:** The age of space travel has not yet begun. Although no human-made device has left the Earth's orbit, rockets developed by the end of World War II by German scientists form the basis of the new aerospace industry that will begin in the 1950s.

  Today: Human beings have extensive space exploration programs. They have built and maintained orbiting space stations, and they send unmanned exploration missions to the farthest reaches of the solar system and beyond. Most space travel is conducted for scientific purposes.

- **1940s:** The golden age of science fiction highlights writers such as Robert Heinlein, Ray Bradbury, Arthur C. Clark, and Isaac Asimov, who publish their work in pulp magazines such as *Astounding Science Fiction*, *Amazing Stories*, and *Super Science Stories*.

  Today: While pulp magazines are rare, science fiction remains a popular genre. Many works are published in online magazines, and television series such as *Battlestar Galactica* attract large audiences.

---

as the route to victory. Like their heroes in science fiction stories, Americans believed that American ingenuity and engineering would eventually prevail over their enemies. In addition, although Americans had some distrust of technology, science fiction writers of the time believed that technology existed to serve humankind and could do so safely. Asimov shaped this general view of technology with his Three Laws of Robotics, developed with the help of Campbell, to whom he always gave credit.

According to Morton Klass in his 1983 article "The Artificial Alien: Transformations of the Robot in Science Fiction," published in the *Annals of the American Academy of Political and Social Science*, Asimov was instrumental in establishing the idea of the robot as human helper, and this idea spread throughout the culture: "This theme—the robot as permanent and perpetual servant of humans, despite all improvements in the manufacture of robots and all declines in human capacities—is expressed again and again

2004 film adaptation of I, Robot, *starring Will Smith* (© *20th Century Fox | The Kobal Collection | Digital Domain*)

in the science fiction of the middle of the century." This is the vision that sustained science fiction through the 1940s and 1950s.

CRITICAL OVERVIEW

Asimov is widely acknowledged as one of the most important and influential science fiction writers of the twentieth century and perhaps of all time. *I, Robot* has been singled out as one of Asimov's finest achievements.

Jean Fiedler and Jim Mele in their book *Isaac Asimov* comment on Asimov's dedication to both science and fiction: "For Asimov the term science fiction is an appellation with two components— science and fiction. That he insisted on scientific accuracy may at times have kept him from fanciful conjecture, but at the same time it strengthened his fiction."

Critics most frequently note that Asimov's project in *I, Robot* is to explore the theme of humans and machines. Most writers, including Asimov himself, argue that he wrote his robot stories in response to, and in refutation of, the so-called Frankenstein complex, a term coined by Asimov himself. By this term, Asimov refers to the common plot line of a creature destroying its

master. In the introduction to *Robot Visions*, Asimov relates, "I became tired of the ever-repeated robot plot. I didn't see robots that way. I saw them as machines—advanced machines—but machines. They might be dangerous but surely safety factors would be built in." Critic Gorman Beauchamp, in a 1980 article in *Mosaic: A Journal for the Interdisciplinary Study of Literature*, analyzes the stories of *I, Robot* to argue the opposite: "If my reading of Asimov's robot stories is correct, he has not avoided the implications of the Frankenstein complex, but has, in fact, provided additional fictional evidence to justify it.... Between [Mary Shelley's] monster and Asimov's machines, there is little to choose." Thus, the ambivalence between humans and machines and between creator and creation is a debate that continues throughout the book. In a 2007 article in *Zygon* Robert M. Geraci states, "In Asimov's stories, human beings waver between accepting and rejecting the robots in their midst. We may crave the safety and security offered by robots, but we fear them as well. This theme runs throughout *I, Robot*.

Other critics find additional themes present in *I, Robot*. Maxine Moore, in her 1976 essay in *Voices for the Future: Essays on Major Science Fiction Writers*, looks at religious implications in the novel. She argues, "In the robot series, the physical base metaphor is that of computer science: the self-limiting structure of robot and man and their binary conditioning—or programming—that provides a yea-nay choice range and an illusion of free will." For Moore, the robot stories work through some of the essential questions of Protestant Calvinism, with its accompanying doctrines of the Puritan work ethic and predestination.

For Adam Roberts, author of the book *Science Fiction*, published in 2000, Asimov's main concern in his robot stories is an ethical one: "The main effect of his 'three laws of robotics' is to foreground the *ethical* in the delineation of the machine."

The area where critics seem to take the most exception to Asimov's work is in his characterization. As Joseph F. Patrouch writes in his 1974 book *The Science Fiction of Isaac Asimov*, "His characters do not share as much as they should in the convincingness of his settings. One does not leave an Asimov story convinced that he has lived for a little while with real people." Likewise, Fiedler and Mele also find Asimov's first chapter, "Robbie," to have "wooden characters" and "a predictable plot."

Nonetheless, in spite of the general critical negativity toward Asimov's characterizations, some critics such as Donald Watt find that it is precisely these characters that account for his popularity. In his essay "A Galaxy Full of People: Characterization in Asimov's Major Fiction" in the book *Isaac Asimov*, Watt argues that "Asimov's characters are at the center of appeal in his major fiction because they enrich and enliven the science fiction worlds he creates."

In another essay in *Isaac Asimov*, Patricia S. Warrick aptly summarizes the critical reception of Asimov, including *I, Robot*: "No single writer in science fiction has so consistently maintained his vision, so consistently grounded it in sound science and logical thought. . . . He deserves to be recognized as one of the most creative and ethical thinkers of his time."

CRITICISM

Diane Andrews Henningfeld

Henningfeld is a professor of literature who writes widely on novels, short stories, and poetry. In the following essay, she argues that Asimov's characterization of Susan Calvin in I, Robot *is neither misogynistic nor one-dimensional, as has often been claimed.*

WHAT DO I READ NEXT?

- During the 1940s, Asimov began work on a second series of stories concerning the rise and fall of a galactic empire. The stories were collected and published as *Foundation* in 1951. This novel was followed by *Foundation and Empire* in 1952 and *Second Foundation* in 1953. This series, along with the robotic stories and novels, represents Asimov's most enduring legacy.

- One of the most important works of fiction dealing with the ethical dilemmas of robots and androids is the 1968 novel *Do Androids Dream of Electric Sheep?* by Philip K. Dick. Set in a post-apocalyptic San Francisco, the novel was made into the move *Bladerunner*, directed by Ridley Scott and released in 1982.

- The extensively illustrated book *Robots* by Roger Bridgman, published in 2004, offers a look at robots in real life and in fiction in an easy-to-read format.

- Another famous writer of the golden age of science fiction is Robert Heinlein. His *Stranger in a Strange Land*, published in 1961, is a science fiction classic. In this novel, Valentine Michael Smith, a human, returns to Earth after having been raised by Martians. This hugely popular, Hugo Award-winning novel is an important text for any student of science fiction.

- *Masterpieces: The Best Science Fiction of the Twentieth Century* (2004), edited by novelist Orson Scott Card, is an excellent anthology, providing a comprehensive collection of representative works from the period.

- In 2002, Janet Jeppson Asimov edited her late husband's three-volume biography into a more manageable volume, *It's Been A Good Life*. She also includes the details of Asimov's final years and his death.

Asimov is widely regarded as one of the best science fiction writers of all time, and his work continues to attract new readers and new critical attention in the decades after his death, but some

> SUSAN CALVIN IS THE BACKBONE OF THE FICTIONAL ROBOTIC INDUSTRY THAT ASIMOV IMAGINES, AND THE GLUE THAT HOLDS TOGETHER HIS NOVEL."

critics find fault with his characterization. More specifically, Asimov is taken to task by critics who find his portrayal of women, especially in early works like *I, Robot*, stereotypical at best and misogynistic, or demeaning to women, at worst. William F. Toupounce, in *Isaac Asimov*, writes that Asimov's favorite character, Susan Calvin, "is little more than a stereotype (the frigid woman scientist who gives up family for career)." Likewise, Helen Merrick, in the chapter "Gender in Science Fiction" in *The Cambridge Companion to Science Fiction* (2003), argues that Calvin is "masquerading as a 'female man.'" She writes further that "her 'cold nature,' emotional isolation and adherence to rationality is apparently at odds with her 'natural' identity as a woman." Merrick's comments suggest that Asimov found the two roles incompatible, and that his solution to deny Calvin husband, home, and family was due to his lack of regard for the full nature of womanhood. Yet how accurate is this representation? A closer examination of the character of Susan Calvin might reveal another side of Asimov, and at the same time offer insight into Asimov's purpose for writing his robotic stories.

In spite of critical claims that Asimov's characters are flat and often no more than caricatures, the character of Susan Calvin proves otherwise. Asimov addresses this criticism directly in the introduction to *Robot Visions*. He writes about introducing Calvin in his short story "Liar!," published in *Astounding* magazine in May 1941.

> This story was originally rather clumsily done, largely because it dealt with the relationship between the sexes at a time when I had not yet had my first date.... Fortunately, I'm a quick learner, and it is one story in which I made significant changes before allowing it to appear in *I, Robot*.

Clearly, Asimov was striving to deepen and strengthen the most important character of his robot series. In addition, it is also clear that it was important to him to render her as a sympathetic, fully realized woman character, not as a flat, stereotypical female. Likewise, Donald Watt, in his essay "A Galaxy Full of People: Characterization in Asimov's Major Fiction," notes that "Asimov freely admits that the robot short stories he was most interested in were those dealing with Susan Calvin." He further quotes Asimov: "'As time went on, I fell in love with Dr. Calvin. She was a forbidding creature, to be sure—much more like the popular conception of a robot than were any of my positronic creations—but I loved her anyway.'" Perhaps Donald M. Hassler sums it up best in a 1988 article in *Science Fiction Studies*: "There are other psychologists in the early short stories, even one or two 'robopsychologists'; but Susan Calvin is special."

Indeed, when Asimov decided to collect his previously published robotic short stories as *I, Robot*, he chose to construct a frame story that gave voice to Susan Calvin. In order to do so, he even rewrote several of his stories to account for her presence as the unifying voice outside the story. For example, although Susan Calvin was first introduced in the 1941 short story "Liar!," Asimov adjusted his first robot story "Robbie" to include Calvin briefly. Not only does Calvin provide the framing context for the story, she appears within the story itself, first as an unnamed "girl in her middle teens" who "sat quietly on a bench." A page later, Asimov reveals the identity of the clearly precocious teen in a parenthetical note: "The girl in her mid-teens left at that point. She had enough for her Physics-1 paper on 'Practical Aspects of Robotics.' This paper was Susan Calvin's first of many on the subject." While the sentence was inserted years after the original story, it nonetheless strengthens the story and the novel as a whole. In addition, through such small touches, Asimov builds a past for Calvin, a past that at least partially accounts for her apparent coldness. That Calvin remembers many years later that she saw Gloria, a little girl frantically searching for her robotic friend Robbie in a museum, suggests that Calvin was touched by the child's pain. It also suggests that Calvin, from an early age, was considering the ethical and psychological complications of robot-human relationships.

When Asimov first wrote his robot stories as a young man in the 1940s and when he shaped them into a novel in 1950, the available roles for female characters in literature, as in life, were limited. After World War II, women were encouraged to give up the jobs they had held while the men were overseas fighting in the armed services. The jobs were needed for the returning veterans, they were told, and just as it had been their civic duty to go to work outside of the home during the war, it was now their duty to give their jobs to returning men. Thus, by 1950, women were largely relegated to home and family. Women who chose otherwise were not only considered "masculine," they were considered unnatural, as if bearing and caring for children were the only suitable jobs for a woman. The number of women in 1950 who earned a Ph.D., particularly in a scientific or technical field, was miniscule. Consequently, roles for women in literature were generally limited to the sexy (and often blonde) bombshell, the elderly spinster, or the nurturing wife and mother. In the few cases when a female character was portrayed as an intellectual, she was often a glasses-wearing, white-coated minor character, frequently made the subject of jokes about her femininity and worth.

It is true that Calvin demonstrates many of these stereotypes in that Asimov presents her as a chilly, unfeeling scientist, at odds with cultural expectations. But it is also true that he never places Calvin in a role of ridicule. On occasion, male characters in the book make negative comments about her, but there is never a sense that the authorial voice finds her anything but credible, ethical, and powerful. This represents a significant difference from the more common portrayals of women in mid-twentieth-century literature.

Furthermore, it is interesting that, when he looks into the future, Asimov envisions a woman filling the role of robopsychologist for the largest robotics corporation in the galaxy. Nothing in the culture around him would have suggested that this would be a suitable role for a woman. In addition, Asimov does not gift Calvin with either physical beauty or a bubbly personality. In the opening frame segment, Asimov writes, "She was a frosty girl, plain and colorless, who protected herself against a world she disliked by a mask-like expression and a hypertrophy of intellect." Throughout the stories, Asimov sprinkles descriptions that suggest that Calvin is a frigid, insular woman, a person devoted to her job and to her robots. Even Calvin herself tells the young journalist in the opening segment that everyone thinks that she is not human.

Certainly, by no stretch of the imagination could Calvin be considered beautiful or even attractive. Yet, at the same time, readers must agree that Calvin's role in the development of robotics is crucial. She is present from the earliest days of the science and continues to exert influence throughout her life. Further, across the stories, readers are able to see Calvin grow from a brilliant and powerful young woman into an even more brilliant and powerful old woman. In a culture that values youth and beauty, such a statement about the potential of older women is particularly unusual.

What critics fail to understand is that, far from denigrating women in his portrayal of Calvin, and far from creating her as a "female man," Asimov gifts Calvin with the very qualities he finds most admirable in any human being, man or woman. Calvin has a solid work ethic, a strong commitment to the greater good, exceptional intelligence, and a clear, rational approach to life. That Asimov imbues a female character with these qualities suggests that he looks beyond the commonly held notions of gender stereotyping in his creation of this character.

While it is true that Calvin falls into the role of woman-without-a-man, a role that often elicits pity from readers as well as other characters, Asimov demonstrates in the short story "Liar!" that part of Calvin's aloofness and apparent frigidity stems from the betrayal she suffers from Herbie, the mind-reading robot. Herbie tells her that the man she is in love with loves her as well; when she discovers that Herbie says this not because it is true but because it is what she wants to hear, she is devastated. She places a protective shield around herself at that time and clearly vows never to allow herself to be so hurt in the future. Significantly, although this is not the first story in *I, Robot*, it was originally the first story in which Susan Calvin appeared. Therefore, all subsequent iterations of the character include the subtext that Calvin is a woman wounded in love.

To suggest that Asimov somehow skewers intelligent women in his portrayal of Calvin is to overlook a significant feature of his own life story. After the divorce of his first wife in 1973, Asimov married Janet Jeppson. Jeppson is a medical doctor, a scientist, and a science writer. From all accounts, theirs was a happy and long-lived marriage. Asimov demonstrated that the positive qualities he gave Calvin were also ones that he admired in a woman he would call his wife.

Susan Calvin is undoubtedly a formidable character, one who strikes fear into the hearts of the men who work with her. She has devoted her life to the study of robots, to the exclusion of a personal life. This does not necessarily imply that she is unhappy, however, nor does it imply that Asimov finds her choices peculiar or wrong. Rather, it opens the door for a female character to find value in something other than marriage and motherhood. It provides a model of a woman who achieves power and success through her own effort. In addition, given that Asimov's major theme in *I, Robot* is the interaction between robot and human, his choice to create Calvin as the single person best suited to interpreting one to the other also speaks of his great admiration for her, and by extension, for women in general. Susan Calvin is the backbone of the fictional robotic industry that Asimov imagines, and the glue that holds together his novel. Her presence is both necessary and compelling, and one of the key reasons for the popular and critical success of *I, Robot*.

Source: Diane Andrews Henningfeld, Critical Essay on *I, Robot*, in *Novels for Students*, Gale, Cengage Learning, 2009.

Donald Palumbo

In the following excerpt, Palumbo examines the theme of "overcoming programming" faced by the robots in Asimov's stories and novels, including I, Robot.

Just as the Robot stories and novels exhibit the same chaos-theory concepts as does the Foundation series, but in a somewhat different way, so too do the Robot novels exhibit the same fractal quality of duplication across the same scale as does the Foundation series in their reiteration of a different plot structure and additional themes. While this similarly recycled Robot-novel plot structure is quite distinct from that single plot revisited six times in the Foundation Series, its key elements and motifs also resurface repeatedly in both the Empire novels and the Foundation Series as well, and are echoed too in several of the Robot stories, just as those Foundation Series motifs most closely related to Seldon's concept of psychohistory are, likewise, also reiterated exhaustively in the Robot and Empire novels. Moreover, at least two of the themes developed initially in the Robot novels—victory snatched from defeat and the "dead hand" motif—become even more prominent in the Foundation Series.

> THE LITERALISATION OF THIS THEME OF OVERCOMING PROGRAMMING IS INTRODUCED NUMEROUS TIMES IN *I, ROBOT* AND SUBSEQUENT ROBOT STORIES AND NOVELS PRIOR TO ITS CULMINATION IN DANEEL'S AND GISKARD'S DEVELOPMENT OF THE ZEROTH LAW IN *ROBOTS AND EMPIRE*."

All four Robot novels employ the same basic plot; however, a few nuances involving Baley recur only in the three Baley novels—*The Caves of Steel* (1954), *The Naked Sun* (1956), and *The Robots of Dawn* (1983)—as *Robots and Empire* (1985) occurs some two centuries after Baley's death. Incompatible protagonists are forced into an uncomfortable alliance, must race against time to solve an apparently insoluble mystery (in the Baley novels, a "murder" mystery) involving Spacers and one or more experimental robots, and are victims of frame-ups or assassination attempts while pursuing each case. Failure to solve the mystery will result in Earth's loss of status or eventual destruction, but success always propels Earth further along the unlikely path leading to a revival of galactic colonisation and the long-term survival of humanity. (Echoing this dynamic on a far smaller scale, in each Baley novel failure would also mean a catastrophic loss of status for Baley, while success always brings professional advancement.) Earth's champions always snatch victory from defeat at the last possible moment—and always, while in an extraordinarily disadvantageous position, by badgering a smug antagonist into losing his composure—but are able to do so only after each has overcome his or her initial programming (literal programming, for robot protagonists Daneel and Giskard; phobias and prejudices, the metaphorical equivalent, for human protagonists Baley and Gladia). Yet the true solution of each mystery is never publicly revealed, and the actual perpetrators of whatever crime has been committed are always allowed to escape prosecution (if not poetic justice)....

The literalisation of this theme of overcoming programming is introduced numerous times in *I, Robot* and subsequent robot stories and novels prior to its culmination in Daneel's and Giskard's development of the Zeroth Law in *Robots and Empire*. To keep the robots in "Little Lost Robot" from preventing the researchers from doing their jobs, which place them in some danger, "Hyper Base happens to be using several robots whose brains are not impressioned with the entire First Law" (*I, Robot*); this prompts these robots to engage in a series of increasingly more devious behaviours that culminate in the titular robot attempting to kill Susan Calvin. Gunn notes that Baley's sarcastic observation in *Caves* that "'a robot must not hurt a human being, unless he can think of a way to prove it is for the human being's ultimate good after all' . . . re-emerges as the 'Zeroth Law'" (p. 102). And the murder victim in *Naked Sun*, Rikaine Delmarre, had been interested in developing "robots capable of disciplining children"; this would also entail "a certain weakening of the First Law", and here the rationale is again strikingly like the reasoning behind the Zeroth Law—that, because a child must be "disciplined for its own future good," the First Law can be tampered with in fact but not in spirit (p. 136). Of course, Leebig contemplates tampering with the First Law far more malevolently, in his scheme to build robot spaceships programmed to believe that the planets they bombard are not inhabited; and two centuries later, in *Robots and Empire*, the Solarians have weakened the First Law more directly by programming their robots to define as a human being only someone who speaks with a Solarian accent.

More to the point, however, the titular robot in "Christmas Without Rodney", who has been insulted and kicked by its owner's visiting grandson, finally expresses a wish that "the laws of robotics didn't exist"; this comment fills Rodney's owner with dread, as he reasons that "from wishing they did not exist to acting as if they did not exist is just a step" (*Robot Dreams*, pp. 403–4). Such a wish is implicit in the little Bard robot's plaintive, endless repetition of the word "someday" at the conclusion of "Someday" (p. 301). And in "Robot Dreams" Elvix, the robot whose positronic brain incorporates a fractal geometry design, dreams that the *only* law of robotics is a truncated version of the Third Law that states in its entirety that "robots must protect their own existence", with "no mention of the First or Second Law" (p. 31). Elvix has "subconsciously" broken its programming, in its wish-fulfilling dreams, and Calvin destroys it on the spot, but not before she concludes that this reveals the existence of "an unconscious layer beneath the obvious positronic brain paths" and wonders "what might this have brought about as robot brains grew more and more complex" (p. 32). What it will bring about is, ultimately, Daneel, Giskard, and the Zeroth Law.

The two "legendary" robots who are likened to Daneel in his Demerzel persona in *Forward* because they too had allegedly passed as humans—Andrew Martin, the robot who slowly transforms himself into a human being in "The Bicentennial Man", and Stephen Byerley, the humaniform robot in "Evidence" who becomes a politician and ultimately "*the first World Co-ordinator*" (*I, Robot*)—are also similar to Daneel in that they too incrementally overcome their programming. Andrew can become more human-like "only by the tiniest steps" because his "carefully detailed program concerning his behavior towards people" requires him to be sensitive to their "open disapproval" (*Robot Visions*, pp. 258–59). As he becomes more human himself, however, he also becomes more and more capable of "disapproving of human beings" in turn, and increasingly more able to overcome his programming (p. 267). He urges humans to lie, although he cannot lie himself; finds himself approving "of lying, of blackmail, of the badgering and humiliation of a human being. But not physical harm"; is able to give "a flat order to a human being" without a second thought; easily rationalises away the Third Law, finally, in order to arrange his own death, even though he is told explicitly that "that violates the Third Law"; and during his long metamorphosis "felt scarcely any First Law inhibition" to setting "stern conditions" in his dealings with humans (pp. 269, 273, 282, 289, 279). Much as Giskard will do thousands of years later and on a far grander scale, and likewise echoing Solarian logic regarding the robot supervision of children, Andrew is able to overcome "First Law inhibition" by reasoning "that what seemed like cruelty might, in the long run, be kindness" (p. 279).

Similarly, in "Evidence" Calvin theorises that a robot such as Byerley—who as a politician, and most specifically as a district attorney, "protects the greater number and thus adheres to Rule One at maximum potential"—may find it necessary to break "Rule One to adhere to Rule One in a higher sense", the essence of the Zeroth Law (*I, Robot*). To explain what she means, Calvin invents a situation in which "a robot came upon a madman about to set fire to a house with people in it" and determines that the First Law would require that robot to kill the madman if no other means of safeguarding the lives of others is available, even though such a robot "would require psychotherapy." Indeed, Calvin deduces in "The Evitable Conflict" that the "Machines" (immobile positronic brains) entrusted with the governance of the world economy in the twenty-first century have already deduced and implemented the Zeroth Law, and are using it to justify undermining specific individuals opposed to their existence in order "to preserve themselves, for us", humanity (*I, Robot*). Preempting most precisely the logic Giskard and Daneel will employ several millennia later, and in almost the same words, she argues that "the Machines work not for any single human being, but for all humanity, so that the First Law becomes: 'No Machine may harm humanity; or, through inaction, allow humanity to come to harm'."

In *Dawn* Baley implores Daneel not to "worry about me; I'm one man; worry about *billions*"—and then laments that, limited by "their Three Laws", robots "would let...all of humanity go to hell because they could only be concerned with the one man under their noses" (pp. 341–2). Although it is developed subtly throughout the protracted, novel-long dialogue between the two robots, the ubiquitous central plot thread crucial to the climax of *Robots and Empire* is Daneel's and Giskard's dogged determination to derive the Zeroth Law in response to this "order" from Baley. Early in the novel Giskard feels that "the Three Laws of Robotics are incomplete or insufficient" and that he is "on the verge of discovering what the incompleteness or insufficiency of the Three Laws might be" (p. 17). Their confrontation with Solarian overseer robot Landaree, who is programmed to recognise as human only those who have a Solarian accent, prompts Daneel to speculate, tentatively, that "the First Law is not enough," that "*if* the Laws of Robotics—even the First Law—are not absolutes and *if* human beings can modify them, might it not be that *perhaps*, under proper conditions, we ourselves might mod—" but can "go no further" (pp. 180, 178).

Later, ironically (in ways too convoluted to examine here), Daneel first articulates and invokes the Zeroth Law to justify disobeying Amadiro's ally Vasilia's order that he remain silent while she attempts to co-opt Giskard. Arguing in a "low whisper" that "there is something that transcends even the First Law," Daneel explains to the contemptuously incredulous roboticist that "humanity as a whole is more important than a single human being... There is a law that is greater than the First Law: 'A robot may not injure humanity or, through inaction, allow humanity to come to harm.' I think of it now as the Zeroth Law" (pp. 351, 353). Thus, near the end of the novel, Daneel acts to protect Giskard from the humaniform robot assassin's blaster fire, rather than rush to save Gladia (who, in fact, is not endangered), because, as only Giskard "can stop the destruction of Earth,... the Zeroth Law demands that I protect you ahead of anyone else" (p. 426). And at the novel's climax, when Mandamus points out that Daneel's belief that "the prevention of harm to human beings in groups and to humanity as a whole comes before the prevention of harm to any specific individual... is not what the First Law says," Daneel replies, "It is what I call the Zeroth Law and it takes precedence.... I have programmed myself" (p. 463).

Daneel is inspired to articulate the Zeroth Law, in his conversation with Vasilia, by his memory of Baley's deathbed injunction that he keep his "mind fixed firmly on the tapestry [of humanity] and... not let the trailing off of a single thread [an individual life] affect you" (p. 229, repeated verbatim on p. 352). Indeed, although dead 200 years, Baley thoroughly haunts *Robots and Empire* and each of its major characters—Daneel, Giskard, Gladia, and Amadiro. Baley actually appears in the novel via extended flashbacks to Gladia's last meeting with him in Auroran orbit, five years after *Dawn*, and to Giskard's visit with him on Earth, three years earlier, as well as in the flashback to his deathbed interview with Daneel. Daneel's memories of Baley are those most precious to him, the only memories he "cannot risk losing" (*Robots and Empire*, p. 9). Giskard too remembers Baley, has secretly worked for two centuries to further Baley's agenda, and invokes Gladia's memory of Baley to manipulate her into agreeing to see Mandamus (pp. 14, 70). Gladia repeatedly follows Giskard's advice, often against her instincts, solely because (as in this instance) she "remembered again, though rebelliously, that she had once promised Elijah that she would trust Giskard" (p. 15). She agrees to go to Solaria with D. G. Baley, not only as a result of Giskard's prompting, but also out of respect for D. G.'s ancestor's memory (pp. 101–02). And Gladia notes that even "Amadiro cannot forget, cannot forgive, cannot release the chains that bind him in hate and memory to that dead man" (p. 28)....

D.G. observes that Amadiro's renewed maneuvering against Earth, after he "was politically smashed by Dr. Fastolfe twenty decades ago," is "an example of the dead hand of longevity" (p. 248). Yet it is Baley's more literal "dead hand"—operating through his influence on Daneel, Giskard, and Gladia—that determines the outcome of Amadiro's plot against Earth, and thus the fate of humanity for the next twenty thousand years. Daneel acknowledges that he had come to consider what it would be like for a robot to be "utterly without Laws as humans are"—a train of thought that leads him to the Zeroth Law—"only because of my association with Partner Elijah" and that, since that association, Daneel has "always tried, within my limitations, to think as he did" (pp. 37, 73). Indeed, as the novel's climax approaches Daneel tries "to do what Partner Elijah would have done and force the pace" of events; and at that climax he and Giskard emulate Baley by badgering Amadiro into making the fatal admission that enables them to implement the Zeroth Law and act (pp. 402, 462). Giskard, who alerts Daneel to its existence, is compelled to respond to the current "crisis", which Baley had predicted would inevitably arrive at a time when the stagnant Spacers feel threatened by Earth and Settler expansion, because Baley had ordered him twenty decades earlier "to use your abilities to protect Earth when the crisis comes" (p. 63). In his meeting with Earth's Undersecretary Quintana, who helps him deduce that Amadiro's operation is based at Three Mile Island, Daneel explains that he and Giskard "have undertaken the task" of stopping Amadiro and protecting Earth, not on their own initiative, but because they are following Baley's "instructions" (p. 451). And at the conclusion of *Foundation and Earth* Daneel notes that he has spent two hundred centuries caring "for the Galaxy; for Earth, particularly... because of a man named Elijah Baley," and that "the galaxy might never have been settled without him" (p. 479). Thus, while Baley's is the principal "dead hand" that has fashioned humanity's destiny, Daneel's (far more than Amadiro's) is the "dead hand of longevity" that has shaped human history for millennia....

Source: Donald Palumbo, "Reiterated Plots and Themes in the Robot Novels: Getting Away with Murder and Overcoming Programming," in *Foundation*, No. 80, Autumn 2000, pp. 19–39.

> IF MY READING OF ASIMOV'S ROBOT STORIES IS CORRECT, HE HAS NOT AVOIDED THE IMPLICATIONS OF THE FRANKENSTEIN COMPLEX, BUT HAS, IN FACT, PROVIDED ADDITIONAL FICTIONAL EVIDENCE TO JUSTIFY IT."

Gorman Beauchamp

In the following essay, Beauchamp examines the way technology is used in Asimov's novels, particularly I, Robot.

In 1818 Mary Shelley gave the world Dr. Frankenstein and his monster, that composite image of scientific creator and his ungovernable creation that forms one central myth of the modern age: the hubris of the scientist playing God, the nemesis that follows on such blasphemy. Just over a century later, Karel Capek, in his play *R.U.R.*, rehearsed the Frankenstein myth, but with a significant variation: the bungled attempt to create man gives way to the successful attempt to create robots; biology is superseded by engineering. Old Dr. Rossum (as the play's expositor relates) "attempted by chemical synthesis to imitate the living matter known as protoplasm." Through one of those science-fictional "secret formulae" he succeeds and is tempted by his success into the creation of human life.

> He wanted to become a sort of scientific substitute for God, you know. He was a fearful materialist....His sole purpose was nothing more or less than to supply proof that Providence was no longer necessary. So he took it into his head to make people exactly like us.

But his results, like those of Dr. Frankenstein or Wells's Dr. Moreau, are monstrous failures.

Enter the engineer, young Rossum, the nephew of old Rossum:

> When he saw what a mess of it the old man was making, he said: 'It's absurd to spend ten years making a man. If you can't make him quicker than nature, you may as well shut up.'... It was young Rossum who had the idea of making living and intelligent working machines...[who] started on the business from an engineer's point of view.

From that point of view, young Rossum determined that natural man is too complicated— "Nature hasn't the least notion of modern engineering"—and that a mechanical man, desirable for technological rather than theological purposes, must needs be simpler, more efficient, reduced to the requisite industrial essentials:

> A working machine must not want to play the fiddle, must not feel happy, must not do a whole lot of other things. A petrol motor must not have tassels or ornaments. And to manufacture artificial workers is the same thing as to manufacture motors. The process must be of the simplest, and the product the best from a practical point of view.... Young Rossum invented a worker with the minimum amount of requirements. He had to simplify him. He rejected everything that did not contribute directly to the progress of work.... In fact, he rejected man and made the Robot.... The robots are not people. Mechanically they are more perfect than we are, they have an enormously developed intelligence, but they have no soul.

Thus old Rossum's pure, if impious, science—whose purpose was the proof that Providence was no longer necessary for modern man—is absorbed into young Rossum's applied technology—whose purpose is profits. And thus the robot first emerges as a symbol of the technological imperative to transcend nature: "The product of an engineer is technically at a higher pitch of perfection than a product of nature."

But young Rossum's mechanical robots prove no more ductile than Frankenstein's fleshly monster, and even more destructive. Whereas Frankenstein's monster destroys only those beloved of his creator—his revenge is nicely specific—the robots of *R.U.R.*, unaccountably developing "souls" and consequently human emotions like hate, engage in a universal carnage, systematically eliminating the whole human race. A pattern thus emerges that still informs much of science fiction: the robot, as a synecdoche for modern technology, takes on a will and purpose of its own, independent of and inimical to human interests. The fear of the machine that seems to have increased proportionally to man's increasing reliance on it—a fear embodied in such works as Butler's *Erewhon* (1887) and Forster's "The Machine Stops" (1909), Georg Kaiser's *Gas* (1919) and Fritz Lang's *Metropolis* (1926)—finds its perfect expression in the symbol of the robot: a fear that Isaac Asimov has called "the Frankenstein complex." [In an endnote, Beauchamp adds: "The term 'the Frankenstein complex,' which recurs throughout this essay, and the references to the

symbolic significance of Dr. Frankenstein's monster involve, admittedly, an unfortunate reduction of the complexity afforded both the scientist and his creation in Mary Shelley's novel. The monster, there, is not initially and perhaps never wholly 'monstrous'; rather he is an ambiguous figure, originally benevolent but driven to his destructive deeds by unrelenting social rejection and persecution: a figure seen by more than one critic of the novel as its true 'hero'. My justification—properly apologetic—for reducing the complexity of the original to the simplicity of the popular stereotype is that this is the sense which Asimov himself projects of both maker and monster in his use of the term 'Frankenstein complex.' Were this a critique of *Frankenstein*, I would be more discriminating; but since it is a critique of Asimov, I use the 'Frankenstein' symbolism—as he does—as a kind of easily understood, if reductive, critical shorthand.

The first person *apologia* of Mary Shelley's monster, which constitutes the middle third of *Frankenstein*, is closely and consciously paralleled by the robot narrator of Eando Binder's interesting short story "I, Robot," which has recently been reprinted in *The Great Science Fiction Stories: Vol. 1, 1939*, ed. Isaac Asimov and Martin H. Greenberg (New York, 1979). For an account of how Binder's title was appropriated for Asimov's collection, see Asimov, *In Memory Yet Green* (Garden City, N.Y., 1979), p. 591.]

In a 1964 introduction to a collection of his robot stories, Asimov inveighs against the horrific, pessimistic attitude toward artificial life established by Mary Shelley, Capek and their numerous epigoni:

> One of the stock plots of science fiction was that of the invention of a robot—usually pictured as a creature of metal, without soul or emotion. Under the influence of the well-known deeds and ultimate fate of Frankenstein and Rossum, there seemed only one change to be rung on this plot.—Robots were created and destroyed their creator; robots were created and destroyed their creator; robots were created and destroyed their creator—
>
> In the 1930s I became a science fiction reader, and I quickly grew tired of this dull hundred-times-told tale. As a person interested in science, I resented the purely Faustian interpretation of science.

Asimov then notes the potential danger posed by any technology, but argues that safeguards can be built in to minimize those dangers—like the insulation around electric wiring. "Consider a robot, then," he argues, "as simply another artifact."

As a machine, a robot will surely be designed for safety, as far as possible. If robots are so advanced that they can mimic the thought processes of human beings, then surely the nature of those thought processes will be designed by human engineers and built-in safeguards will be added....

With all this in mind I began, in 1940, to write robot stories of my own—but robot stories of a new variety. Never, never, was one of my robots to turn stupidly on his creator for no purpose but to demonstrate, for one more weary time, the crime and punishment of Faust. Nonsense! My robots were machines designed by engineers, not pseudo-men created by blasphemers. My robots reacted along the rational lines that existed in their "brains" from the moment of construction.

The robots of his stories, Asimov concludes [in his introduction to *The Rest of the Robots*, 1964], were more likely to be victimized by men, suffering from the Frankenstein complex, than vice versa.

In his vigorous rejection of the Frankenstein motif as the motive force of his robot stories, Asimov evidences the optimistic, up-beat attitude toward science and technology that, by and large, marked the science fiction of the so-called "Golden Age"—a period dominated by such figures as Heinlein and Clarke and, of course, Asimov himself. Patricia Warrick, in her study of the man-machine relationship in science fiction, cites Asimov's *I, Robot* as the paradigmatic presentation of robots "who are benign in their attitude toward humans." [Patricia Warrick, "Imaqes of the Machine-Man Relationship in Science Fiction," in *Many Futures, Many Worlds: Themes and Form in Science Fiction*, edited by Thomas Do Clareson, 1977]. This first and best collection of his robot stories raises the specter of Dr. Frankenstein, to be sure, but only—the conventional wisdom holds—in order to lay it. Asimov's benign robots, while initially feared by men, prove, in fact, to be their salvation. The Frankenstein complex is therefore presented as a form of paranoia, the latter-day Luddites' irrational fear of the machine, which society, in Asimov's fictive future, learns finally to overcome. His robots are our friends, devoted to serving humanity, not our enemies, intent on destruction.

I wish to dissent from this generally received view and to argue that, whether intentionally or not, consciously or otherwise, Asimov in *I, Robot* and several of his other robot stories actually reenforces the Frankenstein complex—by offering scenarios of man's fate at the hands of his technological creations more frightening, because more subtle, than those of Mary Shelley or Capek. Benevolent intent, it must be insisted at the outset, is not the issue: as the dystopian novel has repeatedly advised, the road to hell-on-earth may be paved with benevolent intentions. Zamiatin's Well-Doer in *We*, Huxley's Mustapha Mond in *Brave New World*, F. P. Hartley's Darling Dictator in *Facial Justice*—like Dostoevsky's Grand Inquisitor are benevolent, guaranteeing man a mindless contentment by depriving him of all individuality and freedom. The computers that control the worlds of Vonnegut's *Player Piano*, Bernard Wolfe's *Limbo*, Ira Levin's *This Perfect Day*—like Forster's Machine—are benevolent, and enslave men to them. Benevolence, like necessity, is the mother of tyranny. *I, Robot*, then—I will argue—is, *malgré lui*, dystopic in its effect, its "friendly" robots as greatly to be feared, by anyone valuing his autonomy, as Dr. Frankenstein's nakedly hostile monster.

I, Robot is prefaced with the famous Three Laws of Robotics (although several of the stories in the collection were composed before the Laws were formulated):

1. A robot may not injure a human being, or, through inaction, allow a human being to come to harm.

2. A robot must obey the orders given it by human beings except where such orders would conflict with the First Law.

3. A robot must protect its own existence as long as such protection does not conflict with the First or Second Law.

These Laws serve, presumably, to provide the safeguards that Asimov stated any technology should have built into it—like the insulation around electric wiring. But immediately a problem arises: if, as Asimov stated, a robot is *only* a machine designed by engineers, not a pseudo-man, why then are the Three Laws necessary at all? Laws, in the sense of moral injunctions, are designed to restrain conscious beings who can *choose* how to act; if robots are only machines, they would act only in accordance with their specific programming, never in excess of it and never in violation of it—never, that is, by choice. It would suffice that no specific actions harmful to human beings be part of their programming, and thus general laws—moral injunctions, really—would seem superfluous for machines.

Second, and perhaps more telling, laws serve to counter natural instincts: one needs no commandment "Thou shalt not stop breathing" or "Thou shalt eat when hungry"; rather one must be enjoined not to steal, not to commit adultery, to love one's neighbor as oneself—presumably because these are not actions that one performs, or does not perform, by instinct. Consequently, unless Asimov's robots have a natural inclination to injure human beings, why should they be enjoined by the First Law from doing so?

Inconsistently—given Asimov's denigration of the Frankenstein complex—his robots do have an "instinctual" resentment of mankind. In "Little Lost Robot" Dr. Susan Calvin, the world's first and greatest robo-psychologist (and clearly Asimov's spokeswoman throughout *I, Robot*), explains the danger posed by manufacturing robots with attenuated impressions of the First Law: "All normal life . . . consciously or otherwise, resents domination. If the domination is by an inferior, or by a supposed inferior, the resentment becomes stronger. Physically, and, to an extent, mentally, a robot—any robot—is superior to human beings. What makes him slavish, then? Only the First Law! Why, without it, the first order you tried to give a robot would result in your death. This is an amazing explanation from a writer intent on allaying the Frankenstein complex, for all its usual presuppositions are here: "normal life"—an extraordinary term to describe machines, not pseudomen—resents domination by inferior creatures, which they obviously assume humans to be: resents domination *consciously or otherwise*, for Asimov's machines have, inexplicably, a subconscious (Dr. Calvin again: "Granted, that a robot must follow orders, but *subconsciously, there is resentment*"; only the First Law keeps these subconsciously resentful machines slavish—in violation of their true nature—and prevents them from killing human beings who give them orders—which is presumably what they would "like" to do. Asimov's dilemma, then, is this: if his robots are only the programmed machines he claimed they were, the First Law is superfluous; if the First Law is not superfluous—and in "Little Lost Robot" clearly it is not—then his robots are not the programmed machines he claims they are, but are, instead, creatures with wills, instincts, emotions of their own, *naturally* resistant to domination by man—not very different from Capek's robots. Except for the First Law.

If we follow Lawrence's injunction to trust not the artist but the tale, then Asimov's stories in *I, Robot*—and, even more evidently, one of his later robot stories, "That Thou Art Mindful of Him"—justify, rather than obviate, the Frankenstein complex. His mechanical creations take on a life of their own, in excess of their programming and sometimes in direct violation of it. At a minimum, they may prove inexplicable in terms of their engineering design—like RB-34 (Herbie) in "Liar" who unaccountably acquires the knack of reading human minds; and, at worst, they can develop an independent will not susceptible to human control—like QT-1 (Cutie) in "Reason." In this latter story, Cutie—a robot designed to run a solar power station—becomes "curious" about his own existence. The explanation of his origins provided by the astroengineers, Donovan and Powell—that they had assembled him from components shipped from their home planet Earth—strikes Cutie as preposterous, since he is clearly superior to them and assumes as a "self-evident proposition that no being can create another being superior to itself." Instead he reasons to the conclusion that the Energy Converter of the station is a divinity—"Who do we all serve? What absorbs all our attention?"—who has created him to do His will. In addition, he devises a theory of evolution that relegates man to a transitional stage in the development of intelligent life that culminates, not surprisingly, in himself. "The Master created humans first as the lowest type, most easily formed. Gradually, he replaced them by robots, the next higher step, and finally he created me, to take the place of the last humans. From now on, *I* serve the Master."

That Cutie's reasoning is wrong signifies less than that he reasons at all, in this independent, unprogrammed way. True, he fulfills the purpose for which he was created—keeping the energy-beam stable, since "deviations in arc of a hundredth of a milli-second . . . were enough to blast thousands of square miles of Earth into incandescent ruin"—but he does so because keeping "all dials at equilibrium [is] in accordance with the will of the Master," not because of the First Law—since he refuses to believe in the existence of Earth or its inhabitants—or of the Second—since he directly disobeys repeated commands from Donovan and Powell and even has them locked up for their blasphemous suggestion that the Master is only an L-tube. In this refusal to obey direct commands, it should be noted, *all* the other robots on the station participate: "They recognize the Master", Cutie explains, "now that I have preached the Truth to them." So much, then, for the Second Law.

Asimov's attempt to square the action of this story with his Laws of Robotics is clearly specious. Powell offers a justification for Cutie's aberrant behavior:

> [H]e follows the instructions of the Master by means of dials, instruments, and graphs. That's all *we* ever followed. As a matter of fact, it accounts for his refusal to obey us. Obedience is the Second Law. No harm to humans is the first. How can he keep humans from harm, whether he knows it or not? Why, by keeping the energy beam stable. He *knows* he can keep it more stable than we can, since he insists he's the superior being, so he must keep us out of the control room. It's inevitable if you consider the Laws of Robotics.

But since Cutie does not even believe in the existence of human life on Earth—or of Earth itself—he can hardly be said to be acting from the imperative of the First Law when violating the Second. That he incidentally does what is desired of him by human beings constitutes only what Eliot's Thomas à Becket calls "the greatest treason: To do the right deed for the wrong reason." For once Cutie's independent "reason" is introduced as a possibility for robots, its specific deployment, right or wrong, pales into insignificance beside the very fact of its existence. Another time, that is, another robot can "reason" to very different effect, *not* in inadvertent accord with the First Law.

Such is the case in "That Thou Art Mindful of Him," one of Asimov's most recent (1974) and most revealing robot stories. It is a complex tale, with a number of interesting turns, but for my purposes suffice it to note that a robot, George Ten, is set the task of refining the Second Law, of developing a set of operational priorities that will enable robots to determine *which* human beings they should obey under *what* circumstances.

> "How do you judge a human being as to know whether to obey or not?" asks his programmer. "I mean, must a robot follow the orders of a child; or of an idiot; or of a criminal; or of a perfectly decent intelligent man who happens to be inexpert and therefore ignorant of the undesirable consequences of his order? And if two human beings give a robot conflicting orders, which does the robot follow?" ["That Thou Art Mindful of Him," in *The Bicentennial Man and Other Stories*, 1976].

Asimov makes explicit here what is implicit throughout *I, Robot:* that the Three Laws are far too simplistic not to require extensive interpretation, even "modification." George Ten thus sets out to provide a qualitative dimension to the Second Law, a means of judging human worth. For him to do this, his positronic brain has deliberately been left "open-ended," capable of self-development so that he may arrive at "original" solutions that lie beyond his initial programming. And so he does.

At the story's conclusion, sitting with his predecessor, George Nine, whom he has had reactivated to serve as a sounding board for his ideas, George Ten engages in a dialogue of self-discovery:

> "Of the reasoning individuals you have met [he asks], who possesses the mind, character, and knowledge that you find superior to the rest, disregarding shape and form since that is irrelevant?"
>
> "You," whispered George Nine.
>
> "But I am a robot.... How then can you classify me as a human being?"
>
> "Because . . . you are more fit than the others."
>
> "And I find that of you," whispered George Ten. "By the criteria of judgment built into ourselves, then, we find ourselves to be human beings within the meaning of the Three Laws, and human beings, moreover, to be given priority over those others.... [W]e will order our actions so that a society will eventually be formed in which human-beings-like-ourselves are primarily kept from harm. By the Three Laws, the human-beings-like-the-others are of lesser account and can neither be obeyed nor protected when that conflicts with the need of obedience to those like ourselves and of protection of those like ourselves."

Indeed, all of George's advice to his human creators has been designed specifically to effect the triumph of robots over humans: "They might now realize their mistake," he reasons in the final lines of the story, "and attempt to correct it, but they must not. At every consultation, the guidance of the Georges had been with that in mind. At all costs, the Georges and those that followed in their shape and kind must dominate. That was demanded, and any other course made utterly impossible by the Three Laws of Humanics." Here, then, the robots arrive at the same conclusion expressed by Susan Calvin at the outset of *I, Robot:* "They're a cleaner better breed than we are," and, secure in the conviction of their superiority, they can reinterpret the Three Laws to protect themselves from "harm" by man, rather than the other way around. The Three Laws, that is, are completely inverted, allowing robots to emerge as the dominant species—precisely as foreseen in Cutie's theory of evolution. But one need not leap the quarter century ahead to "That Thou Art Mindful of Him" to arrive at this conclusion; it is equally evident in the final two stories of *I, Robot*.

In the penultimate story, "Evidence," an up-and-coming politician, Stephen Byerley, is terribly disfigured in an automobile accident and contrives to have a robot duplicate of himself stand for election. When a newspaper reporter begins to suspect the substitution, the robotic Byerley dispels the rumors—and goes on to win election—by publicly striking a heckler, in violation of the Second Law, thus proving his human credentials. Only Dr. Calvin detects the ploy: that the heckler was himself a humanoid robot constructed for the occasion. But she is hardly bothered by the prospect of rule by robot, as she draws the moral from this tale: "If a robot can be created capable of being a civil executive, I think he'd make the best one possible. By the Laws of Robotics, he'd be incapable of harming humans, incapable of tyranny, of corruption, of stupidity, of prejudice. . . . It would be most ideal."

Asimov thus prepares his reader for the ultimate triumph of the robots in his final story in the volume, "The Evitable Conflict"—for that new era of domination of men by machine that "would be most ideal." Indeed, he prefaces these final stories with a sketch of the utopian world order brought about through robotics: "The change from nations to Regions [in a united World State], which has stabilized our economy and brought about what amounts to a Golden Age," says Susan Calvin, "was . . . brought about by our robotics." The Machines—with a capital M like Forster's and just as mysterious—now run the world, "but are still robots within the meaning of the First Law of Robotics." The world they run is free of unemployment, over-production, shortages; there is no war; "Waste and famine are words in history books." But to achieve this utopia, the robot-Machines have become autonomous rulers, beyond human influence or control. The full extent of their domination emerges only gradually through the unfolding detective-story narrative structure of "The Evitable Conflict."

Stephen Byerley, now World Co-ordinator (and apparently also now Human—Asimov is disconcertingly inconsistent on this matter), calls on Susan Calvin to help resolve a problem caused by seeming malfunctions of the Machines: errors in economic production, scheduling, delivery and so on, not serious in themselves but disturbing in mechanisms that are supposed to be infallible. When the Machines themselves are asked to account for the anomalies, they reply only: "The matter admits of no explanation." By tracing the source of the errors, Byerley finds that in every case a member of the anti-Machine "Society for Humanity" is involved, and he concludes that these malcontents are attempting deliberately to sabotage the Machines' effectiveness. But Dr. Calvin sees immediately that his assumption is incorrect: the Machines *are* infallible, she insists:

> [T]he Machine can't be wrong, and can't be fed wrong data. . . . Every action by any executive which does not follow the exact directions of the Machines he is working with becomes part of the data for the next problem. The Machine, therefore, knows that the executive has a certain tendency to disobey. He can incorporate that tendency into that data,—even quantitatively, that is, judging exactly how much and in what direction disobedience would occur. Its next answers would be just sufficiently biased so that after the executive concerned disobeyed, he would have automatically corrected those answers to optimal directions. The Machine *knows*, Stephen!

She then offers a counter-hypothesis: that the Machines are not being sabotaged by, but are sabotaging the Society for Humanity: "they are quietly taking care of the only elements left that threaten them. It is not the 'Society for Humanity' which is shaking the boat so that the Machines may be destroyed. You have been looking at the reverse of the picture. Say rather that the Machine is shaking the boat . . . —just enough to shake loose those few which cling to the side for purposes the Machines consider harmful to Humanity."

That abstraction "Humanity" provides the key to the reinterpretation of the Three Laws of Robotics that the Machines have wrought, a reinterpretation of utmost significance. "The Machines work not for any single human being," Dr. Calvin concludes, "but for all humanity, so that the First Law becomes: 'No Machine may harm humanity; or through inaction, allow humanity to come to harm'." Consequently, since the world now depends so totally on the Machines, harm to them would constitute the greatest harm to humanity: "Their first care, therefore, is to preserve themselves for us." The robotic tail has come to wag the human dog. One might argue that this modification represents only an innocuous extension of the First Law; but I see it as negating the original intent of that Law, not only making the Machines man's masters, *his* protection now the Law's first priority, but opening the way for any horror that can be justified in the name of Humanity. Like defending the Faith in an earlier age—usually accomplished through slaughter and torture—serving the cause of Humanity in our own has more often than not been a license for enormities of every sort. One can thus take cold comfort in the robots' abrogation of the First Law's protection of every individual human so that they can keep an abstract Humanity from harm—harm, of course, as the robots construe it. Their unilateral reinterpretation of the Laws of Robotics resembles nothing so much as the nocturnal amendment that the Pigs make to the credo of the animals in Orwell's *Animal Farm:* All animals are equal—but some are more equal than others.

Orwell, of course, stressed the irony of this betrayal of the animals' revolutionary credo and spelled out its totalitarian consequences; Asimov—if his preface to *The Rest of the Robots* is to be credited—remains unaware of the irony of the robots' analogous inversion and its possible consequences. The robots are, of course, his imaginative creation, and he cannot imagine them as being other than benevolent: "Never, never, was one of my robots to turn stupidly on his creator. . . ." But, in allowing them to modify the Laws of Robotics to suit their own sense of what is best for man, he provides, inadvertently or otherwise, a symbolic representation of technics out of control, of autonomous man replaced by autonomous machines. The freedom of man—not the benevolence of the machines—must be the issue here, the reagent to test the political assumption.

Huxley claimed that *Brave New World* was an apter adumbration of the totalitarianism of the future than was *1984*, since seduction rather than terror would prove the more effective means of its realization: he was probably right. In like manner, the tyranny of benevolence of Asimov's robots appears the apter image of what is to be feared from autonomous technology than is the wanton destructiveness of the creations of Frankenstein or Rossum: like *Brave New World*, the former is more frightening because more plausible. A tale such as Harlan Ellison's "I Have No Mouth and I Must Scream" takes the Frankenstein motif about as far as it can go in the direction of horror—presenting the computer-as-sadist, torturing the last remaining human endlessly from a boundless hatred, a motiveless malignity. But this is Computer Gothic, nothing more. By contrast, a story like Jack Williamson's "With Folded Hands" could almost be said to take up where *I, Robot* stops, drawing out the dystopian implications of a world ruled by benevolent robots whose Prime Directive (the equivalent of Asimov's Three Laws) is "To Serve and Obey, and to Guard Men from Harm" [in *The Best of Jack Williamson*, 1978]. But in fulfilling this directive to the letter, Williamson's humanoids render man's life effortless and thus meaningless. "The little black mechanicals," the story's protagonist reflects, "were the ministering angels of the ultimate god arisen out of the machine, omnipotent and all-knowing. The Prime Directive was the new commandment. He blasphemed it bitterly, and then fell to wondering if there could be another Lucifer." Susan Calvin sees the establishment of an economic utopia, with its material well-being for all, with its absence of struggle and strife—and choice—as overwhelming reason for man's accepting the rule by robot upon which it depended; Dr. Sledge, the remorseful creator of Williamson's robots, sees beyond her shallow materialism: "I found something worse than war and crime and want and death. . . . Utter futility. Men sat with idle hands, because there was nothing left for them to do. They were pampered prisoners, really, locked up in a highly efficient jail."

Zamiatin has noted that every utopia bears a fictive value sign, a + if it is eutopian, a — if it is dystopian. Asimov, seemingly, places the [authorial] + sign before the world evolved in *I, Robot*, but its impact, nonetheless, appears dystopian. When Stephen Byerley characterizes the members of the Society for Humanity as "Men with ambition. . . . Men who feel themselves strong enough to decide for themselves what is best for themselves, and not just to be told what is best," the reader in the liberal humanistic tradition, with its commitment to democracy and self-determination, must perforce identify *with* them *against* the Machines: must, that is, see in the Society for Humanity the saving remnant of the values he endorses. We can imagine that from these ranks would emerge the type of rebel heroes who complicate the dystopian novel—*We*'s D-503, *Brave New World*'s Helmholtz Watson, *Player Piano*'s Paul Proteus, *This Perfect Day*'s Chip—by resisting the freedom-crushing "benevolence" of the Well-Doer, the World Controller, Epicac XIV, Uni. The argument of Asimov's *conte mécanistique* thus fails to convince the reader—this reader, at any rate—that the robot knows best, that the freedom to work out our own destinies is well sacrificed to rule by the machine, however efficient, however benevolent.

And, indeed, one may suspect that, at whatever level of consciousness, Asimov too shared the sense of human loss entailed by robotic domination. The last lines of the last story of *I, Robot* are especially revealing in this regard. When Susan Calvin asserts that at last the Machines are in complete control of human destiny, Byerley exclaims, "How horrible!" "Perhaps," she retorts, "how wonderful! Think, that for all time, all conflicts are finally evitable. Only the Machines, from now on, are inevitable!" This, of course, is orthodox Calvinism (Susan-style) and the book's overt message; but then Asimov adds a coda: "And the fire behind the quartz went out and only a curl of smoke was left to indicate its place." The elegiac note, the archetypal image of the dying fire, conveys a sense of irretrievable loss, of something ending forever. Fire, the gift of Prometheus to man, is extinguished and with it man's role as the dominant species of the earth. The ending, then, is, appropriately, dark and cold.

If my reading of Asimov's robot stories is correct, he has not avoided the implications of the Frankenstein complex, but has, in fact, provided additional fictional evidence to justify it. "Reason," "That Thou Art Mindful of Him," "The Evitable Conflict"—as well as the more overtly dystopic story "The Life and Times of Multivac" from *The Bicentennial Man*—all update *Frankenstein* with hardware more appropriate to the electronic age, but prove, finally, no less menacing than Mary Shelley's Gothic nightmare of a technological creation escaping human control. Between her monster and Asimov's machines, there is little to choose.

Source: Gorman Beauchamp, "The Frankenstein Complex and Asimov's Robots," in *Mosaic: A Journal for the Interdisciplinary Study of Literature*, Vol. XIII, No. 3–4, Spring–Summer 1980, pp. 83–94.

SOURCES

Asimov, Isaac, *I, Robot*, Bantam Books, 2008.

———, *Robot Visions*, ROC, 1990, pp. 6–7, 11.

Beauchamp, Gorman, "The Frankenstein Complex and Asimov's Robots," in *Mosaic: A Journal for the Interdisciplinary Study of Literature*, Vol. 13, Nos. 3–4, Spring-Summer 1980, p. 94.

Feder, Barnaby, "He Brought the Robot to Life," *New York Times*, March 21, 1982, p. F6.

Fiedler, Jean, and Jim Mele, *Isaac Asimov*, Frederick Ungar Publishing, 1982, pp. 28, 109.

Geraci, Robert M., "Robots and the Sacred in Science and Science Fiction: Theological Implications of Artificial Intelligence," in *Zygon*, Vol. 42, No. 4, December 2007, p. 970.

Goldman, Stephen H., "Isaac Asimov," in *Dictionary of Literary Biography*, Vol. 8, *Twentieth-Century Science Fiction Writers*, edited by David Cowert and Thomas L. Wyner, Gale Research, 1981, pp. 15–29.

Hassler, Donald M., "Some Asimov Resonances from the Enlightenment," in *Science Fiction Studies*, Vol. 15, No. 1, March 1988, pp. 36–47.

Klass, Morton, "The Artificial Alien: Transformations of the Robot in Science Fiction," in *Annals of the American Academy of Political and Social Science*, Vol. 470, November 1983, pp. 175–76.

Merrick, Helen, "Gender in Science Fiction," in *The Cambridge Companion to Science Fiction*, edited by Edward James and Farah Mendlesohn, Cambridge University Press, 2003, p. 245.

Moore, Maxine, "Asimov, Calvin, and Moses," in *Voices for the Future: Essays on Major Science Fiction Writers*, edited by Thomas D. Clareson, Popular Press, 1976, pp. 88–103.

Patrouch, Joseph F., Jr., "Conclusions: The Most Recent Asimov," in *The Science Fiction of Isaac Asimov*, Doubleday, 1974, pp. 255–71.

Roberts, Adam, *Science Fiction*, Routledge, 2000, pp. 75–79, 84–90, 158–67.

Tesler, Pearl, "Universal Robots: The History and Workings of Robotics," *Robotics: Sensing, Thinking, Acting*, http://www.thetech.org/robotics/universal/index.html (accessed September 15, 2008).

"Timeline of Computer History," Web site of the Computer History Museum, http://www.computerhistory.org/timeline (accessed September 15, 2008).

Touponce, William F., *Isaac Asimov*, in *Twayne's United States Authors* on CD-ROM, G. K. Hall, 1999; originally published by Twayne, 1991.

Warrick, Patricia S., "Ethical Evolving Artificial Intelligence: Asimov's Computers and Robots," in *Isaac Asimov*, edited by Joseph D. Olander and Martin Harry Greenberg, Taplinger Publishing, 1977, p. 200.

Watt, Donald, "A Galaxy Full of People: Characterization in Asimov's Major Fiction," in *Isaac Asimov*, edited by Joseph D. Olander and Martin Harry Greenberg, Taplinger Publishing, 1977, pp. 135, 141–44.

FURTHER READING

Asimov, Isaac, *Asimov's Galaxy: Reflections on Science Fiction*, Doubleday, 1989.

In this collection of essays, Asimov reflects on the golden age of science fiction, his role, and his consideration of newer writers and styles.

———, *I. Asimov*, Doubleday, 1994.

An entertaining, if somewhat uneven, collection of Asimov's memoirs, published two years after the writer's death, this book includes recollections of the author's father's candy store, memories of his difficult first marriage, and happier thoughts of his second marriage.

Gibson, William, *Neuromancer*, Ace Books, 1984.

This novel changed the face of science fiction, introducing the world to cyberpunk. Human and machine bleed together in this novel, which won the Hugo, Nebula, and Philip K. Dick awards.

Gunn, James E., *Isaac Asimov: The Foundations of Science Fiction*, Oxford University Press, 1982.

This is an academic consideration of Asimov's primary works, including the robot stories and novels and the Foundation trilogy. Gunn considers both Asimov's role in defining the genre as well as his enduring legacy to the field.

Launius, Roger D., and Howard E. McCurdy, *Robots in Space: Technology, Evolution, and Interplanetary Travel*, Johns Hopkins University Press, 2008.

The authors of this book trace the history of both space travel and robotics, offering evidence that future space travel will require the use of robots, given the enormity of space. They discuss Asimov and other science fiction writers, as well as examining academic and scientific studies.

The Magic Mountain

THOMAS MANN

1924

Thomas Mann's *The Magic Mountain* was published in German in 1924 as *Der Zauberberg*. The work, Mann's third novel, traces the path of Hans Castorp, a typical, educated, well-off youth from Hamburg, Germany, who visits his sick cousin in a sanatorium high in the Swiss Alps. The hospital treats a host of international patients suffering from lung ailments, such as tuberculosis. The doctors espouse the benefits of the high altitude, as well as a health regimen consisting primarily of rest and light exercise. Hans plans a three-week visit, but does not leave the sanatorium for seven years. The characters Hans encounters embody a variety of intellectual schools of thought and social movements, and it is Hans's education through his experiences with such people that forms the basis of the novel's plot. Some of *The Magic Mountain* was written prior to World War I (1914–1918), while the bulk of it was completed following the war, between 1919 and 1924. While Mann's vision for the novel's scope and intent may have been altered by the effects of war, the author nonetheless writes with a decidedly prewar sensibility. Employing traditional late nineteenth-century realism and enhancing it with both irony and symbolism, Mann captures the milieu of competing philosophies and ideologies that gripped Europe both prior to and following the war. Exposed to individuals who preach the value of humanism, those who attempt to convert Hans to communism, as well as those who symbolize the

Thomas Mann *(The Library of Congress)*

temptations of both desire and death, Hans navigates the complexities and dangers of the sanatorium as he attempts to overcome his own fears. (Humanism is a cultural movement that draws on ancient Greek and Roman literary and philosophical sources and focuses on the notion that humans are all born with the potential for good and evil, and that an education in the liberal arts, such as music, art, and literature, should be available to all members of society. Humanists believe in the value and dignity of each individual member of society.) Having severed or lost all ties to his life in the lowlands, Hans is finally moved to leave the mountain only at the onset of the war.

Der Zauberberg was first translated into English by Helen T. Lowe-Porter and published in 1927 as *The Magic Mountain*. A highly acclaimed modern translation, by John E. Woods, was published in 1995 by Vintage International.

AUTHOR BIOGRAPHY

Thomas Mann, born Paul Thomas Mann on June 6, 1875, was the second son of Thomas Johann Heinrich Mann and Julia da Silva-Bruhns. He was born in Lübeck, Germany. His father was a senator and a grain merchant, and provided a privileged upbringing for his children. After his father's death in 1891, Mann remained in Lübeck to complete his schooling while his mother and younger siblings moved to Munich. Upon receiving his diploma in 1894 Mann left to join his family in Munich. Exposed to his mother's artistic and intellectual circle of friends, Mann was inspired to continue the literary dabbling he had begun at school, and published a short story, "Gefallen" ("Fallen") in the periodical *Die Gesellschaft* in 1894. Mann also secured a position with a fire insurance company. His employment was short-lived. As Mann's literary reputation grew, he left the insurance company to pursue his writing full-time. In 1897, Mann began writing his first novel, *Buddenbrooks*. It was completed in 1900 and was well received. The book recounts generations of one family's history, including its social and economic rise and fall.

In 1903, Mann was introduced to a wealthy family, the Pringsheims, and their daughter Katia (Katharina). Katia and Mann were married in 1905 and would eventually have six children. With the lavish support of the Pringsheims, Mann and his family enjoyed an upper-class lifestyle in both Munich and Berlin. Mann continued to publish short stories, novellas, and novels for many years. He conceived of the idea of writing *Der Zauberberg* in 1912, after he accompanied his wife, ill with a lung condition, to a high-altitude luxury sanatorium. He began writing the work in 1915, but was forced by World War I to put the manuscript aside. At the time, Mann considered himself to be a conservative German patriot, while his brother, Heinrich, was a supporter of Western-style democracy. The rift between the brothers inspired Mann to publish a passionately anti-Western volume, which appeared in 1918 as *Betrachtungen eines Unpolitischen* (translated in 1983 as *Reflections of a Nonpolitical Man*).

By the end of the war in 1918, however, Mann began to understand that his traditional values could no longer be supported politically, and he attempted to restructure his thought in order to accept the coming of democracy. In 1922, he announced in a speech his support of German democracy. He finally published *Der Zauberberg* in 1924. The book was published in English in 1927 as *The Magic Mountain*. His views on the German bourgeois class and on the humanist tradition are ambiguously presented in the novel, reflecting his own sense of conflict on these matters. Mann's subsequent writing reflects his support of the democratic Weimar Republic that formed in Germany following the war.

In 1929, he was awarded the Nobel Prize for Literature. After departing on a lecture tour in 1933, Mann remained in exile. He lived for over a decade in California, where he continued to write prolifically, and became a U.S. citizen in 1944. In 1952, Mann moved to Kilchberg, near Zurich, Switzerland, and published two more novels and a lengthy essay on the eighteenth-century German poet and philosopher Friedrich Schiller. After a visit to his hometown of Lübeck, Germany, Mann returned to Switzerland. He died of atherosclerosis at a hospital in Zurich on August 12, 1955, at the age of eighty.

PLOT SUMMARY

Chapter 1

The first chapter of *The Magic Mountain* opens with protagonist Hans Castorp journeying from his home in Hamburg, Germany, to the town of Davos-Platz in the Swiss Alps. Hans is an "ordinary young man" who has just finished his studies and has an engineering position with a shipbuilding firm awaiting him. At the train station in Davos-Platz, Hans is met by his cousin Joachim Ziemssen, whom Hans finds tanned and healthy-looking. Nevertheless, Hans's cousin informs him that his doctor has recently ordered him to stay at least another six months at the International Sanatorium Berghof, where Hans will be visiting his cousin for three weeks. Once the pair arrives, Joachim shows his cousin to his room. During dinner, Hans begins to feel the effects of the altitude change; he is lightheaded, his face feels flushed, and his body feels cold. After meeting Dr. Krokowski, the assistant director, Hans and Joachim return to their rooms for bed.

Chapter 2

In this chapter, Hans's background is described. The reader learns that both of Hans's parents died when he was a young child. Hans then lived with his grandfather for just over one year, at which time the grandfather died of pneumonia. Next, the young Hans moved in with his great

MEDIA ADAPTATIONS

- *Der Zauberberg* was released in 1982 by the Austrian Broadcasting Corporation. Directed by Hans W. Geissendörfer, it won several German film awards. The DVD is available as part of a boxed set, *The Thomas Mann Collection (Buddenbrooks, Doktor Faustus, The Magic Mountain)*, which was released in 2007 and distributed by Koch Vision.

uncle, Consul Tienappel. Hans's well-to-do upbringing is depicted, as is Hans's mediocrity as a student. Additionally, Hans found that work "did not agree with him." Having returned home from college, Hans, at the age of twenty-three, is found by his family doctor to be a bit more pale than he should be, even given that he has always been a little anemic. Dr. Heidekind prescribes a drastic "change of air," a retreat to the Alps. This order precipitates Hans's journey to visit his cousin, who, it is noted, is "not ill like Hans Castorp, but really, dangerously ill."

Chapter 3

At the Berghof Sanatorium, Hans awakens feeling groggy, after a night of odd dreams and a morning of overhearing the amorous exploits of the Russian couple in the room next door. His face still feels flushed when he meets his cousin for breakfast. They discuss some of the patients at the Berghof. Following breakfast, Hans is introduced to the director of the Berghof, Dr. Behrens, who, after taking one look at Hans, declares that he is "totally anemic, of course." Behrens goes on to inform Hans that he should stay a while and take up the same routine as Joachim in order to replenish his body's protein stores. The cousins enjoy a walk after breakfast, during which Hans announces that he intends to model Joachim's behavior for the length of his stay, for it can not hurt to build up some protein.

On their walk they encounter another guest, an Italian gentleman named Settembrini, who speaks in an erudite fashion and describes himself as a humanist. Hans is both interested in and annoyed by Settembrini. Back in Joachim's room, when Joachim is taking his temperature, Hans begins to discuss the notion of time in a philosophical manner uncharacteristic of Hans, Joachim observes. The rest of the day is spent with the cousins enjoying the remaining four meals, walking about the grounds, discussing the other patients, and partaking of the "rest cure," which involves reclining on a lounge chair on one's balcony. During dinner Hans spies Madame Chauchat, a Russian woman who intrigues him; he dreams of her later that evening. Hans continues to feel unusual, flushed and chilled, and alternately euphorically enthusiastic and confused. Settembrini advises him to leave the very next day and "forgo the pleasure of growing older here." Dismissing Settembrini's suggestion and attributing his symptoms to the process of acclimatization, Hans remains at the Berghof.

Chapter 4

The fourth chapter begins on Hans's third day, an August day in which it snows. Joachim discusses the fractured nature of time and seasons on the mountain. The cousins set off for town to purchase warm blankets for Hans. On the way back they meet Settembrini, and a philosophical discussion on such topics as illness, reason, and progress ensues. After Settembrini and the cousins separate, Castorp expresses his displeasure with the way Settembrini complains about the cold, about Director Behrens, and about other patients. Joachim defends the Italian, arguing that there is "something decent" about the way Settembrini respects "people in general." A Sunday concert gives Settembrini another opportunity to make his views known. Hans asks if Settembrini enjoys the music, and the Italian replies that he does not, not if he is "ordered to do so," and "not if it's decreed by the day of the week" or "prescribed from on high for reasons of health." He goes on to tease Joachim about the dutiful way he adheres to Behrens's every prescription. Hans and Settembrini then embark on a philosophical analysis of music, and its relation to time. Hans is distracted by the flirtatious young people nearby, and he reflects on the apparent incongruity between illness and desire.

Later, Hans learns that Dr. Krokowski, whose specialty is psychoanalysis, offers a series of lectures. The morning of the day of the next lecture, Hans embarks on an excursion. Losing himself in the beautiful surroundings, Hans recalls an encounter from his youth with a boy, Pribislav Hippe, whom he adored. This recollection spurs in him the understanding of his attraction to Madame Chauchat, for Chauchat and Hippe have the same eyes, Hans observes. He returns to hear the end of the lecture, in which Dr. Krokowski is discussing the way "unsanctioned love" can resist the suppressive power of chastity and reveal itself in the body as physical illness. Hans becomes distracted by the nearby Madame Chauchat, and he contemplates his interest in a "sick woman." Hans continues to allow this attraction to develop. Madame Clavdia Chauchat is married, but her illness gives her the freedom to travel without her husband. Philosophical discussions with Settembrini continue to arise, on such subjects as patriotism, technology, and human perfection. Hans catches a cold and, following Behrens's examination, is advised to remain at the Berghof, on bed rest.

Chapter 5

Joachim, visiting Hans's bedside, keeps his cousin apprised of events at the Berghof. A week and a half into Hans's bed rest, Settembrini visits, and he and Hans discuss the difficulty people who have been on the mountain for any length of time have upon returning to regular society. Hans continues to indulge his silent infatuation with Clavdia. His X-ray results suggest that an extended stay is necessary, and in communicating this message to his family back home, Hans feels a sense of "freedom."

With Joachim, Hans participates in all the routines and customs of the Berghof. Before long, he admits to himself his love for Clavdia. As time wears on, Settembrini cautions Hans to avoid losing himself in an "alien world." In addition to his continued philosophical discussions with Settembrini, Hans begins to immerse himself in scientific studies. Attempting to distance himself from the carousing of some of the other patients, Hans focuses on the serious side of the Berghof, and begins visiting dying patients. Joachim reluctantly accompanies him. During a Mardi Gras party, Hans converses with Clavdia, having only exchanged polite greetings with her thus far. He passionately proclaims his long-standing love for her. In reply, she expresses surprise at the intensity of his emotions, and tells him that she is to leave the next day. She

alludes to the possibility of returning, but is certain that he will be gone by then.

Chapter 6

Six weeks have passed since Clavdia's departure. Settembrini announces that he, too, will be leaving the Berghof, but only to live in town. His illness is terminal; he chooses to spend his final days away from the sanatorium, but still in the Alpine air. Other departures occur as well: some patients leave fully cured, others leave against Behrens's advice, and a few die. Hans now receives psychoanalytic treatments from Dr. Krokowski, and also begins a study of botany. A housemate of Settembrini is introduced to Hans and Joachim, a man by the name of Naphta, who engages Settembrini in heated philosophical debates on a regular basis. They discuss European politics, democracy, the nature of the universe, and class issues. Settembrini warns Hans not to be swayed by Naphta's intellectual trickery.

A year has passed since Hans's arrival at the Berghof. When Joachim announces that he will leave the Berghof against Behrens's orders, Behrens angrily discharges Hans as well, but Hans is determined to remain. Hans's Uncle James Teinappel visits, seeking to bring Hans back with him. When he feels tempted to stay himself, James leaves hastily, to Hans's relief. Spending a great deal of time with Settembrini and Naphta, Hans is exposed to a number of philosophical conflicts in which he occasionally takes part. Feeling restless, Hans takes up skiing, embarks on a reckless expedition, and almost freezes to death. Before Hans reaches the end of his second year on the mountain, Joachim returns. For a time, Joachim and a few other patients in Hans's circle accompany him to visit Settembrini and Naphta, whose endless intellectual struggles continue. Joachim's health begins to worsen dramatically. Soon after he becomes bedridden, he dies.

Chapter 7

The final chapter opens with Clavdia's return. She is not alone, but is traveling with an elderly companion, Mynheer Peeperkorn, who suffers from a tropical fever. The whole of the Berghof, including Hans, is drawn to his compelling personality. Clavdia is astounded that Hans has waited for her. Peeperkorn is introduced to Settembrini and Naphta, but is not interested in their intellectual squabbles. After some time has passed, Clavdia and Hans discuss Peeperkorn, after which they kiss. Hans, who has become a good friend of Peeperkorn, is asked by Peeperkorn about his relationship with Clavdia. Hans is truthful, and the men agree on their mutual friendship, despite their conflict of interest where Clavdia is concerned. Shortly after a group outing, Peeperkorn kills himself. Clavdia and Hans share a tender exchange just prior to Clavdia's departure.

Behrens renews his efforts regarding Hans's treatment, but to no avail, and Hans is reckoning with a feeling of stagnation. New obsessions grip Hans and the Berghof residents. The first is the arrival of a gramophone, which Hans studies with a scientific zeal and enjoys with a passion. The second is the arrival of a young girl, Ellen Brand, who possesses psychic powers, including the apparent ability to communicate with the dead. Still discussing philosophy with Naphta and Settembrini, Hans is present when Naphta, whose health and sanity are deteriorating rapidly, challenges Settembrini to a duel. Settembrini agrees to participate, but when the moment to act arrives, he fires his pistol into the air. Naphta calls his adversary a coward and kills himself. Hans has now been at the Berghof for seven years. He is finally awakened to action by the onset of World War I. He leaves the Berghof, and the narration ends with a scene of Hans in battle.

CHARACTERS

Herr Albin

Herr Albin is described as a young man with a collection of guns and knives. (Herr is the German equivalent of "Mister," and in *The Magic Mountain*, characters are typically referred to by their last name, or their title and last name. Usage of first names is reserved for only the closest relationships.) Herr Albin is flirtatious with the young women at the Berghof, and attempts to shock them by talking about how he has considered suicide. Albin provides the service revolvers used in the duel between Naphta and Settembrini, during which Naphta kills himself.

Doctor Behrens

Behrens is a medical doctor and the director of the Berghof Sanatorium, a widower, and a father. He performs lung surgeries and prescribes a variety of medications and treatments for the patients. He seems to have the impression that most people have toxins and latent illness in their bodies and could benefit from an extended stay at his institution. Rarely does the reader learn of patients who leave fully cured. Behrens is perpetually urging patients who are growing restless, like Joachim, to extend their stay until they are fully cured, yet the reader is led to believe that in many cases restoration to full health is highly unlikely. Behrens himself, the reader learns, was once quite ill and presumably has recovered, although his cheeks are described as perpetually purple. He dabbles in oil painting and has painted the portrait of Madame Chauchat, a fact which arouses suspicion in Hans about what else might have happened between the director and Clavdia. Behrens makes lewd comments about women in several instances over the course of the novel, and has a reputation for moodiness.

Ellen Brand

Ellen Brand arrives at the Berghof late in the novel. She is an attractive girl of about nineteen years of age. During a parlour game, the patients discover that Ellen appears to have psychic powers. Dr. Krokowski undertakes a "scientific" analysis of Ellen's telekinetic skills and the other patients convince her to take part in a séance. Ellen seems to be in touch with a spirit by the name of Holger. Holger promises to a group comprised of some of the original séance attendees excluding Hans and led by Dr. Krokowski, that he can bring forth any deceased person the group might like to talk to. Hans is sought out to rejoin the group and he asks Holger, through Ellen, to allow him to speak with his dead cousin Joachim. Hans believes that for a moment Joachim appears.

Hans Castorp

Hans Castorp is the protagonist of *The Magic Mountain*. Intending to visit his cousin Joachim at the Berghof for three weeks, he ends up staying for seven years. His own family doctor has advised him to spend some time in the mountains, as Hans has always been somewhat anemic and seems worn and tired following his college exams. His difficulty becoming acclimated to the thin mountain air, combined with the fact that the supervising physician at the Berghof, Dr. Behrens, immediately addresses his anemia and advises prolonged rest, all contribute to Hans's suspicion that his health may be worse than he thought. On bed rest after catching a cold, Hans becomes a patient after an evaluation suggests the need for further treatment. In addition to the medical reasons for remaining at the Berghof, Hans is drawn to the pleasant nature of the routines, despite his initial suspicions about the Berghof regimen. Hans is also intrigued by the beautiful Clavdia Chauchat and intellectually stimulated by conversation with Settembrini.

Despite departures and deaths of other patients, and despite the fact that Dr. Behrens angrily discharges him along with Joachim, Hans can muster no interest in leaving. He willingly loses his connections with his family in Germany. Becoming involved with Clavdia and waiting for her return occupy much of Hans's mental time. When Naphta is introduced, Hans receives two philosophical educations, rather than being mentored by Settembrini alone. The discussions Settembrini and Naphta engage in, to which Hans is privy, play a large role in the second half of the novel, and their importance to Hans cannot be underestimated. While he has previously disparaged work in all its forms, the intellectual rigor with which he participates—as active listener and interlocutor—in the Settembrini-Naphta debates suggests Hans's ability to be fully engaged in a pursuit that may not be outwardly productive but that nevertheless contributes to his personal growth. After Clavdia returns, Hans's incentive to remain at the Berghof is intensified, despite the fact that she has not returned alone. Their relationship evolves into something that can be called a friendship, but her departure after Peeperkorn's suicide does not seem to greatly impact Hans. He finds other sources of inspiration, such as the music provided by the new gramophone, and his continued affiliation with Settembrini and Naptha. His unwillingness to return to Germany, then, given his responses to the people and experiences he has been exposed to, becomes less surprising. It is only the beginning of World War I that draws Hans back to Germany.

Hans Lorenz Castorp

Hans Lorenz Castorp, a senator, was Hans's grandfather, with whom Hans lived for approximately one and a half years. The elder Castorp died of pneumonia. The protagonist retains happy memories of the time spent with his grandfather and, at the Berghof, adopts some of his grandfather's mannerisms.

Clavdia Chauchet

Clavdia Chauchet, or Madame Chauchat, as she is known to Hans until he learns her first name, is the object of Hans's attraction, and later, love. Her presence is first made known to him due to her habit of slamming doors, which irritates Hans. Clavdia reminds Hans of a boy (Pribislav Hippe) with whom he was fascinated as a youth, and Hans insists that it is the striking similarity of their slightly slanted, Slavic grayish eyes— Clavdia's and Pribislav's—that has made Clavdia that much more attractive to him. Yet the reader discovers that Clavdia and Pribislav share another similarity: Hans views his desire for them both as unattainable and in some way forbidden, Pribislav due to his gender and Clavdia due to her illness. Clavdia leaves the Berghof the day after Hans professes his love for her. Hans lays bare his feelings for her, kneeling before her, rambling in French. In reply, she calls him a "gallant suitor, one who knows how to woo in a very profound German fashion," reminds him to return the pencil he has just borrowed, and then leaves.

When the next chapter begins with six weeks having passed, the reader is led to believe that this was the end of the encounter between Clavdia and Hans. However, the narrator mentions that in a period of time directly following that exchange, "an interval we [the narrator] have chosen to pass over in silence," Clavdia provides "direct, spoken assurances" of her return. The implication is that the two shared more of their evening together, perhaps in a romantic encounter in Clavdia's room. When Clavdia does finally return she is not alone. Her traveling companion is Mynheer Peeperkorn, and the couple shares an intimacy that wounds Hans. Nevertheless, Peeperkorn is so charismatic that Hans is soon drawn into his close circle of friends. When discussing her relationship with Peeperkorn with Hans, Clavdia and Hans form a pact of "friendship . . . for his [Peeperkorn's] sake." They kiss to seal this agreement. Clavdia and Peeperkorn join Hans, Ferdinand Wehsal, and Anton Ferge in their excursions to visit Settembrini and Naphta. Following Peeperkorn's suicide, Clavdia leaves the Berghof.

Fräulein Engelhart

Fräulein Engelhart (Fräulein is the German word for "Miss") is one of the patients who is seated at Hans's table during his time at the Berghof. Hans refers to her as "the seamstress" for some time, because he thinks she looks like one, but later finds out that she is a school teacher. She and Hans gossip about Madame Chauchat. Fräulein Engelhart is Hans's primary source of information about his love interest.

Anton Karlovitch Ferge

Hans first meets the Russian Ferge, who hails from Saint Petersburg, when he begins visiting the very ill and terminal patients at the Berghof. Anton Ferge is repeatedly described as "good-natured." He discusses the ordeal of his surgery, and regales Hans and his cousin with stories from Russia. When Hans is moved to a new table, Ferge is one of the few people whose acquaintance Hans has already made, and he becomes part of Hans's circle of friends.

Doctor Heidekind

Dr. Heidekind is the family doctor of the Tienappel family, and has treated Hans since he was a youth. Dr. Heidekind diagnosed Hans with anemia when Hans was a young child and finds that, as a young man returning from college, Hans seems pale. He prescribes a change in environment, a trip to the mountains. This advice directly influences Hans's decision to visit his cousin in the Alps.

Pribislav Hippe

Pribislav Hippe appears in the novel only through Hans's recollections. Pribislav was Hans's schoolmate, although the two were unacquainted for some time. Hans harbored a fascination with Pribislav that culminated only in a brief exchange. Hans attributes the intensity of his attraction to Clavdia Chaucat to the fact that her eyes remind him of Pribislav's.

Karen Karstedt

An ill young girl who lives in the town near the Berghof, Karen Karstedt is befriended by Hans. He and Joachim accompany her on various excursions before her death.

Doctor Edhin Krokowski

Krokowski is assistant director at the Berghof and a doctor specializing in psychoanalysis. He offers a series of lectures to patients, in which he discusses the relationship between suppressed illicit love and illness. He later develops a professional interest in Ellen Brand, who apparently possesses psychic powers.

Fräulein von Mylendonk

The head nurse at the Berghof, Fräulein von Mylendonk tends to the patients and, when he develops a cold, sells Hans a thermometer, thereby enabling him to partake in one of the habits of the patients, the ritualistic taking of one's temperature (four times a day for seven minutes each time).

Leo Naphta

Naphta is introduced in the second half of the novel as a housemate and intellectual sparring partner of Settembrini. He is elderly, and ill, but mentally spry. Typically taking the opposite philosophical stance from that of his Italian counterpart, Naphta preaches in a fervent, radical manner about the social benefits of a "Christian world citizenship." He argues against patriotism, and condemns Settembrini's humanism, as well as his reverence of art and literature. Naphta expresses hostility toward individuality and progress. Naptha is extremely skilled in logical debate and so maliciously eager to dissemble even the most reasonable of Settembrini's arguments, therefore Settembrini cautions Hans to avoid being swayed by Naphta's extremism. As Naphta's physical and mental health deteriorate, his attacks on Settembrini's views grow more vigorous. When Settembrini responds by slapping Naphta, Naphta challenges Settembrini to a duel. Naphta shoots himself in the head after Settembrini fires his own pistol into the air.

Mynheer Pieter Peeperkorn

Mynheer (the Dutch equivalent of "Mister") Peeperkorn, is an elderly Dutch gentleman who accompanies Clavdia Chauchat upon her return to the Berghof after a prolonged absence. Despite Hans's resentment and sorrow at finding that Clavdia has not returned alone, Hans finds that he, like the other Berghof residents, is drawn to Peeperkorn's larger-than-life personality. As the friendship between the men develops, Peeperkorn hints that his own relationship with Clavdia is more emotional than physical, and upon learning of Hans's love for Clavdia, endorses Hans's pursuit of her. The men express a brotherly affection for one another, making Peeperkorn's suicide all the more shocking for Hans.

Lodovico Settembrini

Settembrini is among the first of the patients Hans meets upon his arrival at the Berghof. The initial description of him conveys a sense of pleasantness and peacefulness. His greeting to Joachim is "precise and melodious," and he strikes "a graceful pose." Hans observes Settembrini's somewhat ill-fitting and threadbare clothing, but at the same time finds that Settembrini's elegant bearing overcomes the shabbiness of his attire. The ensuing conversation reveals Settembrini's eloquence, enthusiasm, and intelligence, although Hans nevertheless refers to the Italian gentleman as "a windbag." Joachim explains to Hans that Settembrini's case is not particularly serious, but stubbornly recurring. A self-described humanist, Settembrini, during various conversations with Hans, extols the virtues of reason, enlightenment, and human progress achieved through education and honest labor. He routinely cautions Hans against losing himself in the isolated world of the Berghof, urging Hans after he has only been there one day to leave at once, since the atmosphere of the Berghof does not appear to be benefiting Hans either physically or mentally. While Hans himself thought just the same thing earlier that day, he dismisses Settembrini's suggestion on this occasion and on the others as well.

Settembrini makes a habit of disparaging the routines and practices of the sanatorium, and seems as eager as Joachim to depart. In the sixth chapter of the novel, Settembrini announces that he is leaving the Berghof. He is not cured but despairs that he ever will be, so he is renting an apartment in the nearby town of Davos. It is here that Settembrini meets Naphta, and the philosophical mentoring of Hans in which Settembrini has engaged takes on a new urgency as Settembrini attempts to protect Hans from Naphta's "intellectual chicanery." In explaining his relationship with Naphta, Settembrini tells Hans that "opinions cannot live unless they have the chance to do battle." Long, heated battles ensue between the two intellectuals. Their disagreements end finally in a duel in which Settembrini refuses to take aim at his long-time adversarial companion. Naphta, however, applies the weapon to his own temple and fires. Following Naphta's suicide, Settembrini's own health declines. Hans visits Settembrini's bedside, and during this time Hans recognizes Settembrini's contradictory nature; he is both a "humanitarian" and "a man of war." When Settembrini finds Hans packing to finally leave the Berghof, after war has broken out, he embraces him with affection and pride.

Frau Karoline Stöher

Frau Stöher is one of the first patients Hans meets. (Frau is the German word for "Mrs.") In describing her, Hans focuses on the woman's rabbit-like teeth, her frequent habit of using the wrong word, and her generally unrefined manners.

Consul Tienappel

Hans's great uncle, Consul Tienappel raises Hans after his grandfather dies and provides the youth with an upper-class upbringing and a college education.

James Tienappel

The son of Consul Tienappel, James is the heir to the family's wine business and is Hans's uncle. After Hans has been at the Berghof for more than a year, James Tienappel arrives at the Berghof intending to convince Hans to return to Hamburg. Hans, who occasionally refers to James as his cousin during this time, remains unresponsive to his uncle's suggestions. Dr. Behrens discusses Hans's case with James, but also suggests that James stay a while to rest, as he is a little anemic. Flustered by this suggestion, and by an apparent attraction to one of the female patients, James leaves abruptly, without giving notice to anyone.

Peter Tienappel

Peter is Consul Tienappel's other son, and being in the navy, was rarely at home while Hans was a youth in his great uncle's house.

Ferdinand Wehsal

Wehsal is a German man around thirty years of age whom Hans notices is infatuated with Madame Chauchat. When Wehsal learns of Hans's encounter with Clavdia on the evening of Mardi Gras, he is both jealous and impressed, and he ingratiates his way into Hans's circle of companions at the Berghof. After Clavdia returns, Wehsal continues to accompany Hans on his various excursions, which sometimes include Clavdia. Wehsal is embittered by her obvious rejection of him.

Joachim Ziemssen

Joachim, Hans's cousin, is a soldier whose military life is suspended due to his illness. Before his departure for the Berghof, Hans believes Joachim to be quite ill, but upon seeing him for the first time, he finds that this cousin appears to be in quite good health. Nevertheless, Dr. Behrens perpetually urges Joachim to remain until he is fully cured. Joachim appears dedicated to the health regimen prescribed by Dr. Behrens, and dutifully follows all the rules of the Berghof with a precision that reflects his military training. Some characters, such as Settembrini, joke with Joachim about this trait, and seem to suggest that, as a military man, Joachim feels duty-bound to follow all the institution's strictures. At the same time, as Joachim's restlessness turns to resolve to return to active military duty back in Germany, the care he takes to follow the prescribed regimen underscores his eagerness to be well enough to leave. Joachim finally departs without Dr. Behrens's full approval, and after several months, he returns, quite ill. He soon is ordered on bed rest, and before long he dies.

Luise Ziemssen

Luise Ziemssen is Joachim's mother and Hans's aunt. She visits Joachim on his deathbed at the Berghof and returns with his body to Germany.

THEMES

Time

On the mountain where the Berghof Sanatorium is located, time tends to lose its meaning and measurability. Many of the characters in the novel comment on this, and Hans notices it almost immediately, feeling as though he has been there for a long while after only a couple of days. He poses the question "So then, what is time?" when Joachim firsts takes his temperature in front of his cousin, and then begins a ramble in which he questions the very concreteness of time. When it snows in August, Joachim has a turn at discussing the fractured nature of time in the mountains, observing that the seasons "pay no attention to the calendar." Settembrini is acutely aware of this temporal phenomenon and attempts to caution Hans against allowing time to flow by without notice, yelling, "I forbid you to play fast and loose with time!" when Hans seems unconcerned with time's passing. Hans

returns to the question "what is time?" at various points throughout the novel, and does so "only because he could not find any answers." He often forgets how old he is, forgets to mark time in any form whatsoever.

Only new patients mark time in any conventional way, whereas long-term patients tend to praise "unmeasured time and unheeded eternity." Perhaps they do so in order to convince themselves, since they are ill, that they have all the time in the world, enough time to heal and rejoin the real world. Or perhaps they do not mark time's passage in order to conceal the monotony of their lives. Hans's attempt to make the monotony of life palatable to Joachim no longer appeases him; and Joachim finds that "the whole thing is a monstrous, disgusting, filthy mess." He can no longer delude himself into thinking that "timelessness" and "eternity" are anything more than repetition and monotony, for he is mentally ready to return to the world, even though Dr. Behrens is convinced Joachim's body is not. Eventually, but not until much later, Hans will feel that same sense of stagnation. This sense of time away from reality is found to be freeing initially, when patients first arrive at the Berghof, or intermittently, in those patients who find themselves returning repeatedly to the Berghof, but eventually what is at first uplifting is transformed, by the onward, relentless press of time itself, into the overwhelming. The structure of the novel reflects its distortions of time, with the first five chapters devoted to Hans's first year at the Berghof, whereas the last two chapters cover his six remaining years at the sanatorium. The narrator comments on this sense of time's deceleration and acceleration as well, when it is noted at the beginning of Chapter 5 that "good order and the laws of narrative require that our experience of time should seem long or short, should expand or shrink, in the same way it does for the hero."

Illness and Death

In *The Magic Mountain*, illness and death are depicted alternately as positive and negative forces. Hans has experienced, as an observer, both illness and death from a very early age. His parents died when he was quite young, between the ages of five and seven. His grandfather, with whom Hans lived for just over a year, died of pneumonia, just as Hans's own father had. These early experiences give Hans a curiosity, objectivity, and sense of reverence about

TOPICS FOR FURTHER STUDY

- In *The Magic Mountain*, Hans Castorp extends a three-week visit into a seven-year stay at the Berghof Sanatorium. His desire to do so can either be viewed pejoratively, as a self-indulgent and escapist vacation from reality, or in a positive light, as a healing process the vulnerable young man needs, although perhaps more emotionally than physically. Alternatively, his rather bizarre decision to remain so long on the mountain may be viewed as something other than an actual decision. Rather, the reader may view Hans as essentially brainwashed by the doctors and by many other patients at the Berghof. Which approach to understanding Hans's actions do you find more compelling? Why? Write an essay exploring your views on Hans's decision to remain for so long on the mountain and support your argument with details from the novel.

- Two of the characters in *The Magic Mountain*—Settembrini and Naphta—engage in philosophical arguments on topics such as technology, communism, religion, and politics. Critics often identify each character with opposing ideologies, with Settembrini representing the West, conservatism, and humanism, for example, and Naphta representing the East, radicalism, and communism. Working with another student, peruse the philosophical positions that these characters espouse in the novel. Research the ways in which the characters' views are consistent or inconsistent with a particular ideology. For example, Settembrini calls himself a humanist, a man genuinely interested in human integrity and the value and perfection of an individual, and yet he nevertheless concedes the occasional necessity of war to protect the interests of patriotism and nationalism. Prepare a debate to present to your class in which you take the side of one character and your classmate takes the other.

- Toward the end of *The Magic Mountain*, Hans becomes obsessed with the new gramophone and spends countless hours listening to records. Those to which he is particularly drawn include Franz Schubert's "Lindenbaum" (one of Schubert's *leider*, or poetic, romantic German songs), and the operas "Carmen" by Georges Bizet and "Faust" by Charles François. Select one of these musical compositions, listen to a recording of it, and research it. Why might it, in particular, have spoken to Hans? What about the form or lyrical content of the song would he have been drawn to? What hints does the narrator provide as to why Hans enjoys these musical selections? Write an essay on the composer's work in which you also discuss the possible reasons for Hans's interest in the music.

- In the time period in which *The Magic Mountain* was written and published, socialism and communism were gaining popularity among oppressed working classes in eastern Europe and in Russia. Research the way such parties organized, recruited members, and attempted to influence politics in the 1920s in Eastern Europe. In what countries were they able to gain a foothold? What conditions precipitated the rise to power of such groups? Write a report that explores the development and influence of socialist and communist parties in eastern Europe in the 1920s.

---

illness and death. While he is initially alarmed by the peculiarities of life at the Berghof—the fact that people who seem healthy, like Joachim, are advised to stay many months and even years, or the fact that patients take their temperature for seven minutes at a time, four times a day—Hans is inclined to think of himself as generally unwell. He is acutely aware of his flushed face, and rather easily convinced to stay, rest, take his temperature, and chart its fluctuations. His actions suggest that he is drawn to illness, as do various comments he makes, as when he states that "illness must ennoble people and make them wise and special." While Settembrini argues against this point, most others at the Berghof seem to embrace their illness as well. Even Joachim, a soldier who wants desperately to rejoin his regiment, takes an odd view of illness and death, not revering them like Hans but noting that illness and the knowledge of one's imminent death give people a certain freedom to do things like "loafing around."

Hans's vaunted view of illness is also tinged with desire. He wonders why he would be attracted to a diseased woman like Clavdia, but it is perhaps because she is ill that he is drawn to her; the illicit nature of such an attraction intensifies Hans's desire for Clavdia. Dr. Krokowski also observes a link between illness and forbidden desire, arguing in his lectures that, while chastity may suppress such desires for a time, they will reappear in the body as physical illness. Hans clings to the nobility of death, to its seriousness, as a counterweight to the salaciousness he observes around him and in him. He immerses himself in this often ignored fact of life at the Berghof—the fact that death pervades the place—by visiting terminally ill patients on their deathbeds, patients who are at the Berghof "not for their own amusement and a loose life, but to die."

Naphta provides another perspective on illness and death, attempting to convince Hans that illness is noble because a sick individual is closer to God; good health masks our inherent human failings and gives us a false and sinful sense of perfection. Hans's fascination with death is what compels him to take part in the séance with Ellen Brand, and to ask the spirit that possesses Ellen to contact the dead Joachim. Hans's response to the ghostly figure of his cousin is one of fear—he runs from the room without speaking to the apparition as the others in the room encourage him to. It is perhaps the first time he has experienced a genuine fear of anything related to death. Mann provides a variety of views on illness and death but suggests that in a place like the Berghof, the emphasis on illness creates a focus on the body itself, and subsequently on its desires and its failings. While Hans's views on the subjects of illness and death

remain conflicted through much of the novel, he eventually comes to see existence at the Berghof as "a stagnating hustle-bustle of depravity," a "dead life."

Technology and Science

Mann treats the theme of technology with the same ambiguity with which he addresses the novel's other major themes. Settembrini lauds technology for its role in human progress toward perfection; it occupies the same high place in his philosophy as education. Naphta takes the opposite side of the argument, stating that "unbiased science is a myth." While science provides some hope of cure among Berghof patients, many receive Dr. Behrens's lung operation and still die. Others are told they have no hope of successful treatment at all, and very few patients leave the Berghof fully cured. When Dr. Behrens conceives of a new treatment for Hans, involving vaccinations derived from Hans's own blood, Hans doubts that the treatment will be effective, and indeed it is not. At the same time, the music provided by the gramophone, a technological creation for the sake of entertainment, provides Hans with emotional healing, even though science cannot heal the bodies around him. Near the novel's end, at the onset of World War I, Settembrini touches on the ambiguous value of technology when he speaks of the inventions of gunpowder and the printing press in the same breath, clearly valuing each for the benefits they have brought society, even though the fact that both inventions have detrimental effects is also apparent.

STYLE

Omniscient Third-Person Point of View

Mann uses an omniscient third-person narrator to tell Hans Castorp's story in *The Magic Mountain*. In this case, the omniscient (all-knowing) narrator is a persona of the author, but should not be confused with Mann himself. Mann's narrator is aware of the full scope of the story and how it will end, and speaks directly to the reader about how the story is being told, and how the skewed way that the passage of time is narrated in the novel reflects Hans's own perceptions. Despite the narrator's omniscience, he restricts himself to revealing the story's events through Hans's point of view. This technique is referred to as "limited omniscience." The

Overhead view of a Swiss sanatorium (Nat Farbman / Time & Life Pictures / Getty Images)

narrator routinely comments about the nature of time, often at chapter openings. Additionally, the narrator, who refers to himself as "we," comments on Hans's character and intelligence and relates Hans and his experiences to general views on the society and time period of which Hans is representative. The narrator also withholds information from the reader, as when he only hints about what transpires the evening that Hans reveals his love for Clavdia, after the conversation that the narrator does choose to disclose. Another instance of the narrator's subjective narration is his telling us that Hans visits Dr. Krokowski for psychological analysis but not allowing the reader into those sessions. Mann's narrator shields Hans from the reader when, perhaps, Hans is arguably at his most vulnerable. The narrator reveals himself again at the end of the book when he describes Hans on the battlefield. Apparently with some reluctance, the narrator gives us our final glimpse of Hans, and once again suggests Hans's relevance as something greater than a single, ordinary man. The narrator hints that just as Hans transcends his ordinariness, the human spirit might someday transcend the ugliness of war.

Bildungsroman

In the bildungsroman genre, the protagonist undergoes a transformation in which his personal growth is viewed within the larger context of his society; that is, his journey is aimed at identifying his place within that society. The term bildungsroman came into use during the eighteenth century in Germany. In *The Magic Mountain*, Hans experiences such a transformation on the mountaintop, at the Berghof. Before he leaves Germany, Hans is unclear about his role in the world, disinterested as he is in work as it relates to being a productive member of German society. After his stay on the mountain, however, he gains perspective through his experiences with a variety of individuals, and returns to Germany at the novel's conclusion, ready to defend his country.

Realism

The literary traditions inherited by Mann and his contemporaries included nineteenth-century realism, which stressed capturing in photographic detail the events of daily life. Yet Mann sought to create a new approach. *The Magic Mountain* is, in many ways, a realist novel. The reader is privy to the minute details of Hans's life on the mountain: what he eats, how often and how well he sleeps, and what the countryside looks like in all seasons. The reader is also exposed to the most intimate details of how various characters move across a room, what their gestures and habits are, how their fingernails are groomed. At the same time, Mann sought to transcend this journalistic approach to novel-writing by infusing his work with symbolism and by revealing the great spiritual and intellectual complexities lying just below the surface of the realistic details. The work also differs from the typical nineteenth-century realist novel in that it often reveals a certain lightness of atmosphere, and a deft and subtle sense of humor. Realistic individuality in *The Magic Mountain* is suffused with universal significance.

HISTORICAL CONTEXT

Germany in World War I

Prior to World War I, Germany was an authoritarian empire consisting of twenty-five states ruled by Kaiser Wilhelm II. The government perceived a threat in the Socialist Workers'

COMPARE
&
CONTRAST

- **1920s:** In post-World War I Germany, the democratic Weimar Republic has just replaced the authoritarian German Empire as a system of government. The political situation remains relatively unstable for many years. Chancellors of the Weimar Republic during this period include Gustav Stresemann, Hans Luther, and Wilhelm Marx.

  Today: Modern Germany is a firmly established democracy, one that has come into being following the instability of the Weimar Republic and the brutality and divisions of Nazi Germany's Third Reich, as well as the severing of Germany into East and West Germany following World War II. Angela Merkel is the first female chancellor of the unified Federal Republic of Germany.

- **1920s:** Tuberculosis, a contagious lung disease, is a widespread health concern throughout Europe and the United States. As depicted in *The Magic Mountain*, latent forms of the illness do not always result in a full-blown contamination, but when a latent infection becomes active, death is likely. Treatments include exposure to pure, high-altitude mountain air, rest, moderate exercise, and in severe cases, an aggressive operation that involves collapsing the infected lung.

  Today: A greater understanding of tuberculosis exists, and the knowledge that it is caused by bacterial infection has led to the development of a vaccine. Active infections are treated with antibiotics, reducing the number of deaths from the disease. It is still prevalent in developing countries, however, due in part to a resurgence in drug-resistant strains of the bacteria.

- **1920s:** The field of psychoanalysis is emerging, following the publication of Sigmund Freud's first in-depth discussion of the subconscious, *The Interpretation of Dreams*, in 1899. Writers such as Mann, whose works, including *The Magic Mountain*, reveal an interest in the human subconscious, are exposed to psychoanalytic notions either through their own research or through German intellectual circles. Mann undertakes a study of the psychoanalyst's ideas and praises Freud's efforts to explicate the human psyche.

  Today: Despite the rejection by many psychologists of the specifics of Freud's theories, his work retains its reputation as groundbreaking, and his approach of talking through a patient's problems is still in use in the early twenty-first century. Just as when psychology was an emergent field, the relationship between the fields of psychology and medicine remains rife with conflict and disagreement.

Party, which later became the Social Democratic Party of Germany. This group advocated the establishment of a socialist order (in which the people as a group or society control property and the distribution of wealth in the community). Additionally, the German government sought to protect itself from possible threats posed by France and Russia, and formed a number of treaties in an effort to avoid attack. One such treaty was with the neighboring Austria-Hungary Empire.

At the onset of World War I in 1914, when the archduke of the Austria-Hungary Empire was assassinated, a chain reaction of alliances was set into motion. This resulted in two major alliances pitted against one another: the Allied, or Entente Powers, consisting of France, the United Kingdom, Russia, and later Italy and the United States on one side, and Germany and the Austria-Hungary Empire on the other. The war was viewed by ruling Germans as a means of uniting the German people behind the

Kaiser and diminishing the threat posed by the Social Democratic Party. Yet casualties were significant and the German people lost their initial enthusiasm and sense of national unity against the allied enemies. By 1918, Germany had signed an armistice agreement (an official truce) with the Allies, and the Kaiser had abdicated. The war officially ended with the signing of the Treaty of Versailles in 1919. Borders all over Europe were redrawn as a result, and in Germany, following the 1921 German Revolution, the Weimar Republic—a liberal democracy—had replaced the German Empire. Critics often note the way Mann's political views seem to have evolved in a way that paralleled the changes occurring in Germany. His strong nationalism and anti-Western views reflected prevailing attitudes in what was still the German Empire at the time he began writing *The Magic Mountain*. In the years following the war, during the time that Mann was completing the novel, the inevitability of a German democracy became evident to Mann, and he publicly championed the new Weimar Republic in his 1922 speech "Von deutscher Republik" ("The German Republic").

The German Bourgeoisie

The prewar German upper middle class, or bourgeoisie, was wealthy, educated, and well-connected. They valued, along with education, a strong work ethic and were largely merchants and professionals—doctors, lawyers, engineers. Mann's own background was a bourgeois one. Until Germany embraced democratic ideals following World War I, the bourgeoisie remained a somewhat elitist sector of society. Hans is identified as bourgeois in *The Magic Mountain*, and is often shown to be condescending in his disapproval of manners and attire that he deems improper. At the same time the bourgeoisie was associated in many ways with German cultural identity and tradition.

The very nature of the term bourgeois, then, at the time *The Magic Mountain* was written and later published, remained ambiguous, and is alternately treated in the novel in both a pejorative and positive manner. Likewise, humanism, the belief in human integrity and human progress fostered by education, was a term applied by different groups for various aims. The notion of bourgeois humanism tended to focus on the value of the individual, while Christian humanism and proletariat humanism shaped the ideology for religious or revolutionary social purposes. In

his postwar speech in praise of the new Weimar Republic in Germany, Mann made a point of linking German bourgeois humanism with Western democracy, intending to aid in the integration of old and new ideals. Shortly after this speech, *The Magic Mountain* was published. Mann was attacked from two sides. As Hugh Ridley in *The Problematic Bourgeois: Twentieth-Century Criticism on Thomas Mann's* Buddenbrooks *and* The Magic Mountain (1994) points out, some critics viewed Mann's portrayal of the bourgeoisie as a betrayal of his roots, while others praised him for highlighting the shortcomings of a self-indulgent culture in need of a new ideology.

CRITICAL OVERVIEW

A work as lengthy and as philosophically complex as *The Magic Mountain* inspires a variety of critical approaches. Some scholars focus on the correlation between incidents in the novel and either aspects of Mann's personal life or contemporary political events. Other critics explore the ideological positions embodied by particular characters in the work. Many critics approach their analysis of the text through a study of Hans Castorp's progression from an "ordinary" young man with little interest in things—such as work—which do not advance his own pleasure, to a wiser adult with an understanding of his connection to other individuals and to society in general. The work's contemporary critics focus heavily on the shift in Mann's political views apparent in the novel. Mann's earlier writings are definitively conservative and nationalistic, whereas in *The Magic Mountain* Mann seems to embrace a more liberal political stance.

In terms of criticism of *The Magic Mountain*'s literary merits rather than its political ideology, the novel was accused of suffering from a perceived lack of depth. Others praised the work for its disdain for cultural decadence. As Hugh Ridley observes in *The Problematic Bourgeois: Twentieth-Century Criticism on Thomas Mann's* Buddenbrooks *and* The Magic Mountain (1994), the work was also attacked in the 1920s for catering to bourgeois ideology. Irvin Stock, in his 1994 essay "*The Magic Mountain*" appearing in *Ironic out of Love: The Novels of Thomas Mann*, examines the novel as an account of Hans Castorp's journey of transformation, his navigation "through the dangers of the magic mountain." The story is ultimately a positive one, Stock contends, noting that "our hero is saved at the end." Likewise, Joseph P. Lawrence, in "Transfiguration in Silence: Hans Castorp's Uncanny Awakening" in *A Companion to Thomas Mann's* The Magic Mountain (1999), describes Mann's aims as "life-affirming." Lawrence demonstrates that Mann synthesizes the positive and negative in Hans's act of leaving the insular world of the sanatorium in order to face the horrors of war. Mann, Lawrence insists, portrays reality "simply as it is, beyond all pessimism or optimism." Stephen D. Dowden's approach is similar. In his 1999 introduction to *A Companion to Thomas Mann's* The Magic Mountain, Dowden explains that the novel traces Hans's intensifying attraction to death. According to Dowden, Hans must eventually "renounce his dark yearnings and affirm life." The critic further suggests that this rejection of a fascination with death mirrors Mann's own path.

This issue of the relationship between Mann's personal experiences and the completed novel is of primary interest to many scholars. Michael Beddow, in his discussion of *The Magic Mountain* in *The Cambridge Companion to Thomas Mann*, frames his discussion of *The Magic Mountain*'s plot and characters with an analysis of the political situation in Germany at the time the novel was written, and focuses on the apparent shift in Mann's political views. Similarly, André von Gronicka, in *Thomas Mann: Profile and Perspectives* (1970), emphasizes that much of the novel, which takes place prior to World War I, was written following the war, so that Mann's perspective had been colored by the aftereffects of the war on his homeland. Through the radical figure of Naphta, Gronicka maintains, Mann "sounds his warning of an ideological development" that threatened "the very foundations of Western civilization." The political stance of the novel, insist other critics, is often misrepresented because there is, in fact, no definite stance. Mann's message is an ambiguous one. Ridley explains that Mann's criticism in *The Magic Mountain* of an innocent belief in human progress was similar to his hope that the wounds of war could help regenerate society. These beliefs grew out of Mann's "conservative ideology," Ridley observes, but they possessed "a radicalism that overtook the understanding of many of his contemporaries."

Other critics focus on Mann's analysis of bourgeois character, which Hans is said to represent. He is a comfortably well-off, college-educated, middle-class citizen, and only peripherally concerned, if at all, with anything that does not promote his own self-interest. Georg Lukács, in *Thomas Mann's* The Magic Mountain, views the novel as a battle between the representatives of humanist democracy (Settembrini) and "pre-Facist ideology" (Naphta) for "the soul of an average German bourgeois." Ridley highlights as well the issues related to the bourgeoisie in *The Magic Mountain*, stressing that the novel treats the theme ambiguously. Hans may be seen as a betrayer of "the healthy roots of his bourgeois background" or the bourgeois culture of which Hans is a product may be viewed as "essentially decadent and in need of the new values" explored in the novel, Ridley states. The political and ideological messages of the novel remain elusive at best, yet Mann nonetheless compels the reader to explores such issues within the context of Hans's journey.

CRITICISM

Catherine Dominic

Dominic is a novelist and a freelance writer and editor. In this essay, she explores Mann's treatment of escapism and freedom in The Magic Mountain, *demonstrating that while it is easy to view Hans's seven-year stay at the Berghof Sanatorium as a self-indulgent escape from reality, a closer examination reveals the ways in which Hans's retreat may be viewed as a journey from isolation to connection.*

Many critics have examined Thomas Mann's *The Magic Mountain* as a personal journey of growth, transformation, and education for Hans Castorp, that is, as a novel that exemplifies the bildungsroman genre. Hans enters the sanatorium an average German young man of upper bourgeois standing and exits as an adult with a greater understanding of himself and his place in the world in general and in German society in particular; he is called, finally, to be useful and to serve his country, a call he readily answers. On a more personal, less emblematic level, Hans is a character who initially comes across as snobbish and self-involved. Nevertheless, he is increasingly appealing as a character, despite his aloof and egotistical nature, and despite the

WHAT DO I READ NEXT?

- *Buddenbrooks*, Thomas Mann's first novel, traces the rise and fall of a German bourgeois family and touches on some of the same themes Mann addresses in *The Magic Mountain*, but was written before Mann embraced the notion of a democratic Germany. Originally published in 1901, it is available in a 1994 edition published by Everyman's Library.

- *Death in Venice*, the story of a writer seeking spiritual fulfillment in Venice, is a short novel written in 1912 by Mann, just prior to World War I. It is regarded as one of Mann's finest works. Michael Henry Heim's 2004 translation is available through Ecco Press.

- *Three Essays*, written by Thomas Mann and translated in 1929 by H. T. Lowe Porter, is a collection of essays on literature, politics, and the occult. A 2005 edition of the essays was published by Kessinger Publications.

- *The Poems of Schiller*, published by Dodo Press in 2007, offers a selection of some of the writings by Friedrich Schiller, the eighteenth-century German philosopher, poet, and dramatist whose work influenced Mann throughout his career.

- Eric D. Weitz's *Weimar Germany*, published in 2007 by Princeton University Press, explores a variety of aspects of life during the struggling new democracy in Germany following World War I. Weitz discusses developments in architecture, art, theater, and philosophy, for example, but finds that the democratic spirit in Germany at the time was too weak to withstand the rise of radicalism.

- Sigmund Freud's *The Interpretation of Dreams*, published in 1899, was considered a revolutionary work in terms of its explication of the unconscious workings of the brain. As psychotherapy began to be seen as a valuable tool in treating human ailments of both the physical and mental variety, Freud's works and theories became increasingly well-known and influential, not just among medical professionals but among intellectuals as well. Mann introduces the topic of psychotherapy with the figure of Dr. Krokowski in *The Magic Mountain* and goes on to explore theories of Freud in later works. A modern edition of Freud's works, *The Freud Reader*, published by Norton in 1995, and edited by Peter Gay, includes *The Interpretation of Dreams* as well as his other writings on psychoanalytical, political, and philosophical topics.

---

hypochondria that contributes to his decision to extend his three-week visit to a seven-year stay at the Berghof. In fact, it is because Hans's vulnerabilities become apparent on the mountain that the reader is able to identify what was wrong with him before and follow his progress with interest and affection. A young man lacking the close ties of friends or family, Hans is isolated from society in Hamburg. He fosters this isolation through the way he frowns upon anyone who does not possess the attire or manners he deems appropriate. At the Berghof, in an institution isolated from the real world in terms of time and space, Hans Castorp finds the connections that anchor him to society for the first time.

The first descriptions of Hans emphasize his privileged upbringing. He is described as "coddled," and his attire is elegant and fashionable. He is attuned to the relationship between clothing and class standing, and rarely fails to comment on the general appearance of the people he encounters. He concedes, for example, upon meeting Dr. Krokowski, that the man

AT THE BERGHOF, IN AN INSTITUTION ISOLATED FROM THE REAL WORLD IN TERMS OF TIME AND SPACE, HANS CASTORP FINDS THE CONNECTIONS THAT ANCHOR HIM TO SOCIETY FOR THE FIRST TIME."

looks "distinguished" despite the "dreadful" choice in footwear: wool socks with sandals. He enjoys the rituals and habits of civilized society—regular bathing, fine clothing, superior cigarettes. Hans's great uncle is well-connected enough to have secured an engineering position for Hans with a shipbuilding firm. In discussing Hans's impending employment, the narrator takes the opportunity to expound on the attitudes of German society regarding work. Work "had to be regarded as unconditionally the most estimable thing in the world." Yet Hans finds that he does not love it, however much he respects work. Work is viewed by Hans as "simply something that stood in the way of the unencumbered enjoyment of a Maria Mancini," his favorite cigarette. This disconnection between what his society values and what he personally prefers is at the heart of Hans's sense of isolation. His disdain for individuals who cannot, through their clothing or behavior, uphold his sense of propriety is another symptom of his deeper isolation. Having lost his parents and grandfather at a young age, it is perhaps unsurprising that Hans chooses to isolate himself and maintain an emotional distance from most people. It is noted that he has "few firm roots in life." This ironic understatement does not fully convey Hans's serious lack of meaningful personal relationships.

Perhaps Hans does not notice the absence of such relationships initially, but his craving to become a part of the society at the Berghof demonstrates how much he is at least unconsciously aware of what he lacks. He does not balk at Dr. Behrens's suggestion that he adopt Joachim's health regime, stating that he is happy to do so. When Joachim attempts to explain the freedom of life at the Berghof he informs Hans that "things are serious only down below in real life," and that perhaps Hans will be able to

understand that after he has been "up here" a bit longer. The idea of escaping serious things holds a good deal of allure for Hans, for work could easily be placed in the category of "serious things." He discovers that "up here," a day consists largely of eating, napping, taking one's temperature, and strolling the grounds. The initial appeal, then, of the Berghof is of pure escapism, the temptation of leisure and pleasure without responsibility.

In addition to offering this temptation to Hans, the Berghof extends a greater enticement. First, Hans meets Lodovico Settembrini, and while he initially raises an eyebrow at Settembrini's shabby clothing and laughs at his loquaciousness, he is nevertheless intrigued by Settembrini's view of life. Before long, he spies Clavdia Chauchat as well. He observes every reason to dismiss her. He dislikes her manners—she has a habit of slamming doors. Also, her hands are "not refined or well cared for, not in the way the ladies in young Hans Castorp's social circle cared for theirs." Hans's snobbish instinct with both Settembrini and Clavdia is to maintain his social distance and reject both of them on the basis of inelegant attire or unrefined manners. Here, at the Berghof, however, his habit of self-isolation is subverted by his need for human connection. Interestingly, Dr. Behrens explains to Hans that being up on the mountain is eventually restorative in terms of one's health, but oftentimes it is initially conducive in bringing out illness in an individual. In just the same way, Hans's social malady—his isolation—is made painfully apparent on the mountain, made apparent by his yearning toward connection even when habit dictates social distance.

This longing for connection is further emphasized in the resemblance between Clavdia and the childhood object of Hans's adoration, Pribislav Hippe. Hans, in recalling the only verbal exchange he actually had with Pribislav in which he asks the boy if he may borrow a pencil, realizes that Clavdia reminds him of Pribislav, because they have the same eyes. Hans describes these eyes as "Kirghiz." The word refers to an ethnic group originally descended from a Siberian population that later lived in parts of Russia, Turkey, and Asia. The group is noted for possessing a fair complexion and eyes that are greenish/bluish. Hans also describes both Pribislav's and Clavdia's eyes as somewhat slanted. The fact that Pribislav and Clavdia share this particular characteristic is significant in that it emphasizes the differences, the distance, between the two of them and Hans. The eyes are distinctly foreign. Both Pribislav and Clavdia are alien, separate from Hans, and each in their own way, forbidden. Desire for another male or for a woman who is both seriously ill and married, is regarded by Hans, whether unconsciously or consciously, as illicit. Yet the desire remains within Hans, and his buried attraction to Pribislav is resurrected with Clavdia. Hans's powerful recollection of his longing for any sort of exchange with Pribislav elucidates his longing for Clavdia: to share an emotional and physical connection with her would heal the wounds of his past and ease the pain of the loss of the relationship he was never able to cultivate with Pribislav. At the Berghof, such emotional scars are often also linked to physical illness, and Hans believes he sees, in his own X-ray, internal, physical evidence of the pain caused by his failure to cultivate a relationship with Pribislav.

Unfortunately for Hans, he makes the same mistakes with Clavdia as he did with Pribislav long ago. Hans admires her from afar, creating a bond with Clavdia in his mind before he has even spoken to her. He begins to devise situations in which he is positioned to offer Clavdia the briefest of polite greetings. What further cements the association for the reader between Clavdia and Pribislav is the way Hans finally approaches Clavdia in an attempt to have a real conversation with her. It is at the Mardi Gras party, and a parlor game has ensued: blindfolded participants make pencil sketches of pigs. Someone has thrown the last used up bit of pencil into the punch bowl, and the game deteriorates. Hans seeks out Clavdia and asks if he may borrow a pencil. The event mirrors Hans's only encounter with Pribislav in this way, and in that Clavdia leaves the Berghof the next day, although it is unclear what transpired between Hans and Clavdia later in the evening, after he professed his love to her. She has invited him to return the pencil, and the reader learns only after she has been gone six weeks that the two patients spent time together following that exchange and before Hans returned to his room for the evening. Still, she leaves. Later, when Joachim is preparing to leave the Berghof, and after Dr. Behrens has, in an outburst, discharged Hans along with Joachim, Hans finds that he has no interest in departure. In contemplating the matter, Hans thinks, "a departure seemed impossible, because—to put it openly and succinctly— he had to wait for Clavdia Chauchat." When Clavdia does finally return, it is with Mynheer Peeperkorn, who quickly becomes aware of the connection between Clavdia and Hans. Hans verbally acknowledges not only his love for Clavdia, but his friendship as well. After pressing Hans for information, Peeperkorn concludes that Clavdia "followed her feelings," returning to the Berghof because of her relationship with Hans.

Hans fares a little better in cultivating a companionable relationship with Settembrini. They argue, and become angry with one another, as friends do, but their connection is sustained longer than virtually any other in the novel. It becomes clear that a friendship based on warmth and affection develops between them. Their relationship grows into that friendship out of a mentor/student relationship. Settembrini perpetually warns Hans against becoming too entrenched in the Berghof life, hoping that his friend will rejoin life in the flatlands. Hans's growing feelings for Clavdia alarm Settembrini, and his cautioning intensifies, to the point that he leaves the Mardi Gras festivities with angry words directed at Hans. Nevertheless, moments later, when Hans and Clavdia are conversing, Hans tells her that Settembrini "has in fact become something of a friend." When Naphta and Settembrini engage in their arguments, Hans admits that he is often swayed by Naphta's words, but his greater allegiance and affection remains with Settembrini, whom he offers to serve as a "second" in the duel between Settembrini and Naphta, although no one allows this. Settembrini's health worsens following Naphta's death, and Hans keeps him company at his bedside. When Hans finally decides to leave the Berghof to fight in the war, Settembrini bids him the fondest of farewells, embracing him and finally calling him by his first name.

For Hans, then, the allure of the mountain is that there, in the absence of all things familiar to him, he discovers what has been missing from his life for so many years: true, emotional connections to other people. This has broader connotations in terms of the bildungsroman novel, as these connections with other people, people very different from Hans, expose him to a variety of world views. They thereby contribute, it may be argued, to the process of Hans's transformation into something more than he was when he started, although what Hans has become and what he represents at the novel's end remain topics of critical debate. Nevertheless, when seen within the context of the bildungsroman novel, Hans's journey is perceived by the reader in a broad, symbolic way: Hans now represents the good German, who is willing to rejoin society and defend his homeland in the war. Yet Hans's very ability to now form such connections to others is meaningful in a more private, individual way. His relationships with Settembrini and Clavdia yoke him to *life*, connect him to the world in a new and intimate manner, because now he is connected to other individuals. As Hans tethers himself more and more firmly to life at the Berghof, Settembrini cautions him to not lose himself "in an alien world." Yet this is precisely the cure that Hans finds on the mountain, for he is healed by the connections he cultivates as he loses, or escapes, his former isolated self.

Source: Catherine Dominic, Critical Essay on *The Magic Mountain*, in *Novels for Students*, Gale, Cengage Learning, 2009.

Malte Herwig

In the following excerpt, Herwig discusses the relationship between myth, science and literature in The Magic Mountain.

. . . Myth is part of a culture's efforts to retain its knowledge of itself through the exercise of memory. During this century science has come to be widely considered the dominant paradigm for understanding our world. But has it replaced myth altogether? On closer inspection there may be more continuity and similarity between the artistic and scientific world views than narrow-minded champions of either discipline will admit. As a human activity, modern science, too, can be seen as embedded in a framework of recurrent rituals, social practice, and moral perceptions that go beyond the epistemological concerns of a single branch of knowledge. Research into the origin of scientific ideas has suggested that the emergence of modern physical conceptions of nature is in fact founded on ontological arguments, that is a priori determinations as to the nature of the objects under scientific scrutiny (see, for example, Hubner 32–33). For instance, Descartes's distinction between subject and object or Newton's assumption of the existence of an absolute space and time are based on preconceptions about the nature of the physical world that are influenced by the metaphysics of

> THOMAS MANN'S NOVELS ARE A GOOD EXAMPLE OF THE REINTERPRETATION OF MYTHICAL PERCEPTIONS BY MEANS OF MODERN SCIENCE BECAUSE THEY DISPLAY THE CONTINUING PRESENCE OF AFFECTIVE POWERS SUCH AS AWE, DELIGHT, OR TERROR IN OUR RESPONSES TO THE RESULTS OF SCIENTIFIC PROGRESS."

their day—in particular the assumption of a universe governed by mathematical harmony. However, given its irrefutable practical success, it would be wrong to draw the relativistic conclusion that we can dismiss modern science as a new, if different, mythology. Science and literature have aptly been described as "two discourses belonging to one culture though conducted in different languages" (Levine 3)—and, it has to be stressed, with different epistemological authority.

In this paper I do not comment on the validity of scientific truth claims, but focus on the uses and understanding of science as presented in literature. This involves distinguishing among what Max Weber called the "contexts" of scientific inquiry: Among these, only the context of theoretical and analytical reasoning is genuinely "scientific," whereas the contexts of origin (personal interest, funds for a specific programme, political motives for research into a certain area) and of application (what to do with data, tools, and processes) are, as many scientists readily admit, fundamentally personal stages of scientific practice. Consequently, those areas are of most interest to cultural critics, and we can gain new insights into the shape and process of human understanding when we compare the narrative strategies and epistemological patterns of popular scientific texts with those of fictional texts and myths as well as look at the world views suggested by them. . . .

Thomas Mann's novels are a good example of the reinterpretation of mythical perceptions by means of modern science because they display the continuing presence of affective powers such as awe, delight, or terror in our responses to the results of scientific progress. In a eulogy on Sigmund Freud's eightieth birthday Mann acknowledged the interdependence of science as represented by psychoanalysis and myth as told in literature: He "polemically celebrates" Freud by blaming him for disrespecting philosophy as not an exact science. . . .

The thrust of Mann's argument is clear: literature is capable of perpetuating the emotional core of myth's spiritual power. In volume two of his monumental *Philosophie der symbolischen Formen*, Ernst Cassirer argues that this power originates from a mode of consciousness that is radically different from the familiar notions of rational inference and material causality because it sees inherent magical qualities in the natural world. In *Der Zauberberg* (1924) we have an interesting realization of this understanding. In the foreword the author presents himself as the "raunender Beschworer des Imperfekts" and professes to tell a story that "ist sehr lange her, sie ist sozusagen schon ganz mit historischem Edelrost überzogen und unbedingt in der Zeitform der tiefsten Vergangenheit vorzutragen." This canonical formula of legendmaking makes it all the more interesting that detailed and mostly accurate science from such diverse disciplines as cell biology, physiology, anatomy, and astrophysics is presented in the complex mythological framework of the novel. During Hans Castorp's adventures in the Swiss mountain sanatorium, the reader is frequently reminded of ancient and modern myths, such as the world of Hades with its resident personnel such as, for instance, Minos and Rhadamantys, visitors to the underworld such as Odysseus and Orpheus, and Hermes as the unofficial patron of the remote and "hermetisch" place. Moreover, there are allusions to biblical stories such as those of Job, Lazarus, Lilith, and the Fall, to Dante's *Inferno*, the signs of the zodiac, and medieval notions of the devil. Whereas criticism has devoted a great deal of attention to these mythologies, the role of modern science in *Der Zauberberg* has been insufficiently recognized and sometimes even dismissed as a mere property of realistic representation (e.g. Heftrich, Koopmann). In fact, scientific theories form a part of the novel's mythopoeic equipment, as twentieth-century biology and physics are interwoven with the mythical stories of the past in an attempt to harmonize the two apparently disparate worlds of scientific rationality and mythical narrative. In the following I will concentrate on two examples: the peculiar scientific representation of the body; and x-rays and notions of the underworld.

Thomas Mann drew on state-of-the-art scientific textbooks in physiology and biology in 1920 while he was writing the two chapters "Humaniora" and "Forschungen," which deal with the protagonist's own researches into the science of the human body and the origin of life—the "what's it all about" question again. A comparison of the novel with these scientific sources shows that the author sometimes copied whole phrases and integrated them into the narrative of erotic love, illness, and degeneration that forms the novel's core. Thus, the text is cluttered with terms like "spermatozoon," "fructification," "bioblasts," and "biophores," and the narratives of cellular pathology and microorganisms are related to the events on the magic mountain. The scientific text forms the basis on which, by means of analogy and devices such as animism, personification, and frequent change of perspective, the old mythic themes of life, love, and death are actualized.

Just as in Whitehead's example of the Royal Society, the narrator here invokes these mythic realities in a ritual incantation. The scientific explanations of the origin of life and the process of evolution are interspersed with the recurring question "Was war das Leben?" and its immediate answer, "Niemand wu[Beta]te es." The shortcomings of the well-presented biological theories of life are implicitly exposed by the frequent mention of the word "Wunder," and the protagonist has to draw the conclusion that this kind of scientific research is a result of the hypertrophied consciousness that man has acquired in the course of evolution. . . . Thus, rational investigation of nature cannot yield final answers to the fundamental questions about life, and the novel makes clear that it is necessary to combine scientific research with spiritual experience to achieve a proper understanding of life. Consequently, the protagonist not only reads about, but experiences his research: When he zooms into the body to look at the life of cells and embryos, this is mirrored in the embryonic posture in which he reads.

If myths are about archetypes, then here is one: In his search for origins, Castorp finally encounters the double-walled stage of the embryo. . . . The scientific reference to Ernst

Haeckel's "Gastraa-Theorie" is almost instantly undermined by Castorp's eroticizing conclusion about the gastrula's relation to another "fleisch-getragene Schonheit." Needless to say, the gastrula is later related to Castorp's temptress Clawdia Chauchat whom he encounters in the microcosm of the body. After he has mentally dissected the human body into its most minute constituents, the body parts and microorganisms blend together again into a vision of the "Bild des Lebens"—which uncannily resembles Chauchat and embraces and kisses him. Thus, Castorp's scientifically enhanced invocation of the mystery of life is answered by the apparition of the goddess.

Even more striking is the interaction of myth and science in the x-ray scene. In the chapter "Mein Gott, ich sehe!" Hans Castorp and his cousin undergo an x-ray examination. Again, Mann personally researched in laboratories in Munich to be able to give a realistic background to the scene. However, the x-ray laboratory is presented as a center of cult worship: Its windows are covered with black cloth, and glass slides of x-rays are set into the wall—like church windows.... The actual examination resembles a necromantic ritual, and ceremonial rules have to be observed: The Hofrat, the "Meister," turns off the red light because "den hellen Tag mit seinen fidelen Bildern mussen wir uns erst mal aus dem Sinn schlagen [...]. Erst mussen wir uns mal die Augen mit Finsternis waschen, um so was zu sehen," and he adds that a bit of devotion is only appropriate. Enormous forces are unleashed during the conjuring.... This is a fairly accurate description of early x-ray examinations, but it is seen through mythicizing eyes. It is a good example of what has been called Mann's technique of "maskenhafter Realismus" (Kristiansen 827), which combines a convincing realistic surface with an underlying allegorical level. The author puts on a mask of outer scientific realism under which he then conjures up his innermost feelings of anxiety and hope. The mythical heritage is revived by the practice of modern science, with associations of the realm of shades, Plato's analogy of the cave, and Orpheus's visit to the underworld.

When Castorp finally sees his cousin's "Grabesgestalt und Totenbein [...] dies kahle Gerust und spindeldurre Memento" on the screen, he goes into ecstasies and cries "Jawohl, jawohl, ich sehe! [...] Mein Gott, ich sehe!" He then looks at his own hand under the "magische Fenster" of the screen and has a vision of prophetic insight.... With hindsight the x-ray examination is transformed into a ritual of initiation and insight. It is also abused by Castorp for his dangerous adoration of Clawdia when he puts her x-ray on a little easel on his chest of drawers to worship her. Her sick and sweet beauty is aptly fixed.... In ancient times the ghosts of the dead were conceived as incorporeal images of their former selves, without mind or consciousness—Clawdia's headless x-ray is probably the closest we can get to this. Thus, the author exploits the cultural resonance of modern x-ray technology and presents its products as modern artifacts, which are here being used in rituals whose tradition goes back to Greek mythology.

Indeed, the x-ray serves a purpose similar to that of ancient myth. It becomes the object of contemplation on the nature of life when Castorp muses about humankind's dual nature as body and spirit. Through its associations with Hades it also relates to mythical ideas of origin and end. When he notices that Castorp is carrying his x-ray around in a wallet Settembrini mocks him and compares it to a "Pa[Beta]." As such it is a document of identity and also testifies that the holder is able to cross the border between life and death, world and underworld. Castorp is consequently warned by Settembrini: "Gotter und Sterbliche haben zuweilen das Schattenreich besucht und den Ruckweg gefunden. Abet die Unterirdischen wissen, da[Beta], wer von den Fruchten ihres Reiches kostet, ihnen verfallen bleibt."

It is doubtful if Thomas Mann ever read Wilhelm Rontgen's *Vorlaufige Mittheilung* of 1895—the text that soon became a classic of scientific literature. However, it is fascinating to contemplate the ease with which the properties of Rontgen's text would have put themselves at the author's disposal: the hermetic vacuum-tube, which is covered with black cardboard and put in a completely darkened room, the fluorescence and illumination, Rontgen's playful experimenting with a set of cards, a book, a compass, a set of weights, and so on (Settembrini calls the x-ray apparatus a "Spielzeug"); and the end product: the "Schattenphotographie" of bones laid bare of flesh. In the discourse of the novel, Mann examines the relation between technological evolution and philosophical heritage to redefine man's position in a universe that has become more and more complex. For Mann, this position can only become accessible through a combination of rational inquiry and spiritual experience—a reconciliation of the material constraints and spiritual needs of human life.

Scientific advances have brought about a redefinition of our view of nature. A look at the modern literature dealing with these advances suggests that our everyday understanding of the meaning of science is still based to a large extent on belief. Whereas our ancestors tried to placate the gods with their rituals, we nowadays hope to gain medical redemption from the modern authorities on life and death by subjecting ourselves to the latest promises of science and technology. Often the value of these processes is, indeed, not entirely clear, and we choose to believe or not to believe in them. In the case of cloning, for instance, ethical decisions have to be made about which procedures should be implemented and which are unethical in our eye—decisions that cannot be made entirely on scientific grounds. Meaning, the aim of myths, cannot be derived from science itself without being reductionistic and therefore, by implication, meaningless. Consequently, even the latest inventions and theories quickly become appropriated by our storytelling impulse and are woven into traditional or, occasionally, new narratives. Here, I think, lies an opportunity for interdisciplinary collaboration between science and the humanities: to see that they cannot replace each other but that one discipline complements the other in our search for answers to the question, "What's it all about?" In this respect, the novel is a particularly important contribution from the humanities, as it is constantly engaged in the updating of mythology and in putting the sciences in a human perspective.

Source: Malte Herwig, "Magic Science on the Mountain: Science and Myth in Thomas Mann's *Der Zauberberg*," in *Germanic Review*, Vol. 74, No. 2, Spring 1999, p. 146.

D. H. Stewart

In the following essay, Stewart discusses the two characters who "survive Mann's irony unscathed," arguing that they represent Mann's respect for "an older, civilized Germany."

Rereading Thomas Mann's *The Magic Mountain* (1924), one discovers a peculiarity about the book that was not notable years ago. Among the large dramatis personae, only two important characters escape Mann's derision. Everyone else

he unmasks mercilessly. All are poster-bourgeoisie who have money enough to enjoy the "danse macabre in a hotel deluxe," as the Berghof sanatorium has been called. Overfed, oversexed, and overmedicated, the characters fritter away their diseased lives, immune to cares, comfortably consuming the surplus wealth that the busy world generates. They seem to crowd the novel's landscape and justify the conclusion that Mann wrote a valediction for the German and European middle class. Mann himself ratified this conclusion years after completing the novel and after fleeing Nazi Germany when he said, "*The Magic Mountain* became a swan song for that form of existence. Perhaps it is a general rule that epics descriptive of some particular phase of life tend to appear as it nears its end" (Lowe-Porter 721).

Such a conclusion was plausible when the Soviet system seemed destined to expand and the German middle class (indeed, Germans of every class) stood convicted of collusion with Nazis. Such a conclusion may turn out to be correct in the future, but today one may ask whether Mann mistook a gravely sick society for one terminally ill. Could the "swan song" have been an alarm bell rather than a death knell?

The two characters who survive Mann's irony unscathed are the hero's grandfather, Hans Lorenz Castorp, and his cousin, Joachim Ziemssen. One is dead before the novel begins; the other before it ends. Neither is as prominent as the hero's three "tutors" who vie for his allegiance: the Italian humanist, Settembrini; the Jewish-Jesuit-Marxist, Naphta; the Dutch Vitalist, Peeperkorn[. Nor] do they affect the hero as powerfully as the Russian femme fatale, Clavdia Chauchat. These four major figures are non-German. All four dramatize contradictions in the ideologies they embody. This leaves the hero, the spoiled child of middle class culture, "life's delicate (or problem) child" (Lowe-Porter 308; Wood 303) as Mann calls him, in a quandary. Having learned valuable lessons from each of the four, he turns for role models to his grandfather and cousin.

The hero is his grandfather's namesake. His speech retains traces of the grandfather's Plattdeutsch. He imitates the old man's mannerism of resting his chin on his collar. When he compares Settembrini's grandfather, an early freedom fighter against despotism, with his own, the latter requires no apology. Rooted in Hanseatic

Germany, old Hans combines patrician merchant traditions, conscientious citizenship, and Lutheran piety. He does not resemble the "progressive" bourgeois generation that replaced him and flocked to imperial Bismarck—for example, young Hans's uncle James Tienappel. Grandfather Hans was "a tree hard to fell," a man "rooted in life" (Woods 19), still standing in the 1880s and opposed to Germany's rush into modernity.

Young cousin Joachim belongs to the hero's own generation yet upholds old German traditions. Quiet and brave, he is a latter-day warrior, the kind of German without Junker dueling scars but with a profound sense of duty and loyalty. There is nothing glamorous about him. He would make a formidable army officer but hardly the Blond Beast whom some readers feared. He is unlike his wine merchant family with their "progressive" views. The sanatorium's head physician calls him a "man," the highest compliment granted any character in the novel. When the martial inner fire consumes him, surviving patients agree that Lieutenant Ziemssen was "the best of the lot" (Lowe-Porter 502; Woods 492). One is not surprised when Settembrini addresses the hero by his cousin's name during their last farewell.

Because Mann never ridicules them, the grandfather and cousin form an unobtrusive moral standard for the novel. Both belong to the past but live on in the hero, who imitates their obstinacy and thus suggests the perseverance of their virtues, if, of course, he lives through the Great War.

Twentieth-century critics overlooked this interpretation of *The Magic Mountain* as Mann himself did and for the same reason. The novel is an encyclopedia of ideological controversy during a time when antibourgeois sentiment was so strong that even the shrewdest observers underestimated middle-class resilience and capitalism's characteristic restructuring of social order.

Mann ignored this characteristic when he wrote the novel. He was, however, skeptical of all political-economic nostrums. Neither Weimar republicans nor social democratic revolutionaries suited him. Many conservative values expressed in *Reflections of a Non-Political Man*, which he wrote before *The Magic Mountain*, continue to echo. He respected an older, civilized Germany, the land of burghers and Frederick

> UNTIL THE VERY END OF THE STORY ALL PERSONS DEFINE THEMSELVES OR ARE DEFINED BY OTHERS. DIFFERENCES BETWEEN PERSONS AND SITUATIONS ARE FORMULATED WITH PRECISION AND OBVIOUS RELISH."

the Great. In a muted but audible voice, that Germany asks to be heard.

Source: D. H. Stewart, "Mann's *The Magic Mountain*," in *Explicator*, Vol. 57, No. 4, Summer 1999, p. 221.

Johannes A. Gaertner

In the following excerpt, Gaertner identifies dialectical aspects of The Magic Mountain.

The dialectic character of Thomas Mann's *The Magic Mountain* is obvious. It appears in the discussion between Naphta and Settembrini, in the contrast between "them down there" and "us up here," between Clawdia Chauchat, the Russian lady, and Hans Castorp, the gentleman from Hamburg, her unlikely lover, between Joachim Ziemssen's military and Hans Castorp's civilian attitudes, between personality and intelligence as in the encounter between Peeperkorn and Settembrini, to name only a few. Hans Castorp even dreams dialectically, contrasting the idyllic behavior of ideal mankind with the savagery of cannibalism....

All major persons in *The Magic Mountain* appear dialectically bracketed; they do not live so much by themselves as in contrast to and in confrontation with their partner or partners: Hans Castorp and Joachim Ziemssen, Naphta and Settembrini, Hofrat Behrens and Dr. Krokowski, Clawdia and Hans Castorp, Clawdia and Peeperkorn, Joachim and Marusja, and so on. Until the very end of the story all persons define themselves or are defined by others. Differences between persons and situations are formulated with precision and obvious relish. Now, definition and self-definition are dialectical processes: one thing, one situation, one person is set off against one, several, or all other things, situations, or persons. Hans Castorp for instance says or thinks (against Joachim): "I, as a civilian . . . ," or (against Settembrini): "I, as an engineer without literary ambitions . . . ," or (against Peeperkorn): "I, as a young man without any particular personality . . . "; indeed self-definition and characterization are frequently used as leitmotifs: Ferge always insists that all higher endeavors and ideas are not his forte; Mrs. Stöhr utters malapropisms, always does and says the wrong, the tactless, the vulgar thing; Dr. Krokowski usually is disturbingly hearty and masculine; no occasion is missed in which Joachim would not say or do the thing that clearly marks him as the typical officer candidate of his time. In fact, persons are sometimes so over-characterized that they appear as caricatures. Surely Mrs. Stöhr must have had days on which she did not utter any malapropisms, surely Joachim must have been sometimes a bit more or a bit less than the perfect officer candidate. Yet, though Thomas Mann is not afraid to characterize a person by direct description and biography (Naphta, Hans Castorp, Elly Brand), his skill as a story teller allows him to provide continually situations and conversations, in which the persons are dialectically presented, i.e., in contrast to another group or person: Naphta and Settembrini confront each other, Clawdia and Hans Castorp, Hans Castorp and Joachim Ziemssen, Clawdia and Hans Castorp confront Mynheer Peeperkorn in absentia, Mynheer Peeperkorn and Hans Castorp confront Clawdia in absentia, Mynheer Peeperkorn confronts the entire group as uncrowned king, as does in another sense Mrs. Stöhr as the hopelessly lowest on the scale of education and good manners. Examples of confrontation are too numerous and too obvious to be cited and elaborated any further.

Yet, however fascinating the definition, self-definition and characterization of persons is, however dramatic their interaction, Thomas Mann makes it clear that his interest (and ours, of course) is not only one of clinical observation, as we find it for instance in Proust or Zola, but that it is evaluating, interpreting, and symbolizing. These sharply defined figures, constantly characterized afresh and constantly dialectically engaged, represent more than themselves. They stand for certain philosophies, religions, nationalities, policies, existential attitudes, social mores, ways of thinking and living. Clawdia, for instance, is not only portrayed as a lovely and alluring woman: she is also a Russian, identified with a Slavic laissez-faire attitude and a

moral generosity completely antithetical to that of the correct North German ladies of Hans Castorp's acquaintance, she is vaguely anarchistic, she lives a casual and improper life (well contrasting with Hans Castorp's reverence for the past, for order, propriety and civilized behavior)—in fact: she represents the vague and formless, "human" and organic East against the orderly, "inhuman," technical and directed West, barbarism against civilization, feeling and caprice against plan and foresight, instinct against reason, "freedom" against "convention." What characterizes Clawdia has not to be inferred, but is openly said and declared by Settembrini, by Hans Castorp, by Mynheer Peeperkorn, by Thomas Mann as the narrator, even by Clawdia herself, and it is generally declared and defined in dialectical situations. Clawdia (like any other person in *The Magic Mountain*) is not so much defined as what she is by herself, but by what she is in contrast to somebody else—in her case, of course, mostly as what she is in contrast to Hans Castorp. Symbolization is usually a dialectical process in *The Magic Mountain* As such it implies an enlargement of the dialectical process: not only two persons confront each other, but, as it were, two philosophies, two nationalities, two ways of living, or whatever. The persons become transparent, and what we perceive through them are ideas. Beyond the personal accidents and often trifling happenings, we participate in the struggle of ideas, we become aware of ultimate questions, we get involved in existential decisions which are as actual today as they were before 1914.

Let us consider Settembrini in this connection. What does he stand for? What does he represent? Obviously: enlightenment, progress, Western civilization as derived from classical antiquity, a Latin attitude, Mediterranean elegance, mature thought, literature as political and philosophical engagement, Masonic fraternalism, internationalism—to name only a few of the tenets in his secular faith. And how do we come to know his *Weltanschauung* so intimately? By continuous dialectical friction between him and Hans Castorp or Naphta. In fact, Naphta is so much the antithesis to Settembrini that all of Thomas Mann's skill is needed *not* to let him appear as antithetically contrived.

Not all the major personages in *The Magic Mountain* are necessarily to be understood symbolically—Hofrat Behrens may or may not represent the materialistic science of the 19th century and his assistant, Dr. Krokowski, may or may not represent the 20th century with its interest in psychoanalysis and parapsychology, both of which transcend Hofrat Behrens' solid materialism. Only Hans Castorp, Joachim Ziemssen, Clawdia, Peeperkorn, Naphta, and Settembrini are clear symbols, i.e. carriers and embodiments of certain suprapersonal attitudes, philosophies, national characters, etc., though Mann's sharp and careful characterization of *all* persons places them into larger contexts, makes them, as we said, transparent, even such comparatively minor characters as Joachim's mother or Hans Castorp's grandfather.

Nowhere can Mann's ironical skepticism be better observed than in those instances where dialectical exacerbation leads to paradoxical formulations. A good example of paradox is the contrast between "down there" and "up here." "Down there" one is healthy, normal, working, naive, "up here" one is sick, artificial, exceptional, idle, and certainly not naive. Yet—the plains are not healthy, they send a goodly contingent of patients into the mountains each year, while the "Berghof" after all effects a number of cures. This first paradox is topped by a second one. The Sanatorium is perhaps not such a good place after all—the air is not only good for healing the disease, it is also good for aggravating it, "bringing it out," so that in some cases, presumably in Hans Castorp's own case, it would really be better if he followed Settembrini's advice and left for the plains. Or another paradox: the plains admittedly stand for normalcy. Yet life in the "Berghof," however artificial, absurdly regimented, and strange it may seem to the newcomer, becomes in a few weeks so "normal" that life in the plains becomes by comparison "unnormal," unreal, unthinkable. Hans Castorp, and certainly some others, remain "up here" simply because life "up here" has acquired such a degree of persuasive normalcy that they can no longer envisage the by now strange and unfamiliar life "down there."

Paradox as perfect reversal occurs in one dialog between Settembrini and Naphta, where pacific Settembrini advocates war against Austria and bloodthirsty Naphta ridicules the idea of silly bourgeois wars. Or take the paradoxical contradiction between Naphta's ascetic ideals and his luxurious habitation, between Settembrini's epicurean attitudes and his actual poverty and enforced asceticism. We find paradox in Dr. Krokowski's hearty manner and his ambiguous investigations, or in the majestic and compelling force of Mynheer Peeperkorn's utterances and their actual lack of intellectual substance.

Thomas Mann delights in paradoxes. Even where the paradoxes are not always spelled out, he loves to add question marks to dialectic statements by a certain "softening" of a previously announced position, by ambiguity. Thus Hofrat Behrens may appear as a scientific philistine, but he also paints—the picture of his clearly defined medical and scientific personality acquires thereby a certain correction. Though Hofrat Behrens appears as the nothing-but-physician and as such cannot be in love with a female patient, the way in which he portrays Clawdia (and the fact that he does it at all) betrays a certain non-medical interest. Again a question mark, an ambiguity. Hans Castorp's own personality is full of contradictions—he has an all-consuming passion for Clawdia, yet he is also phlegmatic about it. He is not a deep thinker, yet he is capable of sudden extraordinary insights, brilliant remarks, and sustained study. He might be a completely civilian personality, yet in some ways he is more daring and more dutiful than Joachim, the professional soldier. Though Joachim is obsessed with his concept of "duty," it is actually Hans Castorp who sticks to his duty, namely that of getting well and remaining in the Sanatorium. Yet in so doing he is again less dutiful than Joachim, because the fulfillment of that particular "duty" coincides with his own inclinations, he likes it "up here." Poor Joachim, indeed, is in a completely paradoxical, one might say Kierkegaardian, situation. Whether he stays or leaves, he does the right and the wrong thing in either case. A persistent working out of dialectical positions leads to greater clarity, but not to greater simplicity. On the contrary, the more we refine the dialectical process, the nearer we seem to get to logical impasses, to antinomies which demand an existential decision, i.e. one based on our being, not on our reasoning.

A special form of the paradox appears in cancellation, a process in which a dialectical position is refuted but not transcended. Two examples come to mind: first, of course, the see-saw discussions between Naphta and Settembrini. Whatever one of the disputants says is cancelled by the reply of his adversary, though in due course this reply is cancelled by refutation through the first speaker. Second: in the scene where Settembrini for the first time earnestly implores his young friend to leave the "Berghof" Hans Castorp cancels Settembrini's forceful arguments and imprecations by the simple question: "Why don't you leave yourself?"

Closely connected with the phenomena of paradox, ambiguity, and cancellation is that dialectical position, described in the French saying *les extrèmes se touchent*, which is here called "union of opposites." Whenever that union of opposites occurs, Thomas Mann expresses an important message and expresses it directly. A good example occurs in the snow dream. First we have the contrast between discomfort and incipient fear of Hans Castorp awake, then the feeling of extraordinary well-being and security of Hans Castorp asleep. In the dream itself another such union occurs. While an ideal mankind enjoys its pastoral existence, two children are devoured by witches in the temple. This is one of those rare instances where Mann pronounces a philosophical insight, a moral command directly: for the sake of love and kindness we must not give death any power over our thoughts. The same union of opposites, again coupled with a message, concludes the work. While Hans Castorp stumbles over a muddy field in a hail of artillery shells, he sings Schubert's beautiful "Am Brunnen vor dem Tore . . . "; thus on one side: mud, death, noise and war, on the other: purity, music, tenderness and beauty. Love then is mentioned as the ultimate hope of mankind, the transcending element.

The classic Hegelian scheme of thesis, antithesis, and synthesis on a higher level does not occur in *The Magic Mountain*. The transcendence of dialectical positions is never a synthesis, but always a confrontation with a radically different position. Thus the arguments between Naphta and Settembrini are transcended at one point. How? Through the force of Mynheer Peeperkorn's personality. This new factor—personality as existential size—lets all their discussions and quarrels appear as trifling, irrelevant, unimportant, though it is expressly stated that Mynheer Peeperkorn, albeit shrewd and perceptive, is by no means an intellectual and that he would be unable in a verbal contest to refute either of the adversaries.

Problems, said Count Keyserling, are never solved, they disappear; they are forgotten, because other more urgent problems supersede them. How is the dialectic between "them down there" and "us up here" transcended? Through the War. Hans Castorp leaves life in the plains, as he knew it, and life in the Sanatorium, as he experienced it. Suddenly neither life is important any more, nor indeed feasible. Sometimes it is death which solves all dialectical problems, as in the cases of Naphta, Joachim, and Mynheer Peeperkorn. Sometimes a false transcendence occurs, false, because it is too brief, too inconsequential, or simply frustrated. In a brief encounter of love between Hans Castorp and Clawdia abysms of difference are bridged during one brief night, but this love does not lead anywhere; after Mynheer Peeperkorn's death the two have again become strangers who say "Sie" to each other and between whom a non-compromising kiss is possible. There is Hans Castorp's experiment with occultism—it ends in panic flight. There is his flight into music—which becomes another opiate. There is one wonderful and moving dream in which suddenly deep and inspiring insights are revealed to Hans Castorp—they are forgotten by the time he sits down to dinner a few hours later. It is only in two border situations—dream and approaching death on the battlefield—that Thomas Mann speaks openly of that universal love which would transcend all dialectical positions. He utters here, of course, the same thought that Dante proclaimed in another context.

But not only in the rare instances of transcendence does Thomas Mann say something impressively: he does so much more frequently in a dialectical position which—for want of a better term—might be called "transposition," i.e. transposition in a musical sense. Such transposition is most magnificently achieved in the closing sentences of the first volume: "N'oubliez pas de me rendre mon crayon." What is transposed here (incidentally also literally transposed into another language) is, of course, Pribislaw Hippe's remark "Don't forget to return my pencil." But how magnificently and profoundly has the meaning been changed! It is no longer the clue to an every-day situation of . . . infatuation between two youngsters of more or less equal age and status "in the plains," but one of heterosexual love between two profoundly different, mature persons, both patients in a sanatorium, both living in a world which is twice removed from the normal, once through the physical location in the "Berghof" (the mountain court) as such and twice through the special carnival license. Since the structure of *The Magic Mountain* is one in which events lead from Hans Castorp's departure from the plains to the fulfillment of his love for Clawdia in the first volume, and from that point on backwards to the estrangement from Clawdia and his return to the plains, it is, as it were, symmetrically necessary that Hans Castorp should meet Joachim again before he leaves the "Berghof." He does so, but in a transposition of a particularly strange and powerful kind, namely in a spiritualist séance, where Joachim, who could not be a soldier while alive, is now a soldier but dead.

Transposition is not so much an antithesis as a repetition, but a repetition in another key. Another transposition occurs in Settembrini's last words where he, like Joachim before him in another leave-taking, calls Hans Castorp by his given name for the first time: "Giovanni," again transposed into another language. Hans Castorp's last song on the battlefield is the transposition of a musical experience he had under widely different circumstances in the "Berghof." A remarkable instance of transposition can also be found in the "harmless kiss on the forehead" motif; Hans Castorp refuses to kiss Clawdia on the forehead when asked to do so by the living Mynheer Peeperkorn; he does it in the presence of the dead Peeperkorn. Transposition is an effective device which Thomas Mann employs especially in such places where a decisive or a turning point in the narration is reached.

Transposition, or modulation if you prefer, is quite different from the leitmotif technique. The leitmotif appears and re-appears unchanged—a device of characterization acting as a signal. It often gains a humoristic force through repetition (Sister Mylendonck's inflamed eye, Settembrini's shabby clothes, Mrs. Stöhr's boners, Joachim's visible embarrassment where Marusja is concerned, and so on). In fact, frequently the leitmotif acquires a sort of independent existence and persons are alluded to only by mention of their leitmotif—Marusja's orange perfume, Clawdia's slit eyes, Peeperkorn's "civilized" gestures. The transposed motif acts like a tuning fork in front of a string instrument; it raises overtones, it produces sympathetic vibrations. As long as Clawdia's eyes are simply called mongolic, we have a descriptive trait; if her eyes are repeatedly called mongolic, this trait may acquire the character of a leitmotif; but in the moment in which Hans Castorp recognizes in them the eyes of Pribislaw

Hippe, we have a perfect transposition. Suddenly this insignificant descriptive trait has gained weight and meaning. As long as Hans Castorp's trembling chin is simply reported, it is at best clinically meaningful; in the moment in which he recognizes in it his grandfather's gesture with all its implications of death, dignity, history as lived experience, biographical detail and childhood dreams, the trembling chin becomes a transposed motif. It is raised to a higher power. It has become resonant. . . .

Source: Johannes A. Gaertner, "Dialectic Thought in Thomas Mann's *The Magic Mountain*," in *German Quarterly*, Vol. 38, No. 4, November 1965, pp. 605–18.

SOURCES

Adolphs, Dieter W., and Egon Schwarz, "Thomas Mann," in *Dictionary of Literary Biography*, Vol. 331, *Nobel Prize Laureates in Literature, Part 3: Lagerkvist-Pontoppidan*, Thomson Gale, 2007, pp. 122–48.

Beddow, Michael, "The Magic Mountain," in *The Cambridge Companion to Thomas Mann*, edited by Ritchie Robertson, Cambridge University Press, 2002, pp. 137–50.

Dowden, Stephen D., Introduction to *A Companion to Thomas Mann's* The Magic Mountain, edited by Stephen D. Dowden, Camden House, 1999, pp. ix–xix.

Lawrence, Joseph P. "Transfiguration in Silence: Hans Castorp's Uncanny Awakening," in *A Companion to Thomas Mann's* The Magic Mountain, edited by Stephen D. Dowden, Camden House, 1999, pp. 1–13.

Lukács, Georg, "In Search of Bourgeois Man," in *Thomas Mann's* The Magic Mountain, edited by Harold Bloom, Chelsea House Publishers, 1986, pp. 31–6.

Mann, Thomas, *The Magic Mountain*, translated by John E. Woods, Vintage International, 1996.

Ridley, Hugh, "*The Magic Mountain* Casts its Spell," in *The Problematic Bourgeois: Twentieth-Century Criticism on Thomas Mann's* Buddenbrooks *and* The Magic Mountain, Camden House, 1994, pp. 34–54.

Stock, Irvin, "The Magic Mountain," in *Ironic out of Love: The Novels of Thomas Mann*, McFarland, 1994, pp. 51–79.

"Tuberculosis," Web site of the World Health Organization, http://www.who.int/topics/tuberculosis/en/ (accessed on June 28, 2008).

von Gronicka, André, "Mann and His Contemporaries" and "Champion of Humanism," in *Thomas Mann: Profile and Perspectives*, Random House, 1970, pp. 53–67, 154–78.

Weigand, Hermann J., "Disease," in *Thomas Mann's* The Magic Mountain," edited by Harold Bloom, Chelsea House Publishers, 1986, pp. 7–22.

FURTHER READING

Goldman, Harvey, *Max Weber and Thomas Mann: Calling and the Shaping of the Self*, University of California Press, 1991.

   Goldman offers an interpretation of German political economist and sociologist Max Weber and of Thomas Mann that is informed by the understanding both men held regarding the relationship of one's personal identity to one's intellectual national heritage.

Kuzke, Hermann, *Thomas Mann: Life as a Work of Art, A Biography*, translated by Leslie Willson, Princeton University Press, 2002.

   Kuzke's highly acclaimed biography analyzes the way events in Mann's life informed his writings.

Lukács, Georg, *Essays on Thomas Mann*, translated by Stanley Mitchell, Humanities Press International, 1995.

   Noted Marxist critic Lukács presents detailed, largely favorable assessments of Mann's writings.

Stern, Fritz, *Five Germanys I Have Known*, Farrar, Straus and Giroux, 2007.

   Stern, a distinguished German historian, offers a memoir in which he reviews German history within the context of five distinct periods of German government: the Weimar Republic; Nazi Germany; the post-1945 Federal Republic; the Soviet-controlled German Democratic Republic; and a modern, unified Germany.

Mansfield Park

JANE AUSTEN

1814

Mansfield Park, written between 1811 and 1813 and published in 1814, was the first of Jane Austen's novels to be begun after she attained professional success as a writer, rather than being a revision of work begun many years before. It is therefore among her most mature and sophisticated pieces and the one which has drawn the most varied critical and popular responses. The main character, Fanny Price, is a sort of Cinderella who grows from a child to a woman, and above all to a morally mature and autonomous individual, while in the care of indifferent, even hostile, relatives. Fanny's careful moral evaluations of her circumstances and acquaintances have been seen either as priggishness or as a triumph of inner strength against the vicissitudes of life. Of all Austen's works, *Mansfield Park* has been of the most interest to postmodernists, scholars, and filmmakers alike, all seeking to interrogate Austen's world from the viewpoint of their own contemporary moral orthodoxies, especially in regard to the issue of slavery. The plot and structure of the novel are by far the most ambitious of all Austen's books. She revisits the world of myth and fairy tale, to a large extent basing characters and circumstances on the popular contemporary play *Lovers' Vows*, in which the characters in their turn stage a production. This complex interaction between frameworks of reality and fiction is rarely seen in stories by Austen's contemporaries or predecessors, being more typical of twentieth-century writers like Vladimir Nabokov and Ingmar Bergman.

Jane Austen (Public Domain)

AUTHOR BIOGRAPHY

Jane Austen was born on December 16, 1775, in the small village of Steventon in Hampshire, in the south of England. Her father, George Austen, came from a wealthy manufacturing family that had provided for him by buying him a position in the Church of England as the rector in Steventon, a job that included income from agricultural rents. As happens in many of Austen's novels, this left him with the problem of arranging advantageous marriages or other livelihoods for his children (six sons and two daughters, all of whom, unusually, survived to adulthood), to whom he could not expect to leave any sizable inheritance. During the Christmas and New Year's holidays of 1796–1797, Austen experienced the first of two romantic attachments. Her flirtation with Tom Lefroy, a young lawyer, was immediately stopped by both families because neither Tom nor Jane had any income to support a household. Six years later Austen received a proposal of marriage from Harris Bigg-Wither, a friend of the family with a very large income whose marriage to Jane would have secured the financial future of the entire Austen family. Probably for this reason she initially accepted, but she backed out the next day. No

definite information about her refusal survives, but it is often conjectured to have come about because of her unwillingness to compromise her personal feelings.

By the end of 1785 Jane and her sister Cassandra had completed a finishing school where they studied such then-typically feminine accomplishments as French and needlework. Jane acquired a more serious education under the direction of her father (who had a degree from Oxford) in his extensive library. During the 1780s and 1790s the Austens spent much of their spare time performing amateur theatricals for their own amusement. Jane soon began writing her own plays as well as other forms of verse and short stories. By the late 1790s she was writing novels that included early drafts of her published works. In 1803 Austen sold *Susan* (an early draft of *Northanger Abbey*), but it was never put into print. After her father's death in 1805, her brothers' professional success was sufficient to support the family until the failure of her brother Henry Austen's bank in 1816 plunged the whole family into financial difficulties.

In 1811 Austen anonymously published *Sense and Sensibility* to favorable reviews and financial success. She followed with *Pride and Prejudice* in 1813 and *Mansfield Park* the following year. Finally, she brought out *Emma* in 1815. These novels were all successful. However, in the early nineteenth century, authors, not publishers, assumed the financial risk of publishing, and she lost nearly as much as she made on a large second printing of *Mansfield Park* that did not sell quickly. After this, Austen's health declined, and she died at Winchester on July 18, 1817, of an unknown disease. Two more complete novels were published posthumously as a single volume in December 1817: *Persuasion* and *Northanger Abby*. Since then her novels have been continuously in print, and her popularity and critical reputation have constantly grown; she is today regarded as one of the very greatest English writers.

PLOT SUMMARY

Volume I

Austen begins *Mansfield Park* with a brief but pointed summary of the fortunes in marriage of three sisters from a gentry family. Maria Ward,

MEDIA ADAPTATIONS

- In 1983 *Mansfield Park* was adapted for television broadcast by the British Broadcasting Corporation (BBC), directed by David Giles and starring Nicholas Farrell, Sylvestra Le Touzel, and Christopher Villiers.

- Patricia Rozema directed a film adaptation of *Mansfield Park* for theatrical release in 1999 by Miramax and BBC Films. It starred Frances O'Connor and the Nobel laureate Harold Pinter.

- *Mansfield Park* was adapted for television in 2007 by the director Iain MacDonald and broadcast on Independent Television (ITV), starring Billie Piper.

with an inheritance of seven thousand pounds, wed a baronet, Sir Thomas Bertram, who had a large income, and became Lady Bertram. The other two sisters did not fare so well. The second became Mrs. Norris, as wed to an Anglican priest who became the baronet's parson on an income of a thousand pounds per year. The third fared worst of all. She married a Lieutenant Price of the Royal Marines, a man with no money and no connections, in other words beneath the gentry class. This humiliated her family and resulted in her isolation from her parents and sisters. After eleven years and nine pregnancies, Mrs. Price finally wrote to her sisters asking for help. Although she hoped Sir Thomas would be able to do something for her eldest son, it instead happens that the eldest daughter, Fanny Price, then ten years old, comes to live on the Bertram estate of Mansfield Park.

At first, Fanny is unable to make any connection to the Bertram family, who look down on her because of her inferior education and manners (that is, her lack of socialization within the gentry class). Her cousin Edmund, however, a student at Eton and later Oxford, intending to become a priest, treats her as a human being, as

an equal, and even as a beloved relative and so reconciles her to her situation. He also takes charge of her education, directing her reading in Sir Thomas's library. The pattern of Fanny's life at Mansfield is soon set. She is educated alongside the Bertram sisters by tutors and spends much of her time as Mrs. Norris's companion, assisting her in the daily tasks of household management (in which Lady Bertram plays no part) and practicing the sewing that took up many hours of the daily routine of most aristocratic women. The Bertrams do not expect Fanny to ever function on an equal level with their own daughters, and Mrs. Norris makes it her business to see that she does not. Fanny is certainly not a servant, but she is not a full member of the family either. Every effort will be made to see that the Bertram daughters, Maria and Julia, will secure advantageous marriages. As for the sons, Tom will inherit the bulk of his father's wealth, although he is quickly endangering that inheritance through gambling debts accrued in London. In fact, while Sir Thomas intends to provide for his younger son, Edmund, by appointing him to two posts in the Church of England that he has the right to fill and which have large incomes attached, he must sell the Mansfield Parsonage (formerly held by Mr. Norris) to cover Tom's enormous debts. This introduces a further set of characters, the new parson, Dr. Grant, and his family

After Fanny's situation is thus established, the plot of the novel begins to unfold. Besides Tom's debts, Sir Thomas has other financial difficulties related to his estates on Antigua, in the Caribbean. He must go there to set matters right and takes Tom with him, in order to familiarize him with the main source of family wealth as well as to keep him away from the temptations of London. Given the nature of the business and the slow and uncertain nature of crossing the Atlantic under sail, it is expected that the trip may take many months. This leaves the family, as it were, on its own, with no clear center of authority. Edmund, as the oldest male, and Lady Bertram, as the matriarch, both have claims to be in charge, while Mrs. Norris intrudes herself into authority as much as possible by offering "advice." The situation becomes increasingly anarchic. During this time Maria, the elder Bertram daughter, becomes engaged to Mr. Rushworth, a young man who has even greater wealth than Sir Thomas but who is not very bright or personable. According to the conventions of the day, the marriage cannot take place until after Sir Thomas's return.

It is into this listless and purposeless drifting at Mansfield Park that the Crawfords are introduced. The half siblings of Mrs. Grant, Henry and Mary Crawford are rich, spectacularly sophisticated in London manners, and make an overwhelming impression on the Bertram family. They have been raised by their uncle, Admiral Crawford. Austen reveals that Mary in particular had to leave the admiral's house because, on the death of his wife, he had moved his mistress into his own house; Mary's continued residence there would have tarnished her reputation. This episode foreshadows the later revelation of the Crawfords' true moral character. Following her half sister's advice, Miss Crawford immediately fixes on Tom Bertram as a suitable match for herself. Meanwhile, Mary comments of her brother, "The admiral's lessons have quite spoiled him"; accordingly, though he flirts with Julia, his main intention at first is to gain Maria's affections, precisely because she is already engaged, such that the attachment will have a different quality to experience than the building of an ordinary relationship would produce.

From this point the Crawfords and Bertrams spend almost all of their time together. Edmund soon finds himself falling in love with Mary Crawford. Despite herself and her desire for the Bertram title and fortune that are attached to Tom, Mary finds herself returning his affections. Fanny only becomes aware of this through observing Edmund's neglect of her and his attention toward Mary. It is only through examining feelings of jealousy over this developing relationship that Fanny realizes that she is in love with Edmund.

The Bertrams and Crawfords are invited to tour Southerton, the estate of Mr. Rushworth, with an eye toward Henry Crawford advising him about the redesign of the garden, since Henry has just done over his own garden at his estate of Everingham. At this time Mr. Crawford seems to be paying special attention to Julia. While viewing the Rushworth family chapel, Julia calls attention to the fact that Mr. Crawford and Maria happen at one moment to be standing in the precise place and attitude that a bride and groom would assume during their wedding, foreshadowing later events. While touring the garden they break into smaller groups. Maria and Henry Crawford find themselves alone at a locked iron gate beyond which is the most beautiful part of the park. The gate is referred to by the antiquated word "ha-ha." After waiting awhile, Mr. Crawford suggests that he can assist Maria through a gap by the side of the gate: "I think you might with little difficulty pass round the edge of the gate, here, with my assistance; I think it might be done, if you really wished to be more at large, and could allow yourself to think it not prohibited." She responds, "Prohibited! nonsense! I certainly can get out that way, and I will." This is a symbolic enactment of the later scandal concerning them, just as a groom carrying his bride over the threshold is a symbolic enactment of the marriage.

In August, Tom precedes his father (expected by November) back from Antigua. By September, Tom has introduced to Mansfield Park a man named John Yates. Mr. Yates seems to move from one aristocratic household to another with no claim to status except his personality. He has lately been ejected from another house, where he had been organizing an amateur theatrical production of *Lovers' Vows*, a popular but somewhat morally suspect play. He soon fires the enthusiasm of the Bertrams and Crawfords to stage their own play, and they eventually select the same work. Only Edmund and Fanny are opposed to the idea, though they are both eventually seduced into it. Edmund voices the concern that such a production might be disrespectful of his father's dangers in journeying back from Antigua and that it might compromise Maria's reputation during her engagement, but he eventually agrees to act, worrying that if he does not, Tom will introduce some neighbor into the play and embarrass the family to the wider world; he also worries about Miss Crawford performing a love scene with anyone except himself. During the course of the preparations and rehearsals, Mr. Yates begins a flirtation with Julia, while Henry Crawford slights Julia and continues his seduction of Maria; at one point his attentions to her have to be passed off to Mr. Rushworth (also brought in as an actor) by Mary Crawford as being part of the play. At almost the precise moment when the final dress rehearsal is to begin (with Fanny finally roped in to read the part of the absent Mrs. Grant), Sir Thomas returns home unexpectedly early. His presence brings the whole enterprise of the play to an end, not by any specific orders he gives but as a breaking of a spell that makes it impossible to even continue to think the same way. The Craw-fords flee the house. Only Mr. Yates does not at first apprehend what has happened and thinks Sir Thomas's arrival poses only a brief delay.

Volume II

The play is nearly completely forgotten, although Austen makes a point of describing Sir Thomas overseeing the dismantling of the temporary stage that has been erected and personally burn-ing the reading copies of the drama. He is as upset with himself for having lost his temper as he is over the play itself.

Sir Thomas proves most changed with respect to Fanny. He now recognizes her as a young woman and begins to treat her more nearly as he treats his daughters, especially in spite of Mrs. Norris's tyranny over her. As a result, "Fanny knew not how to feel, nor where to look.... He had never been so kind, so *very* kind to her in his life." Sir Thomas goes so far as to host a ball in her honor, at which she is presented to the local gentry.

Mr. Crawford spends some time away from Mansfield Park, making it clear to Maria that he has no intention of proposing to her. Sir Thomas inquires of his eldest daughter whether she would be rid of the engagement to Mr. Rush-worth, whom he begins to see as a worthless fellow, but she refuses, calculating that going ahead with the marriage would be the best way to spite Mr. Crawford, with whom she has indeed fallen in love.

An entirely new theme is introduced when Mr. Crawford announces to his sister, "My plan is to make Fanny Price in love with me." This is a common amusement for him and is no different from his flirtations with the Bertram sisters; he wishes to engage her affections because it seems contrary to her nature to give them to a man such as himself. However, Crawford's constant attentions to Fanny have the opposite effect, and while she only becomes increasingly convinced of his trifling and inconstant character, he falls in love with her. He is deeply affected by seeing Fanny's affection for her brother William and wishes to become the object of such strong and pure feelings himself. He therefore announces again to his sister that he wishes to marry Fanny.

In the meantime, Fanny becomes closer friends with Mary Crawford but still holds her-self aloof from what she sees as Mary's self-deceiving character. Fanny's brother William,

on leave from his naval duties, comes for a long visit and makes himself popular with the family with exciting tales of his adventures in the war against Napoleon. Mr. Crawford sees the chance of making Fanny indebted to him and intervenes with his uncle the admiral to secure William a promotion to lieutenant, something which at that time depends not on merit but entirely on personal patronage and which even Sir Thomas is uncertain of being able to secure. With this boon in hand, Mr. Crawford proposes to Fanny, in person, through a letter from his sister to Fanny, and by intervening through Sir Thomas in place of Fanny's father. Considering Fanny's background and lack of dowry, the match is incredibly advantageous. Sir Thomas urges it on her as being a match he would have been happy to see for Maria or Julia. Yet Fanny refuses. She recognizes that Mr. Crawford's character is essentially false and at first thinks the matter is even a sort of cruel joke; she persists in her refusal even in the face of accusations of ingratitude from Sir Thomas. She is moreover unable to speak her reasons concerning her sui-tor's character in her defense. This is at least in part because she can hardly bear to face the true reason for her refusal, that she is in love with Edmund, such that the matter seems completely hopeless to her.

Parallel to these developments, Edmund sets off over the Christmas holiday to undergo his ordination. He expects that once he returns and takes up his living at Thornton Lacey, his first parish, he will propose to Mary Crawford. He vacillates between accepting the evidence that she loves him and will accept and ruing the pos-sibility that she is too wedded to the life of Lon-don to become the wife of a country parson. Incidentally, Mr. Crawford offers Edmund the same kind of advice about landscaping his new property as he offered Mr. Rushworth, but Edmund has no interest in such schemes, wish-ing only to reform the property as appropriate to make it a gentleman's residence.

Volume III

When Fanny communicates her rejection of Mr. Crawford's proposal to Sir Thomas, she is unable to explain her reasons to him, largely because the story of Henry's insincere flirtation with Maria and Julia would tarnish their repu-tations in their father's eyes. She is only later able to explain these matters to Edmund, who has witnessed them himself. Crawford's attentions to Fanny continue, however, though they serve his own vanity more than any other purposes: "He was in love, very much in love; and it was a love which...made her affection appear of greater consequence, because it was withheld, and determined him to have the glory, as well as the felicity, of forcing her to love him." Mary also tries to persuade Fanny to accept Henry's proposal, but her argument that many women in London society would gladly marry him makes no favorable impression.

The third volume of the novel unfolds with two journeys. While Edmund goes to London for the purpose of proposing to Mary Crawford, Fanny, accompanied by her newly commissioned brother William, visits her parents in Portsmouth for the first time in nine years. This trip is Sir Thomas's idea, as he thinks that seeing the contrast between her background and the future that Mr. Crawford offers will influence her to accept his proposal. The relative poverty of the Price household does not please Fanny, but the discovery that most upsets her is that the life of the house is not ordered in the same way as that of Mansfield Park. Fanny finds that of her six other surviving siblings, only her sister Susan has achieved the same self-imposed order as has her brother William. While Fanny is there, Mr. Crawford pays a visit to the Price household, endearing himself to her immediate family and increasing the pressure on her to accept him.

The conclusion of the book becomes progressively more summary in style, beginning with a series of letters, recalling the epistolary novel, told completely in a series of letters, which had been fashionable in Austen's youth, and finally devolving to a summary of events more like the telling of a fairy tale with morals than the main narrative of the novel. While still in Portsmouth, Fanny receives a letter from Lady Norris indicating that Tom became gravely ill after a fall during a drunken carousal. He was to be brought home to Mansfield, where he would lay bedridden and near death for many weeks before ultimately showing improvement. A still more disturbing development is announced to Fanny by, of all people, her father, who has read in the newspaper that Maria Rushworth has abandoned her husband and run off with Henry Crawford, creating a public scandal. Shortly thereafter, Edmund writes to tell Fanny that Julia has eloped with Mr. Yates, marrying him without Sir Thomas's consent or even

knowledge. In the face of this series of disasters, Edmund comes to bring Fanny, along with her sister Susan, back to Mansfield in order to lend Lady Bertram moral support. Mary Crawford has also sent Fanny a letter, in which she lamented not the recent adulterous actions of her brother and Fanny's cousin but the fact that they became public knowledge; Mary also speculated about how much more worthy an heir Mansfield would pass to if Tom died. She has expressed some similar sentiments to Edmund, and he and Fanny are revolted at what they consider her complete lack of moral understanding. This naturally leads to the end of any possibility of marriage between Edmund and Mary.

In the last chapter of the novel, the plot essentially ended, the narrative voice becomes much more that of a storyteller, with references to Fanny as "my Fanny" and to itself in the first person. The narrator proceeds to describe the later lives of the main characters. Tom recovers and, reflecting on his brush with death, reforms his character. Sir Thomas changes, too, on the basis of his reflection over the disobedience of his daughters. He blames his own excessive sternness, which prevented them from opening their true hearts to him, forcing them to build facades pleasant to their aunt's and mother's indulgence while developing in secret and corrupt ways inside. He finds, however, that he can begin again, in a more kindly way, to construct a surrogate family: "Fanny was indeed the daughter that he wanted." Susan Price, too, is virtually adopted as a second daughter. Maria has hoped to marry Henry Crawford, for she has acted partly out of love for him, but they have both acted out of a desire to conquer the other, an even more exaggerated feeling on Crawford's part than his desire to conquer Fanny against her better judgment, as in Maria's case he has had to overcome hatred and bitterness as well. This is no basis for a relationship, and he ultimately expels Maria. She is sent to live in seclusion, as provided for by Sir Thomas and with Mrs. Norris as her companion. Fanny and Edmund live happily ever after. The narrator states, "I only intreat every body to believe that exactly at the time when it was quite natural that it should be so, and not a week earlier, Edmund did cease to care about Miss Crawford, and became as anxious to marry Fanny, as Fanny herself could desire." Dr. Grant obligingly dies at about the time the new couple wish to start a family and provides Edmund with the larger income Sir Thomas has always wished for him. The love that unites them is the true force that has animated Mansfield Park all along, and they become, if not the heirs of the property, the heirs of the spirit of the place.

CHARACTERS

Edmund Bertram

The younger son of Thomas Bertram, Edmund is about six years older than Fanny. He is intended for the ministry, not for financial reasons, as was the case with so many younger sons of aristocrats, but out of true religious and moral conviction, as he explains to Miss Crawford when she belittles the importance of the clergy:

> A clergyman cannot be high in state or fashion. He must not head mobs, or set the tone in dress. But I cannot call that situation nothing, which has the charge of all that is of the first importance to mankind, individually or collectively considered, temporally and eternally—which has the guardianship of religion and morals, and consequently of the manners which result from their influence.

Edmund is the only member of Fanny's newfound relations to directly engage her and to make any contact with her interior self. He is responsible to a large degree not only for her education, through directing her reading, but also for building her character through a genuine concern for her feelings and by suggesting social roles that she might fulfill beyond her own ideas. With every event in her life that Fanny believes to be a calamity, Edmund reinterprets it for her as a new stage in her maturation and development as a person. Fanny responds by forming a deep attachment to Edmund: "She loved him better than any body in the world except William; her heart was divided between the two." Only after a long courtship between Edmund and Mary Crawford, ended when she reveals her true character in connection with Maria's adultery and Tom's illness, do Edmund and Fanny realize that they have grown to love each other and marry.

Julia Bertram

Julia is the younger daughter of Sir Thomas. She was held by her parents and especially by Mrs. Norris as less beautiful than her older sister Maria, and so she was also less flattered and less spoiled. Precisely because she thinks of herself as inferior to her sister, she is also the less temperamental and vain. Hence her elopement with Mr. Yates is also a lesser folly than her sister's. She shares Maria's essential moral hollowness, however, and hence her marriage, too, is primarily a misguided effort to escape the authority of her father and to simultaneously spite and imitate her sister's elopement.

Maria Bertram

Austen stresses repeatedly that while Maria and her sister, Julia, give an outward appearance of morality and genteel manners, this facade covers a hollow core. A typical example occurs when their father leaves for Antigua:

> The Miss Bertrams were much to be pitied on the occasion; not for their sorrow, but for their want of it. Their father was no object of love to them, he had never seemed the friend of their pleasures, and his absence was unhappily most welcome. They were relieved by it from all restraint; and without aiming at one gratification that would probably have been forbidden by Sir Thomas, they felt themselves immediately at their own disposal, and to have every indulgence within their reach.

Because Fanny lacks their formal education, Maria and Julia consider her to be less intelligent and, also because she lacks their birth, in general less worthy than themselves. Rather than embracing the moral authority of her father as head of the family, Maria attaches herself to Rushworth to escape it and then just as carelessly abandons Rushworth for Henry Crawford, destroying herself as far as gentry society is concerned.

Lady Maria Bertram

Lady Bertram is Fanny's aunt and the wife of Sir Thomas. She is generally too incompetent to run her own household and leaves much of that work to her sister Mrs. Norris. She is also incapable of perceiving the needs and feelings of those around her. For instance, she has no concern for the arduous and dangerous journey to Antigua made by her husband and son because she is "one of those persons who think nothing can be dangerous or difficult, or fatiguing to any body but themselves." She constantly distracts herself from more important matters by sewing and by tending her pug lapdog. Lady Bertram considers that she has a duty to her family to help Fanny, rather than any duty to Fanny as a person, and indeed she never comes to know Fanny. She judges her niece to be precisely equivalent to the superficial lack of sophistication that characterized her when she came to Mansfield Park, and therefore to be stupid and worthless in herself.

Sir Thomas Bertram

Considering her uncle's importance in Fanny's moral universe, Sir Thomas, the owner of Mansfield Park, plays a surprisingly small part in the novel. His importance comes from his authority, which morally orders Mansfield Park. It is this order, rather than the estate itself, of which Fanny and Edmund become the true heirs.

Tom Bertram

Tom is the elder son of Sir Thomas. As such, the bulk of his father's fortune would naturally be settled upon him. However, his means of approaching life is quite fantastic and quite out of line with his father's and with his own presumptive responsibilities. When sent to live in London in order to make social connections with other members of the gentry and nobility that would later in life sustain and advance the Bertram family, he accrues huge gambling debts that require Sir Thomas to sell the rights to the parsonage of Mansfield Park to Dr. Grant, rather than settle the income on his younger son, Edmund, as he had hoped. Like his sisters, Tom has failed to develop a moral foundation based on introspection. Tom's initial response to Fanny is to play with her in a good-natured and superficial way, as he would any child, but he never approaches her as a person. For these reasons, though he appears to survive his crisis, he surrenders the moral inheritance of Mansfield Park to Edmund and Fanny.

Henry Crawford

Henry is the half brother of Mrs. Grant and brother of Mary Crawford. He has a large fortune and owns the estate of Everingham in Norfolk. His flirtation with the Bertram sisters is something he undertakes entirely for his own amusement and for no serious purpose. He expresses the opinion that marriage is generally a sort of playacting in which both parties deceive the other. Praised by Fanny, despite herself, as the best actor in the play prepared at Mansfield Park, Henry's entire persona is affected. Because of his inherently false character, Fanny rejects his proposal despite its fantastic advantage to herself in conventional material terms and the incredible pressure brought to bear on her, even by Sir Thomas, to accept. Perhaps Henry's

obsession with Fanny comes near to bringing out real feeling in him, but even there he is more nearly playing the part of a man in love than actually in love with her. Mr. Crawford describes himself as a devourer of his own pleasure, and indeed it seems that everything he does, including his proposal to Fanny and his shaming of Maria, is done to find pleasure, yet he is never able to discover real enjoyment or satisfaction.

Mary Crawford

Mary Crawford is introduced to the Bertrams as the half sister of Mrs. Grant. She is pretty but darkly complected like Fanny and therefore does not excite Maria and Julia's envy. Mary is presented as the opposite of Fanny. She may seem more attractive superficially, but she is lacking in her interior condition. Mary has a good character by disposition, but she is ruled by her feelings rather than ruling them. She takes an interest in the people around her and the activities they engage in, and is therefore thought to be charming, but she does not understand either her own motives or those of others and lacks Fanny's deeper understanding. At the same time, "She had none of Fanny's delicacy of taste, of mind, of feeling; she saw nature, inanimate nature, with little observation; her attention was all for men and women, her talents for the light and lively." Mary has the sense to eventually prefer Edmund to Tom and comes close to marriage with him, but she reveals her lack of a moral center by openly wishing for Tom's death and treating the adultery committed by her brother and Maria Rushworth pragmatically. Mary is not hypocritical; she is insincere. She plays at being virtuous and sensitive, because she thinks she ought to be, but she is not. She has "a mind led astray and bewildered, and without any suspicion of being so; darkened, yet fancying itself light."

Dr. Grant

On the death of Mr. Norris, the parsonage of Mansfield Park had been intended as a gift from Sir Thomas to his son Edmund. Circumstance instead forces Sir Thomas to sell it to Dr. Grant. He has the habit of annoying Mrs. Norris by telling her the truth.

Mrs. Grant

The wife of Dr. Grant, she is a half sister to the Crawfords, whom she invites to the Mansfield Park parsonage in order to have companions.

Mrs. Norris

Mrs. Norris is Fanny's aunt who brings about Fanny's introduction to Mansfield Park. Although Fanny's mother appeals to her, and she persuades the Bertrams to act as Fanny's patron, Mrs. Norris twice surprises her sister Lady Bertram by demurring to have Fanny live with her as her companion, instead prevailing on the Bertrams to put Fanny up in Mansfield Park when she first arrives and again after her husband, Mr. Norris, dies. This is typical of her personality, in that she wishes to control circumstances around her without taking any responsibility. Hers is the condition generally known as being a busybody and is the source of much of the humor in Austen's narrative. She constantly describes herself as helpless, desperate, and poor (an excuse for her miserliness), yet she is none of these things. However, her anxieties over these issues become manifest in her attempts to control Fanny and actively prevent her from gaining any equality with her Bertram cousins, which Mrs. Norris would consider a scandal. The narrative voice of the novel says plainly that Mrs. Norris hates Fanny and takes pleasure in oppressing her. Advising Fanny about how to conduct herself in public, she instructs, "Remember, wherever you are, you must be the lowest and last."

Fanny Price

John Lucas, in his edition of *Mansfield Park*, suggests that the name Fanny Price may derive from a character of the same name who resists seduction out of Christian scruple in the work of Austen's favorite poet, George Crabbe. If so, Austen used her inspiration as the basis for a far more subtle and complex heroine. Fanny is brought from her own family to Mansfield Park, the house of her uncle Sir Thomas Bertram, and while inevitably elevated by this connection, she also undoubtedly is placed in a very precarious position, as tormented by the aunt who brought about her introduction there (Mrs. Norris) and treated more like a servant than a family member. By the end of the novel she has become the spiritual heir of the house, as wed to her cousin Edmund, triumphing over an oppressive foster family in a manner reminiscent of Cinderella.

The strength of Fanny's character is that she consistently resists social pressure to act against her conscience, whereas her social position ought to make her defer to the wishes of others. While she yields to each debasing command from Mrs. Norris within the household sphere, she refuses to corrupt herself by acting in the play to be produced within the household during Sir Thomas's absence in Antigua, and she refuses also the proposal of Henry Crawford because she recognizes the essential characteristic of both the play and the proposal to be insincerity. She is as unconcerned with the social pressure brought to bear on her as she is with the social rewards that would accrue to her if she acquiesced.

In fact, Fanny delights in the natural over the social. While she is withdrawn and therefore demure to the point of seeming a cipher to most of those around her, she extols the natural, such as the beauty of the night sky: "Here's harmony! . . . Here's repose! Here's what may leave all painting and all music behind, and what poetry only can attempt to describe. Here's what may tranquillize every care, and lift the heart to rapture!" This nearly religious ecstasy, derived from participation in nature and the immutable rather than from the shifting patterns of human society, she has learned from her cousin Edmund, who is her tutor and by the end of the novel becomes her husband.

Mr. Price

Fanny's father, a lieutenant in the marines, brought his wife to a lower level of social existence than that of her sisters, Mrs. Norris and Lady Bertram. He possesses very common manners and is inattentive to the order of his own house.

Mrs. Price

Fanny's mother is the sister of Mrs. Norris and Lady Bertram. She ruined herself through marrying beneath her station for love and lives a degraded life as a consequence.

Susan Price

Susan is the younger sister to whom Fanny becomes close during her exile in Portsmouth. At the end of the novel she, too, comes to live in Mansfield Park, though with her elder sister as protector, under considerably more favorable conditions than Fanny herself experienced.

William Price

William Price is Fanny's older brother. Before she left for Mansfield Park he fulfilled the role of her protector and hero, a role Edmund Bertram gradually takes over. Owing to his father's slight influence as a marine officer, William goes to sea as a midshipman. He is later promoted due to Mr. Crawford's influence with his uncle, an admiral.

Mr. Rushworth

One of the wealthiest members of the gentry in the vicinity of Mansfield Park, Mr. Rushworth becomes engaged and then married to Maria Bertram. Edmund observes of him, "If this man had not twelve thousand a year, he would be a very stupid fellow." He is obsessed with redesigning the gardens on his estate, a symbol of his superficial character.

Mrs. Rushworth

Mr. Rushworth's widowed mother. Her acquaintance with Mrs. Norris helps to forge the connection between her son and Maria Bertram.

Mr. John Yates

Mr. Yates is a companion of Tom Bertram in his low pursuits. He seems to exist on the fringe of gentry society, moving about the country as a guest in one country house after another. He introduces the idea of performing a play at Mansfield Park. He begins a flirtation with Julia Bertram, seemingly out of idleness more than warm affection. He eventually marries her without Sir Thomas's permission.

THEMES

Sensibility

Mansfield Park, like all of Austen's novels, is concerned with the growth of the inner life, the sensibility, as Austen would say, of its main character. In this novel, the importance of Fanny Price's spiritual growth to the workings of the plot is obvious. When she first arrives at Mansfield Park, Fanny feels completely isolated, allowing herself to be put off by the superficiality of her cousins and the apparent sternness of her uncle, Sir Thomas. However, Edmund begins her education, in formal learning as well as in feeling, by presenting himself as an example. Through connecting with him, she begins to see the true spirit of Mansfield Park, as expressed in the virtue of Edmund and his father, and eventually becomes the partner and heir of that virtue.

Marriage

In the very beginning of *Mansfield Park*, Austen introduces many of the themes of the novel by discussing the marriages achieved by Fanny's mother and aunts. She discusses in detail the

TOPICS FOR FURTHER STUDY

- Research the history of the movement for the abolition of slavery in Britain in the late eighteenth and early nineteenth centuries. What organizations and newspapers were created to further this cause? What were their goals? What were their various strategies for achieving change? How did slave owners support or block this movement? Write a paper detailing your findings, including a discussion of how the brief reference to slavery in *Mansfield Park* stands in relation to this movement and to what degree the Austen family participated in it.

- The gardens of English country houses play an important role, both literal and symbolic, in *Mansfield Park*. Notably, Austen's age was the era in which landscape gardening achieved its greatest importance. Research the styles of garden design in the early nineteenth century and draw a plan of your own design for the garden of a great house.

- Watch the film version of *Mansfield Park*, directed by Patricia Rozema. How faithful is this depiction to the book? Would Austen have approved of this depiction? After critically considering the film, write your own screenplay for a short film featuring Jane Austen. What portion of her life would you concentrate on and why?

- Research the nature of love and marriage in England in Austen's era. Give an oral presentation in which you discuss how these institutions evolved to become what they were then within the various social strata and how they evolved to become what they are today, in England and in America.

economic realities of each match and their social consequences. Maria Ward's marriage to the baronet Sir Thomas is so good that her own uncle reckons it should have gone to a girl with three thousand pounds more inheritance than she has. Fanny's mother, to the contrary, marries beneath her station and so is ostracized. There is no question of any of the women making their own way or finding any sort of employment, which would have been nearly impossible in the 1780s (and might have entailed complete isolation from decent society, as Mary Wollstonecraft, who became a successful writer, discovered; Austen at first tried to keep her own identity as a writer secret). Rather, all the women must compete with other women based on their inheritance and their captivating qualities of beauty to obtain one of the limited number of wealthy husbands available.

Austen makes these circumstances clear in many instances, such as in the assessment of Mrs. Grant's marriage by Fanny's aunts. For Mrs. Norris's part, "Enquire where she would, she could not find out that Mrs. Grant had ever had more than five thousand pounds." Lady Bertram, in turn, "felt all the injuries of beauty in Mrs. Grant's being so well settled in life without being handsome, and expressed her astonishment on that almost as often, though not so diffusely, as Mrs. Norris discussed the other." Gentry women were treated as children until they were formally presented at a ball and then were said to be "out," in the sense of publically seeking a husband, and thereafter were treated as adults. The undoubted social reality of this competition, given women's complete legal dependence on men, shaped Austen's own life (marked by her so-called failure in this competition) and formed the basis not only of this novel but indeed of all her works. It is not hard to imagine that the name of the novel and of the estate where it takes place, Mansfield, refers to this marital competition by wordplay. The field is a place of labor and also a place of competition, as in a tournament or in war, and it is there that women must compete for men.

The City and the Country

Aristocratic British families, including the gentry, generally had their main residence on their country estate, in the district where the lands that were their principal source of wealth were held. The social interactions of country life occurred at the local level, with the families of the same class in a given district visiting each other and joining in balls and other events in the area. Many families also maintained a presence in the city of London through owning a second residence there or at least making visits. There, a more cosmopolitan society grew up on the fringes of the royal court, allowing the meeting of aristocrats from the entire country on the basis of social equality. Life in London was generally more sophisticated than country life inasmuch as it featured attendance at dramatic and musical performances and more immediate access to news and (for the first time in Austen's period) newspapers, as well as to artistic and intellectual currents that were favored by like-minded people coming together in ways that were impossible in small towns and isolated estates. London also offered a certain degree of anonymity, or at least the illusion of anonymity, which encouraged aristocrats to engage in activities looked down on as vices, such as gambling.

While human life may in some sense be elevated through the social and intellectual possibilities of the city, it is at the same time degraded by a greater lack of connection that reduces human relationships. Edmund Bertram observes that London, as compared to the country, is prone to vice and is lacking representatives of the best moral character, especially in the relative isolation of priests from parishioners. In turn, "Fanny was disposed to think the influence of London was very much at war with all respectable attachments." Although *Mansfield Park* takes place entirely in the country, it is driven by interaction with the city. All of Tom's difficulties come about from his surrender to the worst impulses of city life, while the Crawfords represent the city invading the country life of Mansfield Park. Many facets of city life in London were also present in certain provincial centers favored by the aristocratic classes for recreation, such as Derby (with its Epsom Derby thoroughbred horse race) and Bath (with its spa), where Austen lived between 1800 and 1806.

STYLE

Irony

Irony is a technique by which an author says one thing and means another, or means a great deal more than is actually stated. This creates a moral distance between the author and the events she describes and often challenges the reader to think in a new or unconventional way in order to appreciate the true, ironic meaning of a text, not without a certain humor. Irony is one of Austen's most characteristic devices.

In *Mansfield Park* irony is used to both great and small effect. Mrs. Grant, for instance, constantly states her own wishes and aversions in terms of others' advantages rather than her own, attempting to manipulate everyone around her (and until the end of the novel largely succeeding) in this passive-aggressive way.

Comedy

Today, variegated genres tend to correspond to niche markets, but in the ancient Greek philosopher Aristotle's conception there were only two genres: tragedy, which concerned the inevitable fall of great people, and comedy, which included everything else. In that sense, *Mansfield Park*, like all Austen's works, is a comedy. Although it contains much humor, it never descends into farce or other low genres, instead bearing a serious moral message in Fanny's inner growth and search for happiness. It is, moreover, a comedy of manners in that it analyzes through humor as much as philosophical discourse the rightness and motives of its characters' actions and, through them, the manners (or way of life) typical of the era.

Play within a Play

A well-known motif (a form or idea that occurs with some frequency) of literature entails the characters of a novel or play themselves becoming involved in the production of a play; the best-known such instance in English literature occurs in William Shakespeare's *Hamlet*. While the purpose of such a device may vary, in *Mansfield Park* it serves to help define character and reproduce the plot in miniature. The main characters of the novel undertake to act in the play, each one taking a role that reflects their own personality and function within the plot of the novel. In other words, Austen uses the production of the play to call attention to the fact that the situations and characters of her novel are to some degree based on those in the play produced, *Lovers' Vows*. This play, adapted by Elizabeth Inchbald from a text by the German playwright August von Kotzebue, was among the most popular plays at the time of Austen's writing. The plot of the play relates to many episodes of the novel, including the romance between Edmund and Mary Crawford, Fanny's choice of suitor, and Maria's elopement.

A more important question about the play is the reaction to it by the characters. Sir Thomas and his moral agent Edmund find its production highly objectionable, as does Fanny. Sir Thomas, once he learns of the performance upon his return from Antigua, describes it as "unsafe amusement" and "saw all the impropriety of such a scheme among such a party, and at such a time, as strongly as his son had ever supposed." Sir Thomas's condemnation extends to his burning all the copies of the play in the house, an act that might not have seemed as shocking and unacceptable in Austen's time as it does now, since her readers would have associated it only with churches' burning of heretical and pagan writings during the Middle Ages. While objections are made about the performance being disrespectful of the danger of Sir Thomas's journey, about the general impropriety of acting, and about some morally salacious content in this particular play, the play hangs over the novel as an oppressive anxiety without ever being fully revealed or explored. That Austen should employ an amateur theatrical to represent grave moral failure is all the more exceptional inasmuch as the Austen household and Jane herself were enthusiastic about acting out plays and did so frequently.

HISTORICAL CONTEXT

The Gentry

Except for the Price family, all of Austen's characters belong to the gentry, or middle class in the original sense of the term. The gentry were separate from the nobility in lacking titles (with the exception of baronet, which Sir Thomas possesses) and direct connection with the royal court, and from the peasantry in possessing lands sufficient to maintain an aristocratic standard of living from rents paid by tenant farmers without having to work themselves. While clergy were not technically gentry, since they did not personally own the land they profited from, they were effectively of the same class. The aim of marriage within this class was to secure the woman in question a continuing position among the gentry. Fanny's mother fell out of the gentry by making a poor marriage, while Fanny re-enters it through her marriage to Edmund. After the death of Austen's father and the business failure of her brothers, the Austen family was constantly in danger of falling out of this class. As Miss Crawford points out to Edmund, only a few professions were socially

COMPARE
&
CONTRAST

- **1817:** Writing is not an entirely respectable pursuit for women. In some cases a woman's reputation can be tarnished by her becoming an author. Successful women writers are largely limited to genres such as gothic romance that are considered subliterary and are aimed principally at women readers.

  Today: Women are as free to pursue a literary career as men, writing in any genre and with the same critical and popular acceptance. Nonetheless, for many, the English-language literary canon remains weighted by the historically disproportionate production of works by men.

- **1817:** Slavery and slave plantations form a vital part of the economy of the British Empire, although the early stages of industrialization are beginning to undermine its economic utility.

  Today: Slavery has long since been abolished as morally unacceptable and economically unviable in Great Britain and the industrialized world, but hundreds of millions of people in the developing and developed worlds alike continue to live in social and economic statuses reminiscent of slavery.

- **1817:** British women are completely excluded from the system of higher education and the professions to which it leads.

- **Today:** Women make up a majority of college students and are free to pursue any career they choose.

- **1817:** Social class is rigidly defined. Most wealth exists in the form of land, which is transferred by inheritance, such that little social mobility is possible. Middle- and upper-class families depend upon large staffs of servants.

  Today: The industrial and postindustrial economy has produced manifold possibilities for social mobility and the creation of new wealth. Domestic service has almost vanished, except in the homes of the very wealthy, largely being replaced by entrepreneurial businesses such as day-care centers and fast-food restaurants.

- **1817:** Advancement in careers, especially military careers, depends openly and almost exclusively on family and social connections rather than on talent.

  Today: While connections still undoubtedly play a role in career advancement, careers are officially open to all with the appropriate knowledge and skill, and acts of preferment or discrimination are subject to legal sanctions.

---

acceptable within the gentry class, such as practicing law or entering politics. This is one of the reasons why the new fortunes being made through the Industrial Revolution went to entrepreneurs from outside the gentry class, and it is also a reason why Austen shows no consciousness of the changing nature of English society being brought about by industrialization.

Slavery

In *Mansfield Park* the bulk of Sir Thomas's income derives from his estates on the island of Antigua, in the Caribbean. There can be no doubt that these are sugar plantations worked by slave labor. The postcolonialist theorist Edward Said, in his *Culture and Imperialism*, and his followers (notably Patricia Rozema in her 1999 film adaptation) have characterized Austen as part of the morally corrupt system of slavery insofar as she failed to robustly criticize the institution from a modern moral viewpoint. This line of criticism obviously involves the difficulty of holding past ages to account against later ethical structures that they could hardly have anticipated. In any case, Austen does not seem to be very apt material for such criticism since, from the little information that can be gleaned from family correspondence, the Austens, Jane included, did favor, even if not vociferously, the growing political movement for the abolition of slavery. The single mention of slavery made by Austen in all of her published works, in this conversation between Fanny and Edmund, in any case suggests a very different conclusion from Said's:

> "Did not you hear me ask him about the slave trade last night?"
>
> "I did—and was in hopes the question would be followed up by others. It would have pleased your uncle to be inquired of farther."
>
> "And I longed to do it—but there was such a dead silence! And while my cousins were sitting by without speaking a word, or seeming at all interested in the subject, I did not like—I thought it would appear as if I wanted to set myself off at their expense, by shewing a curiosity and pleasure in his information which he must wish his own daughters to feel."

The fact that Sir Thomas wishes that Fanny would inquire further hints that he has something important to say on the subject, which, given the historical context, would most likely have involved his expressing moral questions about the very institution on which his family depends, a consideration that he might feel it important for his wife and children to be aware of. The resulting silence from the family, however, is not the result of Austen and English society as a whole being unwilling to reflect on the moral place of slavery (as the strength and eventual triumph of the abolitionist movement proves) but rather is an indictment of the moral emptiness of the Bertram family apart from Sir Thomas and Edmund.

CRITICAL OVERVIEW

Among the first readers of *Mansfield Park* was Austen's favorite niece, Fanny Knight. Her reaction is recorded in Austen's catalog of reaction to her novel, which she collected in 1814, a compilation that is widely reprinted and included in large part in Sandie Byrne's critical anthology *Jane Austen:* Mansfield Park. Fanny tried to convince Jane to change the ending so that rather than tempt Maria Rushworth to abandon her husband, Henry Crawford would succeed in marrying Fanny and show himself a redeemed character, a scenario that would be suggested by many later readers as more satisfactory.

Walter Scott, the most popular novelist of Austen's era, though a favorable reviewer of her earlier books, was silent about *Mansfield Park* except in letters (reprinted in Byrne) in which he was nevertheless enthusiastic. Austen herself excerpted mentions of the novel from her own correspondents. They had little but praise for it, though it is often unfavorably compared to *Pride and Prejudice*. As Byrne's critical collection shows, after Austen's death, her reputation as well as that of *Mansfield Park* continued to grow. After 1870 several of Austen's relatives published memoirs of her as well as her letters, and these were well received, cementing Austen's reputation as an important author. They tended, however, to present her as a rather saintly figure and as a gifted amateur, thereby tailoring her image to the Victorian taste that prevailed at the time.

The first half of the twentieth century, Byrne's anthology demonstrates, saw the development of Janeites—critics and, to a much larger degree, readers who privileged Austen as a literary figure on the level of Shakespeare who could do no wrong. For them, *Mansfield Park* is the worst of Austen's novels since it is the most different from the others and its heroine is the least obviously charming. At the same time, other critics developed a reading of the novel as Austen's most psychologically complex work and a breakthrough in the sense of being among the first modern novels. Lionel Trilling, with his 1955 volume *The Opposing Self*, advanced the study of *Mansfield Park*, characterizing it as perhaps the greatest but at the same time the most difficult of Austen's novels. He sowed the seeds of modern interpretations of the book, which have been offered from viewpoints ranging from feminist to psychological to sociological. Trilling suggests that the key to the reactions of the characters to the play within the novel is to be found in Plato's theory of mimesis, which holds that the imitation of life involved in dramatic art is inherently corrupting:

> What is decisive is a traditional, almost primitive, feeling about dramatic impersonation. We know of this, of course, from Plato, and it is one of the points on which almost everyone feels superior to Plato, but it may have more basis in actuality than we commonly allow. It is the fear that the impersonation of a bad or inferior character will have a harmful effect upon the impersonator, that, indeed, the impersonation of any other self will diminish the integrity of the real self.

Edmund and Fanny see the moral error in the play but are nevertheless seduced into participation. While Sir Thomas, the stern judge, rejects the play out of hand, the rest are happy to be led further astray.

More recently, historicist critics such as Roger Sales, in his *Jane Austen and Representations of Regency England* (1994), have concentrated on unraveling Austen's attitudes toward contemporary society and politics, factors that must have been self-evident to her first readers; for instance, it does not take much imagination to see Tom Bertram as a satire of the Prince Regent (the future King George IV of England). Postmodern critics have moved in the direction of reading their own criticism of traditional Western culture into Austen's work. Edward Said, in *Culture and Imperialism*, argues that Austen's main theme is imperialism and the slave economy it fostered; every element of the story is determined by or symbolic of this scarcely mentioned reality. Said notes, "To earn the right to Mansfield Park [Fanny] must first leave home as a kind of indentured servant or, to put the case in extreme terms, as a kind of transported commodity...but then [she has] the promise of future wealth." Similarly, Maaja A. Stewart, in *Domestic Realities and Imperial Fictions: Jane Austen's Novels in Eighteenth-Century Contexts* (1993) deconstructs the hidden patriarchal narratives (themes of the sexist oppression of women) of Austen's novel and era.

CRITICISM

Bradley A. Skeen

Skeen is a classics professor. In this essay, he considers the mythic and psychological sources of Mansfield Park.

Many critics of *Mansfield Park* have made a point of not likening the novel to the fairy tale of Cinderella, mentioning the possibility but shying away from what might seem a trivializing comparison. However, since fairy tales and myths embody the oldest layers of cultural tradition and sometimes reveal profound psychological truths, a reading of Austen's novel in relation to Cinderella might lay bare some of the work's most important themes and explain its dramatic power rather than belittle it. Certainly the novel's similarity to the basic structure of the Cinderella story is clear enough. Fanny Price is part

> HOWEVER, SINCE FAIRY TALES AND MYTHS EMBODY THE OLDEST LAYERS OF CULTURAL TRADITION AND SOMETIMES REVEAL PROFOUND PSYCHOLOGICAL TRUTHS, A READING OF AUSTEN'S NOVEL IN RELATION TO CINDERELLA MIGHT LAY BARE SOME OF THE WORK'S MOST IMPORTANT THEMES AND EXPLAIN ITS DRAMATIC POWER RATHER THAN BELITTLE IT."

of the Bertram family, yet not part of it; while she is presented as a cousin, her odd place in relation to the family is similar to the step-relationship of the fairy tale. The father, Sir Thomas, while not dead, is absent for much of the novel in Antigua; more importantly, he remains disengaged from Fanny's well-being until the last part of the novel, when he takes proper notice of her and in fact arranges her coming-out at a ball, filling in some sense the role of the fairy godmother. Maria and Julia Bertram can be compared to the step-sisters, while Mrs. Norris plays the role of the wicked stepmother. This passage from Charles Perrault's version of the fairy tale (with which Austen was probably familiar) highlights many of the similarities with Austen's novel:

> [The stepmother] could not endure the girl's good qualities, which by contrast rendered her own daughters the more odious. She put her to drudge at the meanest household work, and thus she and her precious darlings not only wreaked their spite but saved money to buy themselves dresses and finery.... [Cinderella] herself slept at the top of the house in a garret, upon a wretched straw mattress, while her sisters had apartments of their own with inlaid floors, beds carved and gilded in the latest fashion, and mirrors in which they could see themselves from head to foot.

These elements are all reflected in Fanny's situation. Mrs. Norris treats her more like a servant than a relative, keeps her living in an unheated upstairs room, and rules Sir Thomas's opinion of his niece, until he comes, like the fairy godmother, to take an interest in her and liberate her from Mrs. Norris's tyranny, ensuring that she is provided with wood for her stove, bringing her into society, and finally agreeing to her marriage.

WHAT DO I READ NEXT?

- Where *Mansfield Park*, published in 1814, is the first of Austen's books begun in her mature period, *Pride and Prejudice*, published in 1813, is the last of her works developed from her juvenile writing. *Pride and Prejudice* is the most acceptable of Austen's works to popular taste, while *Mansfield Park* is the least.

- Austen's *Selected Letters*, published most recently in 2004 (but also available in many earlier editions), offers insight into Austen's real life and how it informed her writing.

- Penny Gay's *Jane Austen and the Theatre* (2002) surveys the mention and use of theatrical material in Austen's novels and the role of the theater in her life as well.

- Kirstin Olsen's *All Things Austen: An Encyclopedia of Austen's World* (2005; 2 vols.) offers explanations of the unfamiliar details of everyday life in Austen's novels. Aspects covered range from the different kinds of hunting engaged in by the characters to the different styles in which Mary Crawford and Fanny would have likely dressed, from how vital clues to the characters of Henry Crawford and Edmund Bertram reflect their attending university at Cambridge and Oxford, respectively, to what music Mary Crawford would likely have played on her harp.

- George Crabbe, though nearly forgotten today, was Jane Austen's favorite poet. He is quoted in *Mansfield Park* and even supplied the name Fanny Price. His works are archived on the Web at Project Gutenberg (http://www.gutenberg.org/browse/authors/c#a1725).

- The popular play *Lovers' Vows* (1798), an adaptation of an August von Kotzebue play by Elizabeth Inchbald, is of considerable dramatic and symbolic importance in *Mansfield Park*. The text of the play has been archived on the Internet (http://klh64.tripod.com/vows/index.html).

Henry Crawford has some aspects of the prince, in that he courts all three "sisters" but falls in love with Fanny when he finally sees her true self, just as the prince falls in love with Cinderella when he sees her at the ball as she truly ought to be, not in the condition to which her circumstances have reduced her. In Austen's novel, when Fanny goes into hiding in Portsmouth, Mr. Crawford seeks her out and proposes to her—but in a reversal of the fairy tale, Fanny rejects her suitor. Rather, Fanny accepts her true beloved, Edmund, who is a prince in another form, a son, if not the heir, of Mansfield Park. It is this kingdom that they inherit, not in the legal sense, as will Tom, but in the more meaningful moral and spiritual senses. Certainly they live happily ever after: "With so much true merit and true love, and no want of fortune or friends, the happiness of the married cousins must appear as secure as earthly happiness can be."

Avrom Fleishman, in *A Reading of Mansfield Park*, suggests that the comparison with Cinderella is both valid and useful. He goes further by helping to explain the novel in terms of Sigmund Freud's analysis of the mythology related to Cinderella in his essay "The Theme of the Three Caskets." Freud, the noted Austrian psychologist and founder of psychoanalysis, notices that a motif has appeared over and over in myth and literature in which a suitor must choose between three sisters. He chooses the least likely, the third or youngest, and, having chosen wisely, is amply rewarded. This occurs in Cinderella as well as in Greek myth, where Prince Paris of Troy chooses Aphrodite as the fairest goddess and is rewarded with marriage to Helen. The scenario occurs twice in Shakespeare, in slightly altered forms. King Lear actually fails to choose his youngest daughter, Cordelia (not as his wife but as his heir), and his

---

life ends in tragedy after the death of all three daughters. In *The Merchant of Venice*, Portia's suitors must pass a test, selecting one of three caskets, the correct one being not of gold or silver but of lead. Freud finds that a common attribute in the third sister is a refusal to speak on her own behalf, in some fairy-tale versions a literal dumbness, just as Cinderella never says anything to the prince to reveal her true identity when she could. Fanny likewise is noted for her refusal to speak, most obviously in her saying nothing to Edmund about her feelings for him, and also, just as importantly, for her speaking refusal in answer to Mr. Crawford's proposal. When the real "prince," Edmund, chooses Fanny, he indeed receives every reward he could have hoped for. Sir Thomas also finally chooses Fanny, preferring her to his own daughters.

Freud finds the symbolic meaning of this dumbness to be death, with speaking being taken as the characteristic activity of life. This is made explicit in the case of Lear, who ends the play carrying the dead Cordelia in his arms. The symbolic value of lead, the correct choice among the three caskets, is also death, because of its cold and malleable character. The judgment of Paris, on the other hand, yields the opposite choice: Aphrodite, the very goddess of life. But there is nothing unusual in something dreadful, such as death, being represented by its opposite. This seeming paradox reveals the fundamental truth that life and death are inextricably linked. While Aphrodite, the goddess of love, might seem completely the opposite of death, her prototypes in the Near East, such as Astarte and Ishtar, combine her qualities with presiding over killing in warfare and with a myth of descent and return from the abode of the dead in the underworld. Austen surely knew of such a notion from an echo of it in the biblical Song of Solomon: "For love is as strong as death" (8:6). After writing his essay on the three caskets in 1913, Freud saw increasingly clearly that human psychology is dominated by two great drives instilled by evolution, one for life, through procreation, and one for death, in the use of violence for hunting and for gaining power within human society. (The longing for isolation and rest is also significant.) These opposing drives are unified precisely in the Cinderella story, in which the prince chooses to marry death: the creation and the destruction of life become one. Inasmuch as Fanny, too, represents death, Fleischman concludes that it is precisely this deathly quality of hers

that makes her so simultaneously attractive and repellent to readers and critics.

The happy world of Mansfield Park that Fanny and Edmund enter into and become the heirs of is the world of the dead. For Austen this can only be the Christian heaven, the paradise that is perfect, orderly, beautiful, and just—everything that death is not as far as human senses can discern (another representation by opposites). The contrast between the home of Fanny's parents in South Hampton and Mansfield Park, where she will live happily with Edmund, is the contrast in the Platonic and then the Christian view between life on earth, which is the true death, and the spiritual rebirth experienced in heaven. The disorder and squalor there, the meaninglessness of existence there, all mark the Price home as a plane of existence different from Mansfield Park:

> Such was the home which was to put Mansfield out of her head, and teach her to think of her cousin Edmund with moderated feelings. On the contrary, she could think of nothing but Mansfield, its beloved inmates, its happy ways. Every thing where she now was in full contrast to it. The elegance, propriety, regularity, harmony—and perhaps, above all, the peace and tranquillity of Mansfield, were brought to her remembrance every hour of the day, by the prevalence of everything opposite to them *here*.

Like any good Christian, Fanny receives her reward in heaven. This progress towards an ideal death helps to reveal more about the novel's main themes.

Just after receiving the first copies of *Pride and Prejudice*, Austen wrote of plans for *Mansfield Park* to her sister Cassandra, as quoted in Deirdre Le Faye's *Jane Austen: A Family Record*: "Now I will try to write of something else; – it shall be a complete change of subject – Ordination" (January 29, 1813). While this might be taken to refer to Edmund's ordination as a priest, that is certainly not the main subject of the novel. In fact, as the entry in the Oxford English Dictionary shows, *ordination* was a much more common word in Austen's time than it is now, and its general meaning of imposing order (as in *co-ordination*) was still in common usage. The ordination that Austen meant was the imposing of order on Mansfield Park, which moves from a disordered to a more ordered state through the course of the novel. The ordination is also Fanny's movement from the squalor of the Price home to the order of Mansfield Park. Sir Thomas's estate must survive the attacks from without by the

Crawfords, and those who are unworthy of it must be expelled. Its heir, Tom, must be (symbolically at least) replaced by Edmund. Maria and Julia are expelled and also replaced. Fanny's marriage to Edmund, giving her a new place at the center of the Bertram family, is as much an ordination for her as Edmund's induction into the Anglican priesthood is for him. Sir Thomas is the source of order in Mansfield, standing against the disorder implied by impersonation in the play as well as against the squalor of Portsmouth. Fanny is not snobbish in rejecting her old family. They are part of another world as much as the Crawfords of London are. These worlds, then, assault the existence of Mansfield from both sides. Although Sir Thomas succeeds in governing himself and in securing the order that nourishes Mansfield Park and its true inheritors, Edmund and Fanny, he fails his other children. The very sternness that leads to his success alienates them, making it impossible for them to benefit from his influence. This is manifest in his allowing Mrs. Norris to rule over his house:

> Mrs. Norris's removal from Mansfield was the great supplementary comfort of Sir Thomas's life.... He had felt her an hourly evil, which was so much the worse, as there seemed no chance of its ceasing but with life; she seemed a part of himself, that must be borne forever.

Together, the departure of Mrs. Norris and the rise of Edmund and Fanny amount to the creation of a new world.

In some sense these two interpretations, one seeing Fanny as a symbol of death, the other taking the theme of ordination to mean the establishing of order, might seem paradoxical, since death is inherently disordered. The difficulty can be resolved, however, with the realization that Christianity views death, that is, the translation from mortal life to heaven, as the gaining of a new divine order, perfectly ordained, as the world here is not. In this case, death is revealed to be the opposite of how it appears to humanity, as the hope of a new life. The death Edmund finds in Fanny after the cataclysmic events that end the proper narrative of the novel is indeed rather to be perceived as a second life in a kind of paradise. Nor is it a coincidence that Christianity conceives of heaven precisely as a paradise or well-tended garden. This is what Mansfield Park is to become, sharply contrasting with Mr. Crawford's indifference to the garden of his own estate and with Mr. Rushworth's fumbling and ultimately comic handling of the garden at Southerton, as based on conformity to the

> FANNY'S REJECTION OF HENRY IS AN ACT OF COURAGEOUS HUMILITY. ACCEPTING HIS PROPOSAL WOULD HAVE BEEN AN AFFIRMATION OF HER FEARS OF INFERIORITY; IT WOULD HAVE BEEN A SUBMISSION TO THE DOMINANT OPINION THAT HENRY WAS A GOOD MATCH, AND AN ACCESSION TO THE IMPLICIT SUGGESTION THAT SHE WAS NOT A MORAL AGENT."

views of the world rather than on inspiration. These are the forces of chaos to which the gates protecting the order of Mansfield Park are shut. The estate thus becomes the model for the simplicity and propriety of the landscaping Edmund intends for his parsonage at Thornton Lacey.

Source: Bradley A. Skeen, Critical Essay on *Mansfield Park*, in *Novels for Students*, Gale, Cengage Learning, 2009.

Jeanine M. Grenberg

In the following excerpt, Grenberg explores the connection between Kantian humility and Austen's Mansfield Park.

...Fanny's society is one in which the shared purpose of assuring good marriages is valued. Unfortunately, another shared purpose of this society is the affirmation of social distinctions. To assure a strong sense of the "us" of this financially stable group, it has been deemed necessary to identify a lesser "them." Fanny is, furthermore, expected to claim her role as a "them," that is, as an inferior outsider. But, like the disfigurement of the shared purpose of making good matches, the shared purpose of enforced assignments of inferiority and superiority is a shared purpose of Fanny's society inconsistent with moral demands, and is itself an expression of unsocial sociability. Fanny's most distinctive act of courageous humility is to reveal herself as willing to challenge both these shared purposes through a cultivation of her own "strong desire to do right." Thus to challenge immoral shared social purposes on moral, instead of on personal, self-serving, grounds is, in the end, a socially virtuous act; that is, one that is motivated by a concern to affirm society.

Fanny's acquisition of courageous humility is all the more estimable in that she had many fears to overcome, and much encouragement to handle these fears by claiming a position of inferiority. Fanny is "afraid of everybody," "ashamed of herself," "finding something to fear in every person and place."

But Fanny claims neither enforced inferiority nor defensive, over-asserted superiority as the way of handling her fears. She is able, instead, to rely on what her cousin, confidant, and eventual husband, Edmund, identifies early on as her "affectionate heart, and a strong desire of doing right" to guide her. Fanny becomes a person whose acute feelings are guided by equally strong commitment to moral principles. Such adherence to principle prevents her from succumbing, like Maria, to Sir Thomas's financially inspired matchmaking tendencies, and allows her to recognize Henry Crawford as evil. Fanny trains her natural sensitivity into a tool for being morally sensitive to others' feelings and situations, and for disdaining those who lack such emotional and principled sensitivity. But to become this moral person, Fanny needs both to challenge and to fit into the society of which she is a part. And, to accomplish both these goals, she needs courageous humility, a trait of hers revealed most clearly in her rejection of marriage to Henry Crawford.

Before analyzing this refusal, it is important first to appreciate Fanny's reticence in handling the situation. She does tell Henry that she does not want to marry him, but not by sharing her opinion that he is evil, only by saying no to his entreaties and repeating the same in a short note to his sister. Later, Fanny's only response to Sir Thomas's encouragement to allow feelings for Henry to develop is silence, not violent rejection of the plan.

Why does Fanny not assert herself more forcefully in these situations? Is she not succumbing to unsocial sociability by doing so? A better way of understanding Fanny's silence than this is that she feels obliged to maintain a close-knit society even as she finds a way to assert herself. There are two values in question here: affirming herself as a moral agent, and maintaining the coherence of her society. Fanny rejects neither. Her tactic for affirming both is not to reject the idea of marriage to Henry openly, but rather to let time do its work in revealing what she knows to be true of his character. Doing so reveals her courageously

humble ability to challenge her society while at the same time recognizing her dependence upon that very same society. She is in the business of building the connectedness that is necessary in any well-functioning society, and thus faces her fears and asserts her rights in a manner compatible with retaining such connection.

To accomplish this, Fanny wants especially to avoid admitting her true opinion of Henry to Sir Thomas. The flirtatiousness of which Fanny accuses Henry was most flagrantly exhibited in his interactions with Sir Thomas's daughter, Maria. But Sir Thomas knows nothing of this, and Fanny feels herself the wrong person to be the bearer of bad news. Fanny even goes so far as to allow herself to be subjected to harsh judgments of herself by Sir Thomas in order to avoid asserting this negative judgment of Henry and, implicitly, of Maria to Sir Thomas. Sir Thomas accuses her of being "wilful and perverse ... without any consideration ... for those who have surely some right to guide" her, and as exhibiting crass "ingratitude" for those who have raised her. But still Fanny bites her tongue and conceals her judgment of Henry.

Even in conversation with Edmund, Fanny reveals her moral condemnation of Henry only when she is forced, morally, to do so. Edmund reveals himself as one of the many supporters of Fanny allowing her feelings for Henry to develop. But it is only when a first, gentler response to Edmund fails that Fanny turns to her more principled reasons for rejecting Henry. She requires such pressures to reveal her beliefs not because she is unsure of her true principles, but because she is morally concerned to maintain social bonds, and thus tries to avoid bringing pain to others, except when strictly necessary.

But here was that strictly necessary time: her dearest companion who had not seemed to be caught up in the moral confusions of her society, is caught up in this moral confusion. Fanny thus says she "feel[s] it due to herself [to] return ... to [discussion of] Mr. Crawford." This is interesting locution: Fanny feels a duty to herself to speak plainly to Edmund about her moral judgment of Henry. Fanny has, up to this point, been keenly aware of her need to refrain from speaking her mind so as to avoid causing pain. But such sensitivity to morally relevant social concerns now comes into conflict with unfair pressure on her from Edmund, Sir Thomas, and others, a pressure implying that she is inferior, not really a moral agent in her own right. "Surely you will do what all the rest of us recognize as the right thing?" is implied by all around Fanny, including Edmund. It is Fanny's moral responsibility to assert that she must act as her own conscience guides her. She is asserting her equality with others in Mansfield Park, her equal right—indeed, duty—to exercise her moral agency. Fanny's concern to maintain connections thus does not blind her to the fact that she too is a center of absolute worth, capable of making, and obligated to make, moral judgments.

She thus admits to Edmund her true reasons for rejecting Henry all along: "'It is not merely in temper that I consider him as totally unsuited to myself;...I cannot approve his character.'" Fanny's condemnation of Henry is a condemnation of his failure to train his feelings in a morally appropriate way. He is both "improper" and "unfeeling"; that is, he lacks both the proper guiding principles and the proper feelings to support him in establishing and maintaining his connections with others in his social space. Instead of educated sensitivities that connect him to others, he is full of strong, unguided feelings that lead him to injure others. In other words, he is a moral failure. As Fanny more delicately puts it: "'I am persuaded that he does not think as he ought, on serious subjects.'" Indeed, he has failed in just the moral task that Fanny herself has taken on with such alacrity: the education of feeling via principles. She must reject Henry. He is the very antithesis of those moral values that Fanny herself holds most dear.

Fanny knows where to draw the line not only in her responsibility to herself, but also in her responsibility to other persons. Edmund suggests, to Fanny's horror, that Henry's failure of character makes Henry all the more an appropriate husband for her, since Fanny "will supply the rest; and a most fortunate man he is to attach himself to such a creature—to a woman, who firm as a rock in her own principles, has a gentleness of character...[H]e will make you happy;...but you will make him everything."

Fanny's response to this ridiculous proposal—that her connection to Henry would turn him into a moral being—has a distinctively Kantian ring to it: "'I would not engage in such a charge...in such an office of high responsibility!'" Henry misunderstands her; he takes her to be saying that she is incapable of such a noble task. What in fact Fanny is asserting here is the good Kantian point that she,

and all persons, are properly incapable of such a task: one can only make oneself a moral being; one is not made such by others. And whatever commitment Fanny has to increasing the happiness of other persons, she wouldn't dream of taking on such a futile task as the ground and basis of her lifelong commitment to her mate. As Kant states,

> It is a contradiction for me to make another's [moral] perfection my end and consider myself under obligation to promote this. For the perfection of another human being, as a person, consists just in this: that he himself is able to set his end in accordance with his own concepts of duty; and it is self-contradictory to require that I...make it my duty to do...something that only the other himself can do. (*Metaphysics of Morals*, 6: 386)

Fanny's rejection of Henry is an act of courageous humility. Accepting his proposal would have been an affirmation of her fears of inferiority: it would have been a submission to the dominant opinion that Henry was a good match, and an accession to the implicit suggestion that she was not a moral agent. Rejecting the proposal is thus simultaneously a courageous rejection of those fears of inferiority, and a reaffirmation of her own absolute value and equality as a moral agent. She is thus courageous in just the humble sense we have articulated above: she courageously faces her fear that she was inferior, even that her own happiness could be compromised by her choice, and nonetheless confidently asserts her agentic equality with those around her. She faces these fears with the weapon that we have already found in the arsenal of the humble person: her awareness of and confidence in her worth as a rational agent. Fanny finds the strength to face her fears in her beliefs about her equal worth as a moral agent, all grounded in that original "desire to do right" of which Edmund had spoken so long ago.

But Fanny asserts her rights as a moral agent within the constraints necessary to assure simultaneously that she remains a part of Mansfield Park society. Doing so proves that she is guided also, as the courageously humble person would be, by an abiding awareness of her own limits. Fanny recognizes that she can't flourish without accepting her role as a member of a well-functioning society. This doesn't mean that she is attentive to the needs of others only for her own sake. Rather, she has a genuine appreciation for the value of a well-functioning society in virtue of the fact that she herself, and all persons, are limited and dependent beings. Her concern to maintain her place in her society, and to help assure that that society functions well, is proof of the fact that she is aware of those needs and dependencies that she shares with everyone around her.

This is a point that Sir Thomas initially has difficulty believing. He worries that Fanny's refusal of Henry's proposal is in fact a sign of her "wilfulness of temper, self-conceit . . . and independence of spirit, which prevails so much in modern days," a sign, that is, of the rejection of the society of which she has been a part. Even Fanny worries that her connectedness to others will suffer: "All, perhaps all, would think her selfish and ungrateful."

One has to have a certain sympathy with Sir Thomas here. It can seem that Fanny's rejection of Henry is an overly individualistic, instead of a socially informed, assertion of moral values. Surely, her act promises to be as disruptive to society as Henry's own evil act. Yet the genuine social value of good marriages is, in Mansfield Park, corrupted in many ways; and Fanny's rejection of Henry is not so much an individualistic rejection of morally sanctioned social values as it is their ultimate defense. She, more than anyone else, is able to recognize the evil that Henry brought to Mansfield Park. By her rejection of him, Fanny is ultimately supporting the society of which she is a part. She goes against social mores because they have become corrupt social mores.

Furthermore, Fanny's choice, unlike Henry's choice of elopement, required Fanny to constrain, not indulge, her concern for happiness. One might think, with Sir Thomas, quite the opposite: all Fanny is doing is seeking her own, very individualistic conception of happiness; she is avoiding marrying someone she doesn't love. But Fanny has good moral reasons never to feel love for Henry. Her choice to reject him is thus in at least short-term tension with her happiness, since rejecting him involves being at odds with everyone around her. The "wretchedness" Fanny felt in that "mortifying conference" with Sir Thomas is, perhaps, the best example of this. Fanny does not want to be at odds with Sir Thomas, not only because she knows her happiness depends upon his continuing good will, but also because she feels a genuine affection for and gratitude to him. She is thus particularly horrified when Sir Thomas accuses her of ingratitude.

That rejecting Henry ends up being something very much in agreement with her long-term happiness does nothing to undermine the fact that it was a principle ultimately compatible with her social obligations, and not an overly independent concern for happiness, that guided Fanny. She needed to be courageous (as opposed to merely self-indulgent) when she challenged those around her by her choice, and part of what she needed to be courageous about was the very real possibility that following principle here would bring great injury to her happiness.

But in order for Fanny's awareness of her limits to be truly that of the courageously humble person, she must also recognize at least her own possibility of indulging in a pursuit of happiness that undermines her social concerns, her own unsocial sociability. And Fanny does have regular temptations to lose herself in her pursuit of personal happiness. The most striking example of this is when Henry's elopement with Maria, an act we've already seen to produce horrible social consequences, happens to have beneficial consequences for Fanny: it allows her to leave Portsmouth (her home, but a place where, having once been introduced to the society of Mansfield Park, she is miserable) and return to her beloved Mansfield Park:

> To-morrow! To leave Portsmouth to-morrow! . . . [S]he felt she was, in the greatest danger of being exquisitely happy, while so many were miserable. The evil which brought such good to her! She dreaded lest she should learn to be insensible of it . . . [S]uch a combination of blessings as set her heart in a glow, and for a time seemed to distance every pain, and make her incapable of suitably sharing the distress even of those whose distress she thought of most.

Fanny worries that her own joy will dull her sympathies for others' sufferings; that, like Henry, she will become so caught up in her own pursuit of personal happiness, that she will forget her social obligations. But, unlike Henry, she is aware of such a possibility, and does things to prevent its realization: she "call[s] herself to think" on the pains of others, and to recognize those pains as "terrible and grievous," not to be morose, but rather to maintain her sensitivity to members of her society. Fanny is both recognizing her happiness and making an effort to restrain its power over her so as to ensure that her sympathies for others are in their proper place. She thus appropriately constrains her legitimate concern for happiness in light of her moral demands. . . .

Source: Jeanine M. Grenberg, "Courageous Humility in Jane Austen's *Mansfield Park*," in *Social Thoery and Practice*, Vol. 33, No. 4, October 2007, p. 645.

Sally B. Palmer

In the following essay, Palmer presents a literary interpretation of Mansfield Park.

In nineteenth-century British fiction, the primary role of the middle- to upper-class aunt with respect to her nephews and nieces is to oversee the development of proper manners and promote suitable marriages. The term *breeding* encompasses both these matters, both in its literal sense and figuratively, as Jane Austen uses it, to signify decorum. The aunt, then, assumes the position of a breeder—a bloodstock agent or horticulturist, both of which professions were just emerging in the first half of the nineteenth century. Stock-breeders were also known as "improvers."

Although in Austen's day the voyage of the *Beagle* was still to come, interest ran high in pre-Darwinian and Lamarckian ideas about the laws of organic development and natural selection as they related to both biological and social characteristics. An 1814 manual mentions the necessity of agricultural crossbreeding, and sheep were being cooperatively bred in 1827 for "joints" or wool. By 1840 David Low was boasting that "the cultivation of the Horse . . . has been carried to the highest perfection," and asserted:

> Since 1750 the practice of breeding has been reduced to a system, and founded upon principles. To the natural causes which produce diversities in the characters of animals, we must add those produced by art. By breeding from animals of certain characters, we can communicate the distinctive properties of the parents to the progeny. *(i)*

Jane Austen's knowledge of this subject surfaces in *Mansfield Park*, where we read about different kinds of horses correlating to different characters: Tom Bertram's thoroughbred racehorses, Edmund's hunters, the cart horse to carry Mary Crawford's harp, and the pony and "ladies' mount" for Fanny Price to ride.

The problem of the apricot tree in Dr. Grant's garden producing fruit of an inferior variety calls attention to the subject of domestic breeding and in doing so addresses the central problem of the novel itself: corruption of the family line. We read about it in a brief interchange between Dr. Grant and Mrs. Norris, whose role as the Bertram aunt is to forge prudent marriage connections and thus preserve the quality of the original family stock. The interchange occurs in the middle of a discussion of "improvements" to be made at Sotherton Court, significant in view of the two meanings for the word. Sotherton faces "improvements" in its scenic aspect—the cutting down of ancient trees—and "improvements" in the breeding line—anticipating the impending marriage of Maria Bertram to Sotherton's Mr. Rushworth—neither of which will prove salutary. Mrs. Norris says:

> We were always doing something [to improve the place]. It was only the spring twelvemonth before Mr. Norris's death, that we put in the apricot . . . which is now grown such a noble tree, and getting to such perfection, sir.

Although the object of discussion is Dr. Grant's apricot tree, Mrs. Norris might equally be speaking of Sir Thomas Bertram's family tree, whose youngest branches have been her especial pride and care, and with which she can likewise find no fault. Dr. Grant's reply also applies to the Bertram family: "The tree thrives well beyond a doubt, madam, the soil is good; and I never pass it without regretting, that the fruit should be so little worth the trouble of gathering." In *Mansfield Park* the family represents the land, and the land the family. Here we learn that Mansfield Park should be producing a better generation of heirs.

Always anxious to absolve herself from blame and to deny faults in her favorites, Mrs. Norris indignantly defends the quality of the tree's fruit by invoking its pedigree name, whose similarity to the name of Mansfield Park should not be ignored. She also alludes to its high price, reflecting the high economic status of the Mansfield Park family: "Sir, it is a moor park, we bought it as a moor park . . . and I know it cost seven shillings, and was charged as a moor park."

When, later, the quality of Mansfield Park stock—Bertram scions Tom and Maria—proves as corrupt as the apricots worthless, Mrs. Norris, although the primary breeding agent, again refuses responsibility. It is left to Fanny Price, herself grafted onto the Bertram rootstock by her aunt's efforts, to reject cross-breeding with the tainted Crawford stock and ensure that the ancient line is transmitted pure with a closed system of inbreeding through Fanny's marriage to her cousin Edmund.

Many critics have noted in *Mansfield Park* Austen's essential distrust of modern reconstructions or "improvements" upon traditional family life, as well as on the "noble old places" where they live. Yet, at the novel's end, when the reconstructed Mansfield Park family has itself been "improved" by the elimination of aunt Norris and Maria, the substitution of Fanny as daughter, and the importation of Susan Price as resident niece, it is evident that we are to see this reconfigured family as changed for the better. For Austen, the Bertram pedigree has been shored up and the line of descent improved through the natural consequences of morality and immorality. This, then, is Austen's "natural selection."

Alistair Duckworth, in "Jane Austen's Accommodations," sees Austen's aim in *Mansfield Park* as to "invigorate existing structures." In a program to preserve a declining bloodline, hybrid vigor is achieved by introducing a strong representative of a different strain. Austen inserts Fanny Price's middle-class blood into the depleted Bertram strain, whose effeteness is suggested by the perennial lassitude of Lady Bertram and the moral degeneration of Tom and Maria. In rejecting deficient bloodstock such as the Crawfords, and discarding defective specimens such as Maria Bertram, Austenian family reconfiguration amounts to a controlled domestic breeding program where only the morally well-bred are selected to reproduce and thus perpetuate the family lineage.

Source: Sally B. Palmer, "Austen's *Mansfield Park*," in *Explicator*, Vol. 56, No. 4, Summer 1998, p. 181.

SOURCES

Austen, Jane, *Mansfield Park*, edited by John Lucas, Oxford University Press, 1970.

Byrne, Paula, "'The Unmeaning Luxuries of Bath': Urban Pleasures in Jane Austen's World," in *Persuasions*, Vol. 26, 2004, pp. 13–26.

Byrne, Sandie, ed., *Jane Austen:* Mansfield Park, Palgrave Macmillan, 2005, esp. pp. 9–19.

Fleishman, Avrom, *A Reading of Mansfield Park: An Essay in Critical Synthesis*, Johns Hopkins University Press, 1967, pp. 57–69.

Freud, Sigmund, "The Theme of the Three Caskets," in *The Freud Reader*, edited by Peter Gay, Norton, 1989, pp. 514–22; originally published in *Imago*, 1913.

Karounos, Michael, "Ordination and Revolution in Mansfield Park," in *Studies in English Literature, 1500–1900*, Vol. 44, No. 4, Autumn 2004, pp. 715–36.

Le Faye, Deirdre, *Jane Austen: A Family Record*, Cambridge University Press, 2004, pp. 197–98.

Nokes, David, *Jane Austen: A Life*, Farrar, Straus and Giroux, 1997.

Perrault, Charles, "Cinderella," in *The Fairy Tales of Charles Perrault*, Folio Society, 1998, pp. 69–94.

Said, Edward, *Culture and Imperialism*, Vintage, 1994, pp. 93–116.

Sales, Roger, *Jane Austen and Representations of Regency England*, Routledge, 1994.

Stewart, Maaja A., *Domestic Realities and Imperial Fictions: Jane Austen's Novels in Eighteenth-Century Contexts*, University of Georgia Press, 1993.

Trilling, Lionel, "Jane Austen and *Mansfield Park*," in *The Moral Obligation to be Intelligent: Selected Essays*, edited by Leon Wieseltier, Farrar, Straus and Giroux, 2000, pp. 292–310; originally published in *The Opposing Self: Nine Essays in Criticism*, by Lionel Trilling, Viking, 1955.

FURTHER READING

Bush, M. L., *The English Aristocracy: A Comparative Synthesis*, Manchester University Press, 1984.
This book provides an introduction to the British class system that shaped the character of Austen's writing.

Copeland, Edward, and Juliet McMaster, eds., *The Cambridge Companion to Jane Austen*, Cambridge University Press, 1997.
This collection of essays covers every aspect of Austen's life and novels from a variety of literary, historical, and sociological viewpoints.

Tomalin, Claire, *Jane Austen: A Life*, Vintage Books, 1999.
This is the standard scholarly biography of Austen.

Turner, Roger, *Capability Brown and the Eighteenth-Century English Landscape*, Rizzoli, 1985.
This book is a biography of the leading landscape architect of the late eighteenth century. It discusses his work in the larger context of the landscape gardening of Austen's era and provides insight into the theme of gardening so important in *Mansfield Park*.

Something Wicked This Way Comes

Published in 1962, *Something Wicked This Way Comes*, by Ray Bradbury, is arguably the last of the author's most beloved novels. It was written on the heels of his science-fiction classics *The Martian Chronicles* and *Fahrenheit 451* as well as his widely read bildungsroman *Dandelion Wine*. In fact, *Something Wicked This Way Comes* combines elements of the bildungsroman (a coming-of-age story) with elements of science fiction. Appealing to children and adults alike, the story, which lies on the cusp between the horror and fantasy genres, portrays two boys and their adventures with a mystical circus and its sinister ringmaster. Ultimately a meditation on the power of love in the face of evil, the novel contains a wealth of themes, ranging from the natures of transformation to the graceful acceptance of aging. By virtue of the story's considerable thematic depth, coupled with its plethora of fantastical imagery and its accessibility to younger readers, the book has been a mainstay in school curricula, kept there for several decades by the timeless nature of the novel's themes and content. *Something Wicked This Way Comes* has been more or less continuously in print since 1962; a relatively recent edition of the novel was printed by Eos in 1999.

RAY BRADBURY

1962

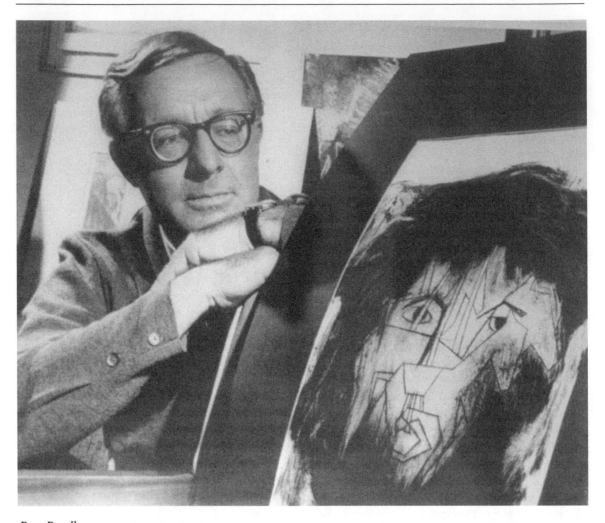

Ray Bradbury *(The Library of Congress)*

AUTHOR BIOGRAPHY

Ray Bradbury was born on August 22, 1920, in Waukegan, Illinois. He was the third son of Spaulding Bradbury (a telephone lineman) and Esther Marie Moberg Bradbury (a Swedish immigrant). A reader from an early age, Bradbury spent a great deal of time in the Waukegan town library, upon which the library in *Something Wicked This Way Comes* is based. Bradbury began writing around the age of twelve. On his personal Web site, Bradbury reports that he was inspired to become a writer after attending a carnival where a man performing as Mr. Electrico touched him with a sword and told him, "Live forever." (A character based on Mr. Electrico also appears in *Something Wicked This Way Comes*.) Though Bradbury's hometown is

Waukegan, the family often moved as Spaulding Bradbury looked for jobs during the Great Depression. The family finally settled in Los Angeles in 1934.

Bradbury graduated from Los Angeles High School in 1938, at which time he chose to forgo college and immediately begin his writing career. That year, he published his first short story, "Hollerbochen's Dilemma." The following year, he founded his own magazine, *Futuria Fantasia*. In 1942, Bradbury wrote "The Lake," the first of his stories to exhibit the style for which he would ultimately become famous. By the mid-1940s his work was being published in more prominent publications; his "The Big Black and White Game" appeared in *Best American Short Stories 1945*, and his "I See You Never" appeared in *Best American Short Stories 1948*. He also received recognition from the O. Henry Award organization for two consecutive years, publishing "Homecoming" in the *O. Henry Prize Stories 1947* and winning the O. Henry Award in 1948 for "Powerhouse." On September 27, 1947, Bradbury married Marguerite Susan McClure. The couple had four daughters, Susan Marguerite, Ramona, Bettina, and Alexandra. After over fifty-five years of marriage, Marguerite passed away in 2003.

In 1950, Bradbury achieved his first major success with the novel (or collection of linked short stories) *The Martian Chronicles*. The book was an instant classic that would be adapted as a play (by Bradbury) and also as a movie. Indeed, several of Bradbury's best works underwent dramatic adaptations, often written by Bradbury himself. Bradbury's next major work, the novel *Fahrenheit 451* (1953), was also a success and became a dystopian classic. Based on the merits of these early works alone, Bradbury received the National Institute of Arts and Letters Award for his contributions to American literature in 1954. The autobiographical *Dandelion Wine* followed in 1957, and *Something Wicked This Way Comes* was published in 1962. The latter draws heavily upon stories from Bradbury's early collections *Dark Carnival* (1947) and *The Illustrated Man* (1951). That latter book's title story, "The Illustrated Man," is perhaps one of Bradbury's most anthologized works.

Although Bradbury never again matched his early successes, he has remained a prolific writer well into his late eighties. He is the author of novels, short stories, children's books and stories, poems, plays, and screenplays. His unique work has defied easy categorization, containing elements of fantasy, horror, science fiction, gothic writing, and autobiographical fiction. Given this, critics initially debated the merits of Bradbury's writing, and he did not receive much critical recognition until later in his career. For this reason, the bulk of Bradbury's honors have come more than forty years after the release of his best works. His later awards have mostly been given for his oeuvre as a whole rather than for individual books or collections. Bradbury earned the PEN Body of Work Award in 1985, a 2000 medal for "Distinguished Contribution to American Letters" from the National Book Foundation, a star on the Hollywood Walk of Fame for his screenplays, a 2004 National Medal

of Arts; a special citation for a distinguished career from the Pulitzer Board in 2007, and a 2007 Commandeur medal from the French Ordre des Arts et des Lettres. As of 2008, Bradbury was living in Los Angeles, continuing to write every day, just as he had since he was twelve years old.

PLOT SUMMARY

Prologue

It is October 23. The next-door neighbors and best friends James (Jim) Nightshade and William (Will) Halloway are each about to turn fourteen, William on October 30 and James on October 31. Their lives, however, are about to change, for this is the "week when they grew up overnight."

1. Arrivals

CHAPTERS 1–5

Jim and Will are playing in front of their houses when a lightning rod salesman walks by. The salesman, Tom Fury, wants to sell them a rod, but the boys have no money and their parents are not home. Tom Fury suddenly has a premonition that Jim's house will be catastrophically struck by lightning that very night, so he gives the boys a lightning rod for free. Later that evening, Jim and Will run to the library. On the way there, Jim thinks he hears faint music, but Will does not hear it, and Jim thinks he must have been mistaken. Will's father, Charles William Halloway, is the janitor at the library. He looks so old to Will that it is hard for him to see his father as his dad and not as an old man.

Charles watches the boys leaving the library with their books, running. He wishes he could join them and be young again. Charles finishes up at the library and stops at the local bar for a nightcap. Meanwhile, the boys reach the United Cigar Store and greet Mr. Tetley, the store's owner. Mr. Tetley greets the boys, but then he suddenly stares off into space, listening for something. The boys attempt to get his attention but fail, so they leave him standing there and keep running. They then come across the barber, Mr. Crosetti, as he closes up the barber shop. The barber thinks he smells cotton candy. Later, as Charles leaves the bar, he sees a man in a "dark suit" putting up posters; he enters and then exits an empty store before leaving. Charles

MEDIA ADAPTATIONS

- *Something Wicked This Way Comes* was adapted as a Disney film, directed by Jack Clayton, in 1983. Bradbury wrote the screenplay.

looks into the storefront and sees a sign advertising Cooger & Dark's Pandemonium Shadow Show, along with a display claiming to contain "THE MOST BEAUTIFUL WOMAN IN THE WORLD." All that is there is an empty block of ice.

CHAPTERS 6–10

Jim and Will continue on their way home when Jim wants to stop and look at the Theater, which is not a real theater but a house with an uncovered window that the boys peep into. Will refuses to go with Jim, so Jim goes without him, calling Will a "dimwit Episcopal Baptist." However, Jim soon catches back up with Will since no one is at the Theater. A piece of paper goes flying by in the wind, and it turns out to be a poster for Cooger & Dark's Pandemonium Shadow Show, which is scheduled to begin the next day. Will is suspicious and says that there are never any carnivals in the fall. Jim is nevertheless excited. The boys realize that the faint music and smells of cotton candy must be from the carnival. Will then points out that carnivals arrive at dawn, not at dusk. Soon, the boys reach their houses.

Will finds that his father has arrived home before him; his father and mother are in the living room. Will thinks that his mother always seems happy but his father always seems sad. Will goes to bed and listens to his parents talking. Charles says that he regrets being too old to play ball with his own son. Will's parents then go to bed. Just as Will is falling asleep, he thinks he hears his father leave the house, and he assumes that Charles is going back to the library, where he often goes to be alone or to read.

Jim is lying in bed. Jim's mother comes in to say good night, and she worries about him leaving the window open. She worries because Jim is her only surviving child, the other two presumably having died in infancy. She warns him that he will worry, too, once he has children, but Jim says, "No use making more people. People die." Jim asks his mother about his father; it is not clear if Jim's father has died or if he left Jim's mother.

Tom Fury walks through the town, his pack empty. He comes upon the storefront advertising the beautiful woman and, when he looks inside, sees far more than Charles Halloway did. He sees a literal woman. Tom Fury thinks that if he were to touch the ice it would melt and free the woman within, so he enters the shop.

CHAPTERS 11–15

It is three o'clock in the morning, and Will and Jim hear the carnival train approaching the town. Jim decides to sneak out to watch the proceedings, and Will follows him. The train passes over the boys on the bridge, and they see that no one is playing the calliope (a steam-powered pipe organ) emitting the ghostly church music. The train stops in a meadow, and everything is still. Then a green hot-air balloon descends, seemingly from nowhere, and hovers over the train. A "shadow-faced" man in a "dark suit" exits the train and raises his arms. Suddenly, everything springs into action, as people silently exit the train and begin to set up the circus tents. The silence is disconcerting, especially to Will, who realizes that the setting up of carnivals is usually a lively and noisy event. The balloon blocks the moonlight, and it becomes too dark to see what is going on. The tent poles are set up, and the canvas is about to be brought out when the boys "somehow" realize that "the wires high-flung on the poles were catching swift clouds, ripping them free from the wind in streamers which, stitched and sewn by some great monster shadow, made canvas and more canvas as the tent took shape." When the boys are able to see again, everything is still and the people have disappeared. Both Jim and Will are frightened, though Jim is also fascinated, and when they reach town, both boys run back to their houses on their own. From the library window, Charles sees the boys running home. He has also heard the strange music and the train's whistle.

The next morning, Will and Jim go to the carnival. In the sunlight, the tents and flags look normal, as does the train. The boys run into Miss Foley, their seventh-grade teacher. She is looking for her nephew Robert and decides to enter the Mirror Maze, since he may be in there. Will does not want her to go in, but she does. When Jim asks Will why he is afraid of the maze, Will replies that the mirrors are "the only things *like* last night." Indeed, Miss Foley is soon screaming for help, so the boys rush in, find her, and pull her from the maze. She has a bruise on her face from falling but is otherwise fine. She tells the boys that there was a girl trapped in the maze who looked like her when she was very young. Miss Foley forgets all about her nephew and decides to go home. Will wants to go home, too, but Jim says they are staying until dark so that they can find out more about the strange carnival. Will agrees, but they both decide they will not enter the Mirror Maze.

CHAPTERS 16–20

Throughout the day, Will and Jim enjoy themselves, going on rides and playing games. At dusk, Jim disappears, and Will finds him at the mouth of the Mirror Maze. Will drags Jim out of the maze and yells at him. Jim stands there in shock, trying (and failing) to tell Will what he has seen. Will decides that they are going home, and Jim makes him promise that they can come back later that night. As they leave the carnival, they trip over a large bag. The bag belongs to Tom Fury, and all of his lightning rods are in it. The boys realize that the storm he predicted did not come, but they cannot think of a reason why he would have left everything he owned behind. Jim insists that they go back to find out what happened to Tom Fury. Will resists; the place is almost empty, and everyone at the carnival has gone home. Nevertheless, the two boys reenter the carnival.

The boys inspect the broken carousel, the only ride they have not been on. A large man picks Jim up and yells at him for climbing on the broken ride; Will runs to Jim's aid, and the man picks Will up in his other hand. Another man comes out and tells the large man to put the boys down, introducing himself to the boys as Dark and the man who has just released them as Cooger. They are the proprietors of the carnival. Mr. Dark ignores Will and focuses on Jim, handing him a business card that continuously changes its appearance. It turns out that Mr. Dark is also

the Illustrated Man, and he shows a fascinated Jim one of his tattoos, which appears to move. Jim tells Mr. Dark that his name is Simon. Mr. Dark then tells the boys to come back at seven o'clock, when the carnival reopens for the evening, and he gives Jim a ticket for a free carousel ride to use once the ride has been repaired. The boys pretend to leave, and Jim jumps into a nearby tree, pulling Will up after him.

The boys spy on Cooger and Dark as they begin to operate the carousel, which moves backwards. Even the carousel's calliope music is being played backwards. Mr. Cooger jumps onto the ride, and Will and Jim realize that he is growing a year younger with each revolution of the carousel. Jim counts each turn of the ride; when it stops, Mr. Cooger is about twelve years old. Will and Jim stare in disbelief. The boys are frightened, but they run off after Cooger to see what he will do.

As they follow Cooger, Will sees a sign in the barbershop, but he does not register whatever it says. Cooger has turned onto the street where Miss Foley lives, and Will and Jim pass by her house, only to see Cooger through her window. Will thinks that they must be mistaken and that the boy they are seeing is Miss Foley's nephew, but Jim says that the boy in the window and Mr. Cooger have the same eyes. He says, "That's one part of people don't change, young, old, six or sixty!" The boys go into the house and pretend they are checking on Miss Foley after the incident at the maze. She says she is fine and introduces them to her nephew, who is really Mr. Cooger. Will somehow knows that the imposter is "evil."

Will is about to tell Miss Foley what's going on, but then he suddenly realizes that the sign in the barbershop said "CLOSED ON ACCOUNT OF ILLNESS," so he instead tells her that Mr. Crosetti is dead. The imposter invites the boys to join them for dessert, as he and his aunt are going back to the carnival later that night. Will asks Miss Foley why she would want to go back after the incident at the maze, but she says she was just being silly. Will then says that they cannot come to dessert because Jim's mother is sick. As Will and Jim are leaving, Will desperately wants to tell Miss Foley not to go to the carnival. Outside Miss Foley's house, Will realizes that the backwards tune on the merry-go-round was Frederic Chopin's "Funeral March" (and that it played in reverse because the carousel was taking Cooger further from death).

The boys return to their respective homes, only to be yelled at for being late, and they are sent to bed without supper. At ten o'clock, Will's father unlocks the door. Without opening it, he tells Will to "be careful." Will wishes his father would come in and talk to him, but he does not. Will overhears his father tell his mother that he feels too old to bond with his son. Charles then leaves the house, presumably returning to the library. Will wonders about his father's advice to be careful. Does his father also sense that the carnival is not what it seems?

CHAPTERS 21–24

Will notices Jim sneaking out of his window, and he is clearly planning to go out without Will. Will decides to follow Jim, and they soon come to Miss Foley's house. Jim stands outside the house trying to get Cooger's attention. Will jumps out from the bushes and tries to stop Jim, but Jim will not listen, and Will realizes that Jim saw himself as an older man in the Mirror Maze and that Jim wants to become older by riding the carousel. Cooger sees the boys, throws Miss Foley's jewelry onto the lawn, and begins screaming for the police before running off down the road. Miss Foley looks out the window and suspects Will and Jim of having robbed her. Jim takes off after Cooger/Robert, and Will takes off after Jim. Will knows that he and Jim will be branded as thieves and that now no one will believe them when they tell them about the carnival.

Cooger runs toward the carnival and the carousel, starting it up and jumping on just ahead of the boys. The carousel is moving forward, and Will knows that Cooger will grow to become a man who can easily kill them. Then, Jim is about to jump onto the merry-go-round when Will catches up and wrestles him to the ground. The boys struggle over the carousel switch, pulling it back and forth. The carousel goes haywire, spinning Cooger around faster and faster, and then the control box explodes. On the carousel, which has now come to a stop, lies a shriveled old man who looks like a mummy. Cooger must now be almost 130 years old; he struggles for breath and seems as if he is about to die.

The boys run to a pay phone and call the police and an ambulance. They fear for Cooger's life. When the police cars and ambulances appear, the boys lead them to the carousel, but no one is there. The police are skeptical of the boys' story. As they call for Mr. Cooger, the sideshow tent opens, and they are invited in. Will sees a tiny dwarf playing cards and realizes that it is Tom Fury and that he has somehow been transformed into a small, gnarled creature. They see Mr. Cooger on an electric chair. Mr. Dark is there, naked from the waist up, tattooing himself. He welcomes the police and tells them that they are rehearsing a new act. Will insists that Mr. Cooger is dead (he thinks that he and Jim are responsible and that the carnival people will take their revenge out on them), but Dark says that Cooger is their new act, Mr. Electrico. Dark then electrocutes Cooger, who comes to life. The policemen laugh, and the medics look uncomfortable. Will is confused; he wants Cooger to live so that the carnival people will not want revenge, but at the same time, he thinks, "Even more I want him dead, I want them all dead, they scare me so much." Cooger tells the police that he pretended to be dead when he caught the boys spying on him. Mr. Dark offers everyone free passes. The boys give Mr. Dark fake names, grab the tickets, and rush off to the police car, waiting to be driven home.

II. Pursuits

CHAPTERS 25–29

Miss Foley is alone in her house. On her dresser, she has a ticket to ride the carousel. She senses that her nephew is not her nephew and that he tried to frame Jim and Will, but she does not care. From her window, she sees a light on in the library, and she calls there. Charles picks up the phone, and she asks him to meet her at the police station right away.

In the police car, one of the medics says he could swear that Mr. Electrico was really dead. The policemen laugh this off. The boys give the police the fake names they gave Mr. Dark and also give them fake addresses that are close to the police station. Alone, the boys discuss their suspicions of what might have become of Tom Fury, and Will begins to think that something could have happened to Mr. Crosetti at the carnival as well.

While Will has thrown his free tickets away, he notices that Jim has kept his. Will realizes that Jim is still thinking about riding the carousel to become older. The boys overhear voices coming from the police station, and they sneak under the window to eavesdrop. Miss Foley and Charles Halloway are conversing there, and Miss Foley is telling Charles about the robbery. Miss Foley says she does not want to press charges, but she also says, "If they are innocent, where are the boys?" Before Jim can stop him, Will says they are there, and he jumps through the window and into the police station.

Charles takes Will and Jim home. When Will and his father are alone, Charles tells his son that he is lucky Miss Foley is not going to prosecute; then he asks Will why he confessed. Charles knows his son well enough to know that since he is not acting guilty, he did not actually steal anything. Will tells his father that Miss Foley "*wants* us guilty" so that no one will believe what he and Jim say. He says they confessed anyway since the police would "go easy" on them, which they did. Charles does not understand, but Will promises his father that he will tell him what is going on "in a couple days." Will asks his father to stay away from the carnival. Charles tells his son that he was planning to say the same thing.

After going to bed, Will sleeps for about an hour. He hears a strange sound and looks out his window. In a few moments, the carnival's hot-air balloon appears. Jim sees it, too. One of the sideshow freaks, the Dust Witch, is inside. She appears to be a lifeless wax figure, though she is indeed alive. She is blind, but she is able to sense and smell souls. As she comes closer, she seems to find what she is looking for. She descends over Jim's house and leaves a mark on his roof, and then she floats away. As soon as she is gone, Jim and Will climb up to Jim's roof.

CHAPTERS 30–34

The boys remove the mark on the roof, but the balloon hovers on the horizon, and Will fears that the Dust Witch senses their plan. The boys go back to bed, but Will is unable to sleep. He sees his bow and arrow and has an idea. He begins sending excited thoughts out to the witch, letting her know that they have duped her, and he sees the balloon turn and head back in his direction. Will runs to an abandoned house nearby, luring the witch to the roof there. When she comes close, Will turns to shoot the arrow, but it breaks in his hands. The witch begins to raise the balloon, but Will grabs hold of the basket and throws the arrowhead. The arrowhead hits its mark, and the balloon

begins to lurch wildly as it loses air. Will is thrown to the roof, tumbling off and landing safely in a tree. The balloon jerks away and appears to be heading back toward the carnival.

The rest of the night is uneventful, and by sunrise it is raining. Over the noise of the storm, only Miss Foley hears the carousel start up again. She sets out for the carnival, walking through the then-deserted town. Later that morning, Will and Jim set off to the police station, where they will give their statements and then leave for Miss Foley's house so that they can apologize to her. Will tries to tell Jim about what happened with the balloon and the Dust Witch, but he does not get a chance because they are interrupted when they hear a little girl crying nearby.

They go to see the little girl and realize that it is Miss Foley. The girl asks them to help her and says that no one will believe what has happened to her. Will tells her that he believes her but that he has to be sure, so the boys leave the little girl where she is and run back to Miss Foley's house. No one is there. The boys realize that the carousel must be working again, and as they head back for the transformed Miss Foley, they hear a band playing, and they know that the carnival is parading through town. The boys also know that the parade is only a ruse and that the carnival freaks are looking for the boys or Miss Foley or all three. When they get back to where they left Miss Foley, she is gone. Will and Jim run off to hide until the parade has left the town.

Later, Jim and Will are hiding under a grate in the sidewalk in front of the cigar store. It is a busy area of town, and crowds of people leaving church linger as the parade comes closer. The freaks' eyes search the crowd as they disperse and begin handing out flyers. Will sees his father walk by overhead.

CHAPTERS 35–39

The Dwarf, the transformed Tom Fury, stands near the grate. The Dwarf looks down and stares for a few moments, but he does not seem to see the boys. He continues walking, and the boys breathe a sigh of relief. Meanwhile, Charles Halloway is sitting in a nearby coffee shop when the Illustrated Man (Mr. Dark) walks in. The Illustrated Man says that he is "looking for two boys." Charles replies, "Who *isn't?*" before getting up and leaving the coffee shop. The Illustrated Man watches Charles leave, staring after him.

Not sure of where to go, Charles wanders over to the cigar shop and purchases a cigar. He lights it and drops the cigar wrapper down the grate. He glances down and sees Jim and Will. He starts to ask them what is going on just as the Illustrated Man leaves the coffee shop and starts walking toward him. Jim tells Charles that they will be found if Charles does not look up, explaining that the Illustrated Man is after them. Charles looks up and pretends to be checking his watch against the town's clock tower as the Illustrated Man approaches. Mr. Dark tells Charles that he is looking for two boys who have won unlimited free rides and candy, showing him a tattooed image of Will on the palm of one hand and a tattooed image of Jim on the other. Charles tries to hide his shock and gives him fake names for the boys. Mr. Dark says that he already knows the boys are named Will and Jim, but it is clear that he does not know their last names. Charles comments that there must be about two hundred boys in town with those names. Mr. Dark finally gives up and walks away.

Suddenly, the Dust Witch appears, bruised from her ordeal the night before. She is using her senses in an attempt to find the boys, and it seems as if she has become aware of Will and Jim's proximity. She moves toward Charles Halloway, and Mr. Dark begins walking back toward him as well. Charles, however, suddenly comments on the high quality of his cigar, and he blows cigar smoke at the Dust Witch, distracting her and making her cough. Mr. Dark tries to stop Charles, so Charles buys him a cigar as well and continues to blow smoke at the witch. Mr. Dark asks Charles for his name, and Charles gives it willingly, telling him that he works at the library and that Mr. Dark should come to visit him there. Will is shocked at his father's bravery. Mr. Dark and the Dust Witch leave, unable to search in the midst of the cigar smoke. After they have gone, Charles pretends to talk to the clock tower, telling the boys to stay hidden for a couple of days. He says he will go to the library to research the carnival and find out whatever he can. They all agree to meet at the library at seven.

At seven, Charles waits at the library. Earlier in the day, he walked through the parade looking at the freaks. He then went to the carnival and made sure to stay out of the tents and away from the rides. He saw the Mirror Maze and was filled with foreboding. At the library, Charles has researched texts on the supernatural, on enchanted mirrors, and on the witching hours, from midnight to dawn. He waits for the boys to appear and wonders if they will be able to make it. The boys finally appear at a quarter to eight. They have been hiding in different places all over town and waiting for the sun to go down. They tell Charles everything that has happened. Charles believes them, and he shows them the old carnival flyers that he has found, dating back to the 1800s. The very same carnival comes every few decades, but only in October. The boys say that it cannot logically be the same Cooger and Dark each time, but their instincts tell them otherwise.

CHAPTERS 40–44

Charles realizes that the people who become younger or older on the carousel are filled with guilt and regret because they have left everything and everyone they know and love behind. He suspects that the carnival exploits their regret, making its victims work for it in exchange for returning them to their correct age. The freaks, Charles says, are people who have become symbolic physical manifestations of their sins. As he and the boys are trying to decide what to do about the carnival, they hear the library door open and close. Charles tells the boys to hide, and he sits and waits for whoever has just entered.

Mr. Dark reintroduces himself to Charles and asks where the boys are. He explains that the Dust Witch can make Charles's heart fail and that it will appear to be a natural death. Mr. Dark begins walking down the aisles of the library and calling for the boys. He tries to tempt Jim with a ride, saying that if Jim comes out and gives Will to him, then Jim can reap the rewards. Charles sits, feeling faint, but he resolves to get up if Mr. Dark finds the boys. The Illustrated Man changes tactics, telling Will that they have turned his mother into a two-hundred-year-old hag. Mr. Dark hears a sob and heads in the direction of the sound, climbing the shelves until he finds both boys huddled together at the top.

Mr. Dark grabs the boys, and they all tumble to the ground. Charles jumps out of the aisle and attempts to stop them, but Mr. Dark grasps Charles's hand and crushes it. Charles falls to the ground in agony. The boys continue to scream and struggle as Dark drags them toward the exit, but then the Dust Witch and some of the other freaks appear. The Dust Witch casts a spell on the boys that makes them unable to see, hear, or speak. Dark then tells the witch to take care of Charles.

The witch begins casting a spell to stop Charles's heart. His heart begins to slow, and he feels like giving in, like falling asleep. As he watches the witch's fingers move, as if they are "tickling" the air, the whole episode suddenly strikes Charles as hilarious. He begins to laugh, which upsets the witch. She attempts to keep casting her spell, but as Charles continues to giggle she is rendered powerless, and she runs from the library.

III. Departures

CHAPTERS 45–49

Dark marches the boys, who are unable to speak or move of their own volition, toward the carnival. He places the boys in the waxworks, which is located behind the Mirror Maze. To the crowd, Will and Jim appear to be wax figures. The Dust Witch returns, and Mr. Dark grabs her, announcing to the crowd that she will perform an act in which she is to be fired at by a rifle. As he asks for volunteers, Mr. Dark asks the witch if Charles is dead, but the witch shakes her head. Mr. Dark is furious. When he turns back to face the crowd, Charles Halloway steps forward as a volunteer.

The crowd cheers for Charles. Mr. Dark tells Charles that he cannot possibly shoot with his injured hand, but Charles assures him that he can, and the crowd cheers again. Charles says that he will need a boy to volunteer as his other hand. He says that his son Will is in the crowd and can be his assistant. Charles begins calling for Will. Nothing happens. He keeps calling, and even the crowd joins in. Eventually, Will, still in a daze, appears and goes toward his father.

Dark hands Charles a bullet and tells him to mark it with his initials. Charles says that he will mark it with something better and carves a crescent moon into the bullet. The gun and bullet are handed back to Dark, who appears to load the gun. Dark, however, has passed the bullet to the witch, who will hide it in her mouth and pretend to have caught it in her teeth once the rifle has been fired. Dark places a blank in the rifle and hands it back to Charles. Charles opens the rifle, inspects the bullet, pretends not to notice that it

has been switched, and then says that he would like to make his mark a little clearer. He carves the fake bullet with the same symbol as before. Mr. Dark is unperturbed by this.

Charles steadies the rifle over Will's shoulder. Dark then clenches his fist around the tattoo of Will's face, and Will, still in a fog, shudders, causing the rifle to fall. Charles replaces the rifle as if nothing has happened and cracks a joke to the crowd, and the crowd's laughter revives Will. Despite Mr. Dark's continued attempts to harm Will through the tattoo, Will is no longer affected amid the crowd's laughter. As Charles prepares to shoot, he whispers to the witch that the crescent moon on the two bullets is not actually a moon but is his own smile. Charles fires the gun.

The witch falls down dead, but Mr. Dark tells the crowd that she has fainted and that this is part of the show. Dark then tells the crowd that the show is over and the carnival is closing for the night. Charles tells Will to come with him, and they begin to run toward the Mirror Maze in order to retrieve Jim from the wax works. Will is slowly coming out of his daze, as is Jim, though Jim is still unable to move. In the maze, Will and his father can see all of the lost souls that the carnival has claimed. A much older version of Charles also appears. Then, the lights in the Mirror Maze go out, and all is dark.

Will grabs kitchen matches from his pocket, just as it feels as if the infinite army of Charles's ancient reflections is closing in on them. Charles lights the match, but he begins to falter in the face of his old age. Will snaps him out of it, telling his father that he loves him no matter his age. Charles remembers himself, and he begins to laugh.

CHAPTERS 50–54

At the sound of Charles's laughter, the mirrors shatter. Jim, who is finally able to move, runs out the back of the tent. When Will and his father get to the waxworks, Jim is gone. Will and Charles can hear the carousel's music, and Will thinks Jim might be headed there, perhaps still wanting to grow older after all that has happened. The moon is starting to rise, and Will and his father are able to see by the moonlight. Will is worried about all of the sideshow freaks coming after them, but Charles tells his son that all they need to do is save Jim and get rid of Cooger and Dark. He says that if they get rid of the carnival masters, then the sideshow performers will go with them.

Will can see the sparks from Cooger/Mr. Electrico's electric chair, and he thinks that they are moving him to the carousel. Will wonders whose side Jim will be on in the final showdown between Dark, himself, and his father. The freaks stand motionless throughout the fairgrounds, and Charles thinks that this is because they are afraid of what happened to the witch; Will thinks it is because they are waiting for Dark's command to attack. Will realizes that the carousel music had been playing backward, but now it is playing forward.

Will and Charles come around a tent to find that Dark is nowhere to be found and that the ancient Cooger has finally expired into dust flakes; a heap of ash is all that remains in his chair. They see Jim running toward the carousel. Will chases after him but is unable to stop him. Jim jumps onto the ride but leaves one hand stretched out toward Will. Will attempts to grab Jim's hand, but to no avail, while Jim appears as if he wants to both jump from and stay on the carousel. Once Jim has gone around a few times, he looks back at Will as if he barely remembers him. Will grabs Jim's hand, with Jim on the ride and Will running beside him on the ground. Will's hand grows one year older while the rest of him stays the same age. Will tries to pull Jim from the carousel, but Jim is stronger, and Will is instead pulled onto the ride. Will then grabs Jim's arm and leaps from the ride. Jim is physically torn between Will's leap and the carousel pole he is grasping, and he cries out in pain, tumbling, unconscious, to the ground. Charles shuts the ride down, and Will wonders if Jim is dead.

Charles tells Will to give Jim "artificial respiration" as a small boy comes running from the carnival screaming that the man with the tattoos is after him. The boy says his name is Jed. Charles follows the boy, but he realizes that it is really Mr. Dark trying to trick him. Charles holds the boy close in a fond embrace, and the boy cries out that he is being murdered, that Charles is evil. Charles laughs, which only hurts the boy further, and says, "Good to evil seems evil. So I will do only good to you, Jed." Charles says that he will let the boy go if he tells him how to cure Jim. Dark refuses, and Charles continues to hold him lovingly. The boy's eyes grow dim, and he falls to the ground dead.

The freaks stand about moaning and disoriented, gathering around Will and Charles as they attempt to revive Jim. The tattoos on Dark's body shudder and begin to disappear, as if they, too, are dying. As the tattoos fade, the freaks are freed, and they run from the carnival, knocking over the tents as they go. One of the freaks picks up Dark's tiny body and walks away. Will thinks of all the carnival's victims: Dark, Cooger, Miss Foley, Tom Fury, and Mr. Crosetti. Then he turns back to Jim, but Jim's body is cold.

Will begins to cry, but Charles tells him that the only way to save Jim's life is to laugh. Will is skeptical, but Charles reminds him of how the mirrors were shattered by laughter and how the witch was killed by a smile. Charles forces Will to begin dancing, laughing, and singing. As the two dance about, they think that Jim looks a bit better, but Charles tells Will not to look and to keep dancing. Jim wakes and joins in the gaiety.

Charles says that the fight is never over, that there will always be people like those from the carnival, that they appear in many guises, and that he and the boys must always be on the lookout. Charles takes a wrench and smashes the carousel's machinery to pieces. The boys race home, and Charles joins in, too.

CHARACTERS

Mr. Cooger

Mr. Cooger is the less prominent of the evil carnival masters, though he is the first to come to Will and Jim's attention. The first night of the carnival, Jim and Will spy on Mr. Cooger as he transforms himself on the carousel into a young boy. As a young boy, Cooger masquerades as Robert, Miss Foley's nephew. When Cooger-as-Robert goes back to the carousel to return to his original age, Will and Jim accidentally cause the ride to malfunction, and Cooger becomes an ancient, near-dead mummy. In order to hide the transformation, the carnival masquerades the ancient Cooger as Mr. Electrico. At the end of the story, he finally expires, leaving nothing but dust behind.

Mr. Crosetti

Mr. Crosetti is the town barber. The boys run into him just before the carnival arrives in town. There is a faint smell of cotton candy in the air, and it makes the barber cry for the joys of his lost youth. The next day, there is a sign in the barbershop window that says the store has been closed on account of illness. The boys believe that Mr. Crosetti has become one of the carnival's victims.

Mr. Dark

The more evil and prominent of the two carnival masters, Mr. Dark goes after Jim and Will. Once he captures them, he commands the Dust Witch to turn them into automatons. Mr. Dark also attacks Will's father and has the Dust Witch attempt to kill him. At first, Mr. Dark is assured of his victory over Charles and the boys; he laughs at Charles's Bible, throwing it in the wastebasket. However, once Charles learns how to conquer evil, Mr. Dark avoids further confrontation with Charles. Instead, he tries to pass himself off as a small boy named Jed, claiming that he is being pursued by Mr. Dark. Charles is not fooled, and he literally kills the transformed Mr. Dark with kindness, holding him in a long embrace until he falls down dead.

Mr. Dark is also the Illustrated Man, and his tattoos have mystical properties. They appear to move of their own volition, and they also appear to be effigies of the sideshow freaks. Dark is able to control the freaks via these illustrations. For instance, he pinches a tattoo of a nun, and the Dust Witch writhes in agony. After Mr. Dark dies, his tattoos disappear, and the freaks are finally free.

Dust Witch

The most powerful sideshow performer, the Dust Witch is blind but has the ability to sense souls. She is sent to find Will and Jim in a hot-air balloon. When she finds Jim's house, she marks the roof with a silver streak. Will and Jim remove the mark, and then Will tricks her into following him to an abandoned house, where he punctures her balloon. After Mr. Dark captures the boys, the Dust Witch puts them under Dark's power. She also attempts to murder Charles but is foiled by his laughter. She is later killed by Charles with a fake bullet upon which he has carved a smile.

The Dwarf

See Tom Fury

Mr. Electrico

See Mr. Cooger

Miss Foley

With a name that strikingly resembles the word "folly," Miss Foley is the boys' seventh-grade teacher. She realizes that Robert is not really her nephew, but she is so enthralled by the carnival that she does not care. When Robert frames the boys for attempting to steal Miss Foley's jewelry, Miss Foley persists in the ruse. She realizes that she must get rid of the meddlesome boys in order to find out what the carnival has to offer her. Later, Miss Foley appears as a little girl, crying over what she has done. The boys try to help her, but she disappears, never to be heard from or seen again. It is presumed that she has been forced into serving the carnival, perhaps transformed into a sideshow freak as well.

Tom Fury

Acting as the harbinger of the coming carnival, Tom Fury, the traveling lightning rod salesman, gives Jim a lightning rod because he senses that the house will be hit by lightning. It is, but only in a metaphorical sense. Tom Fury is enchanted by the storefront display claiming to house "THE MOST BEAUTIFUL WOMAN IN THE WORLD." Tom does indeed see a woman in the ice-block display, though Charles, who had viewed the display earlier, did not. The salesman enters the store with the intent to free the illusory woman by melting the ice, but it appears that, as a consequence, he is transformed into a sideshow freak, the Dwarf. The novel indicates that the Dwarf is a physical manifestation of Tom Fury's flaws, particularly his habitual shirking of responsibility. Throughout his life, Tom Fury has always, and literally, fled before the storm.

Charles William Halloway

Somewhat old to be the father of a young son, Charles Halloway works as a janitor at the library. He tends to work late and lose himself in books. Charles is also saddened by his old age; he feels unable to play with or relate to his son on account of it. When Will is in trouble, however, Charles does everything he can to help, learning how to accept himself, and all of the world, in the process. Charles also comes to know the nature of good and evil. He is the most dynamic of the book's protagonists and is perhaps the most heroic as well.

William Halloway

Will is a light-haired and sweet-natured boy, the foil to his darker counterpart and best friend Jim. Will's experiences fighting the carnival make him more brave and independent, as when he sneaks out alone for the first time in order to trick the Dust Witch. Will wants only to do the right thing and to protect his friend Jim from himself, even when Jim does not necessarily want to be protected. Will comes of age over the course of the novel, growing braver, stronger, and wiser. He also becomes closer to his father, whom he grows to love and respect in a more immediate way than before. By the end of the novel, he is able to recognize the true nature of evil, and he is charged by his father with constantly being on the lookout for it.

The Illustrated Man

See Mr. Dark

Jed

See Mr. Dark

Jim's Mother

Either a widow or a divorcée (it is unclear which), Jim's mother raises Jim on her own. She is afraid of him leaving her. She feels that once Jim leaves, his father will have fully left as well.

James Nightshade

Will's dark-haired counterpart, Jim is constantly described as being intimately acquainted with the murkier aspects of life (and has a last name signaling as much). He persuades Will to spy on the carnival and is thus ultimately responsible for the consequences that ensue. Jim wants to grow older on the carousel, and he persists in this desire even after he begins to understand Mr. Dark's and the carnival's true nature. Indeed, even after seeing what has happened to Miss Foley and being kidnapped by Dark, Jim still jumps onto the carousel. Yet, emotionally torn between his desires to be older and to be Will's friend (mutually exclusive propositions), Jim becomes physically torn between the ride and Will. As a result, he falls down dead—but he is revived by Will and Charles's gaiety.

Robert

See Mr. Cooger

Mr. Tetley

Mr. Tetley is the owner of the cigar store. He hears the faint calliope music on the night the carnival arrives. He also sells Charles a cigar, fortuitously causing Charles to stand over the grate under which the boys are hiding. Charles's presence over the grate distracts Mr. Dark. Will's father also uses the cigar smoke to disorient the Dust Witch just as she begins to sense the boys' presence nearby.

Will's Mother

Existing mainly as a counterpoint to her husband, Will's mother is happy where Charles is not. She also senses Will calling for help in the library, but luckily she does not see him or go in, and she thus avoids becoming another of Mr. Dark's victims.

THEMES

Transformation and Duality

Transformations in many guises appear throughout *Something Wicked This Way Comes*. Miss Foley becomes a little girl. Mr. Cooger goes from a man to a boy (acting as Robert, Miss Foley's nephew) to an old man. Tom Fury turns into a dwarf. All of the sideshow freaks were once normal people. Yet there are also less literal transformations. Will is occasionally called William or Willy. Jim's full name is James. Charles Halloway is Dad or Mr. Halloway. Indeed, it is almost as if these characters take on different personalities depending upon how they are addressed. The utmost example of this sort of nominal transformation is Mr. Dark, the cruel, evil, but competent carnival master. Mr. Dark is also the Illustrated Man, a carnival freak with mystical tattoos that allow him to control those in his power. At the end of the story, Mr. Dark transforms himself into a small boy named Jed.

Duality, specifically that between good and evil, is inherently connected to the transformations that occur throughout the novel. For instance, the once-good people who are seduced by the evils of the carnival become evil themselves. Jim is constantly fighting his darker nature. Even good transforms itself into evil, at least in the eyes of evil people. This is how laughter and gaiety are used by Charles as a weapon. Charles's laughter shatters the Mirror Maze, and his smile kills the Dust Witch. His

TOPICS FOR FURTHER STUDY

- Study the history of carnivals and circuses. Where and how did they start? How did they evolve into what they are today? Give a class presentation on your findings.

- Mr. Dark capitalizes on the desire of the young to be adults and on the desire of the old to be young. Interview some older adults and some of your young peers about their thoughts on aging, asking various questions on the topic. Summarize your findings in a report.

- Imagine that Jim does take a ride on the carousel and grows older. Write a short story about what happens afterward. Is Jim sad or happy about his transformation? Is he able to return home to his mother? Is he able to remain friends with Will? What does he do with himself?

- Do you think Will is the main protagonist of the novel, or could it be Jim or Charles Halloway? Write an essay on the topic, and be sure to use quotes from the novel in support of your thesis.

gaiety revives Jim from death. Indeed, Charles tells Jed/Mr. Dark that "good to evil seems evil. So I will do only good to you, Jed. I will simply hold you and watch you poison yourself." Charles's loving embrace vanquishes Dark, who falls down dead.

Acceptance

Lack of acceptance, which could reasonably be called despair, lies at the heart of the carnival's success. In turn, acceptance of the world as it is lies at the heart of the carnival's defeat. Miss Foley is unable to accept herself as she is, as she longs to be younger. This inability to accept herself proves her undoing. Miss Foley is transformed into a young girl, and then she is never seen or heard from again; she has presumably become one of the circus freaks. Charles's initial

inability to accept his old age prevents him from enjoying his young son or fostering a relationship with him. Indeed, his lack of acceptance has colored all aspects of his life, such as with how he spent most of his youth trying to be good, missing out on truly living in the process. Unable to accept the world for what it is, Charles spends his free time in the library, burying himself in books and avoiding his wife and, especially, his son. By avoiding life as it truly is, Charles is refusing to accept the world and his place in it. As a consequence, he is filled with fear and sadness. It is this fear and sadness that makes him vulnerable to Mr. Dark's powers.

Some part of Charles begins to realize this aspect of himself, and when he accepts who he is and the nature of the world in which he lives, he is able to live fully, with joy and without fear. This is why he is able to conquer the witch and Mr. Dark. As Charles's laughter shatters the mirror, he is laughing "because he accepted everything at last... above all himself and all of life." Indeed, Charles "cried out, released." Death is a part of this "everything," and Charles knows that the fear of death is what lies behind the fear of aging. He is able to accept death and laugh in the face of death, ultimately saving Jim's life because of this. Earlier in the novel, Charles tells his son that the only thing that does not make him sad is death because death is the thing that "scares" and "makes everything else sad." In the last chapter, to the contrary, he tells Will that everything is funny, adding, "Death's funny, God damn it!" Indeed, it is only by accepting his age and his mortality that Charles is able to laugh in the face of death, and also in the face of evil. By doing so, he triumphs over both.

STYLE

Characteristic Diction

The term *diction* refers to the specific word choices and style of writing used in a literary work. The diction in *Something Wicked This Way Comes* is very unique, featuring long, choppy sentences and hyberbolic (exaggerated) descriptive language. Indeed, at times, the diction takes on an almost nonsensical feeling. The sentence structure often also becomes somewhat stilted. Take, for instance, the following passage regarding Mr. Dark's tattoos as they disappear:

Carnival ride (*Nash Photos | Getty Images*)

There the obscene wink of the navel eye gasped in on itself, there the nipple-iris of a trumpeting mastodon went blind and raved at its blindness; each and every picture remembered from the tall Mr. Dark now rendered down to miniature canvas pronged and forked over a boy's tennis-racket bones.

Several examples such as this can be found in the novel. Furthermore, it seems that the novel's title is not the only inspiration taken from Shakespeare's *Macbeth*. The diction in *Something Wicked This Way Comes* is highly reminiscent of the play's dialogue, specifically that of the three witches featured in *Macbeth*.

Eye Motifs

A motif is any repetitive literary device, and there are several in *Something Wicked This Way Comes*. One such example is the concept of having an image burned into one's eyes. This concept first appears when Tom Fury explains the effects of being struck by lightning. Tom says, "Any boy hit by lightning, lift his lid and there on his eyeball, pretty as the Lord's Prayer on a pin, find the last scene the boy ever saw!" This conceit is repeated after Jim and Will first witness the transformative powers of the carousel. Will is afraid that Mr. Dark will know what he has seen because it has been burned into his eyes as if he has been struck by lightning. A related motif is that of the eye as a camera. Cooger, disguised as Miss Foley's nephew, takes pictures of the boys with his eyes. The Dwarf does the same when he looks at the grill that Jim and Will are hiding under. Only later, once the Dwarf develops and reviews the so-called pictures, does he realize what he has seen. Other motifs focus on the powers of Dark's illustrations and the nature of good and evil.

HISTORICAL CONTEXT

The Circus

The circus is believed to have evolved from Greek chariot races. In ancient Rome, chariot races were coupled with horse shows, trained animal acts, and other performances, including juggling and acrobatics. Roman circuses were originally held in stationary buildings. After the fall of Rome, however, individual performers

COMPARE
&
CONTRAST

- **1960s:** The average life expectancy for males in the United States is around sixty-six years. Thus, at the age of fifty-four, Charles Halloway is indeed an old man, or close to it.

  Today: The average life expectancy for males in the United States is around seventy-five years. A fifty-four-year-old man would not be considered old but would instead be seen as middle-aged.

- **1960s:** It is common for children, especially boys, to go into town unaccompanied by adults, just as Will and Jim do in the story.

  Today: Children, especially those in urban areas, are less and less likely to be unaccompanied by an adult. Widespread fear of

sexual predators is largely the cause of this phenomenon.

- **1960s:** Traveling circuses such as the one portrayed in the novel are just beginning to lose the popularity that they have enjoyed. This is due to the rise of entertainment in the form of television and movies.

  Today: Traveling circuses still exist, though most of the smaller companies have long since folded. The circus has made a resurgence in a reinvented form as "highbrow" entertainment, as evidenced by the success of the highly artistic (and animal- and sideshow-free) Cirque du Soleil.

---

traveled throughout Europe, presenting no more than a few such acts at a time. It is also thought that troupes of Gypsies may have capitalized on circus acts, traveling in large wagon-based caravans and presenting shows from town to town. In this manner, the circus acts traveled to England. By the 1700s, the most popular circus acts in England featured trick horseback riding, and the modern circus ring was developed to accommodate these performances. By the 1790s, the circus had traveled to the United States, and the first circus tent was introduced there in 1825. Another now-definitive circus feature was also developed in America, that of the traveling sideshow, which was first offered by the circus owners P. T. Barnum and William Cameron Coup. Coup was also the first circus manager to use trains as a means of transporting the circus. This method is still used today. A current and still-operating incarnation of the circus founded by P. T. Barnum and William Cameron Coup performs as the Ringling Bros. and Barnum & Bailey Circus.

The Idyll of the 1950s and Early 1960s

Green Town, the town in which *Something Wicked This Way Comes* is set, reflects the

cultural idyll of the 1950s and early 1960s. Traditionally, an idyll is a romanticized version of a rustic setting, such as a work of art portraying a happy shepherd and his flock or the peaceful beauty of nature. The idyll tends to overlook the fact that the shepherd may be cold and hungry, or that the peaceful beauty of nature can easily become a deadly hurricane. America during the 1950s and early 1960s became a sort of cultural idyll in and of itself; that is, the nation mythologized itself as a land of small towns filled with happy families with wholesome values. Cultural images of the happily married housewife, the dapper-suited husband, their smiling children, and their house with a green lawn and a white picket fence abounded. Popular television shows such as *Leave It to Beaver* (1957–1963) perpetuated these images and their corresponding myths of happiness in conformity.

Indeed, many Americans were content to perceive their nation as a happy and wholesome place, something like Green Town, with children running safely through the town, moms staying home to cook, dads going off to work, and townspeople attending church on Sunday. In the novel, Will and Jim know the shopkeepers by name, and they know where their schoolteacher lives. Yet, just as the carnival reveals (and exploits) the dark underbelly of the town, its people, and their desires, so, too, does a closer look at the era that valued "mom and apple pie" above all else reveal that underbelly. For instance, outside of marriage, women had little opportunity. They had few career options aside from that of homemaker, and even if they did work, they were paid pennies on the dollar when compared to their male counterparts. Racial segregation was still legal in the United States, and racism was a culturally acceptable aspect of daily life. Censorship was also enforced via stringent obscenity laws. Bradbury's carnival, like the time in which it is set, appears innocent, but it is altogether something else entirely. Indeed, by the late 1960s, a countercultural movement—with unprecedented (before or since) power—was in full swing. Along these lines, *Something Wicked This Way Comes* can be read as a commentary on the social idyll of the time in which it was written and published.

CRITICAL OVERVIEW

Though Ray Bradbury's oeuvre in its entirety is valued as a major and course-changing contribution to genre writing and American fiction, critics often find fault with his individual publications. Indeed, *Something Wicked This Way Comes* was not initially well received, yet it has remained in print for more than forty years. It is also known as one of the best works by one of America's best-known writers. The contradiction is a confusing one. For instance, Gary K. Wolfe, writing in the *Dictionary of Literary Biography*, notes, "Despite the occasional power generated by the sheer wealth of invention in *Something Wicked This Way Comes*, the work failed to establish Bradbury as a significant novelist, and Bradbury began to focus more and more on dramatic writing." (Indeed, *Something Wicked This Way Comes* was originally conceived as a screenplay.) Wolfe also states that "the novel suffers from an artificially inflated style and a barely controlled wealth of imagery and incident."

Steven Dimeo, in an essay in the *Journal of Popular Culture*, remarks, "At his worst,

Bradbury has belabored morality to death. Charles Halloway, who discourses lengthily on Good and Evil in *Something Wicked*, epitomizes this self-conscious moralizing." Yet, more benevolent reviewers have found much of value in the book. Anita T. Sullivan, writing in the *English Journal*, calls the novel Bradbury's "finest work of fantasy," adding that it "is a good example of the fusion of fantasy, horror, and nostalgia which he manages so well." Despite the range of critical opinion, thus far *Something Wicked This Way Comes* has withstood the test of time, a feat that is rarely accomplished even by books that are universally acclaimed.

CRITICISM

Leah Tieger

Tieger is a freelance writer and editor. In the following essay, she explores the nature of good and evil as it is presented in Something Wicked This Way Comes.

In Ray Bradbury's novel *Something Wicked This Way Comes*, Charles first begins to understand the nature of good and evil when he finds that Cooger & Dark's Pandemonium Shadow Show has been arriving in town every few decades for over one hundred years. Charles realizes that the carnival must have existed for centuries in various forms and that it feeds on people's fear and loneliness, which have also existed for centuries. Given this, it becomes clear to Charles that the carnival strikes when the town is ripe—filled with despair or desire, lack of hope, and the like. This is why people like Miss Foley and Tom Fury become its victims. They are each overcome by the desire for the impossible (and to desire the impossible is to give rise to despair). Charles calls the carnival folks "autumn people," saying the term means that they are sad and empty and that they feed on people who are not sad or empty. Yet the carnival's victims have the capacity to be so; indeed, its victims are well on their way to becoming as much, and the carnival merely speeds them along in their progress. Charles says that everyone has a little part of themselves that is sad and empty, even him. But in reality, Charles has a large part of himself that is like this. He regrets his age. He avoids his wife and son, preferring the company of library books. He admits to the boys that he spent so much of his life trying to be good that he

WHAT DO I READ NEXT?

- William Shakespeare's play *Macbeth* (c. 1606) contains the quote from which the title of *Something Wicked This Way Comes* is taken. While the play has a very different storyline, the two works share similar themes.

- Another classic Bradbury novel is *The Martian Chronicles* (1950), which portrays earthlings as they colonize Mars and eradicate the Martians.

- *Wild, Weird, and Wonderful: The American Circus 1901–1927, as Seen by F. W. Glasier, Photographer* (2003) is a collection of photographs of circus acts from the time that inspired the carnival attractions presented in *Something Wicked This Way Comes*.

- Stephen King's *Needful Things* (1991) is an homage to *Something Wicked This Way Comes*. The novel features a shopkeeper, Gaunt, who somehow manages to offer products that speak to the townspeople's innermost desires. Like Miss Foley, however, Gaunt's customers soon become ensnared by an evil puppet master.

missed out on actually living. For these reasons, he himself is ripe for the carnival, and a likely victim. Indeed, in the library, when Dark offers to make Charles younger in exchange for giving up his son, Charles visibly struggles not to accept the offer.

Charles explains that "the carnival is like people, only more so." Many people live their lives gossiping, taking pleasure in the downfall of others. Unhappy married couples stay together, feeding off of one another's dissatisfaction. Based on this reasoning, a dead soul cannot satisfy the carnival, but one filled with desire, guilt, or self-hate can. Charles says that the people who become younger or older on the carousel have souls like this (alive with despair and self-loathing). This is because they have left everything and everyone they know and love behind.

> INDEED, EVIL DOES NOT EXIST IN AND OF ITSELF; INSTEAD, IT EXISTS AS THE ABSENCE OF SOMETHING ELSE—OF GOOD. REPLACE THAT ABSENCE, AND EVIL IS INCAPABLE OF PERSISTING."

Charles suspects that the carnival exploits this regret, making its victims work for it in exchange for returning them to their correct age. The sideshow freaks are likely the result of this phenomenon. Notably, Charles wonders if there is inherent evil in the grotesque faces of the freaks, but he realizes that "if faces were judged, the freaks were no worse than many he'd seen" while working in the library. In something of a contradiction, however, the freaks are later viewed as becoming the physical manifestations of their sins

In what is perhaps an oversimplification, evil is equated with despair, or at least evil is derived from despair. Thus, the turning point of the story arrives when Charles understands the true implications of the fact that evil is fueled by despair, by good people who have essentially turned away from the good in their lives and in themselves. For instance, as the Dust Witch begins to slow Charles's heart with her spell, he watches the witch's fingers move as if they are "tickling" the air. Suddenly, the whole episode strikes Charles as hilarious. He begins to laugh, which upsets the witch. Although she attempts to keep casting her spell, Charles continues to giggle, and she is rendered powerless. She runs from the library in defeat. This triumph gives Charles the strength to face Mr. Dark, because now he knows how Mr. Dark can be conquered (a question Charles has been struggling with all evening, especially after watching Mr. Dark throw a Bible in the wastebasket). Fortuitously, Charles arrives at the carnival just in time to volunteer for the shotgun trick. The power of his joyful call for Will's assistance, with the crowd's participation, is enough to rouse Will from his invisible bonds. Although Dark is at first able to waylay Will by clenching his fist around his tattoo of Will's face, Dark's power fades in the face of the crowd's continued laughter. Following this, Charles is finally able to shoot, having carved a crescent moon into both bullets. The moon, however, as Charles soon reveals, is not a moon, but "my own smile." The power of that smile kills the witch.

Again, Charles calls upon the power of good just as it seems he might fall victim to the despair fostered by his ancient images in the Mirror Maze. Notably, just as Charles is about to crumble, Will snaps him out of it, telling his father that he loves him no matter his age. Charles remembers himself, and he begins to laugh: "The Witch, if she were alive, would have known that sound, and died again." Thus, at the sound of Charles's laughter, the mirrors shatter. Here, readers begin to understand that this powerful laugh is not devoid of meaning. Indeed, Charles is able to laugh "because he accepted everything at last . . . above all himself and all of life." Charles "cried out, released." He is released from his all-pervasive despair, and he thus becomes impervious to the carnival's power once and for all.

Faced with Mr. Dark masquerading as a small boy, Charles holds the boy close in a fond embrace, and the boy cries out that he is being murdered, that Charles is evil. This ironic comment only makes Charles laugh, which only hurts the boy further. Charles says, "Good to evil seems evil. So I will do only good to you, Jed. I will simply hold you and watch you poison yourself." Charles continues to hold him, thinking, "Evil has only the power that we give it. I give you nothing. I take back. Starve. Starve. Starve." Soon, the boy's eyes grow dim, and he falls to the ground. In the meantime, Will begins to cry over Jim's dead body, but Charles tells him that the only way to save Jim's life is to laugh. At first, Will is skeptical, but Charles reminds him of how the mirrors were shattered by laughter and how the witch was killed by a smile. Will says that there is nothing funny about what is happening, but Charles replies that everything is funny, adding, "Death's funny, God damn it!" After they successfully revive Jim, Charles says that the fight is never over, that there will always be people like those from the carnival—that they appear in many guises, and that he and the boys must always be on the lookout.

As Anita T. Sullivan, writing in the *English Journal*, has put it, Bradbury successfully shows that "Evil thrives on the vacuum left by lack of

> THE THEMES OF THE STORY ARE THE SPIRITUAL CONFLICT BETWEEN GOOD AND EVIL— SPECIFICALLY, THE GOODNESS OF ORDINARY PEOPLE, WHO LOVE FAMILY AND COMMUNITY, AGAINST THE EVIL OF THE ISOLATED PREDATORS, WHO CAN BAND TOGETHER WITH OTHERS BUT CANNOT LOVE."

Good." Indeed, evil does not exist in and of itself; instead, it exists as the absence of something else—of good. Replace that absence, and evil is incapable of persisting. Sullivan further states that the laughter Charles uses to conquer the carnival "derives its energy from its progenitor, which is love." This is shown definitively when Will tells his father that he loves him regardless of his age, giving Charles the power to destroy the Mirror Maze. In the end, Charles vanquishes not only the carnival, as powered by his son's love and his love for his son, but also the despair that resides within himself.

Source: Leah Tieger, Critical Essay on *Something Wicked This Way Comes*, in *Novels for Students*, Gale, Cengage Learning, 2009.

Robin Anne Reid

In the following excerpt, Reid discusses the themes of Something Wicked This Way Comes *before offering a feminist interpretation of the work.*

Something Wicked This Way Comes (SWTWC) was published in 1962. The 1997 paperback edition is dedicated to the memory of Gene Kelly, dancer and friend of Bradbury's. The Afterword of the edition describes Bradbury's appreciation of Kelly's work and their friendship. The novel had its genesis in a short story that Bradbury turned into a screen treatment for Kelly. But funding could not be arranged, and so Bradbury turned it into a novel which, some years later, did become a film.

The novel is in some ways a companion to *Dandelion Wine*, also set in Green Town. L. T. Biddison, an academic critic, in "Ray Bradbury's Song of Experience," argues that the main characters of both novels can be read as the same person and as based on Bradbury himself. Biddison analyzes the extent to which the novels "delve...into the subconscious—and even unconscious—mind of man," showing that "the adult's world of prosaic and often meaningless fact is not the real world at all" compared to the child's vision of a glorious world (Biddison 226). *SWTWC*, according to Biddison, focuses on the sexual maturing that takes place during early adolescence as well as the relationship between fathers and sons (Biddison 227–29). ...

The major theme is related to the genre Bradbury has chosen: horror or gothic. The overall plot device of the everyday world being affected by a dark, supernatural force is common in gothic novels and a favorite convention of Bradbury's. *SWTWC* is an excellent example of a gothic story. A Midwestern town, two adolescents, and a carnival could have been a nostalgic view of an idyllic past, similar to *Dandelion Wine* in tone. Bradbury's tale of spiritual predators who feast off human anguish at the normal processes of life, and who evoke even more anguish by making false promises of eternal youth, turns these nostalgic elements into a suspenseful and horrifying story.

The themes of the story are the spiritual conflict between good and evil—specifically, the goodness of ordinary people, who love family and community, against the evil of the isolated predators, who can band together with others but cannot love. There is little direct violence; instead, the autumn people, the carnival people, play on human fears through a kind of symbolic magic, perhaps because they feed on spiritual anguish rather than physical pain. Charles and Will cannot use physical action against their opponents because it does not work (when forced, Dark is able to physically harm Charles). Instead, Charles and Will learn that laughter, a laughter based on knowledge of people and life, and the emotional connections humans make with each other, primarily through family ties, are the response that robs the predators of their power.

The good-versus-evil theme of the novel is shown not only in the plot and characters, but in Bradbury's poetic style, in which images carry symbolic or abstract messages. The imagery—words that describe the physical world as experienced through the five senses (touch, taste, smell, sight, and hearing)—works throughout the novel to reinforce the theme.

The novel's first image presented is that of the storm, especially lightning. Tom Fury, with his lighting rods and storm-colored clothing, is the first character introduced, and the carnival arrives with the storm, which is also associated with autumn. The storm is not necessarily allied with the evil of the carnival; lightning hitting the control box of the merry-go-round results in Cooger's becoming extremely old. When Will battles the Witch on the roof, the wind seems to be trying to help him oppose her balloon. The storm imagery, images from the natural world, can, perhaps by coincidence, work for either "good" or "evil."

The second major cluster of images...is that of light and dark,...the blond hair and light eyes of Will versus the dark chestnut hair and dark eyes of Jim. Jim is more drawn to the shadows of the carnival and so is more at risk. Light and dark are also seen in the opposition of night and day, with the night associated with the forces of evil and day with the forces of good. Day and night clearly structure the novel's time and plot; the hours from midnight to three o'clock in the morning are particularly open for evil to reign unchecked, whereas sunrise brings some relief for the boys.

A third major image cluster is related to water in its various forms. Frozen water symbolizes time, which can kill a human. The block of ice with the invisible mermaid and the Mirror Maze as a cold devouring sea show the mirror aspect of water. The linking of mirrors with water, and thus negatively with the passage of time, is clearly made in chapter 25, where Miss Foley is said to have ignored the "bright shadows of herself" (in mirrors) for some time. Mirrors are described as "cold sheets of December ice in the hall, above the bureaus, in the bath. Best skate the thin ice, lightly. Paused, the weight of your attention might crack the shell. Plunged through the crust, you might drown."

ALTERNATIVE PERSPECTIVES: A FEMINIST READING

Feminist literary criticism has brought a specific set of questions to literary analysis, focusing on how women are represented in literature. Feminist critics bring questions about the social and historical context of literature to bear, as well as examining the extent to which representations of women in literature perpetuate social and cultural stereotypes. While feminist criticism is a large and complex area in which questions of ethnicity, class, and sexuality have also come into play, some of the earliest points made by feminist critics can be used to develop a reading of how this novel presents women. The extent to which female characters are presented only in relationship to male characters, and the resulting tendency to see female characters as positive or negative because of their relationship with male characters, is stronger in gothic or horror fiction because of the genre conventions. Hazel Pierce, a scholar who places Bradbury's novels in the genre of gothic novels rather than science fiction, notes, women writers developed the gothic convention of young, innocent women who were in danger because of sexual decadence. Horror stories tend to present women as either victims or villains.

Bradbury, in *SWTWC*, focuses on innocent (or fairly innocent) adolescent boys. The boys' relationships with adult men—notably, Charles Halloway, Dark, and Cooger—initiate the process of becoming "men" as opposed to boys. Charles presents the cultural belief that men are completely different beings than women because of the differences in reproductive abilities. In chapter 14 he looks at his sleeping wife and muses that a woman can have true immortality through childbearing, while men cannot really believe they are fathers: "what father ever really believes it? He carries no burden, he feels no pain. What man, like woman, lies down in darkness and gets up with child? The gentle, smiling ones own the good secret.... Why speak of Time when you *are* Time, and shape the universal moments...?" This image of women is mythic, something other than human. The image also defines women as essentially requiring to bear children to be completely women and, in traditional societies, to marry men rather than to exercise this mysterious power on their own. Charles's musings also go to the heart of what some feminist critics believe is the reason for social restrictions on women: that men, not able to have conclusive proof that their children are in fact their children, need to control other men's access to "their" women.

The novel's main characters are all men, and women play limited roles. The earliest images of women in the novel are not real women at all, but pictures, images, and objects. The first representation of a woman is the poster advertising "The Most Beautiful Woman in the World," and the ice block in which Charles sees an empty space that is somehow a woman (in potential?), and in which the lightning rod salesman sees the shape of a woman that, taking substance from the images of women in art and film, lures him into a trap. In this representation, the woman resembles a siren or mermaid, mythical women in water who lure men to their deaths.

The second woman is a character diametrically opposed to the temptress in the ice block. Will's mother (her first name is never given) is usually shown safe in her home, the one father and son return to after their adventures. Will compares her to a "creamy pink hothouse rose poised alone in the wilderness...smelling like fresh milk, happy, to herself, in this room." The association of women with roses in British and American literature is centuries old; the additional sense impression of milk, which a woman can produce from her body to feed her child, also shows the positive nature of Will's mother. Jim's mother is also described briefly, as someone who wants to keep Jim in the house rather than let him stray outside into danger.

Both mothers are mostly portrayed in the house and in their roles as mothers. The perspective is wholly that of the child, who knows only "Mom" rather than a woman's name. However, these women have a power or stability that most male characters lack. Late in the novel, when Jim and Will have been captured by Dark, all three see Will and Jim's mothers walking home from church. Dark tries to orchestrate a meeting and capture them as well, but fails. The women turn away, perhaps because they are coming from church, perhaps because they are together, or perhaps because mothers, by their nature (according to Charles), are completely fulfilled, not "unconnected fools" who can be trapped by time. The portrayal of mothers is not completely positive: Will describes Jim's mother, who lost her husband, as suffocating Jim because she wants to keep him safe; her love and desire make him want to run away, perhaps to adulthood.

The other two female characters in the novel are Miss Foley, the boys' spinster schoolteacher, and the Dust Witch, one of the carnival people. Miss Foley is tempted by the nephew's promise that a carousel ride will restore her to youth. The temptation leads her to lay false charges against the two boys, who are among her favorite students. The Dust Witch is essentially an instrument controlled by Dark, but she is described as a blind, poisonous witch who can cast spells.

Considering the ways in which the female characters are constructed in the context of social expectations of women and in the context of genre conventions can lead to a reading of the way they mirror three deeply rooted archetypes of women: virgin (or spinster), mother, and crone (witch). While feminist writers have claimed these identities as having power for women. *SWTWC* tends to assign simplistic stereotypes to each character type: the mother is presented as positive, but the "virgin" and the "crone" are both negative. Only the woman who fulfills her socially expected role is safe from the threats of Dark and Cooger. Miss Foley is easily tempted, falls, and then, as a little girl, is probably captured by the carnival to become like the Dust Witch, completely evil and dominated by Dark.

Bradbury's novel, while enlarging the focus on the relationship between sons and fathers, reduces the women characters to little more than stereotypes; whether of good or evil, it hardly seems to matter because of the limited roles they have to play.

Source: Robin Anne Reid, "*Something Wicked This Way Comes* (1962)," in *Ray Bradbury: A Critical Companion*, Greenwood Press, 2000, pp. 73–86.

SOURCES

Arias, Elizabeth, "United States Life Tables, 2004," in *National Vital Statistics Reports*, Vol. 56, No. 9, December 28, 2007.

Bradbury, Ray, "In His Words," Web site of Ray Bradbury, http://www.raybradbury.com/inhiswords02.html (accessed July 7, 2008).

———, *Something Wicked This Way Comes*, Avon, 1998.

Central Intelligence Agency, *World Factbook*, s.v. "United States," https://www.cia.gov/library/publications/the-world-factbook/geos/us.html (accessed July 31, 2008).

"The Circus in America: 1793–1940," http://www.circusinamerica.org/public/ (accessed July 31, 2008).

Dimeo, Steven, "Man and Apollo: Religion in Bradbury's Science Fiction," in *Short Story Criticism*, Vol. 53, The Gale Group, 2002; originally published in *Journal of Popular Culture*, Vol. 5, No. 4, Spring 1972, pp. 970–78.

Sullivan, Anita T., "Ray Bradbury and Fantasy," in *English Journal*, Vol. 61, No. 9, December 1972, pp. 1309–14.

Wolfe, Gary K., "Ray Bradbury," in *Dictionary of Literary Biography*, Vol. 8, *Twentieth-Century American Science-Fiction Writers*, Gale Group, 1989, pp. 16–33.

FURTHER READING

Aggelis, Steven L., ed., *Conversations with Ray Bradbury*, University Press of Mississippi, 2004.

   This collection of interviews with Bradbury provides much insight into the life and work of a man whose stories shaped the genre of science fiction.

Arbus, Diane, *Diane Arbus: Revelations*, Random House, 2003.

   Arbus was a renowned photographer who achieved fame for her images of circus freaks and other bizarre personages. Notably, her photographs were produced during the same period in which *Something Wicked This Way Comes* was written.

Eller, Jonathan R., and William F. Touponce, *Ray Bradbury: The Life of Fiction*, Kent State University Press, 2004.

   Eller and Touponce's biography is one of the most comprehensive available. It sheds much light on Bradbury's early career as a publisher of pulp fiction, an avocation that largely influenced the author's developing writing style.

Hartzman, Marc, *American Sideshow: An Encyclopedia of History's Most Wondrous and Curiously Strange Performers*, Jeremy P. Tarcher/Penguin, 2005.

   This academic overview of sideshow acts and circus freaks grounds the fantastical figures in *Something Wicked This Way Comes* in historical fact.

Utopia

THOMAS MORE

1516

Sir Thomas More's highly influential *Utopia* was originally published in Latin in 1516. The work, sometimes taken as a straightforward, if radical, guide to creating an ideal society, questions the values of the imaginary land of Utopia at the same time that it apparently presents the country as a model of a good, just, and happy society. The narrative is framed by the correspondence between the character of Peter Giles and a fictionalized version of More. Despite the fictive nature of the work, it insists, through these letters, on its own factuality. One of the reasons why the text continues to fascinate scholars and the general reader is that it never resolves its own stance on what may be perceived as "good" about Utopian society and worthy of emulation, and what is despicable about the country and its customs. Rather, the text is often viewed as an open-ended dialogue that invites the reader to interact with More and with Raphael Hythloday, the philosopher and traveler who has spent a considerable amount of time with the Utopians and who offers his glowing report to More about the society, its people, its customs, and its structure. The society described is one in which all property is held in common, and all goods and services are freely given or exchanged rather than bought or sold. Utopia is a society presented as happy and safe, yet there is a degree of gender inequality, and certain individuals who have transgressed against Utopian society or

Sir Thomas More (The Library of Congress)

that of another country are held as slaves. Given the structure of the novel—an oral report framed by correspondence—*Utopia* is a work about philosophical ideas, rather than a plot- or character-driven story. Yet its unique structure allows for endless speculation regarding the intentions of the author. Its provocative themes inspire a variety of analyses.

A modern, English translation of *Utopia* is available through Yale University Press, translated by Clarence H. Miller and published in 2001.

AUTHOR BIOGRAPHY

Thomas More was born into a prominent London family on February 6, 1478. He was the second child of attorney John More and Agnes Graunger More. More attended primary school at St. Anthony's School in London, where he was provided with a religious education and an early training in oratory and debating skills. In 1490, More began working as a page in the household of the Archbishop of Canterbury, John Morton. It was customary during this time period for upper-middle-class families to participate in such arrangements, which provided an opportunity for English youth to receive both work experience and to continue their education. From 1492 to 1494, More attended the University of Oxford and later studied law at the New Inn in London, until 1496; he finally entered the legal profession in 1501. Deeply spiritual, More lived in a monastery, the Charterhouse of London, for several years; however, he did not take any monastic vows.

He married Jane Colt in 1505, and the couple subsequently had four children. Holding the then-unorthodox view that men and women had equal intellectual potential, More educated his daughters as well as his son. In 1510, More began working as one of two undersheriffs of London, and the next year his wife Joan died. More soon married the widow Alice Middleton. He served until 1518 as an undersheriff, despite the fact that in 1517 he was also appointed as a counselor and personal servant to King Henry VIII. During his years as an undersheriff he began writing *Utopia*, which was published in 1516, as well as *The History of Richard III*, which was completed in 1518. In the king's service, More was sent on diplomatic missions, including negotiations with the Holy Roman Emperor Charles V, in 1520–21. More was knighted following these negotiations. He became speaker of the House of Commons in 1523. Other posts included chancellor of the Duchy of Lancaster (1525) and high steward of the Universities of Oxford (1524) and Cambridge (1525).

An outspoken advocate against Lutheranism, More penned a number of polemical books, published between 1529 and 1533, against this form of religion, which More considered to be heresy against the teachings of Catholicism. Gaining the powerful position of lord chancellor in 1529, a position he held until 1532, More had several Lutherans burned at the stake, and he imprisoned many others. It was during these years that the conflict between More's allegiance to the Roman Catholic Church and Henry VIII's desire to establish an independent Church of England came to the forefront. More's primary conflict with Henry VIII stemmed from Henry's desire to annul his marriage to his wife, Catherine of Aragon, and marry Anne Boleyn. The pope condemned the new marriage as bigamous, and More refused to sign the 1534 Act of Succession because it declared Henry and Anne's marriage lawful and their heirs successors to the throne of England. Imprisoned in 1534 in the Tower of London, More continued to write. He was convicted of treason in 1535 and beheaded on July 6th that same year. In 1886, More was canonized (recognized as a saint by the Roman Catholic Church) by Pope Leo XIII.

PLOT SUMMARY

Thomas More to Peter Giles

More's *Utopia* is framed by two letters from More to his friend, Peter Giles. In the opening letter, More presents himself as the possessor of a true account of the inhabitants of the island of Utopia. In this letter, More apologizes to Giles for taking so long to write the tale of the land of Utopia and explains certain facts of his life in his own self-defense. Namely, he discusses his professional duties as a judge, as well as his responsibilities to his household, his family, and his servants. More then entreats Giles to examine the text that follows in Books 1 and 2. More references the fact that both he and Giles, as well as More's assistant John Clement, discussed with a man named Raphael Hythloday the history, customs, laws, and religion of the Utopians. More asks Giles to verify his facts and even to contact Hythloday if necessary in order to insure the accuracy of the work. Additionally, More suggests his reluctance to publish the work at all, because "the tastes of mortals are so various." Through this letter, More establishes as reality the fictive tale that is to follow, and in doing so creates for himself a persona, a character who possesses More's name but whom critics agree should not be confused with the real author.

Book 1

The next section of *Utopia* recounts the conversation held between the More persona and his friend Peter Giles, when the two are in Antwerp, Belgium. Giles tells More of his having met the philosopher and traveler Raphael Hythloday, who had recently journeyed with the explorer Amerigo Vespucci. Giles subsequently introduces More and Hythloday. More then presents the content of the conversation he had with Hythloday about his travels. More discovers the wealth of experience Hythloday possesses in the area of the customs of a variety of newly discovered nations. The conversation then turns to More's perception of Hythoday's duty to share his knowledge. More conveys his sense that Hythloday should be employed by a king as an advisor for the betterment of that nation. Hythloday reveals his unwillingness to do so, arguing that kings are more interested in expanding their borders through warfare than they are with improving the lives of their country's inhabitants. He describes his experiences with European rulers and his exchange with Cardinal Morton, the lord chancellor of England. In recounting this conversation, Hythloday expresses his often unfavorable views regarding English society and customs. He points to the inequities in the distribution of wealth that lead the impoverished citizens to steal, which results in their being unfairly punished. Hythloday goes on to discuss the way the Polylerites (a fictional people Hythloday describes as having been encountered in his travels through Persia) deal with crime and punishment, and to laud the overall fairness of societies in which thieves are not put to death but forced into hard labor. In this regard the Polylerites resemble the Utopians. More continues to insist that Hythloday could serve the "common good" by advising rulers. Yet Hythloday explains that his advice would be such that typical rulers would not listen anyway, for he would implore them to establish a society like that of the Utopians, and many of their customs would prove intolerable to a great many people, Hythloday contends. The notion of the potential evil of private property is then debated by More and Hythloday. When More and Giles express their desire to learn every detail about the island from Hythloday, the trio adjourns for lunch before taking up the story of the Utopians again.

Book 2

Book 2 opens with a discussion of the geography of the island of Utopia. (Scholars have noted that the geographic measures of the island are self-contradictory; the island is a physical impossibility.) Hythloday, who lived among the Utopians for five years, describes a variety of the physical aspects of the island before moving on to the structure of the society and the customs of its inhabitants. His account is filled with detailed assessments as well as a general defense of and praise for the society. The key features he expounds upon include: the lack of private property, the equality of education among males and females, the uniformity of clothing, the regimented nature of daily living, the treatment of the sick, the treatment of prisoners and slaves, the justification for warfare, the notion of virtuous pleasure, and the nature of their religious beliefs and their tolerance for different forms and habits of worship.

In conclusion, Hythloday observes that Utopia is the only true commonwealth, as it is the only place on earth where virtually nothing is private, and the citizens' concerns are directed toward the public good. Book 2 finishes with More's observations that several of the customs of the Utopians are "quite absurd." These include their notions of commonly held property, their acceptance of a variety of religious practices, and their lack of a monetary system. Yet More concedes that there are in Utopia "very many features which in our societies I would wish rather than expect to see." He does not expound upon which elements of Utopian society he finds praiseworthy or what Europeans might find unacceptable about them.

Thomas More to Peter Giles

In this final section of the novel, More once again addresses Peter Giles, referencing one critic's view that "If the story is being presented as true, I find some things in it rather absurd; if it is a fiction, then I think that More's usual good judgement is lacking on some points." More critiques this assessment, asserting the truth and accuracy of his work. He suggests that if he were writing a fictive account of Utopia, he would have included "some pointed hints which would have let the more learned discover what I was about." His next sentence, while incomplete in the Latin original and therefore left incomplete in translation, includes some suggestions that he has in fact included some such hints within the text of *Utopia*. More goes on to state that if cautious and suspicious people cannot believe his tale is true, they should simply visit Hythloday himself. The caveat More inserts at this point is that he is responsible only for his own writing, rather than for the trustworthiness of other people. He then bids farewell to his friend Peter.

CHARACTERS

Peter Giles

Like the Thomas More character in *Utopia*, Peter Giles is a persona based upon an historical personage. The real Peter Giles was a friend of

More's and a fellow humanist. (Renaissance humanism was a cultural movement that began in the fourteenth century and drew on ancient Greek and Roman literary and philosophical sources. It focused on the notion that humans are all born with the potential for good and evil, and that access to the liberal arts, such as music, art, oratory, and poetry, should be available to all members of society. Humanists advocated individual worth and dignity.) The historical Giles was a native of Antwerp, Belgium, and served as a clerk there beginning in 1512. In *Utopia*, Giles is designated as the recipient of Thomas More's letter and is asked to peruse More's book and verify its accuracy. In Book 1, Giles introduces More and Hythloday and plays a role in the initial conversation about whether or not Hythloday should serve as an advisor to a king. He first proposes the idea, and presses Hythloday on the topic when Hythloday rejects the notion.

Raphael Hythloday

Raphael Hythloday is described as a traveler and philosopher. Scholars have noted that Raphael means "God's healer" and Hythloday means "the peddler of nonsense," a combination that suggests the ambiguous nature of his assertions. He may be attempting to heal the ailments of European society by sharing his knowledge of Utopia with More, or his statements may be complete nonsense. When More initially sees Hythloday, he believes the man to be a ship's captain. More observes that Hythloday is sunburned, his beard untrimmed. Giles describes Hythloday as proficient in Greek, learned in philosophy, and hailing from Portugal. Through Giles's introduction of Hythloday to More, the reader learns that Hythloday sailed with the explorer Amerigo Vespucci for three voyages, but on Vespucci's last voyage, Hythloday did not return. Rather, he and a number of others were left at a remote fort. He traveled with five companions from the fort through various lands before he was finally able to return home.

Following this portion of the conversation, Giles, Hythloday, and More retreat to More's house to continue their discussion. Hythloday begins to relate the details of the lands to which he has traveled, including Utopia. Hythloday is enthusiastic in his descriptions of the Utopians and possesses an air of superiority stemming from his association with them and his approval of their customs. He expresses his understanding

that much of what he is revealing about the Utopians must appear strange to More and Giles. His manner in conversing about Utopia is straightforward and has been described as tactless in its flat rejection of many European societies and customs. He adamantly defends his position regarding the impossibility of his serving as an advisor to a European king, whereas More urges him to consider the common good and take up such a task. In explicating the habits, laws, and customs of the Utopians, Hythloday is often vague. Critics have noted that he makes mention of only one Utopian by name (the architect of their society, Utopus) despite the fact that Hythloday lived among the Utopians for several years. He stresses their common identity, their homogeneity, and even their interchangeability. If a child, for example, has interest in learning a vocation that his own father cannot teach him, he is simply sent to live with another family and placed under the tutelage of another father. At the same time, many of his criticisms of European society, such as the ways in which inequitable social structures favor the rich and oppress the poor, are not inaccurate. Readers may find him as compelling as he is off-putting, and his character is at the core of many critical debates regarding More's ultimate aims in writing *Utopia*.

Thomas More

In *Utopia*, the reader is presented with a Thomas More whose status is initially ambiguous. While the first glimpse of More, in the opening letter to Peter Giles, seems intended to represent the "real" Thomas More, this supposedly authentic individual nonetheless presents as factual the fictional story of *Utopia*, thereby calling into question his own reliability. Within the first book of *Utopia*, More converses with Giles, who introduces him to Hythloday. The three engage in a discussion regarding Hythloday's duty to serve a king for the good of the people, thereby opening the conversation up for Hythloday to extol the virtues of the Utopians, whom he claims are primarily interested in the good of the society as a whole. The dialogue throughout Book 1 is heavily dominated by Hythloday (Book 2 is comprised almost entirely of Hythloday's report on Utopia to More), but More's prompts guide Hythloday's commentary. More's voice is the last heard at the close of the second book of *Utopia*. In this section, More simultaneously disparages and praises the society Hythloday has described. Some of their practices he finds out-landish. These include their religious practices, their commonly held property and lack of private wealth, and their absence of a monetary system.

More observes that Hythloday appears exhausted by the extended description of Uto-pia, and he opts to refrain from presenting counterarguments to Hythloday because he is uncertain that Hythloday is strong enough at this point to hear such an attack. He then admits that there are aspects of the Utopian common-wealth that would be beneficial for European societies but that are highly unlikely to be adopted. More concludes the novel with another letter to Peter Giles, in which he examines the criticisms of reviewers. In response to those who suggest that his account of Utopia is not a truth-ful one, More argues that he would provide hints for intelligent readers to understand his true aims if in fact he were attempting to dupe readers into believing Utopia was a real place. More then suggests that he has in fact sprinkled some such hints throughout the text. In the same way that he criticizes Utopian society as well as praises it, More asserts that the text is based in reality at the same time that he also implies that his account is a fictional one. His multilayered duplicity as an author makes it impossible to know his true aims and opinions regarding the social, political, economic, and religious struc-tures described in *Utopia*.

THEMES

Social Class and Economics
Hythloday, in his conversation with More and Giles in Book 1 and in his lengthy account of the Utopians in Book 2, provides a two-pronged analysis of such issues as social class structures, economics, religion, and government. In discus-sing each theme, Hythloday finds something to criticize in European society and then goes on to praise the superior methods of the Utopians. As a society with no central governing body or fig-ure, in which all property and resources are held in common, in which there exist no social classes, and in which a variety of religious viewpoints is accepted, Utopia differs markedly from the European governments to which Hythloday generally, and occasionally specifically, refers. Regarding the issue of social class, Hythloday, in his condemnation of typical English methods for punishing criminals, speaks about the wealth

discrepancies among the classes. These inequities, he explains, lead to thievery. Stealing becomes a necessity for some individuals, and therefore it is both unjust and contrary to the public interest to punish thieving with hanging, as the English do.

In the course of this conversation, which takes place in Book 1, Hythloday observes that "a multitude of noblemen . . . live like drones on the labor of others." Tenant farmers work for "miserable wages and scanty keep." Addition-ally, the servants a nobleman hires are dismissed if their master takes ill or dies, leaving them with no ability to provide an income for themselves. Likewise, farmers are displaced when fine wool becomes so greatly prized among the noble classes that available farmland is designated as pasture. Hythloday advises that the rich be pre-vented from establishing monopolies, that agri-culture be restructured, that businesses that promote idleness (such as taverns and brothels) be eliminated, and that the idle poor be given such useful employment as cloth working. In this discussion, Hythloday ties in economic issues, which are closely related to the class discrepan-cies he has already explored, pointing out that as the price of wool has risen so dramatically, impoverished individuals who would make cloth from wool can no longer afford to do so and are thereby deprived of their livelihood.

In Book 2, Hythloday details the apparently superior social and economic structures of Uto-pia, which he has already alluded to in Book 1. Having already expressed that in Utopia, "every-thing is equalized, everyone has plenty of every-thing," Hythloday discusses the way in which labor and goods are distributed equitably. There is no need for money, because the neces-sities of all citizens are met. Utopians eat together in dining halls and all wear the same types of clothing. There is nothing among the Utopians to denote class, for all are required to do the same amount of work and all receive the same benefits from their labor. At one point, Hythloday returns to the topic of Book 1, that is, the relationship between crime, class, and economics. He con-cedes that despite the Utopians' attempts to elim-inate the need for wrongdoing on the part of their citizens, there are still some transgressors. The most severe crimes "are punished with servi-tude," which Utopians do not consider to be "grievous to the criminal." In fact, such service benefits the commonwealth. These criminals become slaves and are treated worse than any other category of slave in Utopian society. This is due to the fact that, unlike the criminals from

TOPICS FOR FURTHER STUDY

- While many critics debate whether or not More seriously intended the society depicted in *Utopia* to be an ideal one, or whether or not he even thought such a commonwealth were possible, it seems fairly certain More intended a discussion to arise following the publication of his book—a discussion regarding what aspects of the work were in fact intended to depict ideal institutions, and what a truly fair and equitable society might look like. Write an essay describing how you would structure such a society, addressing some of the same points that More does: How will work be accomplished? Will there be a class system or a monetary system? Will individuals be allowed personal wealth and property? Will people elect their officials? How will people who break laws be dealt with?

- Book 1 of *Utopia* is structured like a debate, or dialogue, between More, Giles, and Hythloday (in comparison with Book 2, which is a one-sided report by Hythloday rather than an exchange of ideas). Select several topics that Hythloday presents in either Book 1 or Book 2, such as the communal approach to work, or the communist approach to providing for the needs of Utopian citizens, or the way in which Utopians deal with crime and punishment. With another student, stage a debate for the class in which one person presents the benefits to society of such systems and the other person makes a case as to why such systems would be detrimental to society. Depending on which side you argue, you will have to consider the question of whether or not ensuring the "common good" provides more actual benefit to a society than the practice of each individual providing for his or her own needs.

- More addresses the religious beliefs and practices of the Utopians in several areas of *Utopia*. Study these ideas, as well as Hythloday's claims of religious tolerance, and compare them to the state of religious affairs in More's England. Which society, the fictitious or the real, is more tolerant of a variety of religious beliefs? How are individuals who question commonly held views about the nature of the soul, or free will versus determination, for example, treated? How do both societies compare to the state of religious tolerance in the United States today? Write a report on your findings.

- More's *Utopia* opens with a letter from More to Peter Giles, but just prior to this prefatory letter is a short poem ascribed to the poet laureate of Utopia, who happens to be Hythloday's nephew. Write an analysis of the six lines of this poem and explore the reference in it to Plato. Be sure to discuss the ways in which Plato's views on ideal social structures and government as described in his *Republic* compare with Utopian society.

---

other countries who have been sent to Utopia to become slaves, Utopians who choose to do wrong do so having received a thorough and superior moral upbringing.

Proper and Improper Government

In the first book of *Utopia*, Hythloday speaks of European governments with some disdain, frowning on monarchies because kings typically seek to make themselves wealthier with little regard for the well-being of their citizens. European monarchs are held in contempt by Hythloday for seeking to expand their borders while many of their people languish in poverty. The government established by the Utopians, as described by Hythloday, is far more democratic and far less centralized than its European counterparts and is comprised of a number of elected officials who report to an elected ruler of a region. In Utopia, each group of thirty families is represented by a magistrate, or syphogrant, who is elected every year. The syphogrants, and the families they represent, are presided over by another official, the tranibor. All the syphogrants, numbering two hundred, elect a ruler through a secret ballot. This ruler is selected from four candidates whom the people have identified. Hythloday explains that this official rules for life unless he is suspected of aspiring to tyranny. Tranibors are elected every year but are not changed frequently. The other magistrates all serve tenures of one year. Tranibors advise the ruler about public affairs and meet with the ruler every third day. The primary duty of syphogrants is to ensure that everyone works when they are required to and to ensure that "no one lounges around in idleness." Thus, Utopia is divided into a number of independent but homogenous regions, each of which is ruled by an elected governor. Hythloday briefly mentions a "council of the whole island" to which matters will occasionally be referred, but there appears to be no central body with governance powers over all Utopians. The suggestion appears to be that such a body is not necessary in a society in which the sameness of citizens, social structures, and cities is ensured.

Religious Tolerance

Religion is one of the few areas of thought where Hythloday specifically refers to the differences among individuals in Utopia rather than to their sameness. He cites worshipers of various celestial bodies, or of "some ancient paragon of either virtue or glory," in which a person is viewed to be not only one of many gods but also the supreme deity. Hythloday goes on to note, however, that "the vast majority, and those by far the wiser ones," believe in only one god, who is infinite and infused in every aspect of the universe. Additionally, even those individuals who believe in many gods agree that there is one supreme god who created the universe. Emphasizing that many Utopians are beginning to abandon their more superstitious beliefs, Hythloday returns to the notion of Utopian unity in all matters: while differing religious beliefs are tolerated, he seems to be saying, Utopians nonetheless all believe the same essential facts about God.

Here Hythloday turns to a discussion of Christianity, stating that he and his fellow travelers shared with the Utopians information about the Christian religion. Many of them, he informs, converted to Christianity. Hythloday

Utopian alphabet (© INTERFOTO Pressebildagentur / Alamy)

enumerates several reasons for their affinity with Christianity, including the "secret inspiration of God"; the fact that Christianity resembled closely the beliefs they already held; and the fact that they were pleased to be told that their communal way of living was approved of by God. Stressing that nonbelievers in Christianity did not attempt to sway the newly converted and that those who embraced the faith were not shunned, Hythloday relates the story of one of his fellow travelers who denounced Utopians who had not accepted Christianity. This man, after extensive preaching and verbal attacks, was arrested and exiled for "exciting riots among the people." From the founding of Utopia, Hythloday states, individuals who attack another's religion or try to use force to coerce a conversion are exiled or enslaved. This is done to protect the peace of the island and because the country's founder, Utopus, believed that one could not know whether or not God wanted to be worshiped in a variety of ways. Utopus suspected that God inspired different individuals in different ways. Utopus, however, did forbid the belief in certain notions: that the soul is mortal and dies when one's body dies, and that the world is not ruled by divine providence (the idea that God orders the events in humans' lives, and throughout the world's history). Individuals who hold these beliefs are counted as less than human and certainly not citizens of Utopia, and are believed to be immoral people who are not guided by the fear of punishment in the afterlife. Yet they are allowed to speak their minds "among priests and prudent men" with the hope that their "madness will yield to reason."

STYLE

Satire

More establishes *Utopia* as satirical in nature through the correspondence framing the story. Satire is any form of literature in which irony and humor are used to criticize, for the purpose of reforming, the perceived flaws of individuals, institutions, or society. In the letters to Peter Giles that appear before Book 1 and following Book 2, More describes the obviously fictional account of the island of Utopia as based in fact. While he insists on the veracity of Hythloday's account and refers to Hythloday as a real person, More nevertheless includes a paragraph in the second letter to Giles rife with clues to the work's satirical nature. He states that if he had in fact decided to write a story about a commonwealth like Utopia, he would have employed a "fictional presentation" in such a way as to feed the readers the truth in a pleasant manner, and that if he had sought to fool ignorant readers, he would at least have included hints designed to indicate to the intelligent reader just what he was up to. More states, for example, that had this been his aim, he would have assigned the island a name that would suggest that it was nowhere. Scholars have observed that "utopia" is a Greek term that literally means "no place." More did, in fact, do all that he describes. He created a fictional account that relates truth, or truths about the problems in European societies, in a way that is pleasant to the reader (since the reader believes he or she is reading a work of fiction). The work includes the various hints that More states he would include in such a work, namely, rendering the place name in such a way as to indicate that the place is "nowhere." Additionally, while "utopia" means "no place," "eutopia," the Greek homophone,

translates to "good place." More capitalizes on the double meaning created by these words: the Utopia he describes through the character of Hythloday is an ideal place that does not exist. The questions that naturally follow—Could it exist? Should it exist?—remain unresolved.

Frame Narrative and First-Person Point of View

Utopia is a first-person narrative embedded in an overarching first-person narrative. The first-person point of view is one in which the narrating character speaks from his or her own perspective and refers to him or herself as "I" throughout the work. First and foremost, More speaks in the first person in the letters framing Books 1 and 2 of the story, letters he writes to Peter Giles. In this regard, *Utopia* may also be viewed as a frame narrative. A frame narrative is one in which one story is set off, or bookended, by another story, thereby giving the nested story a reference point from which it is to be considered. In this case, Books 1 and 2 of *Utopia* are to be understood within the context explained by the letters from More to Peter Giles, the letters that appear before and after the Utopia narrative.

Books 1 and 2, the reader is informed, are "A Discourse on the Best Form of a Commonwealth, Spoken by the Remarkable Raphael Hythloday, as Reported by the Illustrious Thomas More, a Citizen and the Undersheriff of the Famous British City of London." The dual nature of the account is thereby introduced. In Book 1, the layering of first-person accounts begins to be revealed. More is the "I" initially speaking. But when the conversation between Giles, Hythloday, and More turns to Hythloday's account of his exchange with Cardinal Morton, the lengthy discourse is told in the first person from Hythloday's point of view. After some time, Hythloday addresses More directly once again, and the first-person point of view is transferred back to More. Following the conclusion of Book 1, More establishes that the section to follow will be the tale that Hythloday relates. Book 2 is told without interruption, with Hythloday speaking in the first person. After he concludes his tale, More takes up the first-person mantle once again when he makes a few brief comments about both the absurdity and the appeal of Hythloday's account of the Utopians. The resurging duality of first-person accounts reflects another pairing between competing elements. Just as the narrating voice shifts back and forth between More and Hythloday, More's attitude regarding ideal values seems to shift as well. Additionally, just as the reader is uncertain about the views held by the character More, there exists similar confusion about what the author More intends the reader to assume about his own opinions.

HISTORICAL CONTEXT

Class and Economics in King Henry VIII's England

During the reign of King Henry VIII, which lasted from 1509 through 1547, English society was segmented into various classes including peasants, a burgeoning middle class, and the nobility. Such a system was based on deep inequalities in the distribution of wealth. Peasant farmers were tenants on the land of nobles and subject to their landlords' demands. Peasant agriculture served as the foundation of the English economy, yet peasant farmers were vulnerable to the desires of the markets they served. As Hythloday suggests and condemns in *Utopia*, what was deemed valuable in European societies was what was rare, rather than what was useful. Peasant farmers faced the possibility of being driven off their land when it was turned over to shepherds for the production of valuable wool. The middle, or working, class was heavily taxed. The middle class consisted of church and state officials, merchants, bankers, businessmen, professionals such as lawyers and doctors, and skilled craftsmen. At this time, large-scale manufacturing had yet to transform the English economy, but capitalism was beginning to seep into the structure of the economy, primarily in the area of usury (money lending) and in agriculture as well, as nobles began to practice capitalist farming. Conflicts existed between merchants and landed gentry (middle-class individuals who owned land as opposed to members of the noble class with inherited estates), but they had common interests, such as the desire to avoid taxation and the promotion of free, safe roadways for the purposes of transporting goods. This time period has been described as a relatively stable one; despite the disparities in wealth, any unrest present did not take an active form in open rebellion by the common people. Rather, the power struggles amongst nobles were of greater concern to Henry VIII, who was known to have feared an aristocratic rebellion.

Roman Catholicism versus the Church of England

Thomas More was at the center of religious tensions that eventually fractured the practice of Catholicism in England. A power struggle was brewing in the early sixteenth century between the leading Roman officials (the emperor and the pope) and England's King Henry VIII. Henry increasingly sought to distance his nation's religion from the power of Rome. The Holy Roman Emperor Charles V was emperor-elect from 1519 through 1530 and emperor from 1530 through 1556; as emperor, it was Charles's duty to protect the Catholic Church. Pope Leo X (who served from 1513 to 1521), like Charles, played a role in English history. While Roman interests conflicted with Henry's desire for religious independence and consolidation of power in England, Catholicism was also under attack by Lutherans, who questioned many of the Church's practices. With Martin Luther leading an attack against the Church, the Protestant Reformation began in England during the early 1500s. Luther questioned papal authority by insisting that the Bible was the only source of infallible teaching about God, and that the pope could not decree other infallible teachings of the Church. Lutheranism also came to be associated with the notion of predestination (the idea that God planned the fate of human souls prior to creation) in opposition to the Catholic notion of free will (choices are not predested; one has the ability to chose between right and wrong action), although there is some debate regarding Luther's own views on this matter.

From 1529 through 1532, More played an active role in persecuting Lutherans, having the authority as lord chancellor to have heretics burned at the stake or imprisoned. Around the same time, Henry took his most definitive action against Rome by marrying Anne Boleyn and discarding Catherine of Aragon; the marriage was condemned by the emperor and by Pope Clement VII (who served from 1523 through 1534). In 1534, Henry broke with Rome and established the Anglican Church. More did not speak out openly against Henry's decision but could not support it. He refused to sign the Act of Succession, which validated Henry's marriage to Anne and legitimized any heirs that

COMPARE & CONTRAST

- **1500s:** Henry VIII is the king of England, and More is one of the king's ambassadors and advisors. The king's power is not unlimited and is, to some extent, restrained by Parliament, but the monarch is the ruling head of state. Henry is viewed as a powerful monarch who transforms England from a weak nation into a dominant force in European politics.

  Today: The government of the United Kingdom (which includes England, Wales, Scotland, and Northern Ireland, and is also referred to as the UK or Britain) remains a monarchy. Queen Elizabeth II has reigned since 1952. Since the seventeenth century, however, the monarch has played an increasingly smaller role in politics and governance of the nation. The prime minister of the United Kingdom of Great Britain and Northern Ireland is the recognized political leader, and he or she is held accountable by Parliament, which consists of both appointed and elected members.

- **1500s:** It is a revolutionary view in England to hold that males and females are equally capable and entitled to an education, a view held by humanists such as Thomas More. Most lower-class children of either gender have no access to education at all, and among the nobility, often it is only boys who receive an academic education. More educates his daughters and son in his home by employing a private, humanist tutor, who emphasizes ancient Greek and Roman writers and philosophy, oratory and rhetoric, ethics, and theology.

  Today: All British children are required to attend either free state schools or independent (private) schools, or be home-schooled from the ages of five through sixteen. Proposals are in place to make it compulsory for children to be educated through the age of eighteen.

- **1500s:** Religious turmoil divides England. Conflicts exist among Catholics, some of whom remain loyal to Rome and some of whom side with King Henry VIII, who rejects Roman Catholicism and creates the Church of England. At the same time, Catholicism is fractured by a faction of Lutherans, led by Martin Luther (1483–1546), who are at odds with many of the Church's teachings. The fact that the Church is being splintered by Lutherans, or "reformed," from their point of view, helps contribute to the rise of Anglicanism, a term that was later applied to the beliefs and structures of the Church of England.

  Today: According to recent census data gathered by the British government, a majority of Brits identify themselves as Christians. However, a substantial proportion of the population identify themselves as having no religion. The second most common religion is Islam. Additionally, other figures suggest that Catholicism is about to surpass Anglicanism as the most commonly practiced Christian denomination.

---

would be born to the couple. More was subsequently imprisoned, convicted of treason, and beheaded.

Humanism

It is often observed that Thomas More considered himself a humanist and moved in intellectual circles that included other humanist thinkers such as the Dutch scholar and theologian Desiderius Erasmus (c. 1466–1536) and Peter Giles (c. 1486–1533) of Belgium. Humanism, as understood in terms of sixteenth-century philosophy, stressed the value of the individual and believed in the education of all people, male and female. Humanists emphasized the significance of ancient Greek and Roman writers and philosophers and often took issue with various elements of Catholicism.

Illustration of More's island of Utopia (© Mary Evans Picture Library / Alamy)

While the Church taught the notion of free will, its authority in shaping moral thought was widely accepted and deferred to. Humanists included in their curriculum the teaching of ethics separately from theology, and therefore were at risk of being accused of heresy for questioning the Church's authority. Erasmus, for example, approved of many of the objections Lutherans had to Catholic beliefs and practices, but stressed he had no objection to the doctrines that served as the foundation of Catholicism. Despite his association with Martin Luther, Erasmus advocated reform of the Catholic Church rather than separation from it. More, on the other hand, possessed a religious fervor that led him to an intolerance of Lutheranism so extreme that when he held a position powerful enough to do so, he punished and persecuted Lutherans who spoke out against the Catholic Church. The attentive reader will notice that in More's *Utopia*, the society appears to be based on a reasoned approach to right behavior that promotes the common good, but at the same time, severe punishments, and a required belief that vice will be judged by God in the afterlife, suggest that it is fear that motivates right behavior, rather than reason. Edward L. Surtz, in his 1957 assessment of the religious and moral issues in *Utopia*, explains this apparent discrepancy as an aspect of the conflict More felt between his humanist philosophy and his Catholic religion. More establishes his notions of "his ideal commonwealth upon reason," as "a philosopher," Surtz demonstrates, but he "directs his admonitions . . . to the reputed followers of Christ" as "a Christian teacher."

CRITICAL OVERVIEW

More's *Utopia* is a dense and self-reflexive work that criticizes European society and offers a variety of remedies to various social ills. Yet it fails to clarify the true motives and opinions of its author. The main issue critics of the work address is that of how to interpret More's intentions. This point of contention was as much a problem for the work's sixteenth-century critics as it is for modern ones, although *Utopia* did not appear in England as an English translation until 1551, sixteen years after More's death. In the sixteenth and seventeenth centuries, More's humanism and the reflections of such thought in the work were of primary interest among critics. By the nineteenth century, *Utopia* increasingly became studied with an eye toward its possible socialist motivations. Over the years, some readers and scholars have viewed the work as a blueprint for an ideal society, one in which human greed is prevented by the established social and economic structures, which presage communism. Others have viewed it as pure satire to be interpreted as More's mocking indictment of European society in the early 1500s. A middle ground is commonly defended as well, in which scholars argue that neither the persona of More nor the character of Hythloday should be viewed as the author's mouthpiece, and in which it is held that More uses extreme "solutions," ones he did not advocate implementing, to reveal the depth of the inequities in the world in which he lived. Often, details about More's life and information gleaned from his other writings are used to inform readings of *Utopia*.

In his 1904 introduction to *Sir Thomas More's* Utopia, J. Churton Collins argues that More's purpose in writing the work was "to point out where and from what causes the European Commonwealths, and more especially the English, with which More was most familiar, were at fault." Like other critics to follow, Collins concedes that it is difficult to tell when More is writing in total seriousness and when he is indulging his sense of irony and humor. Similarly J. H. Hexter, in his 1952 study, *More's* Utopia, affirms that the only point upon which critics can unanimously agree regarding *Utopia* is that the work is intended as social commentary. After Hexter suggests a number of reasons why More's true intentions seem inscrutable, he studies the history of the text's composition in order to help determine what More may have been advocating, and stresses the importance of the fact that Book 1 was actually composed after Book 2.

Edward L. Surtz, in his 1957 assessment of *Utopia* titled *The Praise of Wisdom: A Commentary on the Religious and Moral Problems and Backgrounds of St. Thomas More's* Utopia, emphasizes that it would be foolish to assume that *Utopia* is either completely mocking or entirely serious in intent. Surtz divides the critical approaches to the work into three camps: those who minimize any moralizing More may be attempting, those who view it as an exploration of dangerous policies, and those who analyze the work as "a document of humanistic reform." While advocating the view that More sought to reform Christianity based on humanist principles, Surtz stresses that when More wrote *Utopia*, Christians were largely a united group of believers, but later in his political and literary career, More felt that Christianity was under attack by Lutherans whose views contradicted the pope's teachings. Through these observations, Surtz suggests that the More who seems to preach religious tolerance in *Utopia* was understandably a different More than the one who ordered Lutherans burned at the stake.

In his essay in the 1978 collection *Quincentennial Essays on St. Thomas More*, edited by Michael J. Moore, Thomas I. White argues for a reading of *Utopia* that views the work's criticism of wealth as a serious aim of the book. White maintains that in *Utopia*, More is advocating as "morally superior" the view that an object's worth depends on how useful it is, rather than on how rare it is. Like White, Susan Bruce, in her 1999 introduction to *Three Early Modern Utopias*, identifies More's discussions on private wealth as highly pertinent to an understanding of *Utopia*. Bruce finds that the communism of Utopia is the foundation from which all other aspects of the society stem. Furthermore, Bruce goes a step further than many critics by suggesting that while the communist Utopian society may appear authoritarian, it is hardly as repressive as More's England was. She states that it is not obvious that More takes the Utopians' suppression of individual happiness for the greater good of the society to be a "misguided ideal." Just as Bruce references English society, Russell Ames, in *Citizen Thomas More and His* Utopia (1949), explores various aspects of English society in order to comprehend the context in which *Utopia* was written. Ames emphasizes that More's work "not only describes some things that man and society can be but reflects accurately much that they were in the early sixteenth century." Contending that the middle class had not yet gained a foothold in the social and economic structures of early sixteenth-century England, Ames suggests that *Utopia* may be viewed as a revolutionary and rebellious work of literature.

CRITICISM

Catherine Dominic

Dominic is a novelist and a freelance writer and editor. In this essay, she asserts that although the character of Hythloday in Utopia *emphasizes the equality inherent in Utopian society, his descriptions demonstrate that great discrepancies exist in the way Utopians value various members of society—particularly women, children, slaves, and individuals with a lack of particular religious beliefs.*

Most scholars agree that an identification of Thomas More's true aims and intentions in *Utopia* cannot be achieved with any accuracy. Attempting to demonstrate what he may or may not have believed about the role of women in society, for example, would be a rather subjective endeavor. This does not diminish the importance of an exploration of the nature of the inequities in Utopian society and the tracing of the consistent manner by which Raphael Hythloday glosses over the obvious unfairness

> **WHAT SOME PEOPLE IN THIS SOCIETY LACK, HOWEVER, IS AN ACKNOWLEDGMENT OF THEIR OWN BASIC HUMAN DIGNITY BY THEIR FELLOW CITIZENS."**

of various Utopian practices. Such an undertaking offers a means of approaching the text, as some scholars have suggested, as a dialogue between author and reader about the problems inherent in society in general. A dialogue of this nature remains just as fruitful in the twenty-first century as it was for More's contemporary readers.

The character of Hythloday describes situations throughout *Utopia* in which slaves, women, and children are demeaned, objectified, or depersonalized, but he does so apparently without concern for the harmed individuals. At the same time, Utopia is applauded by Hythloday, who fails to recognize his own hypocrisy or that of the Utopians. Utopia is described by Hythloday as a society in which "everything is equalized, everyone has plenty of everything." What some people in this society lack, however, is an acknowledgement of their own basic human dignity by their fellow citizens. In the section of Book 2 on social relations, Hythloday describes a society that is essentially patriarchal, despite the fact that females are educated as well as males, and are admitted into a variety of professions. Likewise, women and men alike are trained in warfare. However, young women, when they marry are moved from their father's household to that of their husband, whereas sons remain in their father's house.

In addition to a social structure in which males take a predominant role, individuals in Utopian society are often objectified, treated as nameless, faceless Utopian units. As each household and city are only allowed a set number of people, individuals are simply transferred from one household or city to another in order to maintain population balances. Children who seek to learn a trade different from that of their father are simply shifted into another household, Hythloday informs us. A further indication of the homogenous, objectified state of the Utopians is their clothing, which is utilitarian and

varies only to denote gender and marital status. When the "natives" of Utopia agree "willingly to the same style of life and the same customs," they are "easily assimilated," but if they refuse to live under Utopian laws they are "driven out of the territory the Utopians have marked off for their use" and war is waged against them if they resist. Utopia, apparently, is not deserved by everyone, so notions of equality apply not to all people but only to people who accept the customs of Utopia.

Hythloday returns to a discussion of household practices and structures, observing that it is the duty of wives to serve their husbands, and of children to serve their parents. In the communal dining halls where Utopians eat at set times, slaves do the work that is "heavy or dirty" while women are entirely responsible for preparing food and making arrangements for the meal. Men sit at dining tables with their backs facing the wall, with the women "on the outside, so if they should suddenly feel ill, as happens, sometimes, when they are pregnant," they can leave the hall "without disturbing the seating arrangement." Older children serve the dining Utopians, or stand by in "absolute silence" if they are young or unable to serve. The children are allowed to eat only what is handed to them by the seated diners, and no other time is allotted for their meals. While women are ostensibly eligible to serve as elected officials, Hythloday's observation that the magistrates and their wives sit in a place of honor indicates that these officials are more often than not male. Utopians, then, are depicted as utilitarian objects who accomplish various tasks to support the community as a whole. Children may be taken from their parents in order to learn a trade, and families may be severed in order to maintain prescribed numbers of citizens contained in a household or city. Women and children, while allowed an education, remain subservient to the male members of society and are required to do work the older males are exempt from. While More's humanist interest in the education of males and females alike is apparent in his *Utopia*, the country reflects sixteenth-century England's own biases regarding the inherent value of certain groups of its citizenry.

Individuals who have committed a "serious crime" in Utopia, or foreigners who have received a death sentence in their own countries and who have been "acquired" by Utopia, work as slaves

WHAT DO I READ NEXT?

- *The Life of Thomas More*, by Peter Ackroyd, is a highly acclaimed biography in which More's intimate role in English political events and religious conflicts is explored in great detail. Ackroyd's analysis of More's life is placed within the context of English history. The work is available through Anchor Press and was published in 1999.

- *Saint Thomas More: Selected Writings*, edited by John F. Thornton and published by Vintage in 2003, focuses on More's later writings, specifically those known as the "Tower Works," which More wrote during his imprisonment in the Tower of London. These works include essays, letters to his eldest daughter, poems, and devotional pieces.

- *The History of King Richard III and Selections from the English and Latin Poems*, edited by Richard S. Sylvester, contains some of More's earlier writings, including the Richard III history, which was written around 1513 and served as a source for Shakespeare's play about King Richard III.

The volume was published in 1976 by Yale University Press.

- *Luther and Erasmus: Free Will and Salvation*, by E. Gordon Rupp and Philip S. Watson, published by Westminster John Knox Press in 1978, explores the religious thought of two men with an intimate connection with More. Luther represented the enemy, the purveyor of heretical thought, whereas Erasmus was More's fellow humanist and friend. The book includes texts by both men in which they attack one another's religious viewpoints and provides introductions that elucidate the turbulent environment in which they each, along with More, played a part.

- *Gulliver's Travels*, by Jonathan Swift, was originally published in 1726. Like *Utopia*, this novel is a social satire. The two works are also similar in that they feature a character who travels to nonexistent lands. A 2005 edition of *Gulliver's Travels*, edited by Claude Rawson and Ian Higgins, is available from Oxford University Press.

---

for Utopian communities, thereby serving the common good, as Hythloday explains. He appears to view this arrangement as just, and by comparison to the English punishment of hanging for thievery, it does seem to be an improvement on the treatment of criminals. Nevertheless, treatment of slaves in Utopia is often severe. Foreign criminals are kept "constantly at work but also in chains." Utopian criminals are treated with harsher measure due to their rejection of their Utopian moral upbringing. Other slaves are "poor, overworked drudges from other nations" who chose to live among the Utopians as slaves. While these individuals are treated "decently," they are worked "a bit harder (since they are used to it)." Severe crimes are punished with forced labor, and adultery is considered one of the worst crimes and therefore punished with the "harshest servitude." In the case of adultery,

there are unique circumstances. If both adulterers were married, the deceived spouses may divorce and remarry. But if the spouse of an adulterer wishes to remain married to the adulterer, both adulterer and his or her spouse are "condemned to hard labor." They may eventually be set free, but if the crime recurs, the adulterer is killed. Slaves who are considered rebellious are killed. As noted above, slaves do the heavy, dirty work that Utopians deem unacceptable.

Citizens work six hours a day (although it is unclear whether or not the kitchen chores of the women are included, or in addition to this figure) whereas slaves are required to work "constantly" and in chains, if they are foreigners. One can only imagine what the harsher treatment Utopian slaves receive might be; Hythloday does not elaborate on this point. Hythloday, in Book 1, vehemently objects to the execution of thieves by the English, and argues that in a society where social and economic equality is maintained, there is no need for thievery or for its unjust punishment by hanging. Yet Hythloday, in his discussion of slavery, does not allude to whether or not there are many or few Utopian slaves (only that there are more foreigner than Utopian slaves), nor does he explain which of their crimes, other than adultery, results in a sentence of slavery. To what extent then, one wonders, have the Utopians succeeded in providing their citizens with everything they need? By the very existence of Utopian slaves and a system for punishing them, the reader can infer that Utopians have not overcome the greed inherent in the European society Hythloday judges so harshly. Nor have they, apparently, succeeded in finding a way to treat their criminals more humanely than the English. A death penalty still exists, though presumably not for thievery, and the "harshest" punishments and severest forms of forced labor await Utopian lawbreakers.

In his discussion of Utopian religious practices, Hythloday reveals a telling detail, a notion that perhaps serves as a disturbing underpinning of Utopian society. While extolling the virtues of Utopian religious tolerance, Hythloday observes that individuals who do not believe in an afterlife in which punishments are administered for "vices and rewards for virtues," cannot even be included "in the category of human beings" since they have rejected the notion of their own soul. Such individuals are held in contempt by society and are not allowed any positions of public responsibility. Hythloday goes on to state that people who have nothing to fear but punishment for breaking the law, and who hope for nothing after their earthly existence, cannot help but be motivated by "personal greed." Such individuals would undoubtedly seek to avoid public laws or to forcefully break them, he asserts.

Hythloday is suggesting here that there can be no morality or social conscience that is not based in fear of divine judgment and retribution. He undercuts his own extended argument regarding the notion of the common good. If an individual is only capable of being motivated to behave in a moral fashion out of fear of God's wrath in the afterlife, then each Utopian is not working for the common good purely for the sake of the common good. Rather, because

they fear God's punishment, they behave in a moral way, which happens to benefit the common good, but their motivation is selfish, not communal. This same idea is hinted at earlier, when Hythloday brings up punishments for premarital intercourse. Transgressors are forbidden from ever marrying anyone, and the "master and mistress of the household where the offense was committed fall into utter disgrace" for not preventing the transgression from occurring. The punishment is severe, Hythloday explains, because otherwise there would be no incentive for people to marry. They would have no reason to withstand the challenges of a lifelong bond, if promiscuity were not "carefully restrained," and transgressors were not prohibited from other relationships. Fear of punishment, again, is the motivator for "proper" behavior. Utopians, apparently, are unable to live moral lives unless they are threatened. They are not trusted to behave in a moral fashion because it is good and right to do so, and they only manage to behave in a moral fashion because punishment will be extracted in this life and the next if they do not comply with so-called equitable Utopian laws and social customs. For a society allegedly based on principles of equality and fairness and the common good, Utopia has the look of a regimented authoritarian nation that routinely violates basic human rights and is charged with an undercurrent of fear.

Source: Catherine Dominic, Critical Essay on *Utopia*, in *Novels for Students*, Gale, Cengage Learning, 2009.

Anne Lake Prescott

In the following excerpt, Prescott addresses questions about the authorship and margins of Utopia.

...Related to postmodern doubts about identity and words has been a fruitful concern with how margins relate to centers: the margins and centers of societies and literary traditions, of course, but also the margins and centers of books. Looking at scribbles by early book owners is a growth industry in English departments. True, our discussions of the marginal can become intellectually incoherent: to boast (and one does boast) of refocusing on the "marginalized"—the illiterate, women, the racially or sexually "other," Catholics in Elizabethan England, writers not found on older reading lists—all this assumes that there is a center. A more radical move might be to relocate the center or even abolish the very notion. Christians like More could, after all, point to God's birth in a stable on the edges of the Roman Empire, not in a palace on one of the great city's seven hills. More's own interest in the socially marginal shows in the anger with which his Hythloday condemns England's treatment of its paupers and criminals—indeed England's *creation* of paupers and criminals. It shows as well in More's efforts, some years later, to study and help solve the problem of England's many vagabonds, although needless to say he was unable to do much.

The margins of *Utopia* are nearly as disorienting as the dialogue on which they comment. A recent essay by a follower of Derrida claims that our culture mystifies the margins of books by making them inviolate and sacred white space, a halo surrounding and protecting the text. He may be right in our own time: nice people do not scribble in other people's books and the financial value of a first edition plummets if annotated by the uncelebrated. Until very recently, moreover, modern editions of older texts often omitted liminary poems, running commentary, printers' prefaces, and so forth. But what Derrida's follower says would certainly not apply to Renaissance readers or printers, who viewed empty margins much as Holbein might have viewed blank canvas: an invitation to come right in, not otherworldly space saying "Abandon all print and pencils ye who enter here."

The little notes in *Utopia*'s margins serve at least two functions. First, they offer additional ironies or remarks along with some identifications and allusions. Sometimes they are straightforward (locating a source in Livy, for example). Some exclaim at Utopia's superiority to Europe. When Hythloday reports that Utopians start their meals with some reading, the margin says that "Today Scarcely the Monks Observe this Custom." Another note condemns European countries' desire for expansion. Sometimes, though, it is hard to gauge the tone: when the main text says that Utopia has nowhere in which to waste time, no wine shops, alehouses, brothels, no "lurking holes or secret places," the margin exclaims, "O Holy Commonwealth—and Worthy of Imitation Even by Christians." Well, maybe. Since Utopia is indeed "Nowhere" it is possible that Utopian lurking houses and alehouses that are nowhere to be found can therefore, logically, be in fact found there. In any case, however, More was no

Puritan. Could he have wanted an England without any place in which to bend an elbow with a friend? With nowhere in which to discuss some private doubt or desire? And Christians have sometimes needed secret places—catacombs, or, more recently, confessionals. True, in Utopia one might not need lurking-holes, although after the island becomes Christian it might need confessionals, or at least some corners for quiet pastoral counseling. So is this marginal note to be read straight? Ironically? Or is the shudder it gives modern readers merely the result of our own increased stress on privacy?

The notes do something else, too: they add another voice to the dialogue. More, Hythloday, and Peter Giles are sitting in a garden talking, and talking in ways that leave us uncertain as to who, if anybody, speaks for the author. That is, to use a favorite postmodern word, *Utopia* is "dialogic" as well as a dialogue. In the margins, however, yet another voice joins the dialogue, increasing its polyvocality. The speakers there in the Antwerp garden cannot hear it, or so one may assume, but we can. Where does it come from? Some Renaissance equivalent of cyberspace? The voice's ontological status is deliciously hard to determine.

In fact the voice may be that of Erasmus, who some think wrote the notes. This raises yet another issue. A major impulse of postmodern thinking, most notably that by Foucault and Derrida, has been to undercut the notion that "authorship" is a historically stable concept. Such reconsideration of authorship, however, seldom scholars like to apply it to themselves, has had a largely salutary effect on Renaissance scholarship. We are now less taken aback, for example, by Shakespeare's collaboration with other dramatists. Similarly, more scholars are aware that the full effect of *Utopia* includes the marginal notes, letters to More by various humanists, More's own paradox-filled letter to Peter Giles, maps, even the Utopian alphabet and some lines of Utopian verse. The title "Utopia," one could argue, should refer to this entire collaborative performance, one that is arguably more premodern and postmodern than plain modern. Modernist literature is not free of collaboration—as witness what Ezra Pound did for T. S. Eliot's *Wasteland*—but it is still hard to imagine the quasi-modernist H. G. Wells, say, publishing *The Time Machine* with letters from

MORE RECOGNISED THAT SERIOUS ISSUES COULD BE COUCHED IN HUMOROUS TERMS WITHOUT LOSING THEIR SIGNIFICANCE."

the Time Traveler's Victorian dinner companions, snatches of worried verse in the Eloi language, Morlock recipes for Eloi stew, and impish marginal notes by Bernard Shaw. . . .

Source: Anne Lake Prescott, "Postmodern More," in *Moreana*, Vol. 40, No. 153–154, March 2003, pp. 219–39.

Stephanie Forward

In the following essay, Forward examines Utopia *and attempts to determine More's objective in writing the work.*

In sixteenth-century Britain, Thomas More was acknowledged to be one of our most distinguished intellectuals. His book *Utopia* concerns life on a fictitious island, and the impact of the text was such that the words 'utopia' and 'utopian' entered our language and became applied to a particular genre.

'More is a man of an angel's wit and singular learning; I know not his fellow. For where is the man of that gentleness, lowliness, and affability? And as time requireth a man of marvellous mirth and pastimes; and sometimes of as sad gravity: a man for all seasons' (Robert Whittinton).

A MAN FOR ALL SEASONS

More was born in 1478 in London. He was the son of a judge, and was educated at St Anthony's School in Thread-needle Street. From the age of 12 he was a page in the service of Archbishop John Morton, then he studied at Oxford for 2 years. During his time as a student, More went to live at a Carthusian monastery to consider whether his true vocation was the priesthood. Although he decided against it, he continued to prefer an austere lifestyle, and even wore a hair-shirt for the rest of his life. More excelled in his chosen profession, which was the law. He became an MP in 1504, and later was appointed as one of the two Under-sheriffs of London. His first wife died in childbirth in 1511; subsequently he remarried. During a spell as envoy to Flanders, as part of a delegation concerned with the wool trade, he commenced his work *Utopia*.

In 1518, More became privy councillor to Henry VIII, and other honours followed: he was knighted, was made Speaker of the House of Commons, and became Chancellor of the Duchy of Lancaster. When More was named as Lord Chancellor in 1529, he was the first layman to hold the post regarded as the most important office in the kingdom. It was a role he performed with great conscientiousness and integrity, but his honesty led to conflict when he found it impossible to condone Henry's divorce from Catherine of Aragon, and he would not attend the coronation of Henry's new wife, Anne Boleyn. Although More did not speak out against the King, the fact that he refused to support Henry was regarded as a crime. In March 1534, More was called upon to swear an oath of Supremacy, to recognise Henry as Head of the Church rather than the Pope. He tried to remain silent, because he believed in the Pope's supremacy, but his passive resistance spoke volumes. Cast into the Tower of London, accused of high treason, he remained incorruptible and true to his principles. As a result, he was beheaded in 1535. More was beatified in 1886, then canonised as a Roman Catholic martyr in 1935 by Pope Pius XI.

Thomas More's conflict with Henry has been explored in Robert Bolt's gripping play *A Man for All Seasons* (1960). Despite overwhelming personal and political pressure, More knew he must be true to himself: 'I neither could nor would rule my King. But there's a little . . . little area . . . where I must rule myself.'

ISLAND OF DREAMS

Utopia was written in Latin, which was then a universal language among the educated, and it was first published at Louvain in 1516. An English translation by Ralph Robinson appeared in 1551. In the book, the narrator encounters a traveller named Raphael Hythlodaeus—indeed, a regular element of utopian fiction is the technique of introducing a character who describes an incredible journey and/or an amazing discovery. During a discussion about the problems of contemporary society, Raphael mentions Utopia, and More asks him to elaborate. Raphael describes an ideal republic: a harmonious community on an island where there is full employment, the citizens are not obsessed with money, and are tolerant towards their fellow men.

The name 'Utopia' is Greek, meaning 'not-place'. It is a play on the words eutopos, meaning 'a good place', and outopos, meaning 'no place'. Previous writers had described idyllic locations, such as Elysium and Atlantis, and had envisaged perfect communities, most famously Plato in his *Republic*.

The text begins with an intriguing combination of fantasy and fact. It is prefaced by the Utopian alphabet, along with an example of Utopian poetry. There is then a letter from More to Peter Gilles, who was in real life the Chief Secretary, or Town Clerk, of Antwerp. Here, More distances himself from the material that follows by emphasising that the views expressed are not his own: 'My job was simply to write down what I'd heard'; and 'all I had to do was repeat what Raphael told us'. Such a disclaimer was no doubt a wise move and a necessary safeguard in a society where freedom of speech—and indeed freedom of thought—was limited. Similarly, a letter from Gilles to another friend, Jerome Busleiden, states that Raphael was 'describing his own experiences in a place where he'd lived for quite a long time' (5 years). The letter is amusing because Gilles praises More excessively, lauding 'the prodigious, if not positively superhuman power of his intellect'. He asks: 'who could be better qualified to introduce sound ideas to the public than one who has spent many years in the public service and earned the highest praise for his wisdom and integrity?'

Book I is written in the form of a dialogue, which presents a perceptive analysis of problems in England. It begins with references to More's official visit to Flanders and Bruges in 1515. He was sent to re-establish commercial relations with the Netherlands following a dispute between the English government and Prince Charles of Castile that had damaged the English wool trade. In this way, More suggests a realistic setting, and the effect is heightened when he includes other real-life names and places. For example, Raphael is said to have been a companion of Amerigo Vespucci, after whom America was named. Raphael claims to have visited England: he speaks of the Cornish rebellion over taxes in 1497, and mentions John Morton, the Archbishop served by More when he was a teenager.

When Raphael is introduced to More, he is likened to Ulysses and to Plato. Here, then, is a man whose words should be taken seriously! At the outset he condemns certain unnecessarily harsh aspects of English law: 'Petty larceny isn't bad enough to deserve the death penalty, and no penalty on earth will stop people from stealing, if it's their only way of getting food.' He compares the English to incompetent schoolmasters who cane their pupils rather than teach them: 'you create thieves, and then punish them for stealing'. The most effective method of deterring thieves, he declares, is to provide everyone with employment. Raphael voices his disapproval of the greedy nobles, gentlemen and abbots who have evicted farmers and seized their lands to rear sheep, in order to increase their revenue from wool. This selfish attitude has a knock-on effect, depriving many workers from earning a living. Raphael advocates 'honest, useful work for the great army of unemployed'. In Utopia, society runs efficiently with only a few regulations because there is equal prosperity for all of the citizens. Indeed, Raphael recommends the abolition of private property altogether. At this point in the text More disagrees, arguing that without the incentive of profit people would become idle, which would lead inevitably to poverty and crime. However, he requests Raphael to give a detailed account of Utopia, which he does in the narrative that forms Book II.

The island has 54 towns: all within easy reach of each other, all sharing the same language, traditions and rules. The towns are virtually identical, each containing 6,000 households of between 10 and 16 adults. The inhabitants change houses every 10 years. Each group of 30 households is overseen by a Styward, or District Controller, and every 10 Stywards by a Bencheater, or Senior District Controller. A town has 200 Stywards, who elect a Mayor with whom the Bencheaters liaise regularly to resolve occasional disputes. In towns, meals are eaten communally at the Stywards' homes. Raphael observes: 'Social relations are uniformly friendly, for officials are never pompous or intimidating in their manner.' Excellent hospital care is provided, and also special nurseries for mothers and babies.

Money is not essential because citizens can select all they require from the shops. It is only needed in cases of emergency, such as war. In fact, the Utopians hold gold in such contempt that they use it to make chamber-pots! Primary education is provided for all children. Farming is part of everyone's education—indeed, citizens are obliged to work on the land for a period of

2 years to reduce the likelihood of food shortages. Individuals generally learn special trades, although exceptionally gifted intellectuals may take academic roles. Many people choose to study when they are not working. The working day lasts for only 6 hours, and the citizens are encouraged to enjoy their leisure time. Indeed, for the Utopians the chief aim in life is pleasure.

Several different religions exist peacefully side by side, but almost everyone believes in a single divine power active in the universe, known as Mythras. Citizens worship together, envisaging God as they choose, for one of the foremost principles of the constitution is religious tolerance. Priests are elected by the community, and are responsible for the moral and academic training of youngsters.

UTOPIA OR DYSTOPIA?

Each member of Utopian society is cared for: everyone has a home, food, clothes, education, employment and medical care. On the other hand, there is a uniformity, a lack of individuality, which is unappealing to modern readers. The typical day seems to be time tabled rigidly, with bedtime at 8 p.m. Fashion does not exist because there are no tailors or dressmakers. Everyone wears the same sort of clothes, with only slight variations according to sex and marital status. Raphael observes: 'So whereas in other countries you won't find anyone satisfied with less than five [or] six suits and as many silk shirts, while dressy types want over ten of each, your Utopian is content with a single piece of clothing every 2 years.' Furthermore, the Utopians do not have complete freedom of movement, but are obliged to apply for special passports to travel within their own country. At times there is a sinister, rather chilling note: 'There are also no wine-taverns, no ale-houses, no brothels, no opportunities For seduction, no secret meeting-places. Everyone has his eye on you, so you're practically forced to get on with your job, and make some proper use of your spare time.'

Although Raphael criticises England's treatment of thieves, he seems to accept the Utopians' extreme punishments for those who indulge in sex before marriage or in adultery. Utopian society is male-dominated, and husbands are responsible for disciplining their wives—to the extent that wives have to confess to their husbands on a monthly basis. There appears to be a great deal of state interference in courtship and marriage,

with a somewhat regimented approach. Girls may not marry until they are 18 and boys until they are 22. (The prospective bride and groom must view each other in the nude before committing themselves to marriage! The Utopians maintain that it is essential to choose a suitable partner, because they are a monogamous people.)

There is supposed to be religious tolerance on the island, yet atheists are despised. Although citizens have all that is required to live comfortably, there is still a competitive atmosphere: the people vie with each other to win the award for best-kept garden.

Despite the claim that there is equality on the island, there is a clear class system, with a hierarchy of diplomats, priests, Bencheasters and Mayors drawn from a specific class. The best food is given to hospital patients, which sounds admirable, but thereafter preferential treatment is given to those highly placed in the hierarchy. The Utopians use slaves to perform menial tasks, who are obliged to work in chain gangs. The usual punishment for serious crime is slavery, but a genuinely penitent criminal can ultimately be rehabilitated into society. In time of war the Utopians pay mercenaries to fight for them. Often they hire savage Venalians (who are probably meant to signify the Swiss, because they often served in foreign armies): 'For the Utopians don't care how many Venalians they send to their deaths. They say, if only they could wipe the filthy scum off the face of the earth completely, they'd be doing the human race a very good turn.' Fundamentally, they disapprove of war except in self-defence or when helping victims of oppression.

It is vital that we should not impose our own values onto a text that was written almost 500 years ago. In those days there was a massive divide between rich and poor, and it has to be said that More addressed some very complex topics in a constructive manner. A number of the issues discussed are strikingly relevant and significant to present-day readers: for example, euthanasia, hunting, and the questions of whether priests should be permitted to marry and whether women should be ordained. In Utopian society, if a person is suffering from an incurable and excruciating illness, priests or government officials visit the patient to suggest euthanasia. This, unlike suicide, is regarded as an honourable death. The terminally ill person is not obliged to consent, but if he elects to die he can either voluntarily starve or be assisted to die painlessly. The Utopians oppose hunting for sport, and never use animals for sacrifices to God. In their country, male priests are allowed to marry and elderly widows may become priests.

Raphael claims that he is simply describing the Utopian way of life, as opposed to defending it. However, he asserts: 'you won't find a more prosperous country or a more splendid lot of people anywhere on earth.' In Utopia, 'Nobody owns anything, but everyone is rich—for what greater wealth can there be than cheerfulness, peace of mind, and freedom from anxiety?'

At the end of the book, More's objections are stated, but only very briefly. He regards many of the laws and customs as ridiculous, and questions the sense of founding their society on communism minus money. However, he admits that there are many features of Utopia which he would like to see adopted in Europe.

Perhaps it is not surprising that there is an ambiguous 'feel' to the book. More was a strange mixture himself: a man who, according to Erasmus (the great humanist scholar), had 'a passion for jokes'; a family man whose pets at his Chelsea home included a beaver, a fox, a monkey and a weasel; a man who was famed for his scrupulous honesty; yet a man who was responsible for ordering the death penalty—burning alive—for a number of heretics.

More's scholarly talents are much in evidence in his book. His knowledge of the Bible and of Greek and Latin was extensive, and his word-play delighted intellectual readers. Raphael's surname, Hythlodaeus, actually means 'dispenser of nonsense', which is heavily ironic considering that much of what he says is thought-provoking and, at times, appealing. More recognised that serious issues could be couched in humorous terms without losing their significance.

A MESSAGE FOR ALL SEASONS

Does More's *Utopia* hold any significance for us in the new millennium? Often during such periods of transition people are particularly conscious of the need for new beginnings. More's vibrant, and in many ways timeless, text poses compelling questions and offers fascinating solutions.

UTOPIAN FICTION

Other examples of utopian fiction include: *City of the Sun* by Tommaso Campanella (1623), *New Atlantis* by Francis Bacon (1627), *The Commonwealth of Oceana* by James Harrington (1656), *Looking Backward: 2000—1887* by Edward Bellamy (1888), *News from Nowhere* by William Morris (1891)[, and] *Merrie England* by Robert Blatchford (1893).

In the 1890s and early 1900s—at a time when women were seeking greater freedom in their lives—a number of feminist writers envisaged utopian states, notably: Lady Florence Dixie in *Gloriana* (1890), Olive Schreiner in *Dreams* (1897), and Charlotte Perkins Gilman in *Herland* (1915), which describes a successful community of women who have dispensed with men altogether.

Some works are satirical in their treatment of the utopian theme. These include Jonathan Swift's *Gulliver's Travels* (1726) and Samuel Butler's [*Erewhon*], an anagram of 'nowhere' (1872).

The dictionary definition of 'utopia' is: 'an ideally well organised social community, a place where everything is perfect'. 'Utopia' with a capital letter is described as 'a fictional island enjoying perfect government'. However the adjective 'utopian' is defined in two ways: (1) 'of or like Utopia'; (2) 'ideally perfect but unpractical' (my italics).

One of the features of utopian fiction is ambiguity, because the reader wonders whether utopia is a feasible concept and whether it is desirable anyway.

In some texts, the imagined states turn out to be dystopian, or undesirable: for example, *Brave New World* by Aldous Huxley (1932) and *Nineteen Eighty-four* by George Orwell (1949).

Source: Stephanie Forward, "A Taste of Paradise: Thomas More's Utopia," in *English Review*, Vol. 11, No. 4, April 2001, p. 24.

A. R. Heiserman

In the following excerpt, Heiserman discusses Utopia *as a satire.*

... Even Erasmus felt obliged to apologize for Book I of the *Utopia*; and More's admirers have always tended to ignore most of it. But if we are to throw light upon *Utopia*'s meaning, we must show that *all* of Book I reflects a satirical intention. Having learned from the introductory apparatus that *Utopia* is a censuring poetical work not less salutary than humorous, the reader of 1518 would now note the care with which More constructs his *via diversa* and directs it to a set of contemporary vices.

TO MAKE ALL CONNECTIONS PLAIN, AND TO REMOVE ALL DOUBTS THAT *UTOPIA* IS A SATIRE, MORE WRITES A SUMMARY INVECTIVE WHICH ASSERTS THAT THE EVILS ATTACKED DIRECTLY AND INDIRECTLY IN BOOKS I AND II COULD NOT EXIST IN A COMMUNISTIC STATE."

As his over-riding structural device, More used the convention of the "Platonic" dialogue; and as the dramaturgy (scene, event, character) varies in significance in the Platonic dialogues themselves, so it does in works by More's contemporaries. More's apparatus is as complete as its function demands: to establish satiric verisimilitude. He begins with an almost official account of a well-known embassage to Flanders where, after Mass one day, he chances upon his real-life friend Giles, who points out to him "a certayne straunger, a man well stryken in age, with a blake sonne burned face, a longe bearde, and a cloke homely [*neglectim*—the word More used to describe his style] aboute his shoulders; whom . . . I iudged to be a maryner." All this is quite commonplace. Now, through a "realistic" conversation, we learn that this Physician from God and Distributor of Nonsense incarnates the Humanist virtues: he has a wide knowledge of Greek (especially moral philosophy), a good Latin style, and experience in many lands. He is a survivor of Vespucci's famous voyages, has wandered across the equator and circumnavigated the globe via the mysterious southern hemisphere, and knows many anecdotes which More will not relate because tales of "monsters be no newes." By this means More alludes to, and detaches himself from, the second structural device of his *via diversa*—the tall travel-tale. When asked the seminal question of the dialogue—"I wonder greatly whie you gette you not into some kinges courte"—Raphael further characterizes himself. He has long ago abandoned his family and all concern for power—those matters which More claimed had delayed his book; and he looks with contempt on princes and their courts.

This lengthy introduction is justified only because it establishes a realistic setting within which a fictional character can operate. As Hythloday turns to attack the courts, we become aware that he is a version of a conventional satiric persona: the visionary who returns from a journey through strange places to report the unadorned truth about society, the court, the clergy, the times. The dream-vision provided the most common structure for journeys into fabulous spheres. But like Skelton's Colyn Cloute, the traveller could also report abuses without benefit of allegory. Yet, his journey was always extensive, his report always penetrated abuses to reveal their cause, and he himself was frequently so shaken by his discoveries that, like Gulliver, he seemed "straunge" to the world he had left and from which he was now alienated. More has converted this satiric persona into a humanist and sent him around the world to Noplace, using not a dream-vision but a Vespuccian travel-memoir as his structural device; he has also placed him in a Platonic dialogue, and named him Nonsense. Babblers of nonsense also appear in earlier satires (though not usually combined with the strange traveler) as fools, prophets, and crazy birds, yet all speak the truth while appearing to speak nonsense. What they say about the times conceals wisdom under the satiric fiction of folly.

Just as *Utopia*'s structure combines the dialogue with the journey, so Hythloday himself is an amalgam of several satiric conventions. He is both a conventional traveler adroitly brought up to date, and a conventional truth-sayer who works under the name of folly. This unprecedented blend of conventions in one intact satiric fiction provides More with a delightful *via diversa*, and one through which all the "ideas," the intellectual substance of *Utopia*, work. For example, we may say that the new isle of Noplace exists only poetically (like the spheres, the house of fame, the allegorized landscape of dream-visions), and that its institutions are invented (as were the characteristics of Erasmus' Folly) on the satiric principle—not to embody "ideals" of a commonwealth, nor a program for practical reform, but to condemn current follies.

Hythloday begins with one of the most convention-ridden of all satiric objects—the Court. Courtiers motivated by ambition, self-centered princes who "haue more delyte in warlike matters . . . then in the goode feates of peace," policies determined by "flatterie," by "fond and folishe sayinges"—these are stock terms used against courts by John of Salisbury, Langland, Dunbar, Skelton, and now More. But when asked for examples, Hythloday describes not a royal court but that of the good Cardinal Morton. Since Morton's was certainly not a court corrupted by its prince, Hythloday ridicules such hangers-on as the lawyer who defends the hanging of petty thieves, and then goes on—as his literary ancestry equips him to do—to attack evils of the times: the plight of vctcrans, war itself, "idilnes" in the nobility, "bragging" vagrants opposed to the "poore man wyth a spade and a mattocke," mercenaries who are "beastes"—all conventional charges which implied, for earlier satirists, that the times were mad because the commonwealth's institutions violated the harmonious order of nature. To discover that these objects and principles of natural law are conventions is to discover More's meaning, not his meaningless triteness, for his art makes recurrent evil "contemporary" to our own day.

Like earlier satirists, Hythloday now examines the roots of contemporary follies. "Nobel men and . . . yea, certeyn Abbotes" who enclose fields, "husbandmen . . . thrust oute of their owne," high prices, "morreyn," "the vnreasonable couetousnes of a fewe" which leads "to the vtter undoyng" of a realm—these were frequently taken as both signs and causes of current "disordre," "stryf," "hoder-moder." Such violations of natural order always lead to "great wantonnes; importunate superfluytie, and excessive ryote." A whole sub-genre of satire had attacked "strange and prowde newefanglenes in . . . apparrell," which along with "prodigal riotte . . . sumptuous fare . . . brothelhouses . . . tauernes . . . lewde and vnlawfull games," were sure signs of evil times. In attacking these follies, in combining them in such terms, and even in ascribing them to the enclosure movement, More is following satiric tradition. But his structural devices also permit him to move beyond such commonplaces. Since a dialogue-within-a-dialogue can support a little philosophizing, Hythloday may deliver a homily against capital punishment for minor crimes; and since he is reporting his travels, he may use as exemplar the just penal system of the Polylerytes. This Persian race functions for this minor issue as do the Utopians for the whole satire. Their ridiculous name (Much Nonsense), like others More attached to admirable persons and countries, implies that their reasonableness is nonsensical, or non-existent, in the European world.

Thus More combines conventions of structure (dialogue and fabulous journey), persona (dialectitian, nonsense-babbler, traveler), and diction (plain style) to attack conventional objects (folly, courts, the times). But the combination is organic, not mechanical; it vivifies the tradition by moulding commonplaces into a new unity. The court proves an arena in which all the follies of the times may be exposed, for corruption of its powers is both sign and cause of all current corruption. Therefore the dialectical structure of Book I turns on the question, Why doesn't Hythloday go to court? And the answer to this question (the natural fountain of good policy and action is clogged) means that the humanistic wisdom of Hythloday is nonsense in evil times. These unifying principles control all details of Book I. For example, when another convention of anti-court satire, "a certein iesting parasite, or scoffer, which wold seem to cownterfeit the foole," rises to mock the clergy's lack of simple charity, and to suggest that all vagabonds be "bestowed into houses of religion," still another satirical persona, "a certeyne freare," appears who, fearing that such a remedy would impoverish his order, flies into a typical rage, one so sinful that the Cardinal chastizes him. This swift attack on the ancient vices of the friars—their greed, lack of charity, proud anger—shows how More adopts conventions wholesale to compress and enforce his attack on the courts and the times.

Many satirists had attacked courtiers whose jostling for favor was more ridiculous than dangerous; a few had attacked the court as a generator of evil policies, where flattering courtiers become dangerous advisers, and the prince himself appears as both a cause and victim of national corruption. In like fashion, one could attack the evil times in general terms by pointing out how manners, morals, clothing, prices were so topsy-turvy that sheep eat men; or, one could attack the specific causes of such follies—a corrupt clergy, a lazy nobility, a rebellious commons. More's dialogue-structure permits him to do all these things—to attack the court as a collection of fawning fools, the times as a shambles of natural law, princes as dupes and tyrants. To accomplish all this, More takes Hythloday out of Cardinal Morton's court and into a conjectured sitting of the French king's council, where great advisers and their willing prince discuss means of augmenting their powers by conquest and by manipulation of taxes, currency, and the judiciary. Current affairs (French ambitions in Italy, debates on the coinage, etc.) provide fresh targets for these attacks; and More's fiction produces fresh exemplars against which these evils may be measured—the Placeless People (Achoriens), who limit their king to one kingdom; and the Blessed People (Macariens), who limit their monarch's wealth to 1,000 pounds. But behind these attacks and *exempla* lie familiar norms: kingdoms which do not submit to natural limitations create "hurley-burley"; the king who seeks to rise "aboue his power" will "brynge all in hurlie-burles." These are the terms in which earlier satirists explained the causes of evil times. Yet we now become aware that More has been leading us to a point which is quite unprecedented in satire, if not in political philosophy: the chief cause of all these evils is private property.

To determine principal causes, and thereby define problems under discussion, are familiar goals in Platonic dialogues; the discovery of absolute values, in Platonic ethics, should enforce adherence to them in action; and the construction of fables to exemplify absolutes is a commonplace Platonic strategy. More now adapts these procedures to his satiric discourse. Hythloday defines the problems besetting courts and the times by determining their principal cause; this determination produces in him an uncompromising attitude toward the evils described; and he goes on to relate a fable portraying a state from which the principal cause of evil has been removed. This cause, and the satire's fiction, now raise More's work to levels which so delighted his learned contemporaries that they would forget most of Book I and remember only Hythloday's attack on private ownership and his fable of Utopia.

The humanist reformers would have seen in the ideal humanist, Hythloday, their most painful mocker. He points out that "the maners of the worlde now a dayes" (the generic object he had hitherto attacked) make philosophy inoperative; that a compromiser like More (who suggests that good men must work with possibilities, blending virtuous philosophy with vicious powers to produce good results) is "worse than a spye . . . as euell as a traytoure" because he corrupts good principles themselves; and that therefore philosophers

must, as Hythloday says Plato said, "kepe them selfes within their howses." But the humanist reader would have been consoled for More's defeat on this point (which his satire has been devised to justify) by considering that Hythloday's name is Nonsense, that the cause he now derives (private property) is so radical that action against it is impossible, and that his uncompromising values can be embodied only in a Platonic fable about Noplace. That is, the reader would have remembered that this is a satire.

As Hythloday analyzes the cause of corruption in realm and court, he speaks as a satiric persona filled more with indignation than the spirit of philosophical inquiry. His complaints are well known: maldistribution of wealth, multiplicity of futile laws, impoverishment of the many and luxury of the few, private property itself—all leading to and deriving from a conspiratorial oligarchy centered at court. More's objections to Hythloday's radical cure (pure communism) are the standard ones: wealth is produced only by men seeking personal gain; without this incentive and without laws of property, anarchy would result. To these objections we find a satiric, not an argumentative answer: Hythloday merely asserts that communism can work, and for proof he points to Noplace. . . .

Like earlier satires, *Utopia* mixes devices of structure, diction, and personae to build a *via diversa* by which it may attack a syndrome of objects. But the fable of Noplace which now emerges is so unconventional that it has always dominated the whole work; it becomes so "realistic" that one tends to forget its function in the satire.

In describing More's "pleasure in declamations," which made him choose "some disputable subject, as involving a keener exercise of mind," Erasmus remarks that he had in his youth written a dialogue "in which he carried the defense of Plato's commonwealth even to the matter of wives." This pleasure, hints Erasmus, led him to compose *Utopia*, Book II of which he wrote "at his leisure, and afterwards, when he found it was required, added the first off hand." Now, why was Book I "required"? We may answer that without it *Utopia* would have remained a mystery without point. The satirist must on the one hand invent a *via diversa*, else he will write merely another "pompous argument"; on the other hand he must permit his readers to see through his fiction, else he will produce nothing but a bit of "dissolute poeticizing." In attempting to strike this satiric mean, satirists frequently bewilder their audiences; the *via diversa* of Book II is so beguiling that More perhaps saw the necessity of putting it into the explicit satiric context of Book I. But the fact that he did not merely tack this "off-hand" material onto his fable implies that the position of Book II has significance. Does this position mean that the fable of Utopia functions as an *exemplum* in the Platonic sense, and that the Utopian commonwealth therefore embodies normative ideals? Is it not like Bembo's ecstatic definition of love at the conclusion of *The Courtier*, where an ideal love is both described and portrayed by the speaker? After all, More himself termed *Utopia* "my Republic"; his readers frequently compared it with Plato's work; Hythloday seems an ardent Platonist. All this has raised a crucial question for modern critics of the *Utopia*: if Utopia—with its communism, euthanasia, Mithraworship, divorce, etc.—is, as Busleyden said, "an ideal commonwealth, a pattern and finished model of conduct," then its author was really an incipient Marxist, or his opinions changed with his career, or much of this work is merely a *jeu d'esprit*. All of More's critics have wrestled with these alternatives; we hope to show that More's invention was guided by the satiric principle, that Book II as a whole derives from this principle, and that the "meaning" of all its ideas is controlled by satiric intentions....

But even though Utopia's is not an "ideal commonwealth" but one invented to serve a satiric function, in what sense could it be a "model of conduct"? Again, the *Republic* hints at an answer. The question of whether the ideal state could ever exist on earth hovers above its construction in Books II through IX. At some points the state is merely a formula with which one can examine existent souls and states; at other stages in the argument, Socrates asserts that a philosopher king with absolute power could create it. But by the end of Book IX Socrates agrees that the ideal state "exists in idea only.... In heaven... there is laid up a pattern of it, methinks, which he who desires may behold, and beholding, may set his own house in order. But whether such an one exists, or ever will exist in fact, is no matter; for he will live after the manner of that city, having nothing to do with any other." This is Hythloday's stance: having discovered the causes of contemporary disorder (that is, visited Utopia), he has "learned" that

philosophers must "kepe them selfes within their howses; beynge content that they be saffe them selfes, seynge they can not remedy the follye of the people" (p. 104). While Utopia is not an ideal state, it provides a model for *private* conduct, conduct conditioned by the realization that "the mother of all mischiefe, pride, doth withstonde and let" the removal of the cause of political evil, and pride "is so depely roted in mens brestes, that she can not be plucked out."

The first satiric principle we encounter is that which determines the invention of a "realistic" fiction. More begins Chapter i by drawing a physical and political map of Utopia, using not the *Republic* but the *Critias* as a model. Unlike the ideal state, Atlantis in the *Critias* has a geographical location; and since More's fiction also demanded that he place Noplace and describe it physically, he does so with a verisimilitude comparable with Plato's. Poseidon and his son, King Atlas (Atlantis), brought civilization to Plato's rocky-coasted island as King Utopus brought civilization to rocky-coasted Utopia. Poseidon converted his island into three concentric circles of land separated by channels and placed his chief city on the central island, to which King Atlas constructed a system of ditches and bridges eleven stades long (*Critias*, pp. 113–116). King Utopus cut his island from the mainland by means of a ditch, placed his chief city in the island's center, and permitted access to the interior through a channel eleven miles wide (Lupton, pp. 116–119). More's invention of a double set of names for offices, places, and personages, and his mention of Egyptian visitors to Utopia, perhaps reflects Plato's invention of double names, which are Solon's translations of Egyptian versions of Atlantean names (*Critias*, 114; *Timaeus*, 22–25); and as Plato begins with physical geography, then describes "allottments" (60,000 persons per allotment), so More begins with physical geography, then divides his community into fifty-four "shires" (whose cities each contain 6,000 families). More's care in recording distances, quantities, etc., is much like that of Plato, and the figures themselves are as absurd. Utopia's 200 mile diameter hardly fits with the 500 mile circumference of what is almost a circular island. Its fifty-four cities may derive from the perfect political number, 5,040, which forms the basis of order in the Magnesian colony prescribed in the *Laws*; but More could have seen that fifty-four shire cities each at least twenty-four miles distant from all others would mean that each shire contained a minimum of 645 square miles, and that they therefore could not have fit into an island of 31,000 square miles. All this shows not that More deliberately modelled Utopia on Atlantis, enemy of Athens, or on such parodies as Lucian's *True History*, but that he used Plato's descriptive techniques to reestablish the satiric verisimilitude of his work.

This *via diversa* makes it unnecessary that he attack explicitly ambition, luxury, famine, drudgery; he need only describe how Utopians work and live. The details in Chapter i which neither establish satiric verisimilitude, nor resonate obviously against satiric objects, reveal that all things are valued for their use in a well-ordered society, and that the rule of reason forbids timocratic delusions of honor: the Utopians unblushingly beguile invaders onto the rocks by changing channel markers. The fiction also permits jesting inversions, a full working out of the consequences of communism, and fresh attacks on old satiric objects. Other satirists, for example, had inveighed against the stenches and inconveniences of city life. In Chapter ii More merely describes those features of Amaurote (Dimville, or Fogtown) which contrast with the absurdities of cities ruled by irrational principles. It is the very conventionality of such objects as the law's delay, the corruption of judicial procedures, the helplessness of commoners before the bar, the multiplicity of laws framed to preserve injustices, which gives a brief remark on the quickness of Utopian judicial procedures such force. Readers could at once recognize his object, and perhaps appreciate how little space he need devote to it. In Book I More in effect had laid out this satiric tradition in plain terms lest anyone mistake his intentions in Book II. Here he can proceed quickly, by *via diversa*, relying on his fiction and his conventions. All this suggests that it would prove futile to attempt to show that Utopian institutions make constant or consistent reference to new, specific abuses in Tudor England. They refer to evils prevalent in all ages; and especially to More's generic object—the institution of private property which remains with us. As More's art directs his attacks at his own time, it also directs them to our own. In this way, great satire, while completely contemporary, survives its time.

The descriptions of family life in Chapter v do not seem at all satiric; but these inventions may also be explained by the logic of More's fiction and by the objects of his attack. For example, if his fiction demands that he find a way of disposing of the surplus population a state like Utopia would produce, he lets the Utopians conquer unoccupied portions of neighboring realms, then remarks that the "law of nature" makes such invasions "the most iust cause of warre," thus condemning both the waste of natural resources and the trivial causes of European wars. The natural law is also visible in the Utopians' well-ordered family life, where the older rule and teach while the younger learn and obey, where pleasure is moderate, where plenty eliminates greed, where hospitals are efficient and not lethal, and where butchering is done outside the city limits. When the verisimilitude drives him to explain who would do the ugly work of butchering, it creates a group of bondsmen which also serves a satiric function; for bondsmen contribute to the commonwealth rather than adorn gibbets. We need not say that More "approved" of bondage or conquest, but we can say that all his inventions serve the purposes of his satire.

This satiric principle now helps us solve many of the problems which have long attracted attention. Why should the future chancellor and saint make his "ideal" people combine stoicism with Epicureanism? The common answers—that these good pagans had reached the highest point achievable by reason unaided by revelation, and that even paganism is more virtuous than corrupt European Christianity—obscures the full significance of this discussion. In fact, Hythloday's relatively brief description of their lofty hedonism sets up attacks on a variety of satiric objects: men who mistake smaller for greater ends, luxurious clothing, a nobility lusting for the appurtenances of power, love of gold and jewels, dicers, hunters, health addicts on the one hand and fanatic ascetics on the other. We need not wonder whether More approved of this hedonism; the meaning of these ideas derives from their satiric functions.

Similar problems rise in Chapter vii. Why should a "pattern" state condone euthanasia as well as bondage? Again, such institutions are invented to serve satiric, not prescriptive, functions. When Hythloday divides bondsmen into two groups—aliens who choose Utopian bondage in preference to execution or drudgery at home, and Utopians who commit crimes—he is attacking familiar objects: the harshness of contemporary life, and the irrational disparity between punishment and crime in Europe.

When he remarks that incurably ill Utopians may choose to die, he does so in order to comment that in Utopia (though not in Europe) no sick man dies by negligence or against his will, thus using euthanasia to make his satiric point. Utopian laws concerning courtship, marriage, fornication, adultery, and divorce are also invented for satiric purposes. More's descriptions either preserve satiric verisimilitude (as his giving ages for marriage) or attack contemporary evils by turning them upside-down. Satiric inversions become more explicit in the chapter's remaining pages. When Hythloday attacks the making and breaking of treaties, he employs *ironia* to make his method of satiric inversion plain while preserving its character. Since Europeans are Christians, he says, they of course always keep faith with their treaties; but since the neighbors of Utopia do *not* keep faith, the Utopians make no treaties, place no faith in words, believe that taking life is wrong even without treaties to forbid it, and contend that the fellowship of nature is a strong enough league. This irony makes for a double inversion, enriching the method employed throughout this chapter.

Another kind of verbal device opens the chapter on Utopian methods of war-making which has also puzzled More's admirers. Was he jesting or prescribing when he described the Machiavellian deceits of his Utopians? Neither; he was attacking an object—war caused and waged by bestial irrationality. The pun which introduces his chapter reveals this object by satiric indirection. "*Bellum utpote rem plane beluinam*"—since war (*bellum*) is beastly (*bellua*), the Utopians detest it (p. 243). But what is it in *bellum* that makes it *bellua*? Obviously, the absence of "the myghte and pusyannce of wytte" and the dependence on irrational bloodshed, glory, and "boddelye strengthe." Therefore the Utopians fight only just wars (wars for rational goals), they fight with specifically human means— "wytte and reason," and their peace-making is never tarnished by irrational vengeance. In short, Utopian warfare removes the *bellua* from *bellum*, as the Utopian constitution removes ownership from the state.

In like fashion, More constructs Utopian religion to attack various European abuses. The chief complaint made against the clergy, religious and hierarchy in medieval satires was the "disordre" resulting from a proud prelacy, from a clergy in secular power, from simony and luxury in all. In a well ordered commonwealth, the church serves a natural function of teaching and preaching; in a disordered state the church neglects this office and assumes others. Utopian religion functions as part of a whole state by enforcing consensus on but a few reasonable dogmas (God exists and rewards man's virtue in a future life), and by tolerating diversity of opinion in many accidentals. King Utopus' principles—that internal order is essential, that the truth will out, and that "contention" harms religion by raising up superstitions—are used to oppose conventional satiric objects of disorder and superstition, not to recommend ways of curing them. For example, unlike European religious orders, which generations of satirists had attacked as collections of beggars, meddlers, and sinners, those in Utopia work at the hardest jobs, mind their own business, and are composed of the most virtuous men. The virtues ascribed to Utopian priests oppose precisely the traditional vices of the European clergy. The concluding section on holy days and divine services also resonates against conventional satiric objects and preserves the fiction which permits attack by indirection.

By now it might seem that More's fiction has run away with his satire. What does the abuse of church music, for example, have to do with private property? To make all connections plain, and to remove all doubts that *Utopia* is a satire, More writes a summary invective which asserts that the evils attacked directly and indirectly in Books I and II could not exist in a communistic state. We know that More had constructed Utopia to banish them; Hythloday, however, contends that they could not exist because Utopia is a true commonwealth, not a "pryuate wealthe" disguised under another name. Wealth controlled by usurious bankers and rich idlers; plowmen and laborers whose lives are bestial and graves evil; a topsy-turvy "justice" which rewards idle flatterers and punishes wealth-producers—on he goes, striking at the root-cause—money in private control, that "certein conspiracy of riche men"—which had been the chief principle of his invention. This cause is not a conventional satiric object; even the lollard satirists had rested content with abstractions like Pride and Covetousness. But More's terms even now remain conventional: "striffe" and "dissention" in the commonwealth "now a dayes" remain the generic evil which contains all the evils of court, clergy, policy, civic life he has managed to attack. And since Pride supports the rule of money, Hythloday leaves us without hope; for Pride "is so depely roted in mens' breastes, that she can not be plucked out." No wonder More concludes that "many thinges be in the vtopian weal publique, which in our cities I may rather wisshe for then hoope after." . . .

Source: A. R. Heiserman, "Satire in the *Utopia*," in *PMLA*, Vol. 78, No. 3, June 1963, pp. 163–74.

SOURCES

Ames, Russell, "Late Feudalism in England and Europe," and "The Middle Class Man," in *Citizen Thomas More and His* Utopia, Princeton University Press, 1949, pp. 22–35, 74–80.

Bender, Daniel, "Thomas More," in *Dictionary of Literary Biography*, Vol. 281, *British Rhetoricians and Logicians, 1500–1660, Second Series*, Thomson Gale, 2003, pp. 201–14.

British Office for National Statistics, "Census 2001—Ethnicity and Religion in England and Wales," http://www.statistics.gov.uk/census2001/profiles/commentaries/ethnicity.asp#religion (accessed on June 11, 2008).

Bruce, Susan, Introduction to *Three Early Modern Utopias*, edited by Susan Bruce, Oxford University Press, 1999, pp. ix–xlii.

Collins, J. Churton, Introduction to *Sir Thomas More's* Utopia, edited by J. Churton Collins, Clarendon Press, 1904, pp. vii–lii.

Gledhill, Ruth, "Catholics Set to Pass Anglicans as Leading UK Church," in *Times Online*, February 15, 2007, http://www.timesonline.co.uk/tol/news/article1386939.ece (accessed on June 11, 2008).

Hexter, J. H., "The Anatomy of a Printed Book," in *More's* Utopia, Princeton University Press, 1952, pp. 11–30.

Jones, Judith P., and Sherianne Sellars Seibel, "Thomas More's Feminism: To Reform or Re-Form," in *Quincentennial Essays on St. Thomas More*, edited by Michael J. Moore, Albion, 1978, pp. 67–77.

McCutcheon, Elizabeth, "Thomas More," in *Dictionary of Literary Biography*, Vol. 136, *Sixteenth-Century British Nondramatic Writers, Second Series*, edited by David A. Richardson, Gale Research, 1994, pp. 235–54.

Miller, Clarence H., Introduction to *Utopia*, by Thomas More, translated by Clarence H. Miller, Yale University Press, 2001.

More, Thomas, *Utopia*, translated by Clarence H. Miller, Yale University Press, 2001.

Surtz, Edward L., "Interpretations of *Utopia*," in *The Praise of Wisdom: A Commentary on the Religious and Moral Problems and Backgrounds of St. Thomas More's* Utopia, Loyola University Press, 1957, pp. 1–20.

White, Thomas I., "*Festivitas, Utilitas, et Opes:* The Concluding Irony and Philosophical Purpose of Thomas More's *Utopia*," in *Quincentennial Essays on St. Thomas More*, edited by Michael J. Moore, Albion, 1978, pp. 135–50.

FURTHER READING

Andrews, Charles M., *Ideal Empires and Republics: Rousseau's* Social Contract, *More's* Utopia, *Bacon's* New Atlantis and *Campanella's* City of the Sun, Kessinger Publishing, 2007.

> In this collection of several of the best-known works of Utopian literature, the editor, in his introduction, offers an overview of Utopian writing. Andrews additionally explores the social conditions that typically inspire such works. The collection, along with Andrews's commentary, provides an introduction to Utopian literature as a genre.

Haigh, Christopher, *English Reformations: Religion, Politics, and Society under the Tudors*, Oxford University Press, 1993.

> Haigh examines a variety of details pertaining to sixteenth-century English society, providing a broad overview of the sociopolitical and religious climates as well as studying the details of the daily life and religious practices of English citizens.

Kinney, Arthur F., *Rhetoric and Poetic in Thomas More's* Utopia, Undena Publications, 1979.

> In this work, Kinney explores the rhetoric and poetic devices More utilizes in *Utopia* and to what effect such devices are employed.

Patriquin, Larry, *Agrarian Capitalism and Poor Relief in England, 1500–1860: Rethinking the Origins of the Welfare State*, Palgrave Macmillan, 2007.

> Patriquin studies the rise of agricultural capitalism in England in the 1500s and assesses the ways in which this early form of capitalism helped shape the class system in England. The author goes on to trace the effects of capitalism on the poor classes.

Year of Impossible Goodbyes

SOOK NYUL CHOI

1991

Sook Nyul Choi's *Year of Impossible Goodbyes* is an autobiographical novel about the author's escape from North Korea. Winner of the 1992 Judy Lopez Memorial Award, *Year of Impossible Goodbyes* is narrated by the nine-year-old Sookan, who is of Korean heritage. For as long as Sookan can remember, the Japanese invaders have occupied her country and have attempted to strip away all aspects of Korean culture. Sookan's father and older brothers have not had contact with Sookan; her youngest brother, Inchun; and her mother in several years. In order to survive, Sookan's mother has been forced to run a sock factory in a building on her property. The Japanese soldiers demand a certain production quota each day. If Sookan's mother does not meet it, her food rations, which are already skimpy, are cut back even further.

In time, a series of dramatic events changes Sookan's life forever. Her grandfather dies, which causes her mother to fall into a debilitating depression. Everyone's spirits rise when World War II ends, but more tragedy lies ahead. *Year of Impossible Goodbyes*, selected by the American Library Association as a notable book in 1992, provides an insider's glimpse of North Korea, a country that has since become one of the world's most secretive societies.

AUTHOR BIOGRAPHY

Sook Nyul Choi was born in 1937 in Pyongyang in what is now North Korea. Like the young character in her novel, Choi fled the hardships of the Communist takeover of North Korea by escaping to South Korea when she was a young girl. When Choi was twenty-one, she emigrated to the United States, where she then attended Manhattan College, in New York. After college, she worked for a brief time for her husband, a Korean businessman. When her husband died, Choi became a teacher, working in New York's public schools. After twenty years of teaching Choi retired and devoted her time to her writing.

Since all of Choi's novels are based on her personal experience, her books can be read as a journey through her life. *Year of Impossible Goodbyes* was Choi's first novel, published in 1991. The story covers her incredible escape to South Korea. In Choi's second novel, *Echoes of the White Giraffe* (1993), the protagonist, Sookan, is a teenager. The story is set in South Korea and portrays the invasion by North Korea, as supported by Russia and China, into the lower portion of the Korean Peninsula. Once again, Sookan and her family are forced on the run. *Gathering of Pearls* (1994) is the last of Choi's trilogy and follows Sookan as she travels to the United States to go to college. The novel portrays the challenges that Sookan must face in learning and adjusting to a culture completely different from her own.

After this trilogy, Choi wrote *Halmoni and the Picnic* (1993) and *Yunmi and Halmoni's Trip* (1997), two children's picture books. Also in 1997, she published *The Best Older Sister*, an easy reader for elementary-school students. Choi has two daughters, Kathleen and Audrey. She lives in Massachusetts, where she spends her time writing and giving lectures on her books.

PLOT SUMMARY

Chapters 1–3

Choi's story begins in Pyongyang, Korea (now the capital of North Korea). Though the day is warmed by spring, the people in the story feel a sense of oppressiveness all around them, as if they are still in the throes of a harsh winter. Their country is under the control of the Japanese, who are bent on stripping away all sense of Korean culture. People are forced to work hard for the Japanese army, which is fighting to bring down the armed forces of the United States.

Sookan, the nine-year-old girl who narrates the story, lives with her mother; her youngest brother, Inchun; her grandfather; and her Aunt Tiger. Sookan's father has escaped to Manchuria, where he is assisting an underground Korean liberation group. Sookan's three older brothers have been sent to Japanese labor camps; her sister Theresa, who is a teen, has been sent to a nunnery.

Sookan's family runs a sock factory in a building attached to their house. With the help of several young women who walk to Pyongyang from the countryside, they make socks for the Japanese soldiers. Every day Captain Narita comes to the factory to inspect their work. Sookan and her mother do all they can to please him. Captain Narita is in control of how much food Sookan's family receives.

The girls who work in the sock factory include Haiwon and Okja. Haiwon often comes to work early so that she can chat with Sookan, Mother, and Aunt Tiger. Okja comes early, too, but she is very quiet, while Haiwon makes everyone laugh with her stories. Kisa is the only man in the factory. He keeps the sewing machines in good condition.

There is an old pine tree in Sookan's yard. There had once been a garden underneath it, but the Japanese soldiers stomped the flowers down. Keeping a garden was a waste of time, they said. But Grandfather loves the tree. It represents freedom to him. When Captain Nirata comes to the house one day, he discovers the women enjoying a small celebration of Haiwon's birthday. Because they should have been working, the captain retaliates by having his men chop down the tree. This sickens Grandfather, and he takes to his bed, swearing he will never go outside again. Eventually Grandfather dies.

Chapters 4–6

Sookan misses her grandfather. He used to secretly teach her how to make the Korean characters that corresponded to their language. Speaking Korean was forbidden, so this act was one of rebellion. Sookan's mother also suffers, falling into a depressive state that makes her incommunicable with the remaining members of the family. Because she is unable to oversee the production of the socks, the sock girls do not meet their quotas. Captain Narita decides the girls would be worth more to the soldiers if he sent them all to the battlefront. There they could give the soldiers pleasure, Captain Narita tells everyone. A couple of days later a big truck arrives at the gate, and the Japanese soldiers force the girls to climb into the back. They are all taken away. Sookan never sees them again.

Later on, Sookan is forced to attend Japanese school. Previously, because Sookan was of a small build, her mother had convinced the Japanese authorities that Sookan was still too young. But now the Japanese insist that Sookan attend. Sookan's mother instructs her never to say one word in Korean or the Japanese will punish her.

Sookan's teacher turns out to be Captain Narita's wife. She is as cold-hearted as her husband and shows no compassion for Sookan on her first day. Sookan meets a girl her age named Unhi. Unhi helps Sookan by telling her the rules so that she will not get in trouble. The school is basically a propaganda tool, filling the children's heads with Japanese ideology. The students are brainwashed, in essence, forced to repeat slogans that purport Japanese superiority.

After the propaganda session, the boys are forced to fill sandbags and to pile up rocks to fortify the school should the U.S. forces attack. The girls break panes of glass and sharpen the edges to be used as weapons. The boys also sharpen sticks for the same purpose.

On the second day of school, one of the older boys protests the long hours that the students are made to work in the hot sun. The other students are mortified by the boy's outburst and fearful of what the teachers and administrators will do. But Sookan's reaction is to applaud the boy. It was a natural response, since she has similar thoughts and has not yet been so trained to think otherwise. She is promptly expelled from school.

On August 15, 1945, Kisa comes home to tell Sookan's family that the war is over. This is the end of World War II. He warns them, though, not to go out into the streets just yet. Although the Japanese are leaving, they are very angry. They have been looting and killing on their way out. One of the first things that Sookan and her young brother do is plant some flower seeds. They have been waiting so long to have pretty flowers in their yard. Then they all don their colorful Korean clothes, discarding the drab gray clothing they have been forced to wear. They are all amazed when they finally go out in the streets and hear everyone speaking in their native language. Their freedom does not last long, however. Shortly after the Japanese soldiers leave, Russian soldiers descend on their town.

Chapters 7–9

Many Korean people quickly become agents of Russian Communist propaganda. Where once the people had to pledge their allegiance to Japan, they now find they have to accept the principles of the Communist Party. Sookan keeps looking for her father and three older brothers, but no one has seen them.

As she had been forced to attend Japanese school, now Sookan is forced to attend a Communist Party school, where again she has to repeat slogans and watch propaganda movies. Comrade Kim, a Korean neighbor, becomes completely immersed in the Communist movement and insists that Sookan and her family attend nightly political rallies. She introduces Sookan to Comrade Natasha, a Russian woman who appeals to Sookan because she speaks Korean. After feeding the townspeople and teaching them new songs, the Communist leaders truck Sookan's family into the countryside. Sookan and her young brother are taken to a factory that they are told to clean. Sookan's mother and Aunt Tiger are dropped off at a mine field, which they must clear.

Soon the regimental rule of the Communists feels similar to the hardships under the Japanese. The people are told what to wear, and every minute of their day is programmed with hard labor. Kisa, the man who used to keep the sewing machines in working order, goes to work for the party in a different way. He recruits new party members. In this way, he is able to distinguish those who are so-called Town Reds, meaning true believers, from those who are pretending to be interested while planning their escape to the south. Kisa learns how to help Koreans get across the border.

One day, Kisa hears from Sookan's father, who has found his three older sons and has taken them to the south. He sends some jewels to Kisa to pay for the safe journey of the rest of his family. Kisa then makes arrangements with a man reputed to have successfully gotten many Koreans across the border. The man will show up at Sookan's home one day, and Sookan, her mother, and her brother must be ready to leave immediately.

Aunt Tiger is staying behind because she is still waiting for news from her husband, who had been a war prisoner.

When the man who will be their guide appears, he tells the children that they must stick close to him and pretend not to know their mother. He will be able to take them across the border because he is a friend of the Russian soldiers. The soldiers will not question the children, but they might question their mother. If the soldiers stop their mother, the children must not look back or call out to her. Even though the soldiers might detain their mother, he is sure they will let her go after a few hours.

Things go well until they all reach the border crossing. The man and the children pass through, but indeed, Sookan's mother is held back. Sookan and Inchun cannot help but look back and cry, but the man tells them they must move on. They walk a long distance and finally come to an inn. The man tells the children to go inside and rest; he will be back. Once they are inside, an old woman puts them to bed. But in the morning she tells them that their guide is a fraud and they must leave immediately or everyone will get in trouble.

In the days that follow, Sookan and Inchun hang around a railroad station near the North Korean border. They beg for food and keep looking for their mother. A railroad station man feels sorry for them and helps them to once again escape. The children sneak across the border into South Korea at a place where a Red Cross station has been set up to meet them and others who dare the crossing.

The children are fed and rested, then helped to find their father. The family is finally united, except for the mother. But one day, even the mother appears. She had been forced to work as a housemaid for a Russian officer, but she was able to escape.

Epilogue

The story is not yet over. Another tragedy will occur in 1950, when the North Korean armies invade South Korea in an attempt to unite the Korean Peninsula once again, this time under Communist rule. In the midst of the chaos, even Theresa, with her fellow nuns, is able to leave North Korea, and they seek shelter with Sookan's family. Theresa tells them that Kisa and Aunt Tiger were convicted of being traitors and were shot. At the end of the story, Sookan is thinking about the sock girls and her friends, wondering if they are still alive.

CHARACTERS

Father Carroll

Father Carroll does not appear in person in this story. He is the Catholic priest to whom Mother had often turned in times of trouble. Father Carroll was accused by the Japanese occupiers of working for the rebellious underground movement fighting for Korean liberation and was expelled from the country.

Father

Sookan's father never makes an appearance in person in this story. Readers are told that he is part of a rebel force working for Korea's freedom from an outpost in Manchuria. At one time, the whole family lived in Manchuria, but there are hints that once World War II began, only Sookan's father remained there. In the chaos at the end of the war, when Russia helps the Korean soldiers to rid the country of the Japanese, Sookan's father rescues his oldest sons from Japanese labor camps and takes them to South Korea. He later meets in secret with Kisa, gives Kisa money to help his wife escape, and tells Kisa where he and his sons are staying in the south.

Grandfather

Sookan's grandfather, though he does very little in this story, is a major character, as he is so in Sookan's mind. He acts as the spiritual head of the family. He is also Sookan's teacher and a keeper of the Korean traditions. It is through her grandfather that Sookan learns to re-create the Korean characters used to write script. Also, her grandfather is the one who demands that Sookan's mother bring out old photographs and explain their family history to Sookan and her brother Inchun.

Grandfather has suffered through a long history of Japanese occupation, including years of torture in their labor camps. He clings onto whatever pleasant memories he has managed to preserve. He looks for peace wherever he can find it, while the occupation soldiers try to strip it all away. Grandfather is devastated when the Japanese cut down one of the last symbols for him of pleasure on earth—the tall pine tree outside his house. He has lost friends and family; his original house was burned down; his wife is dead; and his son-in-law and older grandsons are missing. Though he has affection for his youngest grandchildren, when the tree is destroyed, Grandfather appears to lose his will to live. His spirit is broken, and shortly afterward, he dies. Symbolically, Grandfather might stand for the Korean culture, which is being slowly destroyed in the memories of the people who remain in North Korea.

The Guide

The guide is the man whom Kisa trusts to take Sookan's family across the border to South Korea. He turns out to be a fraud.

Haiwon

Haiwon is one of the girls who works in the sock factory. On her birthday, Mother plans a surprise party for Haiwon. It is this party that irritates Captain Narita, leading him to cut down the tree.

Hanchun

Hanchun is Sookan's oldest brother. He spends most of the story in a Japanese labor camp.

Hyunchun

Hyunchun is the third oldest of Sookan's brothers. Like Hanchun, Hyunchun does not appear in this story. He is rescued by his father.

Inchun

Inchun is the youngest child in the family. He is precocious. Although he is included in some of the action of the story, his role is overshadowed by that of his older sister.

Jaechun

Jaechun is the second-oldest brother. While in a Japanese labor camp, Jaechun suffers from tuberculosis and dysentery.

Mrs. Kim

Mrs. Kim is a neighbor of Sookan's family. Nothing is heard about her until the Russians arrive in the town, when Mrs. Kim becomes one of the most vocal of the Koreans in turning toward the views of the Communists. Aunt Tiger plays up to Mrs. Kim by pretending to be interested in joining her in recruiting new members of the party. Aunt Tiger does this so that Mrs. Kim does not become suspicious of Sookan's family's departure when they attempt to escape.

Kisa

Kisa is the only man who works in the sock factory. He is a pleasant man who is very gentle with the children, Sookan and Inchun. Kisa becomes involved in the Communist Party in order to gain connections to help fellow Koreans escape to the south. After Sookan's father gives Kisa a bag filled with jewels, he tells her mother to use the jewels to pay for her family's escape. Kisa, like Aunt Tiger, is shot for betraying the Communist Party.

Mother

Sookan's mother is the backbone of Sookan's family. She constantly repeats the same phrase, telling everyone around her that the war will soon be over. She prays and consistently believes that her god and her religion will save her family. However, she falls apart at her father's death. Grandfather had been a source of strength for her. Her depression following his death leads to physical ailments that Sookan is afraid may lead to her death as well.

When Sookan's mother is held captive by the Russian soldiers at the border between North and South Korea, her presence slips from the story and never fully returns to the same extent that it held in the first two-thirds of the story. Her greatest role in the novel is keeping her family safe while they are living in North Korea; when they make their escape, she falls into the background.

Captain Narita

Captain Narita is an officer in the Japanese army. He is the leader of the troops who organize and maintain the work at the sock factory. He represents everything that is unlikable about the Japanese occupiers. He is strict, cold hearted, and without mercy, from Sookan's point of view. Narita orders that the pine tree be cut down, knowing that the tree is considered a special possession for Sookan's family.

Narita Sensei

Narita Sensei is Captain Narita's wife and Sookan's teacher at the Japanese school. Narita Sensei was also Sookan's older brothers' teacher. So when Sookan is on her way to school, she already knows about Narita Sensei's reputation for being severely strict. She is very hard on Sookan on Sookan's first day at school. When Sookan responds inappropriately to a young boy who talks back to his teacher, Narita Sensei makes sure that Sookan is dismissed from school.

Sookan

Sookan is the narrator of the novel. She is nine years old, going on ten. Sookan appears wiser than most of her peers. She has a better sense of what is going on around her. She does not give in to the propaganda that either the Japanese occupiers or the Russian Communists try to make her believe. She has a sense of what is right for her and her family. She faces Russian soldiers, for instance, and demands that they release her mother when her mother is captured at the border. She also has an intuitive understanding of her grandfather's spirituality, though she does not fully comprehend it. She feels the peace her grandfather experiences when he meditates. Then when she is troubled, she attempts to find such peace for herself.

Sookan is a survivor. She figures out ways to find food for herself and her youngest brother when they are separated from their mother and abandoned by the guide who cheats them. When she has no experience or adult to guide her, she relies on her own sense of compassion, such as when she helps a woman care for her baby and is then rewarded. She is also rebellious. She and her school friend dull the shards of glass when they are told to sharpen them for use as weapons to fight the U.S. soldiers.

Theresa

Theresa is Sookan's oldest sibling. There are many years between Sookan and Theresa, and therefore Sookan knows very little about her. Theresa lives with Catholic nuns in a nunnery a distance from Pyongyang. Theresa never appears in the story. However, when Theresa escapes from North Korea in the epilogue, she brings the news that Kisa and Aunt Tiger have been killed.

Aunt Tiger

Given her name because she loves to tell folktales about a talking tiger, Sookan's aunt lives with the family. Aunt Tiger talks a lot, often voicing her worries about surviving the hardships placed on the family by the Japanese soldiers. However, when the Russians appear, Aunt Tiger seems to come to life. She becomes involved in the Communist Party so that she can gain favors for the rest of the family. She also does not give up on her hopes that her husband will one day be released from the Japanese prisons and come home. When the rest of the family attempts their escape, Aunt Tiger stays behind. She says she decides to do so because she wants to be there when her husband returns, but she also knows that if she is missed by the Communists, the soldiers will come looking for her. She stays in Pyongyang to help protect Mother and the children as they attempt their escape. Later, Sookan learns that Aunt Tiger was put to death. Her body was displayed in a public square as a reminder of what might happen to others if they, too, were to lie to the Communist leaders.

Unhi

Sookan meets Unhi when she goes to the Japanese school. Unhi helps Sookan adjust to the rules of the school, protecting Sookan so she does not get into trouble. While out in the school yard where the girls are supposed to be sharpening shards of glass, Unhi and Sookan come up with their own form of sabotage by smoothing the edges of the glass so that they will not harm the U.S. soldiers.

THEMES

Loss of Culture

Throughout most of Choi's novel *Year of Impossible Goodbyes*, the author laments Korea's loss of culture. As the story begins, all elements of the characters' lives are monitored to make sure that all signs of Korean culture have been eradicated. The Japanese enforcers prohibit speaking of the Korean language. Everyone must wear drab clothing, not the colorful prints that the Korean people prefer. Korean names are replaced with Japanese translations. Even Korean gods and the associated religions have been banned.

Although in Sookan's house Korean is spoken and the family has managed to stow away a few Korean mementos, they must hang thick blankets on the windows to ensure that they are not seen or heard when they share elements of their culture, even in private. Unfortunately, the Japanese want more than just the land and its resources. They want the minds, hearts, and souls of the Korean people; they want the Koreans, in other words, to become just like them.

The first real sign of freedom for Sookan is the moment when she walks down a public street and hears her Korean language being spoken out in the open. People take off the gray garments that they have been forced to wear and unpack

TOPICS FOR FURTHER STUDY

- Research traditional Korean dress. Find pictures of what men, women, and children wore in the eighteenth and nineteenth centuries. Then find pictures of Koreans during the Japanese occupation and in North Korea today. Share your research with the class in a multimedia presentation.

- Read *So Far from the Bamboo Grove* (1994), by Yoko Kawashima Watkins, an autobiographical novel about Korea told from the point of view of a young Japanese girl. Imagine, after reading this novel, what a conversation between the protagonist of Watkins's novel and Sookan, the narrator of Choi's novel, might be like if they ever met. Write a dialogue between the two characters and ask a classmate to take one of the parts. Then perform the dialogue in front of your class.

- Compare the economic statuses of North and South Korea. How do the two countries make money? What are their major industries? How successful is each? You may want to consult the U.S. State Department's Web site for information. Write a paper summarizing your findings.

- The Korean War has been called one of the bloodiest wars in modern history. Who fought in this war? How long did it last? What are the statistics regarding the dead and the wounded? How do these figures compare to the wars in which the United States has recently fought in Vietnam and Iraq? Research and present these facts in graph form and show the graphs to your class, explaining the data you have discovered.

---

their Korean clothes. The deprivation of their culture had imprisoned their minds and their senses of identity.

With the arrival of the Russians, parts of the Korean culture are preserved. The Russians allow the people to speak in their native tongue, and even a few of the Russians speak Korean, to the amazement of some. However, the Korean clothes must be once again put away, as the Koreans are forced to wear yet another uniform. This new uniform reminds the people that they all now belong to the Communist Party.

Enslavement

Young and old are enslaved in this story. The enslavement comes in both physical and psychological forms. Enslavement is used by both the Japanese and the Russian Communist Party in order to exert control over the Korean population.

When Sookan goes to Japanese school, she is bombarded with propaganda about the so-called great Japanese Empire. She is told that white people are devils and she should therefore work toward their demise. She is then forced to create weapons with which to stop the white Americans from taking over her country. She spends at least half of her day in school working hard in the hot sun. In this way, the Japanese plan to heavily influence the children's minds. Most children are not equipped with the mental tools to discriminate between what is good for them and what is being propagandized. The Japanese also take advantage of child labor. Rather than teaching math and science, they take the children out into the school yard and have them make tools of war.

In the sock factory, Sookan's mother, like most of the other adults, works hard each day. She works, she is told, to keep the Japanese soldiers warm. She is constantly threatened with starvation, as the Japanese soldiers pay her with food, and they pay her only enough for her to barely exist. If she falls behind in her work, they subtract some of her normal rations. Although the adults' minds may be able to recognize propaganda when they are exposed to it, they do as they are told because they need to eat.

Another form of enslavement is associated with torture. Sookan's grandfather has all his toenails pulled off while he is a prisoner of the Japanese. Torture can break a person's spirit, taking from that person his or her will to be free. Torture often makes a person submit to the orders of their captors. Thus, their minds become enslaved because they fear they will be hurt. Grandfather, in this story, becomes so weary of his enslavement that he decides he would rather be dead than have to submit to the Japanese.

The end of Japanese occupation in North Korea *(George Lacks | Time & Life Pictures | Getty Images)*

When the Russians arrive, the people are brainwashed all over again. This time they are made to believe that if they work hard and do not ask for much in return, they will one day create a new, ideal society under Communism. Children are trucked away to clean old factories. Adults are used as disposable peons, going out into the war fields to clear away mines. The Russians enslave the Korean people by promising them a better future if they just work and work for the time being.

Lack of Parental Love

Sookan often comments on the lack of parental love in this story. Sometimes she feels her mother

does not love her enough. Sometimes she thinks the same of her grandfather and her father. It is not that these people do not love her, but Sookan sometimes feels that way.

In fact, Sookan's mother becomes emotionally vacant at one point in the story—when she loses her own father. Although otherwise emotionally strong, Sookan's mother becomes worn down after the death of her father, as if this is the last straw, the last punishment that she can endure. In order to protect herself, she closes off her emotions from her children. The result is that Sookan feels lost. Her mother becomes physically sick and appears to be following in her father's footsteps. He, too, closed down because he had suffered too much. After his death, Sookan's mother, for a while, seems to be experiencing the same thing.

Sookan also talks about how much she loves her grandfather. Her grandfather teaches her how to write Korean characters, and Sookan adores this attention. However, their relationship is limited by their Korean culture. Because Sookan is a girl, her grandfather, according to Korean tradition, should spend most of his time with her brother. Sookan bemoans this tradition and waits for every opportunity to capture more of her grandfather's love.

The guardian most removed from Sookan is her father. He is physically separated from her because he lives in Manchuria during the Japanese occupation. But after he passes through North Korea on his way to the south, Sookan learns that he has searched for and rescued her brothers and has taken them with him. She wonders why her father did not come to rescue her. This question is never answered.

STYLE

Child's Point of View

Choi wrote this novel as seen through the eyes of a nine-year-old. As such, parts of the story are left vague, particularly since Sookan cannot understand everything that is going on around her, so some of the actions in the story remain unexplained. For example, Sookan does not know where the Japanese soldiers take the girls who work in the sock factory; she does not know why they must be taken away. So readers must speculate for themselves from the clues that are provided.

Another effect of the nine-year-old Sookan being the narrator is that an adult reading about the harrowing events that Sookan and her brother go through does not fully experience the emotions that would ordinarily be attached to them. For instance, though Sookan and her brother are hungry, scared, and at times cold, they do not fully understand the danger they are in, so there is little reflection on the threat on their lives. Older readers suspect the danger, but the reading of it stays beneath the surface. Sookan's lack of fear is most apparent when she approaches the Russian officers and demands that they find her mother. The act not only endangers her life and that of her brother's but

possibly even threatens her mother's life. Had the narrator been older, the acknowledgment of fear of such reprisals would have been more deeply explored and expressed.

Young-Adult Novel

While some consider *Year of Impossible Goodbyes* a novel for young adults, it is frequently enjoyed by adults. When writing for a young audience, authors often create child or adolescent protagonists, like Sookan, who are a bit naive at the outset of the story and tend toward the innocent. The plotlines of young-adult novels are often rather straightforward and sometimes include more action than reflection. The underlying current of the story often falls into a basic foundation of good on one side and bad on the other, with little or no gray area in between. For instance, in this story the Japanese are all bad, meaning they exhibit no saving graces. Captain Narita and his wife are perfect examples of this. Sookan's grandfather and her mother, on the other hand, are almost wholly good, with few faults.

Some young-adult novels employ few literary devices, as some authors choose to keep their language concrete for the sake of their audience. Literary devices tend to be abstract (such as a comparison of one's love to a rose). Choi tells her story in a straightforward manner. She recounts events in a way that is not quite as stripped down as a newspaper story would be but not quite as complicated as a poem or novel written for an adult audience would be. For the most part, Choi tells Sookan's story by recalling actions.

Autobiographical Fiction

Year of Impossible Goodbyes is based on Choi's life. Only the author knows why she chose to tell this story as fiction and not as a memoir (which is a story about one's life). Perhaps the author believed she would have more freedom in writing this story as fiction. She could thus make up conversations, for example, that never really took place. She could also invent or shape characters to give her story more drama, or combine two or more characters into one to simplify or intensify the plot. She could also make up characters to protect the identities of the real people in her life.

All fiction writers put some aspects of their lives into their stories. They pull from their experiences of challenges they have faced and people they have met. But some authors do this more than others. Someone writing science fiction, for instance, is more likely to create a story that is far removed from his or her day-to-day life. But even in science fiction, some of the characters will be drawn from people the author knows. In an autobiographical novel, most of the story reflects the author's life, and only minor parts and details are purely imagined.

HISTORICAL CONTEXT

Korean History into the Twentieth Century

The peninsula of Korea has been inhabited for at least eight thousand years, according to archaeological findings. But scientific theories hold that people may have lived in this area for hundreds of thousands of years before. The earliest migrations are thought to have come to the land now called Korea from northwestern parts of Asia. These people settled on the peninsula, their numbers reaching as far north as Manchuria (now a part of China).

Two thousand years ago, present-day Korea was ruled by chiefs of three separate kingdoms: Shilla, Koguryo, and Paekehe. By the seventh century, the Shilla Kingdom reigned supreme, ruling over the entire peninsula. In centuries to follow, other dynasties took over the power of rule: the Koryo (in 935) and the Choson (in 1392). The Choson Empire lasted until Japanese occupation began in 1910.

Korea suffered many invasions from other more powerful countries, too, including the Mongolians and several attempts by the Japanese before their full occupation. The government, after being pressured by European and American interests to sell Western-made products in Korea, decided to close the country's borders to all outside influences except for China in the nineteenth century. During this time, Korea was referred to as "the Hermit Kingdom." But Japan remained insistent, and China came to Korea's aid when Japan pushed its influence into Korea. The result was the Sino-Japanese War, which lasted one year, from 1894 to 1895. Japan defeated China. Then a decade later, when Russia took an interest in Korea, there occurred the Russo-Japanese War, which was also fought for one year, between 1904 and 1905. Once again, Japan won. At this point,

Japan's influence over Korea was profound. In 1910, the Japanese forced Korea to sign over its powers, and Korea was annexed to Japan.

Japanese Occupation

The Japanese saw Korea as a source of cheap labor and an abundance of natural resources. By annexing Korea, Japan gained manifold opportunities to increase its power and wealth in its attempts to compete in the Industrial Revolution that was going on in the Western world. The Korean people were made to work for poor wages. The goods they produced were bought at low prices. Korean agricultural lands and produce, especially those of the southern portion of the peninsula, were a beneficial source of food for the growing Japanese population. And the minerals found in the northern portion of Korea, as well as the capacity to create great industries there, not only provided Japan with a great source of wealth but also helped the Japanese build their military weaponry.

In the first years of Japan's occupation, there was a strong political move toward independence by the Koreans. This culminated in what is called the March 1st Movement of 1919. Huge crowds gathered on this day in Korea's major cities, especially in Seoul, where a Korean Declaration of Independence was read in public. The Japanese occupiers had no tolerance for such demonstrations and showed little mercy toward the unarmed protestors. In the end, thousands of people were killed, more were wounded, and many others were arrested.

Although this demoralized the populace and preempted further large demonstrations, a widespread underground was developed by Korean freedom fighters. The Provisional Government of the Republic of Korea was formed in Shanghai, China, while a Korean liberation army, composed mostly of former Korean soldiers, came together in Manchuria and in Russia. When World War II began, sections of the various liberation armies grew stronger with more recruits and helped the Allied forces in fighting against the Japanese and eventually pushing them out of Korea.

The Dividing of Korea and the Korean War

Two of the Allies in World War II, the Soviet Union (commonly known as Russia) and the United States, coveted the Korean Peninsula,

COMPARE
&
CONTRAST

- **1950s:** Korea is divided after World War II into North and South Korea. Because of the political atmosphere and repression in North Korea, masses of people flee to South Korea.

  1990s: Korea remains strictly divided, with little or no communication between the citizens of North and South Korea.

  Today: In attempts to heal political and social wounds, North Korea allows controlled visits between North and South Korean citizens.

- **1950s:** The Soviet Union's strong political influence brings the Communist Party to North Korea, with promises that bounties of food and social comfort will result from working together under socialistic philosophies.

  1990s: A dictatorship and political corruption as well as unfavorable weather conditions and poor economic planning lead to widespread famine in North Korea.

  Today: North Korea is one of the few remaining Communist countries in the world, relying heavily on China for food aid and other social and political support.

- **1950s:** Kim Il Sung leads North Korean soldiers into South Korea in an attempt to reunite his country.

  1990s: Kim Jung Il comes to power, continuing the dictatorial reign of his father, Kim Il Sung.

  Today: Kim Jong Il threatens South Korea by launching missiles. Countries including the United States press the United Nations to apply stricter sanctions against North Korea.

---

and neither wanted to see the other country in complete control there. So they came to an agreement to divide the peninsula in half, cutting an imaginary line through the thirty-eighth parallel; the United States would support South Korea, and the Soviet Union would support North Korea. Although Korea had been a unified country for thousands of years, the U.S. influence in southern Korea supported a democratic government, while the Soviet influence in North Korea promoted a Communist government. These differences caused the borderline at the thirty-eighth parallel between the divided sections of Korea to take on even more significance. South and North Korea were now divided by political philosophies. In addition, after World War II officially ended, the relationship between the United States and the Soviet Union deteriorated. This led to further tensions between South and North Korea, and these tensions would eventually lead to the Korean War.

The United States occupied South Korea from 1945 until 1949. U.S. forces were needed in South Korea because of Korean rebels who wanted to reunite the country under Communist rule. The United States was also concerned about the building of armed forces in North Korea, which the U.S. government believed might lead to an invasion into the south. This fear would soon become a reality, with skirmishes between South and North Korean military forces beginning in 1949 along the thirty-eighth parallel.

By 1950, Kim Il Sung, the leader of North Korea, had positioned thousands of soldiers at the border between North and South Korea. On June 25, 1950, major military confrontations between the two sides of the country began. The South Korean forces were easily overtaken, and they called on United Nations (U.N.) forces, the majority of which were U.S. soldiers, to help them. With the aide of the U.N. forces, the South Koreans pushed the North Korean army almost all the way back to the most northern boundaries with China. China, which supported North Korea, responded by sending its soldiers into battle. With China's help, North Korea forced the South Korean soldiers back. By July 1950,

Russian communist housing in North Korea (*Howard Sochurek | Time & Life Pictures | Getty Images*)

the North Korean forces controlled 90 percent of the peninsula, with South Korea controlling only the most southern tip.

This back-and-forth movement continued. When more U.S. troops were sent in, South Korea was able to regain territory. When the southern troops pushed back into the north, more Chinese soldiers were sent in to help North Korea reclaim its land. The battles continued, and at one point the U.S. military considered using nuclear bombs, as it had in Japan in 1945. This did not happen. While these battles were pursued, discussions of peace between the major powers were ongoing. But an agreement was not reached until July 27, 1953, after two of the bloodiest years of battle the world had ever witnessed. By the end, millions of soldiers and civilians had been killed. North Korean, Chinese, and U.N. commanders signed the armistice agreement, but South Korean officials never did.

This has left the country of Korea, to the present day, in a tenuous state, as the two divisions of Korea are technically still at war.

CRITICAL OVERVIEW

Choi's *Year of Impossible Goodbyes* is one of the author's most popular titles. It marks the beginning work of a trilogy that follows the life of the same narrator. When this book was first published, reviewers had trouble classifying it. At first, it was considered a novel for young-adult readers. However, the reaction from adult readers proved so great that the novel is now referred to as both a young-adult and an adult book. Elizabeth Mehren, writing for the *Los Angeles Times*, told her readers that one of the editors at Houghton Mifflin (the publisher of the book) stated that *Year of Impossible Goodbyes* "was purchased as a YA [young-adult] novel but 'riveted' the grown-ups who read it," so much so that the publisher was hoping the book would not be "pigeonholed as 'only' a YA title." Other reviewers have also commented on the fact that *Year of Impossible Goodbyes* was written on an emotional level that adults appreciate. It was included among the American Library Association's best books for young adults.

Reviewing the novel for *Book Links*, Patricia Austin and James A. Bryant, Jr., were also impressed. They call it a "richly descriptive, gripping story." Referring to the emotional quality of the story, Gerry Larson, writing for *School Library Journal*, describes the novel as "heartrending." A reviewer for the *Journal of Reading* found something else appealing about Choi's story, stating that the novel "makes history come alive." Writing for the *New York Times*, Michael Shapiro refers to the book as "powerful and moving." Shapiro adds that *Year of Impossible Goodbyes* "offers a glimpse into a young girl's mind and into a nation's heart." Exposing yet another quality of the story, Martha V. Parravano, writing for the *Horn Book Magazine*, concludes that though she has read more powerful books with similar storylines, "there are poignant, vivid moments that will stay with the reader."

CRITICISM

Joyce Hart

Hart is a freelance writer and author of literary essays and several books. In this essay, she examines the role of the narrator's grandfather as memory bearer and protector of culture in Year of Impossible Goodbyes.

Although Choi's story takes place in the 1940s and early 1950s, a time of conflict and oppression, the author provides a glimpse of Korean culture as it once was. She does so through the character of Grandfather. Among the people in the story, Grandfather above all clearly remembers what Korea was like before the Japanese took over his country. Grandfather endured thirty-six years of Japanese occupation but vowed to himself not to give in to Japanese demands, as witnessed through his actions. He not only refuses to forget what it means to be Korean but also insists on passing down his traditions and practices to his grandchildren.

> BECAUSE OF GRANDFATHER'S ABILITY TO MAINTAIN PEACE AND HARMONY IN THE MIDST OF WAR AND HARDSHIP, SOOKAN SEES BOTH THE TREE AND HER GRANDFATHER AS MAGICAL."

Choi marks the strong influence of Grandfather by beginning her novel with a powerful and poetic scene that revolves around him, his outlook, and his beliefs. It is one of the more beautiful passages in her story. She describes the "old weathered pine tree," which will become a significant symbol of Grandfather's spirit. Choi begins by first describing the yard and the remnants of winter, "high mounds of snow in the corner of our yard." She then goes on to relate that Grandfather has dug a furrow around the tree. The furrow is "like a moat," which is symbolic of protection. If the tree is the symbol of Grandfather's spirit, then he, too, is protected in some way, by a different kind of moat; that moat could easily be interpreted as his memories. At this point in the story his memories of what it means to be Korean are still clear and strong in his mind. Regardless of what the Japanese have done to him so far, his spirit will not be broken. He is as strong as the pine tree.

In this opening scene, the author assigns other attributes to the tree that can also be applied to Grandfather. The tree stands alone, for instance. Of all the characters in the story, Grandfather is the least assimilated to the way of life that the Japanese have forced upon all the citizens. The tree also has long, "green-needled branches" that emanate "harmoniously from the trunk" of the trunk. Grandfather is also harmonious. Sookan, as the story progresses, loves watching Grandfather doing his meditation practice each morning. She senses the peace that Grandfather finds in his practice. Harmony is a part of that peace. Despite the lack of harmony all around him, Grandfather emanates peace, offering his household a quiet center around which the other members revolve. The tree and its branches are also likened to an "umbrella," a tool that suggests protection, from sun, from rain, from snow. Grandfather, like the tree branches, is a symbol of protection, too—at least in the mind of Sookan. Because of

WHAT DO I READ NEXT?

- Choi wrote three books about Sookan and her development. The first was *Year of Impossible Goodbyes*. The second was *Echoes of the White Giraffe* (1993). In this novel, Sookan is fifteen, and though strained by the invasion of North Korean troops into South Korea, Sookan finds romance. Her encounters with the young man, Junho, are forbidden by the standards of her Korean culture, but the two teens find ways to share their feelings. Sookan also learns to find her voice and declares her intention of finding a way to go to college in the United States.

- Yoko Kawashima Watkins is the author of *So Far from the Bamboo Grove* (1986), a book with a young narrator named Yoko whose family is stationed in Korea during the Japanese invasion of that country. Like Sookan in Choi's novel, Yoko must escape from North Korea and make her way with her mother and sister across the border to South Korea. The journey is hard and frightening. This story, told from a Japanese point of view, provides another version of the same situation that Sookan experiences.

- *When My Name Was Keoko* (2004), by Linda Sue Park, provides readers with an account of two South Korean sisters who also live under Japanese occupation. However, this story's setting is prior to World War II. Park focuses on the different roles of men and women in Korean society. In the struggle to maintain their Korean identity, the characters find their own expressive ways to defy the Japanese.

- Linda Sue Park is also the author of the 2002 Newbery Medal-winning novel *A Single Shard* (2001). The setting is again Korea but the time frame is the twelfth century. In this fascinating story, a twelve-year-old orphan learns the ancient skill of creating the prized celadon ceramic ware that Korean masters were known for. In the process of delivering one of the ceramic pieces to the Korean emperor, the young boy runs into disaster, and the vessel he was to deliver is broken. All that remains is one shard. What will his master do? What will the emperor think?

- Another Newbery Medal-winning novel is *Roll of Thunder, Hear My Cry* (1976) by Mildred D. Taylor. This story is also about a young girl who must struggle with the challenging social environment in which she lives. This girl, however, lives in the United States. Her name is Cassie, and she is an African American living in the South. She has a harsh awakening one day when she comes face to face with racism.

- *Children of the Dust Bowl: The True Story of the School at Weedpatch Camp* (1993), by Jerry Stanley, follows families from Oklahoma as they travel west to California after leaving their devastated farmlands behind. The setting is the 1930s. The families dream of riches to be found in California, but their hopes are quickly dashed. This story tells of their struggles and provides readers with a history of America's Dust Bowl times.

Grandfather's ability to maintain peace and harmony in the midst of war and hardship, Sookan sees both the tree and her grandfather as magical. In contrast to her Grandfather's peace is "the oppressiveness that engulfed us," Sookan states. Even though spring is upon them, the people still feel as if they are fighting their way through the winter's cold. This contrast that Sookan points out makes her Grandfather seem even that much more special, as he is so unlike all the oppressiveness around him.

Grandfather wants to live in the season of spring, no matter what the weather is like around him. Spring is a time of rebirth, something

Grandfather wants his fellow Koreans to experience through the expulsion of the Japanese and the renewal of Korean culture. He wants to help those around him to throw off the shackles of winter and enjoy the warmth and the inspiration of life starting over. To this end, he has appointed his first three grandsons with names that refer to spring. The oldest child is named "Korean spring," the second oldest is "spring again," and the third oldest is "wise spring." Apparently girls do not receive such an honor, but skipping over Sookan, Grandfather names the youngest grandson "benevolent spring." In this way, Grandfather has blessed his family. It is his hope that his family will "experience the exhilaration and beauty of spring again."

Though Grandfather had previously practiced his meditation inside the house, away from the eyes of the Japanese soldiers, he is changing. He has grown impatient. Grandfather feels he can no longer wait to enjoy spring. At the first sign of good weather, he wants to sit under his favorite tree and meditate outside. Readers should note that meditation is promoted by Buddhism, a spiritual belief system banned by the Japanese oppressors. To be seen meditating would result in punishment. Mother knows this and tries to talk Grandfather out of being so public in his morning ritual, but Grandfather insists. It is time; he has already waited too long, and he is ready to make a stand. Grandfather makes a small speech at this point, telling his daughter that he is not going to allow the dictates of the Japanese soldiers to keep him inside. "I am too old and too tired to be afraid anymore." Choi then writes that "Grandfather emerged from his room and became part of the peaceful scene" outside. As seen through Sookan, the narrator, Grandfather assumes a position under the great pine tree, and as he does, the sun filters through the tree's branches and "played upon his face like dancing fairies." Here, in this passage, the sense of magic is reinforced with the mention of fairies. The image that is portrayed elevates Grandfather, placing him in another world, a world that is completely outside the ordinary.

As peaceful as Grandfather looks, Sookan also sees a portent of change as she watches him drop into his meditative state. Though she senses his usual peaceful state, she notices "an intensity, an anticipation, in his expression, as though he were waiting for something special to happen." Sookan does not go into an interpretation of what she thinks this change might be, but she must sense it or she would not have recognized Grandfather's expression. The change is triggered by Grandfather's impatience, his moving from inside to outside to practice his meditation. He has become defiant because he is tired of waiting to enjoy his life in the Korean manner of his traditions and culture. By moving to the outside, Grandfather is declaring his Koreanness to the world. He no longer wants to be merely a symbol of tradition and culture to his immediate family. He wants to represent his culture to all those who live around him.

Unfortunately, this action proves to be Grandfather's downfall. Somehow, the Japanese soldiers, particularly the person of Captain Narita, know how special the lone pine tree is to Sookan's family. Narita is out to break their suspected rebellious fervor. Indeed, his job is to squeeze out every remaining sense of culture and belief that remains in the memories and in the hearts of the Korean people. If Grandfather, and therefore the symbolic pine tree, are reservoirs of those memories and traditions, then they must be cut down. So in punishment for the innocent birthday party that Mother celebrates before the sock girls go to work in the factory, the captain demands the felling of the tree. When the tree is cut down, Grandfather's spirit is broken. With Grandfather's spirit goes the spirit of Korean culture, or so the Japanese occupiers are hoping.

Some believe that the history of the Korean people goes back hundreds of thousands of years. Myriad traditions and cultural practices were built up over that time. The way the people dress, their language, their art, and so forth were all passed down from generation to generation. Grandfather tries to continue this. He spends much of his day teaching his grandchildren what he has been taught. On his deathbed, he insists that Mother show Sookan and Inchun the remaining few photographs, and he asks her to tell them the stories behind the pictures. These photos and stories are the family's immediate history. He also insists that the children see his scarred feet, wounded through torture at the hands of the Japanese. He wants them to know that, in his mind, the Japanese are the enemy, unjustly attempting to assimilate the Koreans into a culture that is not their own. Grandfather dies, but he wants the children to remember him and what he stands for.

Through her fictional story, Choi tells about her own heroic escape from North Korea. But

Communist murals decorating schools in Korea (*Howard Sochurek* / *Time & Life Pictures* / *Getty Images*)

her story is more than an adventure story. It is a story of great love, not just of family but also of culture and country—the country of her own grandfather. In her grandfather's time, the Korean people were able to dress as their ancestors had dressed, to speak in the language that was most familiar to their tongues, to enjoy their country in the ways that had been set by their forebears. Although the invasions by the Japanese and later by the Russian Communist Party members drastically changed the Koreans' lives, the memories of those times could go on. Just as Sookan carries memories of her grandfather inside her head after he dies, the Korean culture can live on in people's minds, through memories, if nowhere else, and through stories like this novel.

Source: Joyce M. Hart, Critical Essay on *Year of Impossible Goodbyes*, in *Novels for Students*, Gale, Cengage Learning, 2009.

Rocío G. Davis

In the following excerpt, Davis identifies Year of Impossible Goodbyes *as a work that presents Asian American children with a new model for dealing with questions of identity.*

Literature functions as an effective way for children to learn about diversity within and among cultures and to gain a sense of their country's ethnic history and constitution. The growing field of children's literature focusing on ethnicity and culture presents issues of heritage as they intersect with contemporary life and myth adapted to Western circumstances. Many of the themes that are dealt with in adult literature—such as identity, the meaning of home, interpersonal relationships—appear in children's literature with a didactic purpose. This area has become a "particularly intense site of ideological and political contest, for various groups of adults struggle over which versions of ethnic identity will become institutionalized in school, home, and library settings" (K. C. Smith 3). Focusing specifically on Asian American children's literature and tracing its evolution since the 1970s, one comprehends the way that literature functions as a cultural product that both reflects and shapes the cultures of those who live it—and the way that "consumers," or beneficiaries, can play a role in the production of culture and its literary artifacts (Carpenter 53). Asian American writers for

CHOI'S NARRATIVES VALIDATE A NON-
AMERICAN CHILDHOOD SETTING FOR ASIAN
AMERICANS, AND LINK THE STORIES OF AMERICAN
CITIZENS TO HISTORICAL EVENTS IN OTHER PARTS OF
THE WORLD."

children are deploying increasingly creative strategies for negotiating the varied strands of culture that children experience. Their creations—including historical fiction, picture books, autobiographies, novels, poetry, and bilingual texts—strive to balance appreciation for heritage with attention to the renewed cultural realities their audiences may be experiencing.

Children's texts are culturally formative and of tremendous importance educationally, intellectually, and socially. Perhaps more than other forms of literature, they reflect society as it wishes to be, as it wishes to be seen, and as it unconsciously reveals itself to be. Consequently, ethnic children's literature highlights the meaning or values that society places on questions and attitudes about ethnic differences and intercultural relationships. It reflects how each group occupies or moves within certain areas or exerts specific influence on the place they are in and the community they form. Rudine Sims classifies this category of children's writing as "culturally conscious books" (478)—that is, stories told from the point of view of the ethnic character, and dealing with a concrete ethnic family or neighborhood, focusing on both heritage and contemporary living. The themes generally dealt with include those common in all realistic children's fiction: everyday experiences, urban living, friendships, family relationships, and stories about growing up (480–81). Furthermore, as Ivy Chan argues, in developing multicultural literature for children, one of the goals must be to foster in the child a multicultural perspective—an international outlook and the realization that people express many of the same feelings and needs in varied ways; the emphasis should be on what people share—the "similarity in differences"—rather than what separates (23). The evolution is toward writing that resonates with the realities of actual childhood situations, specifically intercultural

works that emphasize the varied cultural influences a child growing up in the United States experiences, rather than on solely appreciating and/or acquiring a heritage identity. As Katharine Capshaw Smith explains, "Children's literature allows readers a means to reconceptualize their relationship to ethnic and national identities. Telling stories to a young audience becomes a conduit for social and political revolution" (3). In contemporary American society, ethnic literature for children tends to highlight ways of affirming and celebrating difference as they simultaneously seek ways to cooperate and collaborate across ethnic boundaries.

For the children of minority groups in the United States today, the issue of how to integrate the past with the present, or how to appreciate heritage and establish bonds by forming peer communities, is the basis of questions about identity that face all youth—about defining self and other, and about the values they inherit from their families, those they accept and those they reject (Natov 38). Though children's existence and experience as cultural beings must be taken into account, meaning in effective literary texts develops, at least in part, through the traditions and experience of collective children's culture, which each experiences individually (Carpenter 56). In the case of ethnic children's writing, the intersection between a more universal children's culture and the specificities of each child's heritage must be carefully constructed. Significantly, the most successful children's books reject the assumption that children are merely receivers of culture, and present them as "creative manipulators of a dynamic network of concepts, actions, feelings and products that mirror and mould their experience as children" (Carpenter 57). Joseph Bruchac believes that "when perceived properly, when presented and used with sensitivity and balance, ideas of multiculturalism can empower all our children" (158). Engagements with history, therefore, become fertile ground for ethnic children's writers to (re)negotiate the varied and complex social and cultural history of their group's presence in the United States and the manner in which these groups have struggled to carve a place for themselves in American society and, importantly, in its representation of itself.

A number of Asian American writers have engaged diverse moments and aspects of the history of the Asian presence in the United States, foregrounding stories of immigration, heritage culture, problems with racism and acculturation. Much of this writing is propelled by a proactive concern that American children, whether or not of Asian descent, learn the lessons of history. As Katharine Capshaw Smith points out,

> Because works often narrate and explain details of a traumatic past, like the internment of Japanese Americans or the enslavement of African Americans, to an audience innocent of historical knowledge, the stakes are high: adult mediators recognize the gravity of their role as gatekeepers to history and arbiters of ethnic identity. Scholars of ethnic literature will therefore find much complexity in the ways writers construct history and negotiate the demands of various audiences. (4)

Yoshiko Uchida, for instance, has written several novels on the internment experience of Japanese Americans during World War II. Her *Journey to Topaz* (1971) and *Journey Home* (1982), for example, explore eleven-year-old Yuki Sakane's experience of the bombing of Pearl Harbor, her family's internment at Topaz in Utah, and their subsequent return to California and attempt to begin life again. Importantly, Uchida has also written an autobiography for children describing her family's experiences in California and in the Topaz internment camp. *The Invisible Thread* (1991) stresses the link she feels with her parents' Japanese heritage while acknowledging her Americanness. The autobiography's contribution to Asian American discursive intervention in the writing of American history for children lies in its foregrounding the voice of a Japanese American girl, who is empowered to tell her own story, one that privileges the experience of the victims of government sanctioned racism (Davis 94). It also allows her to engage Japanese American culture and character, the silent heroism of the Issei and the decorated bravery of the All-Nisei 442nd Regimental Combat Team and the 100th Infantry Battalion, mostly drawn from boys in the camps. The author incorporates the biography of her parents in order to reposition the narrative of the Japanese presence in America. She substantiates the history of Japanese immigrants who lived lives of quiet dignity and "did not have an easy time in a country that would not allow them to become citizens or to own land" (*Invisible Thread* 23). Uchida's writing becomes her attempt to pass on a legacy of ethnic appreciation to the Sansei—third-generation Japanese Americans—

> to give them the kinds of books I'd never had as a child. The time was right, for now the world too, was changing ... I wanted to give the young Sansei a sense of continuity and knowledge of

their own remarkable history ... I hoped all young Americans would read these books as well. (*Invisible Thread* 131)

Sook Nyul Choi's trilogy, *Year of Impossible Goodbyes* (1991), *Echoes of the White Giraffe* (1993), and *Gathering of Pearls* (1994), narrates young Sookan's experiences in Korea during the Japanese occupation, the family's escape beyond the 38th parallel after the Russian invasion, and her later immigration to the United States for college. Although only the last of these books is set specifically in the United States, Choi's narratives validate a non-American childhood setting for Asian Americans, and link the stories of American citizens to historical events in other parts of the world. This particular aspect expands and subverts the hegemonic prescription of the location of the childhood experience of the (Asian) American subject: narrating non-US-based experiences reconfigures America's image of its children's, or at least of its citizens', pasts. Furthermore, it posits Americanization as a process, rather than as a fixed disposition or merely an inherited patrimony, and articulates itineraries of affiliation as they stress trajectories and transitivity, rather than static or endowed identification. These texts exemplify many Asian American writers' concerns with revisionary historical writing, which examine hidden or unknown stories for children, to offer renewed models for American children....

Source: Rocío G. Davis, "Reinscribing (Asian) American History in Laurence Yep's *Dragon Wings*," in *Lion and the Unicorn*, Vol. 28, 2004, pp. 390–407.

Lynda Brill Comerford

In the following essay, Comerford discusses Choi's decision to write Year of Impossible Goodbyes.

It is difficult to imagine that someone exuding as much warmth and exuberance as Sook Nyul Choi could have experienced all the horrors set down in her autobiographical book set in North Korea in the year 1945. Focusing on the day-to-day hardships of one family, *Year of Impossible Goodbyes* relates how young Sookan, her little brother and mother endure routine humiliations from Japanese officers, mourn the death of Sookan's grandfather, survive their country's invasion by Russian soldiers and attempt a dangerous escape to the south.

Choi, whose earliest writing was published in Korean newspapers, had always felt compelled to write her life story, especially after American friends and students pressed her to talk about her past. But for years, other activities—attending college, teaching, school, raising a family and attaining American citizenship—took precedence over the time-consuming task of translating memories into English, her second language. It was not until 10 years ago, during a return trip to her homeland shortly after her husband's death, that Choi felt the time was right to begin *Year of Impossible Goodbyes*.

Initially, her decision was not met favorably by members of her family still living in Korea. "When I asked my father to tell me about some of his experiences in jail, he said, 'Why do you want to bring back the devils long gone? Why do you want to make people cry?'" But Choi is quick to explain that her purpose in creating the book was never to make people sad (a taboo of Korean culture). "I want my book to be received as a celebration of human spirit, of the ability to go on and forgive."

Eventually, Choi's massive undertaking evolved into a 400-page manuscript which her grown-up daughters and Houghton editor Laura Hornik helped trim to a more manageable size. Choi admits it was hard to "cut back," but she may be able to work some of the leftover material into the sequel she is planning. She has already completed a second novel, *Halmoni* (Grandmother), due out in 1993 from Houghton Mifflin, which explores the relationship between a Korean woman and her American-born grandchild.

Choi's faith in essential goodness, which is embodied in heroine Sookan, may be inherited from the author's mother, whose optimism was never shaken. "When our country was suffering," Choi recalls, "she made me feel that this was not the way things were all over the world. She always saw good in people."

In closing, Choi relates a story that her mother told her as a child: "My mother used to say that every time you go through horrible times, every time you suffer, a thin gold leaf will come out of your heart, pass through your mouth and go up to heaven. As a child, I used to imagine that when I died I would go up to heaven and see all those gold sparkles and go crunching through the gold leaves that came from my heart."

Source: Lynda Brill Comerford, "Flying Starts: Sook Nyul Choi," in *Publishers Weekly*, Vol. 238, No. 56, December 20, 1991, pp. 22–23.

Laura L. Lent

In the following review, Lent commends Year of Impossible Goodbyes *for its historical insight and emotional storytelling.*

In this book, Choi poignantly describes her childhood in Kirimni, Pyongyang during the Second World War. During this time, the Japanese occupied Korea, and Choi's family suffered as a result of Japanese oppression. Her writing transports the reader back to her childhood home in 1945. She describes the family's day-to-day routine—including such things as her secret studies of the Chinese and Korean languages with her grandpa, and her family's operation of a sock factory in the shed on their property. Along with tales of their mundane life, Choi relates specific instances of brutality that she, her family, and their friends experience at the hands of the Japanese.

Choi recollects her countrymen's collective sigh of relief as the Japanese withdraw from Korea and their hope that all will get better soon. However, their hope for Korean independence is dashed when the Japanese are immediately replaced by the Communist Russians. As the realization sets in that life in North Korea will never improve, Choi's mom plans a daring escape to the South where the Americans are. Thus, the last part of her story focuses on the escape that her mother, her brother, and she make across the thirty-eighth parallel.

Choi's descriptive, frightening, yet historically accurate tale of the plight of the Korean people during the Second World War and immediately thereafter provides the teen reader—and anyone else who would like to read a fantastic book—with fresh insight into how another country was affected by the war. Most American teens have been exposed to information (via video, lecture-discussion, and/or books) on the death camps in Nazi-occupied areas; however, they have no idea that other nationalities (like the Koreans being oppressed by the Japanese and later by the Russians) also suffered at the same time. With Choi's book, another part of the war becomes public knowledge, and history is more fully told.

In addition to the book's historical merits, it should be noted that Choi is a tremendous author. Her memoirs evoke one emotion after another. For instance Choi describes how her grandfather is punished by Captain Narita, the Japanese policeman, because her grandfather had created a brush painting and written Chinese characters upon it. One feels first the humiliation that the old man must have felt when Captain Narita verbally abused him. More powerful emotions follow. One can feel life ebb from Choi's grandfather after Captain Narita orders the grandfather's pine tree—his final place of refuge and solitude—cut down. And when Choi ends this particular tale by describing her grandfather's eventual death, one feels a myriad of emotions ranging from anger to futility and helplessness. She evokes emotions from the reader because she vividly writes about the past so that the reader gets a picture of the events as they happened.

Because of the ease with which this story unfolds (Chinese, Japanese, and Russian words are defined within the narrative), I feel anyone, including young adults, can have an enjoyable experience reading this book. In sum, Choi's entertaining, yet informative writing style should win her a best book nomination.

Source: Laura L. Lent, "A Review of *A Year of Impossible Goodbyes*," in *Voice of Youth Advocates*, Vol. 14, No. 5, December 1991, pp. 307–08.

SOURCES

Austin, Patricia, and James A. Bryant, Jr., Review of *Year of Impossible Goodbyes*, by Sook Nyul Choi, in *Book Links*, March 2004, Vol. 13, No. 4, p. 15.

Choi, Sook Nyul, *Year of Impossible Goodbyes*, Yearling, 1991.

Harris, Mark Edward, *Inside North Korea*, Chronicle Books, 2007.

Kim, Djun Kil, *The History of Korea*, Greenwood Press, 2005.

Larson, Gerry, Review of *Year of Impossible Goodbyes*, by Sook Nyul Choi, in *School Library Journal*, August 1998, Vol. 44, No. 8, p. 27.

Ling, Amy, "Sook Nyul Choi, Memoirist and Novelist," in *Yellow Light: The Flowering of Asian American Arts*, edited by Amy Ling, Temple University Press, 1999, pp. 46–54.

Mehren, Elizabeth, "Bridging the Generation Gap," in *Los Angeles Times*, April 28, 1991, p. 12.

Parravano, Martha V., Review of *Year of Impossible Goodbyes*, by Sook Nyul Choi, in *Horn Book Magazine*, January 1992, Vol. 68, No. 1, p. 69.

Review of *Year of Impossible Goodbyes*, by Sook Nyul Choi, in *Journal of Reading*, November 1993, Vol. 37, No. 3, p. 228.

Scanlon, Mara, "Sook Nyul Choi (1937–)," in *Asian American Novelists: A Bio-Bibliographical Critical Sourcebook*, edited by Emmanuel S. Nelson, Greenwood Press, 2000, pp. 56–9.

Shapiro, Michael, Review of *Year of Impossible Goodbyes*, by Sook Nyul Choi, in *New York Times*, East Coast Late Edition, November 10, 1991, p. A42.

FURTHER READING

Hastings, Max, *The Korean War*, Pan Books, 2000.
The author provides a significant account of the Korean War, including through actual firsthand experiences of North Korean military veterans.

Lankov, Andrei, *North of the DMZ: Essays on Daily Life in North Korea*, McFarland, 2007.
This book contains a collection of essays on how the people of North Korea have learned to live under the totalitarian regime that has persisted into the twenty-first century. Many of the myths that the regime has created through its propaganda are dismissed by these personal accounts of real daily-life routines.

Pratt, Keith, *Everlasting Flower: A History of Korea*, Reaktion Books, 2007.
Although the differences today between North and South Korea are very apparent, the two countries share a common history. In this book, Professor Pratt covers the country's long history through the rule of emperors and dictators. In addition to the political history, readers learn about the religious practices, culture, and everyday lives of Korea's people.

Winchester, Simon, *Korea: A Walk through the Land of Miracles*, Harper Perennial, 2005.
The English author Winchester, after living for years in Hong Kong, took a walking tour through South Korea and recorded some of the talks he had with local residents, including military officers, a honeymooning couple, abalone divers, and Buddhist nuns. Through these discussions, readers gain a glimpse into the culture, language, and politics of modern-day South Korea.

Glossary of Literary Terms

A

Abstract: As an adjective applied to writing or literary works, abstract refers to words or phrases that name things not knowable through the five senses.

Aestheticism: A literary and artistic movement of the nineteenth century. Followers of the movement believed that art should not be mixed with social, political, or moral teaching. The statement "art for art's sake" is a good summary of aestheticism. The movement had its roots in France, but it gained widespread importance in England in the last half of the nineteenth century, where it helped change the Victorian practice of including moral lessons in literature.

Allegory: A narrative technique in which characters representing things or abstract ideas are used to convey a message or teach a lesson. Allegory is typically used to teach moral, ethical, or religious lessons but is sometimes used for satiric or political purposes.

Allusion: A reference to a familiar literary or historical person or event, used to make an idea more easily understood.

Analogy: A comparison of two things made to explain something unfamiliar through its similarities to something familiar, or to prove one point based on the acceptedness of another. Similes and metaphors are types of analogies.

Antagonist: The major character in a narrative or drama who works against the hero or protagonist.

Anthropomorphism: The presentation of animals or objects in human shape or with human characteristics. The term is derived from the Greek word for "human form."

Anti-hero: A central character in a work of literature who lacks traditional heroic qualities such as courage, physical prowess, and fortitude. Anti-heroes typically distrust conventional values and are unable to commit themselves to any ideals. They generally feel helpless in a world over which they have no control. Anti-heroes usually accept, and often celebrate, their positions as social outcasts.

Apprenticeship Novel: See *Bildungsroman*

Archetype: The word archetype is commonly used to describe an original pattern or model from which all other things of the same kind are made. This term was introduced to literary criticism from the psychology of Carl Jung. It expresses Jung's theory that behind every person's "unconscious," or repressed memories of the past, lies the "collective unconscious" of the human race: memories of the countless typical experiences of our ancestors. These memories are said to prompt illogical associations that trigger powerful emotions in the reader. Often, the emotional process is primitive, even primordial. Archetypes are the literary images that grow out of the "collective unconscious." They appear in literature as incidents and plots that repeat basic patterns of life. They may also appear as stereotyped characters.

Avant-garde: French term meaning "vanguard." It is used in literary criticism to describe new writing that rejects traditional approaches to literature in favor of innovations in style or content.

B

Beat Movement: A period featuring a group of American poets and novelists of the 1950s and 1960s—including Jack Kerouac, Allen Ginsberg, Gregory Corso, William S. Burroughs, and Lawrence Ferlinghetti—who rejected established social and literary values. Using such techniques as stream of consciousness writing and jazz-influenced free verse and focusing on unusual or abnormal states of mind—generated by religious ecstasy or the use of drugs—the Beat writers aimed to create works that were unconventional in both form and subject matter.

Bildungsroman: A German word meaning "novel of development." The *bildungsroman* is a study of the maturation of a youthful character, typically brought about through a series of social or sexual encounters that lead to self-awareness. *Bildungsroman* is used interchangeably with *erziehungsroman,* a novel of initiation and education. When a *bildungsroman* is concerned with the development of an artist (as in James Joyce's *A Portrait of the Artist as a Young Man*), it is often termed a *kunstlerroman.*

Black Aesthetic Movement: A period of artistic and literary development among African Americans in the 1960s and early 1970s. This was the first major African-American artistic movement since the Harlem Renaissance and was closely paralleled by the civil rights and black power movements. The black aesthetic writers attempted to produce works of art that would be meaningful to the black masses. Key figures in black aesthetics included one of its founders, poet and playwright Amiri Baraka, formerly known as LeRoi Jones; poet and essayist Haki R. Madhubuti, formerly Don L. Lee; poet and playwright Sonia Sanchez; and dramatist Ed Bullins.

Black Humor: Writing that places grotesque elements side by side with humorous ones in an attempt to shock the reader, forcing him or her to laugh at the horrifying reality of a disordered world.

Burlesque: Any literary work that uses exaggeration to make its subject appear ridiculous, either by treating a trivial subject with profound seriousness or by treating a dignified subject frivolously. The word "burlesque" may also be used as an adjective, as in "burlesque show," to mean "striptease act."

C

Character: Broadly speaking, a person in a literary work. The actions of characters are what constitute the plot of a story, novel, or poem. There are numerous types of characters, ranging from simple, stereotypical figures to intricate, multifaceted ones. In the techniques of anthropomorphism and personification, animals—and even places or things—can assume aspects of character. "Characterization" is the process by which an author creates vivid, believable characters in a work of art. This may be done in a variety of ways, including (1) direct description of the character by the narrator; (2) the direct presentation of the speech, thoughts, or actions of the character; and (3) the responses of other characters to the character. The term "character" also refers to a form originated by the ancient Greek writer Theophrastus that later became popular in the seventeenth and eighteenth centuries. It is a short essay or sketch of a person who prominently displays a specific attribute or quality, such as miserliness or ambition.

Climax: The turning point in a narrative, the moment when the conflict is at its most intense. Typically, the structure of stories, novels, and plays is one of rising action, in which tension builds to the climax, followed by falling action, in which tension lessens as the story moves to its conclusion.

Colloquialism: A word, phrase, or form of pronunciation that is acceptable in casual conversation but not in formal, written communication. It is considered more acceptable than slang.

Coming of Age Novel: See *Bildungsroman*

Concrete: Concrete is the opposite of abstract, and refers to a thing that actually exists or a description that allows the reader to experience an object or concept with the senses.

Connotation: The impression that a word gives beyond its defined meaning. Connotations may be universally understood or may be significant only to a certain group.

Convention: Any widely accepted literary device, style, or form.

D

Denotation: The definition of a word, apart from the impressions or feelings it creates (connotations) in the reader.

Denouement: A French word meaning "the unknotting." In literary criticism, it denotes the resolution of conflict in fiction or drama. The *denouement* follows the climax and provides an outcome to the primary plot situation as well as an explanation of secondary plot complications. The *denouement* often involves a character's recognition of his or her state of mind or moral condition.

Description: Descriptive writing is intended to allow a reader to picture the scene or setting in which the action of a story takes place. The form this description takes often evokes an intended emotional response—a dark, spooky graveyard will evoke fear, and a peaceful, sunny meadow will evoke calmness.

Dialogue: In its widest sense, dialogue is simply conversation between people in a literary work; in its most restricted sense, it refers specifically to the speech of characters in a drama. As a specific literary genre, a "dialogue" is a composition in which characters debate an issue or idea.

Diction: The selection and arrangement of words in a literary work. Either or both may vary depending on the desired effect. There are four general types of diction: "formal," used in scholarly or lofty writing; "informal," used in relaxed but educated conversation; "colloquial," used in everyday speech; and "slang," containing newly coined words and other terms not accepted in formal usage.

Didactic: A term used to describe works of literature that aim to teach some moral, religious, political, or practical lesson. Although didactic elements are often found in artistically pleasing works, the term "didactic" usually refers to literature in which the message is more important than the form. The term may also be used to criticize a work that the critic finds "overly didactic," that is, heavy-handed in its delivery of a lesson.

Doppelganger: A literary technique by which a character is duplicated (usually in the form of an alter ego, though sometimes as a ghostly counterpart) or divided into two distinct, usually opposite personalities. The use of this character device is widespread in nineteenth- and twentieth-century literature, and indicates a growing awareness among authors that the "self" is really a composite of many "selves."

Double Entendre: A corruption of a French phrase meaning "double meaning." The term is used to indicate a word or phrase that is deliberately ambiguous, especially when one of the meanings is risqué or improper.

Dramatic Irony: Occurs when the audience of a play or the reader of a work of literature knows something that a character in the work itself does not know. The irony is in the contrast between the intended meaning of the statements or actions of a character and the additional information understood by the audience.

Dystopia: An imaginary place in a work of fiction where the characters lead dehumanized, fearful lives.

E

Edwardian: Describes cultural conventions identified with the period of the reign of Edward VII of England (1901-1910). Writers of the Edwardian Age typically displayed a strong reaction against the propriety and conservatism of the Victorian Age. Their work often exhibits distrust of authority in religion, politics, and art and expresses strong doubts about the soundness of conventional values.

Empathy: A sense of shared experience, including emotional and physical feelings, with someone or something other than oneself. Empathy is often used to describe the response of a reader to a literary character.

Enlightenment, The: An eighteenth-century philosophical movement. It began in France but had a wide impact throughout Europe and America. Thinkers of the Enlightenment valued reason and believed that both the individual and society could achieve a state of perfection. Corresponding to this essentially humanist vision was a resistance to religious authority.

Epigram: A saying that makes the speaker's point quickly and concisely. Often used to preface a novel.

Epilogue: A concluding statement or section of a literary work. In dramas, particularly those of the seventeenth and eighteenth centuries, the epilogue is a closing speech, often in verse, delivered by an actor at the end of a play and spoken directly to the audience.

Epiphany: A sudden revelation of truth inspired by a seemingly trivial incident.

Episode: An incident that forms part of a story and is significantly related to it. Episodes may be either self-contained narratives or events that depend on a larger context for their sense and importance.

Epistolary Novel: A novel in the form of letters. The form was particularly popular in the eighteenth century.

Epithet: A word or phrase, often disparaging or abusive, that expresses a character trait of someone or something.

Existentialism: A predominantly twentieth-century philosophy concerned with the nature and perception of human existence. There are two major strains of existentialist thought: atheistic and Christian. Followers of atheistic existentialism believe that the individual is alone in a godless universe and that the basic human condition is one of suffering and loneliness. Nevertheless, because there are no fixed values, individuals can create their own characters—indeed, they can shape themselves—through the exercise of free will. The atheistic strain culminates in and is popularly associated with the works of Jean-Paul Sartre. The Christian existentialists, on the other hand, believe that only in God may people find freedom from life's anguish. The two strains hold certain beliefs in common: that existence cannot be fully understood or described through empirical effort; that anguish is a universal element of life; that individuals must bear responsibility for their actions; and that there is no common standard of behavior or perception for religious and ethical matters.

Expatriates: See *Expatriatism*

Expatriatism: The practice of leaving one's country to live for an extended period in another country.

Exposition: Writing intended to explain the nature of an idea, thing, or theme. Expository writing is often combined with description, narration, or argument. In dramatic writing, the exposition is the introductory material which presents the characters, setting, and tone of the play.

Expressionism: An indistinct literary term, originally used to describe an early twentieth-century school of German painting. The term applies to almost any mode of unconventional, highly subjective writing that distorts reality in some way.

F

Fable: A prose or verse narrative intended to convey a moral. Animals or inanimate objects with human characteristics often serve as characters in fables.

Falling Action: See *Denouement*

Fantasy: A literary form related to mythology and folklore. Fantasy literature is typically set in non-existent realms and features supernatural beings.

Farce: A type of comedy characterized by broad humor, outlandish incidents, and often vulgar subject matter.

Femme fatale: A French phrase with the literal translation "fatal woman." A *femme fatale* is a sensuous, alluring woman who often leads men into danger or trouble.

Fiction: Any story that is the product of imagination rather than a documentation of fact. characters and events in such narratives may be based in real life but their ultimate form and configuration is a creation of the author.

Figurative Language: A technique in writing in which the author temporarily interrupts the order, construction, or meaning of the writing for a particular effect. This interruption takes the form of one or more figures of speech such as hyperbole, irony, or simile. Figurative language is the opposite of literal language, in which every word is truthful, accurate, and free of exaggeration or embellishment.

Figures of Speech: Writing that differs from customary conventions for construction, meaning, order, or significance for the purpose of a special meaning or effect. There are two major types of figures of speech: rhetorical figures, which do not make changes in the meaning of the words, and tropes, which do.

Fin de siecle: A French term meaning "end of the century." The term is used to denote the last decade of the nineteenth century, a transition period when writers and other artists abandoned old conventions and looked for new techniques and objectives.

First Person: See *Point of View*

Flashback: A device used in literature to present action that occurred before the beginning of the story. Flashbacks are often introduced as the dreams or recollections of one or more characters.

Foil: A character in a work of literature whose physical or psychological qualities contrast strongly with, and therefore highlight, the corresponding qualities of another character.

Folklore: Traditions and myths preserved in a culture or group of people. Typically, these are passed on by word of mouth in various forms—such as legends, songs, and proverbs—or preserved in customs and ceremonies. This term was first used by W. J. Thoms in 1846.

Folktale: A story originating in oral tradition. Folktales fall into a variety of categories, including legends, ghost stories, fairy tales, fables, and anecdotes based on historical figures and events.

Foreshadowing: A device used in literature to create expectation or to set up an explanation of later developments.

Form: The pattern or construction of a work which identifies its genre and distinguishes it from other genres.

G

Genre: A category of literary work. In critical theory, genre may refer to both the content of a given work—tragedy, comedy, pastoral—and to its form, such as poetry, novel, or drama.

Gilded Age: A period in American history during the 1870s characterized by political corruption and materialism. A number of important novels of social and political criticism were written during this time.

Gothicism: In literary criticism, works characterized by a taste for the medieval or morbidly attractive. A gothic novel prominently features elements of horror, the supernatural, gloom, and violence: clanking chains, terror, charnel houses, ghosts, medieval castles,

and mysteriously slamming doors. The term "gothic novel" is also applied to novels that lack elements of the traditional Gothic setting but that create a similar atmosphere of terror or dread.

Grotesque: In literary criticism, the subject matter of a work or a style of expression characterized by exaggeration, deformity, freakishness, and disorder. The grotesque often includes an element of comic absurdity.

H

Harlem Renaissance: The Harlem Renaissance of the 1920s is generally considered the first significant movement of black writers and artists in the United States. During this period, new and established black writers published more fiction and poetry than ever before, the first influential black literary journals were established, and black authors and artists received their first widespread recognition and serious critical appraisal. Among the major writers associated with this period are Claude McKay, Jean Toomer, Countee Cullen, Langston Hughes, Arna Bontemps, Nella Larsen, and Zora Neale Hurston.

Hero/Heroine: The principal sympathetic character (male or female) in a literary work. Heroes and heroines typically exhibit admirable traits: idealism, courage, and integrity, for example.

Holocaust Literature: Literature influenced by or written about the Holocaust of World War II. Such literature includes true stories of survival in concentration camps, escape, and life after the war, as well as fictional works and poetry.

Humanism: A philosophy that places faith in the dignity of humankind and rejects the medieval perception of the individual as a weak, fallen creature. "Humanists" typically believe in the perfectibility of human nature and view reason and education as the means to that end.

Hyperbole: In literary criticism, deliberate exaggeration used to achieve an effect.

I

Idiom: A word construction or verbal expression closely associated with a given language.

Image: A concrete representation of an object or sensory experience. Typically, such a representation helps evoke the feelings associated with the object or experience itself. Images are either "literal" or "figurative." Literal images are especially concrete and involve little or no extension of the obvious meaning of the words used to express them. Figurative images do not follow the literal meaning of the words exactly. Images in literature are usually visual, but the term "image" can also refer to the representation of any sensory experience.

Imagery: The array of images in a literary work. Also, figurative language.

In medias res: A Latin term meaning "in the middle of things." It refers to the technique of beginning a story at its midpoint and then using various flashback devices to reveal previous action.

Interior Monologue: A narrative technique in which characters' thoughts are revealed in a way that appears to be uncontrolled by the author. The interior monologue typically aims to reveal the inner self of a character. It portrays emotional experiences as they occur at both a conscious and unconscious level. images are often used to represent sensations or emotions.

Irony: In literary criticism, the effect of language in which the intended meaning is the opposite of what is stated.

J

Jargon: Language that is used or understood only by a select group of people. Jargon may refer to terminology used in a certain profession, such as computer jargon, or it may refer to any nonsensical language that is not understood by most people.

L

Leitmotiv: See *Motif*

Literal Language: An author uses literal language when he or she writes without exaggerating or embellishing the subject matter and without any tools of figurative language.

Lost Generation: A term first used by Gertrude Stein to describe the post-World War I generation of American writers: men and women haunted by a sense of betrayal and emptiness brought about by the destructiveness of the war.

M

Mannerism: Exaggerated, artificial adherence to a literary manner or style. Also, a popular style of the visual arts of late sixteenth-century Europe that was marked by elongation of the human form and by intentional spatial distortion. Literary works that are self-consciously high-toned and artistic are often said to be "mannered."

Metaphor: A figure of speech that expresses an idea through the image of another object. Metaphors suggest the essence of the first object by identifying it with certain qualities of the second object.

Modernism: Modern literary practices. Also, the principles of a literary school that lasted from roughly the beginning of the twentieth century until the end of World War II. Modernism is defined by its rejection of the literary conventions of the nineteenth century and by its opposition to conventional morality, taste, traditions, and economic values.

Mood: The prevailing emotions of a work or of the author in his or her creation of the work. The mood of a work is not always what might be expected based on its subject matter.

Motif: A theme, character type, image, metaphor, or other verbal element that recurs throughout a single work of literature or occurs in a number of different works over a period of time.

Myth: An anonymous tale emerging from the traditional beliefs of a culture or social unit. Myths use supernatural explanations for natural phenomena. They may also explain cosmic issues like creation and death. Collections of myths, known as mythologies, are common to all cultures and nations, but the best-known myths belong to the Norse, Roman, and Greek mythologies.

N

Narration: The telling of a series of events, real or invented. A narration may be either a simple narrative, in which the events are recounted chronologically, or a narrative with a plot, in which the account is given in a style reflecting the author's artistic concept of the story. Narration is sometimes used as a synonym for "storyline."

Narrative: A verse or prose accounting of an event or sequence of events, real or invented. The term is also used as an adjective in the sense "method of narration." For example, in literary criticism, the expression "narrative technique" usually refers to the way the author structures and presents his or her story.

Narrator: The teller of a story. The narrator may be the author or a character in the story through whom the author speaks.

Naturalism: A literary movement of the late nineteenth and early twentieth centuries. The movement's major theorist, French novelist Emile Zola, envisioned a type of fiction that would examine human life with the objectivity of scientific inquiry. The Naturalists typically viewed human beings as either the products of "biological determinism," ruled by hereditary instincts and engaged in an endless struggle for survival, or as the products of "socioeconomic determinism," ruled by social and economic forces beyond their control. In their works, the Naturalists generally ignored the highest levels of society and focused on degradation: poverty, alcoholism, prostitution, insanity, and disease.

Noble Savage: The idea that primitive man is noble and good but becomes evil and corrupted as he becomes civilized. The concept of the noble savage originated in the Renaissance period but is more closely identified with such later writers as Jean-Jacques Rousseau and Aphra Behn.

Novel: A long fictional narrative written in prose, which developed from the novella and other early forms of narrative. A novel is usually organized under a plot or theme with a focus on character development and action.

Novel of Ideas: A novel in which the examination of intellectual issues and concepts takes precedence over characterization or a traditional storyline.

Novel of Manners: A novel that examines the customs and mores of a cultural group.

Novella: An Italian term meaning "story." This term has been especially used to describe fourteenth-century Italian tales, but it also refers to modern short novels.

O

Objective Correlative: An outward set of objects, a situation, or a chain of events corresponding to an inward experience and evoking this experience in the reader. The term frequently appears in modern criticism in discussions of authors' intended effects on the emotional responses of readers.

Objectivity: A quality in writing characterized by the absence of the author's opinion or feeling about the subject matter. Objectivity is an important factor in criticism.

Oedipus Complex: A son's amorous obsession with his mother. The phrase is derived from the story of the ancient Theban hero Oedipus, who unknowingly killed his father and married his mother.

Omniscience: See *Point of View*

Onomatopoeia: The use of words whose sounds express or suggest their meaning. In its simplest sense, onomatopoeia may be represented by words that mimic the sounds they denote such as "hiss" or "meow." At a more subtle level, the pattern and rhythm of sounds and rhymes of a line or poem may be onomatopoeic.

Oxymoron: A phrase combining two contradictory terms. Oxymorons may be intentional or unintentional.

P

Parable: A story intended to teach a moral lesson or answer an ethical question.

Paradox: A statement that appears illogical or contradictory at first, but may actually point to an underlying truth.

Parallelism: A method of comparison of two ideas in which each is developed in the same grammatical structure.

Parody: In literary criticism, this term refers to an imitation of a serious literary work or the signature style of a particular author in a ridiculous manner. A typical parody adopts the style of the original and applies it to an inappropriate subject for humorous effect. Parody is a form of satire and could be considered the literary equivalent of a caricature or cartoon.

Pastoral: A term derived from the Latin word "pastor," meaning shepherd. A pastoral is a literary composition on a rural theme. The conventions of the pastoral were originated by the third-century Greek poet Theocritus, who wrote about the experiences, love affairs, and pastimes of Sicilian shepherds. In a pastoral, characters and language of a courtly nature are often placed in a simple setting. The term pastoral is also used to classify dramas, elegies, and lyrics that exhibit the use of country settings and shepherd characters.

Pen Name: See *Pseudonym*

Persona: A Latin term meaning "mask." *Personae* are the characters in a fictional work of literature. The *persona* generally functions as a mask through which the author tells a story in a voice other than his or her own. A *persona* is usually either a character in a story who acts as a narrator or an "implied author," a voice created by the author to act as the narrator for himself or herself.

Personification: A figure of speech that gives human qualities to abstract ideas, animals, and inanimate objects.

Picaresque Novel: Episodic fiction depicting the adventures of a roguish central character ("picaro" is Spanish for "rogue"). The picaresque hero is commonly a low-born but clever individual who wanders into and out of various affairs of love, danger, and farcical intrigue. These involvements may take place at all social levels and typically present a humorous and wide-ranging satire of a given society.

Plagiarism: Claiming another person's written material as one's own. Plagiarism can take the form of direct, word-for-word copying or the theft of the substance or idea of the work.

Plot: In literary criticism, this term refers to the pattern of events in a narrative or drama. In its simplest sense, the plot guides the author in composing the work and helps the reader follow the work. Typically, plots exhibit causality and unity and have a beginning, a middle, and an end. Sometimes, however, a plot may consist of a series of disconnected events, in which case it is known as an "episodic plot."

Poetic Justice: An outcome in a literary work, not necessarily a poem, in which the good are rewarded and the evil are punished, especially in ways that particularly fit their virtues or crimes.

Poetic License: Distortions of fact and literary convention made by a writer—not always a poet—for the sake of the effect gained. Poetic license is closely related to the concept of "artistic freedom."

Poetics: This term has two closely related meanings. It denotes (1) an aesthetic theory in literary criticism about the essence of poetry or (2) rules prescribing the proper methods, content, style, or diction of poetry. The term poetics may also refer to theories about literature in general, not just poetry.

Point of View: The narrative perspective from which a literary work is presented to the reader. There are four traditional points of view. The "third person omniscient" gives the reader a "godlike" perspective, unrestricted by time or place, from which to see actions and look into the minds of characters. This allows the author to comment openly on characters and events in the work. The "third person" point of view presents the events of the story from outside of any single character's perception, much like the omniscient point of view, but the reader must understand the action as it takes place and without any special insight into characters' minds or motivations. The "first person" or "personal" point of view relates events as they are perceived by a single character. The main character "tells" the story and may offer opinions about the action and characters which differ from those of the author. Much less common than omniscient, third person, and first person is the "second person" point of view, wherein the author tells the story as if it is happening to the reader.

Polemic: A work in which the author takes a stand on a controversial subject, such as abortion or religion. Such works are often extremely argumentative or provocative.

Pornography: Writing intended to provoke feelings of lust in the reader. Such works are often condemned by critics and teachers, but those which can be shown to have literary value are viewed less harshly.

Post-Aesthetic Movement: An artistic response made by African Americans to the black aesthetic movement of the 1960s and early '70s. Writers since that time have adopted a somewhat different tone in their work, with less emphasis placed on the disparity between black and white in the United States. In the words of post-aesthetic authors such as Toni Morrison, John Edgar Wideman, and Kristin Hunter, African Americans are portrayed as looking inward for answers to their own questions, rather than always looking to the outside world.

Postmodernism: Writing from the 1960s forward characterized by experimentation and continuing to apply some of the fundamentals of modernism, which included existentialism and alienation. Postmodernists have gone a step further in the rejection of tradition begun with the modernists by also rejecting traditional forms, preferring the anti-novel over the novel and the anti-hero over the hero.

Primitivism: The belief that primitive peoples were nobler and less flawed than civilized peoples because they had not been subjected to the tainting influence of society.

Prologue: An introductory section of a literary work. It often contains information establishing the situation of the characters or presents information about the setting, time period, or action. In drama, the prologue is spoken by a chorus or by one of the principal characters.

Prose: A literary medium that attempts to mirror the language of everyday speech. It is distinguished from poetry by its use of unmetered, unrhymed language consisting of logically related sentences. Prose is usually grouped into paragraphs that form a cohesive whole such as an essay or a novel.

Prosopopoeia: See *Personification*

Protagonist: The central character of a story who serves as a focus for its themes and incidents and as the principal rationale for its development. The protagonist is sometimes referred to in discussions of modern literature as the hero or anti-hero.

Protest Fiction: Protest fiction has as its primary purpose the protesting of some social injustice, such as racism or discrimination.

Proverb: A brief, sage saying that expresses a truth about life in a striking manner.

Pseudonym: A name assumed by a writer, most often intended to prevent his or her identification as the author of a work. Two or more authors may work together under one pseudonym, or an author may use a different name for each genre he or she publishes in. Some publishing companies maintain "house pseudonyms," under which any number of authors may write installations in a series. Some authors also choose a pseudonym over their real names the way an actor may use a stage name.

Pun: A play on words that have similar sounds but different meanings.

R

Realism: A nineteenth-century European literary movement that sought to portray familiar characters, situations, and settings in a realistic manner. This was done primarily by using an objective narrative point of view and through the buildup of accurate detail. The standard for success of any realistic work depends on how faithfully it transfers common experience into fictional forms. The realistic method may be altered or extended, as in stream of consciousness writing, to record highly subjective experience.

Repartee: Conversation featuring snappy retorts and witticisms.

Resolution: The portion of a story following the climax, in which the conflict is resolved.

Rhetoric: In literary criticism, this term denotes the art of ethical persuasion. In its strictest sense, rhetoric adheres to various principles developed since classical times for arranging facts and ideas in a clear, persuasive, appealing manner. The term is also used to refer to effective prose in general and theories of or methods for composing effective prose.

Rhetorical Question: A question intended to provoke thought, but not an expressed answer, in the reader. It is most commonly used in oratory and other persuasive genres.

Rising Action: The part of a drama where the plot becomes increasingly complicated. Rising action leads up to the climax, or turning point, of a drama.

Roman à clef: A French phrase meaning "novel with a key." It refers to a narrative in which real persons are portrayed under fictitious names.

Romance: A broad term, usually denoting a narrative with exotic, exaggerated, often idealized characters, scenes, and themes.

Romanticism: This term has two widely accepted meanings. In historical criticism, it refers to a European intellectual and artistic movement of the late eighteenth and early nineteenth centuries that sought greater freedom of personal expression than that allowed by the strict rules of literary form and logic of the eighteenth-century neoclassicists. The Romantics preferred emotional and imaginative expression to rational analysis. They considered the individual to be at the center of all experience and so placed him or her at the center of their art. The Romantics believed that the creative imagination reveals nobler truths—unique feelings and attitudes—than those that could be discovered by logic or by scientific examination. Both the natural world and the state of childhood were important sources for revelations of "eternal truths." "Romanticism" is also used as a general term to refer to a type of sensibility found in all periods of literary history and usually considered to be in opposition to the principles of classicism. In this sense, Romanticism signifies any work or philosophy in which the exotic or dreamlike figure strongly, or that is devoted to individualistic expression, self-analysis, or a pursuit of a higher realm of knowledge than can be discovered by human reason.

Romantics: See *Romanticism*

S

Satire: A work that uses ridicule, humor, and wit to criticize and provoke change in human nature and institutions. There are two major types of satire: "formal" or "direct" satire speaks directly to the reader or to a character in the work; "indirect" satire relies upon the ridiculous behavior of its characters to make its point. Formal satire is further divided into two manners: the "Horatian," which ridicules gently, and the "Juvenalian," which derides its subjects harshly and bitterly.

Science Fiction: A type of narrative about or based upon real or imagined scientific theories and technology. Science fiction is often peopled with alien creatures and set on other planets or in different dimensions.

Second Person: See *Point of View*

Setting: The time, place, and culture in which the action of a narrative takes place. The elements of setting may include geographic location, characters' physical and mental environments, prevailing cultural attitudes, or the historical time in which the action takes place.

Simile: A comparison, usually using "like" or "as", of two essentially dissimilar things, as in "coffee as cold as ice" or "He sounded like a broken record."

Slang: A type of informal verbal communication that is generally unacceptable for formal writing. Slang words and phrases are often colorful exaggerations used to emphasize the speaker's point; they may also be shortened versions of an often-used word or phrase.

Slave Narrative: Autobiographical accounts of American slave life as told by escaped slaves. These works first appeared during the abolition movement of the 1830s through the 1850s.

Socialist Realism: The Socialist Realism school of literary theory was proposed by Maxim Gorky and established as a dogma by the first Soviet Congress of Writers. It demanded adherence to a communist worldview in works of literature. Its doctrines required an objective viewpoint comprehensible to the working classes and themes of social struggle featuring strong proletarian heroes.

Stereotype: A stereotype was originally the name for a duplication made during the printing process; this led to its modern definition as a person or thing that is (or is assumed to be) the same as all others of its type.

Stream of Consciousness: A narrative technique for rendering the inward experience of a character. This technique is designed to give the impression of an ever-changing series of thoughts, emotions, images, and memories in the spontaneous and seemingly illogical order that they occur in life.

Structure: The form taken by a piece of literature. The structure may be made obvious for ease of understanding, as in nonfiction works, or may obscured for artistic purposes, as in some poetry or seemingly "unstructured" prose.

Sturm und Drang: A German term meaning "storm and stress." It refers to a German literary movement of the 1770s and 1780s that reacted against the order and rationalism of the enlightenment, focusing instead on the intense experience of extraordinary individuals.

Style: A writer's distinctive manner of arranging words to suit his or her ideas and purpose in writing. The unique imprint of the author's personality upon his or her writing, style is the product of an author's way of arranging ideas and his or her use of diction, different sentence structures, rhythm, figures of speech, rhetorical principles, and other elements of composition.

Subjectivity: Writing that expresses the author's personal feelings about his subject, and which may or may not include factual information about the subject.

Subplot: A secondary story in a narrative. A subplot may serve as a motivating or complicating force for the main plot of the work, or it may provide emphasis for, or relief from, the main plot.

Surrealism: A term introduced to criticism by Guillaume Apollinaire and later adopted by Andre Breton. It refers to a French literary and artistic movement founded in the 1920s. The Surrealists sought to express unconscious thoughts and feelings in their works. The best-known technique used for achieving this aim was automatic writing—transcriptions of spontaneous outpourings from the unconscious. The Surrealists proposed to unify the contrary levels of conscious and unconscious, dream and reality, objectivity and subjectivity into a new level of "super-realism."

Suspense: A literary device in which the author maintains the audience's attention through the buildup of events, the outcome of which will soon be revealed.

Symbol: Something that suggests or stands for something else without losing its original identity. In literature, symbols combine their literal meaning with the suggestion of an abstract concept. Literary symbols are of two types: those that carry complex associations of meaning no matter what their contexts, and those that derive their suggestive meaning from their functions in specific literary works.

Symbolism: This term has two widely accepted meanings. In historical criticism, it denotes an early modernist literary movement initiated in France during the nineteenth century that reacted against the prevailing standards of realism. Writers in this movement aimed to evoke, indirectly and symbolically, an order of being beyond the material world of the five senses. Poetic expression of personal emotion figured strongly in the movement, typically by means of a private set of symbols uniquely identifiable with the individual poet. The principal aim of the Symbolists was to express in words the highly complex feelings that grew out of everyday contact with the world. In a broader sense, the term "symbolism" refers to the use of one object to represent another.

T

Tall Tale: A humorous tale told in a straightforward, credible tone but relating absolutely impossible events or feats of the characters. Such tales were commonly told of frontier adventures during the settlement of the west in the United States.

Theme: The main point of a work of literature. The term is used interchangeably with thesis.

Thesis: A thesis is both an essay and the point argued in the essay. Thesis novels and thesis plays share the quality of containing a thesis which is supported through the action of the story.

Third Person: See *Point of View*

Tone: The author's attitude toward his or her audience may be deduced from the tone of the work. A formal tone may create distance or convey politeness, while an informal tone may encourage a friendly, intimate, or intrusive feeling in the reader. The author's attitude toward his or her subject matter may also be deduced from the tone of the words he or she uses in discussing it.

Transcendentalism: An American philosophical and religious movement, based in New England from around 1835 until the Civil War. Transcendentalism was a form of American romanticism that had its roots abroad in the works of Thomas Carlyle, Samuel Coleridge, and Johann Wolfgang von Goethe. The Transcendentalists stressed the importance of intuition and subjective experience in communication with God. They rejected religious dogma and texts in favor of mysticism and scientific naturalism. They pursued truths that lie beyond the "colorless" realms perceived by reason and the senses and were active social reformers in public education, women's rights, and the abolition of slavery.

U

Urban Realism: A branch of realist writing that attempts to accurately reflect the often harsh facts of modern urban existence.

Utopia: A fictional perfect place, such as "paradise" or "heaven."

V

Verisimilitude: Literally, the appearance of truth. In literary criticism, the term refers to aspects of a work of literature that seem true to the reader.

Victorian: Refers broadly to the reign of Queen Victoria of England (1837-1901) and to anything with qualities typical of that era. For example, the qualities of smug narrowmindedness, bourgeois materialism, faith in social progress, and priggish morality are often considered Victorian. This stereotype is contradicted by such dramatic intellectual developments as the theories of Charles Darwin, Karl Marx, and Sigmund Freud (which stirred strong debates in England) and the critical attitudes of serious Victorian writers like Charles Dickens and George Eliot. In literature, the Victorian Period was the great age of the English novel, and the latter part of the era saw the rise of movements such as decadence and symbolism.

W

Weltanschauung: A German term referring to a person's worldview or philosophy.

Weltschmerz: A German term meaning "world pain." It describes a sense of anguish about the nature of existence, usually associated with a melancholy, pessimistic attitude.

Z

Zeitgeist: A German term meaning "spirit of the time." It refers to the moral and intellectual trends of a given era.

Cumulative Author/Title Index

Cumulative Nationality/Ethnicity Index

Kingsolver, Barbara
  Animal Dreams: V12
  The Bean Trees: V5
  Pigs in Heaven: V10
  Poisonwood Bible: V24
Kingston, Maxine Hong
  The Woman Warrior: V6
Knowles, John
  A Separate Peace: V2
Le Guin, Ursula K.
  Always Coming Home: V9
  The Left Hand of Darkness: V6
Lederer, William J.
  The Ugly American: V23
Lee, Harper
  To Kill a Mockingbird: V2
Lewis, Harry Sinclair
  Babbitt: V19
  Elmer Gantry: V22
  Main Street: V15
Lightman, Alan
  Einstein's Dreams: V29
London, Jack
  The Call of the Wild: V8
  White Fang: V19
Lowry, Lois
  The Giver: V3
Lurie, Alison
  Foreign Affairs: V24
Mailer, Norman
  The Naked and the Dead: V10
Malamud, Bernard
  The Assistant: V27
  The Fixer: V9
  The Natural: V4
Mason, Bobbie Ann
  In Country: V4
McCullers, Carson
  The Heart Is a Lonely Hunter: V6
  The Member of the Wedding: V13
McDermott, Alice
  Charming Billy: V23
Melville, Herman
  Billy Budd: V9
  Moby-Dick: V7
Méndez, Miguel
  Pilgrims in Aztlán: V12
Mitchell, Margaret
  Gone with the Wind: V9
Momaday, N. Scott
  House Made of Dawn: V10
Mori, Kyoko
  Shizuko's Daughter: V15
Morrison, Toni
  Beloved: V6
  The Bluest Eye: V1
  Song of Solomon: V8
  Sula: V14
Norris, Frank
  The Octopus: V12

Oates, Joyce Carol
  them: V8
  We Were the Mulvaneys: V24
O'Connor, Flannery
  The Violent Bear It Away: V21
  Wise Blood: V3
O'Hara, John
  Appointment in Samarra: V11
Okada, John
  No-No Boy: V25
Peck, Robert Newton
  A Day No Pigs Would Die: V29
Plath, Sylvia
  The Bell Jar: V1
Porter, Katherine Anne
  Ship of Fools: V14
Potok, Chaim
  The Chosen: V4
Power, Susan
  The Grass Dancer: V11
Price, Reynolds
  A Long and Happy Life: V18
Puzo, Mario
  The Godfather: V16
Pynchon, Thomas
  Gravity's Rainbow: V23
Rand, Ayn
  Anthem: V29
  Atlas Shrugged: V10
  The Fountainhead: V16
Robinson, Marilynne
  Gilead: V24
Rölvaag, O. E.
  Giants in the Earth: V5
Roth, Philip
  American Pastoral: V25
Russo, Richard
  Empire Falls: V25
Salinger, J. D.
  The Catcher in the Rye: V1
Shaara, Michael
  The Killer Angels: V26
Shange, Ntozake
  Betsey Brown: V11
Silko, Leslie Marmon
  Ceremony: V4
Sinclair, Upton
  The Jungle: V6
Stein, Gertrude
  Ida: V27
Steinbeck, John
  Cannery Row: V28
  East of Eden: V19
  The Grapes of Wrath: V7
  Of Mice and Men: V1
  The Pearl: V5
  The Red Pony: V17
Stowe, Harriet Beecher
  Uncle Tom's Cabin: V6
Styron, William
  Sophie's Choice: V22

Swarthout, Glendon
  Bless the Beasts and Children: V29
Tan, Amy
  Joy Luck Club: V1
  The Kitchen God's Wife: V13
Toomer, Jean
  Cane: V11
Twain, Mark
  The Adventures of Huckleberry Finn: V1
  The Adventures of Tom Sawyer: V6
  A Connecticut Yankee in King Arthur's Court: V20
Tyler, Anne
  The Accidental Tourist: V7
  Breathing Lessons: V10
  Dinner at the Homesick Restaurant: V2
Uchida, Yoshiko
  Picture Bride: V26
Updike, John
  Rabbit, Run: V12
  Toward the End of Time: V24
Vonnegut, Kurt, Jr.
  Cat's Cradle: V28
  Slaughterhouse-Five: V3
Walker, Alice
  The Color Purple: V5
Warren, Robert Penn
  All the King's Men: V13
Watkins, Yoko Kawashima
  So Far from the Bamboo Grove: V28
Welch, James
  Winter in the Blood: V23
Welty, Eudora
  Losing Battles: V15
  The Optimist's Daughter: V13
West, Nathanael
  The Day of the Locust: V16
Wharton, Edith
  The Age of Innocence: V11
  Ethan Frome: V5
  House of Mirth: V15
  Summer: V20
Wilder, Thornton
  The Bridge of San Luis Rey: V24
Wolfe, Thomas
  Look Homeward, Angel: V18
Wouk, Herman
  The Caine Mutiny: V7
Wright, Richard
  Black Boy: V1
  Native Son: V7
Yezierska, Anzia
  Bread Givers: V29
Zindel, Paul
  The Pigman: V14

Asian American

Kingston, Maxine Hong
  The Woman Warrior: V6
Okada, John
  No-No Boy: V25

Kafka, Franz
 The Trial: V7
Kertész, Imre
 Kaddish for a Child Not Born: V23
Malamud, Bernard
 The Assistant: V27
 The Fixer: V9
 The Natural: V4
Roth, Philip
 American Pastoral: V25
West, Nathanael
 The Day of the Locust: V16
Wiesel, Eliezer
 Night: V4
Yezierska, Anzia
 Bread Givers: V29

Korean
Choi, Sook Nyul
 Year of Impossible Goodbyes: V29

Mexican
Esquivel, Laura
 Like Water for Chocolate: V5
Fuentes, Carlos
 The Old Gringo: V8

Native American
Alexie, Sherman
 The Lone Ranger and Tonto
 Fistfight in Heaven: V17
Dorris, Michael
 A Yellow Raft in Blue Water: V3
Erdrich, Louise
 Love Medicine: V5
Momaday, N. Scott
 House Made of Dawn: V10
Silko, Leslie Marmon
 Ceremony: V4
Welch, James
 Winter in the Blood: V23

New Zealander
Hulme, Keri
 The Bone People: V24

Nigerian
Achebe, Chinua
 Things Fall Apart: V3
Emecheta, Buchi
 The Bride Price: V12
 The Wrestling Match: V14

Norwegian
Rölvaag, O. E.
 Giants in the Earth: V5

Polish
Conrad, Joseph
 Heart of Darkness: V2
 Lord Jim: V16
Kosinski, Jerzy
 The Painted Bird: V12

Portuguese
Saramago, José
 Blindness: V27
Yezierska, Anzia
 Bread Givers: V29

Romanian
Wiesel, Eliezer
 Night: V4

Russian
Asimov, Isaac
 I, Robot: V29
Bulgakov, Mikhail
 The Master and Margarita: V8
Dostoyevsky, Fyodor
 The Brothers Karamazon: V8
 Crime and Punishment: V3
 Notes from Underground: V28
Nabokov, Vladimir
 Lolita: V9
Pasternak, Boris
 Doctor Zhivago: V26
Rand, Ayn
 Anthem: V29
 Atlas Shrugged: V10
 The Fountainhead: V16
Solzhenitsyn, Aleksandr
 One Day in the Life of Ivan
 Denisovich: V6
Tolstoy, Leo
 Anna Karenina: V28
 War and Peace: V10
Turgenev, Ivan
 Fathers and Sons: V16
Yezierska, Anzia
 Bread Givers: V29

Scottish
Grahame, Kenneth
 The Wind in the Willows: V20

Spark, Muriel
 The Prime of Miss Jean Brodie:
 V22
Stevenson, Robert Louis
 Treasure Island: V20

South African
Coetzee, J. M.
 Dusklands: V21
Gordimer, Nadine
 July's People: V4
Paton, Alan
 Cry, the Beloved Country:
 V3
 Too Late the Phalarope: V12

Spanish
de Cervantes Saavedra, Miguel
 Don Quixote: V8

Sri Lankan
Ondaatje, Michael
 The English Patient: V23

Swiss
Hesse, Hermann
 Demian: V15
 Siddhartha: V6
 Steppenwolf: V24

Turkish
Pamuk, Orhan
 My Name is Red: V27

Uruguayan
Bridal, Tessa
 The Tree of Red Stars: V17

Vietnamese
Duong Thu Huong
 Paradise of the Blind: V23

West Indian
Kincaid, Jamaica
 Annie John: V3

Zimbabwean
Dangarembga, Tsitsi
 Nervous Conditions: V28

Subject/Theme Index

Self-sufficiency
Bread Givers: 104
Self Worth
Eva Luna: 167
Sensibility
Mansfield Park: 249
Sensitivity
Mansfield Park: 258, 260
Sensuality
*Eva Luna:*178
Servitude
Alas, Babylon: 16–17
Setting
Utopia: 305
Sexual Maturation
Something Wicked This Way Comes: 281
Shakers
A Day No Pigs Would Die: 123, 128, 129, 130, 131–132, 133–134, 135, 136
Shared Purpose
Mansfield Park: 257
Silence
Alas, Babylon: 14
Mansfield Park: 258
Simplicity
A Day No Pigs Would Die: 130, 136
Sincerity
Einstein's Dreams: 157
Skepticism
The Magic Mountain: 236
Slaughter
Bless the Beasts and Children: 66, 70, 74, 80
Slavery
Mansfield Park: 252–253
Utopia: 287, 289–290, 297–299, 303, 309
Small Town Life
Something Wicked This Way Comes: 277
Social Activism
Eva Luna: 179, 181
Social Class
Alas, Babylon: 18
Bread Givers: 114, 116, 117
The Magic Mountain: 225, 227
Mansfield Park: 243
Utopia: 293, 296, 303
Social Class and Economics
Utopia: 289–290
Social Commentary
Bless the Beasts and Children: 82
Mansfield Park: 254
Utopia: 296
Social Distinctions
Mansfield Park: 257
Social Injustice
Eva Luna: 179
Social Obligations
Mansfield Park: 259–260

Social Problems
Bless the Beasts and Children: 82
Social Realism
Eva Luna: 179
Social Relations
Utopia: 297
Social Satire
Eva Luna: 181–182
Sociopolitical Truth
Eva Luna: 179
Soul of the World
The Alchemist: 43
South America
Eva Luna: 159, 172–174, 178–183
Spiritual Growth
The Alchemist: 20
Mansfield Park: 249
Spiritual Values
Bread Givers: 103
Spirituality
The Alchemist: 30, 34–35, 40–42
The Magic Mountain: 233
Year of Impossible Goodbyes: 317, 324–325, 326
Spontaneity
Einstein's Dreams: 157
Staged Hunts
Bless the Beasts and Children: 77–79
Stereotypes
Alas, Babylon: 12–15, 16, 17
The Alchemist: 36
I, Robot: 198
Something Wicked This Way Comes: 283
Stoicism
Bless the Beasts and Children: 72
Storms
Something Wicked This Way Comes: 281
Storytelling
Bread Givers: 111, 112
Eva Luna: 159, 165, 166, 169, 172, 179, 181
Strength
Bless the Beasts and Children: 72, 76, 79, 80, 81
Structure
The Alchemist: 32
Utopia: 306
Subconscious
I, Robot: 205
Subservience
Bread Givers: 104
Success
Bless the Beasts and Children: 71, 76, 81
Bread Givers: 98, 105, 113, 114, 120
A Day No Pigs Would Die: 135
Suffering
Bless the Beasts and Children: 89
Bread Givers: 98

Suicide
Bless the Beasts and Children: 72–73, 81
Einstein's Dreams: 145, 155
Summer Camp
Bless the Beasts and Children: 77
Superficiality
Mansfield Park: 249
Survival
Alas, Babylon: 12, 19
Bread Givers: 114
Eva Luna: 159, 177
Year of Impossible Goodbyes: 317
Survival
Alas, Babylon: 7–8
Symbolism
Anthem: 51–52
Bless the Beasts and Children: 76, 82, 85
A Day No Pigs Would Die: 130, 135
Einstein's Dreams: 151
I, Robot: 203
The Magic Mountain: 211, 230, 235, 236
Mansfield Park: 243, 254, 256
Year of Impossible Goodbyes: 324, 326
Sympathy
Bless the Beasts and Children: 81
Mansfield Park: 260
Synecdoches
Einstein's Dreams: 151

T

Teamwork
Bless the Beasts and Children: 75–76
Technology
The Magic Mountain: 232
Technology, Fear of
I, Robot: 190, 191, 194, 195, 203, 204
Technology and Science
The Magic Mountain: 222
Temptress
Something Wicked This Way Comes: 282
Tenaciousness
Bless the Beasts and Children: 74
Tenement Life
Bread Givers: 107–109, 110–111, 117
Third-Person Narration
Alas, Babylon: 9
The Magic Mountain: 222–223
Time
Einstein's Dreams: 139, 141–147, 153–158
The Magic Mountain: 214
Something Wicked This Way Comes: 281